TRANSITION ECONOMICS

Two decades on

Gerard Turley and Peter J. Luke

Routledge
Taylor & Francis Group

LONDON AND NEW YORK

First published 2011
by Routledge
2 Park Square, Milton Park, Abingdon, Oxon OX14 4RN

Simultaneously published in the USA and Canada
by Routledge
270 Madison Avenue, New York, NY 10016

Routledge is an imprint of the Taylor & Francis Group, an informa business

© 2011 Gerard Turley and Peter J. Luke

The rights of Gerard Turley and Peter J. Luke to be identified
as authors of this work has been asserted by them in accordance with sections
77 and 78 of the Copyright, Designs and Patents Act 1988.

Typeset in Times New Roman by Keystroke, Station Road, Codsall, Wolverhampton
Printed and bound in Great Britain by TJ International, Padstow, Cornwall

British Library Cataloguing in Publication Data
A catalogue record for this book is available from the British Library

Library of Congress Cataloging in Publication Data
Turley, Gerard.
Transition economics : two decades on / By Gerard Turley and Peter J. Luke.
p. cm.
Includes bibliographical references and index.
1. Mixed economy–Case studies. 2. Structural adjustment (Economic policy)–Case studies.
I. Luke, Peter J. II.Title.
HB87.T87 2010
330.12'6–dc22
2010017830

ISBN 978–0–415–43881–0 (hbk)
ISBN 978–0–415–43882–7 (pbk)
ISBN 978–0–203–84291–1 (ebk)

**This publication was grant-aided by the Publications Fund of
National University of Ireland, Galway.**

TO MONICA AND KIERAN
TO LIWEI AND AIDEN

CONTENTS

ILLUSTRATIONS

Tables

Figures

Boxes

Maps

ACKNOWLEDGEMENTS

We wish to thank the following people (in no particular order) for their support and assistance in the writing of this book.

Tom Boylan of the Economics Department at NUI Galway, for the initial idea of a book on transition; Michael Cuddy and Pauric Brophy (both of Galway Development Services International, GDSI) for giving us the opportunity to work, and most particularly, live, in Russia; Jimmy Browne and everyone at NUI Galway for granting one of the authors sabbatical leave in what were very tough economic times for the university sector, Ireland and elsewhere; to colleagues and students at the J.E. Cairnes School of Business and Economics, NUI Galway for their dedication and interest in learning and knowledge, and to the NUI Galway Grant-in-Aid of Publications Committee for granting one of the authors a subvention to help in the publication of the book.

In Scotland a debt of thanks is due to Pam Siler, for many years Head of the Economics Department at Abertay University; also to Peter Romilly, a Reader in Economics at the same institution. Both individuals patiently over the years gave Peter Luke a deep appreciation of economics. In Russia, Peter Luke would like to acknowledge the debt owed to the late Professor Yuri Belkin who for many years was the Dean of the Marine Technical University on Leninski Prospect, St Petersburg. Yuri provided many insights into modern-day Russia as well as a guiding hand to everyday living within Russia. Also in St Petersburg, thanks to Professor Gennady Malyshev, Head of the Faculty of Russian Language at the N.A. Rimsky-Korsakov St Petersburg State Conservatory for conveying to me a deep appreciation of the Russian language and the insights to be gleaned from Russian proverbs (пословица) and sayings (поговорка).

To Gérard Roland and Paul Ruud of the Economics Department at Berkeley for very kindly facilitating Gerard Turley at the University of California, Berkeley. Likewise, to Roger Craine and Emil Schissel (both of UC, Berkeley) for granting me an office with a view of San Francisco and the Golden Gate Bridge. While at UC, Berkeley I taught a course entitled Econ 161: Economics of Transition: Eastern Europe, and used our (at the time) incomplete book as recommended reading. For all the Cal students who took this course in spring 2009, I thank you for the genuine interest shown in the course, in transition, and in the drafts of the book chapters. Indeed, to all at Cal (staff, faculty and students alike), I am eternally grateful.

To Mark Schaffer and Alan Bevan who, it is fair to say, mentored both of us in the sub-branch of transition economics when we were 'young' PhD students at the Centre for Economic Reform and Transformation (CERT), Heriot-Watt University, Edinburgh. In addition, one of the authors wishes to thank Hartmut Lehmann, also of Heriot-Watt, for his assistance and insights into labour markets in transition economies. Hartmut's inimitable style of mentoring will always be recalled fondly!

We wish to thank our university colleagues for providing feedback on the book and its contents. We wish to give special thanks and gratitude to Paul Hare of Heriot-Watt University, Edinburgh who, at short notice, provided invaluable and scholarly comments and suggestions to us. We look forward to working with Paul again in the near future. Words of appreciation must also go to John McHale of the J.E. Cairnes School of Business and Economics at NUI Galway for his positive comments on the final draft of the book. Thanks to anonymous referees who provided favourable comments when the book proposal was initially reviewed. To all those at Routledge who agreed to publish the book, provided worthwhile suggestions, and professional help in the design and printing of the book (particularly Louisa Earls). Thanks also to Keystroke, and to Maggie Lindsey-Jones, Emma Wood, Ann King and Rictor Norton. Thanks to the library staff at both NUI Galway and UC, Berkeley, and to Gill McColl for the design of the two maps. As always, she did an excellent job. A number of organisations and individuals have kindly allowed us to reproduce their material. In particular we wish to thank the European Commission, the International Labour Organisation, the European Bank for Reconstruction and Development (and, in particular Lead Economist Peter Sanfey), the International Bank for Reconstruction and Development (The World Bank), the International Monetary Fund, US Department of Health and Human Services, Oxford University Press, Cambridge University Press, Allen and Unwin, Wiley–Blackwell, the Herb Block Foundation, the American Economic Association, the National Centre for Health Statistics, the *Journal of Comparative Economics*, *The Economist*, the *Washington Post, China Daily*, Alan Gelb and David Henderson.

Most especially, we wish to thank our editor and senior publisher at Routledge, Robert Langham, for his excellent advice, thoughtful and insightful comments and outstanding editorial stewardship. Despite a very busy schedule, Rob took the time to read our entire manuscript, offer helpful suggestions and nudge us along when we fell behind. Rob was there from start to finish and we are very grateful for his not insignificant contribution. For us as authors, it was both a pleasure and a privilege to work with Routledge and, in particular, with Rob.

We bear full responsibility for any errors and all ommissions.

Finally, we both wish to thank our respective families for the time and space they gave us when writing this book. The final 'product' is as much their 'accomplishment' as it is ours.

ABBREVIATIONS

BEEPS	Business Environment and Enterprise Performance Survey
BRIC	Brazil, Russia, India, China (economies)
BUR	Belarus, Ukraine, Russia
CBR	Central Bank of Russia
CCP	Chinese Communist Party
CDOs	Collaterised Debt Obligations
CEB	Central and Eastern European and Baltics
CEE	Central and Eastern European
CIA	Central Intelligence Agency
CIC	China Investment Corporation
CIS	Commonwealth of Independent States
CIT	Corporate Income Tax
CMEA	Council for Mutual Economic Assistance
CPE	Centrally Planned Economy
CPI	Corruption Perceptions Index
CPSU	Communist Party of the Soviet Union
EBRD	European Bank for Reconstruction and Development
EC	European Community
ECA	Europe and Central Asia
EU	European Union
FDI	Foreign Direct Investment
FES	Federal Employment Service
FIE	Foreign Invested Enterprise
FIGs	Financial Industrial Groups
FSU	Former Soviet Union
GDP	Gross Domestic Product
GDR	German Democratic Republic
GKOs	Government Short-Term Treasury Bills
GNI	Gross National Income
GNP	Gross National Product
HDI	Human Development Index
HRS	Household Responsibility System
IFIs	International Financial Institutions
IMF	International Monetary Fund (the Fund)
MEBOs	Management and Employee Buyouts

MPP	Mass Privatisation Programme
NBS	National Bureau of Statistics
NEP	New Economic Policy
NIC	Newly Industrialised Countries
NIS	Newly Independent States
NLTS	Neo-Liberal Transition Strategy
NMP	Net Material Product
OECD	Organisation for Economic Cooperation and Development
OFZs	Federal Loan Bonds
OPEC	Oil Producing and Exporting Countries
PLA	People's Liberation Army
PPP	Purchasing Power Parity
PRC	People's Republic of China
RLFS	Russian Labour Force Surveys
RMB	Renminbi
ROH	Revolutionary Trade Union Movement
RSDLP	Russian Social Democratic Labour Party
SAFE	State Administration of Foreign Exchange
SAG	Soviet Shareholding Company
SAL	Structural Adjustment Loan
SAPs	Structural Adjustment Programmes
SASAC	State-owned Assets Supervision and Administration Commission
SBC	Soft Budget Constraint
SDTS	State-Directed Transition Strategy
SEZ	Special Economic Zones
SFRY	Socialist Federal Republic of Yugoslavia
SME	Small and Medium-sized Enterprise
SOE	State-Owned Enterprise
SPC	State Planning Commission
TEs	Transition Economies
TFP	Total Factor Productivity
TIs	Transition Indicators
TVEs	Township and Village Enterprises
ULC	Unit Labour Costs
UN	United Nations
UNDP	United Nations Development Programme
UNECE	United Nations Economic Commission for Europe
US	United States
USSR	Union of Soviet Socialist Republics
WB	World Bank (the Bank)
WDI	World Bank Development Indicators
WGI	World Bank Governance Indicators

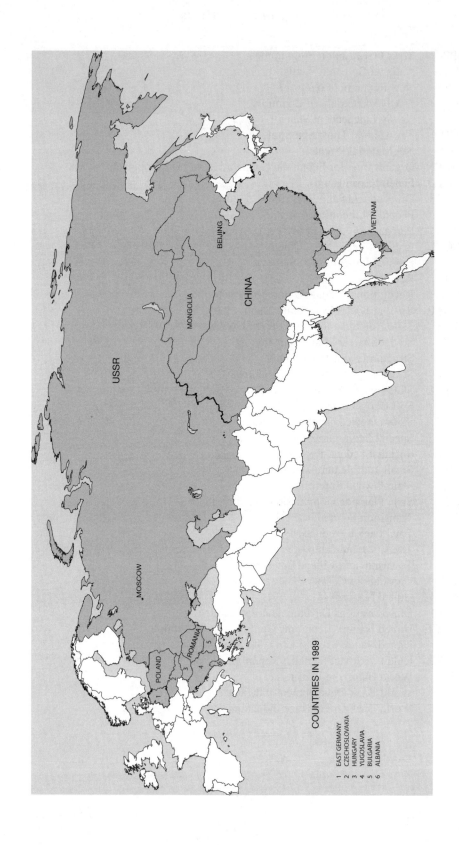

USSR

MOSCOW

POLAND

ROMANIA

1

5

3

4

6

MONGOLIA

BEIJING

CHINA

VIETNAM

COUNTRIES IN 1989

1 EAST GERMANY
2 CZECHOSLOVAKIA
3 HUNGARY
4 YUGOSLAVIA
5 BULGARIA
6 ALBANIA

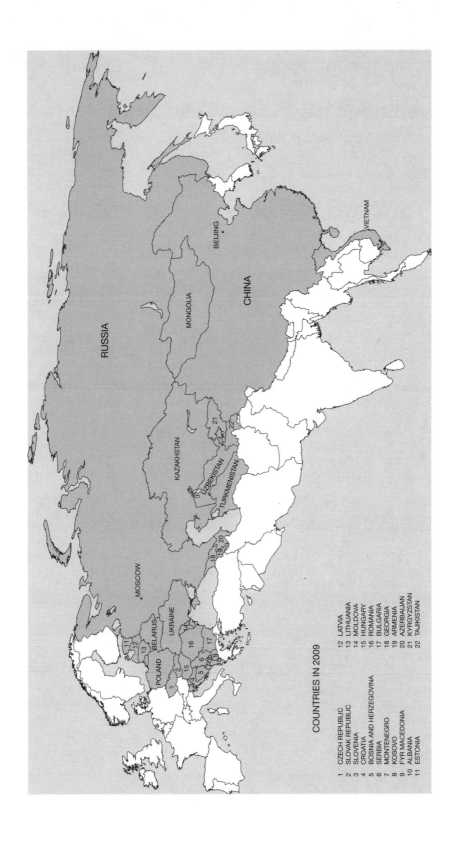

COUNTRIES IN 2009

1	CZECH REPUBLIC	12	LATVIA
2	SLOVAK REPUBLIC	13	LITHUANIA
3	SLOVENIA	14	MOLDOVA
4	CROATIA	15	HUNGARY
5	BOSNIA AND HERZEGOVINA	16	ROMANIA
6	SERBIA	17	BULGARIA
7	MONTENEGRO	18	GEORGIA
8	KOSOVO	19	ARMENIA
9	FYR MACEDONIA	20	AZERBAIJAN
10	ALBANIA	21	KYRGYZSTAN
11	ESTONIA	22	TAJIKISTAN

RUSSIA

MOSCOW

MONGOLIA

CHINA

BEIJING

KAZAKHSTAN

UZBEKISTAN

TURKMENISTAN

POLAND

BELARUS

UKRAINE

VIETNAM

INTRODUCTION

A new sub-branch of economics emerged at the end of the twentieth century. It arose from the collapse of the Soviet socialist system and the subsequent transition from a centrally planned economy to a market economy. It is known as transition economics where transition is defined as the social, political and economic transformation from a command system characterised by state ownership, collective action and central planning to a market system characterised by decentralised decision-making arrangements and private sector market transactions. Although it overlaps with other branches of economics, most notably comparative economic systems and development economics, the study of transition economics (and transition countries) is sufficiently distinct to warrant its own sub-branch within the discipline of economics.

Our motivation for writing this book now is to commemorate the twentieth anniversary of transition for former Soviet or Eastern Bloc countries. Indeed, in the case of China, we can observe over 30 years of reform and transition (despite China's reluctance to use the word 'transition'). Given the passage of time, *Transition Economics: Two Decades On* is our attempt to review and account for the outcomes in the so-called transition economies (TEs) and, from an academic perspective, to take the reader through developments and issues in the 20 years of transition. Although we confine our book to *economic* transition, the interplay between politics and economics (that is, the political economy of transition) and the social upheaval that followed transition are themes which are repeated throughout the book.

This transition from plan to market and from socialism to capitalism has been described as one of the most important economic, social and political experiments of modern times. Indeed, many view the transition from plan to market as one of the two – the other being the Great Depression of the 1930s – most important economic events of the last century.[1] Just as the causes, consequences and lessons of the Great Depression are still matters for ongoing discussion and research (particularly since the onset of the global economic crisis in 2007 to 2009), the transition experience from plan to market is likely to attract debate and controversy for decades to come. At the peak of the socialist system, one-third of the world's population lived in socialist countries. However, within a short space of time (beginning for the most part in 1989 to 1991), these countries had abandoned state socialism – or communism as it was often called – and embraced the capitalist system with its market economy. Although the transformation was remarkably peaceful, it has proved to be both costly and painful for many countries, regions and sections of society. Many citizens in transition economies witnessed an erosion of living standards and public services. For others, it has been a time of extraordinary opportunities, in both political and financial terms. From the economist's and policy maker's perspective, there are many lessons that can be learnt from the transition experience. These lessons have implications for other countries, irrespective of their current status, socialist or otherwise. This makes the study of transition economics both interesting and worthwhile.

Transition Economics: Two Decades On is a textbook on transition aimed primarily at undergraduate economics and business students taking a course in the economics of transition. It may, however, also be used by graduate students wishing to understand the plan to market transition process and experience, and by other third-level students of economics and business who are interested in comparative economic systems, emerging markets, European and Asian economies (particularly Russia and China) and economic policy reforms (whether it is liberalisation and macroeconomic stabilisation or enterprise restructuring and privatisation, or institutional reform and structural change).

Why study transition? And if so, why now, more than two decades after transition began? Is transition not over for some of the ex-socialist countries of Central and Eastern Europe (CEE), and, in particular, the most advanced former socialist countries that have acceded to EU membership?[2] Are the least advanced transition countries of the former Soviet Union (FSU) not similar to other emerging or developing countries of Africa, Central and Latin America, and Asia? Are the lessons of transition not unique to the former centrally planned socialist countries? Aside from intellectual curiosity and the need to record, for posterity, the plan to market transition experience, the authors believe that there are a number of reasons why the study of transition is both timely and valuable for students of economics, business and emerging markets.

First, it gives us a rare insight into the two main economic systems: plan and market. Second, we gain a better understanding of what is involved in systemic and large-scale institutional change. Third, it offers an insight into policy reform and the politics of economic reform. Fourth, it allows for a timely reappraisal of some key economic debates such as the Washington Consensus, the debate over markets versus states, the importance of institutions and contracting, and the role of privatisation and SME development. Fifth, concepts and economic ideas studied in transition such as state capture and corruption, asset stripping and tunnelling, the soft budget constraint and ratcheting, mass privatisation and dual-track price liberalisation, shock therapy and incrementalism have relevance far beyond economic transition and transition countries. Indeed, transition economics as a sub-branch of economics has itself stimulated and spurred on theoretical advances in the wider discipline of economics and political economy. Finally, it is now generally accepted that the economics profession has a great deal to learn from the transition experience and that these 'lessons' influence and, over time, improve our understanding of economic systems and provide a valuable insight into other areas of economics (whether, to name but a few, it is public finance, labour economics or corporate governance).

Unlike many other transition books that are either single-topic-related or country/ region-specific, this book aims to be more comprehensive in its coverage of transition. It also has the advantage of drawing upon the vast transition economics literature that has evolved over the past two decades since transition began. We focus on some of the most important aspects of economic transition, including the socialist system and its demise, the initial conditions at the outset of transition, the paradigms of transition, the main transition policies and economic reforms, the performance of transition countries (and firms) and the lessons to be learned from transition. The textbook covers a wide range of both contemporary microeconomic and macroeconomic issues.

The range of transition economies (see Box 0.1 and Tables 0.1–0.3 below) is wide, extending from the EU accession countries of Central Europe and the Baltic States to the countries of the former Soviet Union and to the East Asian countries of China, Mongolia and Vietnam. Using the World Bank classification of countries (by income, where income is defined as Gross National Income per capita), Table 0.1 lists all 210 countries (for comparative purposes), with the so-called transition countries, 31 in total, in bold.

Table 0.1 Gross national income (GNI) per capita[a, b]
(Transition countries are in BOLD BLOCK LETTERS)

Low income economies (43 in total, 4 transition)

Afghanistan	Guinea-Bissau	Rwanda
Bangladesh	Haiti	Senegal
Benin	Kenya	Sierra Leone
Burkina Faso	Korea, Dem. Rep.	Somalia
Burundi	**KYRGYZSTAN**	**TAJIKISTAN**
Cambodia	Lao PDR	Tanzania
Central African Republic	Liberia	Togo
Chad	Madagascar	Uganda
Comoros	Malawi	**UZBEKISTAN**
Congo, Dem. Rep	Mali	**VIETNAM**
Eritrea	Mauritania	Yemen, Rep.
Ethiopia	Mozambique	Zambia
Gambia, The	Myanmar	Zimbabwe
Ghana	Nepal	
Guinea	Niger	

Lower middle-income economies (55 in total, 9 transition)

ALBANIA	Honduras	Paraguay
Angola	India	Philippines
ARMENIA	Indonesia	Samoa
AZERBAIJAN	Iran, Islamic Rep.	São Tomé and Principe
Belize	Iraq	Solomon Islands
Bhutan	Jordan	Sri Lanka
Bolivia	Kiribati	Sudan
Cameroon	*KOSOVO*[c]	Swaziland
Cape Verde	Lesotho	Syrian Arab Republic
CHINA	Maldives	Thailand
Congo, Rep.	Marshall Islands	Timor-Leste
Côte d'Ivoire	Micronesia, Fed. Sts.	Tonga
Djibouti	**MOLDOVA**	Tunisia
Ecuador	**MONGOLIA**	**TURKMENISTAN**
Egypt, Arab Rep.	Morocco	**UKRAINE**
El Salvador	Nicaragua	Vanuatu
GEORGIA	Nigeria	West Bank and Gaza
Guatemala	Pakistan	
Guyana	Papua New Guinea	

Upper middle-income economies (46 in total, 12 transition)

Algeria	**BULGARIA**	**FYR, MACEDONIA**
American Samoa	Chile	Gabon
Argentina	Colombia	Grenada
BELARUS	Costa Rica	Jamaica
BOSNIA AND HERZEGOVINA	Cuba	**KAZAKHSTAN**
	Dominica	**LATVIA**
Botswana	Dominican Republic	Lebanon
Brazil	Fiji	Libya

(Continued)

3

Table 0.1 Continued

LITHUANIA	Panama	St Kitts and Nevis
Malaysia	Peru	St Lucia
Mauritius	**POLAND**	St Vincent and the Grenadines
Mayotte	**ROMANIA**	Suriname
Mexico	**RUSSIA**	Turkey
MONTENEGRO	**SERBIA**	Uruguay
Namibia	Seychelles	Venezuela, RB
Palau	South Africa	

High income economies (66 in total, 6 transition)

Andorra	France	Netherlands Antilles
Antigua and Barbuda	French Polynesia	New Caledonia
Aruba	Germany	New Zealand
Australia	Greece	Northern Mariana Islands
Austria	Greenland	Norway
Bahamas, The	Guam	Oman
Bahrain	Hong Kong, China	Portugal
Barbados	**HUNGARY**	Puerto Rico
Belgium	Iceland	Qatar
Bermuda	Ireland	San Marino
Brunei Darussalam	Isle of Man	Saudi Arabia
Canada	Israel	Singapore
Cayman Islands	Italy	**SLOVAK REPUBLIC**
Channel Islands	Japan	**SLOVENIA**
CROATIA	Korea, Rep.	Spain
Cyprus	Kuwait	Sweden
CZECH REPUBLIC	Liechtenstein	Switzerland
Denmark	Luxembourg	Trinidad and Tobago
ESTONIA	Macao, China	United Arab Emirates
Equatorial Guinea	Malta	United Kingdom
Faeroe Islands	Monaco	United States
Finland	Netherlands	Virgin Islands (US)

Source: World Bank.

Notes

a. Based on current US$ (2008), per capita GNI, formerly referred to as Gross National Product (GNP), is gross national income, converted to US dollars using the World Bank Atlas method, divided by the mid-year population. GNI is the sum of value added of all resident producers plus product taxes (less subsidies) not included in the valuation of output plus net receipts of primary income from abroad. Source: World Bank.

b. According to the World Bank Atlas method, low income is $975 or less, lower-middle income is $976–$3,855, upper-middle income is $3,856–$11,905 and high income is $11,906 or more.

c. Kosovo is not included in our analysis as it is an independent state only since 2008 (but whose statehood, at the time of writing this book, is still in dispute).

The socialist countries of the Soviet bloc (often referred to as the CEE/FSU countries; see below) that embarked on transition over two decades ago were not, for the most part, developing countries. Developing economies tend to be, on average, low-income countries, with a mix of (predominantly small in size) private and public enterprises (albeit majority state owned), rural and agrarian where agriculture is the primary source of income, with rapidly growing populations, witnessing high levels of poverty and inequality, and low indicators of socio-economic well-being (measured by, *inter alia*, literacy rates, school enrolment rates, life expectancy at birth rates and mortality rates). Markets in developing countries (most of which were former colonies) exist but they tend to be underdeveloped, as with the institutional framework. In contrast, socialist countries tended to be, on average, middle-income countries, with predominately state enterprises (large in size), over-industrialised, with moderate – and even negative – population growth (with the exceptions of China and Vietnam), witnessing low levels of poverty and inequality (indeed, more equal than most countries in the world), and characterised by high levels of human capital and socio-economic welfare (reflected in a well-educated, highly literate workforce, and a healthy population with a different demographic structure). Markets were replaced by the plan, with its own distinct institutional setting.

The implication of this contrast between socialist countries and developing countries is that transition economics is different from development economics.[3] If we assume, for the sake of argument, that the end point for both socialist countries and developing countries is the same (that is, the goal of transition and development is a well-functioning market economy with high living standards and welfare for the population) the starting point and, consequently, the path or route taken – involving macroeconomic, structural and institutional reform – from beginning to end is not the same. This is why we view transition economics as a sub-branch in economics separate from the long-established sub-branch that we know as development economics.

Box 0.1

Transition economies

by Anders Åslund[4]

From 1989 to 1991, communism foundered throughout the former Soviet bloc in Europe and Asia. From Prague to Vladivostok, 28 countries in the former Soviet Union and Eastern Europe abandoned similar political and economic systems.

Differing programs of economic transformation

At the beginning, the transition's direction was clear, but its final aims were not. Overtly, everybody advocated democracy, a normal market economy with predominant private ownership, a rule of law, and a social safety net, but their eventual goals ranged from the American-style mixed economy to a West European-style welfare state to market socialism. Instead of arguing about aims, people argued over whether the transformation to a market should be radical or gradual. A radical program, 'shock therapy' or 'the Washington consensus', became the main proposal for how to undertake the systemic change. It amounted to a comprehensive and radical market reform. Key elements were swift and far-reaching: liberalization of prices and trade, sharp reduction of budget deficits, strict monetary policy, and early privatization, usually coupled with international assistance conditioned on reform measures. The program's main advocate was Jeffrey Sachs of Harvard University, but mainstream Anglo-American macroeconomists; the International Monetary Fund (IMF); the World Bank; the Ministries of Finance of the G-7; and leading policy makers in Poland, the Czech Republic, the Baltic states and Russia also supported it. Radical reform became the orthodoxy. Advocates used many arguments. The success of reform was in danger if a critical mass of market and private enterprise was not formed fast enough. A semi-reformed system would maintain major distortions that would cause people to seek

---

5

privileges and subsidies, and would deter investment. The social and political costs of slow reform would be much greater because a semi-reformed system could not perform well. People were prepared to accept only a limited period of suffering (Fischer and Gelb 1991a; Lipton and Sachs 1990; Shleifer and Vishny 1998). Shock therapy was applied in Poland, the Czech Republic, and the three Baltic states (Estonia, Latvia and Lithuania). In opposition to the radical reform program, numerous gradual reform programs were formulated. Some favored more gradual deregulation of foreign trade or prices. Others wanted more gradual reduction of inflation rates, budget deficits and monetary expansion. Many argued that the quality of privatization was more important than its speed. The opponents of radical reform were diverse. Some were theoretical economists who believed that more gradual reform would minimize social suffering. Others, ranging from social democrats to communists, wanted to minimize the role of the market. The most important protagonists, however, were state enterprise managers, state officials, and political economists in the former Soviet Union. All gradualists maintained that the state was strong and capable of social engineering. Gradual reform came to dominate in Hungary, Southeast Europe and most of the former Soviet Union. Late in the day, Professor Joseph Stiglitz of Columbia University became the leader of the gradualists (Murrell 1992; Roland 2000; Stiglitz 2002).

Dramas of reform

Debate is one thing and implementation is another. In practice, radical reformers were opposed initially by state enterprise managers and later by new businessmen, who were benefiting from transitional market distortions. Many of the anticipated stumbling blocks did not materialize. For instance, labor unrest and popular unrest were minimal, and the large military-industrial complex was timid. Paradoxically, the problem was not the losers but the winners, who made fortunes on the large short-run subsidies garnered during the transition (Hellman 1998). Postcommunist transition is best understood as strife over these subsidies (Åslund 2002a). Many economists have undertaken ambitious multi-country regression analyses. Although statistics remain poor, economists widely agree that certain major market reforms increase real growth (Berg *et al.* 1999). Although the effects are often hard to disentangle because various reforms often occur simultaneously, decontrol of prices and foreign trade appears to have had the greatest impact. In addition, inflation needs to fall below 40 percent a year to allow growth, and privatization is unequivocally beneficial. Governments that pursue such sound economic policies adopt more market-oriented legislation than do less ambitious reformers. The liberalization of consumer prices and imports was surprisingly easily accepted, and many transition countries – for example, Poland, Estonia, and Russia – abolished all import tariffs to overcome the massive shortages. What proved harder was deregulating prices and exports of commodities because well-connected people wanted to purchase oil, metals and grain at low prices fixed by the state and to sell them on the free world market at a multiple, making a huge profit. Usually, such decontrol was possible only after a major crisis. Inflation was the main economic problem in the early transition. Thirteen countries had 14 instances of hyperinflation, almost as many hyperinflations as had been registered in prior world history.

Privatization has been the most controversial reform because it is a conspicuous distribution of wealth, and all vie for a larger share. Moreover, privatization has been monumental and unprecedented in scope. Small-scale privatization of small shops has usually been undertaken relatively easily by selling them cheaply to their employees. Similarly, much of public housing has been sold for a nominal price to tenants. Agricultural land has been restituted in the Baltics and Central Europe. Land reform occurred early where agriculture is vital to the national economy, but later in other countries. The privatization of large enterprises has been most controversial. The objectives have varied, including privatization for its own sake; for enterprise performance; for state revenues; for the attraction of foreign capital; for the satisfaction of employees, managers or other domestic stakeholders; and for corporate governance. The debate has been polarized between advocates of early mass privatization and protagonists of piecemeal case-by-case privatization. The Czech Republic and Russia pioneered the mass privatization of large enterprises through vouchers, which were distributed to all citizens and could be used to purchase shares of large enterprises. Hungary, Poland, and Estonia, by contrast, focused on case-by-case sales (Boycko *et al.* 1995; Stiglitz 2002). Economic analyses increasingly show that privatization has been beneficial. Start-ups and enterprises with foreign capital have performed the best to date, but enterprises that have participated in mass privatization are swiftly improving their records. Private ownership seems to matter in the long run. The officially measured declines in output have been shocking. Fortunately, these huge drops are not credible because communist statistics exaggerated output, while capitalist statistics fail to cover much of what is going on in the economy. The quality of produce has radically improved, as substandard goods no longer find takers. Major structural changes have occurred. The prior over-industrialization has disappeared, and service sectors have expanded sharply. The huge military-industrial complex has shrunk to West European dimensions. In Russia, for example, military spending is now about 5 percent of GDP, falling from almost 25 percent of GDP in the former Soviet Union. Millions of new small enterprises have been created. The decline in the standard of living has been much less than the real contraction in output because consumption has grown sharply as a share of GDP and because much of the prior investment was forced and, therefore, not very valuable. A major concern, however, is that income differentials have risen sharply: in East-Central Europe to a West European level, in Russia to an American level, and in some post-Soviet countries even to a Latin American level. Curiously, pensions initially increased sharply as a share of GDP, while families with children have suffered disproportionate poverty. Complaints about deteriorating education and health care are standard, but in most transition countries their share of GDP has actually risen while these government-run systems appear to be in great disarray (Milanovic 1998).

A great divide

Outcomes have varied remarkably in terms of political system, economic system, and economic growth. Three trajectories are apparent. Radical reformers in Central Europe and the Baltics have built democratic and dynamic market economies with predominantly private ownership. Gradual reformers in Southeastern Europe and most former Soviet republics have had greater problems achieving democracy. Their market economies are still marred by bureaucracy, though most property has been privatized. Three countries – Belarus, Turkmenistan, and Uzbekistan – have maintained their old dictatorship, state control and dominant public ownership, doing little apart from ejecting the Communist Party. These contrasting outcomes can be explained by the different goals of these regimes. While their dominant slogans were to build democracy, a market economy, and rule of law, post-communist countries followed three starkly different policy paths. Radical reformers really wanted democracies and dynamic market economies. At the other end of the spectrum, a few autocrats desired little but the consolidation of their power. In the middle, countries pursued policies imposed by dominant elites who wanted to make themselves wealthy on transitional market distortions. Not surprisingly, the correlation between democracy, marketization, and privatization has been very strong. Since 1999, economic development has taken another turn. By cutting government spending and introducing low or even flat tax rates, the former Soviet countries have excelled, with an average growth of 6 percent per year for five years and almost balanced budgets. The early successful reformers in Central Europe have stopped at a mediocre growth rate of 3 percent per year, with large budget deficits, current account deficits and unemployment. Their public expenditures have stayed at a West European share of GDP. These countries have become, as Hungarian economist János Kornai put it, social welfare states 'prematurely', with excessive taxes and social transfers impeding economic growth (Kornai 1992). The picture of success appears to be partially reversed. Yet the post-Soviet countries are lapsing into more authoritarian systems, while East-Central Europe remains democratic. Much of East-Central Europe acceded to the European Union in 2004, and this appears to have stimulated democracy rather than economic growth.

Transition economics have brought a few new insights to economics. How to launch the transition mattered so much not because the workers or the people objected, but, it turns out, because the elite were the strong interest group that had to be mollified. Because much output under socialism was of so little value, whether real output declined during the transition is still in dispute. Privatization and enterprise restructuring have been the most pioneering areas, and the final verdict on their success is not yet in. Corruption is widespread, but this tends to happen in all countries where government officials have a large amount of discretionary power, not just in transition economies. Macroeconomic stabilization and liberalization hardly offered anything very unexpected, apart from technicalities such as barter. As time passes, the peculiarities of transition economies wane.

Source: Åslund, www.econlib.org/library/Enc/TransitionEconomies.html.

Reprinted by permission from David R. Henderson, ed., *The Concise Encyclopedia of Economics*, Liberty Fund, 2008.

Some basic socio-economic (and reform) data for the 31 transition countries, categorised into three broad regional classifications, may be found in Tables 0.2 and 0.3.[5]

China, Mongolia and Vietnam are generally referred to throughout this book as the East Asian countries. As for the former Soviet Bloc countries, we use different classifications depending on the issue and timeframe involved. Generally, it was common in the early years of transition to use the CEE versus FSU groupings. Later, when it became evident that the

Table 0.2 Transition countries, 2008[a]

	Population estimate (millions)	GDP per capita PPP (US$)[b] /WB income group classification[c]	Industry share of GDP, per cent	Private sector share of GDP, per cent	Rates of inflation / unemployment / General Government Balance (−/+)[d]	Life expectancy at birth, years 2007
Central and Eastern European and the Baltics (CEE/CEB)						
Albania	3.1	$7,195 / lower-middle income	20	75	3 / 13 / −5.7	76
Bosnia and Herzegovina[e]	3.8	$7,514 / upper-middle income	22	60	7 / 41 / −3.0	75
Bulgaria	7.6	$11,259 / upper-middle income	31	75	12 / 5 / 3.0	73
Croatia	4.4	$17,219 / high income	28	70	6 / 9 / −1.4	76
Czech Republic	10.2	$23,341 / high income	38	80	6 / 4 / −1.4	77
Estonia[e]	1.3	$18,639 / high income	30	80	10 / 6 / −2.7	73
FYR Macedonia	2	$8,837 / upper-middle income	28	70	8 / 34 / −1.0	74
Hungary	10	$18,040 / high income	29	80	6 / 8 / −3.4	73
Latvia[e]	2.3	$15,592 / upper-middle income	22	70	15 / 8 / −4.0	71
Lithuania[e]	3.4	$17,467 / upper-middle income	33	75	11 / 6 / −3.2	71
Montenegro	0.6	$10,683 / upper-middle income	18	65	9 / 18 / 1.5	74
Poland	38.1	$16,388 / upper-middle income	30	75	4 / 7 / −3.9	75
Romania	21.5	$11,761 / upper-middle income	34	70	8 / 4 / −4.9	73
Serbia[e]	7.4	$10,741 / upper-middle income	28	60	12 / 29 / −2.4	73
Slovak Republic	5.4	$20,546 / high income	41	80	5 / 10 / −2.2	74
Slovenia[e]	2	$26,941 / high income	34	70	6 / 4 / −0.9	78
Commonwealth of Independent States (CIS)						
Armenia	3.1	$5,611 / lower-middle income	45	75	9 / 6 / −1.4	73
Azerbaijan	8.7	$8,102 / lower-middle income	71	75	21 / 4 / 25.5	67
Belarus	9.7	$11,333 / upper-middle income	39	30	15 / 1 / 1.4	70
Georgia	4.4	$4,526 / lower-middle income	24	75	10 / 17 / −6.4	71
Kazakhstan	15.7	$10,458 / upper-middle income	42	70	17 / 7 / 1.1	66

(Continued)

Table 0.2 Continued.

	Population estimate (millions)	GDP per capita PPP (US$)[b] / WB income group classification[c]	Industry share of GDP, per cent	Private sector share of GDP, per cent	Rates of inflation / unemployment / General Government Balance (–/+)[d]	Life expectancy at birth, years 2007
Kyrgyzstan[e, f]	5.3	$2,023 / low income	19	75	25 / 8 / –0.1	68
Moldova	3.6	$2,704 / lower-middle income	15	65	13 / 4 / –1.0	68
Russia[e]	141.8	$14,917 / upper-middle income	38	65	14 / 8 / 4.8	68
Tajikistan[f]	6.8	$1,761 / low income	23	55	20 / 3 / –6.1	67
Turkmenistan	5	$6,138 / lower-middle income	..	25	15 / .. / 11.3	63
Ukraine	46.3	$6,721 / lower-middle income	37	65	25 / 6 / –3.2	68
Uzbekistan	27.3	$2,455 / low income	33	45	13 / .2 / 10.5	67
East Asia						
China[g]	1,326	$5,511/ lower-middle income	49	60	6 / 4 / –0.3	73
Mongolia[e]	2.6	$3,297/ lower-middle income	41	75	27 / 3 / –5.0	67
Vietnam[g]	86.2	$2,574/ low income	40	65	23 / .. / –3.2	74

Sources: EBRD, United Nations, World Bank.

Notes

a. All data are 2008 unless otherwise stated.

b. Constant 2005 International US$.

c. Based on 2008 GNI per capita, using the World Bank Atlas method (whose purpose it is to reduce the impact of exchange rate fluctuations in the cross-country comparison of national incomes) where low income is $975 or less, lower-middle income is $976–$3,855, upper-middle income is $3,856–$11,905 and high income is $11,906 or more.

d. Consumer prices (annual average, per cent) / persons unemployed as a percentage of labour force, end-year / estimated general government deficit or surplus as a percentage of GDP.

e. Industry share is for 2007.

f. The unemployment rates are for 2007.

g. The private sector share of GDP data for China and Vietnam are for 2003 and 2007 respectively.

Table 0.3 Transition economies: income, development and reform

Country/indicator	GNI per capita 2008[a]	Human Development Index (HDI), 2007[b]		Transition indicator, 2009[c]
		Index	Rank	
Low-income countries				
Tajikistan	$600	0.688	127th	2.41
Kyrgyzstan	$740	0.710	120th	2.93
Vietnam[d]	$890	0.725	116th	..
Uzbekistan	$910	0.710	119th	2.15
Lower middle-income countries				
Moldova	$1,470	0.720	117th	3.00
Mongolia	$1,680	0.727	115th	3.07
Georgia	$2,470	0.778	89th	3.11
Turkmenistan	$2,840	0.739	109th	1.44
China[d]	$2,940	0.772	92nd	..
Ukraine	$3,210	0.796	85th	3.07
Armenia	$3,350	0.798	84th	3.18
Azerbaijan	$3,830	0.787	86th	2.63
Albania	$3,840	0.818	70th	3.07
Upper middle-income countries				
FYR Macedonia	$4,140	0.817	72nd	3.26
Bosnia and Herzegovina	$4.510	0.812	76th	2.78
Belarus	$5,380	0.826	68th	2.07
Bulgaria	$5,490	0.840	61st	3.56
Serbia	$5,700	0.826	67th	2.89
Kazakhstan	$6,140	0.804	82nd	2.96
Montenegro	$6,440	0.834	65th	2.85
Romania	$7,930	0.837	63rd	3.44
Russia	$9,620	0.817	71st	3.04
Latvia	$11,860	0.866	48th	3.63
Lithuania	$11,870	0.870	46th	3.70
Poland	$11,880	0.880	41st	3.78
High-income countries				
Hungary	$12,810	0.879	43rd	3.96
Croatia	$13,570	0.871	45th	3.55
Estonia	$14,270	0.883	40th	3.93
Slovak Republic	$14,540	0.880	42nd	3.78
Czech Republic[e]	$16,600	0.903	36th	..
Slovenia	$24,010	0.929	29th	3.41

Sources: EBRD, UNDP, World Bank.

Notes
a. World Bank Atlas method where low income is $975 or less, lower-middle income is $976–$3,855, upper-middle income is $3,856–$11,905 and high income is $11,906 or more.
b. Developed by the United Nations (Development Program, the UNDP), this is a summary measure of human development combining indicators of income, life expectancy and educational attainment. In 2007 out of a total of 182 countries the highest HDI was 0.971 (Norway) and the lowest was 0.340 (Niger).
c. EBRD's measure of progress in reform, in areas of markets and trade, enterprise restructuring and privatisation, financial institutions reform and infrastructural reform. The scale is 1 to 4.33.
d. There is no transition indicator for Vietnam or China as these East Asian countries are not covered by the EBRD.
e. There is no 2009 transition indicator for the Czech Republic as it 'graduated' from the EBRD at end 2007.

Baltic States, at least in terms of performance and outcomes, more resembled Central and Eastern European countries, the groupings CEE (to include the Baltic States) or CEB versus CIS were commonly used. Later still when it was evident that the countries of South Eastern Europe were, again in terms of performance, distinct from the rest of Central and Eastern Europe, the country groupings CEE (or CEB), SEE and CIS were used.[6] The data in this book are the most up-to-date available at the time of writing, with a cut-off date of November 2009, to coincide with 20 years of transition since the *annus mirabilis* 1989 and the subsequent demise of the *ancien régime*.

Transition Economics: Two Decades On is more than just a book about a particular part of the world and the transformation that was experienced at a particular time in history. The authors believe that the study of the economics of transition gives the reader an insight into theories, policies, reforms, legacies, institutions, processes and lessons that have application and relevance – beyond the specific transition from plan to market – to other parts of the world and to other times in history.

In Chapter 1, the pre-transition socialist system is examined. The central features of the administrative command economy or the centrally planned economy (CPE) as it was commonly referred to, most notably state ownership, central planning, collectivised agriculture, rapid industrialisation and extensive economic growth are discussed, as is the history of the socialist system in the Soviet Union. Chapter 2 briefly outlines the main stylised facts of economic transition. These relate to trends in output, inflation, private enterprise, industry and services, investment and consumption, corruption, informal activities, inequality and poverty, trade, foreign direct investment (FDI), labour, taxation, public expenditure, demographics and institutions. The conditions (incorporating country-specific factors) at the outset of transition are covered in Chapter 3. Understanding these cross-country variations in circumstances is useful when addressing, at a later stage, the issue of the major differences in economic performance and the outcomes that emerged once transition began. Differences in initial conditions may also partly explain the different reform policies adopted by the various transition economies, acknowledging that other factors, including political constraints, electoral support, ideologies, institutions and pressure (or support) from the West, also played a part. The economics literature on transition indicates that the role of the inherited conditions or historical legacy is an important factor in the complex transition process. Not surprisingly, transition countries, to varying degrees, are burdened with the legacy of the past.

The two main paradigms or theories of economic transition are outlined in Chapter 4. The standard paradigm of economic transition, often referred to as the Washington Consensus approach, dominated in the early years of the 1990s and had the support of the International Financial Institutions (IFIs), i.e. the World Bank and, more notably, the International Monetary Fund. We begin Chapter 4 with this neoclassical approach to economic transition. In contrast, the alternative approach, namely the institutional-evolutionary paradigm, views transition from a different perspective. This paradigm, and its implications, is also examined. Chapter 5 examines transition reforms and economic policies. We outline the trinity of liberalisation, stabilisation and privatisation, as well as the structural and institutional reforms needed for a successful transition from plan to market. Progress in economic reform, as well as the major policy debates that dominated transition in the first two decades, is also presented.

Chapter 6 examines enterprise reform and restructuring. Elements of enterprise reform include ownership change and privatisation, corporate governance, competition and demonopolisation, SME development and entrepreneurship. The literature on the determinants of enterprise performance is presented. Chapter 7 outlines the economic record of transition countries, the collapse in output and the determinants of cross-country performance. The labour market during transition is the topic for discussion in Chapter 8. Here we examine how labour markets have developed from one of allocating labour to specific jobs under state planning to one where the market and the role of education and training play a more dominant role. In particular, we focus on labour markets in Russia and China.

Chapter 9 outlines the differences between the transition experience in Russia and China. For obvious geopolitical reasons, the economic performance of Russia versus China is analysed with respect to the initial conditions, political changes and reform paths. The final chapter is a tentative assessment of the transition experience and outlines the main lessons that can be learnt from this 'unique' transition experience. After two decades of economic transformation in the so-called transition economies, what lessons can be learnt from transition? What can the economics profession learn from the experience of transition countries? Can other countries, Cuba or North Korea, for example, undertaking similar changes in economic systems, rules and behaviour, learn from the transition experience? Chapter 10 presents a brief overview of lessons that have relevance beyond transition.

It has been said in relation to the transition from plan to market that 'Nobody said it would be easy, and nobody was right.' But we did, almost all of us, whatever our preconceptions and viewpoints, and we were wrong. The economic transformation of former socialist countries, and most particularly the FSU republics, has proved much more arduous and costly than we expected. Moreover, and not unrelated, transition is rife with ideologies and often clouded with partisan claims, and as social scientists we need to separate the facts from the myths in as dispassionate and balanced a way as possible. We leave it for the reader to judge the success, or otherwise, of our undertaking!

To conclude, in writing a book on the first 20 years of transition we feel it may be a little premature to review the facts, processes and lessons of transition. What we are attempting to do in parts of the book can only be described as tentative work. It was János Kornai, in his Preface to *The Socialist System: The Political Economy of Communism*, who quoted the historian Simon Schama's classic book on the French Revolution, when he wrote, 'Zhou Enlai, the Chinese Prime Minister, when asked what he thought of the significance of the French Revolution, is said to have replied, "It's still too early to say." ' The same caveat applies to any review of the first two decades of transition. We hope that our book is an addition, however modest, to the literature on transition and that the reader will appreciate some of the significance of what is a truly historic event, namely transition from plan to market, and from socialism to capitalism.[7]

1

PRE-TRANSITION:
THE SOCIALIST SYSTEM

An economic and historical description

In August 1991 Boris Yeltsin, President of the newly self-declared independent Russian Federation, hauled himself atop a Russian armoured vehicle, shook the hand of the slightly bewildered Russian soldier inside and declared, 'Soldiers, officers, generals: the clouds of terror and dictatorship are gathering over the whole country. They must not be allowed to bring eternal night.' In doing so he thereby helped to bring to an end one of the greatest social experiments in human history. (See Box 1.1, *Attempted Coup d'état in the Soviet Union, 1991*, for a description and an explanation of this failed Communist coup d'état.)

Before examining this social, economic and cultural experiment we first give a primer in Russian revolutionary history and the ins-and-outs of the various factions that conspired to take power in Tsarist Russia. Later we describe in more detail the actual mechanisms by which the economy under Soviet-style socialism operated. Some of the historical material which follows may seem initially a little archaic but we demonstrate that apparently forgotten disputes still resonate even today when we come to look at the debate as to whether governments have any role to play within the market economy. We also look at the socialist economic system in Central and Eastern Europe after the Second World War (WWII). We leave details and discussion of the other great socialist economic experiment in the People's Republic of China until Chapter 9 when we make a comparison of the transition paths followed in both China and Russia.

Box 1.1

Attempted coup d'état in the Soviet Union, 1991

The attempted coup d'état by hard-line members of the Communist Party of the Soviet Union (CPSU) was staged in order to prevent the Soviet Union from disintegrating. The irony is that the coup plotters far from saving the Soviet Union merely speeded up its ultimate demise.

Mikhail Gorbachev as General Secretary of the CPSU and as President of the Union of Soviet Socialist Republics (USSR, or simply the Soviet Union) had instigated a series of reforms to reverse the declining state of the economy. These reforms on the economic front had not succeeded; on the political front, however, Gorbachev's reforms had increased the democratisation of the country and allowed far greater freedom of expression both for the individual and the media (see Chapter 9 for more details). The

---

coup participants argued that this set in motion 'centrifugal forces' which were starting to rip the USSR apart. Indeed, up until the time of the coup some Soviet Republics had already declared independence, such as the Baltic States. In addition, while the Russian Federation was still formally a part of the USSR at the time of the coup, it had already in June 1990 declared its sovereignty from the USSR, placing Russian federal law above that of Soviet law where conflicts arose between the two sets of laws. The goal of the coup participants was ultimately to take the country back to pre-Gorbachev times despite their declared commitment to free enterprise and elections at the time of the coup itself.

The attempted coup ran for three days over 19 to 21 August 1991. Perhaps the greatest 'technical' failure of the coup participants was not to arrest Boris Yeltsin when they had a chance. By allowing him to remain at large he acted as a rallying point against the coup. Gorbachev himself was on holiday in the Crimea at his dacha at the time of the coup. Prior to the coup Valeriy Boldin, Oleg Baklanov, Oleg Shenin and Deputy USSR Defence Minister General Valentin Varennikov flew to the Crimea for a meeting with Gorbachev, hoping that he would either side with them or formally resign: he did neither, claiming later that he refused utterly to be involved or to resign.

On their return from the Crimea they formed the State Committee of the State of Emergency (GKChP) consisting of eight members in total. As with attempted coup d'états the world over, at the start of the coup newspapers were banned (except for the Communist Party newspapers), troops and tank divisions were rallied, prisons cleared to make way for anticipated new inmates, and an address to the nation made on both radio and television initiating the start of the coup was broadcast early in the morning of 19 August. Moscow citizens began to gather spontaneously around the Russian Federation Parliament building, the White House; cracks began almost immediately to appear in the military when the head of one tank battalion guarding the White House declared his loyalty to the Russian Federation (strictly speaking, the Russian Soviet Federative Socialist Republic, i.e. the body led by Yeltsin). This was the moment when Yeltsin (his finest moment) climbed atop a tank and addressed the crowds. Unbelievably for a coup that had months to prepare, Yeltsin's address went out on the evening television news broadcast!

Two armed detachments of troops were to storm the White House in the early hours of 21 August. However, the units concerned made no decisive move to do so, perhaps ultimately because they realised that while they could have taken the White House the bloodshed of ordinary Russian civilians would have been too great. Learning of their failure to act, the GKChP members met at the Defence Ministry on 21 August to discuss their next move. They decided to send a delegation to Gorbachev in the Crimea to negotiate. With this decision the coup was effectively over. On their return from the Crimea they were arrested at the airport.

After the coup the very thing the coup leaders were trying to avoid was accelerated: on 24 August the Supreme Soviet of Ukraine declared its formal independence from the USSR and announced that a referendum would be held to ratify the move. In quick succession – all by the end of August 1991 – Moldova, Azerbaijan and Kyrgyzstan all declared their independence. Finally – and unbeknown to Gorbachev – on 8 December 1991 the leaders of the three 'Slav' nations within the remnants of the USSR (Boris Yeltsin, Leonid Kravchuk and Stanislav Shushkevich of the Russian Federation,

Ukraine and Belarus, respectively) met in Minsk. (The leaders of Kazakhstan and Uzbekistan had not been invited.) At this meeting it was decided to establish the Commonwealth of Independent States (CIS) consisting of the former republics of the USSR and to formally annul the 1922 treaty which established the USSR. The flag of the Soviet Union was lowered at the Kremlin for the last time on 25 December 1991, the same day that Gorbachev formally resigned as President of the USSR.

What's in a name (and a date)?

For those not steeped in Soviet history, the Bolshevik Party was founded and led primarily by Vladimir Ilyich Lenin (1870–1924, born V.I. Ulyanov). The name Bolshevik derives from a split in socialist forces inside the Marxist, Russian Social Democratic Labour Party (RSDLP) of pre-revolutionary Russia in 1903 when the Tsar still reigned supreme. The Bolsheviks were so called because when the forces of Russian socialism split, Lenin's faction was in the majority and the rival faction was in the minority. The Russian words for (man of the) majority and (man of the) minority are Bolshevik and Menshevik, the name given to the rival faction. The Bolshevik Party proper only emerged in 1912 when attempts at unity came to nothing.

Although the original split had been over issues such as who should or should not be considered a party member (in short, a core professional group of cadres versus a broad party-based membership), deeper divisions between the two rival groupings became more apparent only with the passing of time. In brief, one of the main differences concerned the mechanics of achieving socialism in Russia. The Mensheviks believed that for the new socialist dawn to arrive in Russia one needed to be patient. The need for patience arose, it was claimed, because Russia had not reached the right 'stage'. Karl Marx and Friedrich Engels, they went on, had shown in their theory of 'Historical Materialism' that human society had evolved through various stages – ancient slave societies, feudalism, capitalism – and then would come socialism's turn, building on the efforts of capitalism which had raised human society to a higher level compared to all previous 'isms'. Russia, they concluded, was still at the stage of feudalism personified by the Tsar.

True, nascent capitalism had started to develop in the major cities (see below) but the proletariat or working class was still in a minority with the bulk of the population still living on the land. Factory life gave the proletariat a collective consciousness, it was argued, which was lacking in the peasantry. Time was needed to allow capitalism to take root, build up industry and consequently the natural supporters of socialism – the working classes – would emerge in sufficient numbers. Then, and only then, could a successful onslaught against the prevailing order commence.

It followed that any revolutionary movement in Tsarist Russia would be characterised as *bourgeois-democratic*; it would be for the rising capitalist class within Russia to lead the way, establish a democratic framework within which socialist forces could operate and prepare for the future.[1]

In addition, to struggle for socialism now would be futile since the 'material conditions' for socialism did not exist. A successful assault on the ruling order would inevitably be derailed since even if such an assault was successful, then, to put it succinctly, if the working man and woman were in the running of society (what Marx had called the

16

dictatorship of the proletariat) they could not very well do that if they spent 12 hours a day at the factory bench, returning home exhausted, and having to feed themselves and their children before being expected to go out to attend meetings on running society. Let us allow capitalism to develop first, argued the Mensheviks; let us allow the rising capitalist class to build up the economic prosperity of the country – and, just as importantly – the cultural, social and educational levels of the workers, and then we can think about establishing a socialist order.

It may be a bit harsh but Lenin's view may be characterised as having taken a more direct view of the situation: let us overthrow the established order first and then worry about all of the above. In particular he believed that it was necessary to form a 'vanguard party' to lead the working class since, on their own, the working class at best would concentrate on trade unionism.[2] As Lenin put it himself in his pamphlet *What is to be Done?* written between 1901 and 1902:

> We have said that there could not have been Social Democratic consciousness among the workers. It would have to be brought to them from without. The history of all countries shows that the working class, exclusively by its own efforts, is able to develop only trade-union consciousness, i.e. the conviction that it is necessary to combine in unions, fight the employers, and strive to compel the government to pass necessary labour legislation, etc.[3]

The party was needed to focus the minds of the 'masses' on the struggle for political power.

In addition, Lenin, like Mao Zedong who was to follow in China later, had a more optimistic view of the peasantry, seeing their potential for revolutionary action. Unlike Mao, however, Lenin did not see them in the forefront of the struggle to overthrow Tsarism. True, in 1905 Lenin had put forward the slogan of the *Democratic Dictatorship of the Proletariat and the Peasantry* without fully explaining what this implied; and in 1917 the Bolshevik slogan of *Land, Bread, and Peace* was to encapsulate the desires of the three main disaffected sections of Tsarist society – the peasantry, the urban workers, and the soldiers at the front.[4]

Finally, Lenin justified a concerted attack on the citadels of Tsarist power by his belief that he was helping to break the weakest link in the chain in the European assortment of capitalist and semi-feudal regimes. Once Russia fell – ran the logic – then, domino like, more advanced capitalist countries such as Germany would follow. Workers inspired by events in Russia would follow the lead of the Russian workers. Once the isolation of the Russian Revolution was ended, Germany and other newly established socialist orders would come to the material aid of the new workers' state in Russia.

Developments in the Russian social democratic movement echoed developments in all major parties of social democracy throughout Europe at the end of the nineteenth and start of the twentieth centuries and, indeed, other parts of the world where parties of the Left had taken root. This evolution versus revolution debate is one that still continues to this day.

The irony is that initially the term social democratic was one which implied a belief, in part or in whole, in much of the writings of Karl Marx and Friedrich Engels. As this profound difference between the parties of the Left developed, in 1918 Lenin's Bolsheviks changed their party name to the Communist Party in order to distinguish themselves from what they saw as the 'revisionist' social democratic parties in Europe and beyond which had increasingly moved away, as Lenin saw it, from the true path.

The key turning point had been the outbreak of the First World War; it was this event that burst asunder the loose alliance of Left political parties. The Second International formed in Paris in 1889 was a collection of labour and socialist parties having replaced the dissolved First International of similar bodies.[5] This organisation had openly declared that they would resist the coming war in Europe and elsewhere by using their influence over the trade unions and workers in general to lead strikes that would stop what was seen as a war between imperialists. As it turned out, virtually all parties belonging to the Second International fell into line with their own respective governments, overcome as they were by a groundswell of nationalistic and patriotic fervour in each country. Each socialist party helped the war effort of their country to mobilise the population for war. As a result, in 1916 the organisation was dissolved.

In 1919, the victorious Bolsheviks formed the Communist International, an organisation of like-minded communist parties throughout the world to replace the defunct Second International. This organisation – at least initially – was dedicated to the worldwide overthrow of the capitalist system. With the rise of Stalin as the supreme ruler within the Soviet Union it became an arm of Soviet foreign policy.

The preceding description greatly simplifies the history and endless debates between the Left parties of pre-revolutionary Russia but hopefully captures the essence. However, one more view is worthy of note. Leon Trotsky (1879–1940) who led the first Russian Revolution in 1905 and with Lenin jointly led the Bolshevik Revolution of 1917, argued that the Menshevik position was 'formalistic' or 'mechanical'; it would be possible to 'skip stages of historical development' and proceed directly to socialism but only if the 'advanced capitalist countries' also have their own revolutions which could then 'come to the material aid' of the new workers' state within Russia.

Echoes of this idea may be found even today in development economics and the policies of emerging market governments as regards the processes by which developing nations should beat a trail to the promised land of modernity. Not, of course, in the sense of having socialist revolutions but of climbing up the value chain of modern manufacturing and not simply relying on the production of labour-intensive goods where the country has a comparative advantage through cheap labour.[6]

Returning to our discussion on which way forward for social democrats in Tsarist Russia, Trotsky, while disagreeing with the Mensheviks, did make a prophetic comment in relation to Lenin's idea of a vanguardist party if it were to lead the revolution. Inevitably a political party would substitute itself for the proletariat and in turn the ruling party body (the Central Committee) would substitute itself for the party; finally one individual would substitute himself for the Central Committee; the dictatorship of the proletariat would be replaced by the dictatorship of one person. Notwithstanding this prophecy, Trotsky eventually signed up with the Bolsheviks in the run-up to the 'Great October Revolution'.

The Bolshevik Revolution took place in November 1917 and established the Russian Soviet Socialist Republic which would comprise the largest component of the Union of Soviet Socialist Republics (USSR) formed in 1922.[7] The word soviet, used in the name USSR, meant 'workers' council'. (See Box 1.2, *What is a Soviet?* for a fuller explanation and description.) Workers' Councils were formed spontaneously in the first revolution in 1905 and then during 1917 whereby workers in factories would elect deputies to represent them at a council meeting of deputies from other workplaces within St Petersburg (then the capital of Russia). The peasantry and soldiers and sailors then fighting in the First World War followed suit. Other all-city soviets would be formed in Moscow and other major centres. These city soviets would in turn send representatives to higher regional bodies and ultimately to an all-country-wide soviet. The revolutionaries of 1905 and 1917 saw in them incipient workers' power which, naturally, would be led by the revolutionary vanguard given that the workers were not ready to govern.

Box 1.2

What is a Soviet?

Writing of the first Soviet established in 1905 during the first Russian Revolution, Leon Trotsky wrote:

> What was the Soviet of Workers' Deputies? The Soviet came into being as a response to the objective need – a need born of the course of events. It was an organisation which was authoritative and yet had no traditions; which could immediately involve a scattered mass of hundreds of thousands of people while having virtually no organisational machinery; which united the revolutionary currents within the proletariat; which was capable of initiative and spontaneous self-control – and most important of all, which could be brought out from the underground within twenty-four hours. . . . In order to have authority in the eyes of the masses on the very day it came into being, such an organisation had to be based on the broadest representation. How was this to be achieved? The answer came of its own accord. Since the production process was the sole link between the proletarian masses who, in the organisational sense, were still quite inexperienced, representation had to be adapted to the factories and plants.
>
> One delegate was elected for every 500 workers. Small industrial undertakings combined into groups for election purposes. The young trade unions also received representational rights. It must be said, however, that numerical norms were not observed too strictly; in some cases delegates represented only a hundred or two hundred workers, or even fewer.
>
> (L. Trotsky, 1905, Chapter 8)

And further,

> The first meeting was attended by a few dozen persons; by the second half of November the number of deputies had grown to 562, including 6 women. These persons represented 147 factories and plants, 34 workshops and 16 trade unions. The main mass of the deputies – 351 persons – belonged to the metalworkers; these played the decisive role in the Soviet. . . . The Executive Committee acted as the Soviet's ministry. It was formed on 17 October and consisted of 31 persons – 22 deputies and 9 representatives of parties. . . . What was the essential feature of this institution which within a short time assumed such an important place within the revolution and marked the period of its maximum power? The Soviet organised the working masses, directed the political strikes and demonstrations, armed the workers, and protected the workers against pogroms.
>
> (L. Trotsky, 1905, Chapter 22)

During the events in February 1917 when the Tsar abdicated, the phenomenon of Soviets – of not only workers but of peasants and soldiers – was established on the model of 1905. It should also not be assumed that Soviets, or workers' councils, are linked solely to communist or socialist revolution. For example, during the Hungarian Uprising of 1956 workers' councils had appeared by the third day of the uprising on 26 October. Peter Fryer, a reporter for the *Daily Worker* – a newspaper ironically of the British Communist Party – was at that time based in Hungary. Despite the hostile stance of the British Communist Party towards events unfolding in Hungary (his despatches were heavily edited), Mr Fryer maintained his journalistic integrity and reported from the provincial area of Gyor:

> The Town Hall (was) the seat of the Gyor national committee. The word 'national' was not intended to imply that this body arrogated to itself authority outside its own region; such committees called themselves indifferently 'national' or 'revolutionary'. In their spontaneous origin, in their composition, in their sense of responsibility, in their efficient organization of food supplies and civil order, in the restraint they exercised on the wild elements among the youth, in the wisdom with which so many of them handled the problem of Soviet troops, and, not least, in their striking resemblance to the workers, peasants, and soldiers councils which sprang up in Russia in the 1905 revolution and in February 1917, these committees, a network of which now extended over the whole of Hungary, were remarkably uniform. They were at once organs of insurrection – the coming together of delegates elected by factories, and universities, mines and army units – and organs of popular self-government which the armed people trusted.
>
> Of course, as in every real revolution 'from below' there was 'too much' talking, arguing, bickering, coming and going, forth, excitement, agitation, ferment. That is one side of the picture. The other is the emergence to leading positions of ordinary men, women, and youths, whom the AVH (Hungarian security service) domination had submerged. The revolution thrust them forward, aroused their civic pride and latent genius for organization, set them to work to build democracy out of the ruins of bureaucracy.[8]

Within the year 1917 itself there were two revolutions – the Bolshevik Revolution of which we have already spoken (although some historians would categorise it more as a putsch or coup) and the so-called February Revolution. The February Revolution was 'unplanned' in the sense of not being led like the October revolution which was initiated and led by the Bolsheviks. The revolutions themselves grew and were fostered by the consequences of the First World War and the disastrous outcome for Russia led by the Tsar. The main outcome of that uprising by workers, soldiers and the peasantry was the abdication of the Tsar and the formation of a provisional government led by Alexander Fyodorovich Kerensky (although he was the second prime minister of this government, history recalls his role and not that of the first).

Nicholas Alexandrovich Romanov, or simply Nicholas II, was the last Tsar of Russia and ruled Russia from 1894 until he abdicated on 5 March 1917. The reason for the abdication is not hard to fathom: almost three years of a disastrous war that had devastated the country leaving the populace ready for change; change that they were willing to take into their own hands. A war which had been entered into by the Tsar against the advice of advisers and where, despite approaches to grant constitutional reform by his uncle to 'head off' possible revolution, the Tsar had again refused, declaring that he had to uphold his coronation oath to keep autocratic power intact for his successors. With Petrograd in revolt, with public buildings being razed to the ground, and, crucially, with army regiments joining the protestors *en masse*, the Russian Duma (Parliament) formed a Provisional government which along with the city-wide Soviet called for his abdication.

When the October revolution took place it was Kerensky's government that was overthrown and the all-Russian Congress of Soviets of Workers', Soldiers' and Peasants' Deputies which assumed control. This body in turn created the Council of People's Commissars which in turn elected Lenin as chair (effectively head of state).

The Russian economy before and after the First World War

What then was the state of the Russian economy before war broke out, and what was its state after the war eventually came to an end? Before answering, it is worth re-emphasising why the question is important, since from the perspective of building the new socialist order, the stronger the economic base of the country, the better. Indeed Marx himself had envisaged that the prospects for constructing a new socialist order were best placed in countries such as Germany or Britain as the most advanced capitalist countries which would be able to provide the 'material foundations for socialism'. He had wrongly anticipated that revolution would break out and be successful in these countries first. The exact opposite was to occur with virtually all – if not all – countries which travelled down the road of communist revolution (and subsequently Soviet-style central planning) being economically backward.

In addition, most of these countries adopted the socialist system following major social, economic and political convulsions within their countries: Russia out of the ashes of both the First World War and the civil war which followed; the People's Republic of China founded in 1949 by Mao Zedong was the culmination of years of war against occupying Japanese forces and civil war with non-communist forces; the satellite states of the Soviet Union (East Germany, Bulgaria, Romania, Czechoslovakia, etc.) out of the turmoil and devastation of the Second World War; Vietnam, Cambodia and Laos out of the successive wars with various colonial powers from France to the US; and Cuba from the insurgency of Fidel Castro against General Batista.

The above may seem a political if not a historical point and so removed from a general discussion on the socialist economic system. However, all economic systems operate within an historical framework of social, political and cultural values. In describing the socialist economic system below, one needs to bear the above in mind when evaluating the achievements, or otherwise, of such a system.

At the same time it perhaps also begs the question why, where parliamentary democracy of one sort or another has operated or operates, sufficient support from the electorate has not been garnered to move in the direction of economic planning on the scale which we describe below. A major theme of this chapter is that the answer lies in the failure of extensive socialist economic planning which, ultimately, was due to the *inherent* features of planning rather than the manner of birth of the regimes that attempted the planning of their economies or indeed their low economic and cultural starting points among the populations they ruled. Such adverse beginnings may make any achievements all the more worthy given the backdrop of so many inauspicious starts, but the ultimate downfall of socialist planning is in the *nature* of the system and not its beginnings.

Returning to the Russian economy before the outbreak of war we present Table 1.1 which shows the relative strengths of the major world powers from 1860 to 1910, i.e. just four years before the outbreak of the First World War. In summary, it is not that industrialisation was completely absent from pre-First World War Russia; it was more that it lagged so far behind the other major powers. As may be seen from Table 1.1, only Japan comes in at a lower ranking than Russia.

One needs some care in interpreting these figures inasmuch as they could give the view that Russia pre-war was *exceedingly* backward. This was not the case. Industry was relatively modern using the latest techniques from Europe and the factories were well equipped to compete in their respective industries. The problem was more one of the unevenness of development and the scale of its development with much of these up-to-date factories being located in St Petersburg, Moscow, Ukraine, and that part of Poland under Russian rule.

Nevertheless, the figures in Table 1.1 encapsulate the problems for a Tsarist state entering into a major European war against a country like Germany. Using a boxing analogy it would be like pairing a lightweight against a heavyweight. It was not that the lightweight could not box but the match would be uneven with a predictable outcome. With the onset of war (and with historical hindsight) if any country was going to buckle it was Russia, the weakest link in Europe.

In addition to the above, the limited development that had occurred within Tsarist Russia up until the outbreak of the First World War was heavily dependent on the penetration of the Russian economy by foreign capital. This was in the form of direct investment in new factories and loans to business and the Russian government and/or part ownership of firms through share acquisition. Figures quoted by Nove (1986a) suggest that in 1900 28.5 per cent of the

Table 1.1 Relative industrial progress of world powers, 1860–1910

	Raw cotton (kg per head)		Pig iron (kg per head)		Railways[a]		Coal (kg per head)		Steam power (h.p. per 1,000 persons)		Ranking list	
	1860	1910	1860	1910	1860	1910	1860	1910	1860	1910[b]	1860	1910
Germany	1.4	6.8	14	200	21	75	400	3190	5	110/130	6	4/5
Belgium	2.9	9.4	69	250	30	102	1310	3270	21	150	2/3	3
Spain	1.4	4.4	3	21	6	58		330		4	8	8
USA	5.8	12.7	25	270	19	122	420	4580	25	150/180	2/3	1
France	2.7	6.0	25	100	18	87	390	1450	5	73	5	6
Italy	0.2	5.4	2	8	6	38	–	270	–	14/46	9/10	9
Japan	–	4.9	–	5	–	14	–	230	–	7/10	11	11
UK	15.1	19.8	130	210	44	69	2450	4040	24	220/240	1	2
Russia	0.5	3.0	5	31	1	24	–	300	1	–/16	9/10	10
Sweden	1.5	3.6	47	110	3	76	90	910	–	55/150	7	7
Switzerland	5.3	6.3	–	–	28	88	–	–	–	85/190	4	4/5

Source: Bairoch (1965) Annales (Paris), November–December. Cited in Nove (1986a).

Notes
a Total length related to population and area;
b The higher figure includes other forms of power – indicates negligible or data not available. All data on a per capita basis.

capital of private companies was foreign owned and in 1913 about 33 per cent. 'During these years foreign capital invested in Russia increased by 85 per cent, while Russian capital increased by 60 per cent.'

The above is important, since profits made in roubles had to be converted into foreign currencies – be it deutschmarks, pounds, francs, etc. – so that the foreign owners of Russian capital could repatriate their profits back to their native countries. In addition, foreign loans taken out by private businesses and the Russian government alike had to pay interest to the foreign banks which had lent the money. This interest also had to be converted into foreign currency. The only way to do this was to ensure that Russia ran a visible trade surplus, i.e. that its exports of goods exceeded its imports. These days in most of the OECD countries one would think of such a surplus in terms of manufactured goods or, indeed, of services. In Tsarist Russia the surplus came about predominantly through the export of agricultural produce. This produce, which the peasantry would have liked to have consumed themselves or sold in local markets for their *own* profit, was made available through taxation; the government of the day taxed the peasants and in order to pay the taxes the peasantry had to sell the agricultural surpluses to generate the cash needed to pay the taxes.

How to boost agricultural production?

The shock of the 1905 revolution in Tsarist Russia eventually convinced the Tsar that reforms should be made to widen the social base of the regime which coincidentally in doing so could also help boost agriculture. Between 1906 and 1911 a series of reforms were initiated by one of the Tsar's more able Ministers – P. A. Stolypin (himself assassinated in 1911). He pushed through, against opposition from conservative elements, measures which would allow the peasantry much greater freedom of movement within the country along with the right to buy and sell the land that they worked. Previously the peasant had not been allowed to leave his or her village without approval. With that approval no longer needed, some two million households left their respective communities and set up private farms. The object of the reforms was to set in motion the formation of a conservative layer within society that would support Tsarism. This had some of its greatest effect in Ukraine where the rise of a prosperous group of peasants known as kulaks was far more pronounced compared to elsewhere in Russia; the divide between landless peasants hungry for land also stood in sharper relief. While the revolutionary movements of 1917 cut across this gradual process of social strata development, that a new social strata was forming which could and would be more supportive of the status quo is shown by a remark of Lenin in 1919. Speaking to a British visitor and observer to the country about the civil war flaring in Russia at that time, Lenin remarked that the civil war was 'likely to be more bitter in the Ukraine than elsewhere, because there the instinct of property has been further developed in the peasantry and the minority and the majority will be more equal' (Ransome 1919, quoted in Carr 1984).

As in many other countries before it and after, the Russian government under the Tsar had consciously embarked on a programme of industrialisation which would be paid for through the toil of the peasantry of the land. The implication was (and allowing for some generalisation) that the surplus grain extracted from the peasantry could be used to pay for the import of foreign machinery to pave the way for the industrialisation of the country. In addition, if not directly as described above, then indirectly by allowing cheaper food for the 'masses' in the towns and cities such that costs could be kept down which in turn would allow exports to gain a foothold in foreign markets.

Later on the Soviet government essentially adopted the same policy towards the peasantry but pursued it using the blunt instrument of forced collectivisation. Many of those peasants who took advantage of the Stolypin reforms were to be labelled as kulaks and face deportation to Siberia. We will see that the peasantry under Soviet rule paid a heavy price for the country's industrialisation.

The emergence of planning via war communism and NEP

Many volumes have been written on Tsarist Russia, its downfall and the subsequent historical course of the Soviet Union.[9] Here we give the briefest of outlines and in particular we focus on how some of the historical events relate to the development of the socialist economic system that took form towards the end of the 1920s in the Soviet Union. This system would be adopted in its entirety in most of CEE after WWII and to a large degree in Mao's China.

In the 'prime' of Soviet economic planning the state planning organ Gosplan would be seen as the body which oversaw the development and implementation of the plan. However, in the early part of the revolution VSNKh (written often as *Vesenkha*) or the Supreme Council or Soviet of National Economy was the body responsible for directing economic affairs of the country.

Despite what might be thought, the Bolsheviks did not immediately set about placing industry after industry in state hands and launching into full-scale planning. As Carr (1984) notes:

> Extensive nationalization of industry was thus no part of the initial Bolshevik programme; and, though powers had been conferred on Vesenkha to 'confiscate, requisition or sequester', the first steps towards nationalization were halting and diffident. The nationalization of industry was treated at the outset not as a desirable end in itself but as a response to special conditions, usually some misdemeanour of the employers; and it was applied exclusively to individual factories, not to industries as a whole, *so that any element of planning was quite absent from these initial measures.* [emphasis added]

Apart from the 'misdemeanours' of employers, spontaneous nationalisations from below took place as workers seized factories and workplaces or local Soviets gave instructions for workplaces to be taken over. These spontaneous local nationalisations accounted for about two-thirds of all nationalisations up until June 1918 when only 487 enterprises had been taken over (Nove 1986a).

In the first year of the revolution, the Bolsheviks were grappling for a coherent industrial policy, often as not spurred on by events around them rather than them controlling events from the centre. Serious thought – if transitory – for example, was given to the notion of leaving the capitalist owners in control and management of their enterprises with the state playing only a supervisory role.

While this notion of state capitalism was eventually laid to rest it was not a fanciful one. A proposal by Meshchersky, an important iron and steel magnate, was discussed by Vesenkha who agreed to negotiate on the basis of his proposal. His proposal amounted to him owning 50 per cent of the shares and the state the remainder; he would manage the concerns on behalf of the partnership. In a further case, Carr (1984) reports that another industrialist by the name of Stakheev suggested that the iron and steel industry in the Urals be owned through share ownership with the state having 40 per cent, himself 40 per cent and an American capitalist 20 per cent; alternatively, he proposed, the state could have 100 per cent ownership and his group would manage the trust on behalf of the state.

The wholesale nationalisation of factories can, however, be dated from 28 June 1918 when a decree was issued taking into state ownership all important branches of industry.[10] Even then, while Vesenkha had responsibility to organise the nationalised industries, instructions were issued to the effect that 'individual enterprises would be regarded as leased rent-free to their former owners, who would continue to finance them and to draw revenue from them; and directors and staff were forbidden under penalties to abandon their posts' (Carr 1984). These last instructions surely tell us that the idea of a command economy would seem to be many years away.

In the initial phase immediately after the Bolsheviks had seized power, Vesenkha was primarily concerned with reconstruction given the devastation of the war period. For example, a detailed plan for the restoration of the railway network was established. Originally intended to be completed over a five-year period, the task was accomplished over a three-and-a-half-year period. While this project can in no way be compared to the 'integrated' five-year plans that were to come later, its success was to raise the popularity of planning within Communist Party circles.

Indeed, when Vesenkha was established in 1918, it spoke of being responsible for 'public works' and not about developing any kind of plan. The most well-known public works – and one with which Lenin himself had almost an infatuation – was the electrification of Russia, and Russian industry in particular. Known as Goelro, this commission established in February 1920 drew up detailed plans for the establishment of power stations in various localities throughout the country. For Lenin, 'Communism is Soviet power, plus electrification of the whole country'.

However, with the commencement of the civil war in 1918, Vesenkha's attention turned to one of exclusively supplying the necessary war materials for the Red Army to the exclusion of all else. It would not be until the civil war had been won by the Bolsheviks that attention could once more turn to the issue of planning.

However, the proposal for a form of 'State Capitalism' ultimately was not taken forward, and far from simply carrying out public works many within the now renamed Communist Party thought it was going to be possible to dive straight into a form of communism during the civil war period. What then caused this apparent about-turn whereby serious consideration is given to working with employers to one where they, the employers, are 'airbrushed' from Soviet society?

The conquest of power by the Bolsheviks in 1917 did not mean the end of the struggle of which party would rule the country but only its beginning. By the summer of 1918 full-scale civil war was raging across Russia. The Bolsheviks created the Red Army from virtually nothing and the 'counter-revolutionaries' or 'patriotic forces', termed the Whites or White Army, took up the struggle against the Bolshevik forces assisted by the international intervention of allied powers.[11]

The period in Russian history during the early part of the revolution that is connected with the volte-face in economic policy of June 1918 is known as war communism. This period was to play a formative role in the evolution of economic planning within the Soviet Union, from the perspective of illustrating to the leadership of the country that they needed to learn to walk before they could run. The walking stage would come about with a New Economic Policy

(NEP) which would officially bring a halt to the war communism period; the running stage would be Stalin's forced industrialisation, and the first five-year plan commencing in 1929.

In some respects war communism had *similarities* to the transformation that took place in the new Russia in the early to mid-1990s. Both periods were times when market relations either collapsed (under war communism) or could not establish themselves on a solid footing (in the early to mid-1990s at the start of transition); in many cases both periods saw money cease to play a role in economic relations between firms; both periods also saw large sections of workers paid in kind instead of in cash; barter in both periods was also common; and while war communism would see widespread nationalisations, the *exact opposite* was to occur in a relative few years with sweeping privatisations under President Yeltsin. While there was no civil war in Russia proper – although in other parts of the FSU that was not the case – at the start of transition it came close with the attempted coup d'état of 1991.[12] This absence of proper or normal market relations was to have an impact on how economic actors conducted commercial relations and from these respective periods new economic and political relations would emerge.

It would be wrong to overplay the similarities between the two periods but equally it would also be wrong not to highlight what appears to be a common response among economic agents during times of severe economic rupture – to impose their theoretical view of how the world *should* look onto how the world actually is. In the 1920s some – indeed many – within the Communist Party thought it would be possible to jump straight to a classless society without the 'material foundations' of which Marx had spoken. In the early 1990s some would argue (see Chapter 9) that it was possible to jump to the theoretical foundations of a 'pure market economy' without the need to build the institutional framework that accompanies market economies.

What then was war communism? Following Nove (1986a) we can usefully summarise war communism as:

- The partial elimination of money from everyday transactions and the use of payment in kind, where possible, instead of wages.

    In part this was due to the collapse of the currency with much of state expenditure being financed by printing money (in the early to mid-1990s the Russian government would also attempt to finance state expenditure through the printing presses leading to large-scale inflation). As money lost its value, and given that many enterprises under state control were exchanging with one another, the call went out that firms should not make payments but simply enter such exchanges into 'the books' as a mere accountancy device. Increasingly, communal services were being provided free of charge – postal services, transport, housing and so on. By 1919 to 1920 wages for workers had by and large been eliminated, and workers received payment in kind.

- Sweeping nationalisation of virtually all of industry; a ban on private manufacture; with state allocation of output mainly for war purposes.

    As mentioned above, in June 1918 there were only 487 nationalised enterprises; at the end of June a decree was issued taking virtually all factories into public ownership. Often this nationalisation was more real than apparent:

> Thus VSNKh claimed that on 1 November 1920 there were 4,420 nationalized enterprises, while another source made it 4,547. Yet in August 1920 an industrial census counted over 37,000 nationalized enterprises. Of these, however, over 5,000

employed one worker only. Many of these 'enterprises' were, apparently windmills! This illustrates the fantastic extremes to which nationalization was pushed in 1919–20, despite the clear impracticality of such action.

(Nove 1986a)

- A ban on private trade which was never completely successful.

Speculators appeared, trading in grain and other foodstuffs that came through official channels varying anywhere between 20 and 30 per cent of the total sold. In other words the vast bulk was still being bought and sold through unofficial private trading activities.

- The seizure of peasant 'surpluses' of food.

With the near collapse of industry the Communist government had virtually nothing to trade with the peasants in exchange for their grain and other harvested products. And yet those who remained in the cities needed to be fed; the Red Army needed to be supplied. Requisitioning of peasant grain began under the name of *prodrazverstka* and, while it lasted, peasants as a natural reaction could see no point in sowing extensively if at the end of the harvest the products of their labour would be requisitioned. As agricultural output fell so it became more and more difficult to find surpluses.

At this point a thought may occur to the reader as to why the civil war was won by the 'Reds' and not the 'Whites' given the requisitioning that took place. Just as Mao, later in China, would need the support of the peasantry to win his civil war against the Chinese Nationalists, so the Communist Party would need at the very least the passive if not the active support of the Russian peasantry. Forced collectivisation of the peasantry was still a good ten years or more into the future. The Communist Party still – on the surface – stood for distribution of land to the peasantry. The Whites, on the other hand, were trying to restore the old order:

> Yet in the end fear of a return of the landlords kept enough peasants loyal to the Bolshevik cause to ensure their ultimate victory in the civil war. For in most 'white' areas the landlords did come back, and peasants who had seized their land were often punished.

(Nove 1986a)

With the White armies defeated, the tenuous glue that had held many peasants to the Communists dissolved completely. Riots became increasingly commonplace with more and more peasants turning to bare subsistence farming. Combined with the total inability of the state apparatus to administer the thousands of scattered tiny productive units, the end result was a collapsing economy. Extreme elements within the Communist Party had convinced themselves that the transition to 'real and actual' communism was a possibility and was being constructed. They, however, mistook emergency civil war measures for something more deep and profound. Eventually a halt was called and a new economic policy was announced. On 28 February 1921 the sailors of Kronstadt rose up in revolt against the government, a revolt generated by their conditions of service and linked in their demands for better treatment for the peasantry. Quickly suppressed, the rising was a shock, given that in the October revolution the Kronstadt sailors had been at the forefront supporting the Bolsheviks. Seeing the writing on the wall that if change was not implemented the regime was finished, Lenin agreed to initiate a New Economic Policy, a period which is known as the NEP period, and which was the opposite of war communism: private trade was now encouraged and the peasantry were allowed to sell their surpluses on the open market. This was a recognition that war communism had failed to deliver the increases in production needed to trade openly (and fairly) with the peasantry (although from the perspective of winning the civil war it *had* been successful). *The significance of this period for planning is that it postponed indefinitely any talk of grand detailed economic plans for the economy.*

March 1921 was the decisive moment when the retreat was announced: *prodrazverstka* was replaced by a tax in kind and set at a level that would imply a substantial reduction on the previous year's forced requisitioning. A year later, with inflation brought under control, the tax in kind was replaced by a monetary tax. After payment of the tax, the peasantry were free to dispose of their surplus as they saw fit. Nepmen, as they were called, flourished given that the peasants themselves could not and did not transport grain to potential markets many kilometres away, middle men were necessary and private trade had resumed. By September 1923, some 75 per cent of all retail trade was in private hands.

Even within industry a retreat of sorts was announced. Large-scale industry would remain in the hands of the state, with the vast majority of those in manufacturing and mining still working for the state, but the wholesale nationalisation of the petty producer was seen to have been a mistake. The decisive date for this was 17 May 1921 when the decree nationalising all small-scale production was annulled. Handicraft production and even light industrial production that did not involve more than 10 to 20 workers would be allowed through leasing. In early 1922, some 10,000 productive units had been leased on the basis of two to five years for the payment of between 10 and 15 per cent of the annual output. As before, many of these units were windmills, but according to Nove (1986a), '3,800 were appreciable enterprises, employing fifteen to twenty persons, and fifty per cent of the lessees were private individuals, some of them former owners'. Seventy-six enterprises were actually returned to their former owners, and in 1924 to 1925 there existed 18 private enterprises employing between 200 and 1,000 workers. Wages were paid to workers again and services were charged for. The NEP policy reached its high point in 1925 with both agricultural and industrial output recovering strongly. But NEP was a retreat, not a commitment to free market capitalism.

While the NEP period had achieved its purpose in stemming the collapse of the economy, both industrial and agricultural, it had not resolved the fundamental weaknesses of the economy. With industry, especially heavy industry, stagnating and unemployment rising, the relations between urban and rural were once more under threat as prices for industrial goods rose and prices for agricultural products fell. This was the so-called 'scissors crisis' of 1923 and was to reignite discussion within Party circles on planning the economy. With calls at the Party congress in January 1924 for Gosplan to draw up a general economic plan, by October 1925 Gosplan had drawn up a base calculation of the situation within the Russian economy upon which to forward-build a plan. This base led eventually in May 1929 to the formal approval of a five-year plan and its introduction.

But what do we mean by a plan? Karl Marx had much to say in his many critiques of capitalism, but he had said very little about how the new socialist society was to be constructed. The Bolsheviks themselves, along with the Mensheviks and the party of the peasantry, the Social Revolutionaries, had themselves very little definitive idea in what direction to head. Under two different conceptions,

> a plan was a broadly defined long-term economic policy, and the main essential of planning was a central organ responsible for the formation of general economic policy (the 'plan') and for the direction of the commissariats engaged in the day-to-day execution of economic policy. According to the second conception, a plan was

a project or a series of projects which, while designed in a general way to promote increased productivity and a revival of the national economy as a whole, contained specific and detailed proposals for stated work to be carried out in stated quantities within a given period.

(Carr 1984)

Under the first conception the proposals from Meshchersky and Stakheev would have been entirely tenable. Not so under the second conception which was to ultimately triumph under Stalin (and, in passing, although we jump ahead of ourselves by several chapters, one could argue that the Chinese government has moved from conception two to conception one). Lenin's pet favourite headed by the Goelro commission would also fall under the first conception. Indeed, Lenin had been quite dismissive of those who had argued in the early 1920s for the formation of a general economic plan that would encompass the whole economy, referring to any idea of a general economic plan other than Goelro as 'ignorant conceit' (Carr 1984).[13]

Lenin, who died on 21 January 1924, had in reality been out of the leadership for some time due to a series of strokes. His third stroke on 9 March 1923 prevented him completely from returning to any involvement in affairs of state until his death. As a result Lenin's opposition to any *immediate* detailed plan, or even the preparation of such a plan, was removed.

The essence of the socialist economic system[14]

With the fall of the Berlin wall and the collapse of the Soviet Union, the economic rationale of communism was laid wide open for inspection; it was not a pretty sight. While some have sought to blame the poor workings of the economy on the lack of democracy (and it certainly did not help the situation), more fundamental reasons for the economic decline of the Soviet Union are explored which would confront even a democratically elected socialist government wishing to have a fully fledged socialist economy.

Box 1.3

Shopping in Russia in the early 1990s

As a mature undergraduate student of economics travelling to St Petersburg, Russia as part of a joint exchange programme between my home university and the partner institution in Russia, the year was 1994 and it was around two years since the collapse of the Soviet Union. Things were changing, but very slowly. In particular the retail sector remained almost the same as it had been in Soviet times.

The experience of shopping for food every other day or so was especially challenging. This would involve queuing three times in a shop to get what you needed. Why three times? Well, first you would queue at one counter to tell the 'assistant' what you required as all goods were kept behind counters; if it was cheese, say, it would be weighed and you would be handed a slip of paper on which was written the cost of the said item. You then joined queue number two where you waited patiently to pay the

---

cost of the item to the cashier, who then provided you with another slip of paper to confirm that payment had been made. You finally joined the original queue, or perhaps another, different queue, where once at the front you handed your receipt over and received your goods which had been packaged and were awaiting your return. God forbid you should suddenly recall that you also needed milk and butter! Then the whole process would have to be repeated. Of course, leaving to one side the inconveniences to the foreigner, it was the inconveniences placed on the Soviet consumer in terms of time lost, not to mention the poor quality and lack of assortment that was the main concern.

The above is a classic example of the customer–producer, or in this case the customer–retailer, relationship being seen through the eyes first and foremost of the retailer/producer; you – as the customer – were there to make life easy for the producer and not the other way around. The division of labour taken to extremes here made it easier for the manager to control his or her staff and security of cash takings but did nothing for your poor legs or the time you had at your disposal. Giving your staff flexibility to do many things – weigh, package, take money and hand out receipts all performed by one person – would have involved risk, and indeed extra training and supervision, so it was better to avoid it. This small episode mirrors the 'logic' of central planning – what will make it easier for the planners to decide on what, when, where and for whom goods should be produced is paramount, and the consumers, well, they came in at a poor second, if that.

For those who are interested in exploring the following material in depth two classic books in this area are *The Socialist System – the political economy of communism* by János Kornai and *The Soviet Economic System* by Alec Nove. We will not reinvent the wheel here and reproduce in detail what these two excellent books have already captured in terms of the detailed workings of the economy under socialism. We will, however, give its essential features and explore some of the inherent contradictions within that system. A first approach to these essential features may be found in Box 1.3, *Shopping in Russia in the early 1990s*.

The economic workings of the system under communism go under several names, most of which are used interdependently. Thus we have the centrally planned economy; the command economy; the socialist economy; the administrative economy; and the communist economy. Our preference is to use either the expression 'centrally planned economy' or 'command economy'. Yes, the proponents of this system saw themselves as socialists or communists. However, such are the multi-varied strands of socialist thought that ministers in a Labour government in the United Kingdom, for example, can announce that they have socialist economic policies but such policies are and were several ideologies removed from those conducted under Soviet-style socialism.

Even the use of a centrally planned economy may cause confusion, since one can look at the development of many successful free market-based economies in Asia and South-East Asia (e.g. Singapore, South Korea, Japan, Hong Kong) which although closest in many respects to an introductory textbook model of free market capitalism, nevertheless may arguably have arrived at the place that they did only through much government *indicative planning*.[15] This indicative planning should not be confused with Soviet-style central planning.

With indicative planning, a government might set central targets for the development of this or that sector (e.g. electronics, car manufacturing) but the means of producing cars or electronic consumer goods lay in the hands of private firms. Governments did not direct resources, as they did under Soviet-style central planning, but they did *enable* resources in the form, for example, of preferential cheap credit to favoured sectors or reduced planning legislation to enable the development of factories to proceed without hindrance. Even under the most extreme *laissez-faire* regimes the claim that government was detached from the economy was always more apparent than real.[16]

In addition, it is worth making the distinction as regards planning that goes on *within* companies in market economies as opposed to planning that took place *between* enterprises under the Soviet-style central planning albeit planning directed to these companies from above. All companies in a market system plan. This planning, of course, is related to surviving in the market through, for example, conducting research and development to develop new or existing products; or carrying out market research to see to what extent there is a demand for a product that the firm believes it can sell; the planning of personnel development to ensure that employees are as fully trained as possible in the latest techniques of production or in standards of service and so on. It is, in short, about surviving the competition within the market to ensure your business does not go bankrupt. The planning between companies à la Soviet central planning is the conscious desire to *avoid* competition in the mistaken belief that such circumnavigation of market competition – and the anarchy of the market – will be superior in terms of output performance and consequently in raising living standards.

So if we had to list the distinctive features of Soviet-style central planning, what would they be?

- Underpinning the more overtly economic points listed below is the monopoly on political power enjoyed by the Communist Party in all Soviet-style command economies: a party system with a fusion or symbiosis between party and state, and between politics and economics (that is, between government and business). 'Elections' of sorts are held but with no real competition between the candidates. Turnout to the polls is usually a remarkable 98 or 99 per cent.
- Private property of the wealth-generating resources within society is in state hands and not in private hands. Thus a toothbrush can still belong to the individual but the machine which produces the toothbrush belongs to the state.
- There are no markets for goods and services or for factors such as labour and capital. Like most of the bullet points listed here this is a slight exaggeration. In particular see the chapter on labour under the socialist system (Chapter 8), where it is pointed out that the hire of labour under central planning had *elements* of market behaviour.
- The price of a good or service, not being determined by a market, is no longer able to act as a signal as to what should be produced, how it should be produced, or for whom it should be produced.
- A centralised bureaucracy determines the answers to the above questions by establishing a 'plan of production' and then proceeds through lower level bureaucracies down to the state-owned enterprise to direct all material resources, both animate and inanimate. See the more extensive notes below on the inherent contradictions of this. This, combined with the 'Party Machine', can seriously stifle innovation and initiative at all levels of the economy and society.

- International trade still takes place under a command economy but it is (1) mainly between other command economies and, in the case of the FSU and the other command economies of CEE, dominated by the needs of the Soviet economy at the expense of the Central and Eastern European peoples (notwithstanding market prices for energy *below* world market levels that the USSR charged its satellite neighbours; more on this below); and (2) trade between command economies and the Western capitalist powers is drastically reduced. New technological advances incorporated in new goods and machinery is banned by Western powers from being exported to the East. Trade that did develop often had a barter flavour to it.[17]

  The main forum through which trade was conducted between countries of the Soviet bloc was through the Council for Mutual Economic Assistance (CMEA), or Comecon. Set up in January 1949 it may be seen as the alternative to the European Community (EC), forerunner to the European Union (EU). Whereas the EC and EU was and is a 'club' of equals (with some member states punching heavier than others), Comecon was definitely a one-sided affair. Famously, or infamously, two ministers of foreign trade from Bulgaria and Czechoslovakia were executed for bargaining too hard over trade issues with the Soviet Union.

  The Soviet Union did extend financial aid to the newly established People's Republic of China in 1949 when under Mao Zedong the Chinese Communist Party (CCP) took power. A $300 million credit at 1 per cent interest was granted in February 1950 (presumably to spend on imports from Comecon). Specialists from the Soviet Union of all hues – planners, engineers, electricians, etc. – also descended on China to help set up China's first five-year plan. Mutual assistance in this came to an abrupt halt when Khrushchev (the Soviet Communist General Secretary and so effective ruler) and Mao had a fallout.

- Money, to an extent, loses its function as a way of signalling preferences among consumers and acts more as a unit of account. That is, while money may be used freely in exchange for goods and services it is only for those goods and services produced under the plan. The planned output may (but often did not) coincide with the spending desires of Soviet consumers. For a brief time from 1919 to about 1921 money actually lost all of its traditional role.

- Linked in with the above, a monobank is developed whereby one bank is responsible for all financially related matters although still subsumed within the general economic plan. While it may have appeared that there were several different banks – the Construction Bank; an agricultural bank – these are in reality under the direct control of the Central Bank. While the monobank does have responsibility for issuing currency, it is also – through its subsidiary banks which it controls – responsible for issuing credits to the various branches of the economy. The importance and routine of banking under the socialist system was summed up by Lenin in 1918 (quoted in Kornai 1992) when he said,

  > A single state bank, the biggest of the big, with branches in every rural district, in every factory, will constitute as much as nine-tenths of the socialist apparatus. This will be country-wide book-keeping, country-wide accounting of the production and distribution of goods.

In addition to these points, which may be seen as being pervasive among all Soviet-style regimes from Cuba through to the People's Republic of China, there were features which were priorities of the leadership of these regimes and so skewed the development of the economy in particular directions. In particular:

• The rapid industrialisation of the country with priority given to heavy industry over the consumer sector. This was exemplified by Nikita Khrushchev's slogan, 'To catch up and overtake the West'. This stemmed from a fear among the leaders of many of these countries of 'capitalist encirclement'; a poorly developed socialist economy was also a weak one militarily. For many of them the invasion of the Soviet Union by Nazi Germany was fresh in their minds when their system and the country had come so close to collapse; for China, years of foreign intervention in the country was also ingrained in the psyche of the leadership. One can also point to other countries such as Vietnam and Cuba where essentially nationalistic movements to free the country of either foreign interference or corrupt dictatorships backed by Western powers were transformed into communist movements as they searched for alternative roads of development. Indeed, before Khrushchev there was also Stalin who prophetically (for him) announced at a party conference in 1931, 'To slacken the pace would mean to lag behind; and those who lag behind are beaten. We do not want to be beaten. . . . We are fifty or a hundred years behind the advanced countries. We must make good this lag in ten years.' Recall that this was ten years before Operation Barbarossa when Nazi Germany invaded the Soviet Union.
• The above desire or – as the leaderships of these countries would have seen it – the need to prioritise military development meant the consumer came a very poor second. In standard economics there is taught the production possibility frontier or production possibility curve. This curve shows the trade-off between different outputs within an economy – any economy, be it capitalist or socialist. Any diversion of land, labour and capital for military expansion implies contraction of production of goods and services for the consumer.
• Further, this expansion came about in large measure at the expense of the large rural populations of many of these countries. Investment – again under any type of regime – can only occur if consumption today is postponed in order to allow investment. This implies using the savings of the people. It would be good if this saving was voluntary but, if not, the state can intervene to ensure the savings are forced. Both the workers in the urban settlements and the peasantry in the countryside in the Soviet Union 'saved' to allow for rapid industrialisation and the buildup of the armed forces. That said, the peasantry tended to make the bigger (non-voluntary) sacrifices especially through forced collectivisation.

Planning – how to plan on one-sixth of the surface of the Earth?

The Soviet Union covered one-sixth of the planet's surface. It would appear that if there was a country that may be able to draw on internal resources to construct socialism then it would have been the former Soviet Union. The bedrock of economic planning that evolved under the Soviet Union was the five-year plan. It would, however, be a mistake to suppose that such an economic tool was up and running on the morrow of the Bolshevik Revolution. The section above on war communism and developments throughout the 1920s has shown how the classic Soviet style of planning 'evolved'. While power was seized by the Bolsheviks in 1917, the first attempt at 'conscious' planning of the economy took place in 1928.

Throughout the 1920s, debate raged within the Soviet Communist Party as to the correct way forward. Relatively speaking, the 1920s in Soviet Russia were a time of openness, relative, that is, to the 1930s and beyond. Stalin by the latter half of the 1920s was in control of the party machine but this did not prevent wide-ranging discussions and debates as to the way forward for the economy. The idea of the CPSU 'suffocating' all debate and dominating all organs of administration and decision making was, again, far from complete compared to later years. In particular Gosplan and VSNKh had within them experts who were former Mensheviks. As Nove (1986a) notes:

> Men like Groman, Bazrov and Ginzburg contributed significantly to policy debates. Ex-populists, ex-SRs, were active too, for example the famous economist Kondratiev, the agricultural experts Chayanov and Celintsev. Even non-socialists like Litoshenko and Kutler, could raise their voices. There was a one-party state, there was no legal means of organizing an opposition, but conditions were far from resembling the monolithic thirties. The communists were very weakly represented at this time amongst the planners. Thus in 1924, out of 527 employees of Gosplan, only forty-nine were party members and twenty-three of these were drivers, watchmen, typists, etc.

Most of the above names will mean very little to the reader in modern times. We include the quote to demonstrate that the adoption of a five-year plan did not fall all at once from the sky. The above is also important, as we will see, in the sense that with the complete suppression of any proper discussion from the early 1930s onward *within* the one-party state, the inherent weaknesses of central planning in the long run were exacerbated by the arbitrary decisions of Stalin at the top in the short run who, in ignoring advice from specialists, would make matters worse within the economy.[18] Later, such would be the terror inflicted on Soviet society that in effect no advice would be proffered that any specialist did not think Stalin didn't want to hear. Achievements from central planning – and these did exist – were made despite the role of individuals like Stalin and indeed those that followed him – a sweeping generalisation perhaps, but one with a large grain of truth within it. In Box 1.4, *How to (sort of) plan an economy using input-output analysis*, we outline an extremely simplified description of the technique used by planners to 'sort of' plan an economy.

Box 1.4

How to (sort of) plan an economy using input-output analysis

This section is inevitably a little harder than some of the main text. However, this (of necessity) simplified explanation of input-output methods for planning purposes should not be dismissed on the basis that it belongs to an archaic period of history with no relevance to today. Governments both at a national and regional level still use – to a degree – these methods to help them anticipate changes in the composition of their economies, the better to enable them to plan *indicatively* or prepare for changes in market economies that they can anticipate rather than simply reacting to them. Input-output analysis is a tool which may be used under both socialist planning *and* market economies. We begin with an excellent account from Montias (1959) to which the reader is recommended for a fairly non-technical, and hence accessible, description of the planning process.

> Material balances may be drawn up for short-run planning purposes (for a quarter of a year) or as the foundation for the long-run plans (five years and upwards). . . . Some six to eight months before the beginning of the plan-year, the planning commission prepared preliminary balances of essential materials, taking into account latest production figures as well as forecasts of productive capacity and labor force. Tentative targets ('control figures') based on these balances were handed down to the various industrial ministries, which subdivided them among their Chief Industrial Administrations (*glavki*). Each *glavk* in turn set specific targets for its subordinate enterprises, which were then expected to calculate the material products they would require to hit these production targets. The enterprise's material requirements, written up in formal applications (*zaiavki*), were transmitted to its *glavk* and eventually to the procurement organization of its ministry. The ministry finally turned over its procurement plan (covering the material requirements of all its enterprises) to the Council of Ministers and to *Gosplan*. Simultaneously with this process, ministries . . . drafted more detailed production plans, modifying and complementing the control figures they had previously received. These plans were also submitted to *Gosplan*, whose specialized industrial departments were now charged with preparing material balances for funded commodities on the basis of these latest production and procurement data. The process of concurrent adjustment of the supply and demand for each balanced commodity ended with the 'closing' of the material balance – when the sum total of allocations earmarked for various consuming groups matched the total supply from all sources planned for the year.
>
> . . . the material balances form an interlocking set which can be arranged as an input-output table. Coefficients are now calculated relating the amount of each material input needed for producing a unit of each of the different outputs and ordered as a square matrix with as many rows and columns as there are balances. Since the balances are all expressed in physical units (e.g. tons of steel, thousands of tractors), the coefficients are 'technological' (e.g. tons of coke per ton of pig iron).
>
> (Montias 1959)

As may be seen from the closing section of our quote from Montias, the input-output method developed by Leontief, named after the economist/mathematician who pioneered the technique, was modified by the Soviet planners but the essential elements of the technique remained. What was this technique? The input-output technique as used under planning tries to answer the question, 'What level of output should each industry within an economy produce so that it will just be enough to satisfy the demand for that product?' Recognising that the output of one industry will be the input into other industries (and even its own) we give the very simplified input-output in Table 1.A by way of demonstration where, unlike the planners, we make use of money in the interpretation of the table.

How to read Table 1.A? For row 2, column 2 of the so-called coefficient matrix we see the number 0.55. With prices in the economy given (i.e. the determination of prices is not the aim of the model and so we take the prices as determined elsewhere) and if we are interested in a euro's worth of output (or equally €100; €1,000; €100,000; €1 million, etc.) then the number 0.55 means we require 55 cents worth of construction goods – as an input – into the construction sector to produce €1 worth of construction goods. (Under Soviet central planning with their use of material balances it would have been so many tonnes of construction material to produce so many tonnes of construction goods.)

The number 0.55 and others like it are referred to as input coefficients. Each column, then, is adding up the value of all inputs needed to produce one (monetary) unit of that column output. (Or quantitative unit under the material balance approach.)

Note that if each sector did not require any of its own sector output then the diagonal coefficients would be equal to zero. In addition, the sum of the input coefficients added up in each column must be less than one. Why? Suppose that the sum of the construction coefficients instead of being $0.25 + 0.55 + 0.05$ which equals 0.85 is, instead, $0.35 + 0.65 + 0.15$ which equals 1.15. This would be telling us that in order to make €1 worth of construction goods, the value of inputs would be €1.15. That is, production would be destroying value! As we show in the main text, many economic sectors within the old Soviet Union towards the latter's end were doing just that – economic activity was, in many cases, not creating value but destroying it.

An open model contains an 'open sector' (for example, households which exogenously determine final demand for the purposes of consumption). True, economic sectors also consume but they consume for the purposes of further production. Final demand as understood here by households is consumption for gratification. Since 'someone' must pay the full value of output – here our €1 of construction goods – then all the factors that produce which include land, labour, capital and entrepreneurship must between them have the necessary €1. Land and capital are implicitly in the model. If we assume entrepreneurship is a specialised form of labour then labour is the only one not included. We instead assume, not unreasonably, that households supply labour. The payment for this labour is the sum of the coefficients in the column subtracted from one. That is,

$$€1 – €(0.25 + 0.55 + 0.05) = €0.15$$

For the other two sectors it is €0.55 and €0.60 for the capital goods sector and the agricultural sector respectively. By such recourse we can begin to see how a central planner could estimate the amount of physical currency necessary to be distributed in

Table 1.A A simplified, hypothetical example of an input-output table

	Outputs		
Inputs	*Capital goods*	*Construction*	*Agriculture*
Capital goods	0.20	0.25	0.15
Construction	0.15	0.55	0.05
Agriculture	0.10	0.05	0.20

the form of wages such that it was just sufficient to cover the stock of goods and services produced each year under the central plan. (In this pedagogical example we have started with a currency; the planner, however, could simply 'allocate' a price to each good to ensure the above.) Naturally, there was many a slip twixt cup and lip. Within market economies the inexactness of the method is not crucial since usually the policy maker is interested in a 'feel' for what is going on in order to assist in the formulation of policy. Not so under central planning where one bottleneck caused by the wrong quantities of good X being supplied to industry Y could then 'ripple' through the entire economy, creating multiple bottlenecks.

Now if the output of an industry, say, construction, is just going to be enough to meet the input requirements of the capital goods sector and the agricultural sector and the final demand in the open sector, i.e. the household sector which we call $d_{CapitalGoods}$, then the following equations must hold true:

$$CapitalGoods_{OutputRequirement} = 0.20(CapitalGoods_{InputRequirement}) +$$

$$0.25(Construction_{InputRequirement}) + 0.15(Agricultural_{InputRequirement}) + d_{CapitalGoods}$$

Similarly:

$$Construction_{OutputRequirement} = 0.15(CapitalGoods_{InputRequirement}) +$$

$$0.55(Construction_{InputRequirement}) + 0.05(Agricultural_{InputRequirement}) + d_{Construction}$$

$$Agriculture_{OutputRequirement} = 0.10(CapitalGoods_{InputRequirement}) +$$

$$0.05(Construction_{InputRequirement}) + 0.20(Agricultural_{InputRequirement}) + d_{Agriculture}$$

The above three equations can be rearranged such that final demand is on one side and all other variables are on the other. Writing them as a series of equations we have a set of equations that can be solved for the input requirements for each sector. Given that outputs will always equal inputs (in our model) we can drop the subscript of output/input requirement and write:

$$(1 - 0.2)(CapitalGoods) - 0.25(Construction) - 0.15(Agricultural) = d_{CapitalGoods}$$

$$- 0.15(CapitalGoods) + (1 - 0.55)(Construction) - 0.05(Agricultural) = d_{Construction}$$

$$- 0.10(CapitalGoods) - 0.05(Construction) + (1 - 0.20)(Agricultural) = d_{Agriculture}$$

The non-mathematical reader will be relieved that we do not pursue a matrix algebra solution explicitly but it may be shown that the above three equations can be written as:

Technology matrix	Output vector	Final demand vector

$$\begin{bmatrix} 0.8 & -0.25 & -0.15 \\ -0.15 & 0.45 & -0.05 \\ -0.10 & -0.05 & 0.80 \end{bmatrix} \times \begin{bmatrix} Capital\ Goods \\ Construction \\ Agriculture \end{bmatrix} = \begin{bmatrix} d_{CapitalGoods} \\ d_{Construction} \\ d_{Agriculture} \end{bmatrix}$$

The first matrix on the left-hand side is known as the *technology matrix*, so-called since the value of these coefficients will ultimately depend on the underlying technology available to an economy at any point in time. Using matrix algebra one can solve for the second matrix by pre-multiplying both sides of the equation by the *inverse* of the technology matrix.

If the central planners (or the development economists in an emerging market advising the government) have decided on a goal of final demand being such and such and given that labour remuneration as a *percentage share* has been worked out (in our example above our calculated coefficients were 0.55, 0.15, and 0.60) then the *total value* of the primary input needed (i.e. labour services) can be estimated. If such labour services are not available then the final demand goals of the central planner or developmental economist will need to be scaled back.[19]

On a connected note to planning the economy, it should be noted that the total value of all goods and services within a Soviet-style economy was not Gross Domestic Product (GDP) – the term used in market economies – but Net Material Product (NMP). NMP excluded the value of the 'non-productive' side of the economy, namely financial services such as insurance and retail banking, education, health care, housing, consumer services, public utilities (such as water), government services, and the social organisations such as residents' groups, and passenger transport. NMP took the value of all production costs at each stage of production and subtracted it from the value of all output at each stage of production; this was done only for the 'material production' sector.

In many respects Box 1.4 is misleading, not simply because it greatly simplifies the mathematics behind the input-output technique. It is misleading because it gives the impression of determination; of accuracy; of the ability to plan ahead in terms of the outputs and inputs needed from and to each sector of the economy down to so many decimal places.

When used in market economies the issues are not as relevant since the aims of using input-output techniques are not to plan the economy in the sense of what transpired under the Soviet Union but merely to come to a rough-and-ready understanding for the current potential of the economy such as to inform policy makers of what might or might not be feasible in the future.

The technique 'works best', that is to say, there are fewer complications for the practitioners of the technique – the planners – when one is purely interested in *quantitative* outcomes. What, however, of *new techniques* of production, *innovations* in how an economic activity is conducted? And, finally, what of the *quality* of production rather than simply the quantitative output measures?

The essence of the problem is that under market conditions entrepreneurs are rewarded through profit (See Appendix 1). The lure of profit, combined with sufficient competition in the marketplace (not always present), acts as the stimuli to encourage risk taking, innovation, the introduction of new products into the marketplace; in short, it pushes forward the economy to new heights, admittedly not always in a linear fashion, but over time in an upward direction. Under the Soviet economic system individuals – managers, directors, shop-floor workers – were rewarded for fulfilling output plans.

Stories are endless of factories producing substandard products which would be rejected by consumers under market conditions (where in general output is *demand led*) but under central planning Soviet-style (where output is determined by the preferences of the planners and so *supply led*) the central bureau of statistics can report another great victory for socialism as output has increased as per the latest five-year plan. Under central planning the needs of the consumer are not paramount, if they even figure at all. The factory manager's survival as a manager depends not on pleasing the end user of his product that he is responsible for producing, but on pleasing the higher echelons of this or that ministry and ultimately within the planning agency Gosplan based in Moscow.

As for the planners in Moscow, and planners at a regional level, the simplest way to make their lives easier was to keep producing more of the same. Having spent months if not years (in the early stages of planning) to devise the plan, the easiest thing to do was to scale up the existing plan 'from the achieved level'. The trouble was that over time the products produced may not have been what people now wanted; or the way in which the product was produced could perhaps have now been produced more efficiently in the sense of requiring less input, so freeing up land, labour and capital to other uses.

Under market conditions this freeing-up process can sometimes be quite brutal and takes the form of (mass) unemployment and unused capacity in factories, lower incomes for both employees and entrepreneurs and in some cases extreme deprivation, at which stage the role of government, of whatever colour, is to step in and ameliorate the worst excesses of the market by offering retraining, temporary unemployment benefits and so on.

Planners and heads of enterprises have, then, at least something in common in the sense of freezing the pattern of production. Why? Well to re-emphasise the point made above, enterprise directors were paid for fulfilling the targets set for them by the planners. Even where a keen employee brought to the attention of the director of the enterprise a new way of producing a product which could be more efficiently produced, this would take time to introduce on to the shop-floor; time to switch over to the new technique; time to train up the employees in how to carry out the technique; time to, perhaps, readjust the inputs from different suppliers who in turn may have to alter their processes of production and hence their inputs; time during which the end user of the current product (which may well be another enterprise and not simply a consumer) has its target disrupted; time, therefore, to acquire permission from both regional and central bureaucrats to go ahead with this innovation during which attention is taken away from the task at hand: meeting the target.

The above was reflected in the so-called *retirement rate* of equipment, buildings and general infrastructure. That is, a proportion of equipment, buildings, etc. were, each year, removed from 'active service' in the productive process. Within the USSR in the 1980s it was 2 to 3 per cent whereas in American manufacturing it was 4 to 5 per cent of all capital stock; and 3 to 4 per cent compared to 5 to 6 per cent in American manufacturing for machinery and equipment.

> Consequently, the major part of gross investment was used not to replace the retiring capital stock (since retirement was low), but to expand it. While in the US manufacturing 50–60% of all investment was replacing retirement, and only 40–50% contributed to the expansion of capital stock, in Soviet industry the proportion was reversed: replacing the retirement required about 30% of gross investment, while over 70% contributed to the expansion of the capital stock or to the unfinished construction.
>
> (Popov 2006)

Why is the above important? To give an exaggerated example, it would be like continuing to run a factory using steam-driven equipment side-by-side with electrified machinery in a factory next door. It is not that the steam-driven machinery could not still produce output, but labour, land and raw materials employed in such a process would not be fully or optimally utilised where it could be the most productive. This also helps to partially explain the labour shortage that existed in mature centrally planned economies; the 'natural' process in market economies would be that such land, labour and raw materials would be freed up to be utilised elsewhere in more profitable sections of the economy.

At best those enterprises which did not meet the targets lost bonuses to be distributed at all levels of the enterprise; at worst the director could be sacked and perhaps be sent to a labour camp depending on the importance of the sector of the economy in which the enterprise operated. Better to keep your head down and meet the target regardless of how it was met. Input-output techniques – what you will often see written as material balances as regards Soviet planning – are by nature conservative.

That said, there is another sense in which the planners and those charged with implementing the plan are at loggerheads. The Politburo of the CPSU set the overall political priorities for the Union.[20] It was then for the lower levels of the party and the administrative machinery of government to translate these political objectives into the realities of the plan. Given that the constant overarching objective was to 'catch up and surpass the Western capitalist powers' this meant growth at all costs and primarily growth of heavy industry. And yet the more successful the enterprise at a lower level was at meeting its target, the more it could expect its target to be increased the following year. (This is Berliner's ratchet effect. See Berliner's 'The Informal Organization of the Soviet Firm' in the *Quarterly Journal of Economics* (1952).) To be successful the enterprise had to run faster and faster so to speak. At each level of the planning and implementation process of the plan, each agent had an incentive to *bargain* with the agent above him- or herself in the chain of command by arguing that resources at his or her disposal were limited, while at the same time arguing with subordinates that they should work harder to meet the targets they had been given.

The above had consequences, one of which was the, at first, paradoxical situation of both hoarding of everything – labour, raw materials – at the enterprise level and the simultaneous shortage of such materials at a regional and national level in the eyes of the planners. Why should the enterprise manager hoard excess labour or excess raw materials? Dictators and authoritarian regimes can often have whims; they can change their minds at short notice as regards what they see as priorities. One of the many slogans of the early years of central planning was, '*Fulfil the five-year plan in four years*'. Just when you thought you were on course to meet your target outputs in the time that had been notified to you several years previously, your superiors went and lopped a year off the schedule! Just as well I stocked up over the last few years with extra employees and raw materials![21]

Open unemployment was eliminated very quickly within the Soviet Union (at a time when the West was suffering from the Great Depression). The system would increasingly attempt to draw other layers of society into the economy to meet its targets which helps explain why female employment and participation rates were so high in all centrally planned economies relative to market economies in the West.[22] This was the *extensive* use of resources – the drawing into economic activity of more and more labour, land and raw materials. As we have seen, this was easier than economising on the existing use of resources by a more *intensive* use of labour and capital by making them more efficient either through reorganising production or introducing new techniques into the production process.

While competition was absent under central planning, as we understand it in terms of market economies, competition existed of sorts – between ministries and indeed between regions within the Russian Soviet Socialist Republic and between union republics within the USSR for scarce resources.

Under the market mechanism resources flow to where they can generate the greatest return. Most of the time this coincides with the desires of the population; businesses demand land, labour and capital because ultimately there is demand for the products and services they sell: demand for land, labour and capital is a *derived* demand. When considering how scarce resources will be allocated, firms under market conditions will try to estimate (sometimes guestimate) a rate of return on each potential project factoring in risk and uncertainty where possible. The project with the greatest rate of return will be prioritised ahead of others.

Under central planning there is no market to act as a final arbiter of which enterprise projects should go ahead. Those ministries, regions or republics with the greatest 'pull' with the centre will see a consequent flow of resources their way. While corruption exists under market economies the scope under a command economy system for largess, bribes, graft, backhanders – call it what you will – is enormous, especially in the absence of any form of accountability through a genuine democratic process.

Indeed, the nature of the beast is that this form of corruption is passively encouraged through the need to establish unofficial channels with suppliers of the inputs that you need to feed into your enterprise. Sometimes this was done through the personal networks of individuals who worked in the enterprise. However, this job of acquiring needed resources turned into a specialised occupation; such a person who found the necessary inputs was known as a *tolkach*. In Russian 'The word means, literally, "pusher," which is also the term applied to the booster locomotive added to a long railroad train to increase its power. The supply expediter is sent out by the firm to "push" for its interests' (Berliner 1952).

Given the bottlenecks that did develop at all levels of the plan's implementation, good networks of suppliers at a local level could help overcome these bottlenecks. It was in your interests (as a director of several factories or a manager of an individual enterprise) to keep back so much output with which to barter with other enterprises that may have something that you *might* need in the future. Often – depending on who was in more desperate need – the bartering would also involve the low level or soft corruption of meals at fancy restaurants, tickets to the best shows in town steadily increasing from free passes to the enterprise's privately run sanatorium on the Black Sea coast to the actual handing over of large sums of money in order to expedite the unofficial transaction of supplies.

In the bargaining that would take place between all levels of the planning mechanism it was always in the interests of plant managers to downplay the capacity of their enterprise unit. This was due not just to anticipated bottlenecks but to the fact that bonuses or premia are based on the ratio of actual output to planned output. Management would always strive for a 'cushion' in agreed output targets or a safety factor called *strakhovka*, which translates as safety or insurance. As Berliner (1952) notes:

> The principal method of ensuring a safety factor in the procurement plan is to inflate the statements of material requirements (*zaiavki*) which are approved by the superior organ and become the basis of the procurement plan. As an accountant in a procurement department said: We always submitted our procurement plans 'with a little bit of fat' and the superior organ always returned them 'with the fat cut off.' In fact the fat is not always 'cut off,' and enterprises frequently succeed in obtaining

larger quantities of certain materials than the central planners would have permitted had they known.

It might be concluded that the system was inherently unstable in the sense of having a tendency to paralysis. It must be said this is with historical hindsight. This was not at all clear in the 1930s right through to the late 1960s. Only with the Brezhnev years did it become ever clearer that the system was seizing up and that 'something' would need to be done (the period of stagnation). Enter Mikhail Sergeyevich Gorbachev as President of the USSR and the last General Secretary of the CPSU. We leave a detailed account of Gorbachev's reform efforts until Chapter 9 when we contrast the transition process in both Russia and China from the perspective of a gradualist approach to transition and a fast-track approach also known as shock therapy. However, in short, Gorbachev's reforms failed to save the system – either economic or political. As Pomer (2001) puts it,

> Gorbachev was intent on revitilizing socialism by decentralizing the economy and introducing market forces. He stumbled, not because of gradualism per se or because of opposition within the Communist Party. Rather his hasty and inconsistent initiatives, along with his blind refusal to allow prices to be market-determined, resulted in an incompatible mix of government and market.

Many of the political abuses of the system of course were apparent for those who wished to see, and many of the follies of central planning were also present again for those who wished to see. One of those who experienced some of the follies of the economic system first hand at the tail-end of the regime was the Scottish baker Peter Ford. In Box 1.5, *How to make bread and money in St Petersburg, Russia*, we present a shortened edited version of an interview conducted with Mr Ford in the summer of 1996.

Box 1.5

How to make bread and money in St Petersburg, Russia

The Ford brothers – Peter and Jim – ran a medium-sized bakery in the Scottish town of Musselburgh before it relocated to the adjacent town of Prestonpans. As successful business people they were awarded a contract by the UK government in the early 1990s which in turn was acting on behalf of the then European Community. The five-year contract they were awarded was to lead a project in St Petersburg, Russia to work with a Russian bakery with the view to upgrading its abilities to produce modern bakery products at both high quality and high volume. The following is a highly shortened and edited account of an interview conducted by one of the authors with Peter Ford at the Ford Bakery, Prestonpans in the summer of 1996. A subsequent request to the Russian bakery in the autumn of 1996 for an interview was unfortunately declined.[23]

Author: How did you come to be operating in St Petersburg and what exactly was it that you were trying to do?

Peter Ford (*PF*): Through the UK government which in turn was acting on behalf of the European Community, we got the contract to give assistance to a bakery in St Petersburg. We had to put a package together and demonstrate to the UK government that we could meet the criteria that they had laid down for the successful firm here in the UK to work out there; that we could, for example, train them in Western ways – product manufacture, product development, accounting, marketing, etc. I'd say we mainly gave our partner management techniques plus we supplied lots of capital equipment. Moving from our base in Musselburgh had left us with some spare capital equipment which obviously helped. The contract itself was for a five-year period with an option to renew. However, with my brother looking to leave the family business we decided in April this year not to renew.

We were the first British company to be involved in a joint venture in St Petersburg. We thought we would go out and take a look, so to speak. This was at a time before Yeltsin and before the attempted coup. There was no traffic on the roads. You couldn't eat in restaurants; there were only about two in town where you could eat anything half decent. Our first contact was in October 1990 and we started trading August 1991 and finished up early this year.

Author: And what did you find, when you went out to take a look?

PF: Oh, the food industry was in a terrible state compared to what we would be used to here in the UK. My brother went out to start up the manufacturing side initially for eight weeks. Then we employed someone from Nottingham on a two-year contract who spoke the Russian language, had the cultural background and also had experience in running a bakery. He was there permanently on a two-year contract. He has since married a Russian and moved to Moscow. We effectively ended up with three firms – our own firm here in Scotland, the Russian partners and the actual joint-venture entity. I went over for a week at a time every quarter. I did the accountancy business side of things.

Author: And how did you operate initially with your Russian partners? How did you move things forward?

PF: We would set ourselves goals and targets; we will be targeting these hotels trying to break into this or that market. Understanding of business ethics was one of the major issues between us and the Russian side – this was a big problem. We were the ones taking the lead as you always get in a joint venture with one firm taking the lead. We would say, no this standard won't do, we want you to bake in this way, sell something in this fashion. They found this hard to deal with. Their accounting practices were alien to us and ours vice versa.

Both sides agreed at the start what each was going to put in. That said, the Russian side's contribution wasn't as great as ours. They refurbished a shop for the joint venture and, although on paper their contribution did not look too bad, you need to remember that the rouble–pound exchange rate at that time was about four to one and we were getting anywhere from 25 to 100 to one in the hotels. So in reality their financial contribution wasn't as great as it seemed on paper.

They were a bit slow on the uptake and yes, with hindsight, they were simply trying to bleed us dry for information that would benefit their own company.

Author: So was there a degree of mistrust?

PF: There wasn't a question of mistrust – more of a misunderstanding. We run a very slick operation here in Scotland, we don't have spare staff, we are very much hands on, and we don't suffer fools gladly. We were trying to apply that to people who had been in a regime for 70 years that didn't really put them under a great deal of pressure.

They wanted for a bakery a quarter the size of our bakery in Scotland three engineers and we have one engineer, and the guy is on call 24 hours, seven days a week. They wanted a full-time accountant which is a nonsense for a firm that size but apparently this was the norm at the time when they should have just called in an outside firm to audit the books. That said, we ended up meeting them half-way as you do with joint ventures.

We had to train the mother company with the true facts of how to run a business and we did that. It's now probably the most progressive bakery in St Petersburg if not Russia.

Author: So you had to keep on your toes to keep them on their toes so to speak?

PF: Absolutely. For example, hygiene practices in the food industry need to be of a very high standard. Some of the actions we saw were blatantly outrageous; for example, smoking, drinking, not wearing proper clothing, even painting machinery when production was taking place and so covering the product. Also some crazy ideas about staffing levels clearly not thinking about profits; they were more concerned about covering their backs to ensure that they could make the product. We got it cut down to a level where 12 people ran the place but they had wanted 24; that said the wage costs in our industry in the UK are about 30 per cent of turnover; over there it was about 12 per cent. At one stage our Russian partners wanted us to employ two people to look after a nuclear bunker.

Author: Excuse me?! What has a nuclear bunker got to do with a bakery? Isn't that a government responsibility?

PF: The bakery had a nuclear bunker in its grounds and it was the bakery's responsibility to look after it. We soon kicked that idea into touch!

Author: Are these practices a thing of the past now?

PF: They are gradually realising that full employment is not realistic. When we first arrived in 1990 they laughed when we made the suggestion that we should make some people redundant.

Author: They literally laughed, management that is?

PF: Yes. 'You don't do those sorts of things' they told us. They even brought in some local councillor to explain to us that in this country we have full employment and that we should transfer anyone we didn't want doing whatever to other duties. This is what we had to put up with.

Author: What was the existing skill level of the workers when you first got out there? You read that while the economy was in trouble, the workforce is highly educated and skilled.

PF: The skill level was appalling. How could it be otherwise if they didn't have the necessary equipment on which to train?

Author: How did you communicate? Through this manager mainly, the one you hired from Nottingham?

PF: The language wasn't a problem because we used superb English speakers – many had been employed by the KGB interpreting radio programmes coming from the UK and many even had an Oxford accent; some had worked in the tourist industry for the KGB to vet people as they came into the country. The going rate at that time for such skilled people was $10 per day.

Author: And did the joint venture become profitable?

PF: Well, we were helped initially by receiving £30,000 as part of the contract with the UK government which we got in two tranches. In four and a half trading years our project has been successful – I'd say we got our money back twice. We were making on average about 20 per cent net return each year on our investment. We consider that if we get 3 per cent in a bakery within the UK we'd be delighted. We were not going over there to make Russian products but to prove to them that Western products could be adapted for the Russian market. We introduced your traditional Scottish products: fruit buns, morning rolls, Scottish buns, doughnuts slabbered in chocolate, etc.[24] We were selling more iced buns in a day than we could sell back home in a month. We were successful in many ways because we took Scottish products and adapted them slightly to the Russian market; we didn't try and sell the existing products already on the market.

Author: And any difficulty in repatriating profits?

PF: No difficulty in repatriating profits. That said, each time we did transfer we were losing 7 per cent of the funds that we were transferring. Given the food industry runs on small margins this was quite a lot. You, of course, have just got to try and build these into costs; to allow padding so to speak. We had the added advantage of being in a joint venture which simplified things. For foreign firms operating on their own they needed to be registered with a Russian bank; prove to them they were a legit company before the bank would issue the necessary certificates; the money could then be sent to Moscow and there changed to dollars; from there it went, if I recall, to the Texas Oil Bank in Moscow who sent it to Texas and then from there back to the UK. These days we do it through Barclays and they send it straight back to the UK all in about four days.

Author: It sounds like it all went relatively smoothly. So doing business in Russia at that time was quite straightforward?

PF: Well, you have got to understand what was happening at the time in terms of all the changes in society. The mayor of St Petersburg at that time was Sobchak. I think he could see the way things were going with the country and he knew that the first priority is making sure people get fed. We met him on our first visit out there. He struck me as quite a far-seeing man although he seems to have lost his way a bit now. They had studied the changes that had taken place in Poland and Czechoslovakia and they knew that food was the priority. Everything else comes after that.

There was also this competition thing between St Petersburg and Moscow. I think Sobchak's personal backing for this project, of course, made life relatively easy for us and so we had access to the best banks and lawyers. But I think there was also an attempt to do better than Moscow. You also have to recall that because there had been such hype in the city about a foreign company coming over then we didn't need to do much marketing. We were like show dogs; everyone wanted to meet us so you had to watch your Ps and Qs. Other businesses weren't necessarily so lucky.

Author: Such as?

PF: Well, because we were the first out there, other businesses used to come to us for advice on what to do. Littlewoods approached us. Littlewoods are retailing out there but they are also manufacturing. They are manufacturing clothing out there to British specifications and then bringing back clothes to UK and selling part out there. They put money into a bank that we advised them not to and the bank closed down. They lost about a day's takings. I don't think that was widely publicised in the UK. They also used lawyers that we advised them not to as they had a bad reputation.

In fairness to the Russians it was also Western firms giving inward investment a bad name. It makes me angry. I have seen so many examples of a small business guy in his own country going in and trying to act as the big businessman. Builders buying up a block of flats and taking out 99-year leases for £5,000 to £6,000 but not going through the proper processes. The Finns, rightly or wrongly, didn't have the best reputation with the Russians when it came to business.

Author: Do you feel you got out of it all you could have? Is there room for firms to go in there now and set up joint ventures?

PF: We could have doubled our profit over there but we'd have to have driven it over the years harder, but our main concern was the business in Scotland. Only someone of a certain calibre could go out there and work – you worked there 24 hours a day. Profit came first on the list but challenge was very high on the list in terms of what we wanted to achieve. We could have taken the option to expand and go deeper but then you expose yourself to risk. You have got to remember where your roots are.

As for joint ventures at this stage then I'd say at the moment it would be better to go in on your own despite the difficulties. The best firms have already linked up with Western firms. You'd have to ask why the ones left haven't already linked up. All the good companies for joint ventures have gone. As for our former Russian partners we exposed them to reality; I'd say we have given that company a three-year start over their competitors.

The economic growth of the USSR and its relationship to other communist countries

One of the claims made by Marxists has been that planning of the economy is superior to anarchy of the market. We have already touched on the fundamental weaknesses of central planning above. However, it could be argued that despite all of this the system still managed to deliver impressive growth. We will show below that apparent impressive growth figures for the USSR were respectable at best, but once one takes into account the 'launching pad' afforded to the USSR through its relationship with its satellite neighbours it is not possible to say that central planning delivered the growth rates claimed.

The questions of growth and economic relations with other communist states may at first glance seem disjointed. However, in linking the above questions we start by considering those countries of Central and Eastern Europe after the end of the WWII. In the European theatre of WWII the main fighting was conducted on the Eastern Front, i.e. between the Axis powers led by Germany and with the forces of the Soviet Union. With the tide of the war in Europe turning in the Soviet Union's favour the Red Army advanced westward, taking Berlin with a formal surrender on 2 May 1945 to Soviet forces.

In the process of marching westward the Red Army 'liberated' the countries in the Central and Eastern European bloc from Nazi domination (and in quite a few cases defeating the allies of Nazi Germany). The future fate of these countries, and indeed many other countries, was in part decided at a meeting between Stalin and Sir Winston Churchill, the British War Prime Minister, in Moscow on 9 October 1944, less than a year before the war in Europe came to an end.

At this discussion with regard to the future of Europe after the war, Churchill scribbled down on a piece of paper some percentages. Writing in his war memoirs, Churchill describes the scene and the 'trade' that ensued between the two war leaders:

> The moment was apt for business, so I said 'Let us settle about our affairs in the Balkans. Your armies are in Roumania and Bulgaria. We have interests, agents and missions there. Don't let us get at cross-purposes in small ways. So far as Britain and Russia are concerned, how would it do for you to have 90 per cent predominance in Roumania, for us to have 90 per cent of the say in Greece, and go 50–50 about Yugoslavia?' While this was being translated, I wrote on a half sheet of paper:
>
> Roumania: Russia 90% – The others 10%
> Greece: Great Britain 90% – Russia 10%
> Yugoslavia: 50:50%
> Hungary: 50–50%
> Bulgaria: Russia 75% – The others 25%
>
> I pushed this across to Stalin, who had by then heard the translation. There was a slight pause. Then he took his pencil and made a large tick upon it, and passed it back to us. It was all settled in no more time than it takes to set down. . . .
>
>   After this there was a long silence. The pencilled paper lay on the centre of the table. At length I said, 'Might it not be thought rather cynical if it seemed we had disposed of these issues, so fateful to millions of people, in such an offhand manner? Let us burn the paper.' 'No, you keep it,' said Stalin.[25]

With the consolidation of the Red Army in the various countries of CEE it might be thought that the centrally planned system prevalent in the Soviet Union would simply be transplanted into these countries. In time, yes it was, but there was at first a delay of two or three years and in some cases longer. The first question to pose, however, is whether it was indeed inevitable that this would happen; why not allow these countries to continue their pre-war path of (limited) market development and then allow the Soviet Union to dominate them militarily?

The answer to this question might be thought to be ideological; nominally Stalin presided over a country that was against 'bourgeois exploitation of the masses'. It would seem logical to move to 'expropriate the expropriators' and institute regimes in the image of Moscow. However, it may be argued that Marxist-Leninist ideology had ceased to be the guiding principle in Soviet foreign policy and ideology had come to play a supporting role in the *nationalist* foreign policy of the Soviet Union; i.e. out of the 15 Soviet Republics of the Union of Soviet Socialist Republics (USSR), the dominant Russian Soviet Federative Socialist Republic adopted foreign policies which advanced the interests of the ethnic Russian majority as opposed to any notion of 'international workers' solidarity' between nations.[26]

Another reason may lie in the desire on the part of the victorious Stalin to demand war reparations from the defeated Axis powers. While workers within the Soviet Union had only briefly exercised any direct controlling influence on (Soviet) government policy after the revolution, the Soviet Union was still – on paper – a 'workers' state'; a state where the interests of the workers were supreme.

Even a fairly simplistic 'class analysis' of the situation might have run along the following lines: the rise of fascism and Nazi Germany in particular reflected the desire of the bourgeoisie of Germany (and other countries) to inflict a mortal blow on the workers' movement with the aim of giving capital unfettered reign in the workplace. Such extreme measures were necessary, from a bourgeois perspective, due to the economic crises that existed in Germany and other countries throughout the 1920s and 1930s. Given the 800,000 German socialists, communists and trade unionists that perished in Nazi concentration camps and the annihilation of the workers' movement in general in Germany, the fraternal hand of international solidarity should now be extended to the workers of these countries through the establishment of socialist states and international trade cooperation.

This, however, would pose a problem: how to then justify the looting and plunder of the defeated powers by the Soviet Red Army and, indeed, any additional war reparations that the Soviet government might wish to extract from these defeated countries?

One cannot help but wonder if the coalition governments set up with minority communist participation in countries occupied by Soviet troops after the war ended were encouraged by Moscow from an economic perspective to allow reparations to be taken from 'bourgeois governments'. How would it look for a socialist state (the USSR) to be seen to be squeezing the economic life out of other socialist states? (There are other additional reasons which we touch on below.)

Why is the above important to our discussion of the socialist economic system and the relationship between the USSR and the other communist countries? The answer lies in the growth rates of the USSR in the post-war period and how those growth rates were achieved, in no small measure, with the infusion of material means from the occupied territories that were to be future communist states.

Many authors have attempted to compare the growth rates of the USSR with Western market economies. Successive US administrations through the Central Intelligence

Agency attempted to glean insights into how the Soviet economy was doing. The cartoon by Herbert Block (Figure 1.1) sums up the importance attached to such statistics in a humorous way.

In a document posted on the CIA website (*Watching the Bear: Essays on CIA's Analysis of the Soviet Union*, edited by Gerald K. Haines and Robert E. Leggett, Chapter II, 'CIA's Analysis of the Soviet Economy' by James Noren[27]), the figures for the percentage growth rates in the Gross National Product (GNP) of the Soviet Union are given in Table 1.2.

In addition, we present estimated figures from the Commission of the European Communities from a report *Stabilization, Liberalization and Devolution: Assessment of the Economic Situation and Reform Process in the Soviet Union* (1990). Note that the Commission's data relate to growth rates of Net Material Product (NMP) alongside adjusted NMP data. For comparison we also include the growth rate of the Gross Domestic Product (GDP) of the United States. Consequently we are presenting data which are approaching the issue of economic growth from two slightly different angles.

Regardless of what data we examine the trend is clear: a continuous slowdown in economic growth. That said, the growth in NMP or GNP for the period of the 1950s looks respectable. However, even where one has some faith in the growth estimates of the former Soviet Union they should be seen especially in the 1950s and early 1960s from the perspective of an infusion of material means into the Soviet Union.

What then was this infusion of material means? While the Soviet government did demand thousands of millions of dollars of reparations from Germany, Germany had no actual dollars to give. The reparations took two distinct forms: first, physically dismantling equipment and moving it to the Soviet Union; and second, as the 1940s wore on, establishing Russian-owned companies, known as Soviet Shareholding Companies or SAGs, which took over existing German firms operating within the Soviet-controlled zone of Germany.

A commission established by the Soviet government in February 1948 to estimate reparations up until that date found that between 2 August 1945 and 1 January 1948 the Soviet Union received the equivalent of $2.68 billion in reparations which took the form of:

- $801 million from the Soviet-controlled zone in the form of factories, goods and raw materials;
- $22.3 million from the zone;
- $603.4 million from current production;
- $355.4 million in German property from outside Germany such as from Poland;
- $127.4 million in the form of transport such as railway cars, trucks, tram cars, etc.;
- $200 million worth of patents.[28]

Naimark (1995) concludes that given that removals of current production (from German industry) remained fairly constant until 1950 the figure of $10 billion reparations seems highly likely. The effect on the Eastern zone of the German economy was devastating, with approximately one-third of all productive capacity removed and transported back to the Soviet Union.

There was an almost feverish haste with which the Soviet forces proceeded to extract their 'repayments', often in many cases dismantling the equipment so badly that it could not be used later, or done in such an unplanned manner that it could lie for months rusting at railway stations waiting to be transported.

HERBLOCK'S CARTOON

"Pst! Want To See Some Hot Statistics?"

Figure 1.1 'Pst! Want to see some hot statistics?'

Source: 'Pst! Want To See Some Hot Statistics?'
—A 1964 Herblock Cartoon, copyright by The Herb Block Foundation.

Table 1.2 CIA and EU estimates of GNP growth rates in the USSR

	GNP growth rates (CIA)	NMP	NMP adjusted	GDP in USA
1900–1913	.	.	3.5	4.0
1913–1921	.	−10.7	−10.7	1.5
1922–1940	.	15.3	8.5	2.5
1941–1950	.	4.7	−0.6	4.5
1951–1960	5.9%	10.3	9.3	3.2
1961–1970	5.1%	7.0	4.2	3.7
1971–1980	2.7%	4.9	2.1	2.8
1981–1990	1.4%	.	.	.
1981–1985	.	3.6	0.6	3.1
1986–1989	.	2.7	.	3.0
1900–1987	.	.	3.3	3.2
1929–1987	.	.	4.0	3.0

Sources: As per the main text.

[D]ismantling needs were often so pressing that additional workers had to be recruited, usually without pay, to disassemble and transport the factories. In one case, Major Orlov of the Ninth Trophy Brigade (Fourth Battalion) used his troops to surround a soccer stadium, stop the game in midmatch, and haul off workers for the dismantling of a factory. In a similar case Russian soldiers stopped a movie in the middle (ironically, the Soviet film *Circus*) and seized workers for dismantling. Dances were stopped to get workers; restaurants and bars were also frequent targets. Even when the Germans went along peaceably with the dismantling teams, they were threatened, cursed, and sometimes pistol-whipped. For German workers, especially those of the KPD/SED or in the zonal trade union (the FDGB), it was hard to understand why the Soviets did not seize former Nazis and government officials for their work. Instead, German workers were forced to labor twelve to fifteen hours a day, seven days a week, sometimes without anything more than vague promises of payment that were seldom fulfilled.

(Naimark 1995)

While the bulk of the dismantling was over by 1947, in total about one-third of all East German industry was owned and run by SAGs. These companies totally dominated the heavy industry of East Germany and were only abolished in 1954. As a result they fitted into the Soviet central planning system with output being directed eastward and not remaining within East Germany.[29]

In Romania the entire war fleet, the merchant navy, half the railway stock, all automobiles, and most of the oil equipment were transported back to the USSR. Estimates vary between about $1bn and $1.8bn in war reparations between 1944 and 1948. In Hungary about 90 per cent of the metalworking and engineering industries in 1945 were seized with reparations, consuming in the late 1940s anywhere between 10 and 25 per cent of the government budget. Even in Czechoslovakia – not allied to Nazi Germany – 60 major industrial enterprises were dismantled and taken by the Red Army.[30]

Finally, we must not forget China. As part of the Yalta Agreement between the Allied war leaders, the Soviet Union declared war on Japan on 8 August 1945 and within one week the whole of Manchuria had been easily overrun by the Soviet Red Army. Manchuria was also the only part of China which was a stronghold of the Chinese Communists who had succeeded in seizing a substantial part of Japanese-occupied territory and Japanese equipment. As with countries newly 'liberated' in CEE countries, Manchuria's industrial plant was systematically dismantled and shipped to the Soviet Union via the Trans-Siberian Railway. As Bianco (1971) notes,

> By this decision the Chinese Communists lost the entire industrial infrastructure of a region indispensable to the building of a modern China, and of socialism. The factories had been installed by the Japanese army, and in the Russian view these were ample grounds for treating the factories, like the gold stored in Manchurian banks, as war booty.

It might be argued that, given the widespread economic destruction inflicted on the USSR by Nazi forces, the growth statistics for the 1950s and 1960s are nevertheless impressive; in short, even with the 'infusion of material means' the Soviet economy had less to build on to achieve these growth rates. As Dutkiewicz and Popov (2006) have pointed out,

> ... the national income [of the USSR] never fell that far during World War II. In 1942, it was 80% of the prewar 1940 level, then climbed back up to the prewar level in 1944, and then once again descended to the 80% mark in 1946 during the conversion of defense industry. But, by 1948, it had already substantially exceeded the 1940 level.

Of course if we broaden our definition of destruction to include human casualties, then the destruction was truly horrific with an estimated loss of life within the Soviet Union of approximately 27 million people.

One area where an apparent contradiction may be found to the arguments above lies in the fact that starting in the 1960s, but intensifying in the early 1970s, oil, and natural gas (along with other goods) produced in the Soviet Union were exported to satellite countries in CEE (through the CMEA, also known as Comecon) at *below* world market prices. Calculations for the years 1971 to 1978 'show that on trade in fuels, non-food raw materials, semi-manufactured goods, and agricultural products combined, the Soviet Union implicitly provided a net cumulative subsidy of about $14 billion to the six East European CMEA countries' (Marer 1984). Marer notes that oil prices for Yugoslavia, which, of course, was far more independent of the FSU, were closer to world market prices. In addition, Romania did not receive subsidies in primary product trade with the FSU again presumably due to its far more independent stance from the FSU. Lévesque (1997) quotes the calculations of American economists estimating the subsidy resulting from various price differentials at the very start of the 1980s as being $18 billion dollars per year.

Whatever the exact amount, given the fundamental nature of oil and other primary products to economies at that time it would have been a relatively easy way for the Soviet Union to extract yet more from these countries by charging at least world market prices if not higher.

It is not unreasonable to contrast the immediate post-WWII period when the outcome of the future face of CEE was *likely* to be dominated by the Soviet Union, but still *uncertain*, to the one where having seen Communist parties take power in CEE it was now a period of consolidation. The initial period was a time to put the Soviet economy first, to demand and take reparations, to dismantle and transport back to the USSR; later as communist regimes tried to rebuild and as the Cold War between the West and the USSR intensified, the Eastern Bloc countries became more and more a strategic buffer to the USSR in the event of an impending war. That buffer would be stronger the more the countries of CEE had built up their industrial base upon which modern armies fight. That in turn would be assisted by primary products below world market prices.

Yet another factor lies in the *internal* security situation for these regimes – 'the enemy within', to borrow a phrase. The threat to the stability of the regimes would come not only from a perceived threat from the West – from 'capitalist encirclement' – but from the very citizens of the regimes. Table 1.3 lists some of the major revolts and incidents that occurred up until 1970.

Given the difficulties these regimes had in providing the basics of modern living – from quality consumer goods to a secure, regular supply of agricultural produce – to charge world

Table 1.3 Some major revolts and movements in CEE post-WWII

Country and year	Description	Outcome
East Germany 1953	A spontaneous uprising starts 16 June from a hospital building site in East Berlin sparked by an increase in work norms and a threat to cut wages. On the morning of 17 June other workers in factories met, went on strike and marched to the centre of East Berlin. Estimated that over 300,000 were on strike in over 250 different locations through the country.	On 17 June 25,000 Russian troops and 300 tanks move into East Berlin; martial law declared; rising crushed – leaders imprisoned or executed.
Poland 1956	On 28 June workers in Poznan, focused on the ZISPO factory, went on strike against being overtaxed and at not being paid the full legal overtime rate. The strike led to a demonstration which drew in others. A mass meeting held 23 June agreed to send a delegation to Warsaw to press their demands. Only two conditions met. Thursday 28 June a demonstration from ZISPO is joined by an estimated one-third of the population of Poznan demanding more bread, higher wages and lower prices.	Fighting broke out when the crowd attacked the Security Police building. The Security Police reply with bullets. Government uses their Internal Security Guard to eventually take back control of the streets. Deep splits and infighting within the Polish Communist Party result. Worker discontent continued to 'simmer' into 1957.
Hungary 1956	On 22 October student meetings called for a mass demonstration the next day 'in solidarity with our Polish brothers'. 100,000 marched some headed and tore down statue of Stalin, others to the radio station. Security police use tear gas and machine gun fired at crowd. Insurrection erupts.	Insurrection only brought to an end when roughly 200,000 Russian troops and 3,000 tanks intervene to crush the uprising.

(*Continued*)

Table 1.3 Continued

Country and year	Description	Outcome
Czechoslovakia 1968	Falling more broadly under the category of movement, the so-called Prague Spring started in January 1968 with the election of reformer Alexander Dubček. Dubček attempted to give the country 'socialism with a human face' by decentralising the economy and more personal freedoms to the citizens.	Spring turned to winter when 200,000 Soviet, Bulgarian, Polish, and Hungarian troops plus 2,000 tanks invaded on 21 August 1968 to put an end to the reform process.
Poland 1970	On 12 December average food prices increased by 20 per cent. As a result workers in Gdansk, Gdynia and Sopot on 14 December draw up a list of demands and march to CP HQ. Fighting breaks out. Partial concessions made; workers preparing to return to work next day fired on. Strike continues and spreads to Szczecin and other areas of Poland.	Gomulka as head of the country removed and replaced by Gierek. He announces two-year freeze on food prices. This 'cools' the situation somewhat but repeated strikes break out in Szczecin and Gdansk throughout January 1971.

Source: Information contained in various chapters of Harman (1974).

market prices for oil and other primary products would surely have sent swathes of Eastern European industries under, with the consequent social explosions that would have resulted.[31]

While Naughton (2008a) has argued that 'Communist systems are arguably hyperstable: up until the point of ultimate collapse, they are far more likely to survive in the face of adverse conditions than are ordinary authoritarian regimes', this is surely from the benefit of much hindsight. During the post-WWII period it was not at all apparent to the successive leaderships of the Soviet Union that the communist regimes of CEE would survive, and yes, with the benefit of hindsight, one might say that if these regimes fell would it not – domino-like – lead ultimately to the fall of the Soviet Union itself? Subsidised primary commodity prices was surely a small insurance premium to pay against the wider considerations of the international Cold War and the intermittent, but regular, internal eruptions of revolt.

The socialist system in Central and Eastern Europe after WWII

Only Yugoslavia started and implemented a Soviet-style five-year plan almost immediately after hostilities had ended in 1945. Given the time it takes to prepare such a plan, commencing such a plan on 1 January 1947 was about as immediate as any country was going to be post-WWII. Yugoslavia also had the advantage of being more independent from Soviet foreign policy having effectively defeated Nazi occupiers without the assistance of the Soviet Red Army. The war against the Nazi occupiers by the Communist partisan resistance had been led by Josip Broz Tito, a larger-than-life character, a man who enjoyed the finer things in life, was fluent in German, Russian and knew some French, married four times to women always much younger than himself. Tito 'made his own decisions and did not consult with Stalin. When it became unavoidable, he did not hesitate to follow his own road and risk an open confrontation with the Soviet Union' (Berend 1998).

Above we mentioned that delays in implementing regimes in the image of Moscow were in part due to the desire to collect reparation payments from ex-enemy countries. In the process CEE countries participated in coalition governments between parties of the Left, including the communists, but also with both agrarian and 'bourgeois parties'. This also allowed the Soviet Union time to prepare the ground for complete domination of a country as well as extracting reparations where appropriate. The reader should not think that simply because Soviet troops occupied a country that it dominated a country; the two are not the same thing.[32] At some stage troops – or the bulk of them at least – would be withdrawn. What then? How to really control a country without the need for a very large presence of troops? The aim was to build regimes in the image of the Soviet Union. To do that required the subservience of the local Communist Party to Moscow, which in turn meant that the local Communist Party needed to have deep roots in all *civil* organisations of the country such as trade unions, factory committees, youth organisations, residents' associations and so on. To be sure, such roots grew quicker with the presence of Soviet troops. Even when such domination eventually took place, most countries proceeded more tentatively than Yugoslavia with two- and three-year plans which were aimed primarily at the basics of reconstruction following the devastation of WWII.

Both before and after the end of hostilities there had been an upsurge from grassroots communists in various CEE countries pushing for a more radical agenda on the part of their respective leaderships towards the economy.[33] The rank and file of the respective Communist parties had themselves felt the heat from the working class who themselves, in many cases, had wanted radical Left measures on the economic front. The Soviet leadership held back and dampened such aspirations for more radical policies. On the surface at least this was to avoid upsetting their Western allies: 'the USSR needed to play down any socialist perspective and to emphasize that only the security factor lay behind its demands for a sphere of influence to the west of its borders' (Brus 1986). Given, however, that the Soviet Union was in a very strong position militarily within the CEE countries it occupied, it is difficult to see Stalin losing too many nights' sleep over more overtly socialist policies being espoused by Communist parties on the ground. At best the above offers a partial explanation.

Another partial explanation may be found in the *independent* workers' movements that developed in many CEE countries, independent from the Communist Party, that is. We approach this through the extensive nationalisations that took place from below since, while the actual planning may have taken a few years to get off the ground, it should not be thought that actual nationalisations were entirely absent. A distinction should also be made between nationalisations in allied countries – which happened quickly, the bulk of industry being nationalised by 1946 – and those in ex-enemy countries where it took longer, namely up until the late 1940s and early 1950s.

As with many social and economic upheavals over roughly the last 150 years workers' councils were formed in some of the CEE countries 'liberated' by the Soviet Union. These formed at a factory level and in many cases spontaneously took over factories, placing them under their own jurisdiction. The situation in Czechoslovakia is instructive of the general tendencies that occurred, although the exact process that unfolded differed from country to country. In the immediate post-war period workers' councils or works councils within factories were at their strongest. On the councils in Czechoslovakia Svejnar (1978) writes:

> In the German owned enterprises the councils actually took over the management and often intervened even in the technical organisation of production. . . . Their role, especially in the early post-war period, was not very clearly defined and therefore varied from factory to factory. Their primary aim was to ensure smooth continuation of production and a speedy reconstruction of enterprises from war devastation. At the same time they strove to institute genuine workers' control over the enterprise administration.

The government of the day, of which the communists were a part, tried to ride this tiger in two ways: first, by supporting official Presidential decree No. 104 of 24 October 1945 which, while essentially recognising the de facto situation of workers' control of many aspects of factory life, also decreed the

> managing of the enterprise to be the task of the management which is also fully responsible for the performance of the enterprise. . . . Secondly, the decree included no reference to the widely accepted prerogative of the works councils to influence . . . the nomination of the managers (and thus create an atmosphere of dependence of the management on the council) [and] was *de jure* suppressed. . . . In practice, the old (pre-decree) situation often prevailed.
>
> (Svejnar 1978)

The second channel through which the communists tried to calm and control this independent movement of workers within Czechoslovakia was through the establishment of the Communist-dominated Revolutionary Trade Union Movement (ROH). Indeed, the ROH had, through a special ROH commission, helped to draft Presidential decree No. 104. Established after the workers' councils,

> the ROH leaders realized the potential dangers of the councils as effective competitors to the unions. . . . Realizing how much general opposition there would be to an outright annexation of the works councils . . . the ROH leaders did not push for annexation, but set themselves the task of making the councils at least highly dependent on the Revolutionary Trade Union Movement.
>
> (Svejnar 1978)

When the Communist Party of Czechoslovakia staged a coup d'état in February 1948, Communist Party members had already been elected to key positions within the works councils between 1945 and 1948 through their control of who would be eligible to stand, a right they obtained through the Presidential decree No. 104. As a result, after the coup, many works councils took over management functions inside factories and 'subsequently participated in purges of outspoken opponents of the takeover' (Svejnar 1978). After that the importance and influence of the works councils waned rapidly, given that – from a Communist Party perspective – they had served their 'function'; the existence of the works councils was officially 'terminated' at a congress of the Czechoslovakian trade unions in 1955.

Apart from the nationalisations that had occurred due to pressure from grassroots workers there was also de facto nationalisation by the state in many countries due to the circumstances that immediately prevailed when the war ended. German assets within many of the countries of CEE had often been excessively enlarged during the war due to the confiscation of allied countries' assets along with that of Jews sent to their deaths in concentration camps. These were in turn now seized by the respective post-war governments. When one adds in German property in Sudetenland (handed back to Czechoslovakia) and territory that was once German, now part of Poland (the Regained Territories), post-war governments held a sizeable chunk of industry already in public ownership.

> At Liberation, furthermore, a substantial part of industrial capacity was found abandoned, i.e. without legal owners or representatives able to put the establishment back into operation. The state took responsibility of restarting such capacities. Together with prewar state enterprises, the two channels of confiscation and administration of abandoned property were the equivalent of gaining the industrial 'commanding heights', for they amounted in Poland and Yugoslavia to two-thirds of industrial capacity.[34]
>
> (Brus 1986)

By the late 1940s and early 1950s most of the CEE countries under Soviet domination had started to implement their own five-year plans: 1949 Czechoslovakia and Bulgaria, 1950 Poland and Hungary, and in 1951 Romania and Albania. As with Gosplan in the Soviet Union, hundreds of people were employed in planning ministries in each country charged with drawing up the plans in great detail: for example, 1,200 staff in the Polish planning commission, and 700 and 500 at the Hungarian and Romanian counterparts respectively (Berend 1998). We do not repeat an explanation of the planning mechanism here since, in essence and indeed much substance, the planning process was identical to what has been described above for the Soviet Union, except on a smaller scale.

Despite the scale being smaller – which one may have thought might have inclined the planning process to be more feasible – there were the same inherent problems with central planning in CEE countries as in the Soviet Union. For example, demands for information from all levels of the productive economy resulted in information overload. Not only was it impossible to get all the *necessary* information to plan effectively, much of the information that was obtained was quite useless. Kaser and Zielinski (1970, quoted in Berend 1998) focusing only on CEE countries estimated that only one-fifth of all information gathered by planning ministries post-WWII was actually used in the planning process.

But we run ahead of ourselves. With hindsight and experience the inherent weakness of state planning was to become obvious. However, after WWII many economists in CEE countries had become disillusioned with free market capitalism due to the economic stagnation of many of their respective countries in the inter-war period (Brus 1986). In addition, that the Soviet Union had turned back the tide of Nazism was in no small measure, it was thought, due to the superiority of planning in its war effort. The Great Depression of the 1930s in Western market economies along with the absence of one in the USSR was also fresh in many minds of the intelligentsia of CEE. The scarcity of goods within society after the ending of hostilities was also suggestive of the state playing a leading role such that there would be a 'fairer' distribution of what was available. All in all, the concept of planning was set to have a good reception. We summarise the implementation of planning in the various CEE countries below for each country.[35]

Yugoslavia

The plan drawn up in Yugoslavia was the only one of the countries briefly reviewed here which tried to follow both the objectives and methodology of the Soviet five-year plans using a form of input-output calculations in physical terms; the first plan aimed to double national income and increase industrial production fivefold. The detailed five-year plan was itself broken down into yearly, quarterly and monthly plans. Some important enterprises even had to report at the end of the working day on what had been achieved! The break with the Soviet Union when Tito refused to become merely another satellite of the Soviet Union effectively ended this first attempt at five-year planning when expected trade deliveries that had been incorporated into the plan failed to be delivered due to a Soviet and East European trade embargo. The five-year plan was quickly amended such that key strategic projects were completed. Enterprises within Yugoslavia then switched from a Soviet form of management to one of workers' self-management.

Czechoslovakia

One must recall that a coalition existed during this time. The Economic Council of Ministers established its own Central Planning Commission, consisting of 13 experts drawn from and selected by each of the political parties in the coalition: Beneš, who had been Czechoslovakia's Foreign Minister at the League of Nations in Geneva before the war, had three nominations through his National Socialist Party; the Czechoslovak Communist Party three; the Slovak Communist Party one; the Social Democratic Party, the Slovak Democratic Party and the People's Party nominated two each. The Planning Commission created 18 Working Commissions for each major branch of the economy. The Working Commissions while heavy with political influence did contain non-political experts and representatives of the trade unions. Individual drafts for each branch of the economy were drawn up with assistance from ministries; the Central Planning Commission then presented a comprehensive plan to the government and then ultimately to the National Assembly for approval. As Brus notes, 'the Central Planning Committee was certainly more akin to a genuine commission than the huge administrative bodies bearing the name "planning commission" or "planning committee" in the Soviet Union and in east European countries in the 1950s' (Brus 1986).

Poland

In October 1945 the Central Planning Board which employed professional civil servants on the Board or in its small research institute was charged not with developing a plan but with distributing scarce raw materials and credits where they were most required. This body also drew up the nine-month investment plan. Real power over the economy, however, lay in the hands of the Economic Committee of the government and the Ministry of Industry and Commerce, both bodies being headed by the chief economist Hilary Minc whom Brus describes as a 'towering figure' (Brus 1986). Interestingly the Central Planning Board was controlled and dominated by the Socialist Party whereas the other organisations were controlled by the Communist Party with Hilary Minc herself being a member of the Politburo.

The above led to what became known as the 'planning controversy'. The Ministry of Industry and Commerce sent a memorandum accusing the Central Planning Board of gross methodological errors:

1   First, the Planning Board had included 'non-material' services when calculating national income which undermined the role and importance of the working class. (Recall that the services sector was perceived by certain Marxist economists as being non-productive.)
2   Second, of ignoring the Marxist 'principle' of production over consumption.
3   Third, of confusing plan targets with forecasts: The Ministry of Industry and Commerce asserted that only nationalised firms/industries could be planned and so have plan targets.

At a special meeting of experts from both sides on 18–19 February 1948, with the leaderships of both parties in attendance, the communists represented by the Ministry carried the day. 'The debate was the pretext for a crushing political blow to the Polish version of social-democratic planning: the Planning Board was purged immediately' (Brus 1986). Ultimately the debate was as much about the communists preparing the ground for ultimate control of Polish society as about the rights and wrongs of this or that planning methodology.

Hungary

The coalition government of the Party of Independent Smallholders, the National Peasant Party, the Social Democratic Party and the Communist Party established the Supreme Economic Council in 1945, although the real power was in the hands of its Secretariat led by a communist, Zoltá Vass. Conflict arose with the Office of Materials and Prices under the leadership of the Independent Smallholders who wanted on several occasions to raise industrial prices to profitable levels. The Supreme Economic Council opposed them by deliberately lowering prices, the power to do so having been 'won' after it successfully tackled the hyperinflation within post-WWII Hungary. As well as ostensibly setting prices to control inflation it also determined credit within the economy to large financial concerns which created dependence of these organisations on the state. As within Poland, two versions of a three-year reconstruction plan were drawn up: one by the Communist Party and one by the Social Democratic Party, the latter with the help of Nicholas (later Lord) Kaldor, then lecturer at the London School of Economics and an adviser to the British Labour Party. While the version drawn up by the Social Democratic Party had envisioned foreign credits being used to buy imported machinery, the refusal of the government to sign up to the American government's Marshall Plan (which made the offer of *grant* payments to governments within Europe to assist with post-war reconstruction) effectively ruled out this plan option. In June 1949, changes in the responsibilities of planning were made whereby the Supreme Economic Council was replaced by the People's Economic Council. Be that as it may, by 1950 all the institutions of centralised planning were firmly in place.

Albania

Given the extremely limited amount of industry that existed in the first place, the job of planning such a small number of enterprises hardly demanded the immediate establishment of a planning commission. Nevertheless, an Economic Council was established in 1945 to draw up a plan for the economy with a Planning Commission as its adviser. The new Albania led by Enver Hoxha took what it could find into public ownership: in April 1946,

> the building materials industry, pharmaceutical laboratories, and chemicals' shops were nationalized; printing, edible oil, soap, and leather and tanning on 27 May; milling and pasta-making on 4 September; and repair shops on 23 October 1946. The cement works at Shkodër was nationalized on 7 February 1947, and in the same month ten garment-making, four footwear, four alcohol, fifteen cigarette, and ten ice-making plants were taken over. All twenty-five cinemas were nationalized on 16 April, two chocolate and sweet factories and a vegetable-oil refinery on 24 September.
>
> (Brus 1986)

Bulgaria

Initially the programme of the Patriotic Front in 1944 was – as per the Soviet Union line – very modest in its aims for industry and the economy after the end of the war. Nationalisation was not mentioned and the programme itself merely called on control of profits, and support to cooperatives. Given, however, that enemy property was taken over and combined with pre-WWII state assets in industry, there existed a sizeable percentage of industry already in state hands even before any formal legislation was passed. The legislation came on 23 December 1947 when almost all private industry was nationalised, taking the share of the socialised sector within the country to 95 per cent. The banks followed into state ownership a few days later.

Romania

In 1945 some enemy and collaborators' property was taken into public ownership, although much of the former was appropriated by the SAG companies dominated by the Soviet Union. Nationalisation progressed slowest in Romania in comparison with other CEE countries. The Nationalisation Act of June 1948 meant that firms employing more than 100 people were now in state hands. A reform of the currency in August 1947 was heavily progressive against business people and those with large savings with the exchange rate between the old and new currency being more favourable to those on low incomes or with little savings to exchange. By 1950 state-owned industry stood at 89 per cent and by 1952 at 97 per cent.

German Democratic Republic

The GDR, probably better known among many in the West as simply East Germany, was formed when at the end of WWII the country of Germany was partitioned between the lands occupied by allied troops and those by Soviet troops. As mentioned above, full-scale nationalisation and state planning were delayed while reparations proceeded. The first five-year plan did start in 1951 but the second (in 1956) ran into difficulties and was replaced in 1959 with a seven-year plan.

In all the above countries, growth rates – as in the USSR in the early years – would start off impressively but as the inherent weaknesses of central planning began to assert themselves growth would slow dramatically by the time of the 1980s.

Collectivisation in the Soviet Union and the 'people's democracies' of Central and Eastern Europe

While the main body of the text has focused on planning of *industry* both within the Soviet Union and by implication within CEE countries, one of the main areas that we have not touched on is within agriculture and the fate of the peasantry. All countries in their development process – whether capitalist or socialist – have gone through the process of the population shifting from rural to urban areas and from employment being predominantly on the land to one where the majority are engaged in industrial and then service activities. In many cases the rural to urban transition has been *brutal* to those who scraped a living from the land.

In the Soviet Union of the 1920s and 1930s or CEE of the 1950s and 1960s, the Communist parties in power at those times naturally posed the question: how to achieve our own transition from rural to urban; from land to factory? (Although the Communist parties of CEE post-WWII had the model of the Soviet Union to follow.) How to achieve our own 'primitive *socialist* accumulation'? How to generate sufficient surplus from the land that it can be used as the bedrock for industrial development?

While a debate had raged within the CPSU in the 1920s as to the way forward, with one faction arguing for a slow and voluntary collectivisation of the peasantry backed up by the ability of state industry to supply the necessary mechanised equipment, by the late 1920s Stalin was firmly in control of the party and the decision was taken to collectivise the peasantry. On the surface this was meant to increase agricultural production by concentrating farming resources into larger units. This would assist in providing the surplus which could be used to expand industrialisation in the towns and cities both through feeding a larger workforce and by earning export credits which could be used where needed to import machinery.

That it was called 'primitive socialist accumulation' should in no way hide the fact that the aim was, in part, what had occurred in Britain and many other Western mature economies in years gone by – to turn agrarian countries into industrial ones. We say in part since Stalin in the Soviet Union had one other important objective: to attack what he perceived as a class enemy; an enemy that he saw as a threat to the power of the ruling Communist Party, a group of well-to-do peasants who were called kulaks. The stated aim was to 'liquidate' them as a class.

Kulaks were simply small-scale capitalist farmers, many of whom, as was mentioned earlier, had taken their chance with the introduction of the Stolypin reforms following the failed 1905 Russian Revolution. What constituted a kulak in the eyes of Communist Party officialdom was arbitrary: the regular hiring of labour; the working of a plot of land above some minimum; the ownership of a piece of equipment. The attack would be conducted through forced collectivisation. That is, the compulsory grouping of independent small peasant farmers into collective farms (*kolkhoz*) that would take place in the late 1920s and early 1930s inside the Soviet Union: 'The events of 1929–34 constitute one of the great dramas of history' (Nove 1986a). The statistics for the collectivisation of the peasantry are shown in Table 1.4 along with measures for agricultural and livestock production.

Kulaks as the better-off peasants in rural society were seen as a potential counterweight politically to the power of the regime. Indeed, to be a kulak at this time was to invite almost certain persecution and deportation to Siberia, if not worse. The persecution of the kulaks also came in useful in forcing the pace of collectivisation: if you resisted collectivisation then you must be a kulak! Deportation started at the end of 1929 and peaked in 1930 to 1931.

According to Ivnitsky a total of about 300,000 kulak households were deported (roughly 1.5 million people). . . . What happened to other Kulaks? Ivnitsky refers to

Table 1.4 Collectivisation of Soviet agriculture

Year	Collective farms (thousands)	Peasant households collectivised of total number of households	Gross agricultural production (index)	Livestock production (index)
1913	–	–	96	87
1918	1.6	0.1	–	–
1928	33.3	1.7	100	100
1929	57.0	3.9	93	87
1930	85.9	23.6	88	65
1931	211.1	52.7	84	57
1932	211.1	61.5	76	48
1933	–	–	82	51
1934	–	–	86	52
1935	245.4	83.2	99	74
1936	–	–	93	76
1937	–	–	116	83
1938	242.4	93.5	107	100

Source: P. R. Gregory and R. C. Stuart (1986). Cited in Kornai (1992).

a 'complex of measures' other than deportations, and their fate is left unclear. What is quite clear is that collectivization went hand in hand with dekulakization, and dekulakization with half-disguised robbery. Poorer peasants seized their neighbours' goods in the name of the class struggle, or with no excuse at all.

(Nove 1986a)

The complex measures referred to included concentration camps for those kulaks actively hostile with families of such kulaks forcibly deported elsewhere. Other kulaks regarded as the least 'noxious' were to be allowed to remain in the region where they had lived and worked but were to be given land of the worse type. Stalin gave strict instructions that under no account should any kulaks be allowed to join the collective farms, fearful as he was that they would then dominate the collective from within.

The results of this adventure are shown in Table 1.4: output plummeted precipitously both in terms of cereals and of livestock of all kinds. Not only did new farms lack the experience in handling collectivised livestock, but the state requisitioning of grain and other agricultural stock left in many cases insufficient fodder to feed livestock, especially within Ukraine. 'In 1931 sowing suffered acutely from the appalling state of the hungry horses' (Nove 1986a). In addition, many peasants faced with losing their meagre possessions in a collectivised farm chose to slaughter their livestock. In some respects this should have been predictable, since this also happened during the war communism period.

Excessive state procurements were so severe in the initial collectivisation drive, and the hunger it generated so bad that even Stalin was forced to relent somewhat, by his standards, and grain in some areas was returned to ensure that there would be sufficient grain for sowing. The procurement plan for 1932 had originally been set at 32 million tons, but this was reduced to 18.1 million tons. With a slight relaxation in the procurement, combined with the vast differences between the official state prices and free market prices, much grain found its way either onto the black market or was stored by the peasants themselves, given that hunger from the previous year's bad harvest was fresh in their minds. Party procurement bodies were now instructed to tighten and expedite the collections and in many cases *all* grain was removed, creating an extreme shortage of food. Given that harvests had been smaller to start with, 'The government tried to take more out of a smaller grain crop. . . . In January 1933 a more orderly system of compulsory procurements was decreed. . . . But the damage had already been done' (Nove 1986a). Estimates vary from one million to five million deaths. Using census information from before and after the famine, Nove estimates that 10 million people 'demographically' disappeared.

As developed in Chapter 9 where we look at agriculture within Mao's China, the problem was primarily one of incentives: if the peasants worked the land, what they produced in a collective farm was not theirs to keep. Indeed, when a concession was eventually made to the peasants that they could own and farm a very small plot of land this turned out to be *the* most productive sections of the land farmed precisely because what was produced was kept by the farmer. Kornai (1992) quotes figures for the FSU that in the mid-1960s 40 percent of all meat and 67 per cent of all eggs were produced on the private plots of land. Even as late as 1983 (less than 10 years before the downfall of the Soviet Union) the respective figures were 29 and 30 per cent respectively. Agriculture within the Soviet Union never really recovered from the collectivisation process, or more accurately, given the size of the country, it never reached the heights of agricultural production it could have done that are enjoyed in, say, Canada, America, New Zealand, etc.

What then were the inherent weaknesses of this form of farming? First, some background. Kolkhozy should not be confused with sovkhozy, although from about the 1960s onward the two were increasingly indistinguishable. A kolkhoz was a collective farm whereas a sovkhoz was a state farm. Individuals who worked on a sovkhoz were paid as agricultural workers in the employment of the state. Moreover, the wage was a guaranteed wage unlike in a kolkhoz. The sovkhoz was established in the 1920s on confiscated land of some landlord after the revolution, whereas kolkhozy were often formed by the uniting of smaller peasant plots of land.

In principle the output of the sovkhoz belonged to the state, unlike a kolkhoz. Individuals who worked on kolkhozy were (on paper) members of a voluntary cooperative with each member of the cooperative entitled to a share of the collective output. Given, however, that each kolkhoz had state procurement orders to fulfil, if it had not been for the private plots many 'cooperative' members would have gone hungry. In Stalin's time the kolkhozy tended to be overcharged for their inputs, if indeed they received the necessary inputs. Nove (1986b) gives the example that in the late Stalin period electricity was often not supplied, with individual kolkhozy generating, if possible, their own supplies. The prices paid by the state for the procurement quotas from kolkhozy tended to be very low, but the price it then charged wholesalers was far higher. By such means socialist accumulation proceeded.

Existing before forced collectivisation, the development of kolkhozy following the revolution had been slow, but voluntary and peaceful. With the coming to power of Khrushchev after Stalin's death, measures were taken to place both forms of farming institutions on an equal footing, with kolkhozy members also receiving a guaranteed wage. The members of both types of farming institutions required internal passports to move around the country. This was to prevent unplanned movement from the land to urban areas which often, nevertheless, proceeded unofficially. Even children born on a collective farm up until 1969 were expected to work the farm unless given specific permission to leave. It is little wonder that the peasantry believed the gains of the 1917 Revolution to them had been lost, and that in reality they now had a form of serfdom.

Ultimately then there was no incentive for the members of kolkhozy or sovkhozy to meet and exceed the plan target. While within industry the financial bonuses of management and workers depended on targets being met, within the farm, 'The farm was very likely to be more prosperous if the [procurements] plan was *not* fulfilled' (Nove 1986a). This led to far greater party supervision of work on farms and a larger number of state-sponsored campaigns to motivate the peasant to greater labours. In addition, as in industry, there was lacking the flexibility for local farms to adjust plan instructions to take into consideration local circumstances relating to the quality of land and what might best be grown.

What of Central and Eastern Europe? Collectivisation would come, but only after the various Communist parties had secured their grip on power. Initially, with the formation of coalition governments, the first stage of the revolution was 'bourgeois-democratic' (see the discussion earlier between Mensheviks and Bolsheviks). The big landed estates were to be broken up and distributed to landless and poor peasants; in doing so the power of that social stratum that based itself on the land would be broken, which would be one less worry for the aspiring communist rulers.

This was initially very easy and *popular* to achieve in many of the countries of CEE. As with nationalisations of ex-enemy-owned factories which were seized by the post-WWII governments, there existed a great deal of land that had belonged to German and Italian landowners, who in most cases had fled with the defeat of the Axis powers. Two extra criteria were also seen as being fair game for state seizure followed by distribution to the peasantry: that of wartime collaborators and in some countries, especially Yugoslavia, the lands of the Church. The land was distributed to families not free of charge but payment was usually calculated on the basis of the value of a year or two years' worth of crops which was then paid over a period of time back to the government.

Only in Hungary and to a lesser extent Romania was the overwhelming source of land for redistribution derived from native landowners. In Albania, although not included in Table 1.5, a similar movement occurred when Italian settlers fled after the war, leaving their land to be redistributed.

As radical as the above sounds, Brus (1986) makes the point that one cannot see all countries as being in the same boat. In the case of Bulgaria, Romania and Yugoslavia and to some extent Czechoslovakia, *non-communist* governments of the *inter-war* period had redistributed *more* land than those after WWII through a series of land reforms. Only in

Table 1.5 Sources of land available for agrarian reforms after the end of WWII

	Total[a] area (000s hectares)	Estates above legal limits (000s hectares)	Per cent	German ownership (000s hectares)	Per cent	Collaborators and war criminals (000s hectares)	Per cent	Other[b] (000s hectares)	Per cent
Czechoslovakia	4,200	1,200	29	3,000	71[c]	–	–	–	–
Hungary	3,200	2,900	90	–	–		10	–	–
Poland	13,100	3,200	24	9,900	76	–	–	–	–
Romania	1,500	1,100	73	400	24	–	–	–	–
Yugoslavia	1,600	400	22	600	41	100	6	500	31

Source: Brus (1986) and sources contained therein.

Notes

a Includes land unsuitable for agriculture, and in the Polish case land owned by Poles in the Regional Territories (not subject to redistribution).

b In the case of Hungry, Czechoslovakia and Poland an amount which should be shown under the heading 'Other' could not be separated from the estates above the legal limit.

c Includes land owned by Hungarians in Slovakia.

Table 1.6 Land reform and collectivisation in CEE in the late 1940s onwards

Country	Description of land reform and collectivisation	
Albania	Act of 30 August 1945 confiscated without compensation (1) all land from those whose income came from non-agricultural sources (2) land in excess of 20 hectares where land worked by labour hired and who had other sources of income (3) land in excess of 7 hectares owned by those letting to tenant farmers, (4) land in excess of 40 hectares from owners without other sources of income. Beneficiaries get 5 hectares of land each and pay 10 metric quintals of wheat over 10 years as price of land.	Second Act 27 May 1946: all those not working on the land lost right of ownership. Leads to 300,000 hectares of land (of which 155,000 arable), 474,000 olive trees, and 6,000 head of working livestock were distributed among 21,500 landless families and almost 49,000 smallholders' families. Series of decrees 1948 starting 12 April led to nationalisation of draft animals, followed by forests, grazing and pasture, and water resources. In 1949 first wave of collectivisation begins; all livestock herds more than 400 head nationalised.
Bulgaria	Act 12 March 1946 sets upper limit of 20 hectares fixed for those working their own land and of 10 hectares for those letting more than 40 per cent of their property. Two per cent of cultivated land confiscated (130,000 hectares) and distributed to 120,000 families. Small compensation paid and beneficiaries pay small price also.	15 April 1945 a decree on Labour Cooperative Agricultural Farms led to organisation of collective farms similar to Soviet TOZ* farms building on a long tradition of cooperative farming in the country 382 collective farms in 1945 and 480 by 1946. No compulsion exerted instead economic incentives offered; e.g. discount on price of land bought during land reform if purchaser will join cooperative.
Yugoslavia	Upper limit for landholding set at 45 hectares or 25 to 35 hectares of cultivated land. An owner not working the land could only retain between 3 and 5 hectares. Of the 6 per cent of national territory available for redistribution, half went to 180,000 smallholders and 70,000 landless peasants with an average size of 2.5 hectares per family.	Collective farming encouraged from the start of Tito's regime through Land Reform Decree of 23 August 1945; 454 'pioneer cooperatives' established in 1946; by 1948 1,318 had been established.
Romania	Law of 22 March 1945 limited size of holdings to 50 hectares. 1.5 million hectares distributed to landless peasants and to those with holdings less than 5 hectares. A Romanian landowner could get compensation for confiscated land over 50 hectares.	A second wave of land expropriations takes place in 1948–1949. Royal lands confiscated in 1948 after the King was deposed in December 1947. In 1949 the remaining large estates taken over including 'model' highly intensive, capitalist farms which hadn't been touched in the initial wave of land reform of 1945. The 900,000 hectares confiscated is held in a State Land Fund which is used to establish state farms and/or promote collective farming

(*Continued*)

Table 1.6 Continued

Country	Description of land reform and collectivisation	
Czechoslovakia	By a law of 21 June 1945 'enemy-owned land' 1.8 million hectares of agricultural land confiscated. Three-quarters distributed to Czech and Slovak settlers. Second law of June 1947 sets rigorous enforcement of upper land holding of 250 hectares of total area and 150 hectares of agricultural land. This provided a further 700,000 to 800,000 hectares of land. March 1948, upper limit reduced to 50 hectares which gave another 700,000 hectares for distribution. Total taken over was 4.2 million hectares of which 1.7 million distributed to 350,000 families mostly landless.	The last wave of land reform after the Communist Party coup d'état used as a 'bridgehead' to collectivisation 200,000 hectares of agricultural land went to private farmers; cooperatives obtained 71,000 hectares; and the state kept 132,000. Of the 2.5 million hectares of land confiscated, 0.5 million was agricultural land which was then used to support collectives.
Poland	Poland redistributed over half its agricultural area: 6 million hectares distributed to 1.07 million families.	The recipients of land paid a price similar to that in other countries: the value of a year's harvest spread over 10 to 20 years. No early attempts made at collectivisation, but policy changed in 1948. Some armed resistance to expropriation
Hungary	Roughly one-third of country's surface land expropriated (3.2 million hectares including 450,000 hectares of Church land). 1.9 million hectares distributed to 600,000 families	The land holdings of richer peasants went unchallenged until a collectivisation drive started (but not completed) in the second half of 1948. There would be several waves of collectivisation before the Central Committee of the Hungarian Socialist Workers Party (i.e. the Communist Party) could announce in 1961 that collectivisation had been completed.
German Democratic Republic (East Germany)	From 1945 to 1949, all farms over 100 hectares expropriated without compensation. This gave the state 3.2 million hectares of land of which 1.9 million used for agriculture. From 1952 to 1960 state put pressure on smallholders to collectivise reaching a number of 12,000 farm operations. Between 1960 and 1975 collective farms fell to 4,600 as the state put pressure on them to merge and increase in size.	By the end of 1988 95 per cent of all agricultural land (5.85 million hectares) was run by 4751 farms (465 state-owned and 3855 collectives). Families on collective farms who also cultivated private plots contributed significantly to national income. In 1985 the farmers privately owned about 8.2 percent of pigs, 14.7 percent of sheep, 32.8 percent of horses, and 30 percent of laying hens in the country.

Source: Brus (1986) and sources contained therein for all countries except GDR. For GDR information from Gross (1996).

Note

* Tovarishchestvo Sovmestnoi Obrabotki Zemli: A much looser form of farming cooperative than the Soviet Kolkhoz.

Hungary, Poland and Albania could the post-WWII land reforms be seen to have had a wider impact. The big impact was obviously to come when all of these countries moved to collectivisation (see Table 1.6).

Relatively speaking, collectivisation did not occur in the communist regimes of CEE in the brutal manner as had happened in the Soviet Union in the late 1920s and early 1930s (which does not ameliorate the hardship to those who did experience rough treatment in the collectivisation process). The extent to which the drive to industrialise – tied in with the collectivisation process – affected the urban–rural split in the countries of CEE can be shown by the population of those working in agriculture given in Table 1.7 in the 1940s and 1950s along with the percentage some years later.

While it is true to say that *in general* labour was directed to job positions by the state from rural to urban areas, as Chapter 8 demonstrates, free movement of labour was not completely absent. As those who worked the land were collectivised, sections of the rural community, especially the young, began to 'take their chances' in the towns and cities where the prospects for social and economic advancement were greater.

As with the Soviet Union then, in general, collectivisation was a disaster economically speaking (not to mention socially). Brus (1986) concludes as regards the outcome of the post-WWII land reforms (and before collectivisation took place) that

> there were enough viable holdings [of land] for economic efficiency and hence, on grounds of agrarian structure alone, no need for collectivization. The similarity in the economic policies of each country in the early fifties suggests that political decisions rather than questions of land tenure determined the drive to collectivize.

In terms of how much collectivisation set back CEE countries, Berend (1998) informs us that

> net agricultural production could not surpass prewar levels for about twenty years. Counting the 1934–8 level as a basis, net production remained behind by 10–20 per cent by the early fifties, and was still somewhat behind by 1956, i.e., during the entire Stalinist period.

In conclusion, whether one studies developments within industry or within agriculture, there were inherent flaws within central planning. The birth of centrally planned economies in backward, predominantly agricultural countries often ravaged by war certainly did not give these countries a good start for developing their economies. However, if one did a 'mental

Table 1.7 Percentage shares of population working in agriculture in CEE post-WWII

Country	Percentage of population working in agriculture 1940s or early 1950s	Percentage of population working in agriculture early 1970s
Bulgaria	80	32
Romania	75	53
Yugoslavia	70	57
Poland	57	38
Hungary	53	24
Czechoslovakia	40	18

Source: Berend (1998).

exercise' and imagined the imposition of central planning on the United States of America – yes, very hard to imagine – if we take the US as the pinnacle to date of capitalist development, then central planning would *retard* the further development of the US.

If one had to justify such a statement then it would be with one word: incentives. In the case of central planning, while one can raise other weaknesses within the system such as the level of information required to coordinate a plan of the economy or the lack of innovation, it was the lack of incentives for people to work hard and the lack of motivation for people to 'rise to the occasion' that would be its ultimate downfall.

The understanding of how a state socialist economic system operated is, however, not simply something of historic interest. How it operated and in particular the transition to a market economy for many of these ex-centrally planned economies would and still does continue to provide rich lessons for economists today (see subsequent chapters). With the downfall in 1989 of six communist regimes within CEE and more to follow in the next two years including ultimately the Soviet Union itself, there was a certain triumphalism in the announcements of many Western politicians and economists about the West's victory in the Cold War. This triumph of Western liberal democracy underpinned by a market economy was taken as read by many and was seen to be the 'End of History'.

With the debacle of the world financial and economic crisis in 2007 to 2009, the self-belief in *laissez-faire*-style markets has taken a severe knock. State intervention in the economy on a massive scale has taken place throughout many countries of the world *within* the confines of markets in order to save markets. However, while the *Financial Times* found it necessary to run an editorial in one edition headed 'In Defence of Markets', no one has seriously suggested that, as an alternative to the 'Anglo-Saxon' style of capitalism which seemed to fail spectacularly in the crisis of 2007 to 2009, one should adopt central planning of the economy. A very valuable lesson was learned over the broken bones and dreams of so many people. Given the extremes of state central planning and the excesses of *laissez-faire* free market capitalism we tend to agree with Joseph Stiglitz, who in an online blog wrote,

> The real debate today is about finding the right balance between the market and government (and the third 'sector' – non-governmental non-profit organizations). Both are needed. They can each complement each other. This balance will differ from time to time and place to place.[36]

Understanding what the correct balance is and having the insight to see that the balance may have changed will require flexibility of both economists and politicians in the years to come.

Summary

In the early part of the twentieth century various Marxist organisations in Europe and internationally started to make headway in gaining the ear of large sections of the labour movement in their respective countries. Through the impact of major events such as the First World War, this Marxist camp split into two broad groupings. These may be called reformist and revolutionary; the revolutionary groupings included Lenin's Bolsheviks who would go on to take power on the back of the chaos and destruction heaped upon Tsarist Russia by the First World War.

Most Marxist organisations that did take power in their countries did so under circumstances that were not the most ideal for building a new society which was to be materially and culturally ahead of that achieved under capitalism. Nevertheless, proceed to build or attempt to build such a society they did. The result was that not one example of such a successful construction can be brought forth before the majority of such regimes collapsed under 'people power' in 1989 and the years after that. (We do not include the People's Republic of China here; the economic success of this country in recent decades has been in *allowing* market forces to operate, not in suppressing them.)

It should not be thought that the achievements of state socialist regimes in CEE and within the Soviet Union were inconsequential. Life expectancy in many countries did increase, and education and health levels rose. Industrialisation did take place but through the exploitation of the peasantry and the marshalling of labour and material resources in the cities. With the eyes of the leadership of the state on the planners, prestige projects (Sputnik, the subway systems of St Petersburg and Moscow, to give two examples) could be accomplished and held up as examples of the superiority of the system. However, the inability to fill the shops with consumer goods would prove far more difficult to achieve and the queues that formed outside shops the ultimate reminder that the system was flawed.

While the inauspicious start to such development (on the back of war, civil war, famine, foreign intervention) did not help, the ultimate reason for the collapse of state socialist regimes must be found in the inherent weaknesses and contradictions of such a system called central planning. As has been said by many: when industry belongs to everyone (i.e. the state), it belongs to no one; the end result being that the necessary incentives for developing the economy were removed. In times of revolutionary fervour or in times of war this would be temporarily suppressed, but in the long march to economic development incentives matter, and the lack of such was to be the ultimate undoing for the system and for the regimes which had implemented central planning.

Key terms

Bolshevik	Menshevik
Central planning	Nationalisation
Collectivisation	NEP
Economic growth	October Revolution
Gosplan	Plan of production
Incentives	Soviet
Input-output tables	Vesenkha
Kulak	War communism

Review questions

1   Are there any features of central planning which you think might be useful in running a company, or a country under market conditions?

2   The forced collectivisation of the peasantry was an attempt by the Soviet Union to develop heavy industry by making use of the surplus grain created by the peasantry. Is there any other way that the leadership within the Soviet Union could have proceeded to industrialise their country?

3   Are authoritarian regimes always a by-product or, indeed, a necessary precursor for an economy to be centrally planned? Or could central planning have existed in the Soviet Union under a Western-style democratic government?

2

STYLISED FACTS OF TRANSITION

Two decades on

After two decades of transition from plan to market, we can now identify some of the most important stylised facts of economic transition. Some of these patterns of transition were expected, such as the rise in private enterprise and services, the fall in government expenditure and revenue, the rise in foreign trade and in unemployment, and the change in investment and consumption patterns. Others happened as predicted but the degree of the change was unexpected, such as the rapid rise in prices, the sudden fall in revenues, and the extreme rise in poverty and inequality. Other developments were, for the majority of commentators interested in transition, surprising. This includes the decline in output, the rise in corruption and informal activities, and most alarmingly, the fall in population associated with the rise in mortality rates (unprecedented in peacetime in industrialised nations).

A number of caveats apply. The stylised facts below are based largely on quantitative evidence; yet data in the early years of transition were often unreliable and should be treated with caution. In addition, these trends apply mainly to CEE and FSU countries, and only in part to East Asian countries. Although China and Vietnam did witness some of these patterns (for example, increase in services, corruption, private enterprise, trade, inequality), many of the most disturbing trends (such as the fall in output and population, rise in prices, poverty and mortality rates) were not witnessed in either China or Vietnam. Third, within the CEE/FSU group of countries there are differences with respect to the output collapse and hyperinflation, the trend in relation to poverty and inequality, the structural changes, and the population trends. There are also differences over time, with the early years of transition recording the worst features of transition with a general improvement in the second decade of transition. The general patterns of transition are outlined in Table 2.1.

We will examine each of these patterns of transition using data from the transition countries for the 20-year period 1989 to 2008. As many other assessments of transition (see Campos and Coricelli 2002; EBRD 1999; World Bank 2002a) covered only the first decade, there will inevitably be differences in terms of the facts and patterns identified. For example, Campos and Coricelli (2002) limited the stylised facts of the first decade to seven, covering output, GDP structure, capital, labour, trade, institutions and social costs (see Box 2.1). Although there are some similarities between our Transition Twelve assessment and the Magnificent Seven of Campos and Coricelli (2002), most notably with respect to output and sectoral changes, trade, social costs and institutions, there are also differences in that we highlight patterns during transition pertaining to prices and inflation, private sector activity, corruption, the hidden economy and the role of the state.

Table 2.1 Stylised facts of two decades of transition: the Transition Twelve

With respect to	*Stylised fact*
Output	Output declines and then recovers
Prices	Inflation soars and then stabilises
Sectoral share of GDP	Major sectoral changes in the composition of GDP, with large increases in services
Private sector activity	Private sector share of GDP rises
Investment and consumption	Investment falls and then recovers, consumption falls and then rises
Corruption and the informal economy	Initial rise in corruption and the informal sector, followed by a decline
Poverty and inequality	Initial rise in both poverty and inequality, followed by a decline
Foreign trade and FDI	International trade initially falls and then increases, FDI flows increase
Labour market	Participation rates fall as does employment, unemployment rises
Government revenue and public spending	Role of the state declines as the share of tax and public spending in output falls
Demographics	Demographics deteriorate, then stabilise
Institutions	Institutions initially collapse and are then rebuilt

---

Box 2.1

The Magnificent Seven

Based on evidence and data available post-1989 and covering the first ten years of transition in CEE and FSU countries, authors Nauro Campos and Fabrizio Coricelli identified what they called the Magnificent Seven Stylised Facts of the Transition. They are outlined in Table 2.A.

The reader should compare these stylised facts, as identified by Campos and Coricelli (2002) for the first decade of transition with our stylised facts as listed in Table 2.1, for the first two decades of transition. Please note both the similarities and the differences between the two lists.

Table 2.A Stylised facts of ten years of transition: the Magnificent Seven

Stylised fact	*Comment*
Output fell	Output fell in all countries of the former Eastern Bloc, in stark contrast with development in China and Vietnam (where growth has been fast and sustained). The exact magnitude of the fall is a matter of controversy, inter alia, because of the sizeable informal sectors that quickly emerged.
Capital shrank	Capital stocks reduced dramatically during the transition, although the expectation is that efficiency has increased.
Labour moved	Labour moved in all senses, but the most obvious one: measures of geographical mobility are very low. Yet we observe large changes in labour market status, sectors and occupations.
Trade reoriented	CMEA trade collapsed and was redirected to industrial countries in a very short period of time, with few exceptions (the slow reorientation in BUR is led by Ukraine and Belarus, not Russia).

Table 2.A Continued

Stylised fact	Comment
Structure changed	The share of value-added in industry in GDP declines rapidly. In the CEEB case, this is due almost exclusively to the increase of the services share. In the case of CIS, the reasons for the slower decline are much less clear-cut.
Institutions collapsed	The fall of communism created an enormous institutional vacuum. Although efforts to understand and measure it are just starting, its effects are sizeable and omnipresent.
Transition costs were high	One of the surprises of the transition was the appearance of unexpected costs. The rise of unemployment and income inequality was expected. The rise in mortality rates and the decline in school enrolment rates were not expected.

Source: Campos and Coricelli (2002).

Output

All of the FSU countries with the exception of Estonia suffered an output decline over the period 1990 to 2000 (with Uzbekistan recording an annual average GDP decline of *only* 0.2 per cent).[1] Whereas Latvia and Lithuania experienced relatively mild declines in output (–1.5 per cent and –2.7 per cent annual averages respectively), Moldova, Tajikistan and Ukraine all suffered average annual declines in excess of 9 per cent, resulting in a GDP level, at the end of the first decade of transition, equal to or more than 50 per cent below what it officially was at the outset of transition. At the other end of the performance table, Poland and Slovenia performed the best of the CEE/FSU countries, recording annual average growth rates of 4.7 per cent and 2.7 per cent respectively.[2] Overall, the performance of other CEE countries in this decade was mixed, with some recording small but positive annual growth rates (the Czech Republic 1.1 per cent, Hungary 1.6 per cent and the Slovak Republic 1.9 per cent) as against those recording negative average annual growth rates (Bulgaria –1.8 per cent, FYR Macedonia –0.8 per cent and Romania –0.6 per cent). Russia's decline was an annual fall of –4.7 per cent, but as with other FSU countries not all of the 1990 to 2000 decline is due to transition, since the former Soviet Union was in economic decline before its demise in late 1991. In contrast, China and Vietnam (both countries had started reforms earlier, in 1978 and 1986 respectively) recorded annual average growth rates of 10.6 per cent and 7.9 per cent respectively. The difference in performance between China/Vietnam and former Soviet bloc countries has attracted much attention with different views cited on the relative importance of determinants such as initial conditions, market versus institutional reforms, foreign trade and external aid, and political change (more later).

As for the 2000 to 2005 period, this is recognised as the recovery phase (with the output decline in CEE countries ending well before 2000). Countries that recorded some of the largest output falls in the previous decade were, not surprisingly, the same countries that recorded the highest annual average growth rates in this period (namely Azerbaijan, Kazakhstan and Tajikistan, albeit countries that were growing from relatively low bases). Georgia, Moldova and Ukraine also performed well (7.4 per cent, 7.1 per cent and 8 per cent respectively) but this only goes some way in recovering the output loss of the previous decade: these annual growth rates, although impressive, must be viewed in this context. Although China and Vietnam continued to perform remarkably well (growth rates of 9.6 per cent and 7.5 per cent respectively), many of the other TEs, both CEE and FSU countries (including Russia), also performed well in terms of average annual growth rates. Not surprisingly, the countries with the initial highest GDP per capita levels (see Table 7.2), most notably the Czech and Slovak Republics, Hungary, Poland and Slovenia, were, more or less, the countries that recorded the lowest annual average growth rates for the period 2000 to 2005. However, we need more data for more years before we can conclude evidence of a 'catch-up' or convergence effect, i.e. where poor transition countries grow faster than richer transition countries.

Table 2.2 Decline and recovery (GDP average annual % growth)

Country	1990–2000	2000–2005
Albania	3.5	5.3
Armenia	−1.9	12.4
Azerbaijan	−6.3	12.7
Belarus	−1.7	7.5
Bosnia and Herzegovina	..	5
Bulgaria	−1.8	5
China*	10.6	9.6
Croatia	0.6	4.7
Czech Republic	1.1	3.5
Estonia	0.2	7.5
FYR Macedonia	−0.8	1.7
Georgia	−7.1	7.4
Hungary	1.6	4.1
Kazakhstan	−4.1	10.1
Kyrgyzstan	−4.1	4
Latvia	−1.5	7.9
Lithuania	−2.7	7.8
Moldova	−9.6	7.1
Mongolia	2.7	5.8
Montenegro	..	..
Poland	4.7	3.2
Romania	−0.6	5.8
Russia	−4.7	6.2
Serbia	..	..
Slovak Republic	1.9	4.9
Slovenia	2.7	3.4
Tajikistan	−10.4	9.6
Turkmenistan	−4.8	..
Ukraine	−9.3	8
Uzbekistan	−0.2	5.3
Vietnam	7.9	7.5
as compared to		
Low-income countries	4.8	6.1
Middle-income countries	3.8	5.2
Lower-middle income	5.3	6.3
Upper-middle income	2.1	3.5
High-income countries	2.7	2.2

Source: World Bank Development Indicators.

Note

* China revised its national accounts data from 1993 onwards. Data before 1993 are linked to the revised data on the basis of earlier growth rates.

Various explanations have been given for this recovery in output. These include the boom in the Russian economy (aided initially by the rouble devaluation of 1998 and the high price of oil and other natural resources), restoration of peace and stability in the Balkans, a boost from the cumulative effects of growth-enhancing structural reforms, the favourable international economic climate (in both developed and emerging markets), continued growth in international trade, CEE benefits from EU accession and, finally, low interest rates and cheap credit. Unfortunately, it is the latter that partly contributed to the global economic crisis of 2007 to 2009, adversely affecting all transition economies but, in particular, many of the smaller Central and Eastern Europe countries whose (banks) and economies had amassed large amounts of (bad) debt.

In terms of comparisons with non-transition countries, we report the annual average GDP growth rates for the two periods 1990 to 2000 and 2000 to 2005 for low-, middle- and high-income countries, as classified by the World Bank. Although the transition countries do well with respect to growth in output, compared to other countries in the 2000 to 2005 period, it is clearly evident from the data that the output performance in the 1990 to 2000 decade was, in relative terms (compared to all other groups of countries, as classified by income), poor, leaving many TEs with very low output levels at the start of the new millennium.

Prices

The trend in inflation during the transition period was one of rising prices (indeed, hyperinflation in some cases where the monthly inflation rate was in excess of 50 per cent) followed by a period when inflation rates fell and then stabilised at, in the majority of cases, single-digit inflation rates. After the initial years of rapid price increases (at a time when inflation rates worldwide were falling in an inflationary environment that was generally benign), inflation had peaked by the early to mid-1990s, and thereafter the rate of price increases decelerated in the majority of countries (see Chapter 7 for more on inflation and its causes). For some countries, a second bout of inflation occurred in the late 1990s, coinciding with the 1998 Russian crisis and its aftermath. Inflation rates were highest among FSU countries and the Balkans with Central European economies recording the lowest inflation rates of CEE/FSU countries in transition.

For the majority of TEs, the peak of inflation was early on in transition and coincided with liberalisation policies. This is evident in Table 2.3. All countries, with the exception of Bulgaria, recorded their highest annual inflation rate in the period 1989 to 1994, with the majority (including all FSU countries) witnessing a peak in inflation between 1992 and 1994. The maximum inflation rate varied from a moderate 24 and 35 per cent in China and Hungary respectively to hyperinflation rates in excess of 4,500 per cent per annum in Armenia, Croatia, Georgia and Ukraine, with Georgia's 1994 inflation rate of 22,286 per cent one of the world's highest rates of inflation in modern times.[3]

Despite the common trend of a peak in inflation in early years, economies in transition experienced much cross-country variation with respect to inflation (acknowledging that this variation was also evident on the eve of transition, as the existence of the monetary overhang and the repressed inflation outlined in Chapter 3 indicate). This is evident in the number of years in which inflation was high (measured at above 40 per cent), ranging from (aside from non-reforming Belarus and Turkmenistan) zero years in China and Hungary to a high of eight years in Romania and Tajikistan.[4] It is also evident in the occurrence of inflation reversals,

Table 2.3 Inflation in transition countries

Country	Inflation rate at outset of transition (Year=1991)	Maximum inflation rate (annual average)	Year in which inflation peaked (1989–2007)	No. of consecutive years (1989–2007) in which annual inflation exceeded 40%	Year in which inflation rate first fell below 40%	Inflation reversal[a]	Year(s) of reversal	Inflation in 2007
Albania	35.5	226	1992	2	1994	Yes	1997/8	2.9
Armenia	274	4,964	1994	5	1996	No	na	4.4
Azerbaijan	107	1,664	1994	5	1996	No	na	16.6
Belarus	94.1	2,219.6	1994	12	2003	Yes	1999/2000	8.3
Bosnia and Herzegovina	..	..	..	..	..	:	:	1.5
Bulgaria	334	1,058	1997	7	1998	Yes	1996/7	8.4
China[b]	0.7	24.1	1994	0	na	No	na	4.8
Croatia	123	6,673.6	1992	4	1995	No	na	2.9
Czech Republic	52	52	1991	1	1992	No	na	2.9
Estonia	211	1,076	1992	4	1995	No	na	6.6
FYR Macedonia	115	1,511	1992	4	1995	No	na	2.8
Georgia	79	22,286	1994	5	1996	Yes	1999	9.2
Hungary	35	35	1991	0	na	Yes	1995/6	7.9
Kazakhstan	78.8	1,877.3	1994	5	1996	No	na	10.8
Kyrgyzstan	85	855	1992	5	1996	Yes	1999/2000	10.2
Latvia	172	951	1992	3	1994	No	na	10.1
Lithuania	225	1,021	1992	4	1995	No	na	5.7
Moldova	98	1,276	1992	4	1995	Yes	1999/2000	12.4
Mongolia	20.2	268.4	1993	5	1997	No	na	8.2
Montenegro	..	..	..	..	..	:	:	4.3
Poland	70.3	586	1990	4	1993	No	na	2.4
Romania	170	255.2	1993	4 / 8 in total	1995 / 2001	Yes	1997	4.8
Russia	92.7	1,526	1992	6 / 7 in total	1997 / 2000	Yes	1999	9.0
Serbia	..	..	..	..	..	:	:	6.7
Slovak Republic	61.2	61.2	1991	1	1992	No	na	2.8
Slovenia	118	1,306	1989	4	1993	No	na	3.6
Tajikistan	112	2,885	1993	8	1999	Yes	1995	13.4
Turkmenistan	103	3,102	1993	7	1998	No	na	6.3
Ukraine	91	4,735	1993	6	1997	Yes	1999/2000	12.8
Uzbekistan	82.2	1,568	1994	7	1998	No	na	12.3
Vietnam*	487	84.4	1991	1	1992	Yes	1995	8.3

Sources: United Nations Economic Commission for Europe (UNECE) Statistical Division Database, compiled from national and international (CIS, EUROSTAT, IMF, OECD) official sources; United Nations Economic and Social Commission for Asia and the Pacific (ESCAP).

Notes
a. Defined as a reversal in a downward trend.
b. Economic transition in China and Vietnam began in 1978 and 1986 respectively. The inflation rates in column 2 are for these respective years.
na = not applicable

defined as a reversal in a downward trend. In the case of the TEs, it is evenly split between countries that did not experience an inflation reversal and those countries (well-known cases include the Bulgarian crisis of 1997 and the Russian crisis of 1998) that did experience an inflation reversal. Half of the inflation reversals were in the years 1999/2000 (all CIS countries, including Russia), relating to the aftermath of the 1998 Russian crisis and the subsequent boost in economic activity and prices.

By 2007, almost two decades after transition began, the average inflation rate for all TEs was less than 7.5 per cent, representing significant progress from the early years of rapid and rising prices and inflation rates. The highest inflation rate in 2007 was a moderate 16.6 per cent, in Azerbaijan, a country that has witnessed extraordinary output growth (oil-related) in recent years. Unfortunately, these numbers do not tell the full story, as events were to unfold a short time later. Many of the TEs, and particularly in Eastern Europe, were overheating by the late 2000s, reflected in large current account deficits and rising debt levels. With fixed exchange rates the preferred currency policy of a number of transition countries (and with the prospect of euro membership for some TEs), short-term inflows and a credit boom led to a surge in money supply growth and inflation by 2008 (see Table 7.3). More than half of the 31 TEs had double-digit inflation rates in 2008. These weaknesses in the transition countries were further aggravated by the global crisis of 2007 to 2009, with financial markets turning their attention to Eastern Europe and, in particular, Hungary, Latvia, Romania and Ukraine, which all had to turn to the IMF for financial assistance. By the end of the decade, output decline, recession and deflation rather than inflation had become the main concerns for many of the CEB transition countries.

Sectoral share of GDP

The sectoral share of output is only one of a number of measures that can be used to capture what we call the 'economic structure' of a country.[5] Indeed, three of our other indicators used to measure discernible patterns of transition (namely investment share of GDP, government size, trade openness) also capture a country's economic structure. We begin, however, with the sectoral composition of output. Given that structural changes are central to the transformation from plan to market, sudden and large changes in the sectoral composition of output were to be expected.

The literature identifies well-established or stylised patterns of development over time; namely as GDP per capita increases, the structure of output changes insofar as the agriculture share falls, and the shares of industry and services rise (Syrquin and Chenery 1989). We now wish to consider the sectoral changes that have taken place in transition countries. This is particularly relevant given the priorities of the socialist system towards investment (over consumption) and the preferences for industry (over services). Based on the Marxist-Leninist ideology of services being nonmaterial and unproductive and the need, in a short period of time, to catch up with the industrialised economies, resources were diverted to industry. Hence, with this bias in favour of industry over services, former socialist countries at the outset of transition found themselves with a large industry share of GDP and a relatively small services share of GDP. Industry shares in excess of 50 per cent were common whereas only Croatia and Slovenia of the socialist countries had a services share in excess of 50 per cent, typical levels of services for upper-middle-income countries. These high industry shares combined with relatively low services shares were viewed as a serious structural distortion (in that they arose from the priorities of central planning to ensure rapid industrialisation) and

Table 2.4 Industry share of GDP*

Country	1989	1990	1991	1992	1993	1994	1995	1996	1997	1998	1999	2000	2001	2002	2003	2004	2005	2006	2007	2008
Albania	45	48	43	23	23	22	22	20	19	16	17	19	20	19	21	21	22	20	20	20
Armenia	..	52	49	39	27	37	32	33	33	31	32	35	33	35	38	38	45	45	44	45
Azerbaijan	..	33	31	40	34	28	34	39	40	36	41	45	47	50	53	55	64	69	69	71
Belarus	..	47	50	48	38	36	37	39	41	41	39	39	37	37	39	41	42	42	42	39
Bosnia and Herzegovina	..	..	..	..	..	26	26	31	31	33	30	24	24	22	23	25	25	25	22	..
Bulgaria	58	49	44	43	37	35	35	33	29	32	29	31	30	29	29	29	29	31	32	31
China	43	41	42	43	47	47	47	48	48	46	46	46	45	45	46	46	48	49	49	49
Croatia	..	36	35	33	36	33	31	30	31	30	28	28	28	27	28	29	28	28	28	28
Czech Republic	..	49	49	51	42	44	38	42	41	39	39	38	38	37	36	39	38	38	39	38
Estonia	41	50	40	35	31	30	33	31	31	29	27	28	28	28	29	28	29	30	30	..
FYR Macedonia	..	44	36	39	35	30	30	30	35	34	33	34	32	30	31	29	30	29	30	28
Georgia	39	33	37	24	22	10	16	24	24	23	23	22	22	24	26	26	27	25	24	24
Hungary	44	39	36	35	33	32	32	32	34	34	33	32	31	30	30	30	30	30	30	29
Kazakhstan	..	..	45	45	40	41	32	27	27	31	35	40	39	39	38	38	40	42	41	42
Kyrgyzstan	..	36	35	38	32	25	20	18	23	23	25	31	29	23	22	22	22	20	19	..
Latvia	44	46	44	35	35	31	30	29	30	28	25	24	23	23	22	22	22	22	22	23
Lithuania	44	31	51	43	41	36	34	32	32	32	31	30	31	30	32	33	33	34	33	..
Moldova	39	37	33	31	44	38	32	31	29	24	19	22	24	23	25	17	16	16	15	15
Mongolia	39	41	34	34	28	28	29	22	27	21	22	20	21	22	25	30	34	42	41	..
Montenegro	..	..	..	..	..	..	..	..	..	..	..	23	25	24	23	22	21	20	18	18
Poland	..	50	47	41	40	39	35	34	33	33	33	32	29	29	30	31	31	31	31	30
Romania	..	50	45	44	42	46	43	42	39	35	34	36	37	38	35	35	35	37	36	34
Russia	50	48	48	43	45	45	37	39	38	37	37	38	36	34	34	35	39	38	38	37
Serbia	..	..	..	..	..	..	..	..	..	..	..	31	28	27	26	28	29	29	28	..
Slovak Republic	58	59	38	33	34	38	39	35	35	35	36	36	35	34	35	36	36	39	40	41
Slovenia	..	42	45	41	39	40	35	36	36	36	36	36	35	35	35	35	34	34	34	..
Tajikistan	36	38	37	46	47	41	39	29	29	27	30	39	40	39	37	32	31	27	28	23
Turkmenistan	34	30	31	12	64	47	63	69	48	42	46	44	44	42	41	40	..	..	..	..
Ukraine	48	45	51	51	38	43	38	35	35	36	36	36	35	35	35	36	32	36	37	37
Uzbekistan	33	33	36	36	34	26	28	30	26	26	24	23	22	23	23	26	23	27	32	33

(Continued)

Table 2.4 Continued

Country	1989	1990	1991	1992	1993	1994	1995	1996	1997	1998	1999	2000	2001	2002	2003	2004	2005	2006	2007	2008
Vietnam	23	23	24	27	29	29	29	30	32	32	34	37	38	38	39	40	41	42	42	40
Average TEs, unweighted	**42**	**42**	**41**	**38**	**37**	**35**	**34**	**34**	**33**	**32**	**32**	**32**	**32**	**31**	**32**	**32**	**33**	**33**	**33**	
as compared to																				
Low-income countries	22																		30	
Middle-income countries	38																		37	
Lower-middle income	36																		41	
Upper-middle income	39																		33	
High-income countries	33																		26	

Source: World Bank Development Indicators.

Note

* Industry comprises value added in mining, manufacturing, construction, electricity, water and gas.

they reflected a degree of over-industrialisation that required correction (by market forces, during transition).

The reallocation of resources during transition did see, as was predicted, a decline in the industry shares in value added and an increase in the services share, reflecting a catch-up with market economies. The evidence indicates that large-scale de-agrarianisation (but not in all TEs) as we will see later), deindustrialisation and tertiarisation did indeed take place in transition countries since 1989 (Landesmann 2000). Prior to transition, the industry share in value added for transition countries was, on average, in excess of 40 per cent. Within five years, the industry share had declined to, on average, 36 per cent and there was a steady but slow decline to the 33 per cent, on average, that transition countries witnessed by 2007. How does that compare with other non-transition countries? In 1989, prior to the demise of the socialist system, industry shares in value added varied from, on average, 22 per cent in low-income countries, 38 per cent in middle-income countries to 33 per cent in high-income countries. By 2007, the 33 per cent industry share of GDP in transition countries was not out of line with similar countries, with middle-income countries reporting a 37 per cent share, on average, and upper-middle-income countries reporting a 33 per cent industry share, on average.

The deindustrialisation that is a common feature in market economies over time as they become more developed appears to have been accelerated in transition countries, i.e. the rate of decline in CEE countries (from, on average, 47 per cent in 1990 to, on average, 32 per cent in 2007) is greater than the rate of decline in either upper-middle-income (from, on average, 38 per cent in 1990 to, on average, 33 per cent in 2007) or high-income (from, on average, 32 per cent in 1990 to, on average, 26 per cent in 2007) countries. With respect to industry shares in China, it remains relatively high, with a 47 per cent share in 1979 when reforms began and, after three decades of transition, the industry share has actually increased, to almost 50 per cent of GDP (making China the 'workshop of the world'), second only to oil-rich Azerbaijan.[6] Vietnam has witnessed an even larger increase (reflecting its lower income per capita standing) since reforms began, from a 28 per cent share in 1987 to a 42 per cent share of GDP in 2007.

As for services, at the outset of transition, the services share of GDP was only 34 per cent for transition countries, as compared with 43 per cent in low-income countries, 45 per cent in middle-income countries and 64 per cent in high-income countries. After two decades of transition and structural change, the services share of GDP in transition countries has increased, on average, to 58 per cent in 2007. Again, this is more in line with the 53 per cent average rate for middle-income countries but still (well) below the figure of 61 (73) per cent for upper-middle (high) income countries. The increase in services over that time has been steady, with a one percentage point increase recorded for most years after the initial first decade when yearly increases in the average services share of GDP tended to be large, not surprisingly given the extent of the services gap between transition and market economies. With respect to regional differences between CEE and CIS countries, the gap that existed between the two groups of countries at the outset of transition has widened after two decades: 39 per cent as against 32 per cent in 1989 whereas in 2006 it was 60 per cent for CEE countries (in line with other upper-middle-income countries) as against a lowly 49 per cent for CIS countries (in line with other low-income and lower-middle-income countries). Indeed, four of the CIS countries, namely Armenia, Kyrgyzstan, Tajikistan and Uzbekistan, all still had, as of 2007, an agriculture share of GDP equal to or in excess of 20 per cent. As for East Asian countries, the services share of GDP was low at the outset of transition, at 22 per cent in 1979 for China and 31 per cent in 1987 for Vietnam. Despite some increases, it remains relatively

Table 2.5 Services share of GDP*

	1989	1990	1991	1992	1993	1994	1995	1996	1997	1998	1999	2000	2001	2002	2003	2004	2005	2006	2007	2008
Albania	23	16	18	25	22	25	22	47	48	51	54	52	53	55	55	55	56	57	59	59
Armenia	..	31	26	30	22	18	26	31	35	35	38	39	38	39	38	37	34	35	36	37
Azerbaijan	..	38	36	32	38	39	39	33	38	45	40	38	37	35	34	33	27	24	21	23
Belarus	..	29	29	29	43	46	44	44	43	46	46	47	51	51	51	49	48	48	48	53
Bosnia and Herzegovina	..	..	..	..	..	..	..	..	..	..	..	..	..	..	..	..	..	..	..	..
Bulgaria	32	34	39	44	52	52	54	50	45	49	54	55	65	68	68	64	61	61	61	61
China	32	32	34	35	34	33	33	33	34	36	38	39	40	41	41	40	40	40	40	40
Croatia	..	53	55	52	50	55	56	56	56	57	59	61	60	59	62	60	61	61	61	65
Czech Republic	..	45	45	44	52	52	57	53	55	57	57	58	58	60	61	61	59	59	59	60
Estonia	38	34	42	52	59	60	61	63	64	65	69	67	67	67	67	68	67	67	67	68
FYR Macedonia	..	47	51	44	53	56	57	57	53	53	54	54	56	57	56	58	58	58	59	60
Georgia	38	35	34	23	19	24	32	42	47	50	51	56	56	55	54	56	56	62	65	66
Hungary	41	46	55	58	60	61	61	61	60	61	62	62	64	65	66	65	65	66	66	66
Kazakhstan	..	..	..	29	43	43	55	60	61	60	55	51	52	53	54	55	53	52	53	52
Kyrgyzstan	..	30	28	23	27	34	37	32	33	38	37	32	34	39	41	43	46	47	47	..
Latvia	36	32	33	48	53	59	61	64	65	68	71	72	72	73	74	73	74	75	75	..
Lithuania	..	42	33	43	44	53	55	56	57	58	61	62	62	63	62	61	61	61	61	74
Moldova	24	27	24	18	23	32	35	38	41	44	53	49	50	54	54	62	64	67	73	..
Mongolia	46	44	52	36	42	39	30	31	34	37	37	47	50	51	51	45	41	36	36	..
Montenegro	..	..	..	..	..	..	..	..	..	..	..	64	63	64	66	67	69	69	69	73
Poland	..	42	46	52	53	55	57	59	60	61	62	63	65	67	66	64	65	65	65	65
Romania	..	26	35	37	35	32	36	37	41	48	51	51	48	49	52	51	55	52	55	58
Russia	33	35	38	50	47	49	56	54	56	57	55	56	58	60	61	60	55	57	57	58
Serbia	..	..	..	..	..	..	..	..	..	..	..	48	53	57	59	58	55	57	59	..
Slovak Republic	32	33	34	57	61	60	56	55	59	60	60	59	60	61	60	61	61	61	61	55
Slovenia	..	52	49	53	56	60	60	60	60	60	61	61	61	62	62	63	63	63	63	59
Tajikistan	32	29	26	27	30	35	22	29	36	46	43	34	34	36	36	47	45	48	51	59
Turkmenistan	37	38	37	78	17	19	20	18	30	32	28	31	31	36	38	40	45	..	51	..
Ukraine	29	30	27	29	41	36	42	48	50	50	47	47	49	51	53	52	57	55	55	55
Uzbekistan	36	34	26	29	35	36	40	43	42	43	42	43	43	44	43	43	49	46	46	43

Vietnam	35	39	36	39	41	44	44	43	42	42	40	39	38	38	38	38	38	..
Average TEs unweighted	**34**	**36**	**37**	**40**	**41**	**43**	**45**	**46**	**48**	**50**	**51**	**52**	**53**	**54**	**54**	**55**	**55**	**58**
as compared to																	
Low-income countries	43																	46
Middle-income countries	45																	53
Lower-middle income	40																	46
Upper-middle income	51																	61
High-income countries	64																	73

Source: World Bank Development Indicators.

Note

* Services comprises value added in wholesale and retail trade (including hotels and restaurants), transport, and government, financial, professional, and personal services such as education, health care and real estate services.

low by international standards: in 2007, the services share in value added is 40 per cent and 38 per cent in China and Vietnam respectively, below the, on average, 46 per cent and 53 per cent share for low-income and lower-middle-income countries, respectively.

Is the progress in structural change complete? Further downsizing in industry, particularly for EU accession countries, is expected. As for the modest changes that have taken place in CIS countries, it remains to be seen whether they will show further signs of catching up or exhibit some other transitory phenomenon that has been a feature of transition in many former Soviet Union republics (Campos and Coricelli 2002; Raiser *et al.* 2003).

Private sector activity

During the period of the socialist system, public or state-owned enterprises – a defining characteristic of socialism – dominated ownership of the enterprise sector. With the exceptions of Hungary and Poland, private sector activities in socialist countries accounted for, on average, no more than 5 to 10 per cent of GDP. With the fall of the Berlin wall in November 1989 and the collapse of socialist governments throughout Eastern Europe, former Eastern bloc countries witnessed a sharp increase in private enterprise. Although the Soviet Union's Law on Cooperatives – placing cooperatives, broadly defined, on a legal par with state ownership – and the spontaneous privatisation that preceded transition did see an increase in private sector activity, it was the dissolution of the Soviet Union in December 1991 and the emergence of 15 successor states that all, to varying degrees, espoused market reforms, that precipitated an increase in the private sector share of GDP in transition countries. By the mid-1990s, the private sector/GDP ratio had risen to in excess of 40 per cent, on average. Given the emphasis on early privatisation in CEE and FSU countries, much of the increase in the early years of transition was due to the rapid implementation of privatisation programmes, albeit of different modes and designs. In other countries, particularly Hungary and Poland, the increase was due largely to *de novo* (start-ups as opposed to spin-offs) new private firms, the vast majority of which were SMEs in the services sector.

By the end of the first decade, the private sector share of GDP was 60 per cent, on average, and rising, with over two-thirds of transition countries having a private sector/GDP ratio of 60 per cent or higher. The exceptions were war-torn Bosnia and Herzegovina, and Serbia and Montenegro and the least advanced reforming countries, notably Tajikistan (where market reforms were delayed largely because of the civil war which only concluded in 1997), Uzbekistan (which followed, it is often cited, a more gradual approach), and, most especially, Belarus and Turkmenistan whose respective leaders, in opposing market reforms, delayed and in some cases halted privatisation. Second- and third-wave privatisations, in addition to new private firms, have seen the private sector account for two-thirds of all economic activity by 2005. In some cases, namely the Czech and Slovak Republics, Estonia and Hungary, private sector share of GDP is 80 per cent, in excess of the equivalent figure for many well-established Western European countries. Even more remarkable, and despite some setbacks, was the extent of the increase in private sector activity in both Russia and China.

In the case of Russia, the most important successor state to the Soviet Union where the ideological opposition to private ownership was the strongest, private sector share of GDP was reported to be 70 per cent at the end of the first decade of transition. Given the history of communism and the Marxist-Leninist ideology with its inherited legacy of public ownership and collectivisation, this level of private ownership is remarkable. Unfortunately, this quite astounding transformation is not the full story, since the quality of the private

Table 2.6 Private sector share of GDP[a]

Country	1989	1990	1991	1992	1993	1994	1995	1996	1997	1998	1999	2000	2001	2002	2003	2004	2005	2006	2007	2008
Albania	5	5	10	10	40	50	60	75	75	75	75	75	75	75	75	75	75	75	75	75
Armenia	10	10	30	35	40	40	45	50	55	60	60	60	70	70	70	75	75	75	75	75
Azerbaijan	10	10	10	10	10	20	25	25	40	45	45	45	60	60	60	60	60	60	75	75
Belarus	5	5	5	10	10	15	15	20	20	20	20	20	25	25	25	25	25	25	25	30
Bosnia and Herzegovina	..	..	..	..	..	..	..	..	..	35	35	35	45	45	50	50	55	55	60	60
Bulgaria	10	10	20	25	35	40	50	55	60	65	70	70	70	70	75	75	75	75	75	75
China[b]	..	..	..	..	..	..	..	55	60	..	..	..	..	55	60	..	..	..	..	..
Croatia	15	15	20	25	30	35	40	50	55	55	60	60	60	60	65	65	65	65	70	70
Czech Republic	5	10	15	30	45	65	70	75	75	75	80	80	80	80	80	80	80	80	80	80
Estonia	10	10	10	25	40	55	65	70	70	70	75	75	80	80	80	80	80	80	80	80
FYR Macedonia	15	15	15	15	35	35	40	50	50	55	55	55	60	60	60	65	65	65	65	70
Georgia	10	15	15	20	20	20	30	50	55	60	60	60	65	65	65	65	65	70	75	75
Hungary	20	20	30	40	50	55	60	70	75	80	80	80	80	80	80	80	80	80	80	80
Kazakhstan	5	5	5	10	10	20	25	40	55	55	60	60	65	65	65	65	65	65	70	70
Kyrgyzstan	5	5	15	20	25	30	40	50	60	60	60	60	65	65	65	75	75	75	75	75
Latvia	10	10	10	25	30	40	55	60	60	65	65	65	70	70	70	70	70	70	70	70
Lithuania	10	10	10	20	35	60	65	70	70	70	70	70	75	75	75	75	75	75	75	75
Moldova	10	10	10	10	15	20	30	40	45	45	45	50	55	55	55	55	60	65	65	65
Mongolia	0	10	25	30	35	40	40	45	50	55	60	60	65	65	70	70	70	70	75	75
Montenegro	..	..	..	..	..	..	..	..	..	65	65	70	70	70	70	70	65	65	65	65
Poland	30	30	40	45	50	55	60	60	65	65	65	70	75	75	75	75	75	75	75	75
Romania	15	15	25	25	35	40	45	55	60	60	60	60	65	65	65	70	70	70	70	70
Russia	5	5	5	25	40	50	55	60	70	70	70	70	70	70	70	70	65	65	65	65
Serbia	..	..	..	..	..	55	60	70	75	75	75	80	80	80	80	80	80	..	55	60
Slovak Republic	5	10	15	30	45	55	60	70	75	75	80	80	80	80	80	80	80	80	80	80
Slovenia	10	15	20	30	40	45	50	55	60	60	60	65	65	65	65	65	65	65	70	70
Tajikistan	10	10	10	10	10	15	25	30	30	30	40	45	50	50	50	50	55	55	55	55
Turkmenistan	10	10	10	10	10	15	15	20	25	25	25	25	25	25	25	25	25	25	25	25
Ukraine	10	10	10	10	15	40	45	50	55	55	55	60	65	65	65	65	65	65	65	65
Uzbekistan	10	10	10	10	15	20	30	40	45	45	45	45	45	45	45	45	45	45	45	45
Vietnam[c]	..	70	70	70	60	60	60	60	60	60	60	60	60	60	60	60	60	65	65	..
Average TEs, unweighted	**10**	**13**	**17**	**23**	**31**	**38**	**44**	**51**	**56**	**57**	**58**	**59**	**60**	**63**	**64**	**65**	**65**	**66**	**67**	**67**

Source: EBRD.

Notes
a. 'Private sector share' in GDP represent rough EBRD estimates, based on available statistics from both official (government) sources and unofficial sources. The underlying concept of private sector value added includes income generated by the activity of private registered companies, as well as by private entities engaged in informal activity in those cases where reliable information on informal activity is available. For ease of exposition, actual numbers are rounded so that reported numbers end in a five or a zero.
b. Using the OECD private sector definition as only firms not identified as being publicly controlled (state or collective).
c. The nonstate sector comprising cooperatives, private and household (IMF).

sector, and subsequent country performance, depends on the legal and institutional framework (more later), how enabling the business environment is, the composition of the private sector into privatised and new private, and whether its emergence is due to privatisation (from above) of SOEs or privatisation (from below) with the organic development of new private firms (Winiecki 2000). Given the insider privatisation of the early 1990s, the much-needed enterprise restructuring and improvement in firm performance that was to follow from the change in ownership did not materialise in all cases. In addition, the loans-for-shares scheme of the mid-1990s amounted to, in the view of many critics, the greatest giveaway sale of the century (Freeland 2000). For many Russians, rightly or wrongly, privatisation became associated with corruption and theft, resulting in ever-rising hostile views towards democracy and declining public support for market reforms. In more recent years, the increase in the share of private sector activity was halted, and possibly slightly reversed, by Putin's efforts to renationalise parts of Russian industry. Despite this recent trend and the oligarchic nature of many sectors that typify Russian industry, the Russian economy today, at least in terms of the division of ownership between private and public, resembles, more or less, other middle-income market economies where private enterprise dominates.

The process was very different in China. For one, reforms initially took place in agriculture with the household responsibility system (HRS), a form of decollectivisation (or some might say privatisation).[7] In contrast, privatisation (of industry, at least) was not formally part of the reform agenda until quite recently. The large SOEs were not initially (and for most of the transition era) slated for privatisation. Indeed, as with the word 'transition', privatisation was not commonly used, for obvious ideological reasons given the persistence of one-party rule and its insistence on socialism with Chinese characteristics. Yet, market reforms did result in an initial increase in private enterprise, although small and often rural in nature. The emergence of small private firms and household business activities, combined later with the privatisation of many township and village enterprises (TVEs), saw the private sector share of GDP in China exceed 50 per cent by the mid-1990s. This privatisation from below (as opposed to the privatisation from above as was common in CIS countries) was initially tolerated by government officials and, later, given the apparent increases in output generated by these private enterprises, even encouraged with the slogan 'To Get Rich is Glorious' and the granting of permission for private entrepreneurs to join the Communist Party. Of course, China has a long tradition of entrepreneurship and private enterprise. Pre-1949 Communist rule, China had a history of small rural private businesses which distinguishes it from Russia where in pre-Soviet Union times, the Russian Tsars ruled over their fiefdoms. In China, as in many Central European countries, what we have witnessed since transition began is simply a revival of the private enterprise that flourished pre-socialism.

Investment and consumption

One of the features of the socialist system was high levels of investment expenditure, at the expense of consumption expenditure. If the socialist countries were to close the gap with the industrialised Western world, resources would have to be devoted, it was argued by proponents of the command economy, to investment goods rather than to consumer goods. High investment from mandatory saving, combined with industrialisation, state ownership and central planning, would ensure, it was argued by supporters of the Marxist-Leninist ideology, high growth rates and levels of economic development necessary to catch up and surpass the capitalist countries of Western Europe and North America. Table 3.1 in the next chapter reports investment/GDP ratios for the socialist countries at the outset of transition, as compared to rates for the industrialised world. As is evident from the table, investment ratios in 1989 were high in socialist countries, at 34 per cent for Russia and CEE countries, 26 per cent in China, and 31 per cent in other NIS and Mongolia. Benchmark rates for the industrialised world were lower, at 25 per cent for middle-income countries and 22 per cent for OECD countries (World Bank 1996). Of course, the socialist countries of Eastern Europe and the Soviet Union are not the only set of countries that have had high investment/GDP ratios: the newly industrialised countries (NIC) of South East Asia, including Japan, Korea and Singapore, all had high investment ratios throughout their early years of development.

Investment rates were at their highest in the early years of socialist development but by the end of the socialist era investment had started to decline, admittedly from relatively high levels. Prior to transition, with the Soviet Union and its satellite states in a deep malaise, and with a looming budgetary crisis across the socialist world, investment expenditure was falling, as was the level of economic growth. Indeed, in the immediate years preceding the dissolution of the socialist system, many of the socialist countries were in economic decline, i.e. economic growth rates were negative. Much of the capital stock on the eve of transition was in need of serious upgrade; some was simply obsolete. With transition looming and economic reforms accelerating, expectations were for a decline in the investment expenditure share (but for an improvement in investment efficiency) and a large boost in the consumption expenditure share of GDP. Private household consumption, suppressed under the socialist system, was forecast to rise, as was the level of output and economic growth. Although consumption expenditure did indeed rise (in relative terms), admittedly from relatively low levels at the outset of transition, the fall in investment expenditure combined with a collapse in foreign trade for socialist countries partly contributed to an initial decline in economic activity, as alluded to in the section on 'Output' (p.72). There is still some debate about the relative declines in both consumption and output in the early years of the transition recession. With a large decline in output, evidence would seem to indicate that the fall in consumption, although significant, was not as large. The trend in both investment expenditure and consumption expenditure for the period 1989 to 2008 is given in Tables 2.7 and 2.8 respectively.

Investment, defined as gross fixed capital formation (that is, gross domestic fixed investment) relative to GDP levels, is reported in Table 2.7. Prior to transition, the investment ratio for TEs was, on average, 28 per cent. This compares to an average rate, in 1989, of 17 per cent for low-income countries, 24 per cent for middle-income countries and 23 per cent for high-income countries. Within TEs there were differences, with a rate of 32 per cent in Russia to only 13 per cent in Vietnam. The last few years of the socialist system witnessed a sharp decline in the investment rate, to an average rate of 20 per cent, with these low levels persisting throughout the early years of transition. Although there was a slight recovery in the mid-1990s, levels for TEs remained, on average, low throughout the first decade of transition and even into the early years of the 2000s. However, in subsequent years investment rates had recovered, so that by 2005 the investment ratio had reached, on average, 25 per cent (close to the average rate for middle-income countries), with further improvements to follow (see Appendix 2). Some cross-country comparisons are worth noting. For example, investment in Russia, as a percentage of GDP, fell from a high of 32 per cent in 1989 to a low of 14 per cent in 1999 before recovering to 21 per cent in 2007. In contrast, investment in China has remained high, from 26 per cent in the late 1980s rising steadily to a peak of 43 per cent in 2006 before falling to 40 per cent by 2008. Investment in war-torn transition countries, both in the CEE and CIS regions, was particularly badly affected.

Table 2.7 Investment/GDP*

Country	1989	1990	1991	1992	1993	1994	1995	1996	1997	1998	1999	2000	2001	2002	2003	2004	2005	2006	2007	2008
Albania	31	29	7	5	13	18	21	21	17	16	19	25	28	24	23	24	24	25	30	32
Armenia	..	44	28	17	12	20	16	18	16	16	16	18	18	21	23	24	30	36	37	37
Azerbaijan	..	20	11	22	21	26	16	29	37	36	29	23	23	34	53	53	41	30	20	23
Belarus	..	22	22	25	34	33	25	21	25	26	26	25	23	22	24	25	27	30	31	33
Bosnia and Herzegovina	..	..	..	..	..	..	12	34	34	33	24	21	19	19	19	17	22	19	23	23
Bulgaria	26	21	18	16	13	14	15	14	11	13	15	16	18	18	19	21	24	26	30	35
China	26	26	28	32	38	36	34	34	33	33	34	34	34	36	39	41	42	43	41	40
Croatia	..	14	10	13	15	14	13	17	21	20	20	19	19	21	25	25	25	26	26	28
Czech Republic	..	25	24	28	28	29	31	32	30	28	27	28	28	28	27	26	25	25	24	..
Estonia	29	24	21	21	24	26	27	26	28	31	25	26	27	30	32	31	31	34	32	21
FYR Macedonia	..	18	19	19	17	15	17	17	17	17	17	16	15	17	17	18	17	18	19	27
Georgia	..	23	19	16	3	3	4	19	18	26	26	25	27	24	27	27	28	26	28	20
Hungary	22	19	21	20	19	20	20	21	22	24	24	23	23	23	22	22	24	22	21	20
Kazakhstan	..	..	..	30	28	26	23	17	16	16	16	17	24	24	23	25	28	30	30	..
Kyrgyzstan	33	23	17	15	13	12	21	23	13	13	16	18	17	16	14	15	14	23	25	24
Latvia	32	23	6	11	14	15	14	17	17	25	23	24	25	24	24	27	31	33	33	32
Lithuania	..	28	22	23	23	23	21	21	23	24	22	19	20	20	21	22	23	25	28	24
Moldova	..	19	17	16	19	16	16	20	20	23	18	15	14	16	19	21	25	28	33	32
Mongolia	45	33	35	28	23	21	27	28	26	34	35	25	22	24	32	31	30	32	37	..
Montenegro	..	..	..	..	..	..	..	..	..	..	..	17	18	15	13	17	18	22	21	26
Poland	16	21	20	17	16	18	18	20	22	24	24	24	21	19	18	18	18	20	22	23
Romania	..	20	14	19	18	20	21	23	21	18	18	19	21	21	21	22	23	24	29	26
Russia	32	29	23	24	20	22	21	20	18	16	14	17	19	18	18	18	18	18	21	22
Serbia	..	..	..	..	..	..	..	10	10	10	11	12	10	12	16	18	17	20	21	21
Slovak Republic	28	31	28	33	30	26	25	32	34	36	30	26	29	27	25	24	27	26	26	..
Slovenia	..	19	21	18	19	20	22	22	24	25	27	26	25	23	24	25	25	26	27	..
Tajikistan	27	22	16	11	11	24	21	18	18	13	17	9	9	11	12	14	14	13	21	19
Turkmenistan	..	..	..	..	35	..	..	41	39	45	40	35	32	28	25	23	23	..	..	..
Ukraine	25	23	..	27	24	24	23	21	20	20	20	20	20	19	22	23	22	25	27	26
Uzbekistan	32	31	25	27	25	26	33	37	34	30	27	24	28	22	22	24	22	21	19	19
Vietnam	13	..	..	..	24	25	25	26	27	26	26	28	29	31	33	33	33	33	37	..

Average TEs	28	24	20	21	21	24	23	24	23	22	22	22	24	24	25	26	27
as compared to																	
Low-income countries	17																24
Middle-income countries	24																27
Lower-middle income	25																33
Upper-middle income	22																21
High-income countries	23																21

Source: World Bank Development Indicators.

Note
* Gross fixed capital formation, or formally gross domestic fixed investment

Table 2.8 Consumption/GDP*

Country	1989	1990	1991	1992	1993	1994	1995	1996	1997	1998	1999	2000	2001	2002	2003	2004	2005	2006	2007	2008
Albania	62	61	91	152	120	96	87	93	99	98	86	85	81	92	92	88	91	90	88	85
Armenia	..	46	61	101	86	99	109	102	108	104	99	97	90	85	83	80	73	70	72	75
Azerbaijan	..	51	73	51	67	67	77	85	77	83	72	64	62	60	58	59	38	32	30	25
Belarus	..	47	46	51	56	59	59	60	59	58	59	59	58	60	58	57	50	53	55	54
Bosnia and Herzegovina	..	..	..	..	..	..	..	..	..	..	..	..	..	104	102	100	99	88	90	85
Bulgaria	52	60	54	66	..	73	74	71	75	73	68	71	69	69	71	70	70	70	69	70
China	50	46	45	45	41	42	44	43	44	45	45	47	44	41	40	36	33	32	33	37
Croatia	..	..	74	57	53	66	63	65	62	62	61	62	63	64	62	61	61	60	60	59
Czech Republic	..	49	47	51	51	51	54	52	53	58	53	52	52	51	52	50	49	49	48	..
Estonia	58	62	55	51	57	54	60	59	58	58	57	55	57	57	56	56	55	56	56	..
FYR Macedonia	..	72	64	64	76	70	72	73	72	82	70	74	77	76	76	79	78	78	78	79
Georgia	63	65	66	98	139	102	66	92	99	82	82	67	74	75	73	71	67	78	70	76
Hungary	60	61	70	73	74	72	66	64	62	62	64	67	67	67	69	67	66	65	66	67
Kazakhstan	..	..	..	52	71	75	68	72	78	78	68	62	61	61	58	53	49	45	47	..
Kyrgyzstan	67	71	64	71	78	68	82	69	88	88	78	66	65	68	78	76	86	96	101	..
Latvia	53	53	46	39	59	63	68	67	65	63	63	63	64	62	62	63	63	65	65	..
Lithuania	..	57	56	68	68	67	67	63	62	65	65	65	64	64	65	65	65	65	65	66
Moldova	..	..	58	24	54	57	67	77	86	86	82	91	89	83	91	90	94	95	95	97
Mongolia	60	62	72	60	60	56	64	64	52	60	60	70	74	76	67	62	55	48	48	..
Montenegro	..	..	..	..	..	..	..	..	..	..	..	70	75	81	74	73	70	77	91	84
Poland	..	48	58	58	63	60	61	62	62	62	62	63	64	66	64	63	62	62	60	66
Romania	..	66	61	63	64	63	68	69	74	83	83	79	79	77	76	77	78	74	69	73
Russia	45	49	47	37	51	52	53	55	60	60	54	46	49	51	50	50	49	49	49	45
Serbia	..	..	..	..	..	..	..	..	73	78	82	89	81	80	74	80	84	82	81	84
Slovak Republic	50	54	51	50	54	52	52	53	55	55	56	56	58	58	57	57	57	57	56	54
Slovenia	..	53	55	55	58	57	60	59	58	58	58	57	57	56	56	55	54	53	52	..
Tajikistan	75	74	70	42	55	62	..	64	70	84	74	82	92	88	89	88	102	110	114	114
Turkmenistan	51	49	44	..	29	..	..	44	76	84	76	36	46	46	57	62	46	53	51	..
Ukraine	54	57	54	46	48	55	58	54	57	57	54	54	57	57	56	53	58	60	61	64
Uzbekistan	78	61	56	75	58	51	55	55	61	60	62	62	60	60	55	51	47	48	54	55
Vietnam	88	84	82	81	77	76	74	75	72	71	68	66	65	66	67	66	62	62	66	..

Average TEs unweighted
as compared to

	60	58	60	62	64	67	66	67	68	70	68	66	66	68	67	67	65	66	66
Low-income countries	79																		74
Middle-income countries	60																		55
Lower-middle income	59																		48
Upper-middle income	62																		61
High-income countries	60																		62

Source: World Bank Development Indicators.

Note
* Household final consumption expenditure, or formerly private consumption

Some commentators on transition subscribe to the view that the collapse in output in TEs in the early years of transition was related to the fall in investment that occurred at that time in transition countries.[8] While acknowledging that the relationship between capital accumulation and growth is essentially a long-run relation whereas transition is a relatively short-run phenomenon, supporters of this view argued for more investment, not just from private sources but also state investment, in order for greater enterprise restructuring and for economic growth to be restored. An economic recovery did indeed emerge by the mid-1990s for CEE countries and somewhat later (following the 1998 Russian crisis) for many CIS countries, and this recovery was associated with a pick-up in investment expenditure, as Table 2.7 reports.

Consumption, defined as household (that is, private) final consumption expenditure, relative to GDP levels, is reported in Table 2.8. Prior to transition, consumption as a proportion of GDP was for TEs, on average, 60 per cent. This compares to an average rate, in 1989, of 79 per cent for low-income countries and 60 per cent both for middle-income and high-income countries. As predicted, transition to the market economy, involving early reforms of liberalisation and marketisation, resulted in a rise in consumption expenditure relative to GDP levels. Throughout the first decade of transition, the consumption/GDP ratio rose steadily, from 62 per cent, on average, in 1992 to 68 per cent, on average, in 1999. Since then, with the main market reforms already in place, and with the reallocation of goods from investment to consumption already completed, the consumption ratio has tended to remain steady, in the 65 to 67 per cent range but with sizeable cross-country variations persisting.

Corruption and the informal economy

Corruption

Since transition began over two decades ago, much attention was given to the growing problem of corruption in transition countries. Despite some misguided claims to the contrary, corruption did not surface out of the transition from plan to market. Corruption was a serious problem during Soviet times.[9] Indeed, in the Brezhnev era the problem of corruption was considered to be endemic. On gaining office, Brezhnev's successor, Yuri Andropov, set about to try to reduce the growing corruption and indiscipline associated with the previous regime. With the disintegration of the Soviet Union a decade later, the hope was that the level of corruption would decline. This does not appear to be the case. Indeed, it seems by all accounts that corruption in many former socialist countries actually increased in the early years of transition (and that the increase was due not only to increased awareness and improved monitoring procedures), with many transition countries, in the words of some commentators, 'infested' with corruption. In this short analysis, we will examine a number of issues relating to corruption in transition countries, including the size, causes, empirical findings and policy options. We begin, however, with a definition.

Given its non-transparent nature, corruption is a difficult concept to define and even more difficult to directly observe and subjectively measure. The standard definition of corruption is the misuse of public office (or, more broadly, entrusted power) for private gain. Examples of corrupt behaviour include bribery, extortion, fraud, nepotism, cronyism and embezzlement. In identifying possible causes, there are both economic and non-economic factors at play. Moreover, many of these factors are interrelated, with causality difficult to establish. Among social scientists, economists are particularly interested in corruption given its negative effects on the economy and society at large. The literature identifies the negative consequences to include its effects on economic growth (and most particularly investment and consumption decisions), income distribution, government budgets, and overall social solidarity and cohesion. Of course, there is a view that not all corruption is bad, i.e. the 'greases the wheel' or 'oils the mechanism' idea. However, in many transition countries, what was witnessed in the 1990s was corruption on a grand scale as many states in the newly established countries of the CIS were captured by narrow vested interest groups and powerful elites.

Measurement

As alluded to already, corruption is a difficult phenomenon to measure. For example, even if we could observe and measure bribes, it is the case that such a measure of bribery alone would not capture all forms of corruption. Accurate and comparable cross-country and time series national data for levels of corruption in the transition countries since the start of the 1990s are difficult to obtain. Firm-level data are sometimes used but the resulting cross-country comparisons are often unreliable.

In general, there are two common measures of corruption. One is the Corruption Perceptions Index (CPI), developed by the global civil society organisation Transparency International. The second measure, highly correlated with Transparency International's CPI, is the World Bank Corruption Index taken from the World Bank Governance Indicators (WGI). Details of this measure are given in Appendix 3.

The CPI is constructed from individual surveys of the business community and several ratings by economic risk analysts and country experts, and measures the degree to which corruption is *perceived* to exist among public officials and politicians: it is a subjective indicator and only measures perceived as opposed to actual corruption. The CPI score ranges from 0 (highly corrupt) to 10 (virtually corrupt-free). As the CPI was only constructed from 1995 onward, we report CPI scores for the years 1996 to 2008, in four-year intervals. In 2008, for example, Slovenia, with a CPI of 6.7, was perceived to be the least corrupt transition country (and was perceived to be the twenty-sixth least corrupt country out of a total of 180 countries) whereas Kyrgyzstan, Turkmenistan and Uzbekistan with a CPI of 1.8 were perceived to the most corrupt transition countries (and were perceived to be the 166th least corrupt – or the eleventh most corrupt – countries out of a total of 180 countries).

As is evident from the above, there is considerable cross-country variation. As highlighted elsewhere in this book there appear to be regional differences, with the CEB countries recording the lowest levels of perceived corruption, followed by the SEE countries and with the CIS countries having the lowest (= worst) CPI scores. The CPI scores for China, Mongolia and Vietnam fall between the SEE and CIS range of scores. How do TEs compare to non-transition countries in terms of levels of perceived corruption? For comparison, we include a small number of non-transition countries, including the UK and US. Of the least corrupt transition countries, Slovenia and Estonia have the highest (= best) CPI scores, placing them between France and Spain in Transparency International's 2008 table of perceived corruption. This indicates that, despite some of the exaggerated claims about the epidemic of corruption in all transition countries, some governments in TEs are relatively honest and compare favourably with governments in many well-established market economies. Many of the SEE countries (and, interestingly, China) are clustered just short of mid-table, along with non-transition countries such as Kuwait, El Salvador, Ghana and Mexico. All the CIS countries with the exception of Georgia (having managed to reduce corruption levels through

Table 2.9 Corruption Perceptions Index (CPI), 1996–2008

Country	1996 (n=54)	2000 (n=90)	2004 (n=145)	2008 (n=180)
CEB				
Czech Republic	5.4 (25th)	4.3 (42nd)	4.2 (51st)	5.2 (45th)
Estonia	..	5.7 (27th)	6.0 (31st)	6.6 (27th)
Hungary	4.9 (31st)	5.2 (32nd)	4.8 (42nd)	5.1 (47th)
Latvia	..	3.4 (57th)	4.0 (57th)	5.0 (52nd)
Lithuania	..	4.1 (43rd)	4.6 (44th)	4.6 (58th)
Poland	5.6 (24th)	4.1 (43rd)	3.5 (67th)	4.6 (58th)
Slovak Republic	..	3.5 (52nd)	4.0 (57th)	5.0 (52nd)
Slovenia	..	5.5 (28th)	6.0 (31st)	6.7 (26th)
SEE				
Albania	..	..	2.5 (108th)	3.4 (85th)
Bosnia and Herzegovina	..	..	3.1 (82nd)	3.2 (92nd)
Bulgaria	..	3.5 (52nd)	4.1 (54th)	3.6 (72nd)
Croatia	..	3.7 (51st)	3.5 (67th)	4.4 (62nd)
FYR Macedonia	..	..	2.7 (97th)	3.6 (72nd)
Romania	..	2.9 (68th)	2.9 (87th)	3.8 (70th)
Serbia and Montenegro*	..	1.3 (89th)	2.7 (97th)	3.4 (85th)
CIS				
Armenia	..	2.5 (76th)	3.1 (82nd)	2.9 (109th)
Azerbaijan	..	1.5 (87th)	1.9 (140th)	1.9 (158th)
Belarus	..	4.1 (43rd)	3.3 (74th)	2.0 (151st)
Georgia	..	..	2.0 (133rd)	3.9 (67th)
Kazakhstan	..	3.0 (65th)	2.2 (122nd)	2.2 (145th)
Kyrgyzstan	..	..	2.2 (122nd)	1.8 (166th)
Moldova	..	2.6 (74th)	2.3 (114th)	2.9 (109th)
Russia	2.6 (47th)	2.1 (82nd)	2.8 (90th)	2.1 (147th)
Tajikistan	..	..	2.0 (133rd)	2.0 (151st)
Turkmenistan	..	..	2.0 (133rd)	1.8 (166th)
Ukraine	..	1.5 (87th)	2.2 (122nd)	2.5 (134th)
Uzbekistan	..	2.4 (79th)	2.3 (114th)	1.8 (166th)
East Asia				
China	2.4 (50th)	3.1 (63rd)	3.4 (71st)	3.6 (72nd)
Mongolia	..	..	3.0 (85th)	3.0 (102nd)
Vietnam	..	2.5 (76th)	2.6 (102nd)	2.7 (121st)
Others				
Finland	9.1 (4th)	10.0 (1st)	9.7 (1st)	9.0 (5th)
Myanmar	..	..	1.7 (142nd)	1.3 (178th)
Nigeria	0.7 (54th)	1.2 (90th)	1.6 (144th)	2.7 (121st)
United Kingdom	8.4 (12th)	8.7 (10th)	8.6 (11th)	7.7 (16th)
USA	7.7 (15th)	7.8 (14th)	7.5 (17th)	7.3 (18th)

Source: Transparency International www.transparency.org.

Note
* The CPI scores for Serbia and Montenegro, split since 2006, were the same in 2008.

various anti-corruption campaigns that followed the 2003 Rose Revolution) have CPI scores of less than three, placing them in the bottom half of the 2008 table. Indeed, there are only 10 countries (with the usual candidates including Afghanistan, Dem. Rep. of Congo, Haiti, Iraq, Myanmar and Sudan) that have a CPI score lower than the TEs that are perceived as most corrupt.

Using firm-level data from the EBRD/World Bank BEEPS for the period 1999 to 2005, there are indications of improvements in many transition countries with smaller incidences of corruption than before (see Appendix 3 for more evidence of declines in corruption). The survey evidence indicates that for many TEs, firms are paying relatively (as a share of revenue) smaller and less frequent bribes, with corruption been viewed by firms as less of a problem than before. Strong leadership, anti-corruption campaigns and other institutional reforms have contributed to falling levels of corruption, most particularly in Georgia, and in Bulgaria, Latvia, Romania and the Slovak Republic where the pull of EU membership has had a positive impact (Anderson and Gray 2006).

Causes

Economists, in tending to use the formal language and models common among social scientists, often describe corrupt acts in terms of expected benefits against expected costs (all costs, not just financial). Indeed, the causes of corruption (see below) may be expressed in terms of benefits and costs. Among social scientists there is no consensus on the precise causes of corruption. Many view it as a function of past conditions (that is, legacy and history) and present circumstances (that is, policy and non-policy factors). Others see it simply as a result of the monopoly power of government officials. We, as do many others, view it as a complex phenomenon with no single determinant. The literature identifies a number of factors, including:

- historical, legal, cultural and religious traditions;
- level of economic development;
- state activities (regulations, tax/spending) and (discretionary) government policies;[10]
- political and democratic institutions (e.g. quality of bureaucracy, strength of civil society);
- resource endowments and openness to foreign trade.

According to the literature, the quality of government is better in rich, common law, predominantly Protestant, ethno-linguistically homogeneous countries compared with poor, civil or socialist law, predominantly Catholic or Muslim, ethno-linguistically heterogeneous countries. Expressed in terms of corruption, albeit perceived, countries that are more developed, have a history of British rule, with Protestant origins, and have a longer exposure to democracy (decades as opposed to years) are less 'corrupt' than countries that are less developed, were not former British colonies, with non-Protestant traditions, and have a shorter history of democracy (La Porta *et al.* 1999; Treisman 2000). The more interesting and controversial questions in relation to the determinants of corruption in transition countries include the following:

- Are TEs more corrupt than other countries of similar levels of economic development?
- Is it a legacy of communism? In particular, is there a legacy of communist institutions and social norms that emphasised personal connections, fused economic and political power, and subordinated the rule of law to party diktat (Treisman 2000)?
- How, if at all, is it related to transition and policy reforms?
- What role, if any, did policy mistakes play in increasing the level of corruption in the early years of transition? Did the emphasis on market reforms over institutional building contribute to the rise in corruption? What role, if any, did privatisation, and, in particular, voucher privatisation, play? What specific policy reforms, if any, contributed to the decline in corruption in the second decade of transition?

- What explains the cross-country variation?
- In the case of the big two (Russia and China), are high corruption levels due to the level of development, lack of democracy and free trade or is it a cultural trait?

Here we present some findings on the determinants of corruption in transition countries.

Some empirical findings and policy options

In this short section on empirical findings, we report results from Treisman (2000, 2003). In his cross-country econometric studies, corruption, a priori, is a function of a number of variables, representing, on the one hand, legacy (a favourite phrase of economists but used parsimoniously in this book) and fixed effects and, on the other hand, post-communist developments. His main findings are that post-communist countries are on average somewhat more corrupt than others. However, their level of corruption does not seem to have much to do with post-communism per se, but, according to Treisman (2003), 'in large part, because the countries are poor and lack a post-war history of democracy'; i.e. economic development and the political system matter in terms of explaining the determinants of corruption in TEs. As between countries, the fixed effect or pre-transition factors (that is, initial income, years of communism, resource endowments, etc.) explain most of the current variation whereas post-communist development and policies explain a relatively small part of the variation. Measures of market reforms were not significant, indicating that government policies are somewhat constrained by a country's characteristics and inherited conditions.

It is interesting to compare this cross-country study to country studies of corruption in transition countries. When corruption arises in discussion in the context of transition in the former socialist countries, Russia inevitably crops up in debate. Since transition began two decades ago, the issue of corruption in Russia (and other former republics of the Soviet Union, including Ukraine and the Caucasus and Central Asian states) has been prominent in media reports and country studies. Russia is often labelled as one of the most corrupt countries in the world. Reasons cited for such high levels vary from a cultural trait (of the Slavic nations) to a legacy of Soviet times. However, evidence from Treisman (2000, 2003) would indicate that although legacy matters, the most significant determinants are the level of economic development and its lack of a history of democracy. In the case of Russia, he writes that the 'level of perceived corruption can be predicted quite accurately from four factors – its low economic development, federal structure, and meagre experience until recently with democracy or free trade. All of these have arguably more to do with the Bolshevik victory in 1917 than any cultural traits of contemporary Russians' (Treisman 2000).[11] The implication here is that Russia has higher levels of corruption than, say, the US, because it is poorer and has a much shorter history of democracy.

In a country study on corruption and institutions in Russia, Levin and Satarov (2000) investigate the high levels of corruption in Russian society. They identify a number of factors that explain the high levels of corruption in Russia. These include the heritage of the totalitarian regime, economic collapse and political instability, underdeveloped legislation and a weak judiciary, inefficiency of state institutions, weakness of civil society, and poorly established democratic political transitions. They conclude by claiming that 'it is a continuation from past norms of behaviour that existed in Soviet times, and indicates absence of change in the basic principles of conduct'. Moreover, it is the intertwining of political and economic power, manifesting itself in 'ill-defined boundaries between politics and private business' that facilitates corruption (Levin and Satarov 2000). Of course, this fusion of government and business is not simply a legacy of the Soviet system but indeed can be traced back to pre-Soviet times and the Tsarist era. This analysis still leaves us with an unanswered question: why is measured corruption – perceived or realised – higher in Russia than in China, a country whose level of development as measured by GDP per capita is much lower than Russia's? One possible explanation for the Russian–Chinese corruption dilemma (and the not unrelated output–corruption nexus) is the difference in political change and control of the respective Communist parties and the institutional checks and balances of the former centrally planned system. Andvig (2006), a critic of the cross-country quantitative analysis as presented above, argues that the loss of power (and the subsequent disorder and institutional dysfunction) by the Communist Party in Russia without (unlike in CEE countries) alternative, established political forces to contest elections and succeed to power at the outset of transition, in contrast to the survival of the Communist Party in China, may go some way towards partly explaining the differences in corruption between the two big transition powers.

If the past – and distant past at that – appears as, if not more, important than current policy, does this mean that countries with serious problems of corruption, including TEs, are limited in what can be done? Can a country grow its way out of corruption? Certainly the evidence is that they can, as the advanced countries of Western Europe and the US clearly show. In that context, what is to be done in transition countries? Reform of the state is important. In particular, there is a need for more transparency of laws and rules, changes in relative wages, reductions in business regulations, simplification of taxes and customs. Accession to the EU will help, as will a reform of how political parties are financed. Greater competition, in both economic and political circles, is required. Further changes in the judicial and legal system, state procurement procedures, banking and financial systems are needed, and with greater transparency and accountability required in all. Commitment and strong leadership is required. Finally, continued monitoring of corruption and bribery, even when the trend is positive, is essential if the TEs are to reach corruption levels common in the advanced market economies to which transition countries aspire.

Informal economy

The informal economy, also known as the hidden, shadow, unofficial or underground economy, is another complex phenomenon. Although there is little consensus in the literature on a precise definition, we define it as unregistered economic activities not included in official GDP, i.e. unreported to the state statistical office. Here we will discuss the measurement and size, causes and consequences of the informal or unofficial economy.

Measurement

Measuring the size of the unofficial economy is a difficult task by virtue of its nature, that is, it is hidden. There is no one commonly accepted method to measure the unofficial economy. One approach is micro-based, using firm-level data. Another approach is macro-based, using the currency demand (cash in circulation) method or the electricity consumption method. With respect to the latter, it is believed that electricity consumption provides a good measure of total economic activity, i.e. the electricity-to-GDP elasticity is close to one: a 1 per cent increase in electricity consumption is associated with a 1 per cent increase in GDP.[12] The difference between total GDP (proxied by electricity consumption) and official GDP gives an estimate of the size of the unofficial economy. Whichever measure is used, the evidence worldwide indicates that the size of the unofficial economy, relative to the official economy, has increased. According to Schneider and Enste (2000), 'the shadow economy has reached a remarkably large size'. This growth is due to a number of factors, some of which are listed below.

The unofficial economy in transition economies is no exception to this trend. Of course, an unofficial economy existed in Soviet times long before the transition of the 1990s. The second economy, as it was called, comprised legal and illegal activities and was associated with shortages in the state sector. Officially, the second economy, although tolerated, was viewed as a corrosive force, damaging the state sector (the first economy). Others saw it as an integral part of the socialist system, an inevitable consequence of the centrally planned administration with its pervasive shortages and perverse incentives. In Soviet times, it was not uncommon for underground factories to coexist inside a state factory, with managers engaging in what Gregory Grossman (a University of California, Berkeley-based scholar and expert on the second economy in the Soviet Union) called the four Bs (barter, black market, bribes and *blat*, i.e. Russian for favours or influence). Despite the enormous difficulties involved in measuring the extent of the second economy in Eastern Europe and the Soviet Union, by the 1980s economists and other social scientists had amassed a great deal of research (helped by Soviet émigrés) on the second economy (Sampson 1987). In general, the second economy varied from sector to sector (largest in agriculture, trade and services), from country to country (biggest in southern Soviet republics), and from ethnic group to ethnic group (large among Jews and non-Russian ethnic groups).

Causes

The economics literature identifies a number of determinants of the unofficial economy. These include the following:

- tax and social security burden;
- state regulation (and discretion) in the official economy;
- labour market restrictions;
- corruption and bribery;
- extortion by mafia and criminal gangs;
- provision of public goods and quality of state institutions (trust and loyalty in public institutions).[13]

A priori, it is argued that burdensome tax and social security contributions, heavy and discretionary state regulation (in the form of licences, permits, etc.), restrictive labour market practices, and high levels of corruption, bribes and mafia activities all contribute to a large and rising unofficial economy. In addition, poor provision of public goods and a general distrust of state institutions may further increase the size of the unofficial economy. It is acknowledged that economic factors only partly explain the unofficial economy. People engage in shadow activities for a variety of reasons, partly based on the costs (including penalties) and benefits of operating in the unofficial economy. A more interdisciplinary approach recognises institutional factors such as tax morale and culture, and for transition countries, the number of years under communism and, indeed, whether the former socialist country was part of the old Tsarist Russian Empire. The likely interaction between the official and unofficial economy, and between the unofficial economy and corruption, makes for a complex and intriguing phenomenon. Indeed, it is not clear whether the twin phenomena of the unofficial economy and corruption are, although clearly related, substitutes for or complements to each other.

The literature identifies features of the unofficial economy in transition countries (some of which appear to be unique, and distinct from the unofficial economies in other emerging markets). Kaufmann and Kaliberda (1996) observe the following characteristics of the unofficial economy in TEs:

- coexistence of state and non-state activities and enterprises;
- visible and not necessarily small;
- mostly non-violent and non-criminal;
- sharp dichotomy between unofficial economy and official economy is absent;
- social services and state subsidies are accessible to unofficial activities;
- shallow (meaning it can be reversed by appropriate policies).

Size

Regarding size, according to Johnson *et al.* (1997), the average unofficial (as measured by the electricity consumption method) 'share in east European countries starts in 1989 at 16.6 per cent, peaks at 21.3 per cent in 1992, and falls to 19.0 per cent by 1995. By contrast, the average unofficial share in former Soviet countries starts at 12.0 per cent and rises to 36.2 per cent in 1994.' Schneider and Enste (2000) concur, stating that 'Transition economies are estimated to often have substantial unofficial activity, many at around one-quarter of GNP. The biggest shadow economies belong to some of the former Soviet Union transition countries (between 28–43 per cent of GDP), like Georgia, Ukraine and Belarus.' In terms of the size of the unofficial economy, this places former socialist countries embarking on transition well above many other countries and comparable to many developing and other emerging countries that typically have large unofficial economies. After over a decade of transition, unofficial economic activity in transition countries, as elsewhere, had increased. Estimates of the size of the unofficial economy in 28 transition countries for the year 2002/2003 are listed in Table 2.10. We only include estimates for a point in time (that is, 2002/2003), as there are no reliable time series data for the size of the unofficial economy throughout the entire transition period.

The transition countries are divided into CEE, SEE, FSU and East Asian groupings, and the similarity, in terms of the size of the unofficial economy, within each grouping is striking. What is also striking is the difference between FSU and non-FSU countries. Table 2.10 also reports the average size of the shadow economy for some non-transition (both developing and developed) countries, as a percentage of official GDP. It is evident that the unofficial economy in transition countries is indeed large as compared to the unofficial economy share in either developing or OECD countries.

Consequences and policy options

Among the costs and consequences of the unofficial economy are considered the following:

- too little investment;
- loss of tax revenue, and erosion of tax and social security bases;

Table 2.10 Estimates of the size of the unofficial economy, 2002/2003

Country	Unofficial economy % of official GDP	Country	Unofficial economy % of official GDP
CEE (5)	**25.0**	Lithuania	32.6
Czech Republic	20.1	Moldova	49.4
Hungary	26.2	Russia	48.7
Poland	28.9	Tajikistan	n.a.
Slovak Republic	20.2	Turkmenistan	n.a.
Slovenia	29.4	Ukraine	54.7
		Uzbekistan	37.2
SEE (7)	**36.9**		
Albania	35.3	East Asia (3)*	**18.0**
Bosnia and Herzegovina	36.7	China	15.6
Bulgaria	38.3	Mongolia	20.4
Croatia	35.4	Vietnam	17.9
FYR Macedonia	36.3		
Romania	37.4	Country Groupings (no.	
Serbia and Montenegro	39.1	of countries)	
		Transition (CEE/SEE/FSU)	
FSU (13)	47.6	Countries (25)	40.1
Armenia	49.1	Mostly Developing	
Azerbaijan	61.3	Countries (86)	
Belarus	50.4	Africa (37)	43.2
Estonia	40.1	Central and South	
Georgia	68.0	America (21)	43.4
Kazakhstan	45.2	Asia (28)	30.4
Kyrgyzstan	41.2	Highly developed OECD	
Latvia	41.3	countries (21)	16.3
		Unweighted average (145)	35.2

Source: Schneider (2006).

Note
* According to the author, these estimates are difficult to interpret and it is questionable whether they can be compared, in any meaningful way, with estimates for the other countries.

• greater distortions, particularly its effects on the official economy (e.g. attracting workers from the official economy);
• policy errors based on official data, hindering the effective management of the economy.

Overall, it is argued, the unofficial economy impedes output growth. On a positive note, the fall in output in the early years of transition was partly mitigated by a growing unofficial economy. Indeed, the transition countries that recorded the largest declines in measured output (e.g. Georgia, Moldova, Ukraine) had some of the largest estimates for the unofficial economy. It also allowed enterprises and start-ups to develop their businesses, and experience the competitive pressures of the market system as opposed to the bureaucratic system that preceded the transition. Currently, policy makers in TEs are engaged in trying to reduce the size of the unofficial economy. Policies such as market liberalisation, reform of tax and social transfers, deregulation and privatisation are just some of the policies advocated in tackling the unofficial economy.

Poverty and inequality

Over two decades ago at the outset of transition, neither poverty nor inequality was a major issue or big concern for policy makers. This may have been due to a number of different reasons. Both were considered low relative to other countries (and particularly countries of similar levels of economic development where poverty and inequality were much higher). Given the heavy investment by socialist countries in social expenditures, the level of educational attainment and the health status, on average, of the population at the start of transition, it meant that poverty and inequality were perceived, at least by the majority of policy makers, as second-order problems in the transition to the market. In addition, given the consensus at the outset of transition that there would be a resumption of growth and a narrowing of the income gap between East and West, poverty and inequality were not considered as priority challenges. Moreover, social issues were not a central element of the reform package advocated by mainstream economists, with, as a priority, a commitment only (at least, initially) to a social safety net and a reorientation of public expenditure (towards health and education).[14]

Here we will examine a number of issues pertaining to poverty and inequality, including the situation pre-transition, and developments since the beginning of transition. In particular we will examine developments in the first decade of transition when, according to the international organisation responsible for reducing global poverty, the 'increase in poverty and inequality in the transition countries of Europe and Central Asia over the past decade is striking as it is unprecedented' (World Bank 2000).

The way it was

Given the socialist principles of equality and redistribution, it is no surprise that, officially at least, socialist countries were different, at least in terms of social services and welfare conditions, as compared to the capitalist world. Again, officially, the social features of the socialist system were:

- universal access to health services and education;
- no official poverty, or unemployment;
- more egalitarian with respect to income distribution;
- high participation rates for women;
- wage differentials were small as wages were compressed;
- wealth accumulation was minimal (even allowing for benefits received by the Party elite and cadres);
- cash transfers (that is, pensions, unemployment benefits, family allowances) were universal (and non-targeted).

Underpinning all of these features was the ideology of socialism and public ownership with the primary objective of boosting economic growth through investment, industrialisation and central planning.

Although pre-transition data are somewhat sketchy and unreliable, the reality was somewhat different, particularly so in the Soviet Union as compared with the satellite states in Eastern Europe. Poverty did exist, especially in the Central Asian states of the Soviet Union. Inequality in the Soviet Union increased significantly in the last few years prior to transition.

Indeed, 'by 1991 the FSU, and Russia as a part, was already a country of substantial inequality with a high incidence of poverty' (Commander *et al.* 1999). Unemployment also existed, albeit hidden and on the job. Hence, at the outset of transition, poverty and inequality in socialist countries, although lower than in the non-socialist world, were beginning to emerge as serious problems. Inevitably (as we will explain later) the transition to the capitalist system and the market economy would bring a further increase in inequality. What was surprising was the extent, in such a short period of time, of the increase in inequality and poverty and most especially in the former Soviet Union republics. Possible causes for this increase are cited below. The interesting policy debate is whether the market reforms adopted by the transition countries contributed to the incidence of poverty and inequality.[15] We will begin our analysis, however, with developments with respect to poverty in the early years of transition.

Poverty

There are absolute and relative measures of poverty. Unlike relative poverty which defines the poor as those whose income or expenditure is significantly below the country's average, we use an absolute measure, as it focuses on those deprived of basic material needs, i.e. the minimum basket of goods that are required in order to survive. In this context, the conventional measure of poverty is income deprivation. We measure it using the poverty headcount index which is the percentage of people who are poor because their income or expenditure is below a certain $ amount. Then the issue is what should the poverty line or threshold (that is, the minimum needed to cover the cost of the basic needs) be? The standard poverty lines used globally are $1, $2 or $4 per capita per day adjusted for purchasing power parity (PPP). These are to be distinguished from the official poverty lines or national subsistence levels common in most countries.

Poverty is a difficult concept to measure, and even more so in the early period of transition when hyperinflation was common and national statistical offices were poorly resourced (both in terms of finances and appropriate technical skills). All we can get is an approximation. Using household survey data and with the $4 per capita per day PPP as the poverty line, the total estimated number of the poor for 18 TEs increased twelvefold, from nearly 14 million (or 4 per cent of the population) pre-transition to 168 million (or 45 per cent of the population) by mid-decade (Milanovic 1998).[16] As alluded to above with respect to other trends in transition, there were large regional differences in terms of poverty numbers. Table 2.11 reports the poverty headcount index for pre-transition and transition years.

On average, for those first few years of transition, Central European countries at one end of the spectrum experienced an increase from 1 per cent to 2 per cent, while Central Asian countries at the other end of the spectrum witnessed an increase from 15 per cent to over 65 per cent, on average.[17] Transition, with all the turmoil of the first few years, appears to have accentuated the trend of rising rates of poverty that were emerging in the last few years of the Soviet Union. The two most populated TEs, namely Russia and Ukraine, witnessed some of the largest increases in poverty numbers, resulting in the two countries accounting for almost two-thirds of the poor in transition countries by mid-decade.

As a rough guide, we can present the following account of poverty for the early to mid-1990s: the further east one goes, the worse, on average, the situation is with respect to poverty, as seen in Figure 2.1.

Table 2.11 Poverty in transition countries, before and during transition

	Poverty Index (%)[a]	
	1987–1988	*1993–1995*
Central Europe	*<1*	*2*
Czech Republic	0	<1
Hungary	1	4
Slovak Republic	0	<1
Slovenia	0	<1
Balkans and Poland	*5*	*32*
Bulgaria	2[b]	15
Poland	6	20
Romania	6[b]	59
Baltics	*1*	*29*
Estonia	1	37
Latvia	1	22
Lithuania	1	30
Slavic Republics & Moldova	*2*	*52*
Belarus	1	22
Moldova	4	66
Russia	2	50
Ukraine	2	63
Central Asia	*15*	*66*
Kazakhstan	5	65
Kyrgyzstan	12	88
Turkmenistan	12	61
Uzbekistan	24	63
Average TEs	**4**	**45**

Source: Milanovic (1998).

Notes
a. Regional averages are weighted.
b. 1989 data.

Poverty Index	Central Europe < Eastern Europe = Baltics < Slavic < Central Asia				
	2	30	30	45	60+

Figure 2.1 Poverty.

Source: Milanovic (1998).

Using expenditure (rather than income), the results are, although somewhat less dramatic, still striking.

In terms of a profile of the poor, the three risk factors identified are the labour market and employment status, demographics and age, and location. These groups with the highest relative risks of poverty were:

• head of household is unemployed or inactive;
• children;
• rural dwellers.

Aside from these three main at-risk groups, there are others, including the less educated and ethnic groups, but somewhat surprisingly there are mixed results for gender (females) and the elderly (pensioners). As expected, there were differences between CEE and CIS countries. For example, in CEE countries the elderly constitute a lower risk than the population whereas in CIS countries it is the reverse, i.e. the elderly have a higher risk. What about the majority of the poor? The typical example is 'aged between 15 and 64 living in an urban area in a household whose head is employed', i.e. urban working poor. Unlike the poor in developing countries, in TEs many of the poor are literate, well educated and have experienced paid employment (although, for the majority, in the former state sector of the socialist system). Overall, the risk of poverty in CEE countries is linked to well-established household characteristics (employment status, number of earners, education, etc.). In contrast, the picture in CIS countries is more unclear. The bulk of the poor are working poor, and they do not look very different from the non-poor. Furthermore, in the first decade of transition there existed a transient poor, with some people moving from poor to non-poor and vice versa. This should not be surprising given the fluidity of economic and social conditions pertaining at that time in these countries (World Bank 2000).

We now consider the causes of the increase in poverty. From a purely accounting exercise, if we treat poverty as a function of income and its distribution, the proximate causes of the rise in poverty in the first few years of transition were the fall in output and household income and the increase in inequality, or, in the words of Milanovic (1998), 'the descent into poverty is the product of two forces: lower income and greater income inequality'. In the early years of transition, former socialist countries experienced a decline in output followed by a worsening distribution of income (and wealth), amounting to sizeable (cross-country) increases in poverty. What specific factors contributed to the rise in poverty? According to the literature (see Milanovic 1998; World Bank 2000), the contributing factors include:

- social and economic upheaval and dislocation;
- fall in output, incomes, employment and wages (and rise in wage arrears);
- high and rising inflation;
- fall in government revenues and expenditures, with a decentralisation of social services without devolved resources;
- social transfers inadequate, regressive in some countries (due to poor targeting);
- deteriorating health and education systems.[18]

Many of these are conditioned by institutional legacies. Equally, using the accounting framework as before, cross-country differences in poverty outcomes may be expressed as a function of income, and income distribution or inequality. In turn, these reflect policy choices which are often the product of political and institutional structures. For example, even when it became apparent, by the mid-1990s, that there was a growing poverty and inequality problem, a commitment to poverty alleviation and income redistribution was absent in many TEs, particularly in the resource-starved CIS countries where, in these newly established states, old elites (part of the *nomenklatura*) retained power or new elites (often powerful, narrow vested private interests) captured the state, at a high cost to the population and society at large. Poverty outcomes were the result of a complex interaction between politics and institutions in the economic and political spheres (World Bank 2000).

We now examine developments in respect of inequality in those early years of transition.

Inequality

Income distribution was more equal in the former socialist countries than elsewhere in the world. Indeed, 'the countries of Europe and Central Asia entered the transition process with some of the lowest inequalities in the world' (World Bank 2000). Yet by the end of the first decade, inequality in some of the transition countries had reached alarming levels, comparable with some of the most unequal countries in the world. How did this dramatic transformation materialise? Before we examine possible causes, we need to begin with some methodological issues.

Inequality can be measured in a number of different ways. One standard approach is the use of the Gini coefficient or index, measured on a scale of zero to one where zero measures perfect equality (all income is perfectly equally distributed) and one measures perfect inequality (all income is concentrated in the hands of one person).[19] Using the Gini index (of income), inequality rose in all regions in the first years of transition. Table 2.12 reports estimates of the Gini index for pre-transition and transition years.[20] As before, data are from the national household budget surveys.

Within a number of years of transition some former socialist countries, namely Armenia, Georgia, Kyrgyzstan, Moldova and Russia, had become, by all accounts, some of the most

Table 2.12 Inequality in transition countries, before and during transition

	Gini index (annual)[a]	
	1987–1988	*1993–1995*
Central Europe	*0.21*	*0.24*
Czech Republic	0.19	0.27[c]
Hungary	0.21	0.23
Slovak Republic	0.20	0.19
Slovenia	0.22	0.25
Balkans and Poland	*0.24*	*0.30*
Bulgaria	0.23[b]	0.34
Poland	0.26	0.28[e]
Romania	0.23[b]	0.29[c]
Baltics	*0.23*	*0.34*
Estonia	0.23	0.35[d]
Latvia	0.23	0.31[d]
Lithuania	0.23	0.37
Slavic Republics & Moldova	*0.24*	*0.40*
Belarus	0.23	0.28[d]
Moldova	0.24	0.36
Russia	0.24	0.48[d]
Ukraine	0.23	0.47[c]
Central Asia	*0.26*	*0.39*
Kazakhstan	0.26	0.33
Kyrgyzstan	0.26	0.55[d]
Turkmenistan	0.26	0.36
Uzbekistan	0.28[b]	0.33
Average TEs	**0.24**	**0.33**

Source: Milanovic (1998).

Notes
a. Regional averages are unweighted.
b. 1989 data.
c. Monthly.
d. Quarterly.
e. Semi-annual.

unequal countries in the world, with Gini coefficients exceeding 0.4 and in some cases approaching 0.5, levels common in the more unequal countries of Asia and Latin America.[21] This all occurred within a relatively short period of only a decade, resulting in 'a change of unprecedented magnitude and speed' with 'the increase in inequality far exceeding anything ever seen before' (World Bank 2000). In contrast, inequalities in Central Europe remain low by world standards, within a (0.19–0.28) range, rates comparable to levels in Western and Northern European countries. This observation of a sizeable cross-country variation, from a low of 0.19 in the Slovak Republic to a high of 0.55 in Kyrgyzstan, is a common feature of the transition experience. As for the range of Gini coefficient values over time, it is noticeable how the range of values has increased sharply with transition, from a relatively low spread of (0.19–0.28) pre-transition to a relatively high spread of (0.19–0.55) in the early years of transition. The unweighted average for the 18 TEs increased from 0.24 to 0.33, and all occurring in less than one decade.

As with poverty, and only as a very rough approximation, we can present the following account of inequality for the early to mid-1990s: the further east one goes, the worse, on average, the situation is with respect to inequality.

	Central Europe < Eastern Europe < Baltics < Slavic = Central Asia
Gini Index	0.25 0.30 0.35 0.40 0.40

Figure 2.2 Inequality.

Source: Milanovic (1998).

As alluded to earlier, an increase in income disparities for countries embarking on transition was inevitable, and indeed, given the compressed wages and poor relative returns to education in the socialist system, welcome, i.e. in the sense that the transition to the market system would see wages and incomes no longer reflecting the ideology and targets of the Communist Party but in the new market environment reflecting individual abilities, efforts and productivities. The positive factors pushing up inequality were the higher returns to education, the dispersion of wages, the risks/returns to entrepreneurship and the impact of non-labour earnings (e.g. capital and property income). Aside from a shift in the composition of income, the increase in inequality was also associated with some negative developments, as listed below.

- fall in incomes and wages;
- wages, pensions and cash transfers arrears;
- lack of employment opportunities;
- weak social safety net.

When taking all factors (both positive and negative) together, it appears that, as in non-transition countries, the inequality of labour earnings (that is, wage earnings and earnings from self-employment) accounts for much of the increase in income inequality. Again, differences between CEE and CIS countries are evident. In the former, rising wage inequalities and increased returns to education are important explanatory factors in explaining rising income inequalities whereas in the CIS countries wage arrears and income from self-employment and entrepreneurship play a much more important explanatory role (World Bank 2000).[22]

With respect to government action in cushioning the negative effects of transition and, more specifically, dampening the effects of rising wage inequalities, the experience in TEs is mixed. In CEE countries, governments managed to use tax and transfers progressively, to partially or fully offset the increased inequality of wage earnings. In other countries, transfers were mainly neutral. However, in some CIS countries, most notably Russia, transfers were often regressive, actually increasing income inequality further.

Both the positive and negative developments listed above can only be described as the immediate causes of the rise in inequality. For the more fundamental reasons behind the increased income distribution, we need to examine the institutional and political factors surrounding transition countries. For former socialist countries of the Soviet Union (namely the countries that witnessed the largest increases in inequality), the historical (both Soviet and Tsarist) and institutional legacy of a fusion between political and economic power and the absence of a history of democracy and accountability gave way at the outset of transition to weak states and poor governance. This, in turn, resulted in stalled reforms, corruption and state capture, i.e. where vested interest groups, the oligarchs and the financial-industrial conglomerates or groups (FIGs), for example, who might see themselves as losers from reform, use their position to capture for their own benefit various elements of state policy. The subsequent outcomes for these transition countries were falling output, rising inequality and increased poverty (World Bank 2000).

Second-decade developments in poverty and inequality

Since the late 1990s, poverty in most countries has declined and the rise in inequality has abated in some countries, and has been partly reversed in countries that experienced the largest increases in the previous decade. The two most obvious explanations for this improvement are the resurgence of economic growth, income and wages (from the mid- to late 1990s onward, associated with the cumulative impact of structural reforms, benefits from EU accession, the ending of conflict in the Balkans, and the Russian boom arising from the increase in oil prices and the devaluation of the rouble following the 1998 crisis) and in some countries, where government revenues have recovered from the collapse of the 1990s, more and better targeted social protection benefits. Using the $2 per day poverty line, there has been a fall from 20 per cent of the population (that is, one in every five) in 1998 to about 12 per cent of the population (that is, one in every eight) in 2003: in actual numbers, it is estimated that about 40 million people (a fall from about 100 million to 60 million) moved out of poverty between 1998 and 2003 (World Bank 2005a). The largest decline in poverty numbers occurred in the Slavic countries of Belarus, Russia and Ukraine.

With respect to changes in distribution, income inequality changes have been modest with a decline in countries where it was previously most acute, i.e. CIS countries. Although no single explanation exists, declining wage and transfers arrears played a significant role in explaining the decline in inequality witnessed in many of the CIS countries. Sizeable cross-country variations still persist.

Table 2.13 reports poverty and inequality estimates for a sample of CEE/FSU countries for 2002. The biggest improvement in income distribution and poverty, as against the inequality and poverty estimates of earlier transition years (as reported in Tables 2.11 and 2.12), is in the Baltic States and the Slavic countries of the CIS (World Bank 2005a). In some Central European countries where poverty was relatively low in the early 1990s (most notably,

Table 2.13 Poverty and inequality in transition countries, 2002

Country	Poverty Index[a]	Gini Index[b]
CEE countries and the Baltic States		
Albania	71	0.32
Bulgaria[c]	33	0.28
Estonia	27	0.33
FYR Macedonia	23	0.37
Hungary	12	0.25
Latvia	18	0.34
Lithuania	30	0.30
Poland	27	0.32
Romania	62	0.29
Serbia and Montenegro	42	0.29
CIS countries		
Armenia	91	. .
Azerbaijan	74	0.36
Belarus	21	0.29
Georgia	84	0.39
Kazakhstan	71	0.33
Kyrgyzstan	97	. .
Moldova	90	0.34
Russia	41	0.34
Tajikistan[c]	96	0.33
Ukraine	31	0.27
Uzbekistan	86	0.33

Source: World Bank (2005a).

Notes
a. $4.30 per capita, per day PPP.
b. Per capita.
c. 2003.

Hungary and the Slovak Republic), poverty levels (as estimated by the poverty index) had actually increased by 2002.

Before we consider policy reforms with respect to poverty and inequality, we will briefly examine China's record on poverty alleviation and income distribution. The main source for this note on China is Naughton (2007a). Since reforms began in 1978, GDP and household income in China have significantly increased, as shown in the section on 'Output' (p. 72) and Table 2.2. Evidence from official Chinese statistics, based on major annual (urban and rural) household surveys of China's National Bureau of Statistics, indicates that there was a very large increase in household income over the past three decades. This increase in national output and household income, arising from market and institutional reforms, and with some additional one-off factors (e.g. an improvement in the terms of trade in agriculture) resulted in a dramatic fall in poverty levels. According to Chinese statistics, based on the – albeit very low – official poverty line of RMB627 (about $76), poverty numbers (most, if not all, in rural areas, unlike most other developing countries where urban poverty is a problem and urban centres are more unequal than rural areas) fell from 250 million in 1978 to 26 million in 2004.[23] Even if we use international comparable data (with a poverty line of RMB850 or about $103), the improvement, although uneven over time and across regions, is still impressive: a decline, in percentage terms, from in excess of 40 per cent (a legacy of the Great Leap Forward and the Cultural Revolution) in the early 1980s to 12.5 per cent in 2001.[24] Although poverty is still a 'serious and persistent problem' with further improvements possibly constrained by the high levels of inequality in today's China, Naughton (2007a) is not afraid to claim that 'Possibly never before in history have such a large number of people climbed out of absolute poverty in such a short time'.

However true this statement is, it may be equally true to say something similar for inequality in China since the start of the reforms. Indeed, the same author makes the following bold assertion regarding inequality: 'there may be no other case where a country's income distribution has deteriorated so much, so fast' (Naughton 2007a). The data on income distribution and inequality for China are certainly stark, if not 'unprecedented'. Using the Gini index, inequality in China rose from about 0.28 – making one of the largest, low-income countries of the world also, unusually, one of the most equal countries in the world – in the early 1980s when China embarked on reforms to about 0.45 in 2001. Inequality increased in both rural (from about 0.25 in 1983 to about 0.36 in 2001) and urban (from about 0.17 in 1982 to about 0.33 in 2001) areas, with China's rural–urban disparity remaining very large by international standards. It also increased between regions, between urban centres and between population groups.[25] Inequality in China, now comparable to the most unequal Asian developing countries, has increased for a number of reasons, including the increase in regional (inter-provincial) inequality as market reforms have, over time, accelerated urban economic growth, the rise of new income sources that tend to be concentrated in urban areas, the rise in the returns to education and changing trends in government subsidies, and non-cash income to urban and rural dwellers. More recent evidence, based on a new independently designed household survey, indicates an improvement in the position of income inequality and a reversal in the trend with respect to the distribution of income in both rural and urban China (taken separately), and may be due to more equity-oriented policies and social protection measures (Khan and Riskin 2005). In sum, although great care needs to be taken when using and interpreting Chinese data, surveys and findings, we can concur with Naughton's (2007a) conclusion on incomes, poverty and inequality in China that 'Chinese society has become much better off, much less poor, but much more unequal'.[26]

Policy options

Despite the improved trends since the late 1990s, poverty and inequality rates are still unacceptably high in transition countries. If the primary cause of the increase in inequality and poverty are institutional and political factors, fundamental change in institutions and governance are required. Only then will accelerated market reforms and a continuation of economic growth, together with government redistributive policies, have the desired impact. World Bank (2000) outlines in detail (reprinted in Appendix 4) the desired institutional and economic reforms needed to tackle poverty and income inequality.[27] Despite the changes and improvements recorded since 2000, and with the global economic and financial crisis making the situation worse for transition countries, many of the policy recommendations outlined in the appendix are as relevant today as they were over a decade ago when formulated by the Bank.

Foreign trade and FDI

External trade relations were very different for socialist economies than for advanced market economies or even developing economies. Foreign trade was managed by a state monopoly and conducted through the planning system, the state Bank for Foreign Trade and specialised foreign trading organisations that were subordinate to the Ministry of Foreign Trade. Trade was subservient to the plan: as imports were a residual source of needed inputs, exports – instead of being viewed as a source of demand, growth and foreign exchange earnings – were considered a necessary evil to pay for imports (Gregory and Stuart 2001). The majority of socialist countries were members of the CMEA. The establishment of CMEA was an attempt by the Soviet Union to create a self-sufficient and regionally interdependent trading bloc. Member states of the inward-oriented CMEA traded with fellow member states, and trade flows outside of the area – to the 'hostile' capitalist world – were low. Within the USSR, for example, inter-republic trade accounted for about 80 per cent of all trade for Soviet Union republics (with Russia as an exception where the share of inter-republic trade was *only* about 65 per cent). Admittedly the satellite states in Central and Eastern Europe did have a more diversified pattern of trade than the Soviet Union republics.

The collapse of the CMEA in 1991 had a detrimental effect on trade flows in the region – a region of the world whose share of global trade was in decline long before 1990/91 – and, in turn, on economic activity, partly contributing to the transformation recession of the early 1990s in the former socialist countries (Kornai 1994; Rodrik 1994). With the disintegration of inter-republic trade links and a collapse of the payments system, and with future international trade involving former socialist countries as partners to be conducted in world market prices and payments in convertible currencies, it is not surprising that trade volumes in TEs fell very early on in transition. Many of the FSU countries, and the Balkans, also witnessed wars and civil strife, events that are not very conducive to foreign trade and settlements.

Once again regional differences emerged with the decline in trade for CIS countries considerably greater than the trade decline for CEE countries. Yet expectations were very different at the outset of transition. Once the central plan and directives were removed, it was expected that this region would open up and integrate with the world economy, with increased and more diversified international trade flows reflecting market forces and comparative advantage, based on well-endowed natural resources, low wage costs and an educated labour force. Nevertheless, by the mid-1990s, there was a recovery in trade volumes across the transition countries, although the 1998 Russian crisis was to prove a further setback for many of the CIS countries. CEE countries began to witness an increase in trade flows and greater diversification of trade, both in terms of export markets (with Germany replacing the former Soviet Union as the largest trading partner) and the commodity composition of exports (with medium-high- and high-tech products increasing in importance). Exports to the rest of the world increased, as did exports to the EU-15. By 1995, 70 per cent of Poland's exports were to the EU: it was 60 per cent in the cases of the Czech Republic and Hungary. Reorientation of trade by CIS countries was much slower. In 1995, for the two big FSU republics, namely Russia and Ukraine, exports to the EU accounted for *only* 33 and 10 per cent respectively. Many of the richer CIS countries still tended to export fuels and primary commodities, while importing mainly manufactured and consumer goods (Brenton and Gros 1997; Hare 2001b).

One of the more significant changes, with respect to reoriented trade flows, has occurred in the Baltic States. Given their membership of the USSR and the CMEA, and the negative consequences for trade (and output) of the dissolution of both, the speed of reorientation of trade in the Baltic States was, according to Campos and Coricelli (2002), 'remarkable'. Using their own calculations, the authors report that the percentage of Baltic exports to industrial countries grew from under 5 per cent in 1991 to more than 50 per cent in 1998 (Campos and Coricelli 2002).

FDI flows to socialist countries were virtually absent prior to transition, largely due to the Communist regimes and associated policies that were in place across the region. One of the expectations of transition was for a flow of FDI to transition countries once reforms had begun. Indeed, FDI did flow to former socialist countries but not by as much in the early years as had originally being predicted. There was also a large cross-country variation, with the Czech Republic, Estonia and Hungary doing best (measured in terms of US$ per capita) and the least reforming countries or countries engaged in civil or international war (that is, Belarus, Bosnia and Herzegovina, Moldova, Serbia and Montenegro, Tajikistan and Ukraine) faring the worst. Despite Russia's great potential, FDI flows in the first decade of transition were low, outstripped by massive capital flight. Political and economic uncertainty, an unfavourable business climate, fears of default, a burdensome government bureaucracy, insecure protection of property rights and weak contract enforcement were often cited as reasons why foreign investors were reluctant to invest in Russia. By the end of the first decade, however, FDI flows to some TEs were relatively large overall, but were still highly concentrated, with just three countries (Czech Republic, Hungary and Poland) accounting for two-thirds of the total FDI investment (Bevan and Estrin 2000).

The two trends identified above, notably the greater trade openness and the increase in FDI flows, are confirmed by the data below. However, as with other data from transition countries, trade statistics, whether it is for cross-country comparisons or country comparisons before and during transition, need to be treated with caution. With transition to the market, the system of collecting trade statistics changed. In addition, the accuracy of trade statistics is undermined by an underreporting of foreign trade, and the practice of barter trade and shuttle trade, not uncommon in TEs. Although we report the data here, confirming the patterns identified above, we stress again the importance of treating the actual numbers tentatively. Table 2.14 reports the openness of TEs, as measured by the trade/GDP ratio (that is, exports and imports as a percentage of national income).

It is evident from Table 2.14 that as transition progressed, the trade ratio for TEs increased to, on average, 110 per cent by the mid-2000s. Although this trade/GDP ratio appears to be high as compared with average ratios for World Bank income classification country groupings, the reader needs to remember that the group of TEs, as compared with low-income or lower-middle-income groups, contains many small countries (16 TEs with a population of 5.5 million or fewer, 16 TEs with an area of 95,000 sq. kilometres or less) and many developed countries (with 18 TEs classified as upper-middle or high-income countries), both of which generally tend to have high trade/GDP ratios.

FDI flows, expressed as a percentage of GDP, are reported in Table 2.15.

Very low levels of FDI pertained at the outset of transition. However, within a few short years, FDI flows in some countries, most notably some of the more advanced, reforming EU accession countries (particularly the Czech Republic, Estonia and Hungary), were close to, and in some cases exceeded, 5 per cent of annual GDP. In addition, both the East Asian countries of China and Vietnam (that had started reforms earlier, including opening up to FDI) and the oil-rich Azerbaijan, Kazakhstan and Turkmenistan fared well in attracting FDI. As stated earlier, FDI flows to Russia, despite the attraction of natural resources and minerals, were low throughout most of the transition period, with some minor improvement in later years. Indeed, China has done consistently better than Russia in attracting FDI and this factor may partly explain differences in performance between the two big transition countries (acknowledging that the causation may be two-way, i.e. high and improving levels of economic activity may lead to higher flows of FDI).

Table 2.14 Trade/GDP*

Country	1989	1990	1991	1992	1993	1994	1995	1996	1997	1998	1999	2000	2001	2002	2003	2004	2005	2006	2007	2008
Albania	39	38	35	100	78	50	47	48	47	45	49	57	59	67	66	65	69	74	82	83
Armenia	..	81	101	101	108	112	86	79	79	72	71	74	72	76	82	70	72	63	58	55
Azerbaijan	..	83	87	141	133	55	69	85	82	77	70	77	78	93	108	122	116	105	97	93
Belarus	..	90	70	117	151	155	104	97	126	123	121	142	137	131	134	142	119	124	128	136
Bosnia and Herzegovina	..	..	..	..	..	..	92	108	101	126	122	107	106	96	98	100	108	103	113	99
Bulgaria	95	70	83	100	84	91	91	105	112	94	95	117	119	111	117	126	137	148	149	144
China	34	35	38	43	49	47	44	38	39	36	38	44	43	48	57	65	69	72	75	63
Croatia	..	..	..	114	106	92	74	78	84	77	79	87	91	90	94	93	92	94	93	92
Czech Republic	..	88	99	108	110	104	106	104	109	110	112	130	133	123	126	140	141	150	154	149
Estonia	..	..	115	137	154	144	135	155	160	146	174	163	150	146	154	166	173	160	..	..
FYR Macedonia	..	49	108	101	87	76	67	88	97	94	112	99	96	93	101	107	115	125	125	133
Georgia	87	86	59	102	119	167	68	46	58	54	57	63	72	78	80	85	90	90	89	90
Hungary	69	60	63	..	61	64	89	96	109	125	131	148	143	128	125	130	134	155	159	162
Kazakhstan	..	..	149	85	84	84	83	71	65	83	106	89	94	83	91	96	98	92	92	101
Kyrgyzstan	79	72	83	75	74	72	72	87	84	95	99	89	74	83	84	96	98	121	135	..
Latvia	97	61	153	130	91	88	101	102	107	90	93	90	93	91	97	104	110	111	109	..
Lithuania	113	51	43	173	117	111	114	116	103	88	96	105	111	108	111	123	128	122	130	..
Moldova	99	66	80	51	82	107	129	129	124	120	125	123	131	141	133	143	137	143	141	..
Mongolia	76	72	163	152	117	117	97	89	112	124	131	127	126	130	133	144	133	125	130	..
Montenegro	..	..	..	..	45	..	46	..	51	57	54	88	100	95	78	100	105	127	131	115
Poland	50	49	46	45	45	44	46	51	57	54	61	58	61	69	77	75	81	81	84	77
Romania	43	39	64	51	52	61	65	65	53	61	71	74	77	81	76	78	75	75	65	65
Russia	36	26	111	69	51	55	48	47	56	69	68	61	60	59	57	55	52	56	..	56
Serbia	43	..	..	..	..	..	..	..	41	52	44	62	57	59	62	69	73	78	81	87
Slovak Republic	61	96	145	116	113	113	117	122	129	127	143	154	149	154	152	157	173	174	154	154
Slovenia	..	158	119	116	115	102	101	104	104	99	111	112	108	117	125	134	142	142	..	..
Tajikistan	85	63	22	70	98	138	157	181	107	134	200	146	142	137	128	121	79	81	87	75
Turkmenistan	..	..	..	146	170	168	150	111	103	140	176	158	122	119	121	115	113	129	111	84
Ukraine	64	56	50	46	52	74	97	94	84	86	102	120	109	106	113	115	102	96	95	90
Uzbekistan	..	77	74	70	64	37	56	62	57	45	37	46	56	60	68	73	67	65	70	73
Vietnam	58	81	67	74	66	77	75	93	94	97	103	113	112	119	127	139	143	152	167	..
Average TEs, unweighted	**65**																			**112**

Source: World Bank Development Indicators.

Note
* Sum of exports and imports of goods and services as a share of GDP.

Table 2.15 FDI/GDP*

Country	1991	1992	1993	1994	1995	1996	1997	1998	1999	2000	2001	2002	2003	2004	2005	2006	2007
Albania	..	2.8	4.7	2.7	2.9	3.0	2.2	1.7	1.2	3.9	5.1	3.0	3.1	4.6	3.1	3.6	4.4
Armenia	..	..	0.1	0.6	1.7	1.1	3.2	11.7	6.6	5.5	3.3	4.7	4.3	6.9	4.9	7.1	7.6
Azerbaijan	0.2	0.0	0.0	0.3	10.8	19.7	28.1	23.0	11.1	2.5	4.0	22.3	45.1	41.0	12.7	-2.8	-15.2
Belarus	..	0.0	0.1	0.1	0.1	0.7	2.5	1.3	3.7	0.9	0.8	1.7	1.0	0.7	1.0	1.0	4.0
Bosnia and Herzegovina	..	..	..	0.0	0.0	-0.1	0.0	1.6	3.8	2.7	2.1	4.1	4.6	7.1	5.6	5.9	13.9
Bulgaria	0.5	0.4	0.4	1.1	0.7	1.1	4.9	4.2	6.3	7.9	6.0	5.8	10.5	10.8	15.9	23.7	22.7
China	1.2	2.6	6.2	6.0	4.9	4.7	4.6	4.3	3.6	3.2	3.3	3.4	2.9	2.8	3.5	2.9	4.3
Croatia	..	..	1.1	0.8	0.6	2.6	2.7	4.3	7.3	5.9	6.8	4.9	6.9	3.0	4.6	8.0	9.6
Czech Republic	..	..	1.9	2.1	4.6	2.3	2.3	6.0	10.5	8.8	9.1	11.3	2.2	4.5	9.3	3.9	5.3
Estonia	..	2.1	4.2	5.4	4.6	3.2	5.3	10.4	5.4	6.9	8.8	3.9	9.4	8.1	21.3	10.9	12.9
FYR Macedonia	0.0	0.0	0.0	0.7	0.2	0.3	0.4	3.6	0.9	4.9	12.8	2.1	2.1	2.9	1.7	5.5	4.2
Georgia	..	..	0.0	0.3	0.2	1.7	6.9	7.3	2.9	4.3	3.4	4.7	8.4	9.6	7.1	13.7	17.0
Hungary	4.4	4.0	6.1	2.8	10.8	7.3	9.1	7.1	6.9	5.8	7.4	4.5	2.6	4.4	6.9	17.4	26.9
Kazakhstan	..	0.4	5.4	3.1	4.7	5.4	6.0	5.2	9.4	7.0	12.8	10.5	6.8	9.6	3.5	7.8	9.7
Kyrgyzstan	..	..	0.5	2.3	5.8	2.6	4.7	6.6	3.6	-0.2	0.3	0.3	2.4	7.9	1.7	6.4	5.6
Latvia	..	0.6	1.0	4.2	3.4	6.8	8.5	5.4	4.8	5.3	1.6	2.7	2.7	4.6	4.4	8.3	8.3
Lithuania	..	..	0.4	0.4	1.0	1.9	3.6	8.3	4.5	3.3	3.7	5.0	1.0	3.4	4.0	6.2	5.3
Moldova	..	0.7	0.6	0.7	1.5	1.4	4.1	4.6	3.2	9.9	3.7	5.1	3.7	3.4	6.4	7.4	11.2
Mongolia	0.6	0.2	1.2	0.9	0.8	1.3	2.4	1.9	3.4	4.9	3.7	6.1	9.1	5.1	8.0	11.0	8.3
Montenegro												5.6	2.6	3.0	21.2	22.9	25.2
Poland	0.4	0.8	2.0	1.9	2.6	2.9	3.1	3.7	4.3	5.5	3.0	2.1	2.1	5.0	3.4	5.8	5.4
Romania	0.1	0.3	0.4	1.1	1.2	0.7	3.4	4.8	2.9	2.8	2.9	2.5	3.1	8.6	6.6	9.3	5.7
Russia	..	0.3	0.3	0.2	0.5	0.7	1.2	1.0	1.7	1.0	0.9	1.0	1.8	2.6	1.7	3.0	4.3
Serbia	..						3.8	0.7	1.0	0.3	1.4	0.9	6.7	3.9	6.1	14.7	7.8
Slovak Republic	..	..	1.5	1.7	1.2	1.7	0.8	2.5	1.7	10.1	..	16.8	1.7	7.2	5.0	7.5	4.5
Slovenia	..	0.9	0.9	0.8	0.7	0.8	1.7	1.0	0.5	0.7	2.5	7.2	1.0	2.5	1.5	1.7	3.1
Tajikistan	..	0.5	0.5	0.9	0.8	1.7	2.0	2.3	0.6	2.7	0.9	3.0	2.0	13.1	2.4	12.0	9.7
Turkmenistan	..	..	2.5	4.0	9.4	4.5	4.4	2.4	5.1	4.5	4.8	6.2	3.8	5.2	5.2	7.0	6.2
Ukraine	..	0.3	..	0.3	0.6	1.2	1.2	1.8	1.6	1.9	2.1	1.6	2.8	2.6	9.1	5.2	7.0
Uzbekistan	..	0.1	0.4	0.6	-0.2	0.6	1.1	0.9	0.7	0.5	0.7	0.7	0.7	1.6	0.6	1.1	1.2
Vietnam	3.9	4.8	7.0	11.9	8.6	9.7	8.3	6.1	4.9	4.2	4.0	4.0	3.7	3.5	3.7	4.0	9.8

Source: World Bank Development Indicators.

Note

* Foreign Direct Investment, net inflows.

Labour market

Transition from plan to market involves, in theory, a reallocation of labour across location, jobs, sectors and occupations. In their account of transition in the first decade, Campos and Coricelli (2002) identify changes in the labour market as one of transition's stylised facts. They summarise the changes in labour market flows with the catchy term 'labour moved'. Ironically, and as acknowledged by Campos and Coricelli (2002) and others, labour in CEE/FSU countries did not move much in the literal sense, that is, geographically. Labour mobility in the first decade of transition was low for a number of reasons, including obstacles in the housing market, market segmentation and labour market regulations, including, for some FSU countries, continued use of residency registration permits and requirements. Although EU accession did see an increase in migration from the EU accession countries to EU-15 member states, labour mobility within former Soviet bloc countries has been relatively low by international standards. Of course, labour mobility within China far from being low can be measured in the tens of millions from countryside and rural areas to cities and urban centres. In other respects, labour in TEs did indeed move, but again, whether it is inter-industry or inter-occupational mobility, worker flows in transition countries were somewhat low as compared with mobility in some other regions. In terms of labour mobility in transition countries witnessing large structural change, we will examine worker flows out of the labour force into unemployment (or inactivity) and later, across sectors, industries and occupations. We begin with labour force participation rates.

In the early years of transition, there were significant labour flows out of the labour force. A feature of the socialist system was high labour force participation rates. This is evident in Table 2.16, compiled from the World Bank Development Indicators (WDI) and reporting the proportion of the population aged 15 or older that is economically active. In 1989, before the start of transition, the labour force participation rate for the TEs was, on average, 69 per cent, well above the average rate for upper-middle (62 per cent) and high-income (61 per cent) countries and similar to average rates for lower-middle and low-income countries (both at 70 per cent). Moreover, female participation rates, by international standards, were high in former socialist countries ranging from, on average, in 1989, the mid-50s per cent in some Central European countries (the lowest being Hungary, at less than 50 per cent) to rates in excess of 70 per cent in some of the Central and East Asian countries. During the first two decades of transition, labour force participation rates fell in all TEs, with the exception of Mongolia. By 2007, the labour force participation rate for TEs, was, on average, almost ten percentage points lower than at the start of transition (with much of the fall occurring in the early years of transition), whereas, in contrast, non-transition upper-middle and high-income countries showed no change in participation rates over the same period. This decline was not uniform across all transition countries, with the smallest decline recorded in the larger, more populated countries (that is, China, Russia, Ukraine and Vietnam) and the largest fall registered in some of the smaller, less populated countries (e.g. Albania, Bosnia and Herzegovina, Moldova, Tajikistan). In many transition countries the fall in participation rates was greater for females than for males, indicating that women, at least in those early years of transition, suffered disproportionately by the deteriorating conditions in the labour market. Excluding China and Mongolia, the fall in the female participation rates during transition ranged from a low of a few percentage points to falls in excess of 15 percentage points. Despite some improvements in some TEs in later years, 'female activity rates in 2001 were everywhere lower than in 1985 except in Romania' (UNECE 2000, 2003). Again there are regional

Table 2.16 Labour force participation rate*

Country	1989	1990	1991	1992	1993	1994	1995	1996	1997	1998	1999	2000	2001	2002	2003	2004	2005	2006	2007
Albania	75	76	62	61	62	62	62	62	61	61	61	61	61	61	61	61	60	60	60
Armenia	73	73	64	62	61	61	61	60	60	60	60	60	51	51	50	50	51	53	51
Azerbaijan	71	72	65	65	64	64	63	63	63	64	64	65	65	65	65	65	65	64	65
Belarus	68	67	66	65	64	63	62	62	61	60	59	59	59	59	59	59	59	59	59
Bosnia and Herzegovina	76	76	63	62	62	62	63	64	63	62	62	61	61	61	60	60	60	60	60
Bulgaria	62	61	58	58	56	55	54	53	52	50	49	47	51	51	50	50	51	53	51
China	79	79	79	79	79	79	79	79	79	78	78	78	77	77	77	76	76	75	75
Croatia	63	63	57	57	56	56	55	55	55	54	54	54	53	53	53	53	53	52	52
Czech Republic	70	70	61	62	62	62	62	61	61	61	61	60	60	60	60	59	59	59	59
Estonia	66	66	64	64	64	63	63	62	61	61	60	60	60	59	60	58	59	59	59
FYR Macedonia	64	64	57	56	55	54	55	54	54	54	53	53	54	53	54	52	53	54	54
Georgia	74	74	68	67	65	64	65	65	66	66	66	64	66	64	65	64	64	64	64
Hungary	56	56	55	55	53	51	50	49	48	49	49	50	50	50	50	50	51	51	51
Kazakhstan	70	70	70	70	70	70	70	70	70	70	70	70	70	70	70	69	69	68	69
Kyrgyzstan	66	66	66	66	66	66	66	66	66	65	65	65	65	64	64	63	63	64	64
Latvia	70	69	68	66	65	63	61	59	59	58	58	56	56	58	58	59	59	61	60
Lithuania	67	66	66	65	65	64	63	62	61	62	62	60	59	58	58	57	56	56	56
Moldova	68	67	66	65	64	63	62	61	60	58	57	55	54	52	51	49	49	49	47
Mongolia	60	60	61	61	62	62	62	62	62	62	62	62	62	61	61	61	60	60	60
Montenegro	:	:	:	:	:	:	:	:	:	:	:	:	:	:	:	:	:	:	:
Poland	64	63	62	61	61	60	59	58	57	57	56	56	56	55	55	55	55	54	54
Romania	61	61	61	62	64	65	67	65	65	64	64	63	62	58	57	55	54	55	53
Russia	68	67	66	65	64	63	62	61	60	60	60	60	61	61	61	61	61	61	63
Serbia	:	:	:	:	:	:	:	:	:	:	:	:	:	:	:	:	:	:	51
Slovak Republic	73	72	66	64	62	60	60	60	60	60	60	60	61	61	61	60	60	59	60
Slovenia	68	67	60	56	53	58	59	58	59	60	58	58	58	56	56	59	59	60	59
Tajikistan	79	79	62	59	57	54	52	48	49	50	50	51	53	54	55	56	57	58	62
Turkmenistan	69	69	64	64	64	65	65	64	65	65	65	65	65	65	65	65	65	64	65
Ukraine	64	64	63	63	62	62	62	63	64	65	56	57	57	57	57	57	58	58	58
Uzbekistan	80	80	62	60	60	59	59	59	60	60	61	61	62	62	62	63	63	63	64
Vietnam	78	78	78	78	77	77	77	77	76	75	75	74	74	74	74	73	73	73	73

(*Continued*)

Table 2.16 Continued

	1989	1990	1991	1992	1993	1994	1995	1996	1997	1998	1999	2000	2001	2002	2003	2004	2005	2006	2007
Average TEs unweighted *as compared to*	**69**																		**60**
Low-income countries	70																		69
Middle-income countries	68																		65
Lower-middle income	70																		66
Upper-middle income	62																		61
High-income countries	61																		61

Source: World Bank Development Indicators.

Note

* Proportion of the population aged 15 or older that is economically active.

Table 2.17 Employment growth

Country	1991	1992	1993	1994	1995	1996	1997	1998	1999	2000	2001	2002	2003	2004	2005	2006	2007	2008
Albania[a]	-1.7	-22	-4.4	11	-2	-1.9	-0.8	-2	-1.8	0.3	-13.9	0	0.7	0.6	0.1	0.3	0	..
Armenia	2.5	-5.6	-2.2	-3.6	-0.8	-2.8	-4.4	-2.5	-2.9	-1.6	-1	-12.5	0.1	-2.3	1.5	-0.5	0.8	1.7
Azerbaijan	0.8	-0.3	-0.2	-2.2	-0.5	2	0.2	0.2	0	0	0.3	0.3	0.6	1.7	1.1	3.2	0.9	..
Belarus	-2.5	-2.6	-1.3	-2.6	-6.2	-1	0.1	1.1	0.6	0	-0.5	-0.8	-0.9	-0.5	0.8	1.2	1.7	2.6
Bosnia and Herzegovina																		
Bulgaria	..	..	..	..	..	..	-3.1	-1	-4.3	-2.4	-0.7	0.2	2.9	2.6	2.7	3.3	2.8	3.3
China[b]	1.4	1.2	1.9	1.0	0.9	1.3	1.3	1.2	1.1	1.0	1.3	1.0	0.9	1.0	0.8	0.8	0.8	..
Croatia[c]	..	..	..	..	..	0.9	3.2	-3	-3.3	4	-5.4	4.2	0.6	1.7	0.8	0.8	1.8	1.0
Czech Republic	..	..	..	..	0.9	0.2	-1.5	-3.4	-0.2	0.5	0.6	-1.4	0.3	1.1	1.6	2.7	1.1	..
Estonia	-2.9	-5.9	-7.9	-3.4	-6.1	-2.4	0	-1.9	-4.3	-1.5	0.9	1.2	1.5	0	1.9	5.5	0.8	0.2
FYR Macedonia[c]	..	..	..	..	..	..	0.2	0.1	0.8	9	-6.3	-2.9	-4.1	4.3	4.6	3.5	..	..
Georgia[a]	-8.9	-21.2	-9.6	-2.4	-1.2	2.7	0.2	0.1	6.2	2.1	0.2	-2	-1.3	-1.7	-2.2	0.2	-2.5	0.3
Hungary	..	..	..	..	-0.5	0.2	0.2	1.7	3.4	1.3	0.2	0	1.3	-0.7	0	0.6	-0.1	-1.2
Kazakhstan[c]	..	-1.8	-8.1	-5.5	-0.5	-0.7	-5.3	-0.4	1.6	8	0.2	4.1	2.8	1.1	2	3.1	3.1	3
Kyrgyzstan[d]	..	4.5	-9.2	-2.2	-0.2	0.6	0.6	2.2	3.3	0.9	1.1	1.1	1.6	2.3	2.8	2	2.7	2.7
Latvia[c]	-0.9	-7.4	-6.9	-10.1	-1.9	4.3	-0.2	-1.8	-3	2.2	2.2	1.6	1.7	1.1	1.8	4.7	3.5	0.7
Lithuania[c]	2.4	-2.3	-4.2	-5.8	-11.6	0.9	0.6	-0.8	-2.2	-4	-3.8	3.6	2.2	-0.1	2.5	1.8	2.8	-0.5
Moldova[c]	..	..	..	..	1.0	0.3	-0.6	3.6	2.7	-0.6	-1	0.4	-9.9	-3	0.2	-4.7	-0.8	0.3
Mongolia[b]	..	..	..	-0.7	1.0	0.3	-0.6	3.6	2.7	-1	2.9	4.6	6.4	2.6	1.9	4.3	1.4	6.3
Montenegro	..	..	..	..	..	..	..	..	..	0.2	-0.7	1.9	0.6	-0.1	5.2	3.7	3.7	2.7
Poland	..	..	..	..	1.8	2.6	2.6	1.3	-0.9	-2.4	-3.2	-1.8	-9.1	1.2	2.2	3.2	4.4	2.7
Romania[c]	-0.5	-3	-1.5	-6.3	-2.3	0	-3.1	-1.8	-2.4	-1.3	-1.9	-4.2	-0.1	-0.7	-0.1	0.4	0.4	0.6
Russia[c]	..	-3.4	-5.6	-1.0	-1.9	-4.6	-2.6	-1.8	-2.5	4.2	0.1	2.4	-0.3	1.3	0.9	1	2.5	-0.1
Serbia[c]	..	..	..	..	..	..	0.1	-0.5	-1.8	-2.6	0.2	-1.7	-1.2	0.5	0.9	1	-1.1	-0.1
Slovak Republic	..	..	..	0.2	2.1	-1	-1.9	-0.2	-1.9	-1.9	0.6	0	1.1	-0.2	1.4	2.3	2.1	2.8
Slovenia	..	..	..	..	-2	-1.9	-0.2	1.4	1.3	0.6	0.4	1.5	-0.4	0.3	-0.1	1.5	3	2.8
Tajikistan	1.6	-3.1	-2.8	0	-0.1	-6.6	3.5	0.3	1.4	0.6	4.8	1.5	1.5	10.8	1.4	1.2	..	..
Turkmenistan	3.5	3.3	3.2	3.9	3.4	1.8	2	1.3	0.7	0.5	2	2.5	2.2	..	1.1	..	..	..
Ukraine[c]	-2.0	-0.1	0	-4.0	0.0	-1.5	-3.3	-3.3	1.1	-1.0	1.7	0.4	0.7	0.7	1.9	0.2	0.8	0.3
Uzbekistan	4	0.2	-0.1	1.4	0.8	1.3	1.4	1.4	1.0	1.1	1.7	2.2	2.7	3.4	2.9	2.7	..	..
Vietnam[b]	2.3	2.7	2.8	2.9	2.7	3.5	3.4	3.8	0.6	1.6	3	2.5	2.8	..	..	..	..	..

Sources: UNECE Statistical Division Database, compiled from national and international (CIS, EUROSTAT, OECD, UN) official sources, CIS Yearbook.

Notes

a. end of period.
b. ILO.
c. LFS-based.
d. CIS Yearbook.

differences, with the fall in female participation rates smaller in CEE countries than in FSU countries.

Labour moved into unemployment (or inactivity), with the subsequent rise in unemployment rates throughout the transition region. With output falling, drastically in some TEs, in the early years of transition, the adjustment in labour markets came in the form of falling employment (and rising unemployment), reductions in real wages, or a combination of both. On average, in CEE countries, employment took the brunt of the labour market adjustment. In contrast, CIS countries witnessed a large reduction in real wages (with marked declines in labour productivity), in excess of 50 per cent over a ten-year period in some FSU countries (UNECE 2000). As a result, joblessness was much more of a feature in CEE countries (and particularly so in Bulgaria, Poland and the Slovak Republic) than in CIS countries in the first decade of transition (see Chapters 7 and 8 for more on unemployment). As for gender differences, once again women were hurt disproportionately, with the decline in female employment considerably greater. Table 2.17 reports the annual employment growth rates for the period 1991 to 2008. Negative growth rates are in bold, and as is evident from the table, employment losses as opposed to gains dominated the early years of transition (but with a welcome reversal of that trend in the second decade of transition, associated with the recovery in output). Aside from Turkmenistan (where data are unreliable) and Uzbekistan (where the output collapse was relatively small), only the East Asian countries of China and Vietnam recorded any significant increases in employment by 2000/2001. Employment reductions in the first decade of transition were very large in some countries, both for male and female. For example, according to UNECE secretariat estimates, reductions for the period 1985 to 2001 (acknowledging that this includes the last few years of the socialist system) were for male (female), in the Czech Republic, 5.2 per cent (15.2 per cent), in Estonia, 19.8 per cent (36 per cent), in Hungary, 26.9 per cent (35.4 per cent), in Lithuania, 18.4 per cent (24.2 per cent), in Poland, 18.4 per cent (28.6 per cent), in Russia, 7.9 per cent (19.2 per cent) and in Slovenia, 13 per cent (16 per cent).

As cited by Boeri and Terrell (2002), Campos and Coricelli (2002) and UNECE (2003), labour moved from the state sector to the private sector (as previously outlined in the section 'Private sector activity' (p. 82), from large enterprises to SMEs and self-employment, and, with respect to sectors (and occupations), from agriculture (but not in all TEs as some FSU countries – mainly Caucasus and Central Asian republics – witnessed an increase in numbers engaged in subsistence farming, on small plots) and industry (and from engineers and trades) to services (to business professions and services). These reflected considerable changes in the sectoral distribution of employment (and by occupation), corresponding to the major sectoral changes in the composition of output already alluded to in the section 'Sectoral share of GDP' (p. 76). The differences between the transition experiences of CEE and CIS countries that we witness throughout this book are again evident here with respect to labour market adjustment trajectories, with the CEE countries witnessing swift structural change, sizeable labour adjustment and high unemployment whereas, in contrast, the CIS countries have seen slower structural change, sluggish employment response to output changes (but with large wage declines and arrears), and a more gradual rise in (official) unemployment (Boeri and Terrell 2002).

Government revenue and public spending

The fiscal system that existed under the socialist command economy was very different from the fiscal system common in market economies that are characterised by codified tax systems, revenue collection agencies, a treasury and an office of budget and expenditure management. With respect to taxation, the tax system in socialist countries, as opposed to the market-based system that collects revenue to finance public spending, was simply an instrument to fulfil the plan. Immediately prior to the Perestroika reforms of the late 1980s, the majority of all budgetary or fiscal decisions were controlled by Gosplan, with the USSR Ministry of Finance also playing a key role in the budgetary process. There was no corporate income tax (CIT) system in the usual sense of the term. State enterprises were subservient to the various ministries and any 'profits' or surpluses made were expropriated by the state. Likewise, losses were made good by arbitrary pricing and subsidies. Often, in respect of taxation, enterprises were treated on an individual basis according to their strategic importance and powers of negotiation. Tax rates were numerous and non-parametric, tax structures were complex and differentiated, and tax liabilities were not based on tax law but were discretionary and negotiable. The main sources of tax revenue were typically enterprise profit tax (i.e. profit remittances or transfers), payroll taxes and turnover taxes; direct taxes on individuals were unimportant.[28] Although revenue as a percentage of GDP was high in socialist countries (at 50 per cent in the Soviet Union up until the mid-1980s), administrative costs were low and tax collection was straightforward as firms tended to be large, few in number, state-owned and closely monitored. The generally accepted principles of modern tax administration, namely voluntary compliance and self-assessment, were absent from the system of revenue administration in Soviet and pre-transition times.[29]

Once the socialist system collapsed, TEs, some lacking an explicit, codified tax system (or culture), had to build a market-oriented, rule-based tax system (including a market-type tax administration) from scratch. The creation of a new tax system involved the introduction of a corporate income tax system. Not only did this involve changes in how enterprises were treated by the state in terms of taxation, but it was also introduced in conjunction with other market-oriented policies, such as price liberalisation, demonopolisation and privatisation. A VAT system to replace the turnover tax was introduced in the early years of transition and was in place, sometimes with little preparation, in most TEs by the mid-1990s. Tax on individuals accounted for a small proportion of the total tax take in socialist countries: the transition to a market economy meant that a personal income tax system as operates in market economies was also to be introduced (Turley 2006).

As for the expenditure side of the budget, there were many unusual features (aside from the absolute level which was very high) as compared to public spending in market economies. Budgetary subsidies were high, often three to five times greater than levels found in market economies. Defence spending was also unusually high, but not surprising given the priority to military spending.[30] Again, with the national priority given to investment as opposed to consumption, investment expenditure was by international standards: SOEs were heavily dependent on the state for funding investment projects, since other sources of finance, such as commercial lending or stock market flotations, were absent. As yet another priority was human development, levels of spending on education and health were high. Of course, with guaranteed job security and virtually, at least officially, no unemployment, there was no need for a social welfare system, as it is normally understood. In practice, the SOE acted as the social safety net. Indeed, unlike in market economies where local government supplies many of the public goods, many of the social functions (such as housing, childcare, etc.) were provided by the enterprise.

The first decade of transition witnessed a sharp fall in government revenues. This is a trend that had started before the demise of the socialist system, with revenues falling (due to the relaxation of the planning system combined with the deterioration in the economy) relative to output in the last few years of the centrally planned economy. In some cases, particularly in the Caucasus and the Central Asian states (with the notable exception of Uzbekistan), tax revenues fell to alarmingly low levels, often below levels observed in the world's least developed countries. Aside from internal strife and the transformational recession (with declining incomes and profits, and the shrinking tax bases that followed) experienced by the CEE/FSU countries, a weakened state appears to be a contributing factor (although not in all cases, as some of the transition countries in Central Asia were renowned for their authoritarian rule). Least-reforming countries, in this instance Belarus and Uzbekistan, that retained Soviet-type state institutions while at the same time suffering a much smaller decline in output, managed to prevent a collapse in revenues. Contributing factors to tax-collection problems in TEs include corruption and bribery, powerful vested interests, ineffective tax administration and other institutional weaknesses, poor intergovernmental fiscal arrangements and low tax effort reflecting political resistance to taxation. The lesson from other non-transition countries is for taxation to be used to raise revenues for the provision of public goods, for income redistribution and for macroeconomic stabilisation rather than, as was the case in many countries throughout the early years of transition, as an instrument to carry out various economic and social objectives, particularly in the enterprise sector – often resulting in low and insufficient tax revenues (Turley 2006).[31]

Table 2.18 shows the trend in government revenue (both tax and non-tax) in all former socialist countries since the beginning of transition up until 2006. The coverage is for consolidated government (that is, budgetary central government and extra-budgetary funds and social security contributions) but, in general, excludes local government revenues which tend to be small in former socialist countries, as fiscal systems in TEs and even more so in socialist times were highly centralised, as compared with market economies where there is, on average, much greater decentralisation.

As alluded to already, the revenue share of GDP was high in socialist times. In the early years of transition, as the former socialist countries found themselves in deep recession, revenues declined. Cross-regional variation was evident, with revenues in CEE countries in some years ten percentage points higher than in CIS countries in the early years of transition. With the SOEs (the traditional tax base or cash cow of socialist governments) losses mounting, and with the more profitable new private firms, mainly SMEs, difficult to tax (due to a weak, under-resourced tax collection agency unable to detect the thousands of new small firms many of which were operating underground in the unofficial sector engaging in informal activities), government revenues fell. The predicament was exasperated by the common phenomena, particularly in CIS countries, of non-payments, tax arrears, non-monetary payments (IOUs, veksels, etc.) and barter (strictly, goods for goods). The fiscal crisis that many CIS countries found themselves in culminated in the 1998 Russian crisis. Revenues did improve somewhat after that (although regional differences still persist), due primarily to the recovery in output experienced by all transition countries. A tax policy change that became popular at that time in some transition countries was the introduction of a flat income tax (see Box 2.2). There is still debate over what impact, if any, the new flat income tax had on government revenues. The increase in revenues that did materialise at that time may have been due to other factors, such as the recovery in output, the higher oil and gas prices, improved collection, etc. The East Asian countries of China and Vietnam tended to have lower levels of government revenue (and expenditure), as one might expect from countries of lower levels of economic development, as measured by income per capita. In China, revenues to central government

Table 2.18 Revenue/GDP

	1991	1992	1993	1994	1995	1996	1997	1998	1999	2000	2001	2002	2003	2004	2005	2006
CEE countries[a]																
Albania	..	..	..	..	21	15	17	24	..	..	..	24	24	24	..	..
Bosnia and Herzegovina																
Bulgaria	37	36	33	39	36	33	32	33	34	34	34	34	36	36	36	40
Croatia	33	34	36	42	43	44	43	46	43	42	40	41	41	40	40	38
Czech Republic	..	..	38	36	33	32	31	30	30	31	32	32	33	33	33	40
Estonia	27	25	29	34	33	30	31	30	28	28	28	31	31	31	31	32
FYR Macedonia	..	..	..	..	36	35	34	35	35	34	35	37	37	36	36	31
Hungary	49	47	48	47	44	42	39	38	38	39	37	37	37	36	36	36
Latvia	..	..	..	26	26	27	29	31	29	27	26	27	27	28	29	30
Lithuania	32	..	22	24	22	22	26	26	25	26	26	28	28	29	30	30
Poland	..	..	..	39	35	34	33	33	30	29	32	32	35	33	34	..
Romania	36	36	32	30	30	28	26	28	31	30	27	26	..	20	21	21
Serbia & Montenegro																
Slovak Republic	..	..	..	..	..	39	36	35	37	36	34	34	35	34	31	30
Slovenia	..	..	42	41	41	40	40	38	38	37	37	36	36	37	34	33
CEE, average	**36**	**36**	**35**	**36**	**33**	**32**	**32**	**33**	**33**	**33**	**32**	**32**	**33**	**32**	**33**	**33**
CIS countries[b]																
Armenia	..	36	34	22	18	15	16	18	19	17	17	17	18	16	17	..
Azerbaijan	39	30	34	27	15	15	16	14	15	15	15	15	17	18	17	..
Belarus	30	32	37	37	29	26	31	34	35	35	33	34	33	..	..	..
Georgia	..	..	..	..	16	16	..	17	16	..	..	..	..	..	28	..
Kazakhstan	42	23	27	25	22	17	17	18	20	23	23	22	22	22	29	..
Kyrgyzstan	19	17	16	17	16	17	17	18	17	15	17	19	19	19	20	..
Moldova	..	23	20	31	31	27	33	30	25	26	23	22	24	24	27	..
Russia	45	28	29	28	31	28	30	26	25	29	30	32	31	32	35	..
Tajikistan	44	35	37	..	14	19	21	18	19	14	15	17	17	17	20	..
Turkmenistan	..	..	20	12	19	..	30	28	..	..	..	..	..	..	..	..
Ukraine	..	..	33	44	38	37	..	..	25	28	27	27	28	27	32	..
Uzbekistan	49	33	36	29	30	32	..	..	..	28	35	34	32	31	23	..
CIS, average	**38**	**29**	**29**	**27**	**24**	**23**	**23**	**22**	**22**	**23**	**24**	**24**	**24**	**23**	**25**	..
Esian Asian countries																
China[c]	14	13	12	11	10	10	11	12	13	14	15	16	16	17	17	18
Mongolia[e]	..	21	25	20	20	19	20	22	22	26	28	29	..	17	15	16
Vietnam[d, e]	15	19	22	24	23	23	21	20	19	20	21	23	24	25	25	26

Sources: IMF, CIS Yearbook, Chinese Statistical Yearbook.

Notes

a. Consolidated central government revenue figures. Source is IMF Government Finance Statistics database.
b. Consolidated budget revenue figures. Source is CIS Yearbook.
c. Total Government revenue only. Source is the All China Data Centre Online.
d. General Government figures.
e. Source is IMF Government Finance Statistics database.

fell to alarmingly low levels in the mid-1990s before tax and other reforms resulted in a rebound of tax revenues, relative to output.

Box 2.2

The flat tax revolution in transition countries

In modern times the idea of a flat tax dates from the early 1980s in the US when Robert Hall and Alvin Rabushka of the Hoover Institution at Stanford University advocated a flat tax to replace the federal income tax system. In their 1985 book *The Flat Tax*, they argued that the then federal income tax failed to meet any of the basic tenets of a good tax system, that is, efficiency, simplicity and fairness. They, as did others, argued that the US income tax system, with all its loopholes and tax deductions, was enormously complex, inefficient and unfair as the rich could use the allowances and shelters to avoid, legally, paying much or any tax. Such a system, they also argued, is not conducive to invest, save or, ultimately, for economic growth. Instead of the graduated tax rates and tax bands, they proposed a uniform or single flat tax with a threshold where no tax on income below the threshold is liable. The basic features of a flat tax include a single flat rate, consumption-based, elimination of exemptions and deductions, and no double taxation of saving and investment. The flat tax, as with tax reductions, it was argued, would increase incentives to work, invest and save. Critics of the flat tax, in addition to claiming that flat single low tax rates can only lead to a race to the bottom, argue that the system is regressive or, at best, less progressive than the graduated system it replaces, and that it benefits the rich at the cost of other taxpayers.

It was the Eastern European transition countries, in continuing their adoption of market reforms, that opted for the flat tax systems, with in later years, lower rates of tax (thus incorporating both flatness and tax reductions into the new tax systems). In 1994 Estonia was the first to introduce a single rate of tax, at 26 per cent, replacing its three rates of 16, 24 and 33 per cent. The other two Baltic States, Lithuania and Latvia, followed in 1994 and 1997, with uniform rates of 33 and 25 per cent respectively. Supporters of the flat tax were euphoric when Russia introduced its flat tax system in 2001, with a single rate of 13 per cent (for personal income tax only) replacing a 'primitive' system of three rates of tax, namely 12, 20 and 30 per cent (Gaddy and Gale 2005). Ukraine, the Slovak Republic, Georgia and Romania were all to follow in 2004/2005. A number of other (smaller, less high-profile) TEs joined the flat tax club in 2007/2008, including Albania, Bulgaria, the Czech Republic, Mongolia and Montenegro, as shown in Table 2.B. Although all countries did adopt flat tax systems, there were significant differences between each system (differences in terms of rates, changes to personal allowance, changes to CIT, treatment of capital income), and, in turn, differences with the original Hall and Rabushka flat tax proposal.

As transition countries adopted flat tax systems it coincided with a pick-up in tax revenues and a recovery in economic activity. However, many of the claims of cause and effect (i.e. it was the introduction of the flat tax that led to increased revenues) are unsupported by what is unfortunately a dearth of empirical evidence in most countries. It is true that revenues did improve as did output, but in many cases the increase in revenues and output preceded the introduction of the flat tax system. These tax changes

---

Table 2.B Flat tax systems in transition countries*

Country	Year flat tax adopted	New rate introduced	Old rates No. of rates	Old rates Rates of tax	Change in personal allowance	Tax rate as of 2009
Estonia	1994	26	3	16, 24, 33	modest increase	21
Lithuania	1994	33	5	10, 18, 24, 28, 33	substantial increase	15
Latvia	1997	25	2	25 and 10	slight decrease	23
Russia	2001	13	3	12, 20, 30	modest increase	13
Ukraine	2004	13	5	10, 15, 20, 30, 40	increase	15
Slovak Republic	2004	19	5	10, 20, 28, 35, 38	substantial increase	19
Georgia	2005	12	4	12, 15, 17, 20	eliminated	20
Romania	2005	16	5	18, 23, 28, 34, 40	increase	16
Others:						
FYR Macedonia	2007	12				10
Kyrgyzstan	2007	10				10
Mongolia	2007	10				12
Montenegro	2007	15				12
Albania	2008	10				10
Bulgaria	2008	10				10
Czech Republic	2008	15				15

Source: Adapted from Keen *et al.* (2006).

Note
* Personal income tax only.

also coincided with other reforms, thus making the claim that the flat tax was the cause of the recovery in both revenues and output difficult to prove. For example, in Russia, many claimed that the new flat 13 per cent single rate was the primary reason for the improvement in revenues. Others, including Gaddy and Gale (2005), argue that the improvement in compliance and revenues was due more likely to improved (and, no doubt, tougher) enforcement procedures, including the introduction of a common taxpayer ID number, withholding tax at source (on all income paid to individuals) and greater powers for the tax authorities, not to mention the broadening of the tax base arising from newly introduced restrictions on allowances and deductions. Indeed, the authors are sceptical of other claims made in respect of the effect that the flat rate had on the Russian economy. They argue that there was little, if any, effect on labour supply based on microeconomic evidence (thus ruling out the much-hyped supply-side effect) and that, from a macroeconomic perspective, the claims of higher tax revenues arising from the lower, single tax are unfounded, and due more likely to higher oil prices and increased wages. These findings are supported by Keen *et al.* (2006) in their study of flat tax in TEs, concluding no evidence of a Laffer effect, that distributional effects are complex and difficult to establish, and that there is no indication of strong work incentives.

What is the current position of the flat tax in Eastern European countries? A paper by staff at the IMF concluded in 2006, prior to the global economic crisis which saw a decline in tax revenues (albeit largely due to the downturn in economic activity), that the future for the flat tax may not be as bright as some had hoped. Keen *et al.* (2006) raised the issue of the sustainability of flat tax systems and, although it is early days, the global crisis may have put further pressure on TEs to revisit the issue of tax design and, in particular, flat versus graduated tax systems (with some TEs, under mounting fiscal pressures, already increasing the uniform tax rate from the level it was when it was first introduced).

With respect to expenditure, as expected, given the level of state expenditure in Soviet times, levels of government expenditure fell in the early years of transition. In many countries (CEE countries in particular) budgetary subsidies and military spending (both of which were exceptionally high in socialist times) fell to levels common in mature market economies. Investment in public goods – infrastructure, education, health – fell in both absolute and relative terms. The fall in government transfers and the failure to target such payments more efficiently meant that the poor were disproportionately affected by the expenditure cutbacks. In the majority of transition countries the fiscal contraction did not materialise from a concerted effort to rationalise spending priorities or a systematic reassessment of government obligations. Much of the fiscal adjustment on the expenditure side, and especially so in CIS countries, came about through sequestration, non-payment and expenditure arrears. Under pressure, central governments also tended to devolve spending to subnational governments (primarily local governments), but, in the majority of cases, without the matching revenues. Aside from the political and electoral pressure that confronts all governments to maintain levels of public spending, governments in TEs were under additional pressure as revenues collapsed and tax bases shrank combined with the added burden of financing social functions that in pre-transition times were the responsibilities of SOEs (Alam and Sundberg 2002; Mitra and Stern 2003).

The trend in government expenditure over the period 1991 to 2008 is evident in Table 2.19. Here the coverage is for general government, including extra-budgetary funds and local government spending, where available. Prior to transition, government expenditure as a percentage of GDP was high (much less in China and Vietnam), close to 50 per cent (as it was in the last few years of the Soviet Union) and 55 per cent (as it was, on average, in Eastern European countries) and in some cases even higher (with rates of close to 60 per cent in Czechoslovakia and Hungary, pre-transition). Given the level of development, that was unusually high (what Kornai called the 'premature welfare state') and comparable to levels found in the high tax, high spending Nordic countries whose level of income per capita is much higher (in general, the higher level of income per capita, the higher the level of government spending).

At the outset of transition, government spending, despite the turmoil of the years preceding the demise of the socialist system, was still high by international standards, with the majority of former socialist countries having a public spending/GDP ratio in the mid-40s. Within a short time, that ratio had fallen below the 40 per cent threshold. After 20 years of transition, government spending as a percentage of GDP has fallen about ten percentage points, on average, to 35 to 37 per cent of GDP, a figure more in line with those found in countries with

Table 2.19 General government expenditure/GDP[a]

Country	1991	1992	1993	1994	1995	1996	1997	1998	1999	2000	2001	2002	2003	2004	2005	2006	2007	2008
Albania	52	47	40	36	33	24	28	34	34	32	32	31	29	30	29	29	29	33
Armenia[b]	28	47	..	44	29	26	26	26	30	26	21	19	19	17	18	20	22	22
Azerbaijan	..	48	56	37	21	17	19	24	24	21	19	28	29	26	23	27	27	28
Belarus	..	48	58	47	42	41	46	45	47	46	47	47	48	46	48	48	49	50
Bosnia and Herzegovina	..	..	..	..	36	47	36	57	63	54	47	49	39	39	40	42	44	45
Bulgaria[c]	41	44	48	46	41	42	33	37	40	40	38	37	38	37	38	35	37	37
China	..	..	17	16	15	17	15	16	18	20	21	22	21	21	21	22	22	..
Croatia[d]	..	39	37	25	42	38	38	47	49	45	44	51	44	43	42	42	42	41
Czech Republic	54	53	..	..	42	41	41	38	39	40	42	44	47	45	44	44	43	42
Estonia	..	..	..	..	41	40	38	40	41	36	35	36	35	34	34	34	35	40
FYR Macedonia	50	49	54	46	39	37	35	35	35	34	40	40	35	33	35	34	33	35
Georgia	..	..	..	..	12	21	21	19	22	19	18	18	19	19	25	29	34	37
Hungary	56	60	60	60	53	53	52	53	50	47	51	51	49	49	50	52	50	50
Kazakhstan	..	..	25	18	21	19	20	26	23	23	23	21	22	23	22	20	24	27
Kyrgyzstan	25	35	39	32	40	29	30	34	34	29	26	28	27	28	28	29	31	30
Latvia[e]	..	..	..	37	39	37	36	40	42	37	35	36	35	36	36	38	36	39
Lithuania[e]	..	..	37	37	36	37	50	40	40	39	37	35	33	33	33	34	35	37
Moldova	23	49	28	50	46	44	49	45	37	35	29	32	33	35	37	40	42	42
Mongolia[f]	47	25	39	33	27	28	30	36	34	36	38	39	37	35	28	33	38	40
Montenegro	..	..	..	..	..	..	..	..	..	..	..	44	45	41	39	42	39	43
Poland	45	50	50	51	48	51	46	44	43	41	44	44	45	43	43	44	42	43
Romania	..	42	34	33	35	34	34	35	35	35	39	40	34	34	31	33	35	38
Russia	..	58	44	45	43	45	48	43	37	34	35	37	36	34	32	31	34	34
Serbia	..	..	..	..	..	61	65	60	57	51	45	45	43	42	42	45	44	43
Slovak Republic	41	44	46	45	54	46	47	48	48	47	48	46	46	46	45	45	42	44
Slovenia	55	58	47	53	54	46	47	48	48	47	48	46	46	46	45	45	42	44
Tajikistan[g]	..	..	17	19	19	16	17	16	18	19	18	19	19	20	23	22	29	28
Turkmenistan	36	30	17	19	20	16	25	19	19	24	21	18	19	19	20	15	13	12
Ukraine	..	58	54	51	43	40	44	38	34	34	34	36	37	42	44	45	44	47
Uzbekistan	..	30	49	34	38	50	40	44	42	39	36	38	33	32	30	29	33	33
Vietnam	..	23	..	..	24	24	24	22	23	25	27	27	27	26	27	27	..	..
Average TEs, unweighted	**45**	**42**	**40**	**36**	**35**	**36**	**37**	**36**	**35**	**34**	**35**	**34**	**34**	**34**	**34**	**35**	..	..
Average TEs, without China and Vietnam	**46**	**43**	**41**	**37**	**36**	**37**	**38**	**38**	**36**	**35**	**36**	**35**	**34**	**34**	**35**	**36**	**37**	**37**
CEE, average	49									40					36	39	37	
CIS, average	46									28					32			

Sources: EBRD, IMF, Chinese Statistical Yearbook.

Notes
a. Includes local government and extra-budgetary funds, incorporated where available.
b. Central government only.
c. 2003 and 2004 includes capital transfers of about 0.4 percent of GDP.
d. Consolidated general government from 2002.
e. Includes net lending.
f. Includes grant and net lending.
g. Includes externally financed public investment programmes.

similar levels of economic development and income per capita. There is still much cross-country variation, with the high-income countries of Croatia, the Czech Republic, Hungary and Slovenia all with government spending/GDP ratios of 40 per cent or higher. Although there may an issue over the sustainability of these expenditure levels, notwithstanding the difficulty in establishing what level might be appropriate, it is nevertheless true that in the first decade of transition these levels of social expenditure and investments were important in maintaining public support for market reforms (often in the face of much criticism from vested interests) and did manage to partly cushion the worst effects of transition. In contrast, at the other end of the government share of GDP spectrum are countries such as Armenia, China and Turkmenistan with a spending/GDP ratio of 20 per cent or less.

The global crisis of 2007 to 2009 saw revenues fall in TEs (as elsewhere), resulting in a re-emergence of rising budget deficits for some transition countries, most especially in Central and Eastern Europe as many of the CIS countries were buffeted by tax revenues arising from high oil and gas prices of earlier years. In addition to continued reform of tax systems (flat and otherwise), governments in TEs are under growing pressure to reassess their levels of public spending with a view to bringing spending more in line with other countries at similar levels of development.

Demographics

One of the surprises, and most alarming trends, of transition has being the change in demographics. Since transition began in CEE/FSU countries over two decades ago, a disturbing pattern (rare in modern peacetime in industrialised nations) of falling fertility rates, rising mortality rates, falling life expectancy at birth rates and, overall, a decline in population has emerged. This compares sharply with transition in the East Asian countries of China and Vietnam where population numbers keep on rising: the estimated population of China has increased by 38 per cent since reforms began in 1978, and by 18 per cent since 1989. The population increases recorded in Vietnam are even greater: 41 per cent since reforms began in 1986 and a 31 per cent increase since 1989. Furthermore, the decline in population in CEE/FSU countries over this period is contrary to what one expects for middle-income countries whose population, on average, tends to rise. Is the trend in population unique to transition? Is it related to market reforms, and, in particular, the speed and intensity of reforms? Or, is it related to initial conditions, or simply convergence with Western and Northern European levels? As the trend of rising mortality rates and declining population numbers seems particularly striking in FSU countries, we will focus on former Soviet republics, especially Russia. We begin, however, with some numbers.

Excluding China and Vietnam (that is, low-income countries that started reforms earlier), the population of CEE/FSU countries on the eve of transition, taking 1989 as a reference point, was 402.4 million. By 2007, the population had fallen to 396 million, a decline of 1.6 per cent. The decline in FSU countries was greater, with a fall of 2.1 per cent between 1991 and 2007. Of the non-war-torn CEE countries, Romania and Bulgaria have recorded the largest declines, 7 per cent and 14 per cent respectively. It is, however, the FSU countries that have witnessed the largest declines in population numbers. Taking 1992 as the start of transition for FSU countries, the majority of former republics of the Soviet Union have seen a fall in population since transition began, including the three Baltic States (whose decline is due to negative rates of natural increase *and* outward migration, mainly of Russians). As seen in Table 2.20, in terms of percentages for the period 1991 to 2007, Georgia suffered a 19 per

Table 2.20 Population changes[a]

Country	1989	1991 (for FSU and Mongolia)	2007	1989–2007, +ive Δ	1989–2007, -ive Δ	Transition period (for FSU and East Asian countries)[d]	Number of years of decline	Year(s) of largest decline	Largest yearly decline	Years of consecutive decline
Albania	3255133		3181326		-2		8	1994	-1.4	1992–1999
Armenia	3542436	3512440	3009161		-15	-14	16	1994	-2.4	1991–2006
Azerbaijan	7085000	7271000	8556378	21		18				
Belarus	10170000	10194000	9702000		-5	-5	14	1998; 2002–2005	-0.5	1994–2007
Bosnia and Herzegovina	4359957		3772964		-13		8	1991–1995	-5.1	1990–1995; 2006–2007
Bulgaria	8877000		7659764		-14		19	2001	-1.9	1989–2007
China[b]	1118650000		1318309724	18		38				
Croatia	4767000		4435982		-7		6	1991	-5.8	1991–1992
Czech Republic	10362000		10334160	no change						
Estonia	1568000	1561000	1341672		-14	-14	17	1993	-2.6	1991–2007
FYR Macedonia	1893408		2037032	8						
Georgia	5469181	5412506	4398588		-20	-19	18	1994	-2.0	1990–2007
Hungary	10398261		10055579		-3		17	1989	-0.4	1989–1990; 1993–2007
Kazakhstan	16249500	16450500	15484200		-5	-6	10	1995	-1.8	1992–2001
Kyrgyzstan	4340000	4495000	5234800	21		16				
Latvia	2684000	2662000	2276100		-15	-14	18	1993	-1.8	1990–2007
Lithuania	3691000	3704000	3375618		-9	-9	16	2000	-0.9	1992–2007
Moldova	4367897	4403088	3803704		-13	-14	14	2001–2003	-1.4	1994–2007
Mongolia	2069173	2141909	2608412	26		22				
Montenegro	582797		599006	3						
Poland	37963000		38120560	no change						
Romania	23152000		21546873		-7		17	1992	-1.7	1991–2007
Russia	147721000	148624000	142100000		-4	-4	14	2003–2006	-0.5	1993–1999; 2001–2007
Serbia	..		7381579							
Slovak Republic	5297000		5397318	2						

(Continued)

Table 2.20 Continued

Country	1989	1991 (for FSU and Mongolia)	2007	1989–2007, +ive Δ	1989–2007, –ive Δ	Transition period (for FSU and East Asian countries)[d]	Number of years of decline	Year(s) of largest decline	Largest yearly decline	Years of consecutive decline
Slovenia	1999400		2018122	1						
Tajikistan	5170562	5418488	6740085	30		24				
Turkmenistan	3570110	3773480	4963332	39		32				
Ukraine	51773000	52000470	46509350		–10	–11	14	2000–2002	–1.0	1994–2007
Uzbekistan	20033394	20952000	26867800	34		28				
Vietnam[c]	64774000		85154900	31		41				
TEs (excl. China and Vietnam)	402411209		396129885		–1.6					
Total for FSU countries		290433972	284362787							

Source: World Bank Development Indicators.

Notes
a. Midyear estimates
b. China's estimated population in 1978 at the start of reforms was 956.2 million
c. Vietnam's estimated population in 1986 at the start of reforms was 60.2 million
d. Only reporting TEs with a transition start date other than 1989.

cent decline with Armenia, Estonia, Latvia, Moldova and Ukraine all suffering population declines in excess of 10 per cent. Although some of these countries did witness conflict early on in transition, neither Estonia, Latvia nor Ukraine experienced any serious strife, indicating that the reason for the decline in population lies elsewhere. The last four columns in Table 2.20 report some more detail for those transition countries that have experienced a decline in population. Although the number of countries is just a little over half the total of TEs, the extent and intensity of the decline is shocking. Aside from the war-torn Balkans which obviously experienced large losses of life, the numbers indicate that other countries have experienced rapid depopulation. For example, eight countries, namely Armenia, Bulgaria, Georgia, Hungary, Romania and the three Baltic States, have all experienced, since 1989, 15 or more years of consecutive population decline, with Bulgaria witnessing a population decline every year since 1989 (up to 2007).

In terms of numbers, the majority of the population decline in TEs was in Russia and Ukraine. The population of Russia, despite the inward migration of ethnic Russians from the other republics, fell from 148.6 million in 1991 to 142.1 million by 2007 (a trend that had started before the breakup of the Soviet Union); in Ukraine, the population declined from 52 million in 1991 to 46.5 million in 2007. Future projections are for further depopulation in the European CIS countries although it is difficult to establish, given the uncertainty over future migration patterns. In contrast, all the most advanced CEE countries (with the exception of Hungary), that is, the Czech Republic, Poland, the Slovak Republic and Slovenia, witnessed over the period 1989 to 2007 either no change in population, or in the case of the Slovak Republic and Slovenia, small increases. Interestingly, of the four least advanced reforming TEs (Belarus, Tajikistan, Turkmenistan and Uzbekistan), only Belarus suffered a decline in population, with the other three countries recording large increases in population (24 per cent, 32 per cent and 28 per cent, respectively). It is difficult to establish for certain how much, if any at all, of the rise in population in these countries is due to delayed reforms (and less subsequent economic disruption and social upheaval) as opposed to other non-policy factors, such as all three having large Muslim populations, as have Azerbaijan and Kyrgyzstan, two other CIS countries that recorded large increases in population during transition.

Birth rates slump, death rates soar

With respect to fertility rates, a downward trend was evident *before* the collapse of the socialist system: aside from the trend in middle- and high-income countries for lower fertility rates (and the spread of Western influence, and family and reproductive behaviour); the decline, accelerating between 1989 and 1991, may have been due to the stagnation and the deepening economic and social crisis emerging in the Soviet Union and its satellite states in the late 1980s. Indeed, the former German Democratic Republic (GDR) experienced what the UN described as 'a fertility decline that has no known parallels' (UNECE 1999). GDR was no exception. By the mid-1990s, many former socialist countries, particularly in Eastern Europe, had some of the lowest fertility rates in the world. The rapid decline in fertility rates continued (as did the fall in marriage rates), with cross-country variations increasing, throughout the early years of transition as the social upheaval persisted and poor economic conditions continued (with future prospects uncertain) for the vast bulk of transition countries and their peoples. Rising unemployment and poverty, falling real wages and declining state supports to family may have depressed fertility further as family circumstances remained uncertain.

However, with the recovery of output well underway in all transition countries by the late 1990s the decline in fertility rates had noticeably decelerated, but to levels that 'by European standards are unprecedentedly low' (UNECE 2000).

We now turn to mortality rates and the question posed in the World Bank Development Report 1996, *From Plan to Market*, namely '*Is transition a killer?*'[32] This was in response to rising mortality rates in FSU countries (as against falling rates in CEE countries, and countries worldwide), particularly in Kazakhstan, Russia and Ukraine, but also in the three Baltic States, indicating that despite much of the media attention directed towards the Russian mortality crisis, it is as much a post-Soviet crisis and post-communist phenomenon, affecting many FSU countries (Kontorovich 2001). Identifying precise causes for falling male life expectancy rates (see Chapter 7) and rising mortality rates is a vexed and highly complex question that many academics (economists, demographers, epidemiologists and others) and practitioners (physicians, medics and others) have tried to address in what is a very fluid environment. As with fertility, we begin with the observation that mortality rates were on the increase in the Soviet Union long before transition, and indeed the upward trend goes as far back as the Brezhnev era. Other than the small reversal in the trend in the mid-1980s (due, it is often claimed, to Gorbachev's anti-alcohol campaign), the trend has been one of rising mortality rates, accelerating from the years 1989 to 1991 onwards. With the rise in death rates particularly prevalent among males of working age, various explanations have been cited in the literature for the rise in mortality rates. Notwithstanding the problems of accessing high-quality data, there is evidence that some or all of the following (often interrelated) factors have played a role in the rise of male mortality in Russia (and other former Soviet republics) up until the mid-1990s when first indications of a reversal appeared (Anderson 1997; Shkolnikov *et al.* 1998). Aside from the change in the age composition of the population (i.e. transition countries have ageing populations), they are as follows:

- substance abuse (e.g. alcohol, smoking, illegal drugs);[33]
- deterioration in the health service and care, and a rise in infectious diseases (e.g. TB, HIV/AIDS);
- stress and loss of security and status (arguably arising from the abrupt and severe transition);
- economic disruption and social upheaval, resulting in a fall in living standards, loss of earnings and rising unemployment.

Although the last two explanations are directly related to transition, neither the Russians' predilection to alcohol nor the country's failing healthcare system (already in crisis before the collapse of the Soviet Union) can be directly traced to post-Soviet transformation.[34] Although the immediate causes are primarily circulatory/cardiovascular diseases (strokes and heart attacks) and accidents/violent deaths, it is probably a combination of the factors listed above (and others, with ecological problems and environmental pollution getting a mention), but ultimately it is a case of state failure and collapse (Ellman 1997b, 2000). It is evident from other patterns of transition (rising levels of unemployment, inequality and poverty) that transition has resulted, particularly in CIS countries, in enormous social problems, some of which were unexpected or, at the very least, not a priority at the outset of transition. Among these social costs, the demographic crisis requires urgent attention.

Institutions

Institutions will be discussed in greater detail in Chapter 5. For now, we will briefly define institutions and comment on the trends with respect to institutional development over the past two decades. Although there are different definitions of institutions, the most common one is taken from North (1990, 1991) where institutions are defined as formal rules, informal constraints and enforcement mechanisms. Examples of formal rules include constitutions, laws and regulations. Norms of behaviour, codes of conduct, conventions and customs are examples of informal rules or constraints. Enforcement mechanisms include the judicial system and third-party arbitration. Institutions, including the organisations that implement the rules and codes of conduct, are important because they facilitate exchange and govern market transactions. Distinct from policies, institutions are the rules and social norms by which agents interact and exchange. Policies affect which institutions evolve, but, in turn, institutions affect which policies are adopted. Institutional structure affects behaviour but, likewise, behaviour may also change within existing institutional structures (World Bank 2002b).

Measuring institutions empirically is a difficult task where despite recent research and some advances there is no consensus on a precise measure. Acknowledging the differences between measuring formal and informal institutions (using 'hard' measures for the former as opposed to 'soft' measures for the latter), a common criticism of the current measures or indicators of institutions is that they measure institutional outcomes (not inputs) rather than institutions per se. In later chapters, we will cite work by scholars (e.g. Campos 2000; Kaufmann *et al.* 2009; Weder 2001) reporting to measure different aspects of institutions (and institutional dimensions of governance). Although not perfect, these are reasonable indicators of institutions (or, more correctly, different dimensions of institutions, including the rule of law) at a point in time (see Chapter 5 for more on measures of institutional quality). Of course with transition we wish to assess institutional change, and the progress, or otherwise, of institutional reform over time.

As of now, there is no universal measure (nor is it clear that there should be) that captures the different aspects (institutions/organisations, formal/informal, de jure/de facto, predatory/developmental, best-practice/transitional) of institutions and institutional change. Although there is great temptation to report some of the actual numerics of the different dimensions of institutional change during transition (as, for example, for the period 1996 to 2008 in Kaufmann *et al.* 2009), we provide, as an alternate, a descriptive account of developments with respect to institutional quality and change. What follows is a brief description (with some citations) of the patterns that have developed in respect of institutions since the fall of socialism over two decades ago. In supporting this account, we reproduce an updated version of a table from Murrell (2003) where, using the World Bank Governance Indicators (WGI) (see Kaufmann *et al.* 2009), the direction of change for each of the six indicators for all TEs is given (where I = improvement and D = deterioration). The overall evidence is mixed, with sizeable improvements in some dimensions (particularly government effectiveness and regulatory quality) and some countries (most notably in Croatia, Estonia, Latvia, Serbia, the Slovak Republic and Tajikistan) but, in contrast, a deterioration in other dimensions (rule of law, and voice and accountability) and other countries (China, Hungary, Kyrgyzstan, Moldova, Mongolia and Vietnam).[35]

In any setting (centralised or decentralised, plan or market) a stable society requires a set of rules and social norms for behaviour. Order in the socialist system was provided by the state and the Communist Party. All else, whether it was public ownership, the central plan, the soft

Table 2.21 Institutional change, 1996–2008[a, b, c]

Country	Voice and accountability	Political stability and absence of violence	Government effectiveness	Regulatory quality	Rule of law	Control of corruption	Number of institutional dimensions improving
CEB							
Albania	I	I	D	I	D	D	3
Bosnia and Herzegovina	I	D	I	I	D	no change	3
Bulgaria	I	I	I	I	no change	I	5
Croatia	I	D	I	I	I	D	6
Czech Republic	I	I	I	I	no change	I	3
Estonia	I	D	I	I	I	I	6
FYR Macedonia	I	D	no change	I	D	D	4
Hungary	D	D	I	I	D	D	1
Latvia	D	I	I	I	I	I	6
Lithuania	D	D	I	I	I	I	5
Poland	D	I	D	I	D	D	2
Romania	I	D	I	I	I	I	5
Serbia	I	I	I	I	I	I	6
Slovak Republic	I	I	I	I	I	I	6
Slovenia	D	I	I	no change	I	D	3
CIS							
Armenia	I	D	I	I	I	I	5
Azerbaijan	D	I	I	I	I	I	5
Belarus	D	I	I	I	I	I	4
Georgia	D	D	I	I	I	I	5
Kazakhstan	no change	I	I	no change	no change	I	2
Kyrgyzstan	D	D	D	I	D	D	1
Moldova	D	D	D	D	D	D	0
Russia	D	I	I	D	D	D	2
Tajikistan	I	I	I	I	I	I	6
Turkmenistan	D	I	I	I	I	I	4
Ukraine	I	I	I	I	D	I	5
Uzbekistan	D	D	I	I	D	D	2
East Asia							
China	no change	D	I	D	D	D	1
Mongolia	D	D	D	I	D	D	1
Vietnam	D	no change	no change	D	I	D	1
Number of TEs for which the institutional score has improved	15	17	23	24	13	16	
% of TEs improving	50%	57%	77%	80%	43%	53%	

Sources: Murrell (2003); Kaufmann et al. (2009).

Notes

a. Choosing 2006 (as opposed to 2008 when the global crisis may have had an impact on the numbers) as the end-year makes little difference in terms of overall results.

b. 1996 is the earliest year for which the WGI are available.

c. No change is when the score moves up or down by 0.03 or less between the years 1996 and 2008.

budget constraint or shortages, followed from the one-party system (Kornai 1992). Although the fall of communism was greeted enthusiastically as a move towards freedom and prosperity, an unanticipated consequence of the collapse of the state and the disintegration of the Party was, at least in the early years of transition (and particularly so in FSU republics), an institutional vacuum filled by disorder, disorganisation and, in some cases, chaos (Djankov *et al.* 2003). As the state apparatus weakened, economic activity and production declined (see Chapter 7). As one commentator remarked, 'the institutional vacuum that followed the fall of socialism is at the root of the successes and failures in economic reform' (Campos 2000). Neither the market nor the market-supporting institutions emerged overnight. Although markets soon evolved (quicker in CEE countries than in CIS countries), the institutions that facilitate and support market transactions were often slow to develop. With a weakened state capacity, many market-supporting institutions were either, at worst, absent or, at best, ineffective.

Over time, with the support of a reconstructed state and international assistance, many of the formal institutions and organisations required for a stable society and a growing economy were developed. However, it was the more informal institutions and social norms – customs, traditions, codes of conduct – that, not surprisingly given the influence of culture and history, evolved more slowly (and often, as a result, undermined the new formal institutions). Aside from differences in how these institutions evolved, there was also significant cross-country or cross-regional variation with respect to institutional change. Whereas many of the CEE countries managed to make good progress with respect to institutional reform (with EU enlargement playing an important role), institution building in CIS countries lagged behind (in many ways, replicating the cross-regional variation evident with respect to policy reform). With the onset of the second decade in transition, more attention was paid to institutions and institutional reform.

After two decades, although much progress has been made, there is still a long way to go in improving the institutional quality in many former socialist countries and, most especially, the CIS countries. Nevertheless, given an earlier view that institution building is inevitably a slow process, many countries did manage their institutional construction 'surprisingly quickly and successfully', and furthermore, judging against countries of similar levels of economic development and per capita income, 'levels of measured institutional development are roughly as expected', with some 'remarkable improvements in institutional measures over the 1990s' (Murrell 2003, 2006).[36] This has led to a further classification of institutions, not just the distinction between formal and informal, as North (1990) made previously, but between institutional change that is slow and continuous as opposed to institutional change that is quick and irregular (Roland 2008a). Another classification made is between best-practice international institutions and imperfect transitional institutions. Whereas many CEE countries, largely owing to EU accession, tended to adopt or transplant best-practice or first-best institutions, China is a prime example of a country adopting, successfully as argued by many, including Qian (2000, 2003), transitional or second-best institutions.

In sum, with the notable exception of China, transition witnessed the destruction of the institutional structures of the socialist system and an institutional vacuum for much of the early years of transition. As time passed and state capacity improved, institutions were developed and rebuilt, with more progress in CEE countries than in CIS countries. By the end of the second decade, a majority of the former socialist countries had many of the market-supporting institutions common in other emerging markets and the more established market economies. Whereas many TEs transplanted best-practice international institutions, others (particularly China) experimented with transitional institutions. Two decades on, transition countries have, on average, the institutional structure that is generally expected, given their level of economic development (Murrell 2003). The question of how the quality of institutions can be improved in the laggard CIS countries remains an outstanding issue.

Summary

1   The main stylised facts or patterns of economic transition from plan to market over the past two decades relate to trends in output, inflation, sectoral share of GDP, private enterprise, investment and consumption, corruption and informal activities, inequality and poverty, trade and FDI, labour flows, taxation and public expenditure, and demographics and institutions.

2   Some of the patterns of transition were expected, such as the rise in private enterprise and services, the fall in government expenditure, the rise in foreign trade and FDI, the increase in unemployment, and the change in investment and consumption patterns. Others happened as expected but the degree of the change was unexpected, such as the rapid rise in prices, the sudden fall in revenues, and the extreme rise in poverty and inequality. Other developments were simply unexpected. This includes the decline in output, the rise in corruption and the unofficial economy, and, most alarmingly, the fall in population associated with the unprecedented, in peacetime, rise in mortality rates.

3   As regards these patterns of transition, there are differences with respect to time and regions/countries. In respect to differences over time, the early years recorded the worst features of transition whereas, in general, the second decade of transition witnessed a recovery. In respect of country and regional differences, the biggest difference is between CEE/FSU countries and the East Asian countries of China and Vietnam. Aside from some similarities (increase in services, corruption, private enterprise, trade, inequality), many of the most disturbing trends (unexpected fall in output and population, big rise in prices, poverty and mortality rates) were not witnessed in either China or Vietnam. Within the Soviet bloc group of countries there are also differences, along the lines of CEE (including the Baltics) versus CIS countries, with the CEE countries doing much better in terms of output, employment and inflation, poverty and inequality, corruption and demographics.

Key terms

Absolute poverty	Gini Index
Arrears	Gross domestic fixed investment
Convergence effect	Hyperinflation
Corruption Perceptions Index	Inequality
Council for Mutual Economic	Informal economy
Assistance	Insider privatisation
Decollectivisation	Institutions
Deindustrialisation	Labour force participation rate
De novo private firms	Patterns of development
Final household consumption	Poverty Headcount Index
expenditure	Structural change
Flat tax	Trade openness
Foreign Direct Investment	

Review questions

1   Outline the differences between the patterns identified by Campos and Coricelli (2002) and those identified in this textbook.
2   Explain how some of the patterns may be interrelated. In your answer, identify cause and effect and provide explanations for the particular causation given.
3   Take any three TEs (one from each of the three groupings listed in the Introduction) and write a short article on each of the three countries (highlighting the differences) as regards the stylised facts of transition.

3

INITIAL CONDITIONS AT THE OUTSET
OF TRANSITION

In this chapter we outline the starting point for socialist countries embarking on transition from plan to market. The chapter identifies a number of initial conditions that reflect the circumstances of these countries at the outset of transition. Differences in these inherited conditions are examined with a view to later explaining differences in cross-country performance during transition. Was it the case that countries with the most adverse initial conditions were indeed the same cohort of countries that were the worst performers? Other explanatory variables, such as reforms and external factors, are also identified. The chapter ends with a summary of the main quantitative studies examining the impact of initial conditions on performance, and the interrelationship between initial conditions, policy reforms and economic outcomes.

Close on 30 countries, from East Germany in the West to China in the East, set out to transform, rather than reform as was the case in the pre-transition era, their economic system at the end of the twentieth century. Table 3.1 outlines some basic data for these transition economies on the eve of transition, and how, with respect to a number of indicators, the transition countries differ from other countries, such as low-income developing countries, middle-income emerging countries or high-income industrialised countries.

A number of observations can be made from Table 3.1. In terms of income per capita, the majority of socialist economies at the beginning of transition were neither low-income countries as was prevalent in the developing world of Africa and Southern Asia nor were they high-income countries as was predominantly found in North America and Western Europe. Many tended to be middle-income countries (classified by the World Bank as having a national income per capita in 1990 of between $610 and $7,620) but often, in later years, with low and declining growth rates. In terms of the economic structure, socialist countries tended to be, on average, urbanised and industrialised with high investment rates and equally high (and often inefficient) energy usage. In terms of human resources and social indicators, although socialist countries had – as compared with countries of similar levels of development and income per capita – extensive welfare systems as characterised by relatively even distributions of income, high rates of life expectancy and high literacy rates, there was evidence of a deterioration in living standards as the economies of the Soviet bloc began to stagnate in the later stages of the Brezhnev era. Despite the early successes of the socialist system, critics of the command economy claimed that these years of economic decline and stagnation were due to the inefficiencies of the centrally planned system and that the dual problems of distorted incentives and lack of information were the main reasons why the countries of the socialist system failed to close the gap with the West and, indeed, by the 1980s, were falling further behind.

Table 3.1 The starting numbers (per cent except where stated otherwise)

Indicator	Transition economies					Comparators			
	CEE	Russia	Other NIS and Mongolia	China^a	Vietnam^a	Low Income^b	India	Middle income	OECD
Population and income									
Population, 1989 (millions)	122	149	139	1,102	64	1,002	850	1,105	773
GNP per capita, 1990^c (1990 dollars)									
From World Bank Atlas	2,268	4,110	2,141	404	188	320	380	2,220	20,170
At PPP	4,647	6,440	4,660	1,000	..	1,086	1,090	4,289	15,615
Growth rate before transition^d	1.5	1.9	2.3	4.9	..	3.4	5.8	2.9	3.0
Economic structure									
Urban population as share of total population, 1991	61	74	58	18	19	28	27	62	77
Investment share of GDP, 1989^e	34	34	31	35	16	21	24	25	22
Industry share of GDP, 1989	51	50	40	48	23	28	29	36	31
Energy use (kilograms of oil equivalent per dollar of GDP)^f	0.81	0.91	0.71	0.38	..	0.14	0.21	0.41	0.31
Human resources									
Gini coefficient, 1989^g	26	24	24	30	36	46	34	45	33
Life expectancy at birth, 1989 (years)^g	71	69	70	70	66	56	60	68	77
Illiteracy rate, 1991	3	2	2	31	12	41	52	17	<5
Monetary and exchange rate indicators									
M2 as percentage of GDP	53	100	75	25	19	33	46	41	78
Black market exchange rate premium, 1989	331	1,828	1,822	..	464	87	12	101	0

Source: World Bank Development Report (1996). The International Bank for Reconstruction and Development, The World Bank retains the copyrights to the data.

Notes
All measures for country groups are averages, weighted by population.
.. = Not available.
a. All data for China are for 1978, and those for Vietnam for 1986, except where specifically noted otherwise (i.e., for GDP growth, energy use. Gini coefficients, and life expectancy).
b. Excluding China and India.
c. Data are for 1991 for NIS and Mongolia.
d. Average annual real GDP growth rate at market prices; data are for 1980–89 for CEE and comparators, 1980–90 for NIS and Mongolia, 1966–78 for China.
e. Gross domestic investment.
f. At PPP using 1992 dollars; data are for 1990 for CEE; 1992 for NIS, Mongolia, and comparators: 1980 for China (staff estimate).
g. Data are for 1980 for China, 1992 for Vietnam.

We know from our discussion of the command economy in Chapter 1 that the socialist system had a number of distinguishing economic features. These included the centrally planned mechanism of resource allocation (as opposed to voluntary exchange within a decentralised system), collectivism and state ownership (as opposed to individualism and private enterprise), the dominance of industry and investment over services and consumption, high literacy rates and a relatively even distribution of income.[1] The common legacy of the command system may be characterised by four main elements, namely coordination through plans (or, in practice, bureaucratic bargaining), macroeconomic balance by direct controls, prices that were administratively fixed and rarely changed (with heavily distorted relative prices), and little private ownership (World Bank 1996). Yet, despite the common legacy of one-party rule, public ownership and bureaucratic coordination, the former socialist countries were not all the same at the outset of transition (despite claims by some to the contrary). In this chapter we focus on the differences in initial conditions at the beginning of transition and the inherited burden confronting transition countries.

Initial conditions varied greatly, not just between the countries of East Asia, Central and Eastern Europe and the republics of the former Soviet Union but even within these groups of countries. Understanding these cross-country variations in circumstances is useful when explaining, at a later stage, the issue of the large variation in economic performance and outcomes that emerged among countries once transition began. Differences in the starting point may also partly explain the different reform strategies adopted by the various TEs (with the important and controversial implication that the reform path was predetermined), acknowledging that other factors including political constraints, electoral support and legitimacy, ideologies, institutions and pressure (or support) from the West also played a role. The economics literature on transition indicates that the role of the initial conditions was indeed an important factor in the complex transition process (De Melo *et al.* 2001; Falcetti *et al.* 2002). We now provide some details on these differences in inherited conditions.

At the start of transition there were a number of important differences between the socialist countries that were embarking on transition. In particular, there were important differences between, first, the degree of economic centralisation and the prevalence of markets, and second, the degree of macroeconomic internal and external imbalances. Fischer and Gelb (1991a) illustrate, using a four-quadrant diagram which is reproduced below (Figure 3.1), key differences between these two indicators for six socialist countries, namely Bulgaria, Czechoslovakia, Hungary, Poland, the USSR and Yugoslavia at the start of transition. With respect to markets and centralisation, Bulgaria, Czechoslovakia and the USSR had relatively centralised economies. In contrast, Yugoslavia, Hungary and Poland were more decentralised, relying more on markets and with a greater degree of autonomy for firms and managers. In relation to macroeconomic imbalances, both internal and external, Hungary and Czechoslovakia were in reasonable shape at the outset of transition. In contrast, Poland and Yugoslavia were in serious trouble, with both countries requiring urgent stabilisation packages to counter rising inflation and, in Poland's case, an overwhelming debt crisis. Although less urgent, both Bulgaria and the USSR also faced the prospect of macroeconomic instability.

Aside from political, cultural and historical factors, there are a range of economic factors that indicate differences between these countries. Cross-country differences in levels of human capital, income distribution, demographics, the extent of pre-transition reform and the size of government existed at the outset of transition. The problem with these and many other

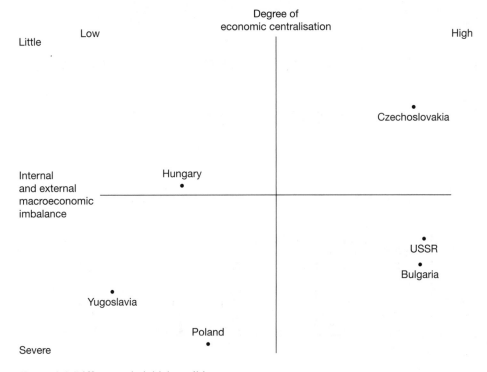

Figure 3.1 Differences in initial conditions.

Source: Fischer and Gelb (1991a).

factors is the difficulty of acquiring accurate and comparable cross-country data. Several studies on transition have identified a list of factors that are both quantifiable and provide a reasonable account of the differences in initial conditions or circumstances on the eve of transition. In particular, a 1997 World Bank study classifies a large number of variables into three categories, namely development and structure, economic distortions and institutional characteristics (De Melo *et al.* 2001).[2] In terms of regions, countries are classified into three groups, namely CEE countries, FSU countries and others. Arising from these categories, 11 country-specific factors were identified and, for the reader's benefit, these variables are reproduced in Table 3.2.[3]

As mentioned throughout the book, there are particular problems with reporting data for transition countries. Aside from the standard caveats that apply with the reporting of economic data, figures for the transition period (and, moreover, for the pre-transition era) are subject to a number of specific problems. For instance, output data were likely to be over-reported – for ideological and methodological reasons – in the pre-transition period, and, thus, at the outset of transition official GDP figures were likely to be overestimates of economic activity. In contrast, since transition began, output data are likely to be under-reported due to official GDP figures not accounting for underground or unofficial private sector activity. There are also difficulties with acquiring accurate estimates of, *inter alia*, price deflators (due to, among other things, the rapid increases in price levels in the early years of transition), public finance figures (as some government activity was off-budget or in the form of barter and/or offsets)

Table 3.2 The initial conditions[a, b, c]

Country	Per capita income at PPP (US$ 1989)	Average % growth 1985–89	Urban isation 1990	Industry share of GDP	Natural resource	Repressed inflation	Black market premium 1990 (%)	CMEA trade 1990 (%)	Years under central planning
CEE									
Albania	1400	3.6	37	0.37	Poor	4.3	434	6.6	47
Bulgaria	5000	2.7	68	0.59	Poor	18.0	921	16.1	43
Croatia	6171	0.2	62	0.35	Poor	12.0	27	6.0	46
Czech Republic	8600	1.6	65	0.58	Poor	-7.1	185	6.0	42
Hungary	6810	1.6	62	0.36	Poor	-7.7	47	13.7	42
FYR Macedonia	3394	0.2	59	0.43	Poor	12.0	27	6.0	47
Poland	5150	2.8	62	0.52	Moderate	13.6	277	8.4	41
Romania	3470	-0.8	53	0.59	Moderate	16.8	728	3.7	42
Slovak Republic	7600	1.6	57	0.59	Poor	-7.1	185	6.0	42
Slovenia	9200	-0.4	62	0.44	Poor	12.0	27	4.0	46
Yugoslavia	n.a.	0.2	..	0.45	Poor	12.0	27	6.0	..
Czechoslovakia	n.a.	1.6	..	0.59	Poor	-7.1	185	6.0	..
FSU									
Armenia	5530	2.7	68	0.55	Poor	25.7	1828	25.6	71
Azerbaijan	4620	0.8	54	0.44	Rich	25.7	1828	29.8	70
Belarus	7010	5.2	66	0.49	Poor	25.7	1828	41.0	72
Estonia	8900	2.7	72	0.44	Poor	25.7	1828	30.2	51
Georgia	5590	2.4	56	0.43	Moderate	25.7	1828	24.8	70
Kazakhstan	5130	4.3	57	0.34	Rich	25.7	1828	20.8	71
Kyrgyzstan	3180	5.2	38	0.40	Poor	25.7	1828	27.7	71
Latvia	8590	3.5	71	0.45	Poor	25.7	1828	36.7	51
Lithuania	6430	2.9	68	0.45	Poor	25.7	1828	40.9	51
Moldova	4670	5.7	47	0.37	Poor	25.7	1828	28.9	51
Russia	7720	3.2	74	0.48	Rich	25.7	1828	11.1	74
Tajikistan	3010	1.9	32	0.34	Poor	25.7	1828	31.0	71
Turkmenistan	4230	5.0	45	0.34	Rich	25.7	1828	33.0	71
Ukraine	5680	2.4	67	0.44	Moderate	25.7	1828	23.8	74
Uzbekistan	2740	3.9	41	0.33	Moderate	25.7	1828	25.5	71

USSR	n.a.	3.8	..	0.44	Rich	25.7	1828	..	..
Mongolia	2100	5.4	60	0.41	Moderate	7.6	1400	31.0	70
China[d]	800	9.0	18	0.49	Moderate	2.3	208	1.0	46
Vietnam[d]	1100	5.0	19	0.23	Moderate	15.0	464	7.2	21[e]

Source: De Melo *et al.* (2001).

Notes

a. The location variable is not reported in the table. It is a dummy variable (1,0) with '1' = geographical proximity (i.e. a neighbour) to a thriving market economy, and '0' = otherwise. The countries with a '1' are Albania, China, Croatia, the Czech Republic, Hungary, Poland, the Slovak Republic, Slovenia, Russia, Vietnam and the three Baltic countries. All others have a '0'.

b. The nationhood variable is not reported in the table. It is a categorical variable with '2' = independent state prior to 1989; '1' = member of decentralised state or core country of centralised federal state; '0' = new nation state. The countries with a '2' are Albania, Bulgaria, China, Hungary, Mongolia, Poland, Romania and Vietnam. The countries with a '1' are Croatia, the Czech Republic, FYR Macedonia, Slovenia and Russia. All others have a '0'.

c. Data for Serbia and Montenegro, and Bosnia and Herzegovina were not included in the original analysis.

d. The data for China and Vietnam are for the years 1978 (and before 1978) and 1986 (and before 1986) respectively.

e. Average for South and North Vietnam.

and foreign trade data (as shuttle trade and the number of international borders in former socialist regions of Europe and Asia expanded).

The variables that proxy for the level of development, resources and growth are income (and changes in income), urbanisation, the sectoral share of GDP, natural resource endowment and location or proximity to well-established market economies. The income variable is measured as GNP per capita in 1989 US$ but reflects purchasing power parity incomes in the base year. As the table shows, this income measure ranges from lows of $800 in China, $1,100 in Vietnam and $1,400 in Albania to highs of $8,600 in the Czech Republic, $8,900 in Estonia and $9,200 in Slovenia. Changes in income, measured as economic growth rates prior to the start of transition (that is, the period 1985 to 1989) for CEE and FSU countries, are reported to gauge the extent of the stagnation that many mature socialist countries were reportedly experiencing. The data appear to validate this claim. Whereas the poorer Southern European and Central Asian countries that were in the early stages of socialist accumulation were recording positive annual growth rates (such as 3.6 and 5.7 per cent in Albania and Moldova respectively, and 5.2 and 5.0 per cent in Kyrgyzstan and Turkmenistan respectively), the richer, more mature socialist countries were experiencing sluggish and, in some cases, negative growth rates (as evident, for example, by a 1.6 per cent growth rate in Hungary and a 0.4 per cent decline in Slovenia). The degree of urbanisation is another proxy for the level of development. This is expressed as the percentage of the population, in 1990, living in urban areas. As expected, the results for this measure correlate strongly with the income data. On average, whereas poorer countries tend to be more rural (for instance, Albania, Kyrgyzstan and Tajikistan), richer countries tend to be more urban (for example, Russia, the Baltic States and the Czech Republic).

A good proxy for economic structure is the sectoral share of GDP. Due to the policies of industrialisation in the early years of communism, socialist countries tended to have high – often overly industrialised – industry shares of national output and, in common with the socialist view that non-material output (that is, services) were unproductive, a relatively low share of services in GDP. Whereas industry shares of GDP in non-transition, middle-income countries are typically below 40 per cent, rates of industry share of national income in excess of 50 per cent were not uncommon in socialist countries, with Bulgaria, Czechoslovakia, Poland, Romania and Armenia all having, in 1990, industry shares of between 52 and 59 per cent of national income. Russia, the most important constituent of the USSR, had an industry share of GDP equal to 48 per cent.

Transition countries, as indeed is the case with non-transition countries, differ greatly in terms of the availability of natural resources. As with other factors, this can be measured in different ways. De Melo *et al.* (2001) treat it as a categorical variable with three categories, namely poorly endowed, moderately endowed and richly endowed. Whereas most transition countries fall into the first two categories, there are, however, a small number of TEs, namely Azerbaijan, Kazakhstan, Russia and Turkmenistan, that have an abundance of natural resources. This factor needs to be treated with a note of caution as natural resource endowment does not, as we know from economic history and the so-called resource curse, guarantee economic success (and likewise, an absence of natural resources does not mean economic despair). For instance, in terms of oil and gas (which are the main natural resources for countries such as Russia and the Central Asian states of Kazakhstan and Turkmenistan), there are often huge exploration and production problems to be overcome before any revenues or profits accrue. In addition, as the evidence will show, an abundance of natural resources can sometimes be used by recalcitrant governments to delay necessary reforms. Others point to the costly rent-seeking attached to government regulation of resources and the likelihood of the Dutch disease – named after the effects of natural gas discoveries in the Netherlands – which refers to the adverse effect on a country's manufacturing industry when rising natural resources' exports cause a real appreciation of the exchange rate (making manufactured goods less competitive internationally).

The final variable measuring economic development and structure that the study examined was location and geographical proximity to thriving market economies. Again, as with other factors, there are different ways to measure this variable. For one, some studies take the distance from Brussels or Frankfurt as a way of measuring the location variable. In this study, the authors use a dummy variable. A 'one' indicates that the country is located close to thriving market economies. A 'zero' indicates otherwise. Central European countries, the Baltic States, China and Vietnam are all located close to well-established market economies. This geographical proximity is likely to benefit these transition countries as it will facilitate greater international trade and allow for the importation of market institutions. Again, outcomes will show that countries located close to the EU (and, in particular, those that sought early EU membership) and countries located close to the newly industrialised countries of South East Asia did better than all the other transition countries.

The economic distortions and macroeconomic imbalances that emerged in the later stages of socialism and were evident in many socialist countries at the outset of transition are measured by the extent of repressed or hidden inflation, the exchange rate premium and the share of CMEA or Comecon trade. In the socialist system, the existence of price controls meant that inflation as it is understood in market economies was, at least in theory, absent. However, socialist countries did experience, particularly following the attempts to reform the system, repressed or hidden inflation. This was evident in the form of the monetary overhang which is the excess of cash (and savings deposits) over goods (that are in short supply), resulting in an excess demand or disequilibrium, i.e. due to fixed prices and the planning process in command economies, households, faced with endemic shortages of consumer goods, hold money balances that are generally higher than desired levels.

The study measures the extent of repressed inflation as the percentage change in the real wage less the percentage change in real GDP from 1987 to 1990. Using this as our indicator, we can see from Table 3.2 that inflationary pressures, on the eve of transition, were most prevalent in the republics of the FSU, and in Central and Eastern European countries of Bulgaria, Poland and Romania. In contrast, Czechoslovakia and Hungary had a more favourable inflationary environment. One consequence of this was that some TEs (the latter group) could confront the inevitable structural change without worrying excessively about macroeconomic imbalances, whereas the former group of countries had to deal with the macroeconomic crisis in conjunction with (and, most likely, in advance of) the structural change required from plan to market. The East Asian countries of China and Vietnam differed with respect to inflationary pressures: China managed to prevent large price increases whereas Vietnam experienced severe inflationary pressures in the mid-1980s.

Another distortion that existed in many socialist countries was the so-called black market exchange rate premium which arose owing to the difference between the official exchange rate (as determined by the authorities) and the free exchange rate (as determined by the 'black market'). The black market exchange rate premium is a measure of foreign exchange rationing (due to the exchange controls and currency non-convertibility put in place by the authorities) and it is often seen as an indicator of the size of exchange rate depreciation expected. Whereas the premium was high in Bulgaria, FSU republics and Romania – countries that had experienced little or no foreign exchange or foreign trade reforms pre-transition – it was relatively low in Hungary and the former Yugoslavia, reflecting relatively low levels of distortions in their foreign exchange markets.

The third indicator of initial economic distortions is the trade dependence on other socialist countries. As alluded to earlier, the CMEA was a self-sufficient and regionally interdependent trading bloc. Given the nature of CMEA, some member states were more dependent on it than others, and the trade data indicate that the smaller republics of the Soviet Union were heavily dependent on inter-republic trade flows, subjecting them to greater disruption once the system collapsed. The study measures the degree of trade dependency by the ratio of the CMEA exports and imports to GDP. As evident from Table 3.2, the republics of the FSU, with the exception of Russia, had, in 1990, trade ratios all in excess of those evident in Central and Eastern Europe where CMEA trade was less prevalent.

There are two variables used to measure the institutional characteristics of transition countries. These are the number of years under central planning (capturing what is commonly referred to as 'market memory') and nationhood prior to transition (since many of the transition countries were not independent states prior to 1989 to 1992, thus making the transition process longer and more arduous). Soviet communism began in Russia and Ukraine, and then spread to the other republics of the USSR. Moldova and the three Baltic States were the last to be integrated into the Soviet Union. With respect to the so-called satellite states of the Soviet bloc, the majority were integrated at the end of the Second World War, and thus had fewer years of communist rule and, it is argued, more of a market memory than the member states of the USSR. Countries such as Poland and Hungary, at the outset of transition, were able to revert to laws and codes that were in place before the Soviet occupation. By contrast, it had been over 70 years since communism took hold in Russia and, moreover, the Soviet system in Russia was preceded by centuries of Tsarist rule where the rule of law and market mechanisms were largely absent.

The other variable, simply identified as 'State' or 'Nationhood' in the study, attempts to capture, at the beginning of transition, the cross-country variation in nation building, or state capacity. The study identifies three classifications: countries that were independent states before the collapse of communism, countries that were members of federal states; and new nation states. New nation states, constituting most of the republics of the former Soviet Union, had to confront, in addition to the transition from plan to market, the building, often from scratch, of state institutions, such as a constitution and laws, a judiciary and a police force, a Central Bank and a tax collection agency and so forth. Their task was inevitably more difficult than for other countries where these institutions, albeit imperfect, had already been in place. Most countries in Central and Eastern Europe had the luxury of such state institutions and could focus on the economic changes involved from plan to market. In terms of the actual measure, the study treats it as a categorical variable with the number 'zero' assigned to new countries, the number 'one' assigned to member states of federal countries and the number 'two' assigned to independent countries prior to 1989. The details are given in the notes to Table 3.2.

Although quite comprehensive in capturing the extent of the initial conditions, a number of points have been raised in the literature with respect to the detail of the variables (Åslund et al. 1996; Krueger and Ciolko 1998). First, some of these measures, notably income per capita and urbanisation, are more likely to reflect relative backwardness and low levels of development (and thus do not distinguish these former socialist countries from 'traditional' less developed countries) whereas others, the industry share of GDP and the repressed inflation indicators, for example, are more likely to reflect the distortions due to central planning and the socialist system. Second, FSU countries differed as compared to CEE countries in terms of the size of defence spending and, in particular, the extent of the military-industrial complex. The military-industrial sector was very important in the USSR and its successor states, particularly Russia, had to confront massive restructuring of this sector at the beginning of transition. Third, a number of other initial conditions have been omitted from this and other studies. Two such indicators are the extent of pre-transition reform and the presence – or absence – of a consensus in favour of economic and political reform.[4] With respect to the latter, due to the history of the Soviet occupation of Central and Eastern Europe in the post-WWII period, it is not surprising that these CEE countries were more open to reform, as compared with many of the FSU republics, once the socialist system collapsed.

By analysing the initial conditions, the World Bank authors of the study identified four broad clusters of countries. The first group comprises the former Soviet Union republics. These all started with severe market distortions, that is, large macroeconomic imbalances and unfamiliarity with market processes. The second group comprises the Slavic countries. They were more developed than the Central Asian republics but had more serious structural distortions, i.e. they were over-industrialised. The third group comprises the more developed Central and Eastern European set of countries, with fewer market distortions, more developed but with more severe structural distortions. The fourth group consists of China, Vietnam and to a lesser extent Albania, and this group is characterised by fewer market and structural distortions.

Similar studies have identified other indicators that reflect cross-country differences at the outset of transition. Fischer and Sahay (2000), in exploring the extent to which initial conditions account for differences in economic performance of 25 CEE/FSU countries, consider seven factors that represent inherited conditions. Of the seven, six are common to the 1997 World Bank study (i.e. industry and agriculture share of GDP, natural resource endowment, trade dependency, location – in this case measured as the distance from the West German city of Düsseldorf – and years under communism). The new variable is secondary school enrolment (as with others, a proxy for economic development). Sachs et al. (2000) use a framework to evaluate transition. In examining the determinants of transition, initial conditions are treated as one of the key determinants (in addition to six other factors, including policies, institutions, donor assistance and external shocks). Twelve factors are listed that capture the initial conditions. Of the 12, six are common to the 1997 World Bank report, namely geography, macroeconomic variables, trade orientation, industrialisation, market memory and wealth/income. The new categories are demographics and health, human and physical capital, culture, infrastructure and the political situation (the latter is often treated separately, as a political constraint or change variable). To assess how each of these categories is measured, see Sachs et al. (2000).[5] Whichever variables are chosen, differences in initial conditions raise the question of the likelihood of conformity, or not, in the reform process, the adoption of similar or diverse policy strategies and the extent of the variation in the performance of transition countries.

The message from Table 3.2 is clear: not all TEs at the outset of transition were the same. Moreover, numerous studies in the past decade set out to analyse the effect of these initial conditions on performance during transition and, in particular, test to see if differences in inherited conditions had an effect on cross-country variation in performance and outcomes; i.e. did country-specific factors matter? Initially, the earlier studies on cross-country performance looked primarily at the relationship between policies and outcomes, and often downplayed the importance of differences in inherited conditions as a factor in explaining cross-country performance. However, from the mid-1990s it was recognised that initial conditions played an important role – although probably diminishing in importance over time – in explaining cross-country differences in economic performance.[6]

Of course, initial conditions were only one of several factors used in the quantitative studies. Others included political change, policy reforms (macroeconomic, structural, institutional), external factors and donor assistance. Various studies, using data from the transition period, have now reported on the account of cross-country performance. The majority of these conclude that inherited conditions had an important explanatory impact. The seminal paper by De Melo *et al.* (2001) concludes that

> Policy reform, represented by economic liberalization, depends on initial conditions, political change and regional tensions. Economic performance, measured in terms of growth and inflation, depends on initial conditions, economic policies, and regional tensions. Cross-section equations suggest that initial conditions are indeed important, both for performance and the speed of economic liberalization.

Fischer and Sahay (2000) found that initial conditions, and in particular two such variables (that is, years under communism and secondary school enrolment), 'explain nearly 50 percent of the growth performance'. The 1999 EBRD Transition Report, *Ten Years of Transition*, in examining the transition recession, acknowledged the importance of four broad sets of explanations. These were stabilisation policies, structural reform, institutional change and initial conditions. With respect to inherited conditions, the report remarked that the

> extent of structural and macroeconomic distortions at the start of transition, the distance to important markets in western Europe (and East Asia), the level of development as well as the extent of national consolidation may all have affected economic performance during the initial transition phase.
>
> (EBRD 1999)

Figure 3.2, reproduced from the EBRD 2004 *Transition Report*, illustrates the significance of the initial conditions. It shows the correlation between the cumulative change in GDP over the period 1989 to 2003 and a summary measure of initial conditions. A country's 2003 GDP, relative to its 1989 level, is measured on the vertical axis. Along the horizontal axis is represented a measure of initial conditions. It includes, *inter alia*, the degree of CMEA trade dependency, the level of development and economic structure, macroeconomic imbalances, and geographical distance from Western Europe and its markets.

As evident from the figure, CEE/FSU countries with better starting points (that is, lower initial conditions index) have higher 2003 GDP index levels, whereas, in general, CEE/FSU countries with the most adverse initial conditions (that is, the CIS countries) have the lowest 2003 GDP index levels. Admittedly, the correlation in 2004 is not as strong as previously found (see Chart 3.6 in EBRD 1999) as the affects of initial conditions decline over time, with other factors (market policies, institutional reform) becoming more important. Nevertheless, an earlier EBRD (1999) did conclude that

> differences in initial conditions play a major role in explaining why some countries fared so much worse than others in the first phase. Both economic distortions and the capacity to adapt rapidly to a changing economic environment have played a role. CEE had an advantage in both of these areas, with less macroeconomic and

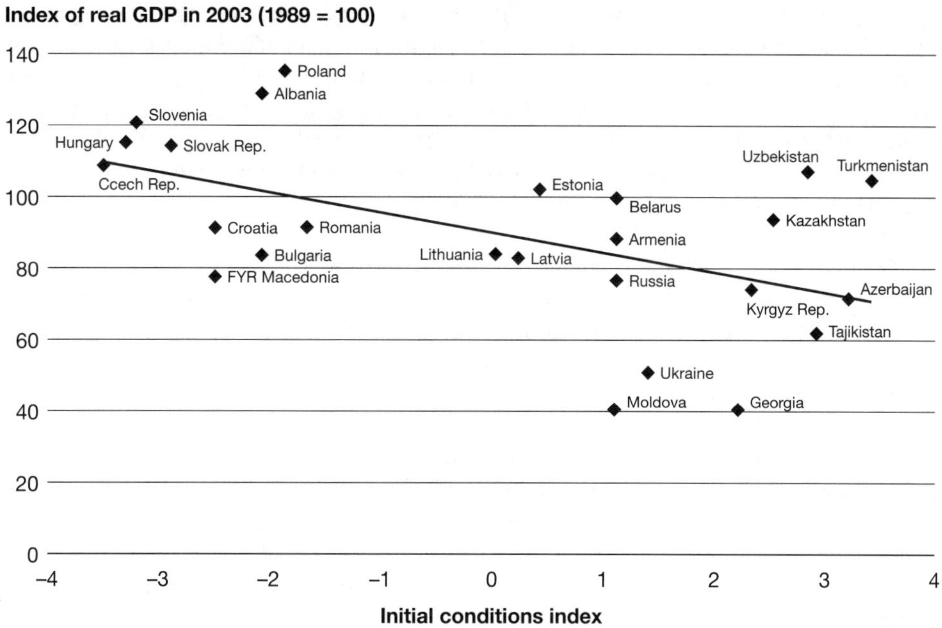

Index of real GDP in 2003 (1989 = 100)

Figure 3.2 Initial conditions and economic growth.

Source: EBRD Transition Report, 2004.

Note: The initial conditions index was calculated using principal components anaylsis on the following set of variables: GDP per capita in 1989, at PPP exchange rates; pre-transition growth, where pre-transition refers to 1985–89 in CEB and SEE and 1987–91 in the CIS: a dummy for wealth in natural resources (ranging from 0 to 2); the share of the population living in urban areas; the distance between the country's capital and the EU (Brussels); the share of employment in industry, agriculture and services, all relative to market economy benchmarks; the value of trade with the Council for Mutual Economic Assistance over GDP in 1989; a measure of repressed inflation (derived from the difference between wage growth and productivity); the black market exchange rate; the number of years a country lived under central planning; the initial private sector share in GDP; a dummy for state capacity, set equal to 2 in all established nation states, 1 in all dominant states in a federation (Czech Republic and Russia) and the ex-Yugoslav republics, and 0 for all new CIS states and the Slovak Republic. A lower value on this index means better initial conditions.

structural distortions to begin with and a higher capacity for change due to more consolidated nation states and the benefits of proximity to EU.

Falcetti *et al.* (2002), in attempting to find out whether countries defied the odds – that is, countries with the more difficult starting conditions did better than expected – conclude that initial conditions had a strong negative impact upon growth and performance. Moreover, in the first decade of transition, the effect of inherited conditions dominates the effect of reforms. This finding was contrary to the 'conventional wisdom' at the time, as many other studies, including Berg *et al.* (1999), had found that policy reforms explain most of the cross-country differences in performance, and indeed, largely explain the economic recovery that was evident in the majority of transition countries by the late 1990s (while acknowledging that it was the adverse initial conditions which primarily explained the initial output decline that occurred in all CEE and FSU countries in the early 1990s). Some of these studies examined the differences between CEE and FSU countries at the beginning of transition. For instance,

Selowsky and Martin (1997) acknowledge the 'FSU countries' more distorted starting point (e.g., a higher share of negative value-added activities . . .)' in addition to their 'intrinsic disadvantages . . . such as physical size and distance to external markets, large and inefficient company-town enterprises located in isolated regions due to strategic reasons, and stronger political and constitutional turmoil inhibiting business decisions'. Others report the difference between CEE/FSU countries and East Asian countries. For example, Parker *et al.* (1997) conclude that

> The first lesson is that initial country conditions determine the output response of a centrally planned economy upon its marketization, be it of the all-out or phased-in variety. The existence of surplus agricultural labour in Vietnam and China, and the over-industrialization of Eastern Europe, are the primary causes of growth in socialist Asia and collapse in post-socialist Eastern Europe.

One of the most detailed studies of the factors explaining differences in economic performance, including the importance of inherited conditions, was by an IMF staff member (see Chapter 7). Havrylyshyn (2001) examined 23 papers that had undertaken quantitative studies of the growth determinants. Of these 23, the empirical evidence relating variation in growth performance to differences in initial conditions varied. Overall, however, the author concluded that the

> evidence is clear that the negative burden of Soviet inheritance (excess industrialization, energy inefficiency, inertia of price distortions, geographical and historical distances from the market, civil wars) does have a hindering effect on growth, albeit not clearly separate from its indirect effect as a brake on speedy reform implementation.
>
> (Havrylyshyn 2001)

This finding illustrates the importance of the interrelationship between initial conditions, policy reform strategies and (cross-country) economic performance, a topic that is revisited in Chapter 7.

In conclusion, it is evident that initial conditions mattered (as we will see later, so do policies and institutions). As Murrell (1995) remarked, 'When . . . the analysis focuses on institutional development, reform and comparative country performance, the historical legacy, in politics and society, as well as in economics, has to be an important explanatory factor.'[7] The evidence of path dependency, country-specific effects and the inherited legacy of the socialist system and central planning is an important element in the transition experience. What varies from study to study is the magnitude of importance given to these initial conditions.

Our next step is to outline the two broad theoretical approaches to economic transition. This is the subject matter of Chapter 4.

Summary

1   The socialist countries that embarked on transition from plan to market had different starting points. The most important initial conditions related to development and economic structure, distortions and imbalances, and institutional characteristics.

2   The CEE countries began transition with initial conditions that were less severe than those in FSU countries. In contrast, the East Asian countries of Vietnam and China had fewer market and structural distortions but were less developed.

3   Differences in initial conditions are an important element in the transition experience and are a significant factor in explaining the different reform strategies, the initial output collapse, the subsequent economic recovery, and the cross-country variation in performance and outcomes of transition countries.

Key terms

Dutch Disease	Market memory
Exchange rate premium	Monetary overhang
Growth determinants	Over-industrialisation
Inherited legacy	Political constraints
Initial conditions	Reform strategies
Macroeconomic imbalances	State capacity

Review questions

1   Identify a number of key initial conditions where TEs, at the outset of transition, differed.
2   In terms of the transition process, why was the starting point, and, more particularly, differences in initial conditions, important?
3   What other factors, aside from initial conditions, explain the variation in cross-country performance during transition?

4

PARADIGMS OF TRANSITION

Strictly speaking, there is no 'theory' of transition from a centrally planned system to a market system. In the late 1980s when change was imminent in the Eastern bloc countries (and was already underway in the East Asian countries of China and Vietnam) there was no theory of transition from plan to market that policy makers and supporters of reform could adopt. What evolved over time, in the period that has passed since then, are two different approaches to understanding the transition process from a centrally planned economy to a market-based economy.[1] The conventional paradigm – which many policy makers did adopt – is, for want of a better title, the Washington Consensus approach to economic transition and the alternative paradigm is the institutional-evolutionary approach. We outline both viewpoints and their respective underlying conceptual framework in this chapter.[2] As a prelude, we begin with the Washington Consensus.

The Washington Consensus refers to a set of policy guidelines for most Latin American countries in the late 1980s for which, it was argued, a consensus was reached among Washington-based international agencies, the US government and mainstream economists. John Williamson of the Institute for International Economics, the person who coined the phrase, viewed these policy reforms as the lowest common denominator (or, as in his own words 'the common core of wisdom') of policy advice by 'Washington' to Latin American countries as of the late 1980s.[3] The ten economic reforms focused primarily on structural adjustment policies of price and trade liberalisation, macroeconomic stabilisation and fiscal discipline, deregulation of entry barriers and privatisation of state-owned enterprises. Table 4.1 lists the ten policy reforms identified by the Washington Consensus.

The recommendations of the Washington Consensus appealed to many because of its simplicity and clarity. This is particularly true of policy makers who, when working in transition countries, were confronted with great upheaval and change. For others, its very simplicity, and its glaring omissions, contributed to its downfall. According to its detractors, the implementation of universal and best-practice market reforms, in an institutional vacuum, contributed to the transformational recession of the 1990s and the disappointing outcomes, and the subsequent disillusionment with market reforms, which were to follow. However, as one might expect from a social science like economics, and particularly from transition economics which is fundamentally about the dynamics of system change, views and debates have moved on. An illustration of this is the World Bank's report on reform and growth in the 1990s (World Bank 2005b). Instead of the case for a standard menu of policy reforms, best practices and the simple mantra of liberalise, stabilise and privatise, Rodrik (2006) notes that the 'emphasis is on the need for humility, for policy diversity, for selective and modest reforms, and for experimentation'. He further remarks that 'this is a rather

Table 4.1 The Washington Consensus

Policy reform item	Policy reform detail
Fiscal discipline	(Operational) budget deficit of no more than about 2 per cent of GDP
Public expenditure priorities	Redirection from politically-sensitive projects to expenditures in education, health and infrastructure
Tax reform	Broadening the tax base, moderate marginal tax rates and improving tax administration
Financial liberalisation	Interest rate liberalisation – market-determined (moderately positive real) interest rates and abolition of preferential rates for privileged borrowers
Exchange rates	Unified and set at a competitive level
Trade liberalisation	Quantitative trade restrictions to be replaced by low and uniform tariffs
Foreign direct investment	Abolish barriers to entry of foreign firms
Privatisation	State-owned enterprises to be privatised
Deregulation	Easing barriers to entry and exit; regulations only to ensure safety, environmental protection and prudential supervision of financial institutions
Property rights	Secure property rights and made available to the informal sector

Source: Williamson (1990).

extraordinary document demonstrating the extent to which the thinking of the development policy community has been transformed over the years' (Rodrik 2006).

In outlining the two broad perspectives on transition from plan to market, we begin with the Washington Consensus approach as this dominated in the early years of transition and had the support of the IFIs (the World Bank and, more notably, the International Monetary Fund).[4] This orthodox or standard vision, especially popular in the Anglo-Saxon world – seen by many as an expression of the neoclassical mainstream – views the transition from a centrally planned economy to a market economy as a reform process emphasising the universality of the laws of the market and the undoubted economy-wide efficiency gains accruing from the standard policy prescriptions of the trinity of liberalisation ('getting prices right'), stabilisation and privatisation (more details on these specific policies are given in Chapter 5). This blueprint for transition, based on the spontaneity of markets and private enterprise, traditional neoclassical price theory and Walrasian general equilibrium theory, promotes the primacy of policy reforms and economic fundamentals and the replication or transplantation of international best-practice institutions – with the emphasis on laws and property rights and the legal and regulatory framework – of the West to the ex-socialist countries of the Soviet bloc and beyond (a kind of utopia based on 'societal engineering').

Although the Washington Consensus emerged from a different set of conditions, it argues that these one-size-fits-all market-oriented reforms are appropriate to any setting, including the post-socialist CEE and FSU countries. A knowledge or experience of the state socialist system and the centrally planned economy is not required. Regional studies and area specialists – those with a knowledge of the Soviet system were known as Sovietologists – emphasising the importance of historical, cultural and socioeconomic factors were dismissed. Instead, liberal economic reform strategies are implemented along a scorched-earth approach, with textbook reforms being designed by technocrats – as the agents of social change – and introduced as rapidly and comprehensively as possible in view of the reform complementarities that exist. Not surprisingly, in terms of the speed of the radical reforms, this approach is often referred to as the 'Big Bang' or 'shock therapy' view of transition.[5] This also applies to the economic role of the state where what is required is a depoliticisation of the economy, a break of the nexus between government and business, and a dismantling of the state, or, according to critics of the Washington Consensus approach, in the extreme case of neoliberal market fundamentalism, state desertion.[6] The country most associated with the shock therapy reforms was Poland. Box 4.1 outlines the details of the Big Bang approach.

Box 4.1

The Big Bang strategy

The first socialist country under a new regime to implement market reforms along the lines outlined above was Poland, starting in 1990. The more controversial Russian shock therapy reforms that were to follow in 1992, and thereafter, were informed by Poland's Big Bang. Leszek Balcerowicz, Finance Minister and Deputy Prime Minister of Poland's first non-Communist government, was advised on how to proceed by Jeffrey Sachs, then Professor of International Trade at Harvard University and the guiding force behind shock therapy. It was Balcerowicz who, when arguing in favour of rapid and comprehensive reforms at the outset of transition when there was an exceptional 'window of opportunity', coined the phrase 'extraordinary politics'. Rapid and simultaneous market reforms were designed, and controversially inspired by the metaphor that a chasm can only be crossed in one leap (as opposed to the metaphor most associated with gradualism, namely 'the wise man tests the stones before crossing the river'). Shock therapy was both an economic and a political strategy, aimed at stabilising the economy and making a clean break from the past. The idea was that bureaucrats, plans and shortages would be replaced by (spontaneous) markets, profits and supplies. As Jeffery Sachs argues in his 1993 book *Poland's Jump to the Market Economy* 'markets spring up as soon as central planning bureaucrats vacate the field'. Contrast this with the views of Grzegorz Kolodko, a critic of the Washington Consensus and Poland's Minister for Finance from 1994 to 1997, who, in 1999, wrote, 'The incorrect assumption that emerging market forces can quickly substitute the government in its role toward new institutional set up, investment in human capital, and development of infrastructure, have caused severe contraction and growing social stress' (Kolodko 1999).

Radical economic reforms were introduced on 1 January 1990. They consisted of five pillars. Below is an extract from Sachs where he describes the 'familiar classical economic medicine':

> Stabilization – ending the high inflation and establishing a stable, convertible currency
> Liberalization – allowing markets to function by legalizing private economic activity, ending price controls, and establishing the necessary commercial law
> Privatization – identifying private owners for assets currently held by the state. These assets might be privatized in the form of entire enterprises, or piecemeal (machinery, buildings, land), depending on the circumstances

---

Social Safety Net – pensions, health care, and other benefits for the elderly and the poor, especially to help cushion the transition
Institutional Harmonization – adopting, step by step, the economic laws, procedures, and institutions of Western Europe in order to be a successful candidate for the European Union.

(Sachs 2005)

Stabilisation was to involve a specific package of tight fiscal and monetary measures aimed at cutting the rate of credit expansion. Under the social safety net, an unemployment compensation scheme was to be introduced. As part of the institutional harmonisation, international financial assistance was to be mobilised.

On 1 January 1990, and despite opposition from many within the Solidarity movement, 90 per cent of prices were freed (albeit some price controls had been lifted before 1990) as public subsidies were slashed. The main exceptions were coal, transport and housing. Monetary policy was tightened; the zloty was devalued, there was a unified exchange rate and the currency was made convertible for trade purposes; trade restrictions were lifted; a zloty stabilisation fund was put in place; and numerous legal changes were made. Price inflation in January 1990 was 77 per cent, slowing to a 16 per cent monthly rate in the following month. For many, this was certainly a shock. For others, the therapy manifested itself in, among other things, a rise in supplies on the shelves of many new stores. In Poland these orthodox reforms were combined with other policies such as wage controls in the form of the excess wage tax (the *popiwek*). In relation to enterprise reform, although there were economic arguments in favour of rapid privatisation, in practice the privatisation programme was to follow stabilisation and liberalisation. For many, privatisation was the greatest challenge facing the transition countries. Mainstream economists advocated a strategy of mass privatisation based on a free distribution of shares in enterprises rather than the adoption of a case-by-case sell-off. Restructuring in advance of privatisation was not favoured by the majority of Western policy advisers.

At the same time that Poland was experiencing its Big Bang, attention turned to the Soviet Union. A report on the Soviet economy, undertaken jointly by the IMF, the World Bank, the OECD and the newly created EBRD, and published in 1991, highlighted the serious decline in economic growth in the Soviet Union over a long period of time and also the failure of the pre-transition policies – aimed at reforming rather than transforming the system – to turn the economy around. The report, entitled *A Study of the Soviet Economy*, outlined the rapid deterioration in the economy by 1990 and advocated a radical approach to reform in three closely related areas where complementarities would arise, namely price and market liberalisation, macroeconomic stabilisation, and ownership reform and privatisation. To complement these policies, longer-term systemic reforms in the area of foreign trade, enterprise ownership, labour and financial markets and the legal system were required to bring about more fundamental structural changes. The report did, however, acknowledge the extraordinary complex nature of the transformation that was required and noted that it would take 'many years to complete'.

Similar to Sachs in Poland (and later in Russia), other mainstream economists, schooled in the neoclassical way of thinking, were not slow to advocate a particular package of reforms for transition economies. As early as 1991, in a symposium on economic transition on the Soviet Union and Eastern Europe, Stanley Fischer and Alan Gelb (both at the World Bank at that time) outlined a bundle of reforms, or, in the words of the authors, a 'prototype reform process' that were necessary. These included 'macroeconomic stabilization, price reform, trade reform, small-scale privatization, new regulations for private investment, the creation of emergency unemployment insurance' (Fischer and Gelb 1991a). In addition, there was a recognition for work to start on 'new tax, legal and regulatory institutions'. In a later article published in 2000, Fischer and Sahay (2000) did acknowledge that 'Rapid policy action was possible in some areas of reform – price and trade liberalization, and inflation stabilization, and perhaps small scale privatization – but in others it was clear that reform would take a long time.' (See Figure 5.1 for more details on the composition and sequencing of these reforms.)

The institutional-evolutionary paradigm, more popular within academic circles, views transition as a large-scale institutional transformation where the focus is on the institutional underpinnings of capitalism appropriate to the specific conditions of each country and in accordance with the initial conditions at the outset of transition (see Chapter 5 for more on institutions). Following in the traditions of Schumpeter and others, this approach is inspired more recently by the evolutionary theorising of Nelson and Winter (1982) and, separately, by North's (1990) work on institutions and the contribution of new institutional economics.[7] It is critical of the revolutionary vision of transition and, instead, views transition as an evolutionary process involving systemic change in the face of great uncertainty and complexity, unlike the competitive neoclassical model and its notion of equilibrium, which arguably is inherently static. As opposed to equilibrium processes, the emphasis of the institutional-evolutionary approach is on the dynamics of institutional change within an evolutionary perspective, based on contracting, non-cooperative game theory in modern microeconomics and the second-best theory. Here, the focus is on the gradual development of the institutional supports or arrangements for a market economy, accepting the dangers of institutional voids and that not all existing or inherited institutions, organisational forms or social capital are redundant. Transitional second-best institutions and the preservation of social capital can be both worthwhile and necessary in order to prevent further economic disruption.

Advocates of this paradigm of transition argue that an appreciation of transition requires an understanding of the constituent elements of the capitalist system and, likewise, of the dynamics of large-scale institutional change (Dewatripont and Roland 1997; Roland 2000). Likewise, a leading transition economist, when reflecting on the success of the reforms in China, wrote that the 'core of the transition concerns institutional transformation, which is complicated and difficult' (Qian 2000).

Whereas the Washington Consensus view of transition is a top-down approach, the institutional-evolutionary perspective is a bottom-up view focusing on the institutional infrastructure of market economies, the importance of social norms and the organic development of the private sector.[8] Markets and economic agents do not exist in a vacuum but in an institutional framework – 'the rules of the game' – that facilitates exchange and interaction. Institution building and the provision of a framework for well-functioning market

gradual, sequred

structures and organisations is the focus of this approach and it argues for the gradual or incremental implementation of sequenced reforms (often through experimentation and learning by doing) in order to ensure growing support for policies (Murrell 1992, 1993).[9] Followers of the institutional-evolutionary perspective were critical of the Washington Consensus emphasis on economic, and particularly, monetary variables at the expense of institutional and social variables. Similar criticisms were made of the mathematical precision and overly scientific nature of the economic orthodoxy and the narrowly defined market reforms that follow. As one commentator put it, 'Within the neo-classical inspired shock approach, the nature of transition is a matter of instantaneous adjustment of rational agents without a past' (Hoen 1996).

In the institutional-evolutionary paradigm, although there is recognition of the need to reduce the role of the state, the emphasis is on a reconstituted state and improving state capacity (so as to, among other things, enhance the market environment) as opposed to a weakened state. It also stresses the path dependency of system development and is mindful of the historical continuity and the communist heritage, unlike the ahistorical, *tabula rasa* Washington Consensus approach. Critics of the institutional-evolutionary perspective claim that the time lost in waiting for the evolution of the institutions will be too costly, both in political and economic terms. Others concede that although history matters, it is not a reason to oppose, delay or reverse reforms. Furthermore, policy makers often argued that the political and administrative collapse that accompanied transition meant that the strategy as espoused by the followers of the institutional-evolutionary approach, namely a gradual, sequenced approach, was not possible.

Jozef van Brabant, in his 1998 polemic *The Political Economy of Transition*, neatly summarises the two approaches as follows:

> Though the various actors involved in debating transformation strategies have voiced a diverse range of 'opinions', there are essentially two stylized strands. One approach – 'shock therapy' – emphasizes the importance of wholehearted commitment to the liberal economic-policy agenda constructed around the so-called 'Washington Consensus.' This encompasses primarily rapid stabilization, liberalization, and privatization at the start of the transition and the introduction of many other elements of the transformation agenda as early as feasible once the process gets under way. The other – 'gradualism' – stresses the importance of proceeding in a more evolutionary fashion, given that the success of constructing markets depends importantly on putting in place the latter's core 'institutions' and making them work reasonably well.
>
> (Brabant 1998)

A useful schematic summary of the differences between the two approaches, and how they differ with respect to various important elements of transition, may be found in Table 4.2.[10]

Several authors, including Ellman (1997b), McMillan (2004) and Easterly (2006), have argued that the two broad approaches identified above are simply a replica of Karl Popper's two modes of reform that he identified in his earlier works.[11] Utopian social engineering (which Popper attacked), with its grand blueprint, is similar to the Big Bang, top-down approach whereas piecemeal social engineering (akin to learning by doing as espoused by Albert Hirschman), with its emphasis on gradual reform and experimentation, is analogous

Table 4.2 The two paradigms of transition

Washington Consensus approach	Institutional-evolutionary approach
Neoclassical mainstream economics	Institutional and evolutionary economics
Traditional price and general equilibrium theory	Institutions and economic change
Macroeconomic stabilisation	Modern microeconomic theory
Conventional wisdom, based on universal market norms	Unconventional, based on country-specific factors
Revolutionary, top-down, holistic, by design	Evolutionary, incremental, by trial and error
Faith in social engineering	Scepticism in social engineering
One-size-fits-all	Different paths
Economics of reform	Dynamic theory of change
Reform complementarities	Sequenced reforms
First generation reforms	Second generation reforms
Rapid, comprehensive, simultaneous, universal reforms	Gradual, experimental, piecemeal, tailored reforms
Privatisation of state-owned enterprises	Organic development of new private sector
Depoliticisation of economy	A reconstructed state
Total break from the past	Use existing conditions and institutions
Transplant best-practice institutions	Transitional institutions

to the incremental reforms outlined above. In a similar fashion, Wagener (1993) cites the writings of the founder of the Austrian School of economics Carl Menger in distinguishing between two paths to institutional development, namely pragmatic-constructivist change and organic-evolutionary change. Along similar lines but from the perspective of administrative decision-making processes and policies, Charles E. Lindblom (1959) over half a century ago advocated an incremental approach or branch method (what became commonly referred to as the 'science of muddling through') as opposed to the more comprehensive and scientific technical analysis approach or root method (which may be, in the words of Lindblom, 'the "best" way as a blueprint or model, but is in fact not workable for complex policy questions').[12]

Many in academic circles claimed that as transition progressed, the criticisms of the Washington Consensus grew, leading to the emergence of the so-called post-Washington Consensus (not only in relation to transition and transition countries but to development and the merits of structural adjustment) while, at the same time, the views of the institutional-evolutionary vision became more popular. By the second decade, arguments in favour of institutional reform had become the norm. Others, including Boenker *et al.* (2002), claim that a paradigm shift, from the radical, neoliberal consensus view to a more interdisciplinary approach focusing on institutional change and evolution, took place at the end of the 1990s. Moreover, others, including Qian (2000), claim that the successful East Asian experience in Vietnam and particularly China is proof that the 'conventional wisdom' of universal market norms and standard economic reforms of liberalisation and privatisation can be challenged by unconventional transition institutions and diverse reform paths based on country-specific conditions and traditions.

Many observers feel that the debate between the two schools of thought and, in particular, the controversy between shock therapy and gradualism and the tendency to label countries as either one or the other, has not been very helpful and has unintentionally diverted attention from some of the more important aspects of economic transition. Some of these important dimensions of transition will be covered in later chapters.

Even after two decades of transition, there is still a dearth of research papers and journal articles on the different paradigms of transition. This may be due to a number of reasons. To begin with, the emphasis in the early years of transition was, not surprisingly given the urgency, on policy-related matters. Later, after years of both micro- and macro-related reforms, empirical papers dominated the international journals and publications. It is also true that the liberal Washington Consensus approach was so prevalent, particularly in the early years among policy makers and Western scholars, that it dominated the transition literature (and, more controversially, the programmes of the IFIs, as outlined in Box 4.2).[13] Although there was a sizeable literature on the shock therapy/Big Bang versus gradualism/ incrementalism debate, this was a rather narrow debate focusing largely on the speed and sequencing of reforms. However, as time progressed and dissatisfaction grew with the standard neoclassical approach (due, in no small measure, to the poor performance of transition countries during the first decade of reform) scholars turned to other interdisciplinary, evolutionary approaches. By the turn of the century there were a number – although still quite few – of publications that outlined the alternative paradigms of transition from plan to market. These include Murrell (1993), Pickel and Wiesenthal (1997), Roland (2000, 2001) and Marangos (2004).

Box 4.2

Economic reform programmes of the IFIs

As with the traditional developing countries of Africa, Asia, South and Central America, the International Monetary Fund and the World Bank have advocated economic reforms for transition countries. IMF reform policies were packaged as so-called stabilisation programmes whereas the policies advocated by the World Bank became known as structural adjustment programmes. More particularly, the IMF stabilisation programmes are meant as short-run, demand-side policies to correct macroeconomic problems of high inflation, rising balance of payments deficits and large budget imbalances. A typical stabilisation package would involve such orthodox policies as reductions in government deficits (through cuts in spending and/or improvements in tax collection) and financing of budget deficits through non-monetary means as ways of reducing inflation. More trade-promotion policies would include reductions in import controls, liberalisation and devaluation of the exchange rate, and opening up the economy to foreign investment. These 'conditions' had to be adopted before countries could qualify for new loans from the IMF. IMF conditionality became hugely unpopular in developing countries, and subsequently in transition countries, although not to the same degree, as it was seen as draconian and 'imperial', while some of the Fund's policies were seen as inappropriate, excessively austere and, at worst, counterproductive.

The Structural Adjustment Programmes (SAPs) of the World Bank are more long term in nature. They provide financial and technical assistance for purposes of structural adjustment and microeconomic reform. The aim of structural adjustment lending is to increase the economy's supply capacity by eliminating structural imbalances and rigidities. Advocates of the SAP argue that they increase economic efficiency and improve long-term economic performance. Critics of the IFIs have noted the growing similarity between the Fund's stabilisation policies and the Bank's structural adjustment policies (despite the distinct roles given to the two organisations at the end of the Second World War).[14] Criticisms of the stabilisation policies and structural adjustment programmes, despite some changes in their implementation in later years, by other international agencies, NGOs and governments and citizens alike of developing and transition countries, continue.

With the passing of two decades of transition, we can now make some tentative assessments of the two approaches. It is clear from the evidence that neither framework provides a full and complete picture of the transition process but rather emphasises different dimensions of transition. Whereas the Washington Consensus approach outlines the importance of the urgent need to stabilise and liberalise the economy at the outset of transition, the institutional-evolutionary perspective emphasises the importance of the institutional environment or underpinnings of the market system. In a review of markets in transition, McMillan (1997) concluded that

> Although some designing and guiding of the transition is necessary, also needed is spontaneous evolution. The starting point for the transition is misaligned prices, unproductive firms, and unfilled market niches. Such an inefficient economy has large scope for improvement, with a few incentives and some competition. But just what will work is hard to predict. It is necessary to be experimental, living for a while with unconventional solutions, if they work.

This view appears to acknowledge, and give credit to, the contribution of both perspectives. It also recognises the complexity of the transition process and that, as economists and social scientists, we have much to learn from the transition experience.

Summary

1 The Washington Consensus paradigm and the institutional-evolutionary paradigm are the two broad approaches to transition from plan to market. Although they have some common features, they differ in their perspective on the transition process.

2 The Washington Consensus approach to transition focuses on the market policy reforms of price and trade liberalisation ('getting prices right'), macroeconomic stabilisation and fiscal discipline, restructuring, and privatisation of state-owned enterprises. In contrast, the institutional-evolutionary approach views transition as an evolutionary process involving large-scale institutional change. It emphasises the importance of the institutional framework ('getting institutions right') that underpins the market system.

3 The difference between the two paradigms manifested itself in the policy debate between Big Bang and gradualism. Although this focus on the speed and sequencing of reforms was not unimportant, other more fundamental issues such as ownership, competition, institutions and governance emerged later.

Key terms

Big Bang	Path dependency
Evolutionary	Privatisation
Gradualism	Restructuring
Institutions	Shock therapy
Liberalisation	Stabilisation
Neoclassical	Washington Consensus

Review questions

1 Outline the main differences between the two approaches to transition from plan to market.

2 Explain the economic theories or schools of thought that underlie each of the two approaches to transition.

3 According to the conventional approach to transition from plan to market, what constituted the main elements of reform?

5

TRANSITION REFORMS AND ECONOMIC POLICIES

The economic policy reforms required for transition from a centrally planned economy to a market economy are outlined in this chapter. The elements of the reform package beginning with the trinity of liberalisation, stabilisation and privatisation are explained. This is followed by the structural and institutional reforms that are also required. Some of the policy debates that dominated transition, including the controversy regarding the speed and sequencing of reforms, are covered. Finally, the chapter outlines the indicators used to measure the progress in reform, how the TEs have fared in terms of progress in reforms, and the patterns of reforms that have been evident since the start of transition.

One of the main problems in respect of devising policies suitable for post-socialist transition was the absence of any historical precedence or theoretical framework. Although there were several examples of countries in the twentieth century that had adopted reforms in the face of systemic change and great uncertainty – Germany and Japan post-Second World War, the developing countries and emerging markets of Latin and Central America or the newly industrialised countries (NICs) of South East Asia – the transition from a centrally planned economy to a market economy was unprecedented (and a reversal of the socialist revolution of 1917) since it required, unlike in many previous cases where dormant or distorted markets had to be revived or corrected, building markets, institutions and the capitalist system from scratch.[1] Although both the starting point – a dysfunctional command economy – and the end point, namely a well-functioning market economy, were known, the path or process from start to finish was unclear. Despite this lack of a blueprint for reforms in TEs (not surprising, given the complexity involved in the dynamics of systemic change) the first decade was dominated by the policies of stabilisation, liberalisation and privatisation, as strongly advocated by the IFIs, and most especially the IMF. It was argued that the distortions and inefficiencies of the old system would be corrected by (rapid and comprehensive) price, trade and free-entry liberalisation combined with the necessary (austere) macroeconomic stabilisation. The other (and what later proved to be the most controversial) part of the 'holy' trinity was the transfer of ownership from state to private hands by a process of privatisation. These three policies formed the basis of the reform package advocated by mainstream economists and the international financial organisations. For example, in their early account of the economic reforms necessary in Poland, Lipton and Sachs (1990) argued that the 'transformation of the Eastern Europe economies into market economies requires comprehensive action on three fronts: macroeconomic stabilization, liberalization of economic activity, and privatization of state-owned enterprises'. Figure 5.1 outlines the list of policies and the timeframe involved.[2]

Although some policies were to be implemented throughout the entire time period (for example, enterprise reform) while others were only implemented at certain stages (for

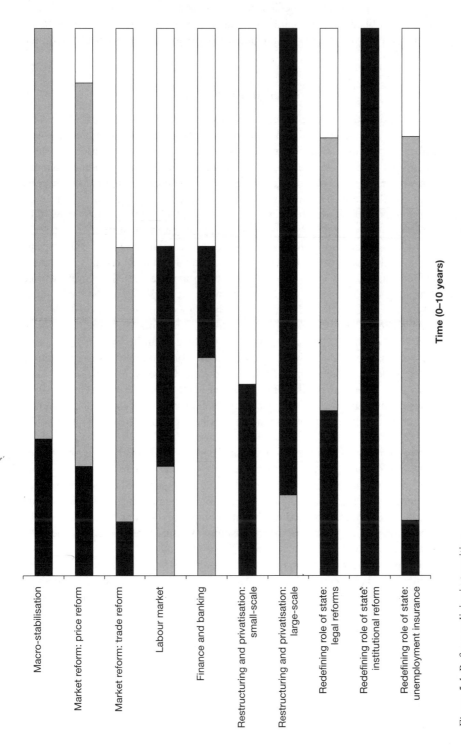

Time (0–10 years)

Macro-stabilisation

Market reform: price reform

Market reform: trade reform

Labour market

Finance and banking

Restructuring and privatisation: small-scale

Restructuring and privatisation: large-scale

Redefining role of state: legal reforms

Redefining role of state: institutional reform

Redefining role of state: unemployment insurance

Figure 5.1 Reform policies in transition.

Source: Fischer and Gelb (1991a).

example, liberalisation was required essentially at the outset), it was argued that the success of the reform agenda hinged on the immediate and simultaneous introduction of the standard policy prescriptions of liberalisation, stabilisation and privatisation.[3] As the emphasis in the early stages of transition was on these standard policies, we begin here with a brief description of each of these reforms.

Liberalisation (price + trade)

Price and trade liberalisation was an essential component of the package of reforms for countries embarking on transition. In the socialist system, prices reflected the preferences and decisions of planners. Taxes, subsidies and monopolies were all part of the pricing system. Queues, infamous in Soviet times, were the main rationing mechanism. By comparison, in a market economy prices reflect costs and scarcity, and steer resource allocation. For domestic trade, the intention of price liberalisation was to bring about a change in relative prices (in order for transactions to be guided by market signals) and to lift the price controls, thus eliminating the shortages and price distortions that plagued the socialist system, and allow prices to be 'freely' determined by the market forces of demand and supply. Once price controls were lifted, the combination of (pre-transition) low fixed price levels, government subsidies and the monetary overhang was likely to result in an increase in the aggregate price level. However, it was also predicted that a rapid response in supply, based on the belief of the spontaneity of markets, would increase the quantity of goods and services available, thus damping down the general price increase. Unlike many other reforms, the implementation of price liberalisation was straightforward, as it could be done with the 'stroke of the pen'. Indeed, this is what happened in the CEE and FSU transition economies as price controls were lifted, state orders abolished and subsidies reduced. There were some exceptions, including energy prices, housing, public transport and basic foodstuffs. In respect of subsidies, most TEs witnessed large declines in budgetary subsidies: in some countries to levels similar to those found in mature market economies where subsidies are tied to the provision of public services.

China, in contrast, followed a more unconventional approach. It implemented a dual-track or two-tier liberalisation strategy. The dual-track pricing system is where the planned output remained (and contracted to the state procurement agency at predetermined planned prices, as previously mandated in the plan) and, at the same time, at the margin, any residual output can be traded at market prices, provided fulfilment of output obligations as specified by the plan. The planned track was, in an incremental fashion, eventually phased out by the early 1990s, to be replaced by the market mechanism (Qian 2000, 2003).

Although the intention of foreign trade liberalisation was similar, i.e. prices of goods and services in the traded sector in line with international prices, the changes involved greater and more difficult choices. Among others, this involved the abolition of licences and the state monopoly on foreign trade, ending favourable access to foreign exchange at preferential rates, the unification of the exchange rate – as multiple exchange rates were common – followed by a devaluation in the early stages of transition (supported by a sufficient level of foreign reserves, and in other cases an internationally funded stabilisation fund to support the domestic currency), current account convertibility (where exporters and importers can freely buy or sell foreign exchange for trade purposes), lifting quantitative restrictions, membership of the IFIs (including the World Trade Organisation) and relaxing laws (and, in other cases, introducing new laws) on FDI flows. Tariffs were expected to remain – often for

160

revenue-generating purposes but also as part of a country's industrial policy in its attempt to support infant industries – as were capital controls (it took many countries in Western Europe decades to move to full convertibility, in the fear that premature liberalisation of capital would lead to large and damaging capital flows). The issue of a regional trading association had already been partly resolved with the abolition of the CMEA in 1991. Again, as these policies were advocated by the international financial organisations, most of the CEE and FSU countries implemented these reforms, with some significant differences across countries.

As with domestic price liberalisation, China's policy in terms of foreign trade did not follow the standard policy prescription of liberalisation. Exchange controls on capital transactions remained and the currency remained non-convertible for current account transactions. Notwithstanding these differences, China did open up its economy to the rest of the world and, by doing so, benefited enormously in terms of trade, capital flows, and, ultimately, greater economic growth and prosperity.

Overall, the purpose of foreign trade liberalisation was to remove barriers to trade, reduce the dependence on intra-regional trade (as former socialist countries that were members of the CMEA conducted foreign trade predominantly with other CMEA member states, highlighting the autarkic feature of the Soviet socialist system) by increasing trade flows with EU member states and other countries, and, ultimately, to reintegrate into the world economy.

Stabilisation

Macroeconomic stabilisation is the second part of the trinity. Macroeconomic policy, as it is understood in the market system, was not required in socialist economies as controls were prevalent at the micro-unit level. Money, interest rates and exchange rates did not play the macroeconomic role that is a feature of market economies. However, by the late 1980s, some of the (pre-transition) reform policies that had been adopted by the socialist countries had unintentionally led to rising fiscal problems. As central authorities had ceded much control to state-owned enterprises (SOEs), wage concessions increased, tax collections declined and inflationary pressures rose, either open or hidden by price controls. In some cases, transition exacerbated the problem with further falls in tax revenue, the emergence of inter-enterprise arrears, an increase in barter transactions and rising pressures on (and, in some cases, sequestration of) public expenditure.

'Orthodox' macroeconomic stabilisation, involving a combination of tight fiscal and monetary policies, was aimed at cutting the rate of credit expansion, reducing budget deficits and lowering inflation rates (in some cases, hyperinflation) as the latter two, when high, are deleterious to economic growth. As was partly the experience of previous stabilisation programmes in the 1980s in Latin American countries and elsewhere, this involved reducing and, in other cases, redirecting government expenditures (and particularly, budgetary subsidies), tax reforms targeted at introducing new taxes such as VAT and corporate tax systems (as the major sources of revenue in former socialist times, namely enterprise profit tax and the turnover tax, had dwindled) and cutting marginal tax rates combined with improving tax collections.

Some argued, contrary to what was considered the orthodox view, that the restrictive fiscal and monetary policies, aimed at reducing inflation, were excessive (in terms of the contraction in demand), and even unnecessary (as inflation, it was argued, was not demand-led) contributing to the output collapse of the early 1990s (see Chapter 7 for more on the output fall). More conventionally, there was some debate over what was the optimal rate of inflation for transition economies, with, in most cases, less debate over the appropriate size of fiscal deficits. Reference was often made to the view that an inflation rate only in excess of a critical figure (ranging from a high of 40 per cent to a low of 10 per cent, according to the literature) is harmful to economic growth and that it was unnecessary, as was the case in many TEs in the 1990s, to insist on getting the inflation rate down to a single-digit figure. Another debate was the choice between exchange rate-based and money-based stabilisation programmes, i.e. using an exchange rate anchor or a money supply anchor to reduce inflation. It was also believed that macrostabilisation was going to be particularly difficult for new states following the breakup of the USSR, Yugoslavia and Czechoslovakia, as most of their successor states were confronted with the establishment, *ab initio*, of a new Central Bank and a new currency, a tax administration office and a Treasury, in addition to the implementation of economic reforms. This issue of state building and economic reforms is raised by a number of authors, including Hare (1999).

In conjunction with these fiscal reforms were a number of important monetary changes. Two such reforms were the non-monetary financing of budget deficits (although difficult when domestic capital markets are in their infancy and access to foreign sources of finance are limited) and a move to positive real interest rates (that is, nominal interest rates above the inflation rate). In many cases, often referred to in the literature as the heterodox programme, a tax-based incomes policy (based on wage controls such as a wage bill tax on excessive wage increases) was also used. The choice of exchange rate policy varied from the extreme of a flexible exchange rate to a currency board (akin to the adoption of a foreign currency but less strict) where the national authorities cede monetary autonomy, and to all types in between these polar extremes. The choice was often subject to a number of factors, including the extent of macroeconomic imbalances, the level of international reserves and the credibility of government policies. Whether it was fiscal or monetary policy, the traditional tools of stabilisation policy, in the context of the early transition experience in some of the former socialist countries (particularly the CIS countries), were often rendered ineffective due to the proliferation of non-monetary exchanges, barter transactions and payment arrears.

In advance of the start of transition, McKinnon (1991a) outlined the appropriate sequence of reforms and, in particular, the ordered sequence of fiscal, monetary and exchange rate policies required for a successful transition to a market economy. The order of economic liberalisation would involve the following steps. At the outset of transition, attention should be paid to domestic financial control and, in particular, fiscal reform and the establishment of a tax administration system to ensure adequate tax collection, and ultimately, macroeconomic stabilisation. Fiscal control needs to precede financial liberalisation. Interest rates should be gradually decontrolled. Indeed, fiscal and monetary control would have to be in place before reform of the banking and financial system is implemented. A similar sequenced approach is required for foreign trade and capital market liberalisation. In particular, convertibility on the capital account would be gradual, with free international capital mobility only after liberalisation and stabilisation of domestic financial markets and prices, and is the final stage in the optimal order of economic liberalisation. In all cases, the speed of liberalisation would depend on the initial conditions (McKinnon 1991a).

Privatisation

For many, privatisation was the key element in transition. State ownership was a central feature of the socialist system. In transition, privatisation was necessary to transfer ownership from public to private hands. It was argued that privatisation would, *inter alia*, eliminate the tendency for SOEs to fulfil political (as opposed to profit-maximising) objectives, improve the quality of managers, encourage greater financial discipline (via, for example, the fear of bankruptcy), raise much-needed revenue for government and, when combined with other reforms, result, eventually, in an efficient ownership structure. As the 1980s saw a worldwide increase in privatisation, it was inevitable that the transition countries would follow the privatisation route. Even before the Soviet Union broke up, enterprise managers were seeking changes in ownership structures (primarily through leasing) during the so-called 'spontaneous privatisation' period.

Aside from differences in the number of enterprises undertaking privatisation (hundreds in the case of non-transition countries as against thousands in TEs), the form or method of privatisation often differed. With inadequate savings, poorly functioning capital markets, 'fuzzy' property rights, underdeveloped legal systems, a plethora of unviable SOEs, a weakened state capacity, public opposition (not to mention the strong vested interests in opposition) to privatisation and reluctant foreign investors (if even allowed to participate, as in some countries foreign investors were excluded from competing), the normal forms of privatisation, including individual sell-offs of publicly owned firms, were inadequate and, in many cases, inappropriate. Other issues at the outset of privatisation were the speed (versus the quality) of a change in ownership, the role (and difficulty) of restitution to pre-communist owners, the sequencing of privatisation vis-à-vis demonopolisation (that is, the breaking up of enterprises into smaller units) and restructuring (and legal and other institutional changes), the role of investment funds and the involvement of foreign investors, and the relevant importance of privatisation (of SOEs) as against the development of *de novo* private firms. There was also some debate on how to deal with the winners and losers that result from privatisation and how to provide adequate protection for minority shareholders.

Given the scarcity of private capital and the difficulty in valuing enterprises on the eve of transition (to help identify and distinguish between viable and non-viable enterprises), a new form of privatisation, called mass privatisation schemes (described by Åslund as 'possibly the only one real invention of postcommunism'), was initiated whereby shares in enterprises were sold for free (or sometimes at a nominal fee) to a country's citizens, via vouchers, coupons or certificates, and tradable at auctions. Many TEs, and, in particular, most of the FSU countries adopted the mass privatisation schemes, since they were viewed as the most politically acceptable.[4] Although supporters of rapid privatisation (through the mass privatisation route or other similar schemes) cited the usual economic arguments for doing so (see above), often the politics of privatisation was invoked. Rapid privatisation would ensure a depoliticisation of economic activity – that is, break the nexus between government (politicians and bureaucrats) and business (firms and managers) – and, in turn, prevent a return to the old state-dominated socialist system, while at the same time create a demand for market-supporting institutions. This argument was particularly evident in the case made for rapid privatisation in Russia (Boycko *et al.* 1995).

However, it became evident in the mid- to late 1990s that all was not well with privatisation and that a change in ownership alone was not sufficient to guarantee improvements in enterprise performance. In particular, there were problems with the process and outcomes of

change of ownership not enough ... also need functioning legal systems + capital markets

form matters

privatisation in many transition countries, including the high-profile schemes in the Czech Republic and Russia.[5] Later, it became clear that, among other things, the form that privatisation takes – direct sales, voucher schemes, management (-employee) buyouts – does matter (despite, in the early stages of transition, advocates of privatisation invoking Coase's Theorem claiming that the question of how to privatise, and the initial allocation of property rights, do not matter).[6] Well-functioning legal systems and capital markets also matter.

Table 5.1 outlines the different modalities of privatisation and their likely impact.

Equally important, in terms of improving enterprise performance, are the related issues of systems of effective corporate governance (and the agency problem inherent in the separation of ownership and control), hardening the budget constraint (see Box 5.1), the discipline of competition (and the business environment) and the development of a new private sector comprising *de novo* SMEs (by, among other things, reducing barriers to entry and exit), some of which will be dealt with in the next chapter. Different results emerged from privatisation depending on whether the process favoured insiders (managers, workers) or outsiders (banks, enterprises, investment funds), dispersed or concentrated ownership, domestic or foreign investors, the absence or presence of enterprise restructuring (including the divestiture of social assets) and the hardening or softening of the budget constraint. For example, in CIS countries, privatisation was often associated with harmful activities such as self-dealing, asset-stripping, tunnelling (that is, the transfer of resources or funds out of a firm to its controlling shareholder), rent-seeking and state capture.

Need:
- institutions
- HBCS
- corporate governance
- competition
- new private sector (SME creation, de novo private firms)

The evidence of enterprise reform in China and Vietnam indicates that contractual incentives (where peasants on the land and managers in state firms were not subject to a change in ownership but who did enter into new contracts with the state) may substitute for ownership incentives. With respect to ownership, again the evidence indicates that a change from public to private may not always be necessary for an improvement in performance. The most obvious example is the TVE in China. Collectively owned and run by local government, TVEs have being largely responsible for China's impressive (earlier) output performance (McMillan 1997). Notwithstanding these observations, it must be acknowledged that for privatisation to take place at all, and in such numbers and in such a short period of time, was indeed a significant achievement (see Chapter 6 for more on privatisation).

TVE's still SOE's

Table 5.1 Methods of privatisation

Method	Objective				
	Better corporate governance	Speed and feasibility	Better access to capital and skills	More government revenue	Greater fairness
Sale to outside owners	+	–	+	+	–
Management-employee buyout	–	+	–	–	–
Equal access voucher privatisation	?	+	?	–	+
Spontaneous privatisation	?	?	–	–	–

Source: World Development Report (1996).

Box 5.1

The soft budget constraint

One of the most important legacies of the centrally planned system that was still prevalent in the early years of the post-socialist era is the soft budget constraint (hereinafter SBC). The SBC is the tendency for loss-making firms to be continually bailed out by the state. The incentive problem inherited from the socialist system known as the SBC takes its name from the budget constraint faced by households in standard microeconomic theory. The budget constraint was first extended to organisations and firms by Kornai (1979, 1980) and applied to the socialist economies of Central and Eastern Europe. The budget constraint is softened when a firm is not held to a fixed budget, but finds its budget constraint non-binding. The enterprise sector is said to exhibit a SBC when there is a recurring or persistent expectation of a refinancing or bailout of loss-making firms; firms receive financial assistance *because* they are loss making and the expectation of aid is close to certainty as the external support is more than just a one-off event. The channels or mechanisms by which the *ex post* rescue of unprofitable firms takes place vary, from budgetary subsidies and tax arrears (by government) to inter-enterprise arrears (by trade suppliers and utility companies) to overdue loans (by banks). Since transition began, the more traditional forms of the SBC, namely arbitrary pricing and direct subsidies, have given way to new and, often, more implicit instruments, such as tax arrears and overdue payables to banks, trade suppliers and utilities. Another mechanism that is evident in predominately FSU countries, where banking intermediation is generally underdeveloped, is non-cash payments (in the form of barter, promissory notes, offsets) by firms to their creditors. Either way, this expectation of a bailout influences and undermines the *ex ante* behaviour and incentives of firms, i.e. current behaviour will be shaped by the expectations of the future.

The objective of the organisation that is bailed out is straightforward, namely survival. The motive of the rescuer varies, depending on the interpretation of the SBC (as there is no consensus on a precise definition of the concept). Kornai's bureaucratic hierarchical model (1980, 1992), as opposed to Dewatripont and Maskin's dynamic commitment model (1995) and Stiglitz's gambling banks model (1994), is one of a paternalistic and benevolent state willing to support unviable firms in order to avoid politically and socially costly layoffs. A fourth interpretation is Shleifer and Vishny's politicians and firms model (1994). Using the Kornai model, the SBC syndrome may be viewed as a theory of exit and, thus, complements Schumpeter's theory of creative destruction (Schumpeter 1942). Whereas Schumpeter focused on the birth or creation of organisations, the SBC phenomenon explains the survival (or demise) of organisations. By saving certain firms from bankruptcy, the SBC alters the natural selection process inherent in a competitive environment (whether it is market socialism, transition economy or market economy).

Since the term first appeared in 1979, there have been a number of different explanations of the SBC. According to Kornai (1979, 1980), the source of the budget softness, in the context of the socialist system, is the paternalism of the state. Firms are not responsible for losses, or for profits, hence the levelling effect. This explanation is system-specific, focuses on political considerations and is based on the vertical relationship between superior and subordinate. In contrast, the explanation advanced by Dewatripont and Maskin (1995) focuses on economic causes, namely the inability to commit to no bailout *ex post* and the centralised financial system. Using a game-theoretic model, the SBC is viewed as a time-consistency problem in the presence of irreversible investment. With asymmetric information and adverse selection, bad projects get refinanced – the phenomenon of 'throwing good money after bad'. A different explanation, espoused by Stiglitz (1994), argues that, in the context of the financial system, soft budgets arise when financial institutions have an incentive to make large gambles when appraising projects. In this explanation, an insolvent bank may be willing to invest in a risky project because the bank will become solvent if the gamble pays off and, in the case of the project turning bad, will be no worse off than it was before the loan was made, i.e. still insolvent. A fourth model is presented by Shleifer and Vishny (1993, 1994), where subsidies are paid to enterprises to retain excess employment. These transfers result from bargaining that takes place between managers of firms and government politicians, the latter driven by non-economic objectives, namely their own narrow self-interest and self-preservation.

In the context of transition and economic theory, there are two broad perspectives on the SBC. One approach is the Washington Consensus view, which treats the SBC as an exogenous variable and a matter of direct policy choice. The implication here is that political will is all that is required in order for the budget constraint of firms to be hardened. The alternative perspective is the institutional-evolutionary approach which views the SBC as endogenous to the institutional set-up. Here, the hardening of budget constraints is possible only as an outcome of institutional change. Credible commitment to hardening budget constraints is a matter of devising suitable institutional mechanisms and arrangements (Roland 2000).

Despite the problems with the short time horizon and the usual data difficulties, the empirical evidence on the SBC is now quite considerable (Kornai 2001; Roland 2000; Schaffer 1998). The evidence appears to indicate that in the early years of transition, trade credit arrears and overdue payables to banks were often the main instruments of budget softness as opposed to the budgetary subsidies and arbitrary pricing mechanisms of earlier pre-transition years. Among other changes, price liberalisation and reform of the public finances ensured that these old channels of the SBC were to disappear (in the case of arbitrary pricing) or to decline in importance (in the case of budgetary subsidies). As transition progressed, banks and trade suppliers imposed hard budget constraints on firms and customers by insisting on payment, and, in the case of late or non-payment, refusing to extend new flows of finance to delinquent firms (Schaffer 1998). These firms, often loss making or unviable, managed to stay afloat by extracting new forms of assistance, either from their workforce (in the form of wage arrears), from utilities (in the form of payment delays or non-cash payments), or, more commonly, from the state (in the form of tax and social security contributions arrears).

In the case where the SBC manifests itself in the form of inter-enterprise arrears or overdue payables to banks, the source of the budget softness is frequently the state. In the case of the former, firms often accumulate trade credit arrears in anticipation of a general government bailout (for example, by means of a clearing scheme). In the case of the latter, banks with large non-performing loans (to non-viable and/or favoured firms) are often state-owned or subject to political interference or operate under a SBC regime, i.e. insolvent banks expect a bailout by government. The empirical evidence on the SBC from the transition era indicates that the tax system was a mechanism commonly used by which the budget constraint of firms can be softened. In particular, late, non-cash, or non-payment of tax liabilities by loss-making firms (although not exclusively, as tax arrears of high-profile profitable firms in Russia and elsewhere were not uncommon) suggests that the hardening of budget constraints, expected in transition countries in the 1990s, did not fully materialise (Kornai 2001; Turley 2006).

This perception of government is particularly true in some of the FSU countries where the state is often viewed as the softest creditor; a perception that is tolerated and sometimes even instigated by the state itself. These forms of budget softness were also evident in CEE countries but have diminished as transition has progressed. In the wider context of the SBC, the relation is between government and firm, with government acting as the supporting organisation or funding source and the firm acting as the budget constraint organisation. Other relations where the SBC is evident include government–government (Wildasin 1997), government–bank (Mitchell 1998) and bank–firm (Dewatripont and Maskin 1995).

Initial phase reforms

In the first decade of transition, 30 socialist countries embarked on a transformation from plan to market. The majority, with the exception of Belarus, Turkmenistan, China[7] and some war-torn Balkan States (and less so Uzbekistan and Tajikistan), implemented a policy mix of macroeconomic stabilisation, domestic price and foreign trade liberalisation, and some form of privatisation (or, at the very least in some countries, enterprise restructuring), in addition to providing a social safety net (and, most especially, unemployment benefits). A list of policies, relating to what is often called first-generation reforms, for a sample of countries (from the three country categories identified earlier in the book) is outlined in Table 5.2.[8]

Second-phase reforms

Aside from the first-generation policies listed above, structural and institutional reforms were also required, to bring about necessary structural adjustments and a change in economic behaviour.[9] Enterprise restructuring and competition policy, banking and financial sector reforms, labour market and fiscal reforms, social security and pension reforms (beyond the initial social safety net provision) tended to take longer and often required a strong state and increasing administrative capacity (as opposed to the earlier reforms which called for a smaller state). Reform of government – everything from civil service reform to new arrangements for intergovernmental fiscal relations – was also necessary, while still recognising the important role of the (reconstructed) state during and after transition.

Enterprise restructuring and labour market reform are dealt with in later chapters. As for banking and financial sector reform, what was initially required was a breakup of the monobank system into the usual two-tier (a Central Bank and commercial banks) system as operates in market economies, liberalisation of interest rates and credit allocation (with a decline in interest rate ceilings, directed credit and subsidised or preferential loans), a new payments system, the need to recapitalise banks and ways to deal with the problems of non-performing loans and demonetisation (reflected in overdue bank credit and the payment arrears

Table 5.2 Initial phase reforms*

Reform policies	Transition country								
	Czech Republic	Latvia	Poland	Croatia	Romania	Georgia	Russia	Kyrgyzstan	China
Macroeconomic stabilisation	Starts Jan 1991	Starts 1992	Starts Jan 1990	Starts late 1993	Starts 1990 but stalled until relaunch in 1997	Starts late at end 1994	Starts Jan 1992 and relaunch from 1995 onward	One of the first CIS countries to start, in May 1993	Moderate inflation controlled periodically by administrative means
Exchange rate	Fixed until 1997 currency crisis, managed float adopted thereafter	New currency (lat) in 1993; initially floating and then fixed rate after 1994	Crawling peg followed by managed float with fluctuation bands	New currency (kuna) in 1994; managed float thereafter	Regulation until 1997 when exchange rate unified and float adopted	New currency (lari) in 1995; managed float changed to free float in 1998	New currency (rouble) in 1993; initially floating, then currency crisis in 1994 followed by crawling peg/currency corridor	New currency (som) in 1993; managed float thereafter	Unified since 1994; managed float thereafter; controls on capital flows
Incomes policy	Excess wage bill tax	None except for minimum wage	Excess wage tax (popiwek)	Heterodox, with a strict incomes policy and wage restraint via administrative control of wages	Excess wage bill tax	..	Excess wage tax	Excess wage bill tax	..
Liberalisation	Most prices liberalised by end 1991; same with foreign trade controls	Almost full liberalisation; some controls on energy prices	Most prices liberalised in Jan 1990; same with foreign trade controls	A relatively late (after 1993) liberaliser	Delay with only most prices liberalised in 1995	Majority of prices liberalised in 1992; as with foreign trade controls	Starts Jan 1992 with most prices liberalised; energy (and some others) price controls remain	Most prices liberalised in 1992	Dual track price liberalisation from 1978, beginning in agriculture and extending to industry

Privatisation	Mass / voucher privatisation begins in 1992; investment funds; direct cash sales	Direct sales and voucher privatisation from 1992 onward	Delayed with a mix of cash sales and MEBOs; National Investment Funds (NIFs)	MEBOs and voucher privatisation from 1992 onward	Slow start with MEBOs and direct sales methods	Slow start with mass / voucher privatisation and direct sales	Voucher privatisation in 1992–94. 'Shares for loans' auctions in 1995/96	Delayed voucher auctions and MEBOs from 1996	Very slow to privatise, particularly large SOEs; focus on new TVEs and foreign joint ventures
Social safety net	Unemployment benefit; minimum wage; partial wages indexation	minimum wage	Unemployment benefit; minimum wage; wages indexation	Unemployment benefit; minimum wage	Unemployment benefit; minimum wage; partial wages indexation	Minimum social transfers. Low Unemployment benefits; arrears.	Low unemployment benefits; minimum wage; arrears	Unemployment compensation scheme (UCS) in place; minimum pension	Unemployment insurance scheme administered by provinces, benefits are low and only to urban workers; minimum wage

Sources: Adapted from Lavigne (1999); various EBRD Transition Reports.

Note

* Croatia, the Czech Republic, Latvia, Poland and Romania are the sample of countries from the CEE region, Georgia, Russia and Kyrgyzstan from the CIS region and China from the East Asian region.

problem). More medium-term issues were the need (or otherwise) for a deposit insurance scheme to protect depositors, improvements in accounting standards and reporting requirements, investment in expertise in screening and monitoring loans, and effective prudential supervision and regulation of banks, non-bank financial institutions and the securities market. There was also some debate over the privatisation of existing banks and the entry of new banks, the role of foreign investors in the domestic banking system and the increased role in corporate oversight. The ultimate aim of reform in the financial sector was to allow banks to enhance their role as financial intermediaries (and, most particularly, to increase lending to the private sector and SMEs) while, at the same time, to guarantee, through regulation and prudential supervision, a sound banking sector. It was Nicholas Stern, a former Chief Economist of the EBRD, who wrote, 'Financial institutions are both central to a market economy and were almost entirely absent under the old regime. They are in many respects the most novel and important aspects of the transition' (Stern 1997).[10]

There was much cross-country variation in terms of these structural reforms. Whereas most CEE and FSU countries implemented many of these second-stage reforms, both China and Vietnam have been slow to adopt structural transformation, particularly in the case of financial sector reform and enterprise restructuring. Table 5.3 outlines country-specific detail on these second-phase reforms for a selected sample of countries.

Policy debates

In terms of reform strategies and the emphasis on initial and second-phase reforms, TEs have often been labelled as following either a 'gradual' or a 'Big Bang' strategy. An overview of the classification, in terms of both the pace and sequencing of reforms, for a selection of transition countries is included in Roland (2000). This is reprinted in Table 5.4.

The experience of transition countries indicates that the radical versus gradual label is not very useful and is often misleading.[11] János Kornai, in his ten-year assessment of his much-celebrated book *The Road to a Free Economy*, regards the emphasis on the speed of reforms as excessive and even obsessive (Kornai 2000a). The evidence indicates that the TEs have varied the speed and nature of reforms depending on the different dimensions of the reform agenda. For example, Poland's – often cited as the best example of a 'Big Bang' reforming country – liberalisation policy may be regarded as radical (or conventional as some would call it) but its privatisation and enterprise reforms were gradual and more unorthodox (for example, restructuring before privatisation) in nature. In contrast, Hungary, often portrayed as an example of a 'gradualist' reformer, adopted a more gradual approach with respect to liberalisation, but its bankruptcy reforms (most particularly, the automatic trigger procedure) were of a 'Big Bang' type. The same applies to the Czech Republic which was very quick to privatise but was slow in initiating the actual restructuring of enterprises (aside, obviously, from the change in ownership aspect).

In practice, and despite the rhetoric of the reformers (advocating Big Bang or gradualism), policy was more often dictated less by ideology and more by factors such as the economic conditions of the time (including the level of social hardship and the state of the public finances), the political constraints and electoral support facing the authorities, and the administrative capacity of government. In reality, it was often a case of what was technically possible and feasible (and eking out second-best solutions) as opposed to what was optimal. To quote one expert on economic reform in emerging (transition and developing) countries,

Table 5.3 Second-phase reforms*

Reform policies	Transition country								
	Hungary	Estonia	Slovak Republic	Bulgaria	Albania	Moldova	Ukraine	Uzbekistan	Vietnam
Enterprise restructuring / competition policy	State Property Agency established 1990 / competition law adopted 1991 (amended 1997, 2000)	Estonian Privatisation Agency established 1993 / competition law adopted 1993 (amended 1998, new Act 2001)	National Property Fund established 1991 /competition law adopted 1991 (amended 1995)	Privatisation Agency established 1992, restructuring programme 1996 / competition law adopted 1991 (amended 1998)	Enterprise Restructuring Agency established 1993 / competition law enacted 1995	Enterprise Restructuring Agency established 1995/ competition law adopted 1991	State Property Fund established 1992/ competition law adopted 1991 (amended 1998)	State Property Committee established 1992 (amended 1996) / competition law adopted 1992 (amended 1996)	Some enterprise reforms in the form of equitisation (non-strategic SOEs), mergers, liquidations and joint ventures; reductions in budgetary subsidies.
Financial sector reform	Banking law adopted 1990 (new 1997) / Stock Exchange established 1990 / SEC established 1995	Banking law adopted 1993 (amended 1994, 1999) / Stock Exchange established 1996/SEC established 1993	Banking law adopted 1992 (new 1994) / Stock Exchange established 1993	Banking law adopted 1992 (new 1997) / Stock Exchange established 1991/ SEC established 1995	Banking law amended 1998 / Stock Exchange established 1996/ SEC established 1996	Stock Exchange established 1995 / SEC established 1994	Stock Exchange established 1992 / SEC established 1995	Banking law adopted 1996 / Stock Exchange established 1994	Incomplete reforms. 2 tier banking system dominated by state-owned commercial banks / banking law adopted 1998
Social protection reform	Pension reform adopted 1997	Pension reform law adopted 1998	Reform of health and pension system initiated 2003	Pension reform 1999	Poverty Reduction and Growth Strategy adopted 2001	Pension reform adopted 1998	Laws on pension reform 2003	Pension Reform 2001	Informal support mechanisms and private contributions have replaced the state system

(Continued)

Table 5.3 Continued

Reform policies	Transition country								
	Hungary	Estonia	Slovak Republic	Bulgaria	Albania	Moldova	Ukraine	Uzbekistan	Vietnam
Fiscal reforms	T-bills market initiated 1992 / all three PIT, CIT and VAT systems by 1989	T-bills market initiated 1993 / all three PIT, CIT, VAT systems by 1993	T-bills market initiated 1992 / all PIT, CIT, VAT systems by 1993	T-bills market initiated 1991 / all PIT, CIT, VAT by 1994	T-bills market initiated 1994 / PIT, CIT, VAT by 1996	T-bills market initiated 1995 / PIT, CIT, VAT by 1992	T-bills market initiated 1995 / PIT, CIT, VAT by 1992	T-bills market initiated 1996 / PIT, CIT, VAT by 1992	T-bills market initiated 1995 / low yield PIT from 1990, CIT (was Profit tax) and VAT (was turnover tax) from 1999
Legal and regulatory reform	Bankruptcy law adopted 1991 (amended 1993); Central Bank law enacted 1991/electricity regulator 1994; telecommun. regulator 1993	Bankruptcy law enacted 1992; Central Bank law enacted 1993/ both electricity and telecommun. regulator 1998	Bankruptcy law adopted 1991 (amended 1993, 1998; new 2000); Central Bank law enacted 1992 /electricity regulator 2001; telecommun. regulator 2000	Bankruptcy law adopted 1994 (amended 1996); Central Bank law enacted 1991 / electricity regulator 1999; telecommun. regulator 2002	Bankruptcy law enacted 1995 (amended 2002); Central Bank law enacted 1992 (amended 1996) / electricity regulator 1996; telecommun. regulator 1998	Bankruptcy law adopted 1992 (amended 1997); Central Bank law enacted 1991 (new 1996) / electricity regulator 1998; telecommun. regulator 2000	Bankruptcy law adopted 1992 (new 2000); Central Bank law enacted 1991 (new 1999) / electricity regulator 2000	Bankruptcy law adopted 1994 (amended 1996); Central Bank law enacted 1992 (amended 1995) / electricity regulator 2000	Bankruptcy law adopted 1994 (new 2004) / Central Bank law adopted 1998 / electricity law 2005

Source: Various EBRD Transition Reports; IMF Country Reports.

Note

* Albania, Bulgaria, Hungary, Estonia and the Slovak Republic are the sample of countries from the CEE region, Moldova, Ukraine and Uzbekistan from the CIS region and Vietnam from the East Asian region.

Table 5.4 The speed and sequencing of reforms

Country	Political reform	Liberalisation	Stabilisation	Tax reform	Entry	Privatisation	Enterprise restructuring	Bankruptcy reform	Banking reform
China	1978	1984 (dual)	1994	1980	1978	1995 (gradual)	1995 (gradual)	–	–
Hungary	1989	1968 (gradual)	1995	1988	1982	1990 (gradual)	1992 (gradual)	1992	1991
Vietnam	–	1989 (Big Bang)	1989	1990	1979	1989 (gradual)	1989	1993	1991
Poland	1989	1990 (Big Bang)	1990	1992	1990	1990 (gradual)	1993 (gradual)	1992	1993
Czech Republic	1989	1991 (Big Bang)	Not relevant	1993	1991	1992 (mass)	1993 (gradual)	1993	1991
Slovak Republic	1989	1991 (Big Bang)	Not relevant	1993	1991	1992 (gradual)	1993 (gradual)	1993	1991
Slovenia	1989	1965 (gradual)	1990	1990	1965	1993 (gradual)	1989 (gradual)	1989	1993
Russia	1991	1992 (Big Bang)	1995	1995	1992	1993 (mass)	1992 (gradual)	1993	1992
Ukraine	1991	1994 (Big Bang)	1995	1992	1992	1994 (gradual)	1995 (gradual)	–	1995
Romania	1989	1990 (Big Bang)	1994	1993	1991	1991 (gradual)	1993 (gradual)	1995	–
Bulgaria	1989	1991 (Big Bang)	1991	1994	1993	1994 (gradual)	1991	1994	1997

Source: Roland (2000).

there will never exist a preferred (let alone optimal) strategy valid for all countries at all times. Country-specific conditions will dominate the choice of the reform strategy. Real-life reform is more a blend of vision, art and science than an abstract blueprint of policy moves developed under well-controlled laboratory conditions.

(Solimano *et al.* 1994)[12]

Throughout the transition era, debate continued over the most appropriate sequence to reforms, and, in particular, the order of enterprise restructuring versus privatisation, enterprise reform versus financial/banking sector reform, institutional reform versus market reforms, (stabilisation versus) liberalisation versus demonopolisation and competition, not to mention the order of economic reform versus democratisation. Inevitably, those reforms that were easiest to implement, attracted less opposition from powerful vested interests and were popular in policy circles (including the IFIs of the Fund and the Bank) were advocated and implemented first. These reforms included price liberalisation and macroeconomic stabilisation. Those reforms that took longer to implement, attracted most opposition from interest groups and were less frequently championed in policy circles were slower to emerge. These included changes to governance (both at national and corporate levels) and financial sector reform. The effect of these reforms, both market and institutional, on performance and economic growth in TEs is covered in Chapter 7.

Other policy debates that raged throughout the transition era include the relative importance of market reforms (as opposed to initial conditions, external factors or institutional arrangements) in accounting for economic performance (and, indeed, whether, market reforms should take initial conditions into account), the importance of political constraints, how to compensate losers and prevent vested interest groups from stalling reforms, the tightness of monetary policy, the methods of privatisation, the validity of the 'uniqueness' argument in designing country-specific policies (and, as we will now examine, institutions),[13] the importance of the lure of the EU (the 'return to Europe' commitment), the role of foreign aid and, not least, the case for and against an investment strategy and an industrial policy.[14] One thing that is clear after two decades of reform in transition countries is that expectations, after the collapse of the socialist system, with respect to policy reforms (and transition in general) were unrealistic and overly optimistic.

Institutions

If we view transition as large-scale institutional change, the role of institutions and institutional reforms becomes paramount. As stated earlier, institutions are defined as humanly devised mechanisms or constraints that structure economic behaviour and interaction (North 1990). They are said to affect economic performance by determining the cost of transacting. In essence, they are the 'rules of the game' that facilitate exchange. According to Olson (1992), 'A thriving market economy is not, contrary to what some say, simply the result of "letting capitalism happen" – not something that emerges, spontaneously out of thin air. It requires a special set of *institutional* arrangements that most countries in the world do not have.' Market reforms can only succeed in establishing a well-functioning market economy if suitable institutions are in place. The Soviet centrally planned system had its own institutional and organisational capital. For transition to succeed, a new institutional order with market-based institutions at best, or transitional institutions at second best, was required. However, by their very nature, the institutional arrangements, including a set of credible and enforceable laws and regulations, required for a market economy take time to evolve.[15] In the words of the late Alec Nove, 'time is needed before market institutions and market culture are in place. They cannot just be decreed into existence' (Nove 1996). They also depend on the norms and patterns of social behaviour. This raised the danger of an institutional vacuum in the early years of transition.

The protection of property rights and the rule of law are generally regarded as two of the most important market institutions. As transition progressed (and the problems of transition became more evident), the role and importance of institutions became more apparent. Well before the second decade, institutional reform had become the key constituent of the reform agenda.[16] This was in contrast to the first decade of transition which was dominated by the Big Bang versus gradualism debate. As stated previously, those in favour of the Big Bang, shock therapy approach argued in favour of early, simultaneous (or at least a critical mass of) reforms in order to, among other things, take advantage of the short 'window of opportunity' for reforms and the reform complementaries, while avoiding a political backlash and a return to the old system. Many of the CEE and FSU countries adopted a reform agenda similar to the radical, Big Bang approach (notwithstanding some differences in reform priorities). Those in favour of the gradual, incremental approach argued, in the context of evolutionary change, the need for sequenced reforms, in order to, among other things, minimise disruptions, aggregate uncertainty and the adjustment costs associated with systemic change, while at the same time building a constituency for reform. This school of thought gave more prominence to the role of institutions, both formal (for example, laws and regulations) and informal (for example, customs and norms). According to North (1997), it was the heritage of informal norms from the pre-communist era, and the subsequent establishment of formal rules, that (partly) explains the success of certain policy measures adopted in some CEE countries as against the failure of such measures in Russia and other former Soviet Union republics.[17]

In summary, although the debate with respect to the speed, nature and sequencing of reforms dominated the early years of transition, second-generation reforms proved more difficult, and, it is now believed by many, were more fundamental to achieving a successful outcome. Transition required, at different stages, macroeconomic, structural and institutional reforms. Stabilisation, liberalisation and privatisation were necessary but not sufficient conditions to guarantee a return to growth and an improvement in living standards.[18] The institutional underpinnings of the capitalist system are needed for market reforms to work and, ultimately, for transition to succeed. Sound policies, to be effective, require a solid institutional setting. Likewise, poor institutions and weak governance will inhibit market reforms. Without these changes, the transition to the market will remain incomplete and the least-advanced transition economies will continue to experience serious coordination problems. To quote a UNECE report on transition, and specifically on the former republics of the Soviet Union where progress is most disappointing,

> The experience of transition in some CIS countries shows that systemic reforms that are not grounded in suitable institutions – including an active and well-organized civil society – are unlikely to deliver successful outcomes. The choice and speed of reforms in individual countries appear to have been closely related to their national institutions, history, economic circumstances and political conditions.
>
> (UNECE 2003)

Using more blunt language, Ofer and Pomfret (2004) summed up the general experience of CIS countries as a case of 'colossal institutional failure'.[19]

Measuring progress in reforms

Acknowledging that reforms may partly explain cross-country variations in economic performance, progress in economic reform is useful to measure but difficult to quantify. However, since the early 1990s, both the World Bank, using its liberalisation index (defined as a weighted average of policy reforms in three areas: domestic market liberalisation, foreign trade liberalisation, and enterprise privatisation and banking reform), and the EBRD, using its transition indicators, have developed methodologies for assessing, quantitatively, the progress in economic reform. Although both measures suffer from subjectivity and other shortcomings and therefore should be treated with caution, they, nevertheless, are useful as proxies for indicators of progress in reform.

Here we report the EBRD transition indicators (TIs). The TIs purport to measure, as judged by the EBRD's Office of the Chief Economist, progress in reform in a number of different policy areas, including markets and trade, enterprise restructuring and privatisation, and financial institutions reform. A score of 1 indicates little progress in market reforms whereas a score of 4+ indicates full market reforms, i.e. standards and performances typical of advanced market economies. Table 5.5 shows a summary of the cross-country progress in transition reforms. We report a simple average of eight transition indicators for the transition countries for the years 1990, 1995, 2000 and 2005.

The countries that have progressed the most in terms of reform are the CEB countries. The countries that have progressed the least are Belarus, Turkmenistan and Uzbekistan. All the other non-East Asian countries have achieved some progress, but in some cases only partial reforms and in other cases reforms have been stalled and, even, reversed (often due to opposition from powerful vested interests). More specifically, countries closer to Western Europe (historically and geographically, with the lure of EU membership playing a positive role) have made most progress in reform. This includes Hungary, Poland, and the Czech and Slovak Republics (that is, the Visegrád-4). Indeed, given such a short period of time, their progress in reform has been very impressive and this is sometimes overlooked by the critics of the reform agenda. This is also true of the Baltic States whose progress (surprisingly, given their membership of both the USSR and CMEA) in reform is, more or less, as impressive as Central European countries.

However, countries further afield such as the Caucasus States (Georgia, Armenia, Azerbaijan) and some of the five Central Asian countries (Tajikistan, Kazakhstan, Kyrgyzstan) have made much less progress. Belarus and Turkmenistan have made little or no change to the old economic system, due largely to the presence of an old-style authoritarian leader. A number of other countries, including the partial reform countries of Ukraine, Russia, Bulgaria and Romania, have made uneven progress (and, in some cases, policy reversals). Many of the successor states to Yugoslavia (namely Bosnia and Herzegovina, Croatia, FYR Macedonia, Montenegro, Serbia) were hampered by war and conflict in the early and mid-1990s but have managed to make progress in reforms since the cessation of fighting. Not surprisingly, China has achieved less progress in these 'orthodox' reforms, but has managed to achieve more in the areas of decentralisation, FDI/joint ventures and sectoral reform (particularly in agriculture where the 'household responsibility system' and the TVEs resulted in accelerated economic growth).

Similar methodological exercises have been carried out to measure institutional change and reform. Weder (2001) has developed one such methodology that purports to measure the institutional quality of various countries, including the TEs.[20] In developing the index, the

Table 5.5 EBRD's transition indicators, 1990–2005[a, b]

Country	TIs 1990	TIs 1995	TIs 2000	TIs 2005
CEB				
Czech Republic	1.0	3.5	3.5	3.9
Estonia	1.0	3.2	3.5	3.8
Hungary	2.0	3.5	3.7	4.0
Latvia	1.0	2.8	3.1	3.6
Lithuania	1.0	2.9	3.2	3.7
Poland	2.0	3.3	3.5	3.8
Slovak Republic	1.0	3.3	3.4	3.8
Slovenia	1.7	3.2	3.3	3.4
SEE				
Albania	1.0	2.4	2.6	3.0
Bosnia and Herzegovina	1.0	1.1	2.0	2.6
Bulgaria	1.0	2.5	3.0	3.5
Croatia	1.7	2.8	3.2	3.5
FYR Macedonia	1.7	2.5	2.9	3.1
Romania	1.0	2.5	2.8	3.2
Serbia and Montenegro	1.0	1.5	1.6	2.7
CIS				
Armenia	1.0	2.1	2.6	3.2
Azerbaijan	1.0	1.6	2.4	2.8
Belarus	1.0	2.1	1.5	1.9
Georgia	1.0	2.0	2.9	3.1
Kazakhstan	1.0	2.1	2.7	3.0
Kyrgyzstan	1.0	2.9	2.8	3.1
Moldova	1.0	2.6	2.7	2.9
Russia	1.0	2.6	2.5	3.0
Tajikistan	1.0	1.6	2.2	2.5
Turkmenistan	1.0	1.1	1.3	1.3
Ukraine	1.0	2.2	2.5	3.0
Uzbekistan	1.0	2.4	2.0	2.2
East Asia[c]				
China	..	..	2.1	..
Mongolia	..	..	2.8	..
Vietnam	..	..	1.9	..

Source: Various EBRD Transition Reports.

Notes

a. Price liberalisation, trade and foreign exchange system and competition policy are grouped into the category named 'Markets and trade'. The category 'Enterprise reform' includes governance and enterprise restructuring and (small-scale and large-scale) privatisation. The category 'Financial institutions reform' includes banking reform & interest rate liberalisation, and securities market and non-bank financial institutions. Infrastructure (including electric power, railways, roads, telecommunications, water and waste water) and legal reform indicators were added later to the EBRD set of transition indicators and for that reason are not included in the calculations above. The definition of the price liberalisation indicator was modified in 2003.

b. As is common practice with the TIs, we linearised the scores by adding 0.3 for a 'plus' and subtracting 0.3 for a 'minus'.

c. The TIs for the East Asian countries are IMF staff estimates and are only for the year 1999.

author aggregates five of the six indicators of governance developed by the World Bank (that is, the WGI). Omitting the most political variable, 'political instability and violence', the five indicators are voice and accountability (i.e. democracy), government effectiveness, regulatory burden, rule of law, and graft, with each indicator based on a combination of various component indicators (see Table 2.21). The resulting institutional quality index ranges from

– 25 to + 25 and was estimated only for the year 1997/1998. IMF (2000) reports that the EBRD TI 1997 and the Institutional Quality Index 1997/1998 are highly correlated with a coefficient of 0.9.

Table 5.6 reports the values for this institutional quality index for the TEs. For comparative purposes, the average for mature market economies is 12.6. It is also worth noting the relatively low scores for both China and Vietnam.

In the same study where the author measures the degree of institutional quality for 170 countries, all the CEB countries (and Mongolia) are in the first two quintiles (as are 59 high-income and upper-middle income, non-transition countries), whereas the CIS countries (except, surprisingly, Moldova), Albania, Bosnia and Herzegovina, FYR Macedonia, Serbia and Montenegro, and Vietnam are in the last two quintiles (with 50 lower-middle-income and low-income, non-transition countries). Moldova, along with China, Croatia, Bulgaria and Romania, is in the third quintile.

When examining the role and design of institutions, it is important to note that there is no one institutional setting that all TEs need to adopt. This point is clearly made in Pickel and Wiesenthal (1997), with one of the authors writing that 'There are as many institutional configurations as there are actually existing market economies'.[21] As in mature market economies, institutions differ, as between, for example, common and civil law, bank-based versus securities-based financial systems, centralised versus decentralised wage bargaining, and so on. Whereas the new EU accession states have tried to replicate the institutions of the EU, it might be more appropriate for the Central Asian states to emulate the institutions of, say, Malaysia and for other Asian TEs to follow the role model of South Korea (Pomfret 2002). A good example of this is China which did not, at least initially, implement the best-practice institutions of the rule of law and secure private property rights, yet has still managed to perform well with respect to growth and development. The key point is to recognise that there are alternative institutional arrangements and that the essential reform is to follow the

Table 5.6 Institutional Quality Index

Country	Institutions Index 1997–1998	Country	Institutions Index 1997–1998
CEB		*CIS*	
Czech Republic	6.6	Armenia	–4.3
Estonia	5.8	Azerbaijan	–8.6
Hungary	8.0	Belarus	–8.3
Latvia	2.2	Georgia	–5.8
Lithuania	2.4	Kazakhstan	–6.8
Poland	6.7	Kyrgyzstan	–5.6
Slovak Republic	2.1	Moldova	–2.0
Slovenia	8.0	Russia	–5.1
		Tajikistan	–14.3
SEE		Turkmenistan	–13.8
Albania	–6.5	Ukraine	–6.4
Bosnia and Herzegovina	–9.6	Uzbekistan	–11.8
Bulgaria	–0.8		
Croatia	–0.5	*East Asia*	
FYR Macedonia	–3.2	China	–3.4
Romania	–1.0	Mongolia	1.8
Serbia and Montenegro	n.a.	Vietnam	–5.9

Source: IMF (2000).

most appropriate institutional framework for each respective circumstance. Related to this debate is the question of what are the most important market-enhancing institutions, and, if so, what constitutes the minimum critical core (in the same way as those who argue in favour of a minimum set of market reforms). Again the experience of TEs would indicate a lack of consensus on this vexed topic. Of course, identifying these core institutions is the relatively easy task. Acquiring them is more difficult.

Figure 5.2 is a reprint of a chart which captures the institutional reform gap that TEs are confronted with. It measures the distance that each country has to go in order to reach the level of institutional quality of the average industrialised country.

Much of what we already know with respect to progress in institutional reform in TEs is replicated here. It is the CEB countries that have the smallest difference with respect to the institutional quality index with the average industrialised country whereas the SEE and CIS countries (and particularly the Caucasus States of Georgia and Azerbaijan and the Central Asian states of Uzbekistan, Turkmenistan and Tajikistan) are the furthest away in terms of the quality of institutions. The East Asian countries of China and Vietnam are mid-table and are in a relatively better position than the large FSU republics of Russia and Ukraine.

One particular institutional change that is necessary, and regarded by many as the key institution required for a successful transition, is the development of the rule of law. Campos (2000) found that of the six institutional dimensions of governance identified by the World Bank, it was the rule of law that was the most important institutional dimension in explaining differences in economic performance in TEs. Table 5.7 reports a World Bank measure for the rule of law (defined as 'the extent to which agents have confidence in and abide by the rules of society, and in particular the quality of contract enforcement, the police, and the courts, as well as the likelihood of crime and violence') for a selected number of countries, including all the transition countries and a small random selection of non-transition countries (Kaufmann *et al.* 2009). The measure is from a point estimate range of –2.5 to +2.5, with higher scores corresponding to better outcomes. For our exercise, if we interpret the rule of law as the existence of well-defined property rights and proper enforcement mechanisms, we can see that the transition countries, and in particular the SEE and CIS countries, fare badly.[22] On a positive note, some of these poor-performing (with respect to the rule of law dimension of governance) transition countries have experienced large positive changes in the rule of law during the second decade of transition. For instance, according to the study, of the seven countries (out of a total of over 200 countries) that witnessed substantial improvements in the rule of law in the period 1996 to 2008, five, namely Albania, Estonia, Georgia, Latvia and Serbia, are ex-socialist transition countries. Kyrgyzstan was the only ex-socialist transition country among the ten nations (others include, not surprisingly, countries such as Zimbabwe, Venezuela and Eritrea) that recorded a large deterioration in the rule of law over the same period.

Finally, we now move to the patterns of reform that have emerged since transition began over two decades ago.

Patterns of reform

We begin by assessing the progress in reform by country. As alluded to earlier in this chapter and as is evident in Figure 5.3, the countries that have progressed the most in terms of reform, as judged by the Chief Economist's Office of the EBRD, are the Visegrád-4 (Hungary, Poland, and the Czech and Slovak Republics) and the Baltic States.[23] These are often labelled as the most rapid-reforming transition countries. The next group of countries, with an average

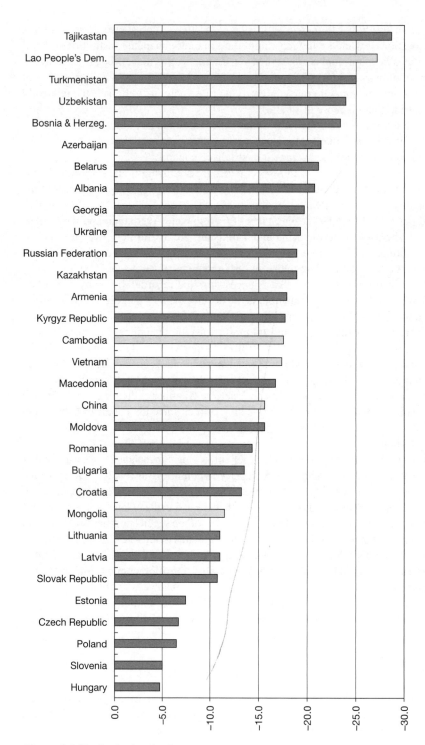

Figure 5.2 The institutional reform gap.

Source: Weder (2001).

Table 5.7 The rule of law, 2008[a]

Country	Rule of law	Country	Rule of law
CEB		*CIS*	
Czech Republic	0.85	Armenia	−0.36
Estonia	1.05	Azerbaijan	−0.76
Hungary	0.82	Belarus	−1.00
Latvia	0.73	Georgia	−0.34
Lithuania	0.58	Kazakhstan	−0.78
Poland	0.49	Kyrgyzstan	−1.26
Slovak Republic	0.52	Moldova	−0.46
Slovenia	0.91	Russia	−0.91
		Tajikistan	−1.12
SEE		Turkmenistan	−1.30
Albania	−0.60	Ukraine	−0.62
Bosnia-Herzegovina	−0.35	Uzbekistan	−1.18
Bulgaria	−0.12		
Croatia	0.08	*Non-transition countries*	
FYR Macedonia	−0.32	Angola	−1.28
Romania	−0.05	Egypt	−0.09
Serbia[b]	−0.46	Guatemala	−1.10
Montenegro[b]	−0.09	Israel	0.88
		Malawi	−0.29
East Asia		Malaysia	0.49
China	−0.33	Mexico	−0.64
Mongolia	−0.54	New Zealand	1.85
Vietnam	−0.43	Senegal	−0.31
		Uruguay	0.50
		US	1.65

Source: Kaufmann *et al.* (2009).

Notes

a. The rule of law is measured by the extent to which agents have confidence in and abide by the rules of society.
b. Serbia and Montenegro formally split in June 2006.

transition score close to 3.5 reflecting significant progress in reform, are the remaining (relatively) conflict-free Eastern European countries of Bulgaria, Croatia, Romania, Slovenia and FYR Macedonia. Below that we have a cluster of CIS countries (including Russia and Ukraine, but also Armenia, Georgia, Moldova, Kazakhstan and Kyrgyzstan) and the former republics of Yugoslavia (namely Serbia, Montenegro, Bosnia and Herzegovina) affected by war and conflict following the breakup of the Yugoslav federation. All of these countries, with an average transition score of between 2.75 and 3.2, have achieved modest but uneven progress. The least-reforming countries comprise, at one end of the scale, Azerbaijan and Tajikistan with transition indicators in excess of 2+ (that is, at least a score of 2.3 or higher) and, at the other end, Uzbekistan, Belarus and Turkmenistan, with average transition scores of approximately 2 or less.

We now consider the different dimensions of reform, as indicated by the transition indicators. In general, most reform has been made in the area of liberalisation and (small-scale) privatisation. The least progress in reform has been made in areas of financial sector reform, corporate governance and enterprise restructuring, and competition policy. The state of progress, in 2009, with respect to the different dimensions of reform, is captured in Figure 5.4.

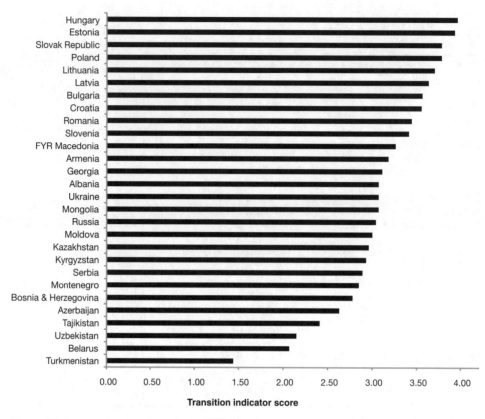

Figure 5.3 Progress in transition reforms 2009, by country.

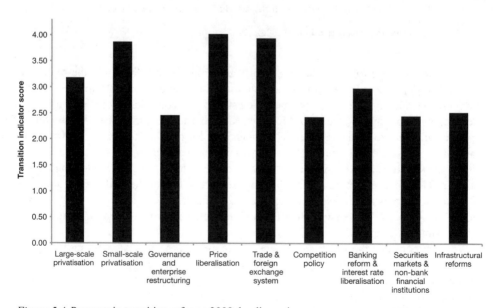

Figure 5.4 Progress in transition reforms 2009, by dimension.

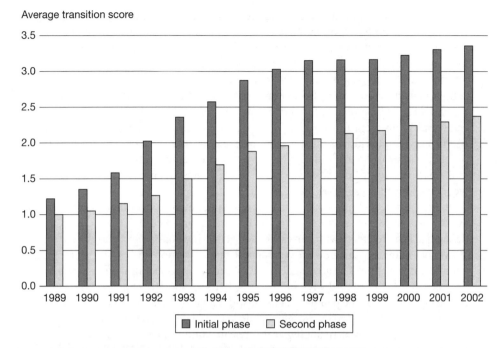

Average transition score

Figure 5.5 Progress in initial and second-phase reforms, 1989–2002.

Source: EBRD (2002).

Note
As per the EBRD definition, initial phase reforms include price and trade liberalisation and small-scale privatisation whereas second phase reforms include large-scale privatisation, governance and enterprise restructuring, competition policy, infrastructural reform, banking and the non-bank financial sector.

Figure 5.5 shows the progress between 1989 and 2002 (the period of most intensive reform) with respect to both the initial phase of reforms and the second-phase reforms.

It is evident that the initial phase of reforms were easier to implement and were completed, for most reforming countries, within the first decade of transition. The second-phase reforms were more complex and required a much longer period to implement. Progress in some respects has been uneven with some setbacks (for example, the 1997 Bulgarian and Czech crises, the 1998 Russian crisis, of which there is more in Box 5.2) during the past two decades.

Box 5.2

The 1998 Russian crisis

The débâcle of August 1998 was described by many commentators as the worst economic and political crisis in Russia since the dissolution of the USSR (Illarionov 1999; Malleret *et al.* 1999; Nagy 2000).

On 13 July, one month before the 17 August crisis, agreement was reached between the international financial organisations and Russia on a loan package worth US$22.6bn

---

in total, of which US$11.2bn was additional monies agreed by the IMF. For many, this was viewed as both helpful and necessary if a financial crisis was to be averted in Russia. For others, it was seen as yet another bailout, with the inevitable consequences to follow. Critics of the package believed that the terms agreed (fiscal and structural reforms, particularly relating to tax) were unlikely to be met by the Russian government and Parliament. Of the total, US$4.8bn was disbursed at the end of July, down from the anticipated US$5.6bn. A further $300m was disbursed by the World Bank, under Structural Adjustment Loan 3 (SAL III). Another measure aimed at boosting market confidence and providing some relief to the Treasury was the swapping of short-term rouble-denominated debt for dollar-denominated debt (eurobonds). The initial reaction to the package was positive, with a fall in interest rates and a rise in share prices. As we now know, this was short-lived.

In its short period in charge, Kiriyenko's government concentrated on the fiscal system, and in particular on reducing the budget deficit. By 1998, the federal budget deficit had been reduced, with current revenue covering non-interest current expenses. However, many of the new government's tax collection initiatives were of an administrative nature. The government did succeed in introducing a much-needed new tax code but there were delays in enacting Parts II and III. Other measures were inevitably rejected by the populist communist-dominated Duma. Some of the remaining proposals had to be passed by presidential decree. By late summer as market sentiment deteriorated further, net financing from treasury bills issues was negative, i.e. the government was making net repayments of treasury bills. The government could no longer roll over treasury bills as holders demanded payment on redemption dates. Matters were made worse by the fact that external reserves continued to fall, forcing the Central Bank of Russia to draw down the IMF monies in order to support the much-maligned rouble. Eventually, the government could no longer meet its financial obligations. On 17 August, the government conceded.

In essence, there were three separate announcements. First, a change in the exchange rate bands was revealed. There was to be a new 'currency corridor'. The existing currency bands (+/−15 per cent) with upper and lower limits of 5.27 roubles and 7.13 roubles respectively around a central parity value of 6.2 roubles per dollar were to be replaced with wider limits of 6.0 roubles and 9.5 roubles respectively. This was a de facto devaluation of the lower band of 33 per cent. Second, a 90-day moratorium on private debt repayments to foreign creditors was announced. Although described by the IMF as a 'temporary restriction on capital payments abroad', it amounted to a unilateral default on private foreign debt. Third, a mandatory debt conversion of GKOs and OFZs maturing on or before 31 December 1999 into longer-term maturity debt instruments and a suspension of trading in the domestic treasury bill market was announced. This amounted to a unilateral rescheduling of rouble-denominated government debt and its aim was to give the government some breathing space in its attempt to meet its obligations. The government also announced that certain restrictions on foreign exchange operations were to be imposed. The combined decision to devalue and default, prompted by an unsustainable fiscal position and excessive public sector debt, brought an abrupt end to Russia's commitment to low inflation, to be achieved by a mix of (possibly prolonged) tight monetary policy and a (seemingly inflexible) exchange rate regime.

The August 1998 crisis was more than simply a case of an overvalued currency, i.e. the Russian rouble. It was a fiscal crisis that had its origins in a weak and ineffective state. As in other countries where regime changes have arisen from major economic and political crises, it was hoped that the events of August 1998 and the subsequent changes in government would provide Russia with the opportunity to rebuild an effective and well-functioning state. Many have argued that this is exactly what former President Putin tried to do in his two terms of office. Others argued that as the Russian State became more authoritarian, the result was more corruption, opportunistic behaviour and abuse. The truth is probably somewhere in between. For a more recent account of Russia post-crisis see Hare *et al.* (2004) and Åslund (2007).

A disaggregation of these initial and second-phase reforms into more detailed dimensions of reform (as per the eight elements of reform that comprise the EBRD transition indicators) for the period 1994 to 1999 is given in Figure 5.6. The difference between progress in liberalisation and privatisation as against progress in the more institutional reforms, already evident in Figure 5.4, is again apparent here. These differences were evident in 1994, when the EBRD first began to quantitatively measure progress in transition reform. Whereas liberalisation and privatisation were easier, since they required a reduction in the role of the state (as was expected in the transition from state socialism), the development of institutions supporting markets and private enterprise requires an administrative capacity that is both strong and effective (which proved to be difficult and often unpopular in transition). The improvement in all dimensions of reform evident in 1994 to 1997 was halted in 1998 with the Russian crisis and its aftermath. After 2000, progress in reform was once again accelerated and this was associated, particularly in CIS countries, with a significant recovery in economic activity.

The final pattern reported here is the regional pattern of reform. Figure 5.7 reports this for six geographical regions (not including the East Asian countries). The average progress in reform score declines the further east the subregion lies; i.e. as we move from left (West) to right (East), less progress in reform is evident. As expected, countries closer to Western Europe and the EU have, on average, made greater progress in reform, or in the words of János Kornai, 'where reforms were most consistent and far-reaching' (Kornai 2006a). In contrast, countries located further away from well-established market economies have, on average, made less progress in reform.

A summary of these patterns of reform, taken from Havrylyshyn (2006), is given in Table 5.8. The reform policies labelled liberalisation are analogous to our initial phase of reforms whereas the group of policies labelled institutions is analogous to our second-phase reforms. Recall that a transition indicator equal to the maximum '4+' (= 4.3) is described by the EBRD as 'standards and performance typical of advanced industrial economies', a '3' is viewed as making 'substantial progress', a '2' reflects 'moderate progress' and a '1' denotes 'little progress' achieved. We can see from the table that the Baltic States have, surprisingly given their starting point, done as well as Central European countries whereas SEE countries lag somewhat behind. As we know from earlier discussion, not all CIS countries are the same with respect to progress in reform. Belarus, Uzbekistan and Turkmenistan have delayed or stalled reforms, both in terms of liberalisation and institutional changes, whereas the other CIS countries have made steady, if somewhat uneven in some cases, progress, reflecting, as

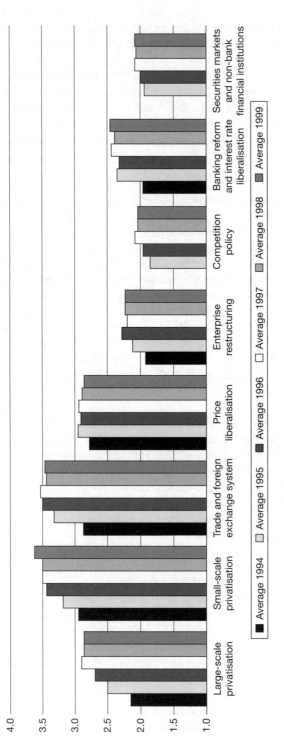

Figure 5.6 Progress in transition reforms, 1994–1999.

Source: EBRD (1999).

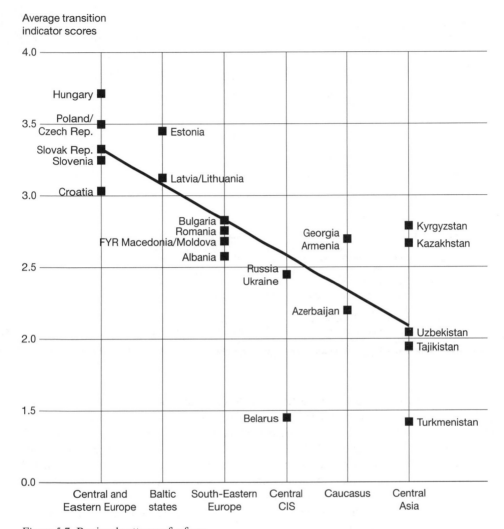

Average transition
indicator scores

Figure 5.7 Regional patterns of reform.

Source: EBRD (1999).

Havrylyshyn (2006) noted, 'reasonable well-functioning market mechanism if not institutions'.

This chapter has outlined reforms in the tradition of neoclassical economics and does not include alternative strategies as described by economists from other schools of thought or from the non-Anglo-Saxon world. However, one such strategy, although still in the tradition of mainstream economics, was expressed by the so-called Economic Transition Group in 1994 when assessing the problems of transition in Russia. Notable US and Russian economists, including Leonid Abalkin, Oleg Bogomolov, Michael Intriligator, Lawrence Klein and Marshall Pomer, argued, in trying to achieve a greater balance between market and government than that advocated by the neoliberals, for a more state-led reform agenda, with an appropriate aggregate demand management policy combined with an active industrial

Table 5.8 Regional pattern of reform[a, b]

Region	Reform	1994	1999	2003
Central Europe [c]	Liberalisation	3.7	4.2	4.3
	Institutions	2.7	3.1	3.3
Baltics	Liberalisation	3.7	4.1	4.3
	Institutions	2.3	2.9	3.3
S.E. Europe [d]	Liberalisation	3.0	3.9	4.1
	Institutions	1.7	2.2	3.0
CISM [e]	Liberalisation	2.2	3.7	3.9
	Institutions	1.4	2.1	2.3
CISL [f]	Liberalisation	1.9	2.0	2.2
	Institutions	1.4	1.6	1.5

Source: Havrylyshyn (2006).

Notes
a. Liberalisation Reform is the average of the following EBRD transition indicators: price liberalisation, trade and foreign exchange system and small-scale privatisation.
b. Institutional Reform is the average of the following EBRD transition indicators: large-scale privatisation, governance and enterprise restructuring, competition policy, infrastructural reforms and financial institutions reforms.
c. Central Europe includes Croatia, the Czech Republic, Hungary, Poland, the Slovak Republic and Slovenia.
d. South East Europe includes Albania, Bulgaria, FYR Macedonia and Romania.
e. CISM (CIS Moderate Reforms) comprises Armenia, Azerbaijan, Georgia, Kazakhstan, Kyrgyzstan, Moldova, Russia, Tajikistan and Ukraine.
f. CISL (CIS Limited reforms) comprises Belarus, Uzbekistan and Turkmenistan.

policy to support industry and viable enterprises, thus ensuring both macroeconomic stability and output growth. Unlike the liberal reformers who made reference to the Latin American experience of the 1980s, the Group drew inspiration from the experiences of Germany and Japan post-World War II, and the NICs of South Korea and Taiwan. Their recommendations centred on a five-point reform agenda, emphasising the importance of institutional infrastructure, decriminalisation, growth-oriented policy, restructuring and competition, and a social contract. Details of these are included in Klein and Pomer (2001).

After two decades of socio-economic transformation, there is a need to reflect on the policy errors of the 1990s. A list of policy mistakes might include the failure early on to recognise the importance of market-enhancing institutions, the urgency of macro-stabilisation, the delay in demonopolisation and a competition policy, the reluctance on behalf of the reformers to advocate active state supports for a new private sector (comprised largely of SMEs), the premature opening of capital markets, the failure to deal adequately with some of the fallouts from privatisation (e.g. asset-stripping and self-dealing) and the delay in recognising the important role of effective corporate governance mechanisms in explaining firm performance.[24] We finish the chapter on a note of caution. Lawrence Klein, the 1980 Nobel Laureate in Economics, entitled his contribution to the aforementioned book on Russian reforms, 'What Do Economists Know about Transition to a Market System?' Despite two decades of regime change, we still need to remind ourselves that, given the complex nature of the transition process, there are few guarantees or certainties with respect to systemic transformation. Although the reforms outlined in this chapter are a necessary part of the transition process, their implementation, enforcement, and ultimate success is often dependent upon, and complicated by, other factors, and, in particular, the political economy element of reform.

6

ENTERPRISE REFORM AND RESTRUCTURING

We now turn our attention to microeconomic reform, aimed at improving enterprise efficiency and performance. Here we examine reform at the enterprise level, and, in particular, issues relating to restructuring and privatisation.[1] The main elements of enterprise reform and restructuring are ownership change and privatisation, corporate governance, hardening the budget constraint, competition and demonopolisation, and SME development and entrepreneurship, and each of these will be discussed separately. The empirical literature on the determinants of enterprise performance is then presented. We begin, however, with the legacy of central planning for enterprise reform and, in particular, we examine the basic production unit of the traditional centrally planned system, namely the state-owned enterprise (SOE).

The state-owned enterprise (SOE)

Under central planning there was a hierarchical bureaucratic structure that comprised vertical relationships between the state planning agency (Gosplan in the case of the Soviet Union), ministries, trusts or industrial associations (i.e. intermediaries between ministries and state enterprises) and SOEs. Subject to this bureaucratic coordination, the objective of the SOE, under the authority of a ministry and managed by an appointed director (a member of the Communist Party elite, the *nomenklatura*), was to fulfil the plan in the form of assigned quantitative output targets. Plans were taut, and set deliberately so by the state in order to exert greater effort from management, as there was a dependency on all links of the production chain working well. In practice, these plans were subject to much bargaining and negotiation (both up and down the vertical chain) between the enterprise and the bureaucracy.

Although it was the basic production unit in the socialist system, the SOE was very different to its equivalent – the firm – in the market system. The SOE was not an autonomous decision-making unit. Indeed, it resembled a production unit within an economy that operated as a single large corporation (e.g. USSR Inc). As Campbell (1966) noted, 'it is helpful to think of the Soviet planned economy as equivalent to one giant corporation which embraces all the units of a national economy under a single administration'. State enterprises were notoriously large, often employing thousands of workers. For example, the average size, in terms of employment, of industrial enterprises in the Soviet Union in 1987 ranged from a low of 314 and 489 employees in food and timber/paper industries respectively to a high of 1,856 and 3,094 employees in chemistry and the metallurgy industries respectively (IMF 1991). These numbers greatly exceed average employee numbers in industrial firms located in market economies. Moreover, in what were called monotowns, the state enterprise was often the only industrial employer. The monotowns were to suffer severe social and economic hardship during the transition when its main employer faced a collapse in state orders and greater competition from home and abroad.

State enterprises were also responsible for the provision of welfare benefits and social services, including housing. As for the enterprise workforce, workers (with some important exceptions) were allowed to choose and change jobs, so a labour market, although an imperfect one, did exist. However, they had very little influence on enterprise decision making, as trade unions were subservient to the Party. As for management, there were both monetary (money bonuses if plans were met or exceeded) and non-monetary incentives (examples include dachas, automobiles, access to state stores and services), in addition to moral motivations (e.g. serving the Party and the state). Likewise, there existed negative sanctions (e.g. removal from the post of director) for poor performance. For the director, more often an engineer rather than a 'manager' in the Western sense, production issues dominated at the expense of all other matters, including marketing, innovation, the product mix, quality and so forth. More particularly, yearly production was based on incremental adjustments to the baseline levels, i.e. the previous year's achieved levels. This created incentive problems, as we will see later.

Due to the problems of securing input supplies – what the eminent Hungarian economist János Kornai called the supply or resource-constrained economy (as distinct from the demand-constrained economy prevalent in the West) – the vertically integrated enterprises often hoarded labour and materials. Arising from this uncertainty of supply and the endemic shortages that prevailed, many state enterprises, in the absence of a SME sector, were forced to meet their own input needs while also operating in fits and starts (so-called 'storming'). At the same time, state enterprises, by employing special supply agents or using personal influence or 'blat' as it was commonly referred to, often procured supplies and materials unlawfully from the black economy in order to be able to fulfil the plan. With no alternative supplier, no competition (domestic or foreign) from other enterprises – as central planners' preferences were for extreme concentration of production in very few large units (or, in many cases, only one producer) as this was easier to control and aimed at reaping economies of scale – and with no attention or concern for consumer choice or product quality (except in the high-priority sectors[2]), SOEs were far removed from the normal competitive pressures and price signals of the marketplace. Self-sufficiency was the rule. Hence, it was not uncommon for commentators, largely from the West, to view all SOEs as dinosaurs and value subtractors (or, as it was called, negative value adders where the value of output is less than the cost of inputs).

Problems at the enterprise level varied from, at best, misdirected (at worst, perverse) incentives to a lack of innovation and risk taking resulting in inefficiencies, inertia and complacency. Prices were distorted with information flows inadequate and often inaccurate: the very same information problem that Friedrich A. von Hayek exposed as far back as the 1940s (Hayek 1944, 1945). Unlike in market economies where consumer preferences guide production, planners' preferences dominate in the socialist system. With no guarantee of a match between demand and supply, shortages were rife.

Other features of the SOE that provide further evidence of distance from the marketplace is that there was direct bureaucratic control of employment and wages, workers were, in some cases, 'tied' to the enterprise and were not subject to layoffs unlike their counterparts in the West, prices were administratively set, and money played only a secondary role in exchange as trade was often facilitated via barter. Entry and exit of enterprises was rare, as planners preferred the existing large incumbents over new entrants and, at the same time, did not allow unprofitable enterprises to fold because of the paternalistic state's concern for employment and security. Furthermore, enterprise transactions, both domestic and foreign, were subject to arbitrary interference as SOEs were subservient to political considerations. So-called 'profitable' state enterprises were subject to arbitrary tax and had their residual income remitted to the state budget in order to subsidise the 'loss-making' state enterprises. This fiscal redistribution from 'profit-making' to 'loss-making' enterprises via taxes and subsidies is known as the levelling effect.

Gregory and Stuart (2001) point to the principal–agent and asymmetric information problems inherent in, but of course not unique to, the enterprise sector of the centrally planned economy. The well-established principal–agent problem is where the interests of the principal and the agent do not coincide. In the context of the SOE, the principal is the state and the agent is the enterprise director. Although bonus schemes were in place to incentivise management to fulfil the plan, in practice the personal interests of the director were often in conflict with those of the state. This problem will be discussed later in this chapter when we consider effective corporate governance mechanisms during the phase of enterprise restructuring. Similarly, asymmetric information arises when one party to an exchange has more or better information than the other party, and this can lead to inefficiencies and market failures. In the context of the state enterprise, the director of the SOE was aware of detail with respect to the operation of the enterprise (e.g. production potential, input requirements) to which the state bureaucracy and central planners were not privy.

Two common incentive problems particularly confronting the SOE were the ratchet effect and the soft budget constraint. The ratchet effect, coined by Joseph Berliner in his accounts of the state enterprise in the Soviet Union, is where output targets are ratcheted up if managers over-fulfil their plans. This provided an incentive for managers of enterprises to under-perform and, more specifically, to overstate their need for inputs and understate their production capacity. Generally, state bureaucrats were aware of this behaviour and employed tactics aimed at preventing adverse outcomes and eliciting high levels of managerial effort. The soft budget constraint (see Box 5.1) is the persistent or recurring expectation of a bailout of loss-making enterprises. Firms that are in financial trouble are consistently bailed out by the state. This provided an incentive for managers to look to the state for external support. As firms were not held responsible for losses (or profits) and where their survival was secure, their behaviour was adversely affected. The SOEs' incentives to cuts costs, generate revenue or innovate were dampened. Under socialism, these two incentive problems reinforced each other, leading to greater inefficiencies. We will revisit the soft budget constraint syndrome later in this chapter.

The extent of central planning was much less in China than in the Soviet Union. SOEs in China were not as large as those in the Soviet enterprise sector. Indeed, the state enterprise industrial sector in China was dominated by small and medium-sized enterprises. Instead of SOEs under the supervision of branch ministries, SOEs in China were under the control of local governments (comprising provinces, prefectures, counties, townships and villages, with some provinces populated by 50 million or more). In the early days of reform in China, SOEs were given more autonomy in an attempt to improve performance. Despite these changes, state enterprises in China continued to be subject to budget softness, either in the form of supports from the state budget or loans from state banks.

In terms of enterprise reforms (of which more later), the big difference between China (where the dual-track approach dominated) and the Soviet Union (where privatisation of state enterprises was the main strategy adopted) was the growth of the non-state sector in China. In particular, rural TVEs – described famously by Deng Xiaoping 'as if a strange army suddenly appeared from nowhere' – have contributed enormously to the success of Chinese reforms. Although there are different types of rural TVEs, they are, in terms of their ownership structure, collectively owned public enterprises under the control of local, as opposed to central, government officials. It is these community-owned local government firms (operating in competition with state-owned enterprises), and not the *de novo* private firms as in CEE countries, that were the engine of growth in China's enterprise sector. In more recent years, many TVEs were subject to substantial restructuring, with many changing ownership into privately owned firms.

Among the many other differences between the enterprise sector pre-transition in the Soviet Union and China, the economics literature has identified the form of organisational structure of central planning as a significant difference, in terms of its legacy on enterprise reform. In the Soviet sphere, enterprises operated along branch or functional lines. This is a system based on industries.[3] In China, enterprises were organised on a geographical basis i.e. a system based on regions. Borrowing from organisational theory, the transition literature identifies the branch organisation structure of the centralised Soviet system as similar to the U-form hierarchy whereas the regional organisation model of the more decentralised Chinese system is more akin to the M-form hierarchy of firms. These differences in organisational structures are used later to explain coordination failures during transition, and variations in enterprise reform (and performance) in Russia and China. In particular, the experimentation (and success) of Chinese reforms is partly due, it is argued, to the flexibility of the organisational structure found in the Chinese system at the outset of transition. In contrast, reform experiments along regional lines were much more difficult to implement in CEE and CIS countries given the organisational structure prevalent in the Soviet system (Qian *et al.* 1999).

There were attempts, in pre-transition days, to decentralise the economic system and, in particular, to reform the SOE. These were mainly targeted at increasing the role of profits, allowing for greater flexibility and autonomy for management, introducing new bonus schemes, establishing Western-style taxes, reducing the number of targets, charging for the use of capital and liberalising foreign trade arrangements. Despite these changes, the enterprise sector (as with the socialist system within which it operated) was in crisis on the eve of transition.[4] Of course, the enterprise reform that took place pre-transition varied significantly from country to country. For example, whereas the authorities in Hungary and Poland did introduce many changes to the SOE pre 1991/1992, countries like Czechoslovakia and East Germany experienced very limited reforms at the enterprise level.

As the socialist system collapsed, it was widely recognised that the transition from a centrally planned system to a market system would inevitably involve a transformation of the enterprise sector and the SOE. Unlike previous attempts at enterprise reform, these changes were aimed at 'greater efficiency in resource use, faster technological progress, more rapid output growth, and improved product quality' (IMF 1991). Although change in ownership dominated the enterprise reform debate, privatisation is only one of a number of key features of the enterprise reform process. We now consider each of these elements.

Elements of enterprise reform and restructuring

The economics literature has identified a number of elements of enterprise reform and restructuring. We will explain each in some detail before we examine the empirical literature on the determinants of enterprise restructuring and performance that follows. We begin, however, with some clarification on the term 'restructuring'.

Although restructuring is a rather vague concept, it is generally interpreted, in the context of transition from plan to market, as changes in the behaviour, structure and operation of the enterprise. Djankov and Murrell (2002) define restructuring as 'the whole process undertaken by enterprises as they adapt for survival and success in a market economy'. In an earlier paper, Pohl *et al.* (1997) are more specific in their definition, with restructuring defined as 'shedding surplus labour, manufacturing higher quality products, finding new markets in Western countries, and spinning off social and unneeded assets'. The primary objectives of enterprise restructuring are greater efficiency, an overall improvement in enterprise performance and, ultimately, an increase in the long-term value of the firm. Although it involves many different changes in the organisation and operation of a firm, the literature identifies two broad types of restructuring. The first involves short-term changes and is termed 'defensive' or 'reactive' whose objective is the immediate survival of the enterprise. The second concerns long-term changes and is coined 'deep' or 'strategic', and involves significant reforms in the operation of the enterprise.

Examples of defensive (cost-reducing) restructuring activities include liquidation of unprofitable product lines, the shedding of labour, cuts in social provision and the sale of excess equipment and non-productive assets. Overall, the aim is to cut costs and scale down unprofitable economic activities. In contrast, strategic (revenue-enhancing) restructuring involves the launching of new products and services, the search for new sources of finance, increased marketing and a drive for new markets, new investments, technologies and greater innovation. Here, the aim is to implement a business strategy that is suitable to the new market environment (Grosfeld and Roland 1997).

The degree of enterprise restructuring varies from firm to firm (whether it is state, privatised or private) and, indeed, from sector to sector. There is also a difference between the degree of defensive restructuring undertaken as opposed to the amount of deep restructuring engaged by firms. Size effects are also evident, with larger firms more likely to close or open plants and shed workers than are smaller firms. Using the Business Environment and Enterprise Performance Survey (BEEPS) 1999 which includes thousands of firms across CEE/FSU TEs (see later section on survey description), we can get an indication of these restructuring activities, and differences by ownership type and size of firm (see Table 6.1).

Aside from observing from the table the differences in restructuring activities (defensive vs. deep; by ownership type; by size), it is abundantly clear that firms in transition economies have, on aggregate, engaged in a great amount of restructuring of one type or another. Later, we will outline the empirical evidence relating to the factors and policy changes that explain such restructuring.

Important policy questions relating to restructuring involve many sequencing issues: should defensive restructuring precede strategic restructuring or can they be done simultaneously? Should privatisation precede restructuring (as was the consensus view) or can restructuring precede privatisation, as argued by others? Should restructuring of existing firms and the development of new firms be implemented simultaneously or, as was the case in most TEs, should, out of a sense of urgency, restructuring (and privatisation) of state enterprises take priority over the development of a new private sector, which, by its very nature, will take time (as it depends on a number of factors, including legal and institutional changes, government assistance and state supports, access to outside finance, etc.)? As with other aspects of enterprise (and indeed broad economic) reform, political factors and events outside the control of government often dictated, although not exclusively, the particular course of action that followed.

Table 6.1 Enterprise restructuring activities in transition economies (by ownership type and size of firm; by proportion of firm type, %)

	Old firms		New firms	All firms
	SOE	*Privatised*		
Employment decreases	47.4	44.2	17.9	30.4
Closure of plant	11.2	10.9	5.6	8.0
Employment increase	15.1	22.3	37.7	29.6
Opening of new plant	15.7	22.7	19.1	19.6
New product line	27.4	33.6	28.4	29.8
Upgrade	42.3	43.1	37.6	40.0
Change supplier	16.6	21.1	21.3	20.5
Change customer	17.6	27.3	24.1	24.0
Change main bank	15.3	18.3	14.3	15.6
Change organisational structure	7.6	12.6	8.4	9.5
	Micro *(< 10)*	*Small* *(10–49)*	*Medium* *(50–199)*	*Large* *(> 200)*
Employment decreases	17.3	24.9	38.0	45.8
Closure of plant	3.7	5.9	10.7	13.2
Employment increase	27.8	39.7	27.3	23.5
Opening of new plant	11.2	18.5	23.7	27.8
New product line	22.1	28.9	31.4	39.9
Upgrade	31.1	38.5	42.7	51.2
Change supplier	21.4	20.0	20.8	19.4
Change customer	24.7	24.3	22.5	24.4
Change main bank	8.4	18.2	18.6	19.2
Change organisational structure	5.5	11.2	10.9	11.3

Source: Carlin *et al.* (2001).

Notes
All restructuring indicators refer to changes in the previous three years. Employment decrease/increase refers to a decrease/increase of employment of more than 10 per cent. 'New product line' refers to the successful development of a major new product line. 'Upgrade' refers to the upgrading of an existing product line. 'Change supplier' and 'Change customer' are changes of identify of the main supplier and the main customers (>20 per cent of sales). 'Change organisational structure' means that firm has had a completely new organisational structure.

We begin our discussion on enterprise restructuring with changes in ownership structure, as it was privatisation – a recent phenomenon in historical terms – that dominated the early debate on enterprise reform.

Ownership structure and privatisation

We define privatisation as the transfer of a majority of ownership rights from state to private hands.[5] State ownership is considered to be an inefficient ownership structure. For one, there is the managerial view that highlights the state's inability to monitor enterprise managers. The lack of a threat of takeover or bankruptcy means that firms are not disciplined. Second, there is the political view that identifies the objectives of SOEs as politicised, away from profit maximisation towards some political objective. Privatisation, in turn, is a response to these failings of state ownership.

From an economic perspective, the objective of privatisation is increased efficiency. The literature identifies two ways for efficiency to increase (Barberis *et al.* 1996). One channel is through better incentives for management as this exerts greater effort. Here, private owners with equity stakes and bearing the financial consequences of their decision have stronger incentives than do government appointees. The second channel is through new human capital. Here, privatisation selects managers who have more appropriate skills at managing enterprises and maximising profits in a competitive marketplace than those managers that were appointed in former times when establishing political contacts and lobbying with ministries were the essential skills required. Quoting from Boycko *et al.*'s (1996) well-publicised paper 'A Theory of Privatisation', 'privatisation works because it controls political discretion'.[6]

State-owned firms fulfil government objectives such as excess employment numbers or the financing of large state projects. Transfer of ownership from such a politically motivated resource allocation model to one where private enterprise and profit motives dominate leads to improvements in profitability and productivity, it is argued. With a change in ownership from state-owned enterprises to private firms, incentives to, for example, cut costs and innovate improve. More specifically in relation to former socialist countries, whereas many argued that the aim of privatisation was the establishment of effective corporate governance structures (a notable economic and financial objective) that would improve firm performance, others argued that the main aim was political and, in particular, the depoliticisation of economic activity. With the focus on politics, the prediction here is that market-supporting institutions will follow private property rather than the other way around. Rather than market failure (where public goods, monopoly power and externalities provide a rationale for state ownership), here the emphasis is on government failure (Boycko *et al.* 1995; Stiglitz 2000).

Privatisation in TEs in the 1990s took its cue from the privatisation in Western Europe in the 1980s. In the latter, however, ownership change took place in well-established market economies (but with a sizeable public sector, comprising large state-owned companies) where property rights were well defined, administrative and state capacity was strong, capital markets were well established and savings were plentiful. There, privatisation involved case-by-case sell-offs and was strictly overseen by government. Because of the legacy of central planning and the socialist system, privatisation in transition countries was inevitably going to be a much more difficult task. A sense of this complexity is given by Lipton and Sachs in an early paper on privatisation in Eastern Europe, and, in particular, Poland. The conclusion of the authors was that

> the most daunting challenge facing the countries of Eastern Europe today is the transfer of state property to private hands in a manner that is rapid, equitable and fiscally sound. To achieve this in the Eastern European context is particularly difficult, because it requires the complete redefinition of property rights and wealthholding in the society, and the creation anew of the basic institutions of a market financial system.
>
> (Lipton and Sachs 1990)

Over time, as the aura of transition waned, a number of concerns were raised with regard to privatisation. Could meaningful restructuring take place before privatisation? In Poland, restructuring and improvements in firm performance did take place in the early years of transition under state ownership. In contrast, in Romania, the enterprise isolation programmes, which were an attempt to restructure and improve performance while under state ownership, were less successful. Did the emphasis on privatisation deflect from the need to foster a new private SME sector? Although not mutually exclusive, the experience of many TEs suggests that the focus on privatisation did indeed detract from the need to develop and support *de novo* private firms. How important were demonopolisation and anti-monopoly laws relative to the push for privatisation? Whereas demonopolisation and a competition policy require a strong (but limited) state to ensure enforcement, the privatisation of SOEs is aimed at reducing the influence of the state. Could privatisation work without a hardening of the budget constraint and effective corporate governance structures, or, put another way, could privatisation alone result in a change in the behaviour of the enterprise? Whereas privatisation, at least in a formal sense, was straightforward, hardening the budget constraint and introducing proper corporate governance mechanisms is less so.

Could privatisation proceed in advance of the required institutional and legal framework? This question raises the issue of the suitability of 'best-practice' institutions as opposed to transitional institutions that better suit the country circumstances. As mentioned elsewhere, many of these sequencing concerns relate to the dynamics of transition and, in particular, the timing of privatisation vis-à-vis institutional reform. Should the building of market-supporting institutions precede privatisation or be introduced simultaneously, or, as was the case in most TEs, follow privatisation? This is one of the most important issues in transition and we will revisit it in the final chapter. However, the opinions of some senior legal advisers to the Russian privatisation scheme post-privatisation are worth quoting here: 'development of a decent legal and enforcement infrastructure must precede or at least accompany privatisation of large firms. If privatisation comes first, massive theft is likely to occur before the infrastructure to control it can develop.' They go on to say that 'Privatisation is not enough. It matters who the owners are, what constraints on self-dealing they face, and the business climate they operate in' (Black *et al.* 2000).

It is also the case that the method of privatisation (case-by-case direct sales, voucher or mass privatisation, management and employee buyouts) and the ownership outcomes that emerged following privatisation (insider, outsider, concentrated, dispersed) matter in terms of improving firm performance. Of course, the pattern of ownership in TEs was partly related to the method of privatisation adopted. Outsiders, comprising institutional investors and foreigners, dominated in cases where direct sales were the primary mode of privatisation (e.g. Hungary).[7] In contrast, where voucher schemes (see Box 6.1) were used to privatise state-owned firms, insider ownership resulted (e.g. Russia). It is also the case that in most TEs the state retained a sizeable share in many large privatised SOEs.

The pros and cons of the different modes of privatisation adopted in TEs are outlined in Table 6.2.

The different methods of privatisation adopted by TEs are given in Table 6.3. Among other things, it highlights the popularity of mass or voucher privatisation in CIS countries, the variety of methods adopted by many countries, the adoption of case-by-case direct sales by many of the leading TEs and the delay in privatisation in a mix of both the most advanced (e.g. Poland, Slovenia) and the least advanced transition countries (e.g. Ukraine, Romania). As for the best method, Havrylyshyn and McGettigan (2000) conclude that 'there is no one method of privatisation that comes out unambiguously superior to others'. The choice, design, implementation and success, or otherwise, depend on a number of factors, many of which are outside the control of the authorities, and some of which are a legacy of the socialist past.

With respect to Western countries, studies such as those by Megginson *et al.* (1994) which compared pre- and post-privatisation performance of privatised firms, and Vining and Boardman (1992) which compared the performance of state firms with private firms, found that privatisation improves performance, or, phrased differently, private firms outperform state-owned firms. Findings from other studies, for continental Europe and elsewhere, were

Table 6.2 Pros and cons of modes of privatisation

	Restitution	Direct sales	Mass privatisation	Management and employee buyouts (MEBO)
Pros	– Seen as fair as it attempts to redress past injustices by compensating former owners	– Revenue generation – Foreign/large investors – Tailored to each case	– Overcome lack of domestic capital – Speedy – Popular	– Prevents blocking by managers and workers – Aligns the interests of owners and workers
Cons	– Difficult to establish rightful owners, and their claims – General population do not benefit	– Difficulty in valuing firms – Hampered by limited private capital – Slow	– Dispersed ownership structure and ineffective corporate governance – Lack of revenues	– Perceived as unfair as general population do not benefit – Entrenched insiders may stall restructuring

Note
Restitution involves the return of state assets to their rightful owners in cases where the previous owners can be verified. Although restitution, in theory, is often viewed as a fair method of privatisation (and redistribution), it often, in practice, creates new injustices.

Table 6.3 Privatisation methods in TEs

Country	Direct sales	Vouchers	MEBO
CEB			
Albania	–	Secondary	Primary
Bosnia and Herzegovina	Secondary	Primary	–
Bulgaria	Primary	Secondary	–
Croatia	–	Secondary	Primary
Czech Republic	Secondary	Primary	–
Estonia	Primary	Secondary	–
FYR Macedonia	Secondary	–	Primary
Hungary	Primary	–	Secondary
Latvia	Primary	Secondary	–
Lithuania	Secondary	Primary	–
Poland	Primary	–	Secondary
Romania	Secondary	–	Primary
Slovak Republic	Primary	Secondary	–
Slovenia	–	Secondary	Primary
CIS			
Armenia	–	Primary	Secondary
Azerbaijan	Secondary	Primary	–
Belarus	–	Secondary	Primary
Georgia	Secondary	Primary	–
Kazakhstan	Primary	Secondary	–
Kyrgyzstan	–	Primary	Secondary
Moldova	Secondary	Primary	–
Russia	Secondary	Primary	–
Tajikistan	Primary	Secondary	–
Turkmenistan	Secondary	–	Primary
Ukraine	Secondary	–	Primary
Uzbekistan	Secondary	–	Primary

Source: EBRD Transition Report (1999).

more uncertain, with very mixed results. Notwithstanding the difficulties in establishing the effects of privatisation on firm performance (and particularly so for TEs which are experiencing massive economy-wide changes), some of the earlier studies in TEs found no clear evidence that privatisation improved performance, or indeed, led to more restructuring. Aside from the possibility that the data from these earlier studies pertained to a period that was too short and too early in the reform process, it is likely that privatisation alone, without changes in corporate governance structures, improvements in the competitive business environment and a hardening of the budget constraint, will not result in improved performance.[8] Even the IMF, the great bastion of market reforms, admitted that on the evidence of the first decade of transition 'privatisation has not always been effective in bringing about enterprise restructuring. Although private ownership activates profit motives, private ownership alone is not sufficient to make firms efficient – complementary conditions are required to make privatisation lead to effective restructuring' (IMF 2000).[9] Indeed, one could argue that, as occurred in many of the institutionally weak and fractured state FSU countries, privatisation in the absence of the necessary legal and institutional changes contributed to the economic decline of the 1990s, further accelerating the already weakened state and breakdown of social harmony.

By the mid-1990s and beyond, studies of privatisation in TEs began to find evidence that ownership change and privatisation matter, in terms of the effects at the microeconomic level.[10] Based on a survey of 500-odd medium-sized state-owned and privatised manufacturing firms in three leading TEs (the Czech Republic, Hungary and Poland), Frydman *et al.* (1999) found that privatisation has different effects on performance depending on whether the firm is insider controlled (no significant effect) or outsider controlled (positive significant effect). The authors found that 'privatisation to an outsider owner adds, on average, nearly ten percentage points to the annual rate of revenue growth and about nine percentage points to productivity growth' (Frydman *et al.* 1999). In terms of restructuring, Pohl *et al.* (1997) found that for over 6,000 state-owned and privatised, industrial firms across seven CEE countries, (rapid and comprehensive) privatisation (leading to concentrated ownership) was the single most important factor in determining enterprise restructuring. The authors found that, on average, a firm privatised for four years will increase productivity three to five times more than a similar state-owned firm.

In a review of a selection of empirical studies over a range of TEs, Havrylyshyn and McGettigan (2000) found that privatised firms generally outperform state-owned firms. With such a finding, the authors then proceed to claim that these results 'bring the findings for TEs into line with earlier findings cited for other developing and advanced economies that privatisation generally leads to an improvement in enterprise performance' (Havrylyshyn and McGettigan 2000). In contrast, a later study, for the Czech Republic, found, contrary to convention, that the performance effects of privatisation and different types of owners is limited, with many types of private owners (with the exception being concentrated foreign owners) having effects on performance no different from those of state-owned firms (Hanousek *et al.* 2007).[11] Likewise, using the BEEPS dataset for 26 TEs, Commander and Svejnar (2007) found that, although foreign ownership has a positive impact on performance, there is, contrary to conventional wisdom, no effect of domestic private ownership on performance.

The findings from country studies vary greatly, and indicate, at best, only modest effects of privatisation. Based on a study of 400-odd manufacturing privatised firms in Russia, Angelucci and Estrin (2003) found no evidence that ownership change (privatisation) had any significant effect on performance, or that outsider-owned firms had outperformed insider-owned firms. Similarly, a study of medium- and large-sized firms in the Czech Republic found that concentrated foreign ownership improves firm performance, but that domestic private ownership, relative to state ownership, does not improve performance (Kočenda and Svejnar 2003). In contrast, and again for Russia, Earle (1998) and Earle and Estrin (1998) found that privatisation improves firm performance, and that outsider-owned firms do better. As for the Czech Republic, a study of 380 firms privatised in the second wave of voucher privatisation found that these second-wave firms, unlike the first-wave firms, experienced a significant increase in profitability and efficiency (Harper 2002). In general, insider privatisation, whether worker controlled or manager controlled, has not led to deep restructuring, or alone, to improved performance. In contrast, privatisation to outsiders has led to better restructuring and per-formance outcomes.[12] There is also some evidence that, as predicted, concentrated ownership (that is, when ownership is transferred to an individual investor or a small group of investors) is better for performance compared to dispersed ownership.

In comparing the most important transition countries, namely Russia with China, Bhaumik and Estrin (2005) found that in China, enterprise performance is associated with increases in factor inputs but is not significantly affected by privatisation or indeed, institutional factors. In contrast, the determinants of enterprise performance in Russia are demand and institutional factors at a regional level (that is, region-specific factors matter), a finding also found in Estrin and Bevan (2003), and are not associated with factor inputs (except for labour). Differences in managerial and institutional quality between China and Russia are, according to the authors, possible explanations for these variations in determinants of firm performance between the two countries.

In terms of regional differences, the record on privatisation differs between CEE and FSU countries. In their impressive survey of empirical studies on privatisation, Megginson and Netter (2001) classify TEs into two groups for the purposes of analysing privatisation results. For CEE countries, the results indicate that private ownership (as opposed to state ownership), outsider control (as opposed to insider control), concentrated (as opposed to diffused), foreign ownership (as opposed to domestic ownership) and new managers (as opposed to original managers) are all associated with improvements in firm performance. Although the authors claim some evidence of similar results for Russia and the other former Soviet Republics, namely improved performance associated with privatised firms, outsider-controlled firms, and firms under new management, they warn of the difficulty of reaching simple conclusions regarding privatisation in the FSU countries given, *inter alia*, the economic turmoil and the data problems of the 1990s. They conclude that results of privatisation in transition countries are not dissimilar to results for developed and developing countries but that there appears to be greater variation in the results for the TEs.

In their equally considerable study of the empirical research on the determinants of enterprise restructuring in transition, Djankov and Murrell (2000), by synthesising results across various empirical studies, conclude that the evidence in terms of microeconomic effects 'is extremely strong that the move from state to private ownership has resulted in greater amounts of restructuring'. However, differences appear once the group of TEs is classified into CIS and non-CIS countries. The above conclusion, namely that privatisation is associated with more enterprise restructuring, applies for the non-CIS countries but the story is more complex for the set of CIS countries. With respect to this regional variation, the authors conclude that 'we have no doubt in the soundness of the conclusion that privatisation has been less effective in the CIS than in other countries' (Djankov and Murrell 2000). As for the effects of different types of owners on restructuring, concentrated ownership and privatisation to outsiders results in far more restructuring than dispersed ownership and privatisation to insiders. Whereas traditional state-owned firms are the worst-performing category, a somewhat surprising result, according to the authors, is that partially privatised firms (retaining some state share) produce more restructuring than ownership by enterprise insiders and non-blockholder outsiders.[13] The authors interpret this difference in performance between CIS and non-CIS countries as caused by institutional factors which, in turn, are related to the length of time the country has spent under communism. For a more general result on privatisation in TEs, Djankov and Murrell (2002) conclude that 'Privatisation done in the right way, or under the right circumstances, can have huge positive effects, but privatisation can also be hugely detrimental.'

A more recent study on the impact of privatisation (on productivity) on privatised manufacturing firms in four TEs, namely Hungary, Romania, Ukraine and Russia, found that privatisation does improve productivity (with cross-country differences in productivity effects of privatisation between all four countries), privatisation to foreign investors has a bigger impact than privatisation to domestic investors, and that for Hungary, Romania and Ukraine, the effect of privatisation is almost immediate (that is, within one year), and continues to grow thereafter, whereas for Russia the impact is negative until the fifth year after privatisation (Brown *et al.* 2006). Drawing from this and other studies, Guriev and Megginson (2007) conclude that privatisation works, but only if the relevant institutions (identified by the authors as protection of private property rights and rule-of-law, competition and hard budget constraints, quality of governance and regulation) are in place. The authors claim that it is the absence of these institutions that explains the disappointing results of privatisation in Russia and other CIS countries.

So, it appears that the further East one travels, the worse the privatisation outcomes. Particularly in relation to many of these FSU countries, Nellis (1999) concludes that 'it is time to rethink privatisation, at least in those transition settings where history, geography and politics have so readily channelled seemingly laudable economic policy into sub-optimal outcomes'. It is fair to say that this is a view espoused by many economists and organisations, including those who supported market reforms in transition countries and other emerging markets. When writing on the gains from privatisation, Jeffrey Sachs (the intellectual leader of radical market reforms) wrote: 'one size (policy) does *not* fit all: privatisation policies must be tailored to the level of complementary reforms in place' (Sachs *et al.* 2001). Similarly, the World Bank, in its 2005 review of economic reform, acknowledged that 'There is no universal appropriate reform model. Every restructuring and privatisation program needs to consider explicitly the underlying economic attributes and technology of each sector and its institutional, social, and political characteristics' (World Bank 2005b). Many others, of course, are far more critical of privatisation, and its effect worldwide, including transition countries. K.S. Jomo, a leading critic of privatisation, writes, 'privatisation in many developing and transition economies has primarily enriched the few with strong political connections who secure most, if not all, of these profitable opportunities, while the public interest is sacrificed and vulnerable to the powers of private business interests' (Jomo 2008).

Privatisation may have been a necessary condition but we now know from the evidence in Russia and elsewhere that it was clearly not sufficient to bring about economic prosperity, not to mention the adverse social impact and negative distributional aspects of privatisation. In hindsight, we now also know that expectations at the outset of transition were too great (for a process that was hugely complex) and that the claims made of privatisation (without the complementary changes to competition and corporate governance) were overstated.

Box 6.1

Voucher privatisations in Russia and the Czech Republic

The most cited case of privatisation is the Russian example. To begin, there is a need to acknowledge the enormous task involved in privatisation in Russia and to further acknowledge the remarkable speed at which privatisation took place. It is also true that, as in other TEs, small-scale privatisation (mainly of retail trade and services units) in Russia, as opposed to the privatisation of medium-sized and large enterprises, was more or less uncontentious and generally successful.

At the outset of transition, state ownership in the USSR accounted for 87 per cent of national income and 84 per cent of the workforce (IMF 1991). With state ownership dominating the enterprise sector and with privatisation popular throughout many countries of the Anglo-Saxon world (and, indeed, in many non-transition developing countries), it was not surprising that ownership change became a central feature of the transition process.

There were a number of stages to the Russian privatisation of the 1990s. Concerned with a possible return to the old system, the designers of the Russian privatisation scheme co-opted managers and workers by offering them preferential treatment of shares in privatised firms (partly in the expectation that secondary trading would result in a better ownership structure, which, in turn, would create the constituency for legal, institutional and governance changes). Although a non-cash privatisation scheme was employed where every Russian citizen was given a voucher worth 10,000 roubles, to be used later in exchange for shares sold at auctions, the end result was insider privatisation where distribution of ownership was dispersed. However, it was the notorious 'loans-for-shares' scheme that was to damage the image of reformers and liberal market reforms in Russia for years to come. Since the Russian government was short of revenue, Russian bankers and the FIGs, owned by the oligarchs, proposed to lend funds to the government, with the government's share in the state-owned enterprises as collateral. In the (most likely) case of non-repayment of these loans, the government would forfeit its share in these enterprises to the banks. This is indeed the way it turned out, with Russia's wealthiest companies, in commodities such as oil, gas and aluminium, sold off to oligarchs at very low prices in what were effectively rigged auctions. An insider's account of the detail of Russia's privatisation and its failure is given by Black *et al.* (2000) who describe Russian privatisation as 'dirty'. This is not the view only of legal experts. In the more moderate words of two economists with an expertise in Russian affairs, 'Russian privatisation was pursued in excessive haste, with poor results in terms of the subsequent enterprise behaviour and performance' (Hare and Muravyev 2002).

Privatisation in the Czech Republic is another often-cited case as it was the first mass privatisation scheme in CEE countries. In 1992 the government of Czechoslovakia issued coupons (for a nominal fee) to all adult citizens which could, in turn, be used to buy shares at national auctions of firms to be privatised. Eventually many of these coupons were bought by investment funds, which became the dominant owners of Czech firms and, in doing so, allowed for greater ownership concentration. Although the Czech authorities did adopt a number of different privatisation schemes (including a combination of the voucher scheme described above, restitution and case-by-case sell-offs), while at the same time retaining a government share in many large enterprises, the outcome in terms of ownership structure was described as privatisation to outsiders. Despite the initial euphoria and claims of an end to transition, the recession and economic crisis that followed in the Czech Republic has been attributed to the voucher privatisation scheme which, according to many, led to little restructuring, much insider looting and tunnelling of firms' profits, and ineffective corporate governance structures. In particular, 'the crux of the problem was that insufficiently regulated privatisation investment funds ended up owning large or controlling stakes in many firms privatised by vouchers. . . . But most of these large funds were owned by the major domestic banks – banks in which the Czech state retained a controlling or even majority stake' (Nellis 1999). Although not uncommon in some developed market economies, where banks play a more central role in the ownership of firms (examples include Germany and Japan), a conflict of interest arose when the (state-owned) banks that were lending to firms were, at the same time, controlling the funds that owned these (privatised) firms. This is a case of a design in a privatisation scheme that failed to properly account for proper corporate governance mechanisms.[14] One possible reason why such behaviour occurred was the minimal regulation of investment funds and securities markets advocated by the free-marketeer Czech authorities responsible for privatisation policy.

Overall, for these and other countries implementing changes in ownership structure, it is worth noting that although economic factors shaped the design of privatisation schemes in developed countries, it was often the case that in TEs the design of privatisation programmes (concerned more with achieving economic efficiency than social equity) was largely dictated by political factors and constraints. We should also note here that although these most controversial privatisation schemes were disappointing (in terms of outcomes) there were a number of successful privatisation programmes in TEs, often where direct sales methods were employed (e.g. Hungary, Estonia). Of course, evaluation of privatisation schemes (including voucher privatisation which was always a second-best solution), and other reforms taken is difficult because the counterfactual remains unknown (Lieberman and Kopf 2008).[15]

We finish our discussion on mass privatisation in Russia and the Czech Republic with some concluding remarks made by the legal advisers to the Russian privatisation scheme.

A central economic lesson of the 20th century is the huge difference between well-run, mostly market-centred economies and badly-run, often government-centred economies. That experience demonstrates the boost that good government can give to economic performance, and the difficulty of escaping from a legacy of bad government. A central lesson from the past decade is that mass privatisation offers no escape from that general lesson. A weak government can't build the institutions that are needed to control self-dealing and support a complex market economy. Yet without that infrastructure, rapid large-firm privatisation won't help the economy much if at all. Initial conditions, especially the quality of institutions, matter more, and privatisation matters less, than we thought in the early 1990s. In the artificial world of the Coase Theorem, neither these institutions nor the manner of privatisation would matter much. Bad owners would quickly sell enterprises to good owners, who would build long-term value. In the real world, bad initial owners loot enterprises instead and corrupt the government while they're at it. Call it the triumph of Hayek over Coase – of Hayekian respect for endogenously developed traditions over the abstract promise of the Coase-influenced mass privatisation schemes.

(Black *et al.* 2000)[16]

Another result from the evidence is the difference in performance between state-owned, privatised and new private firms. Whereas the general expectation was that privatisation would result in improved performance of privatised SOEs (with the result that privatised firms outperform state-owned firms), this is not true for all TEs. However, what is clear from all TEs is that *de novo* private firms outperform both state-owned and privatised firms. Havrylyshyn and McGettigan (2000) concluded that 'de novo firms are overwhelmingly shown to be most efficient and superior to even the best privatised firms'. A number of important issues relating to the development of a new private sector are outlined in a later section. What remains to be said here is to raise the issue of the relationship between the privatisation strategy and the entry of new firms strategy. One view is that these strategies are complementary, and that efforts to privatise can at the same time support new private sector development. Alternately, there is a view that privatisation, in its use of resources, has hindered the entry of new firms. What is clear is that for most TEs in the former Soviet Union, privatisation was the dominant strategy and, likewise, that the number of new private firms is low, relative to other TEs or to other countries of similar income per capita levels. Indeed, for some, privatisation was synonymous with transition.[17]

Whereas transition countries of the former Soviet system adopted the privatisation route, China implemented a very different strategy with respect to state-owned enterprises. First, the ruling Communist Party was ideologically opposed to privatisation per se, even referring to 'restructuring of ownership' or 'transformation of ownership' as opposed to the use of the term 'privatisation'. Second, the success of the TVEs delayed, it is argued, the need for some privatisation of the loss-making SOEs. Third, privatisation of SOEs proved socially difficult as they were still burdened with the responsibility for providing many social welfare services, including social security, housing, and some basic education and health services. However, improvements in the performance of SOEs were sought (in the cautious, gradual, incremental and experimental fashion that Chinese reforms are renowned for) by the authorities through other means, including greater competition (from the non-state sector), improved managerial incentives, downsizing and layoffs, corporatisation, and greater decentralisation of economic decision making. It was close to the turn of the century (after 20 years of economic reform and a deteriorating SOE sector) before the Chinese authorities, which up until then were committed to minimising the costs of privatisation, finally embarked on greater ownership changes (captured in the slogan 'Grasping the large, and letting go of the small') with respect to SOEs and TVEs. China's largest and most strategic industrial firms have remained in state hands as the authorities attempt to foster national and international champions while there has been partial privatisation of other large, less strategic SOEs. As for small and medium-sized enterprises slated for privatisation (often by local government), employee and management buyouts have been widely used, and with that mode of privatisation (but with the Chinese authorities in many cases retaining administrative oversight over the enterprise), not surprisingly, insider privatisation has dominated in terms of ownership outcomes (Lieberman and Kopf 2008; Naughton 2007a). Efforts to diversify ownership of SOEs, including acceleration of privatisation, are likely to continue as China persists with market reforms into the future.

Another aspect of enterprise reform and restructuring, and one that is closely related to ownership and privatisation, is that of corporate governance.

Corporate governance

As with the concept of restructuring, the term 'corporate governance' is not well defined. Yet it plays an important role in the performance of the corporate sector, and the economy (and society) at large. At the level of the firm, the benefits from a good corporate governance structure come primarily, it is often argued, in the form of better access to, and lower cost of, capital, higher returns on equity and greater efficiency (Claessens 2006). This applies to developed and developing countries, as well as to transition countries. To fully understand the concept and its importance in transition from plan to market, we need to begin, from an economics perspective, with some definitions.

The OECD defines corporate governance as 'the system by which business corporations are directed and controlled. The corporate governance structure specifies the distribution of rights and responsibilities among different participants in the corporation, such as, the board, managers, shareholders and the other stakeholders, and spells out the rules and procedures for making decisions on corporate affair' (OECD 1999). This definition is similar to that contained in the *Financial Aspects of Corporate Governance*, or the United Kingdom's 1992 Cadbury Report as it is commonly known, which, in effect, is a code on corporate governance. Along similar lines, Claessens (2006) defines the term as 'a set of mechanisms through which firms operate when ownership is separated from management'. Alternately, Qian (2000) defines it as 'a set of institutional arrangements governing the relationships among investors (shareholders and creditors), managers, and workers. The structure of corporate governance concerns (1) how control rights are allocated and exercised; (2) how boards of directors and top managers are selected and monitored; and (3) how incentives are designed and enforced.' When writing specifically on corporate governance and TEs, Dallago (2007) identifies corporate governance as 'how rights and duties are distributed within and around the firm'.

As the modern corporation, either in a transition or non-transition setting, comprises a number of different stakeholders (most especially shareholders and managers), the concept of corporate governance is often used to capture the problem of the separation of ownership and control. It was Berle and Means' classic book *The Modern Corporation and Private Property* (1932) that brought to prominence the problem of the separation of ownership and control for modern corporations. Unlike small businesses which are often owner-managed, modern corporations are owned by shareholders but controlled by management and boards of directors. This separation of corporate ownership and corporate control is an example of the principal–agent problem where the interests of the hired managers (agents) may not coincide with the interests of the shareholders (owners). When there is a conflict of interest between shareholders and managers, how can shareholders be sure that when they invest, managers will not expropriate their funds, engage in asset-stripping, self-dealing and other costly activities? A solution to the problems of discretionary managerial behaviour is disciplinary devices such as monitoring of managers by owners (which can be costly), management turnover (which requires a pool of skilled managers), corporate takeovers (which need to be credible) or, ultimately, bankruptcy (which needs a sound legal framework). Or, are managerial incentives such as bonus schemes, stock options and higher remuneration sufficient to induce greater efficiency? These issues are as much, if not more, relevant to TEs as they are to developed countries where the concept of corporate governance has attracted a huge amount of interest and a growing literature.

In TEs the agency problem is not new. In the days of state-owned enterprises, directors, ministries and central planners, similar problems prevailed. As alluded to in the opening section on the description of the SOE, the socialist system and the inefficient ownership structure of the SOE (where, in theory, control rights and cash flow rights were aligned but, in practice, these rights were separated) were rife with asymmetric information and agency problems. In transition, where privatisation and restructuring are ongoing, policy makers are confronted with the problem of managerial discretion compared with, as in the socialist era, political discretion and the political control of economic activity (Boycko *et al.* 1995).

There are different categories of owners in transition countries. There are state-owned (traditional or commercialised/corporatised), insider-owned (workers and managers) and outsider-owned (banks, investment funds, foreigners, individuals and institutional investors). With respect to corporate control, and based on having a majority of seats on the board, the control categories are as follows: state-controlled; manager-controlled and worker-controlled (these two together constitute insider-controlled); outsider-controlled and no overall control. As expected, corporate ownership and control has been, and remains, a problem in transition countries. TEs have witnessed a variety of different ownership structures. In many cases, the majority shareholder group is insiders (managers and workers). Unchecked, entrenched insiders may be reluctant to shed labour, can manipulate wages and may fail to attract external finance in sufficient amounts. Contrast this with outsiders who are expected to bring much-needed capital, managerial experience and new technologies and, for these reasons, are considered better owners in term of changing managerial behaviour, improving firm performance and increasing efficiency. Another related issue is ownership concentration. Large block shareholders are normally preferred over dispersed or fragmented ownership as the former allows for easier and less costly monitoring of managers, whereas the latter are not able to exercise control over the corporations they own. However, in transition countries, and especially in FSU countries, voucher schemes were the main form of privatisation and these often resulted, even after secondary trading, in diffused ownership. There is also the issue concerning the role of banks and most particularly stock markets as an important mechanism for corporate control. However, in TEs, stock markets tend not to be very well established, trading is thin and regulation is often insufficient.

With respect to different corporate governance structures and practices, the corporate governance literature identifies two models of corporate governance appropriate to CEE and FSU countries in transition. They are the Anglo-Saxon shareholder model and the Continental European stakeholder model. Table 6.4 highlights the main differences between the two models.

Again with respect to transition countries, the EBRD Legal Indicator Survey assesses TEs' level of compliance with international standards for corporate governance. The survey is based on corporate governance laws and regulations covering five areas (based on the *OECD Principles of Corporate Governance*), namely:

- Shareholders' rights
- Equitable treatment of shareholders

Table 6.4 Corporate governance models

Anglo-Saxon model	European model
Management dominated	Controlling shareholder dominated
Shareholder focused	Stakeholder focused
Wide public share ownership	Narrower public share ownership
Strong shareholder rights	Weaker shareholder rights
Unitary board structure	Two-level board structure
Single powerful leader	Consensus or divided leadership
Shareholder litigation culture	Weaker litigation culture

Source: UNECE (2003).

- Role of stakeholders
- Disclosure and transparency
- Responsibilities of the board.

In 2005, of 27 TEs assessed, eight countries (including, surprisingly, EU accession country Romania) were deemed to have a low or a very low compliance rating. At the other end of the ratings, nine countries (including, surprisingly, Russia) had a high compliance rating, 'indicating a sound legal framework in line with OECD principles' (EBRD 2005).

In terms of improving corporate governance structures in TEs, the corporate governance literature identifies elements (many of which are listed above) that constitute a good corporate governance system. These include:

- A rules-based system of governance, with a legal framework that includes company law, contract law, securities law and so forth.
- Rights of stakeholders (shareholders, investors, creditors, workers, managers, banks) are well defined and enforced.
- Legal protection for minority shareholders, i.e. protecting and enforcing minority shareholder rights.
- Board of directors composition that reflects ownership structure.
- Information disclosure and transparent accounting and financial reporting procedures.
- An independent Regulator.
- Clear rules on stock market listing arrangements and insider dealing.

Some of the questions raised by the corporate governance literature with respect to transition include the following: What constitutes a good corporate governance system? Should TEs replicate international 'best-practice' corporate governance structures (typically as above) or, alternatively, develop a system that is most appropriate to its own needs, culture and circumstances? How exactly does good corporate governance improve firm performance? How does privatisation affect corporate governance?[18] Moreover, which form of privatisation is better in terms of providing effective corporate governance mechanisms?

Later, we will report on the findings into how privatisation and corporate governance (and, in particular, the role of managers) affect restructuring and, ultimately, firm performance. We simply note here that, as with some of the other explanatory variables, researchers investigating governance effects encounter methodological issues. How can we measure corporate governance and, if such measures are constructed, which is the best indicator? For measures of governance, are qualitative indicators superior to quantitative indicators? What is the nature of the causality between corporate governance and enterprise performance and restructuring? If changes in corporate governance complement other enterprise reforms, what are the joint effects? One such microeconomic reform is competition and reducing the market power of monopolies and dominant firms.

Market structure and competition

A core feature of the socialist system, at least in the Soviet Union and its satellite states, was the near-complete absence of competition in the enterprise sector. For many reasons, political, economic and administrative, industrial sectors comprised single, large enterprises that faced no domestic competition. In addition, the industrial enterprise had often only one supplier (state-owned) and the state was often the only buyer. As it was an autarkic state, foreign-based firms were prevented from competing in the domestic market and, likewise, the traditional SOE was prevented from competing abroad as this was limited to special foreign trade organisations. Hence, in this most 'monopolistic' of market structures, there was a high concentration in production.[19]

Barriers to entry and exit were the norm for industrial sectors. New firms were prevented from entering as the planners' preferences were for single large firms, as they were easier to control and monitor, in addition to reaping economies of scale. From the perspective of the enterprise, the incumbent, often in receipt of favours from the state, would lobby bureaucrats to prevent entry of new firms. The overall economic environment was not conducive to entry of new firms which, worldwide, tend to be small and medium-sized enterprises. Barriers to exit also applied, as existing firms were prevented from going under because of security and employment concerns of the paternalistic state. Loss-making enterprises were kept afloat by transfers from profit-making enterprises. In practice, this meant that troubled firms were aided through tax concessions, subsidies and other forms of external assistance. Moreover, this external assistance was conditional on poor performance. This is the soft budget constraint.

Overall, it is widely believed that the absence of competition and the very low rates of entry and exit contributed to the poor performance of socialist countries. As Nickell (1996) argues, 'the low level of productivity in Eastern Europe relative to that in Western Europe is an impressive example of what can be achieved by repressing the forces of market competition'. Yet, and surprisingly so, both the theoretical reasoning (such as the arguments that competition increases effort, sharpens managerial incentives and spurs innovation) and the empirical evidence supporting the virtues of competition are somewhat limited. We will return to this, in the context of determinants of enterprise performance in TEs, in the next section.

In contrast to the socialist system as described above, the market system is typified by, at least in theory, competition, entry (of new and, most often, private SMEs) and exit (of failed firms), price and profit signals that reflect relative scarcities and different market structures, depending on the sector. A limited but strong state combined with market forces allows competition to flourish. Commander *et al.* (2000), when addressing the issue of competition in TEs, neatly express the importance of competitive pressures when noting that 'the intensity of rivalry is the engine that makes market economies work'. Provided that the market-supporting institutions (including secure property rights and rule of law) are in place, competitive forces of demand and supply dominate with competition acting as a disciplinary device on firms (and, indeed, banks and governments). In the face of consumer sovereignty, profit-maximising firms compete with each other and, in doing so, drive down costs and profits. Furthermore, in the competitive market system, the behaviour and actions of self-interested economic agents result in increased welfare for society at large. This is Adam Smith's 'invisible hand'.

In transition, one of the central tenets of enterprise reform is to move towards a more competitive business environment and to reduce the monopoly power of firms given the highly concentrated 'market' structures that existed at the outset of transition. The conventional approach to this transition was the adoption of liberalisation, stabilisation and privatisation policies. Advocates of this mainstream strategy argued that by liberalising domestic and foreign trade, reducing subsidies and introducing a Western-style tax system, and by privatising state-owned enterprises, there would be a spontaneous reaction as markets flourish, new suppliers, driven by the profit motive, emerge and competitive pressures, both domestic and foreign, prevail. As the attention was on these policies, less focus was on demonopolisation, the development of, and supports to, a new private sector, the enforcement of antitrust laws and regulations, and the establishment of competition agencies to promote competitive practices and outlaw monopolistic behaviour and restrictive practices (involving the breakup of cartels, price-fixing, predatory pricing and so forth).

With respect to competition in TEs, some of the earlier studies on competition and performance found no significant effect of competition. However, this may be due to the fact that in the early years competition was limited and enterprise performance data problems were common. Later, in a study of 25 TEs and over 3,000 firms (mix of state, privatised and private) Carlin *et al.* (2001) find evidence that competitive pressures have a positive effect on performance. Competition matters, and is 'much more important than the effect of ownership *per se*' (Carlin *et al.* 2001). This confirms some of the empirical evidence from developed countries.

In their analysis of 125 empirical studies that examine determinants of enterprise restructuring, Djankov and Murrell (2000) conclude that

> The economic effects of competition are large. The studies surveyed here imply that in CIS countries, firms that face near-perfect competition are 40 to 60 per cent more efficient than enterprises that operate in near-monopoly markets, while the efficiency gain is 30 per cent in non-CIS countries.

Brown and Earle (2000) found similar results with regard to Russia, concluding that 'total factor productivity results provide strong evidence that domestic product market competition, import competition and local labour market competition have strong positive effects on efficiency'. Also for Russia (where it is often cited that there is evidence of product market fragmentation), Angelucci and Estrin (2003) found evidence of a positive relationship between competition and restructuring. Of course, there may be a joint effect, i.e. competitive pressures and ownership together affect restructuring and performance. This suggests the existence of complementarities between competition and ownership. This is particularly true at the outset of transition when privatisation without competition would likely have resulted, as indeed did occur in some TEs, in SOEs that formerly operated as state monopolies transformed into private monopolies.

As for advances in competition policy, the EBRD transition indicator measures such progress in terms of competition policy in TEs. Table 6.5 shows progress with respect to competition policy for a selection of TEs. A score of 2 reflects 'legislation and institutions

Table 6.5 EBRD TI on competition policy, 1999–2007

Country	1999	2003	2007
CEB			
Lithuania	2+	3	3+
Poland	3	3	3+
Slovak Republic	3	3	3+
Slovenia	2	3–	3
SEE			
Albania	2	2–	2
Croatia	2	2+	3–
FYR Macedonia	1	2	2+
Romania	2	2+	3–
CIS			
Georgia	2	2	2
Kazakhstan	2	2	2
Russia	2+	2+	2+
Ukraine	2	2+	2+

Source: EBRD.

set up, with some reduction of entry restrictions or enforcement action on dominant firms' whereas a score of 3 measures 'some enforcement actions to reduce abuse of market power and to promote a competitive environment, including breakups of dominant conglomerates'.

Although competition laws have, in general, been introduced in all TEs (as evident from Table 6.5), and compare reasonably well with those in more established market economies, the problem in many TEs has been the enforcement of these laws. In terms of competition policy in TEs, there is much cross-country variation. As with many other reforms, most progress has been made by the CEB countries, with less progress made by SEE and, lower still, by CIS countries.

This section has examined the importance of competition, vis-à-vis ownership, restructuring and performance. Competition is also necessary in transition in order to, it is argued, help harden the budget constraints of firms.

Hardening the budget constraint

As already established in Chapter 5, an important feature of the socialist system was financial indiscipline, or as it was commonly referred to, the soft budget constraint. Although there was much agreement on the existence of and the forms (primarily subsidies) that the SBC took pre-transition, there was no consensus on the cause of budget softness. Whereas Kornai (1980) regarded paternalism and state ownership as the primary cause, i.e. a political explanation, others, including Dewatripont and Maskin (1995) argued that the cause of the SBC was a centralised economy and a dynamic commitment problem, i.e. a purely economic explanation. Accordingly, the source of the budget softness lies in such common economic concepts as adverse selection and asymmetric information, sunk costs and irreversible investments, dynamic commitment and time inconsistency. An alternative model is given by Shleifer and Vishny (1994) who argue that the cause is bargaining between self-interested politicians and firms. These differences in the cause of the SBC are important as it explains why a number of different conditions (and not simply privatisation as was argued in the early days) have to be met for the budget constraint to harden. The pre-transition evidence indicates that partial reforms did not harden the budget constraint. Indeed, pre-transition and early transition reforms may even have softened the budget constraint further. Different and new forms of budget softness evolved, ranging from overdue payables to suppliers, utilities and banks to tax arrears. As the SBC is, in the words of Kornai (1998), 'a behavioural regularity' that interferes with the natural process of market selection, only full reform to a market economy dominated by private ownership and competition can eliminate the SBC. A number of reform measures have been identified that would help to harden the budget constraint of enterprises. They are:

- Legal changes with respect to accounting and taxation, banking and property rights,
- Reduction in government subsidies,
- Privatisation and a new private sector,
- Demonopolisation and greater product market competition,
- Fiscal decentralisation,
- Enforcement of bankruptcy and liquidation,
- Improved screening and monitoring by creditors.

Expressed in terms of the rescuer, these reforms, it is argued, will make it more likely for the supporting organisation to be able to credibly commit to no bailout. With respect to privatisation as a means of hardening budget constraints, the evidence indicates that although privatisation is a necessary condition for budget hardness, it is not regarded as sufficient. It must be combined with other policy reforms, as above.

The evidence of budget hardness, or to be more precise, the persistence of budget softness (acknowledging the difficulty in measuring budget hardness or softness), since transition began seems to indicate that hardening budget constraints is not simply a result of direct choice of action on a exogenous policy variable, i.e. all that is required is the political will of policy makers. Budget hardness is a result of (credible) changes in institutional design, i.e. SBCs are endogenous to specific institutions and hardening the budget constraint requires devising suitable institutional mechanisms (Roland 2000). It is evident that a hardening of the budget constraint is an important element of reform for transition countries (see Appendix 5). Furthermore, other components of reform, both microeconomic and macroeconomic policies, depend on, and indeed impinge upon, budget hardness. This implies the importance of what is generally referred to in the literature as the complementarity of reforms. For example, budget hardness is unlikely to emerge without the necessary legislative changes (e.g. bankruptcy and liquidation laws). Likewise, macroeconomic stability is unlikely to be achieved unless the budget constraint of enterprises (and, indeed, subnational governments) is hardened.

Actions undertaken to harden the budget constraint must, ultimately as with other market reforms, result in changes in enterprise behaviour. More specifically, firms must believe that there is no longer an expectation of a (persistent) bailout or refinancing of loss-making activities. Proof of evidence of a hard budget constraint regime in transition countries would include survival and exit rates of enterprises, number and size of bailouts, and numbers of bankruptcies and liquidations approaching levels common in more established market economies. As for some concluding remarks on the SBC, whereas the next element of reform, namely SME development and entrepreneurship, focuses on the creative part of creative destruction (capitalism's 'essential fact', according to Schumpeter) the SBC and the regime change to a HBC focuses on the destructive (i.e. demise of organisations) element of a capitalist market economy's creative destruction (Kornai 1998).

Entrepreneurship and SME development

It is widely recognised that a key element of enterprise reform in TEs is the development of an enterprise culture and the promotion of a SME sector comparable with levels in more established market economies. Yet, in the early years of transition, much of the focus – and indeed, policy advice – was on the privatisation and restructuring of the SOEs (not surprisingly, given that large state enterprises, in transition and non-transition countries alike, yield disproportionately political clout and public attention) and less on the development of a new private sector, comprising mainly *de novo* private firms. Kornai (2000a) in his *Ten Years after 'A Road to a Free Economy'* outlines these two different strategies. Interestingly, it was Kornai who, in the face of a near-total consensus in support of the privatisation strategy for Eastern Europe, advocated in favour of the strategy of organic development in preference to privatisation. Moreover, the evidence indicates that the different enterprise strategies adopted (privatisation versus new business formation) partly explains differences in performance between transition countries, and, most pertinently, between Russia and China.[20] For instance, McMillan and Woodruff (2002) claim 'the robust economic growth enjoyed by Poland and China is attributable in large part to the substantial entrepreneurial development they have experienced, while the economic stagnation Russia has endured during its transition has, as a root source, its record of relatively sluggish entrepreneurial development'.[21] Indeed, in emphasising the importance of entrepreneurs, the same authors argue that 'the success or failure of a transition economy can be traced in large part to the performance of its entrepreneurs' (McMillan and Woodruff 2002).

One of the features of the socialist system, and particularly in the Soviet sphere, was the large size of enterprises. SOEs tended to be very large, with few small and medium-sized enterprises in operation. This reflected the philosophy and preferences of the ruling Communist Party. Hence, at the outset of transition, TEs and most especially those in FSU countries lacked a SME sector. Once transition took off, SMEs began to emerge in TEs. However, in terms of the size and number of SMEs, there has been a significant variation across TEs (see Table 6.6).

While the SME sector is relatively large in some CEE countries (but still below, not surprisingly, levels found in the majority of the mature market economies of Western Europe), the sector remains relatively small and underdeveloped in some larger CIS countries.[22] Various different explanations have been given for this cross-country variation. It is argued that, unlike in CEE countries, some CIS countries have suffered from a lack of an entrepreneurial culture, have witnessed more years of communist rule (the 'burden of legacy' notion), are geographically located further from established market economies and trading centres (West or East) and have focused more on privatisation and less on small business formation. In supporting this claim, Frye and Shleifer (1997) illustrate, in terms of private firms and their relationship with the state, differences between Poland and Russia.[23] A mix of small private and privatised retail stores were surveyed in the mid-1990s in both Warsaw and Moscow. The results indicate that the regulatory and legal environment was a 'good deal more friendlier to business in Warsaw than in Moscow' (Frye and Shleifer 1997). This may partly explain the differences in small business development in Russia and Poland, and, in general, between FSU countries and CEE countries. In contrast, an earlier study finds that on the eve of transition, attitudes towards enterprise, business and profits in the Soviet Union were not that different to attitudes in the US (or, more precisely, Muscovites as compared

Table 6.6 Share of SME sector in GDP for TEs 2000/2001

Country	SME sector/GDP, %	Country	SME sector/GDP, %
CEB		Romania	55
Czech Republic	33.5	Serbia and Montenegro	46.6
Estonia	52		
Hungary	57	*CIS*	
Latvia	63.2	Armenia	30
Lithuania	32	Azerbaijan	38.6
Poland	49.4	Belarus	n.a.
Slovak Republic	46	Georgia[a]	24.4
Slovenia	56.6	Kazakhstan	n.a.
		Kyrgyzstan	42.7
SEE		Moldova	n.a.
Albania	75	Russia[b]	12
Bosnia and Herzegovina	36	Tajikistan	n.a.
Bulgaria	30	Turkmenistan	n.a.
Croatia	50	Ukraine	6.8
FYR Macedonia	42	Uzbekistan	31

Source: United Nations Economic Commission for Europe (UNECE) SME Databank (2003).

Notes
a. According to legislation in Georgia, self-employed persons are not included in the total number of employees in the economy – mostly 1.1 million people working in the agricultural sector.
b. Official data for incorporated SMEs with juridical personality, registered as legal entities.

to New Yorkers). Shiller *et al.* (1991) claim that although 'Soviets indeed display a somewhat less warm attitude toward business', results indicate that 'on the whole neither country lacks respects for businessmen'. On a specific question relating to profiteering and morals, the authors conclude that 'the Soviets are not dramatically more concerned with profiteering' (Shiller *et al.* 1991).

Notwithstanding the profit opportunities that existed in the early years of transition, the absence of market-supporting institutions has limited the growth of the new private sector. In the face of missing or imperfect institutions, privatised and new private firms adopted many different survival or coping strategies. These ranged from internal finance (as opposed to external sources of finance), barter and delayed payments (often, in preference to trade or bank credit) and reputational incentives, relational capital and private protection (in place of arm's-length transactions and court enforcement of contracts).

In transition, the state needs to reduce its involvement in the economy. However, as the state weakens, its ability to promote and foster small business formation is limited. Yet, even in the most mature market economies it is not uncommon for the state to support and develop, through various different channels, the small business sector. Partly as a result of this, the new private sector and SMEs in TEs are smaller in number than in non-transition market economies of similar levels of income per capita. Factors that prevent the development of a viable SME sector in TEs are the power of the incumbent (often a monopolist, with market power) to obstruct the entry of new firms, lack of sources of external finance and the absence of the rule of law, insecure property rights and an inadequate legislative and regulatory framework (see Box 6.2). In assessing the relative importance of the aforementioned market-supporting institutions (i.e. secure property rights and external finance/access to credit) as obstacles or constraints to entrepreneurship and investment, Johnson *et al.* (2002) conclude from a study of small *de novo* manufacturing firms in five TEs (Poland, Romania, Russia, the Slovak Republic and Ukraine) that 'weak property rights discourage firms from reinvesting their profits' while, in contrast, 'lack of collateral . . . does not appear to have been a binding constraint on firms' investment'.

Box 6.2

Doing business in transition economies

Since 2004, the World Bank has carried out an annual worldwide project of business regulation reform, called *Doing Business*. Its purpose is to produce a quantitative measure of regulations that reflect regulatory reforms aimed at improving the ease of doing business. The survey measures the regulatory environment for domestic small and medium-sized businesses, based on a country's performance in ten indicators (or topics) of business regulation. The topics covered are starting a business, dealing with construction permits, employing workers, registering property, getting credit, protecting investors, paying taxes, trading across borders, enforcing contracts and closing a business. Countries and regions are ranked accordingly, with the rankings on the ease of doing business an average of the ten indicators covered, weighted equally. A high ranking indicates that the regulatory environment is conducive to the operation of business. The rankings do not reflect other aspects of the business environment, including macroeconomic stability, the financial system or the skills of the workforce. The actual data are based on domestic laws and regulations, as well as administrative requirements. According to the *Doing Business 2010* report, covering the period June 2008 to May 2009, the average rank for the CEE/FSU transition countries of the Eastern Europe and Central Asian region (includes Kosovo and Turkey) was 71. This compares to an average rank of 30 for the OECD high-income region (includes Hungary, the Czech and Slovak Republics, as they were reclassified in 2008), 83 for the East Asian and Pacific region (includes China, Mongolia and Vietnam), 92 for the Middle East and North African region, 95 for the Latin America and Caribbean region, 118 for the South Asian region and 139 for the Sub-Saharan region.[24] In terms of individual transition country rankings (out of a total of 183 countries), the majority (23 of 30 countries) of TEs are placed between 24th and 94th place, with only Georgia (11th), Croatia (103rd), Bosnia and Herzegovina (116th), Russia (120th), Ukraine (142th), Uzbekistan (150th) and Tajikistan (152nd) outside this range. Turkmenistan was not included in the survey. Of the top ten reformers in 2008/2009, five were transition countries, namely Belarus, FYR Macedonia, Kyrgyzstan, Moldova and Tajikistan. The world's top business regulation reformer in 2007/2008 was Azerbaijan. Moreover, (transition) countries comprising the Eastern Europe and Central Asia region were the most active reformers for the six years up until 2009, surpassing all other (six) regions.

Source: www.doingbusiness.org.

Other obstacles to private business growth include the following.

Tax system

For a vibrant, flexible, small business sector to develop, it is important that the tax system within which the sector operates does not act as an obstacle. In market economies, tax systems tend to favour small businesses by offering tax breaks either in the form of low tax rates, rebates, allowances or other forms of assistance. In some TEs, the reverse has often been the case. As for the tax system itself, tax rates in the early years of transition tended to be high, there were a plethora of different taxes to be paid and, often, it was the case that the normal allowances applicable to small firms in other countries did not apply in transition countries. In addition, tax administration procedures were often complicated and costly.

Bureaucracy and corruption

It is widely known and recognised that many TEs suffer from high levels of bureaucracy and corruption. With respect to the small business sector, state intervention is often excessive and costly. The legislative and bureaucratic environment hinders small business development. The form of this intervention varies, from the burdensome registration and certification requirements and the excessive number of license regulations to the frequent and arbitrary nature of inspections by tax, fire and safety officials who often use their position to extract bribes from businesses. As the state in Russia and in other former Soviet republics continued to weaken throughout the 1990s in terms of the provision of basic public services, the gap was often filled by the private sector and, within that, the private protection organisations. In return for regular payments, these competing groups would offer certain services to businesses, ranging from debt collection and contract enforcement to security protection.

As discussed in Chapter 2, possible causes of corruption in transition countries include the socialist and post-socialist legacy, low levels of economic development and the limited exposure to democracy and the rule of law. This combination of excessive bureaucracy and corruption contributed to a rise in the cost of business for the small business sector. The result has often been the demise of many small businesses or, in many other cases, the decision of many firms to go underground.

Banking system

In a mature market economy, banks act as financial intermediaries, channelling funds from lenders to borrowers. For start-up businesses and new private firms, the banking sector is an important source of finance. This is particularly true when alternate sources, such as venture capital and equity shares, are not fully developed. In transition, there are many problems with the banking system. With respect to the small business sector and lending, banks have often tended to ignore small firms. Although thousands of banks emerged in the early years of transition, many (particularly in Russia and some other CIS countries) tended not to engage in the normal banking activities of saving and lending but rather, in many cases, acted as clearing houses for large enterprises or engaged in non-lending activities (e.g. foreign exchange speculation). When banks have engaged in lending activities in the past, it has often either been to the government or to large state-owned enterprises rather than to new, small, private firms. In the past, collateral or guarantee requirements have tended to be excessive, interest rates have been high and volatile, and the public's confidence and trust in banks has been low (for reasons that are well documented). For small firms and individual entrepreneurs operating in CIS countries, family and friends, as opposed to the banking sector, were, often, a more realistic source of finance.

Economic conditions and macroeconomic instability

Favourable economic conditions are considered necessary for self-employment and the small business sector to develop. Unfortunately, less than a favourable market environment tended to be the case in the first decade of transition. For example, it is estimated that after the first ten years of transition in Russia, the level of real GDP was only 63 (1989 = 100). It is difficult for firms to operate, let alone take investment decisions, in an environment where real wages are falling, unemployment is rising and domestic demand is stagnant. For most of the first decade (more below on the recovery in Russia), CIS countries, including Russia, were either in a (transitional) recession or, in the few cases when economic growth was recorded, it was often export-led growth, arising from high oil prices (and, in the Russian case, a rouble devaluation) that was primarily responsible. In such circumstances, it is difficult to imagine how a new emerging small business sector can develop, let alone flourish.

In summing up, Berkowitz and DeJong (2005) write:

> In many post-socialist cities, entrepreneurs have thrived although their plants and equipment have been poorly protected; their contracts have been poorly enforced; their taxes have been high and the regulations they face have been burdensome; they have routinely been forced to make extra-legal payments to local mafias and government organs for protection; and they have limited sources of external finance.

In 1999, the EBRD, in collaboration with the World Bank, conducted a large cross-country survey of firms, called the Business Environment and Enterprise Performance survey (BEEPS). Survey updates were carried out in 2002 and 2005. Of the circa 9,100 firms that were surveyed in 26 countries, 90 per cent of the firms were SMEs, with 70 per cent defined as small (2 to 49 employees). As for ownership, there was a mix of privatised and new private firms. The survey uses seven indicators of the business environment, namely business regulation, labour, taxation, institutions and property rights, infrastructure, finance and the macroeconomic environment. Firms were asked to rate, from a low of one (minor obstacle) to a high of four (major obstacle) how problematic these factors or constraints were for the operation and growth of their business. Of those seven, the EBRD (2005) report concludes that, following 15 years of transition, the biggest obstacles to doing business are 'the costs of business regulation, poor-quality institutions, weak property rights and macroeconomic instability'. In the same report, there is evidence that of all the business constraints, it is access to finance that constrains smaller firms as compared to larger firms. The report states that small or micro firms (employing fewer than 50 people) were more constrained than others (medium and large) in access to, and the cost of, finance.

As for a comparison with market economies the report indicates that 'Smaller firms in mature market economies do not face financial constraints to the same extent as those in transition countries. This implies that financial systems in transition countries are still facing problems in identifying and lending to creditworthy smaller firms.' In supporting the earlier claim for greater state supports to small business formation and growth, the report argues that:

> Evidence of the difficulties that SMEs face in access to finance in transition countries indicate the need for supportive measures, including SME credit lines, the establishment of specialised micro-credit institutions and technical assistance for the financial sector with the explicit aim of increasing lending to SMEs.
>
> (EBRD 2005)

This completes our discussion on the various elements of enterprise restructuring. In the context of these reforms, we now examine the empirical literature on the determinants of enterprise restructuring and performance.

Determinants of enterprise restructuring and performance

Within the first few years of transition, there were indications of large-scale variation in enterprise restructuring and performance. While some enterprises managed to successfully restructure and compete internationally, others managed to stay afloat (despite being in distress) only with assistance from the state, while others folded. As Djankov and Murrell (2002) remarked, 'the revolutionary changes in transition countries have been matched by great variation in the degree to which enterprises have responded successfully to events'. One of the important issues in transition (and, of course, non-transition countries alike), and, particularly, in microeconomic reform, is these variations in enterprise restructuring and performance.

The broad purpose of the empirical literature is to determine what policies are required to encourage restructuring and improve enterprise performance. In the large volume of empirical studies carried out on enterprise reform, enterprise restructuring and performance is treated as the dependent variable. In turn, the dependent variable may be in a qualitative (measurement using words) or quantitative (measurement using numbers) form. Quantitative indicators are based on actual accounting or stock market information and measure firm performance or restructuring. It includes such variables as profits, productivity or sales (with no consensus in the literature on which variable is the better measure). In contrast, qualitative variables tend to be softer, and are usually derived from survey responses to managers on performance and restructuring. These might include a forecast of profits or a change in organisational structure or plant size, or a broader rate of restructuring indicator.

Building upon earlier work from Western economies on firm performance and its determinants (see Bevan *et al.* 1999), the literature has identified a number of determinants, including ownership structure and privatisation, market structure and competition, financial discipline and a hardening of the budget constraint, corporate governance, and the business environment. The relationship, in equation form, might resemble the following:

> Enterprise Restructuring and Performance = f (ownership and privatisation; product market competition; corporate governance; access to finance/financial constraints, hardened budget constraints; enabling business environment and entrepreneurship).

Put another way, enterprise restructuring and performance is a function of, or depends upon, a number of factors or reforms, including ownership and privatisation, market competition, corporate governance, the business environment, and entrepreneurship. Using enterprise-level survey data, statistical and econometric techniques (such as regression analysis) are employed to determine the independent effects of these explanatory variables, controlling for firm characteristics such as the size of enterprises, the economic sector of operation and the region or country in which the firm is located. These are the so-called control variables and they are included because economic performance and restructuring are also likely to be influenced by the size of the firm, the sector in which it operates, and the region or country in which it is located. The purpose of the statistical exercise is to try to disentangle the explanatory variables effects from the firm-specific effects so as to arrive at accurate estimates that measure, if possible, the separate effects of these independent variables.

In the literature, the explanatory variables are measured, or proxied, in different ways. For a change in ownership and privatisation, the degree (in percentage terms) of private ownership is often used. In the case of ownership types, a distinction is usually made between state, insiders, outsiders and foreigners. As for market competition, the import penetration ratio is often used to capture competition from imports and foreign trade whereas various different measures are used to proxy domestic competition. With respect to corporate governance, the composition of the board, and board control, is often employed: dummy variables for bonuses and managerial turnover have been used to specifically capture the role of managers. More qualitative measures have been employed to capture the soft budget constraint and the enabling business environment. Legal indicators are often used to measure (formal) institutions.

In trying to isolate the effects of these explanatory variables, a number of methodological problems emerge. First, there are problems with accounting information. Accounting and tax rules, and their reporting, differ from country to country, and do not necessarily conform to international standards. The caveats that usually apply, with respect to data availability, consistency and reliability, apply even more for transition countries given the enormous changes and upheaval that they were subject to at the outset of transition. Of course, in the earlier studies, data were only for the first couple of years, capturing short-run effects but unable to reflect the medium- and long-run effects. Another problem in the early years was that some studies worked with unrepresentative samples of firms. As transition progressed and enterprise-level data became more available, this was less of a problem.

Establishing the direction of causality is not straightforward, as there are problems of endogeneity and selection effects. For example, in examining the relationship between performance and ownership change, improved performance in privatised firms may simply reflect that it is often the better firms that are divested first by governments anxious to make privatisation 'look good'. If there is two-way causality between performance and these explanatory variables, the estimated effects of these variables on performance that the econometrics techniques produce can be severely biased and unreliable. This so-called selection bias can be dealt with through the use of instrumental variables and other approaches. Another issue is that there may be joint effects, i.e. two or more explanatory variables may together affect performance. If so, we say that the variables in question are complementary. We have discussed complementarity of reforms before, both in this chapter and in previous chapters.

To assess the evidence of the factors determining enterprise restructuring and performance in transition countries we use two different sources. BEEPS is an enterprise-level survey conducted by the EBRD and World Bank for over 25 transition countries in the years 1999, 2002 and 2005. EBRD (2005) uses the three BEEPS rounds covering the period 1999 to 2005 to analyse the factors explaining how firms performed. Using the literature on the determinants of enterprise performance, it identifies a number of factors affecting overall performance. These are ownership, competition, export market, business constraints and the business environment. More details on the BEEPS are given below. The second (Djankov and Murrell 2002) is an analysis of over 100 studies examining the determinants of enterprise performance and restructuring. Here the authors employ a meta-analysis to synthesise results across the various empirical papers selected on the basis of sound methodologies adopted and the quality of the empirical evidence.[25] The determinants identified in this survey are ownership, competition, the role of managers (an indicator of corporate governance),[26] hardened budget constraints and institutions. The main findings for both studies are included in Table 6.8.[27]

Business Environment and Enterprise Performance Survey (BEEPS)

The BEEPS is a large survey conducted by the EBRD and the World Bank covering thousands of firms in the former socialist countries and carried out in 1999 (over 3,000 firms in 25 TEs), 2002 (over 6,100 firms in 26 TEs) and 2005 (over 9,000 firms in 26 TEs). The purpose of the survey is to 'investigate the extent to which government policies and practices facilitate or impede business activity and investment in central and eastern Europe and the Commonwealth of the Independent States' (Fries *et al.* 2003). Given the focus on the business environment (that is, the interaction between state and firms), certain types of firms were excluded from the study: large enterprises employing 10,000 or more workers; firms that started operation after 1999; utility companies and banks as these tend to be subject to government regulation and supervision, and agricultural enterprises (farms). A classification of firms that did participate in the study and are included in the dataset is given in Table 6.7.

The distribution between manufacturing industry and services was determined by their relative share to GDP in each country. Foreign-owned firms (defined as having a foreign stake of at least 50 per cent) and state-owned firms (defined as the state owning more

Table 6.7 Characteristics of firms in BEEPS

Characteristics	Percentage
Sector	
Manufacturing	39
Services	61
Firm size (number of employees)	
Small (2–49)	70
Medium (50–249)	20
Large (250–9,999)	10
Ownership	
New private	16
Privatised	75
State-owned	9
Foreign-owned	10
Location	
Capital	32
Large cities (excluding the capital)	21
Small cities	23
Rural areas	24

Source: EBRD Transition Report (2005).

Table 6.8 Evidence on the determinants of enterprise restructuring and performance in TEs

BEEPS (2005)	*Djankov and Murrell (2002)*
Ownership	*Ownership*
The effect of ownership on performance broadly confirms findings from previous studies but with some important qualifications. Foreign-owned firms perform better than domestic firms, but the difference is not increasing. There is little variation in the performance of domestically owned firms, indicating that the privatisation of state-owned firms to domestic owners has not necessarily brought about the expected efficiency gains. New private firms perform better than privatised firms, as shown in research elsewhere on transition countries.	Privatisation is strongly associated with more enterprise restructuring. With respect to the different types of owners, the most effective privatisation, in terms of restructuring, is privatisation to foreign investors whereas the least effective, aside from the traditional state-owned firms, is privatisation to dispersed individual owners. Outsider privatisation is associated with 50 per cent more restructuring than insider privatisation.
Competition	*Competition*
Results indicate that competition generally exerts a positive impact on a firm's performance. The presence of competing producers has helped to improve performance but has had less effect on the level of efficiency, with differences evident across the three regions (CEB, SEE, CIS).	Product market competition has a significant effect in improving enterprise restructuring. In terms of regional differences, import competition is the primary source of improvement in Eastern Europe whereas if there is a beneficial effect in CIS countries it comes from domestic competition (through new private firms or demonopolisation). Overall, competition has a stronger effect in explaining enterprise restructuring in Eastern Europe than in the CIS.
Export market	*Hardening the budget constraint*
When ownership and other factors are taken into account, exporting has a positive impact on the change in a firm's performance. Again, regional differences exist.	There is evidence that a hardening of the budget constraint is effective in promoting enterprise restructuring. However, there is a regional difference. Whereas the beneficial effect of hardening the budget constraint is significant in Eastern Europe, the effects of hard budgets in CIS countries are often insignificant.
Business constraints	*Role of managers*
Results indicate that the identified business constraints (access to finance, infrastructure, macroeconomic instability, corruption, business licensing) faced by individual firms do not have a significant impact on a firm's level of efficiency or improvements in efficiency. Interestingly, corruption, in the form of bribes, which is generally known to have a negative effect on the economy as a whole, has a positive impact on the performance of individual firms, i.e. firms that bribe tend to have a better level of performance (either because firms that bribe gain an advantage over others, or that government officials tend to target better performing firms).	In examining the role of managers and, in particular, the difference between managerial turnover as opposed to managerial incentives, in determining more restructuring, it is management turnover (that is, new human capital) that is associated with improved restructuring. The strengthening of managerial incentives, on its own, is not associated with more restructuring, according to the findings.

(Continued)

Table 6.8 Continued

Business environment	Institutions
A country's business environment has a significant impact on a firm's performance.	The findings here are quite limited due to the relatively small amount of enterprise-level evidence on the relationship between institutional reforms and improved enterprise restructuring. As a result, there is no general conclusion on the effect of institutions on restructuring. More research is needed to identify, *inter alia*, the nature and type of institutions that are conducive to greater restructuring.

than 50 per cent) each account for approximately 10 per cent of the total sample. Although all three ownership groups (state, privatised, private) are represented, and, indeed, all three size categories (small, medium, large) are included in the sample, the majority of those surveyed are small privatised or private firms that are majority owned by domestic investors. The sample of firms included is meant to be broadly representative of the population of firms, according to their sector, size and geographical location within each country. For the sampled firms included, there are both quantitative and qualitative indicators. The TEs excluded from the study are Turkmenistan, China and Vietnam. For analytical purposes, the remaining 26 countries are classified into three regional categories: CEB, SEE and CIS.

In summary, the EBRD (2005) concluded that from the BEEPS evidence, and while acknowledging that the impact of ownership on performance is not as clear-cut as was widely assumed, 'foreign-owned and new private firms tend to be more efficient than privatised and state-owned enterprises.' This difference in performance has remained constant over time.' Djankov and Murrell (2002) concluded that:

> transition policies have had similar effects on the restructuring process in CIS and non-CIS countries in terms of direction, but not in terms of economic or statistical significance. In particular, privatisation, hardened budget constraints, and product market competition all appear to be important determinants of enterprise restructuring in non-CIS countries, while they are much less effective in the CIS.[28]

As we witness the third decade of transition, research in respect of enterprise reform, restructuring and performance will turn to, *inter alia*, a comparison between transition and non-transition countries with respect to how different (or similar) firm performance is, the determinants of firm performance, and the relations between state and firms, i.e. the business environment.

Summary

1   SOEs and firms in market economies are very different production units. Whereas firms in market economies are autonomous decision-making units, state-owned enterprises were part of a hierarchical bureaucratic structure comprising central planners, ministries and

enterprises. SOEs, whose aim was to fulfil the plan (in the form of output targets rather than profits), were notoriously large, faced little or no domestic or foreign competition (as entry and exit was rare) and were responsible for the provision of social services. They were managed by a one-person director and, as vertically integrated enterprises, were engaged in various different stages of production. Although SOEs were subject to reforms pre-transition (primarily in the form of more autonomy), the enterprise sector at the outset of transition faced enormous challenges, including restructuring, demonopolisation and greater competition, and ownership and corporate governance changes.

2   The primary objective of enterprise restructuring is greater efficiency and improved enterprise performance. Defensive restructuring involves short-term changes and comprises cost-reducing activities whose aim is the immediate survival of the enterprise. Strategic restructuring involves long-term changes and revenue-enhancing activities whose aim is the development of a business strategy that is suitable to the competitive market environment. The elements of enterprise restructuring include a change in ownership (privatisation), a hardening of the budget constraint, greater product competition, proper corporate governance mechanisms and supports for a new private sector comprising SMEs.

3   In the empirical studies, enterprise restructuring and performance is the dependent variable. The explanatory variables are ownership structure and privatisation, product market competition, corporate governance, business environment, legal and institutional framework. The conclusions from the literature indicate that ownership *and* institutions matter, reform complementarities exist, and that enterprise reforms with respect to competition policy, hardened budget constraints and SME supports are incomplete. There is also evidence of differences between CIS and CEE countries in terms of enterprise reform and firm performance outcomes.

Key terms

Asymmetric information	Outsider privatisation
Competition policy	Ownership structure
Concentrated ownership	Principal–agent problem
Corporate governance	Privatisation
Defensive restructuring	Ratchet effect
Demonopolisation	Reform complementarities
Dispersed ownership	Restructuring
Enterprise reform	SMEs
Entrepreneurship	Soft budget constraint
Insider privatisation	State-owned enterprise
Mass privatisation	Strategic restructuring
Monotowns	

Review questions

1   Explain the key differences between the enterprise sector as existed in the pre-transition era and the enterprise sector as it currently exists, post-transition. What are the main differences between the SOE as existed in the socialist system and the firm as found in market economies?

2   What is meant by enterprise restructuring? Explain the two types of restructuring as identified in the transition literature. In Table 6.1, identify the restructuring activities as one or other of these two broad forms of restructuring.

3   What are the main determinants of enterprise restructuring and performance in transition countries? What does the literature suggest about the relative importance of these determinants? With respect to ownership change and privatisation, what can we learn from the privatisation experience during transition?

7

PERFORMANCE AND TRANSITION OUTCOMES

We begin this chapter with an account of the performance of former socialist countries during the transition era. The indicators reported here to measure performance are output and price changes (that is, economic growth and inflation rates), unemployment rates and life expectancy at birth rates. We then proceed to examine the output collapse of the 1990s and report on the various theoretical explanations put forward, ex post, to explain the fall in output. We conclude the chapter by reporting on the cross-country variation in economic performance (as measured by economic growth) and present the results of the empirical research on the determinants of economic performance in transition countries. As with variations in enterprise performance, various factors explain cross-country growth and performance differences, and these will be explained in detail in this final section.

There are a number of issues relating to the economic performance of TEs. First, there are data problems, particularly in the first few years of transition when the capacity of national statistical offices to produce reliable, regular and comparable data was limited. Despite technical support from international institutions, the statistical offices of the transition countries were initially ill-equipped to handle the data demands of a market economy, and, in particular, attempts to record the economic activity generated from the large numbers of new (predominately micro or small) private firms. This problem has been more or less resolved with the passage of time. Second, there are a wide range of indicators that can be used to measure the economic performance of transition countries. Some of the most appropriate indicators include GDP growth rates and income per capita, inflation and unemployment rates, consumption levels and investment rates, poverty and income distribution (inequality) levels, population changes and life expectancy rates. We will report on a selection of these indicators for the former socialist countries that embarked on transition.

Third, one of transition's stylised (and surprising) facts is the decline in output that was recorded in CEE and FSU countries (but not China or Vietnam) for much of the first half of the 1990s. Various theories have been given to explain the collapse in GDP, ranging from systemic reasons to policy errors. A brief explanation of the most important theories will be given here. Fourth, irrespective of what indicator is used to measure performance during transition, significant cross-country differences have emerged; some expected (the relatively good performance of Hungary and Slovenia and the relatively bad performance of Ukraine and Tajikistan) and some unexpected (the relatively good performance of the three Baltic States and the relatively poor performance of Bulgaria and Romania). Explanations for these variations in output growth are briefly outlined.

Finally, despite the hardship and poor performance of many countries during transition, there is a need to recognise and acknowledge the fundamental changes that have taken place since transition began. These economies, once characterised by the trinity of collectivisation, nationalisation and industrialisation, are now, more or less, characterised by market-based, private sector activities, market-determined prices, a sizeable and growing services and SME sector, foreign trade activities and integration with the rest of the world. This is a considerable achievement in such a short space of time. However, despite these changes in the economic system, and the recovery in economic growth that eventually followed, there is also a need to accept that in many CIS countries the standard of living and well-being of many of its citizens did not improve in the first decade or so of transition. Accordingly, one 2004 UN *Economic Survey of Europe* report concluded, 'in many cases the ultimate objective of transition – improving the lives of ordinary people – appears to have taken second place to the imperative of economic growth'.[2] We will address these issues in the following sections.

Performance and transition countries

Output

The output fall that in some former socialist countries (including the Soviet Union, according to many estimates) preceded the transition from plan to market did not end with the demise of the socialist system. Indeed, and contrary to most expectations, all former socialist countries, with the exceptions of China and Vietnam, suffered an initial decline in output. This fall in output, often recognised as one of transition's stylised facts, is one of the great surprises in the transition from plan to market (see section on 'Output' in Chapter 2). In his widely acclaimed book on the European economy since 1945, Barry Eichengreen, when describing the recession and adjustment following the collapse of central planning, remarks, 'This was not the measured adjustment anticipated by the apostles of the market economy' (Eichengreen 2007).[3]

Although there were cross-country differences in the output collapse (as is evident in Table 7.1), both in terms of duration and intensity, we can report that for most CEE countries, the output decline was quickly followed by a recovery in output (although there were some setbacks, most notably in Albania, Bulgaria, the Czech Republic and Romania). A decline in output followed by a recovery was also the pattern of output for the Baltic States: although Estonia, Latvia and Lithuania were part of the Soviet Union their performance since transition began more resembles the experience of CEE countries than that of the former Soviet republics. Unfortunately, the Baltic countries were badly affected by the 2007 to 2009 global economic and financial crisis, and this is reflected in negative growth rates in 2008 for both Estonia and Latvia. In contrast, the CIS countries experienced a much greater decline in output. Some of the CIS countries witnessed almost a decade of decline, with the cumulative fall in output often in excess of 50 per cent of initial GDP. However, even within this group of countries, the decline was *eventually* succeeded by a recovery, and in many cases an economic boom, although it must be said that these increases in output recorded were coming from very low bases, and, further, were often related to high commodity, oil and gas prices (see later section in this chapter on the output collapse).

Another measure of output performance is income per capita. Table 7.2 reports GDP per capita (in constant prices, in US$) at five-year intervals.

Again, the decline that was reported in the GDP growth data is evident here. For countries where we have complete data, and aside from China and Vietnam, Poland is the only country

Table 7.1 GDP growth (real change, in %) at PPP prices[a, b]

Country	1991	1992	1993	1994	1995	1996	1997	1998	1999	2000	2001	2002	2003	2004	2005	2006	2007	2008
Albania	−28	−7.2	9.6	8.3	13.3	9.1	−10.8	9	13.5	6.7	7.9	4.2	5.8	5.7	5.8	5.5	6	6.8
Armenia	−11.7	−41.8	−8.8	5.4	6.9	5.9	3.3	7.3	3.3	5.9	9.6	15	14	10.5	13.9	13.2	13.8	6.8
Azerbaijan	−0.7	−22.6	−23.1	−19.7	−11.8	1.3	5.8	10	7.4	11.1	9.9	10.6	11.2	10.2	26.4	34.5	25.1	10.8
Belarus	−1.4	−9.6	−7.6	−11.7	−10.4	2.8	11.4	8.4	3.4	5.8	4.7	5	7	11.4	9.4	10	8.6	10
Bosnia and Herzegovina						54.2	36.6	16.6	9.5	5.4	4.3	5.3	4.4	6.3	3.9	6.9	6.6	5.4
Bulgaria	−8.4	−7.3	−1.5	1.8	2.9	−9.4	−5.6	4	2.3	5.4	4.1	4.5	5	6.6	6.2	6.3	6.2	6
China	9.2	14.2	14	13.1	10.9	10	9.3	7.8	7.6	8.4	8.3	9.1	10	10.1	10.4	11.6	13	9
Croatia	−21.1	−11.7	−8	5.9	6.8	5.9	6.8	2.5	−0.9	2.9	4.4	5.6	5.3	4.3	4.3	4.8	5.5	2.5
Czech Republic	−11.6	−0.5	0.1	2.2	5.9	4	−0.7	−0.8	1.3	3.6	2.5	1.9	3.6	4.5	6.3	6.8	6	3
Estonia	−10	−14.1	−8.5	−1.6	4.5	4.4	11.1	4.4	0.3	7.9	7.7	7.8	7.1	7.5	9.2	10.4	6.3	−3.6
FYR Macedonia	−6.2	−6.6	−7.5	−1.8	−1.1	1.2	1.4	3.4	4.3	4.5	−4.5	0.9	2.8	4.1	4.1	4	5.9	4.9
Georgia	−21.1	−44.9	−29.3	−10.4	2.6	11.3	10.5	3	2.9	1.8	4.8	5.5	11.1	5.9	9.6	9.4	12.3	2.1
Hungary	−11.9	−3.1	−0.6	2.9	1.5	1.3	4.6	4.9	4.2	5.2	4.1	4.1	4.2	4.8	4	4.1	1.2	0.6
Kazakhstan	−11	−5.3	−9.2	−12.6	−8.2	0.5	1.7	−1.9	2.7	9.8	13.5	9.8	9.3	9.6	9.7	10.7	8.9	3.3
Kyrgyzstan	−7.9	−13.8	−15.5	−20.1	−5.4	7.1	9.9	2.1	3.7	5.4	5.3	0	7	7	−0.2	3.1	8.5	7.6
Latvia	−12.6	−32.1	−11.4	2.2	−0.9	3.8	8.3	4.7	3.3	8.4	8	6.5	7.2	8.7	10.6	11.9	10	−4.6
Lithuania	−5.7	−21.3	−16.2	−9.8	5.2	5.1	8.5	7.5	−1.5	4.2	6.7	6.9	10.2	7.4	7.8	7.8	8.9	3
Moldova	−17.5	−29	−1.2	−30.9	−1.4	−5.9	1.6	−6.5	−3.4	2.1	6.1	7.8	6.6	7.4	7.5	4.8	3	7.2
Mongolia	−9.2	−9.5	−3	2.3	6.3	2.4	4	3.5	3.2	1.1	3	4.7	7	10.6	7.3	8.6	10	8.9
Montenegro											1.1	1.9	2.5	4.4	4.2	8.6	10.7	7.5
Poland	−7	2.5	3.7	5.3	7	6.2	7.1	5	4.5	4.3	1.2	1.4	3.9	5.3	3.6	6.2	6.6	5
Romania	−12.8	−8.7	1.6	4	7.2	4	−6	−4.7	−1.1	2.2	5.8	5.2	5.3	8.5	4.2	7.9	6.2	7.1
Russia	−5	−14.5	−8.7	−12.7	−4.1	−3.6	1.4	−5.3	6.4	10	5.1	4.7	7.3	7.2	6.4	7.7	8.1	5.6
Serbia								0.7	−11.2	5.3	5.6	3.9	2.4	8.3	5.6	5.2	6.9	5.4
Slovak Republic	−14.6	−6.5	−3.7	6.2	5.8	6.9	5.7	3.7	0.3	0.7	3.4	4.8	4.7	5.2	6.5	8.5	10.4	6.4
Slovenia	−8.9	−5.5	2.8	5.3	4.1	3.6	4.9	3.6	5.3	4.1	2.8	4	2.8	4.3	4.3	5.9	6.8	3.5
Tajikistan	−8.2	−32.1	−16.3	−21.3	−6	−22.5	1.7	5.3	3.7	8.3	9.6	10.8	11.1	10.3	6.7	6.6	7.7	7.9
Turkmenistan	−4.7	−15	−10	−17.3	−7.2	−6.7	−11.4	7.1	16.5	5.5	4.3	0.3	3.3	4.5	13	11.4	11.6	9.8
Ukraine	−8.7	−9.9	−14.2	−22.9	−12.2	−10	−3	−1.9	−0.2	5.9	9.2	5.2	9.6	12.1	2.7	7.1	8.9	2.1
Uzbekistan	−0.5	−11.1	−2.3	−5.2	−0.9	1.7	5.2	4.4	4.4	4	4.5	4.2	4.4	7.7	7	7.3	9.5	9
Vietnam	6	8.6	8.1	8.8	9.5	9.3	8.2	5.8	4.8	6.8	6.9	7.1	7.3	7.8	8.4	8.2	8.5	6.2

Sources: United Nations Economic Commission for Europe (UNECE) Statistical Division Database, compiled from national and international (CIS, EUROSTAT, IMF, OECD) official sources; United Nations Economic and Social Commission for Asia and the Pacific (ESCAP).

Notes

a. Constant price estimates are based on data complied by the National Statistical Offices, and scaled to the current price value of 2005.
b. Common currency (US$) estimates are computed using Purchasing Power Parities (PPP) which are the rates of currency conversion that equalise the purchasing power of different currencies.

Table 7.2 GDP per capita (in US$)[a, b]

Country	1990	1995	2000	2005
Albania	3323	3118	4094	5320
Armenia	..	1663	2157	3903
Azerbaijan	..	1888	2534	4573
Belarus	6450	4200	5816	8541
Bosnia and Herzegovina	..	..	4348	5392
Bulgaria	7612	7012	6979	9353
China[c]	1626	2731	3940	6014
Croatia	11367	8430	10469	13370
Czech Republic	16231	15513	16794	20254
Estonia	10163	8019	11092	16477
FYR Macedonia	7577	6188	6933	7382
Georgia	5420	1759	2502	3610
Hungary	12421	11165	13735	16970
Kazakhstan	7096	4497	5405	8699
Kyrgyzstan	2524	1232	1510	1737
Latvia	10988	6265	8651	13218
Lithuania	12141	7304	9531	14219
Moldova	3974	1893	1657	2362
Mongolia[c, d]	1768	1419	1523	1899
Montenegro	..	..	6601	7959
Poland	8054	8932	11632	13573
Romania	7757	7160	6916	9376
Russia	12686	7854	8606	11864
Serbia	..	..	6302	8357
Slovak Republic	..	10699	12585	16038
Slovenia	..	15914	19654	23379
Tajikistan	3203	1121	985	1413
Turkmenistan	..	..	..	..
Ukraine	8108	3920	3706	5605
Uzbekistan[e]	4204	3171	3543	..
Vietnam[c]	1153	1551	2040	2737
OECD Countries				
Denmark	25710			33544
Germany	24964			30476
Greece	17889			25348
Ireland	17266			38216
Italy	23553			27853
Japan[c]	23289			27345
Portugal	15230			19983
Spain	19616			27281
Turkey	7277			10242
United Kingdom	23280			32055
United States	32135			41913

Sources: United Nations Economic Commission for Europe (UNECE) Statistical Division Database, compiled from national and international (CIS, EUROSTAT, IMF, OECD) official sources; United Nations Economic and Social Commission for Asia and the Pacific (ESCAP).

Notes
a. Constant price estimates are based on data complied by the National Statistical Offices, and scaled to the current price value of 2005.
b. Common currency (US$) estimates are computed using Purchasing Power Parities (PPP) which are the rates of currency conversion that equalise the purchasing power of different currencies.
c. UN ESCAP, in constant 2000 prices.
d. 1996 figure as 1995 figure is unavailable.
e. Penn World Table Version 6.2, University of Pennsylvania.

where GDP per capita in 1995 exceeded GDP per capita in 1990. Whereas the recovery in output meant that later GDP per capita figures show an increase for many countries, there are still a large number of transition economies where GDP per capita in 2000 was still less than it was at the outset of transition (for example, Bulgaria, Croatia, FYR Macedonia, Romania, CIS countries). Indeed, of the eight CIS countries where we have a full set of data, GDP per capita in 2005 for six of these countries (namely Georgia, Kyrgyzstan, Moldova, Russia, Tajikistan and Ukraine) was less – despite falling population numbers in all but Kyrgyzstan and Tajikistan – than GDP per capita at the beginning of transition. Further, the variation in GDP per capita evident at the outset of transition, from a low of $1,153 in Vietnam to a high of $16,231 in Czechoslovakia, was still as, if not more, sharp 15 years into transition. In 2005, GDP per capita varies from lows of $1,413, $1,737 and $1,899 in Tajikistan, Kyrgyzstan and Mongolia respectively to highs of $16,970, $20,254 and $23,379 in Hungary, the Czech Republic and Slovenia respectively. The observation that the dominant pattern in transition outcomes – both economic and political – has been one not of similarity but of variation has been made elsewhere (see Bunce 1999; Campos and Fidrmuc 2003).[4]

Given this poor overall performance, the income gap between transition countries and advanced market economies (East and West as it was commonly referred to) remains large. Table 7.2 also reports GDP per capita, in 1990 and 2005, for a sample of OECD countries. Given the favourable economic climate that advanced OECD countries experienced throughout most of this 15-year period, and compared with the disappointing and uneven performance of transition countries in this same period, it is not surprising to see the large income gap between transition and advanced OECD countries in 2005. All indications are that it will take decades, rather than years, for this gap to close, if at all.

Inflation

As with output, the record on inflation in TEs, given in Table 7.3, took the majority of the economics profession by surprise.

Given the administrative price controls of the centrally planned system (where prices for many goods were kept artificially low), it was expected that price liberalisation would initially result in a general rise in prices. Predictions were that this one-off increase in prices would be offset, and possibly within a short period of time, by new supplies from the 'liberated' private sector, thus dampening down further price increases. However, in most cases, this rise in prices was followed by successive increases in price levels, leading to hyperinflation (usually defined as a monthly inflation rate of at least 50 per cent) in many countries, and especially, the war-torn Balkans and Caucasus States. Annual inflation rates in excess of 100 per cent, and in some cases in excess of 1,000 per cent, were not uncommon in FSU countries. Explanations varied from monopoly pricing to lax monetary policy and excessive initial devaluations to large fiscal deficits financed by monetary means. In the case of FSU republics, individual countries remained members of the rouble zone even after the breakup of the Soviet Union, and thus availed themselves of extending new credits to enterprises in their respective countries, at the cost of higher inflation across the region.[5] Economic disruption caused by war and civil strife was also a contributing factor in explaining high inflation in many of the FSU republics, and the Balkans.

In the majority of cases, almost a decade passed before inflation rates fell to reasonable levels. This reduction in inflation coincided with more austere (and/or stricter adherence to)

Table 7.3 Inflation (change in annual average consumer price level, in %)

Country	1991	1992	1993	1994	1995	1996	1997	1998	1999	2000	2001	2002	2003	2004	2005	2006	2007	2008
Albania	35.5	226	85	22.6	7.8	12.7	33.2	20.6	0.4	0	3.1	5.5	2.6	2.3	2.4	2.4	2.9	3.4
Armenia	274	1346	3731.8	4964	175.6	18.7	13.8	8.7	0.7	-0.8	3.2	1	4.7	6.9	0.6	2.9	4.4	9
Azerbaijan	107	912.6	1129.7	1663.9	411.5	19.8	3.6	-0.8	-8.6	1.8	1.6	2.8	2.1	6.7	9.6	8.2	16.6	20.8
Belarus	94.1	971.2	1190.9	2219.6	709.3	52.7	63.9	73.2	293.7	168.9	61.4	42.8	28.5	18.3	10.4	7	8.3	14.8
Bosnia and Herzegovina								-0.3	3.4	5	3.2	0.3	0.6	0.4	4	6.1	1.5	7.4
Bulgaria	334	91.3	72.9	96.1	62	121.6	1058.4	18.7	2.6	10.3	7.4	5.8	2.2	6.4	5	7.3	8.4	12
China[b]	3.6	6.4	14.7	24.1	17.1	8.3	2.8	-0.8	-1.4	0.4	0.7	-0.8	1.2	3.9	1.8	1.5	4.8	5.9
Croatia	123	6673.6	1909.9	107.2		4.3	4.1	6.4	4	4.6	3.8	1.7	1.8	2	3.3	3.2	2.9	6.1
Czech Republic	52	11.1	20.8	9.9	9.5	8.8	8.4	10.7	2.1	3.9	4.7	1.8	0.1	2.8	1.8	2.5	2.9	6.4
Estonia	211	1076	89.8	47.6	28.8	23	10.6	8.2	3.3	4	5.7	3.6	1.3	3	4.1	4.4	6.6	10.4
FYR Macedonia	115	1511	352	126.6	16.4	2.5	0.9	-1.4	-1.3	6.6	5.2	2.4	1.1	-0.6	-0.7	3.3	2.8	8.3
Georgia			4084.9	22286	261.4	39.4	7.1	3.5	19.3	4.2	4.6	5.7	4.9	5.7	8.2	9.2	9.2	9.9
Hungary	35	23	22.4	18.9	28.6	23.4	18.3	14.2	10	9.8	9.2	5.5	4.4	6.8	3.6	3.9	7.9	6.1
Kazakhstan	78.8	1381	1662	1877.3	176.2	39.2	17.4	7.2	8.3	13.2	8.4	5.8	6.4	6.9	7.6	8.6	10.8	17.1
Kyrgyzstan	85	855	772	229	40.7	31.9	23.4	10.5	35.9	19.7	6.9	2.1	3	4.1	4.4	5.6	10.2	24.5
Latvia	172	951	90.9	35.9	25	17.6	8.4	4.7	2.4	2.6	2.5	1.9	2.9	6.2	6.8	6.5	10.1	15.4
Lithuania	225	1021	410	72.2	39.7	24.6	8.9	5.1	0.8	1	1.3	0.3	-1.2	1.2	2.7	3.8	5.7	10.9
Moldova[a]	98	1276	789	330	30.2	23.5	11.8	7.7	39.3	31.1	9.6	5.2	11.6	12.5	12	12.8	12.4	12.8
Mongolia[b]	20.2	202.6	268.4	87.6	56.8	46.8	36.6	9.4	7.6	11.6	6.2	0.9	5.1	7.9	12.5	5.1	8.2	26.8
Montenegro					97	80.2	23.4	32.4	67.6	97.1	22.6	18.2	6.7	2.2	2.6	3	4.3	9
Poland	70.3	45.3	36.9	33.2	28.1	19.8	15.1	11.7	7.3	10.1	5.5	1.9	0.8	3.6	2.1	1.1	2.4	4.4
Romania	170	211.2	255.2	136.8	32.2	38.8	154.8	59.1	45.8	45.7	34.5	22.5	15.3	11.9	9	6.6	4.8	7.8
Russia	92.7	1526	874.6	307.6	197.5	47.7	14.8	27.7	85.7	20.8	21.5	15.8	13.7	10.9	12.7	9.7	9.0	14.1
Serbia[a]					78.6	94.3	18.3	30	41.1	70	91.8	19.5	11.7	10.1	16.5	12.7	6.7	11.6
Slovak Republic	61.2	10	23.2	13.4	9.9	5.8	6.1	6.7	10.6	12	7.3	3.3	8.6	7.6	2.7	4.5	2.8	4.6
Slovenia	118	207	31.6	21	13.4	9.8	8.4	7.9	6.2	8.9	8.4	7.5	5.6	3.6	2.5	2.5	3.6	5.6
Tajikistan		822	2884.8	350.3	682.1	422.4	85.4	43.1	27.4	32.8	38.6	12.2	16.3	7.2	7.2	10	13.4	20.4
Turkmenistan[a]	103	493	3102	1748	1005	992	83.7	16.8	24.2	8.3	11.6	8.8	5.6	5.9	10.7	8.2	6.3	15
Ukraine		1485.8	4734.9	891.2	376.8	80.2	15.9	10.6	22.7	28.2	12	0.8	5.2	9	13.5	9.1	12.8	25.2
Uzbekistan[a]	82.2	645	534	1568	305	54	70.9	29	29.1	25	27.3	27.3	11.6	6.6	10	14.2	12.3	12.7
Vietnam[b]	84.4	37.8	8.4	9.5	17.4	5.7	3.2	7.3	4.1	-1.6	-0.4	4	3.2	7.7	8.2	7.5	8.3	23.1

Sources: United Nations Economic Commission for Europe (UNECE) Statistical Division Database, compiled from national and international (CIS, EUROSTAT, IMF, OECD) official sources; United Nations Economic and Social Commission for Asia and the Pacific (ESCAP).

Notes
a. EBRD.
b. IMF.

stabilisation programmes, and a number of fiscal and monetary reforms (interestingly, under widely different exchange rate regimes, ranging from floating exchange rates to adoption of currency boards), including better control of the public finances, tighter monetary policy (than before), non-monetary deficit financing and greater Central Bank independence. Admittedly, many of the leading reforming TEs had succeeded in reducing inflation much earlier (by implementing many of the reforms identified above) and recorded single-digit inflation rates as they continued to seek EU (and eurozone) membership. Indeed, some regarded this pursuit of low inflation rates as disproportionate, and costly in terms of output losses and excessive contractions in demand.

Unemployment

A feature of the socialist system was the absence of open unemployment. In practice, and particularly in later years, many socialist countries experienced hidden unemployment or unemployment on the job. The transition to a market economy was expected to bring a rise in official unemployment, along with the introduction of a social safety net.

Unemployment rates did rise, as is evident in Table 7.4, but in many cases, the rise in unemployment, and particularly in FSU countries (where the real unemployment rate is much higher than the official rate), was not as large as expected given the severe economic transformational recession and the record of the more established market economies whose unemployment rates rose in line with output falls during periods of economic decline. Several factors may account for this, including the observation that, unlike in CEE countries where the labour market adjustment to the output decline was in significantly fewer numbers employed, troubled firms in many FSU countries cut wages (or deferred wage payments in the form of wage arrears) often in preference to laying off workers; the tendency for many enterprises to retain workers (continuing the practice of labour hoarding either out of paternalism or a belief that the economic environment would improve or as a way of bargaining with local and national governments in order to gain supports and/or favours); the reluctance of many former workers (despite wage arrears or being put on compulsory leave without pay) to detach themselves completely from their former employer (as some enterprises continued to provide social benefits, such as housing); and, finally, derisory unemployment benefits (see Chapter 8 for more on this topic). Interestingly, the decline in real wages and the much lower anticipated rise in unemployment that transition countries witnessed are in stark contrast to the labour adjustment experienced in the Great Depression of the 1930s when real wages remained stable but unemployment soared (Milanovic 1998).

In terms of cross-country variation in unemployment, the differences between CEE and FSU countries are not as great (as with some other economic indicators). However, the differences within each respective country grouping are large. For example, within the CEE block of countries, the Czech Republic, Hungary and Slovenia managed to keep unemployment relatively low whereas in Bulgaria, Poland and the Slovak Republic unemployment rates were high, exceeding 12–15 per cent of the labour force for much of the transition era. With respect to the latter category, some features common to the investment climate and labour markets in all three countries may partly explain the high unemployment rates. Aside from some country-specific factors (e.g. the macro crisis in Bulgaria in the mid-1990s, population increases in Poland in the early 1980s, the costly legacy of heavy industry and armaments production in the Slovak Republic) these common factors include an

Table 7.4 Unemployment rate, annual average[a,b]

Country	1991	1992	1993	1994	1995	1996	1997	1998	1999	2000	2001	2002	2003	2004	2005	2006	2007	2008
Albania	9.2	27	22	18	13.1	12.4	14.9	17.7	18.4	16.8	16.4	15.8	15	14.4	14.1	13.8	..	..
Armenia	..	3.5	6.3	6	8.1	9.7	11	8.9	11.5	10.9	9.8	10.5	10.2	9.4	7.6	7.2	7.1	6.3
Azerbaijan	..	0.2	0.7	0.9	1.1	1.1	1.3	1.4	1.2	1.2	1.3	1.3	1.4	1.4	1.4	1.3	1.2	1
Belarus	..	0.5	1.3	2.1	2.9	4	2.8	2.3	2.1	2.1	2.3	3	3.1	1.9	1.5	1.2	1	0.8
Bosnia and Herzegovina	..	..	..	..	..	..	39	38.7	39	39.4	39.9	42.7	44	44.9	46.6	47.7	..	..
Bulgaria	..	..	21.4	20.2	16.5	14.1	14.4	14.1	15.7	16.4	19.5	18.2	13.7	12.1	10.1	9	6.9	5.6
China[e,f]	2	2	3	3	3	3	3	3	3	3	4	4	4	4	4	4	4	4
Croatia	..	..	..	..	..	10	9.9	11.4	13.6	16.1	15.8	14.8	14.2	13.7	12.7	11.2	9.6	8.5
Czech Republic	..	..	4.4	4.3	4.1	3.9	4.8	6.4	8.6	8.7	8	7.3	7.8	8.3	7.9	7.2	5.3	4.4
Estonia	1.5	3.7	6.6	7.6	9.7	9.9	9.6	9.2	11.3	12.8	12.4	10.3	10	9.7	7.9	5.9	4.7	5.5
FYR Macedonia	..	..	..	..	..	..	..	..	32.4	32.2	30.5	31.9	36.7	37.2	37.3	36	34.9	..
Georgia	..	..	..	..	..	..	7.6	14.5	13.8	10.3	11.1	12.6	11.5	12.6	13.8	13.6	13.3	..
Hungary	6.7	7.4	6.8	6.1	5.6	9.6	9	8.4	6.9	6.4	5.7	5.8	5.9	6.1	7.2	7.5	7.4	7.9
Kazakhstan[c]	..	..	..	7.5	11	13	13	13.1	13.5	12.8	10.4	9.3	8.8	8.4	8.1	7.8	7.3	6.6
Kyrgyzstan	..	..	..	..	..	..	..	..	..	..	12.5	12.5	9.9	8.5	8.1	8.3	8.2	..
Latvia	..	..	..	..	..	20.6	15.1	14.3	14	13.7	12.9	12.2	10.5	10.4	8.9	6.8	6	7.3
Lithuania	..	..	..	17.4	17.1	16.4	14.1	13.2	13.7	16.4	16.5	13.5	12.5	11.4	8.3	5.6	4.3	5.7
Moldova	..	..	8.6	9	5.5	6.7	7.7	5.9	11.1	8.5	7.3	6.8	7.9	8.1	7.3	7.4	5.1	4
Mongolia[d]	..	..	..	..	..	..	..	..	4.7	4.6	4.6	3.5	3.5	3.6	3.3	3.2	2.8	2.8
Montenegro	..	..	..	..	..	..	..	..	..	..	..	..	..	27.7	30.3	29.6	19.3	..
Poland	..	..	16.3	16.9	15.4	14.1	10.9	10.2	13.4	16.2	18.3	20	19.7	19	17.8	13.9	9.6	7.1
Romania	..	..	..	8.2	8	6.7	6	6.3	6.8	7.1	6.6	8.4	7	8	7.2	7.3	6.4	..
Russia	..	5.2	6.1	7.8	9.5	10	11.2	13.2	12.6	10.6	9	7.9	8.3	7.8	7.3	7.2	6.1	6.3
Serbia	..	..	..	..	..	..	..	..	..	12.1	12.2	13.3	14.6	18.5	20.8	20.9	18.1	..
Slovak Republic	..	..	..	13.7	13.1	11.3	11.9	12.6	16.4	18.8	19.3	18.7	17.6	18.2	16.3	13.4	11.1	9.6
Slovenia	..	..	9.1	9	7.4	7.3	7.1	7.7	7.4	7.2	5.9	5.9	6.6	6.1	5.8	6	4.9	4.5
Tajikistan	..	0.4	1.1	1.8	1.8	2.4	2.8	3.2	3	2.7	2.3	2.6	2.3	2	2.1	2.3	2.5	..
Turkmenistan	..	..	..	..	..	..	..	..	..	2.4	2.6	2.5	2.5	..	..	..	..	..
Ukraine	..	..	..	..	5.6	7.6	8.9	11.3	11.6	11.6	10.9	9.6	9.1	8.6	7.2	6.8	6.4	6.4
Uzbekistan	..	0.1	0.2	0.3	0.3	0.3	0.3	0.4	0.4	0.4	0.4	0.4	0.3	0.4	0.3	0.3	0.3	0.2
Vietnam[e]	..	..	..	..	..	1.9	2.9	2.3	2.3	2.3	2.1	2.1	2.3	2.1	..	..	..	..

Sources: United Nations Economic Commission for Europe (UNECE) Statistical Division Database, compiled from national and international (EUROSTAT, OECD, CIS) official sources; United Nations Economic and Social Commission for Asia and the Pacific (ESCAP).

Notes
a. The unemployment rate represents unemployed persons as a percentage of the civilian labour force. Data comes from the Labour Force Survey unless otherwise specified.
b. For Albania, Armenia, Azerbaijan, Belarus, Bosnia and Herzegovina, Tajikistan and Uzbekistan, the unemployment rate represents registered unemployed, at end of period.
c. Official Estimates 1994–2000.
d. ILO data, at end year.
e. United Nations ESCAP.
f. Official estimates of unemployment in urban areas, at end year.

Table 7.5 Unemployment rates (%), 2005[a, b]

Region	Rate
Central and South-Eastern Europe (non-EU)+CIS	**9.0**
Developed economies + European Union	6.9
of which	
Baltics 3	**8.3**
Visegrad 4	**12.3**
EU Accession 8	**10.0**
EU Accession 10	**9.7**
Euro area 12	7.5
North America 2	6.0
East Asia (including China)	**3.7**
South-East Asia and the Pacific	6.1
Latin America and the Caribbean	8.4
North Africa	11.6
Sub-Saharan Africa	9.7
Middle East	12.2
World	6.4

Source: Bureau of Statistics, International Labour Organisation.

Notes
a. A listing of the various regional groupings can be found on the ILO website.
b. Numbers in bold are unemployment rates for transition countries only.

unfriendly business environment (at least in the 1990s with some improvements thereafter) combined with inflexible labour laws, labour market rigidities and skills mismatches.

In FSU countries, (official) unemployment rates in Azerbaijan, Tajikistan and Uzbekistan remained extraordinarily low, whereas in the Baltic States, Russia and its neighbouring states (Ukraine, Kazakhstan and Kyrgyzstan) unemployment rates, a decade into transition, were over 10 per cent of the labour force. As always, countries inflicted by internal strife or war suffered very high unemployment rates. With the exception of (not for the first time) Slovenia (see Box 7.1), the other former republics of Yugoslavia is a case in point, with successor states recording unemployment rates in the region of 20 to 30 per cent of the labour force. By mid-decade (2005), unemployment rates in transition countries as compared with unemployment rates in many non-transition market economies were, in general, high. This is evident in Table 7.5 where we report unemployment rates (on a regional basis) for both transition and non-transition countries.

Furthermore, and more worryingly from a policy perspective, two notable aspects of unemployment in transition countries are the low turnover of the unemployment pool caused by the relatively low rates of outflows from unemployment (arising from, among others, a mismatch of skills, insufficient active labour market policies, sluggish economic growth and job creation), and, the relatively high rates of long-term unemployment, i.e. unemployment lasting for more than 12 months (Boeri and Lehmann 1999; Svejnar 2002). Whereas the long-term unemployment rate in the EU-15 has tended to be – with some exceptions – below 50 per cent (of the unemployed), in many transition countries more than half of the unemployed are long-term unemployed (Blanchard 1997). Tackling the increased duration of unemployment must be a priority for the active labour market policies of transition countries.

Box 7.1

A case of a successful transition: the Slovenian way

Slovenia has the highest GDP per capita of any former Eastern bloc country. During the worst years of transition (that is, the early 1990s) it was the second country (after Poland) to recover from the output collapse associated with transition from plan to market. An indication of Slovenia's progress since the collapse of socialism (and the dissolution of Yugoslavia) and its subsequent journey on the road to a market economy can be greatly measured by its accession to the EU in 2004 (alongside fellow transition countries Czech Republic, Estonia, Hungary, Latvia, Lithuania, Poland and Slovak Republic with Bulgaria and Romania joining in 2007). Moreover, it was the first former socialist country to qualify for the eurozone, and was admitted on 1 January 2007. However, partly owing to its size (only c. 20,000 km^2, with a population of 2 million), its story often goes unnoticed. There follows a brief account of the so-called Slovenian Way.

Slovenia's initial conditions at the outset of transition were benign, partly explaining Slovenia's successful transformation to a market economy. It has a favourable geographical location, having borders with Italy and Austria and, although mountainous, it has access to the Adriatic Sea. Over 80 per cent of the population are ethnic Slovenes making it a relatively homogeneous society. Although a constituent entity of the decentralised socialist country that was the Socialist Federal Republic of Yugoslavia (SFRY), it did, however, manage to retain much autonomy and more freedoms than elsewhere in the Eastern bloc. Prior to being a republic of socialist Yugoslavia, it was part of the powerful Habsburg and Austro-Hungarian Empire.

Slovenia was by far the wealthiest and most developed of the SFRY's six republics. Although comprising only 8 per cent of the population of SFRY, it accounted for 20 per cent of production. Although it did face some macroeconomic problems (that is, rising levels of inflation and debt) on the eve of transition, these were quickly dealt with by the use of prudent macro-stabilisation policies. Although fiscal and monetary policies were generally conventional, heterodox policies were also adopted in tandem. In particular, an incomes policy (collective bargaining on the basis of tripartite social agreements) combined with an unorthodox managed float exchange rate policy, with capital controls and only a gradual reduction in capital account restrictions averted the type of macro crisis (and, it is argued, output collapse) experienced in other former socialist countries embarking on transition. Equally, a good record on tax collection meant that, with high and persistent levels of public expenditures, large and costly fiscal imbalances were avoided.

In June 1991 Slovenia declared its independence with the disintegration of the SFR of Yugoslavia. Elections were held in April 1990 and again in December 1992, with successive governments comprising broad-based coalitions noted for their bipartisanship. The most important positions – the President and the Head of Government (the Prime Minister) – for Slovenia's first decade as an independent state (post the demise of Yugoslavia and the self-management socialist system therein) were filled by two statesmen. Milan Kučan was President, running as a non-party candidate, for two terms, and was generally considered a stabilising influence on Slovene politics.

The late Janez Drnovšek (leader of the Liberal Democracy of Slovenia Party and a former member of the Yugoslav Presidium) competently served as PM for over a decade, and then as President for a more controversial five-year term, until 2007. Unlike many other former socialist countries, Slovenia has managed to avoid excessive recriminations about its communist past, and this, combined with its relatively peaceful transition – conflict in 1991 between Slovenian forces and the Yugoslav People's Army resulted in the so-called 10-Day War – and its traditional consensus-building (at least officially) approach to politics has meant that the country has avoided many of the post-socialist upheavals witnessed in other ex-socialist (and particularly other former entitles of Yugoslavia) countries.

Aside from its favourable initial conditions, other factors have contributed to Slovenia's success. Wholesale reorientation of trade to the West and the EU has resulted in making Slovenia one of the world's most open economies, heavily dependent on foreign trade, and particular with high-income Western and Central European countries. Adoption of the EU *acquis communautaire* over a relatively short period of time has resulted in a legal and institutional framework that has given Slovenia a competitive edge over many other former socialist countries. The disciplinary device of EU accession and the broader wish to 'return to Europe' contributed to stable politics, with consistent policies and a certain cohesion to and within society. The more interesting, and controversial, aspect of Slovenia's transition is the speed of its economic reforms. Reforms in Slovenia, often introduced in the face of much Western advice (and criticism), are often described as gradual and cautious as opposed to speedy and radical, but as Slovenia was relatively well placed at the outset of transition (in addition to those conditions outlined above, having trade links with the West while still a socialist country, skilled human capital, and reforms pre-transition), gradualism was an option and policy choice that some other countries (such as Russia) possibly could not afford. Debates between gradualists and rapid reformers were common in the early 1990s with the gradualists – often out of pragmatism rather than any ideological vision – prevailing in the majority of cases.

For political reasons, the privatisation debate (between the gradual, decentralised approach and the speedy, government-led voucher approach) culminated in the compromise Ownership Transformation Act of 1992, and the subsequent slow change in ownership of SOEs. Ownership structures post-privatisation were both diverse and dispersed with different methods used, the most popular mode of privatisation being buyouts (to insiders). This gradual approach also applied to the private and foreign ownership of banks. Overall, consolidation and restructuring in the enterprise sector was gradual and decentralised (at enterprise level rather than government led), and still lags behind other rapidly reforming transition countries (Mrak *et al.* 2004). FDI flows for most of the transition era have been small and, until recently, did not play a role in Slovenia's reforms and transition outcomes. Although gradualism is an undoubted feature of the Slovenian Way, it is still unclear how transposable its particular set (and speed) of reforms are: local circumstances, pre-transition conditions and political constraints often dictate the policies and reforms adopted. Just as radical and speedy reforms are not suitable for all countries, the same applies to the cautious and gradual reforms adopted in Slovenia – the Slovenian Way is not necessarily the Estonian, Polish or Russian Way, not to mention a possible future Cuban Way!

Life expectancy

Socialist countries at the outset of transition were predominantly middle-income countries with relatively impressive scores for many socioeconomic indicators such as literacy and school enrolment rates, mortality rates, labour force participation rates and so on. As for life expectancy, rates in socialist countries were below rates for well-established market economies but above life expectancy rates for many Asian, Central and Latin American countries. There is some evidence that the stagnation evident in the decades preceding transition resulted in a fall in life expectancy in some of the socialist countries, and in particular, in some CIS countries.[6] Whereas transition witnessed, in general, an increase in life expectancy rates in CEE countries, some CIS countries (most notably Russia) witnessed dramatic declines in male life expectancy rates in the early years of transition (but with some improvement in later years). Table 7.6 reports life expectancy rates, both for men and for women, at five-year intervals over the period 1990 to 2005.

Table 7.6 Life expectancy at birth*

Country		1990	1995	2000	2005
Albania	female	75.9	78.3	78.6	78.6
	male	69.6	71.5	72.1	72.1
Armenia	female	75.4	74.9	75.8	76.5
	male	68.6	67.3	70.1	70.3
Azerbaijan	female	74.8	72.9	75.1	75.1
	male	67	65.2	68.6	69.6
Belarus	female	75.6	74.3	74.7	75.1
	male	66.3	62.9	63.4	62.9
Bosnia and Herzegovina	female	75.2	75.1	76.7	77.5
	male	69.7	69.5	71.3	72.1
Bulgaria	female	74.7	74.9	75	76.2
	male	68	67.4	68.4	69
China	female	69.6	71.1	72.9	74.3
	male	66.7	68.2	69.8	71
Croatia	female	76.4	77.2	76.7	78.9
	male	68.7	69.3	69.1	71.9
Czech Republic	female	75.5	76.8	78.5	79.2
	male	67.6	69.7	71.7	72.9
Estonia	female	75	74.3	76.2	78.2
	male	64.7	61.5	65.5	67.3
FYR Macedonia	female	74.5	74.4	75.6	76.2
	male	70.3	70.1	70.9	71.4
Georgia	female	76.6	74.2	74.9	77.4
	male	69	66.3	67.5	69.9
Hungary	female	73.8	74.8	76.2	77.2
	male	65.2	65.4	67.6	68.7
Kazakhstan	female	73.4	70.4	71.6	71.7
	male	63.9	59.3	60.2	60.4
Kyrgyzstan	female	73	69.9	72	71.8
	male	64.4	61.3	63.8	63.8
Latvia	female	74.6	72.9	76.1	76.6
	male	64.2	60	64.9	65.4
Lithuania	female	76.4	75.1	77.6	77.4
	male	66.5	63.3	66.8	65.4

(*Continued*)

Table 7.6 Continued

Country		1990	1995	2000	2005
Moldova	female	72	69.7	71.4	71.7
	male	65	62	64	63.8
Mongolia	female	62.6	64.7	67.5	69.2
	male	59	60.3	61.5	62.8
Montenegro	female	78.2	76.7	76.3	74.9
	male	72.8	71.4	71	70.4
Poland	female	75.6	76.4	78.1	79.4
	male	66.6	67.7	69.8	70.8
Romania	female	73.1	73.5	74.8	75.8
	male	66.6	65.5	67.8	68.8
Russia	female	74.4	71.7	72.4	72.4
	male	63.8	58.3	59.2	59
Serbia	female	74	74.6	74.8	75.4
	male	68.9	69.8	69.7	70
Slovak Republic	female	75.7	76.5	77.5	78.1
	male	66.7	68.4	69.2	70.2
Slovenia	female	77.8	78.5	79.9	80.9
	male	69.8	70.8	72.2	73.9
Tajikistan	female	72.6	69.1	70.3	73.2
	male	67.1	63.6	66.1	68.1
Turkmenistan	female	69.7	67.5	71.8	72.7
	male	62.9	61.9	64.9	65.8
Ukraine	female	75	72.6	73.6	73.4
	male	65.7	61.3	62.3	61.5
Uzbekistan	female	72.4	71.7	73.2	74.1
	male	66.1	66.4	68.4	69.6
Vietnam	female	67.3	71.2	73.8	75.7
	male	63.7	67.8	70.2	71.9

Sources: United Nations Economic Commission for Europe (UNECE) Statistical Database, compiled from national and international (WHO, EUROSTAT and UNICEF) official sources; United Nations Economic and Social Commission for Asia and the Pacific (ESCAP)

Note
* Life expectancy at birth is the average number of years a newborn is expected to live, if the prevailing pattern of mortality at the time of her/his birth were to stay the same throughout her/his life.

Increases in life expectancy over the period 1990 to 2005 are evident in *both* the poor, low-income transition countries (Albania, China, Mongolia, Vietnam) and the most developed, high-income transition countries (the Czech and Slovak Republics, Hungary, Poland, Slovenia). Life expectancy at birth rates fell in the Baltic States but then recovered and were generally higher in 2005 than at the start of transition. Falling life expectancy rates (both male and female) were recorded in Kazakhstan, Russia and Ukraine. In all three countries (and, in addition, Belarus) the extent of the fall in male life expectancy rates is particularly alarming. As with the output decline, this fall in life expectancy is one of the great surprises of transition, as falls in life expectancy in modern times for middle-income countries (with the exception of countries suffering internal strife or at war) are uncommon. Explanations for the sharp decline in male life expectancy in predominantly Slavic countries varied from the stress associated with the economic turmoil of transition, declining living standards (associated with the fall in output), loss of employment, status and security, difficulty in accessing the (in some cases deteriorating or expensive private) health service, and, particularly relevant in the Russian case, high levels of alcohol consumption.

The trends reported above, for both output and life expectancy, are repeated in the broader measure of economic well-being more commonly used by the United Nations, namely the Human Development Index (HDI). The HDI is a composite socioeconomic indicator based not solely on living standards (as measured by GDP per capita in PPP US$) but on a long and healthy life (measured by life expectancy at birth) and on education attainment and knowledge (measured by adult literacy rates and enrolment ratios). Whereas a small number of countries (namely China, the Czech Republic, Hungary, Poland, Slovenia and Vietnam) reported a continuous rise in the HDI over the period 1990 to 2005, the majority of TEs experienced an initial fall, and, subsequently either a recovery (for the majority of countries) or, in a small number of TEs (Moldova, Russia, Tajikistan and Ukraine), a levelling off such that the 2005 HDI was still below the 1990 HDI figure recorded at the outset of transition. By 2005, out of a total of 29 TEs, 16 (the majority of which, not surprisingly, are CEB countries) were high human development countries (defined as with a HDI of 0.8 or above) whereas a further 13 (the majority of which are CIS countries) were medium human development countries (defined as with a HDI between 0.5 and 0.799). Comparable HDI data for the transition countries (reported for the five-year intervals 1990, 1995, 2000 and 2005) can be found in Appendix 6. As a comparison with transition countries, we also report the 2005 HDI values for some regional groupings.

As witnessed across all of these measures, the early 1990s was a difficult time, with huge upheaval. Output collapsed, prices soared, unemployment rose, demographics deteriorated, poverty levels increased and inequalities widened.[7] However, by the mid-1990s in the CEE countries and the late 1990s in the FSU countries there was evidence of a recovery, although uneven and erratic. The pattern or evolution of output in CEE countries is often described as the J-shaped recovery whereas in CIS countries it is referred to as the U-shaped (or, in some cases, the V-shaped) recovery. Others refer to the inverse J-shaped pattern in the worst affected transition countries that suffered a deep and protracted recession. By the beginning of the second decade, the vast majority of TEs were performing well. Output levels recovered, inflation rates fell and unemployment levels stabilised. This was particularly true of the 2004 EU accession states, namely the Czech Republic, Estonia, Hungary, Latvia, Lithuania, Poland, the Slovak Republic and Slovenia. Many experts viewed the transition from plan to market for these countries as over. For others, the data indicate that they have a long way to go. In some cases the level of GDP, over a decade after reforms began, was still below the level of GDP recorded at the start of transition. Many of the Central Asian states (including Mongolia) and Vietnam resemble, in many respects, less developed countries in other parts of the world, as evident in the GDP per capita data in Table 7.2. The legacy of the Soviet system, political constraints, conflicts, corruption, bad governance and policy mistakes all contributed to the poor performance, most notably the severe economic recession, which we will shortly address.

In sum, rating the overall performance of transition countries to date is a difficult task. For one thing, and as we have reported here, there was wide cross-country variation in performance and living standards, not just between China/Vietnam and the former Soviet bloc countries but within the former Soviet Union and its satellite states, between CEE (and within that grouping, between Central Eastern European countries and South Eastern European countries) and FSU countries (and within that grouping, between the Baltic States and the CIS countries). It also depends on what benchmark performance is measured against, or for that matter who is doing the evaluating, as Gregory (1997) notes.

In the context of transition countries, various different benchmarks have been used, including the general expectations (or even aspirations) at the outset of transition, the income gap with advanced OECD or EU countries, the gap with countries of similar levels of development, the degree of structural change and modernisation achieved, a more historical perspective focusing on large-scale institutional and systemic change, or the economic conditions pre-transition. Measured against any of the last three benchmarks listed here, the outcome is generally positive. This is largely the view of János Kornai who, when assessing the transformation of Central Eastern Europe, asserts that it was 'a success story because it established a capitalist economic system within a historically brief timeframe' (Kornai 2006a).[8] Measured against expectations at the outset of transition or against relative income gaps, the outcome is disappointing, and for many the experience, at least initially, was traumatic. For example, Svejnar (2002) concludes, with respect to output changes, 'one may interpret the growth performance since 1989 as having been mildly to significantly disappointing in central Europe and poor to disastrous in eastern Europe and the Commonwealth of Independent States'.

The obvious success stories are the EU accession countries, including the Baltic States, and, surprisingly for some, Vietnam and China. China's economic transformation, despite current problems with respect to many poorly performing state enterprises and banks, has been a great success (Roland 2000; Qian and Wu 2008).[9] In contrast, for the CIS countries and many Balkan States, the period of transition from plan to market will often be remembered for wars and internal strife (although, overall and in a historical context, the transition at the end of the twentieth century was remarkably peaceful), rising corruption, falling living standards, worsening demographics and rising inequalities.

Although transition countries witnessed many surprises (most notably, the rise in corruption and the unofficial economy, the worsening demographics in the form of falling population numbers and deteriorating life expectancy for men in some CIS countries, the extent of different privatisation outcomes and the persistence of the soft budget constraint), the surprise that captured much of the attention of the economics profession (and others) was the collapse in output in the early years of transition.

The output collapse

This section previews the economic theories that explain the output collapse of the early 1990s in transition countries. In the next section we will present empirical findings, and, in particular, the results of studies on the determinants of performance (as measured by changes in national output) of TEs, covering both the recessionary phase and the recovery period that followed.

At the outset of transition, many economists (particularly those unfamiliar with the socialist system) predicted a closing of the gap between East and West. Given the distortions and inefficiencies of the old socialist system, it was argued that implementation of the reform package and improved resource allocation would result in an increase in output levels and higher economic growth rates.[10] More specifically, it was expected that transition economies would move from inside on to their production possibility frontiers and, thereafter, the frontier, with implementation of market reforms, was expected to shift outward. Others were more pessimistic and predicted a difficult transformation. The initial decline in output that occurred in all of the CEE and FSU countries vindicates the latter's position. Few in the economics profession predicted the fall in output. Kornai, writing in 1993, observed that no 'forecast of . . . serious recession [can] be found in the early theoretical writings to outline the program for the transition'.[11] This poses a challenge to the advocates of (one-size-fits-all) market reforms in particular, and neoclassical theory in general. Standard market analysis failed to predict the output decline but this was not surprising given, a priori, the assumption in traditional market and price theory of the existence of markets underpinned by appropriate institutional settings and the spontaneity of private enterprise (not to mention the fact that mainstream textbooks consider marginal changes in variables whereas transition from plan to market is a large-scale systemic and institutional change).

Table 7.7 reports the fall in output during the period 1990 to 2000. Notwithstanding the difficulties in measuring GDP at the outset of transition (as mentioned earlier) and acknowledging the underreporting of economic activity due to the significant size, and growing in the first few years of transition, of the underground or unofficial economy, the collapse in output in the early years of transition was unprecedented in modern economic times and for some countries even exceeded the decline recorded in many capitalist countries during the Great Depression years of the 1930s. A comparison with the Great Depression is depicted in Figure 7.1.

Table 7.7 The output decline in transition countries

Country	Consecutive years of output decline	Cumulative output decline (%)	Real GDP, 2000 (1990 = 100)
Central and Southern Europe and the Baltic States	3.8	22.6	106.5
Albania	3	33	110
Bulgaria	4	16	81
Croatia	4	36	87
Czech Republic	3	12	99
Estonia	5	35	85
Hungary	4	15	109
Latvia	4	51	61
Lithuania	5	44	67
Poland	2	6	112
Romania	3	21	82
Slovak Republic	4	23	82
Slovenia	3	14	105
CIS	6.5	50.5	62.7
Armenia	4	63	67
Azerbaijan	6	60	55
Belarus	6	35	88
Georgia	5	78	29
Kazakhstan	6	41	90
Kyrgyzstan	6	50	66
Moldova	7	63	35
Russia	7	40	64
Tajikistan	7	50	48
Turkmenistan	8	48	76
Ukraine	10	59	43
Uzbekistan	6	18	95
Output decline during the Great Depression 1930–34			
France	3	11	n.a.
Germany	3	16	n.a.
United Kingdom	2	6	n.a.
United States	4	27	n.a.

Source: World Bank (2002a).

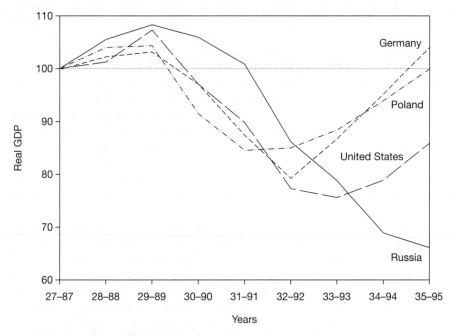

Figure 7.1 The two depressions.

Source: Milanovic (1998); World Bank.

Note
1927 = 100 for the United States and Germany; 1987 = 100 for Poland and Russia.

Poland and Russia are cited because of their size and their significance (both economically and politically) during the transition era. The scale of the depression in Russia, both in terms of duration and intensity, is stark, even compared with the output decline in its fellow transition country, and compared with the output fall in the US and Germany. As Milanovic (1998) states, 'the post-Communist depression in Russia is deeper than the Great Depression was in the United States and Germany'.

As evident from Table 7.7, Poland experienced the shortest and mildest recession. Although other CEE countries witnessed longer and deeper recessions, it was the FSU republics that experienced the steepest declines. Ukraine witnessed ten consecutive years of economic decline while Georgia experienced the largest fall in output, estimated at almost 80 per cent. It is important to note here that for many of these countries, the fall in output, although often associated with the start of liberalisation, had started prior to the collapse of the Soviet system and had originated in socialist times. The surprise for many analysts was that this decline in output was not halted by the economic reforms as part of the transition to the market system and, indeed for some countries (particularly the FSU countries) the output decline accelerated in the initial years of transition before a recovery was evident. With respect to the output decline and economic reforms during transition, the questions that the empirical studies on the determinants of performance will address (see later section) include the following: was the decline in output caused, or accelerated by, liberalisation? How was the change in output related to the speed of reform? In particular, did the rapid reformers suffer

241

least in terms of the extent (as opposed to the duration) of the output decline (put another way, did the least rapidly reforming countries, by not adopting market reforms, simply defer the output fall?), or, did the least rapidly reforming countries manage to avoid the excesses of the output collapse? Is the recovery in the most rapidly reforming countries more robust than that experienced by the least rapidly reforming countries?

There was no output collapse in China or Vietnam. Some argue that this is due to the different starting conditions between China/Vietnam and the CEE/FSU countries. The initial conditions in China and Vietnam, in terms of agriculture and industry shares of GDP, extent of surplus labour, the prevalence of the state sector (in terms of both output and employment) and the size of state enterprises, were not as severe as in the Soviet bloc countries where there was massive over-industrialisation, a colossal state sector and gigantic state enterprises. Although it is true that China and Vietnam did not have the same level of distortions as were evident in the former Soviet bloc countries, they did have to face the dual problem of development and transition which many of the Soviet satellite states did not have to confront.

We now turn our attention to the various explanations given to the output collapse. We begin by acknowledging that there is a view, although a minority one, that most of the output decline was a statistical illusion, largely because output on the eve of transition (and during the socialist era) was inflated as incentives (namely the bonus schemes aimed at fulfilling plan targets) in the Soviet socialist system led to an overreporting of production whereas during transition output was underestimated due to unreported informal economic activity in the private sector, not to mention an end to the negative value-added activities (in the form of unsalable goods) and, at the same time, an improvement in the quality and selection of goods and services that transition brought (Åslund 2001a). It is fair to say that this rather controversial perspective is a minority position within the economics profession. Whereas most commentaries agree that an output decline did occur, they differ on the size of the decline (not withstanding the cross-country differences in output performance). In his review of studies that examine differences in growth performance, Havrylyshyn (2001) concludes that 'the vast majority of analyses concur the decline was large and often say or imply it has been surprisingly large'.[12] We also note here that for TEs, the actual decline in output does not necessarily translate into an equivalent loss in economic welfare. In the transition recession, the fall in consumption (a better indicator of well-being) has tended to be smaller than the decline in output.

The economics literature identifies several explanations for the output collapse, or what is commonly referred to as the transformational recession (Kornai 1994; Popov 2000). Some of the models identify a systemic reason for the fall in output (Kornai 1994; Blanchard and Kremer 1997), others identify (external) trade shocks as the reason (Rodrik 1994; Bevan *et al.* 2001) while others identify policy mistakes or excesses (Calvo and Coricelli 1993; Taylor 1994). A different approach to explaining the decline (and subsequent recovery) in output is to use the, although probably ill-suited, macroeconomic aggregate demand and aggregate supply framework. Whereas the transition recession resulted primarily from a fall in aggregate demand, the output recovery after the initial years of transition was mainly supply driven, it is argued. Others view the transition recession as a supply-side phenomenon resulting from a change in relative prices arising from the need to correct for the distortions in industrial structure and external trade patterns inherited from the socialist system (Popov 2000). Notwithstanding the different contributions of these approaches, a better understanding of the recession can be reached, in our view, by seeking microeconomic foundations or underpinnings to the slump in output. As we now know, mainstream microeconomics with its emphasis on the market mechanism, traditional price theory and resource allocation was not able to predict or explain the unexpected output fall. Rather, modern microeconomics with the focus on transaction cost economics, contracting and property rights provides us with more adequate explanations for the decline in output.

The most cited explanation of the transition recession is the disorganisation theory where disorganisation, as opposed to reorganisation, is when old relationships and organised production break down before new ones are established (Blanchard and Kremer 1997; Roland and Verdier 1999). Disorganisation identifies problems in the traditional domestic supply chain between producers. As transition began with price liberalisation, and in the absence of pre-existing markets, the taut plans resulted in disruption of production and trade. In effect, transition destroyed the organisation of the central planner. Price liberalisation provided firms in these production chains scope for bargaining, i.e. suppliers had the option to switch between buyers. With inefficiencies in the bargaining process between initial buyers and suppliers, output in the state sector collapsed. Here, specificity, where a firm is locked into relationships with a small number of firms, is a key determinant in explaining the fall in output (Blanchard 1997).

The theory of disorganisation works as follows. Under state socialism, enterprises had few suppliers, and for many inputs there was only one supplier (state-owned, of course). The same applied to buyers. These bilateral arrangements meant that relations between enterprises were highly specific. With liberalisation, firms were able to bargain with enterprises up and down the production chain (that is, with firms from which they bought inputs, and firms to which they sold their output). However, under the assumption of asymmetric information or incomplete contracts, there may be numerous bargaining failures. The result is a breakdown in these economic relations and networks. This disruption in the supply chain was evident in the reported shortages of inputs (an indicator of disorganisation). With new institutions, firms and suppliers all in their infancy, and with the coercive power of the central planner waning, the result was a fall in output. The theory of disorganisation is based on core ideas in modern microeconomics, including asymmetric information, hold-up problems and incomplete contracts.

Blanchard and Kremer (1997) concluded that the output decline was larger in countries where, first, the greater the complexity of production, and second, the less liberal the economic regime was at the beginning of transition. The former condition is cited as a possible explanation for why Russia, relative to China where production complexity was lower as agriculture exceeded industry in importance (not to mention the maintenance of political control over production), did so badly in the initial years of transition. The latter condition is cited as a reason why Russia has done poorly relative to the more liberal pre-transition CEE countries. Further, in the worst-performing CEE countries (e.g. Bulgaria and Romania) and the FSU republics (where specialisation during Soviet times was high), the authors claim that, given the incidence of shortages, disorganisation played an important role. Roland and Verdier (1999) also model disorganisation during the transition process. They focus on search frictions and relationship-specific investment where the fall in output is often caused by a failure to undertake investment as long-term partners and repeated interactions are difficult to find and sustain given the new trading environment. As no investments take place during search, and as the capital stock is obsolete, the result is a fall in aggregate output.

Kornai (1994) identifies the transformational recession as caused by the systemic change from a planned, supply-constrained, shortage economy to a decentralised, demand-constrained economy. With a shift from a sellers' to a buyers' market, the decline in output in the state sector was not sufficiently compensated for by the nascent private sector activity. Invoking Joseph Schumpeter, the recession is characterised by a number of features including a sudden shift in relative prices, a change in the composition of output (from industry to services), a coordination mechanism that is no longer central planning but is not quite fully market determined, a hardening of the budget constraint (with the inevitable bankruptcies and layoffs to follow) and an underdeveloped financial sector. Kornai, however, did acknowledge that policy errors and mistakes compounded the transformational recession, as indeed did his fellow Hungarian compatriot, the historian Ivan Berend (see Berend 2009).

Calvo and Coricelli's (1993) credit crunch explanation blames the early recession on high interest rates and tight monetary policy leading to a decline in the demand for credit and subsequent falls in output levels. This arose out of imperfections in credit markets that were absent in the socialist system (as enterprises could only avail themselves of state funds as per their financial and physical plans) and the delay in establishing new private credit markets where banks extend credit based on a firm's creditworthiness. The credit crunch was particularly felt by the new private sector (comprising SMEs) and less so by the large SOEs that continued to trade in the face of liquidity shortages with the help of state supports, inter-enterprise arrears and non-monetary transactions (that is, barter and use of IOUs). In contrast, Amsden *et al.* (1994), while acknowledging that output losses and inflation were inevitable given the socialist institutional legacy and the macroeconomic imbalances that had amassed in the later years of the socialist era, blame the inappropriate radical reform package of the mainstream orthodoxy, and, in particular, the overly austere macroeconomic stabilisation policies that overshot, leading to a slump in output. Attributing the output decline to the excesses of stabilisation alone is, admittedly, in contrast to the experiences of and evidence from many heavily indebted countries in the 1980s that adopted stabilisation programmes to correct, *inter alia*, severe fiscal imbalances and hyperinflation. The difference may be that this group of countries, although heavily indebted, had, unlike the former socialist countries embarking on transition, a market system (although often rudimentary) in place and an institutional setting (although not fully embedded) that allowed the stabilisation programme to succeed.

A much more critical account of the economic policies advocated by market reformers is given by King (2003) who, by employing a sociological perspective on transition, argues that in the post-communist countries of the former Soviet Union where performance was an 'unmitigated disaster', it was the adoption of the neoliberal transition policies (as opposed to a *failure* to adopt the market reform policies, as argued by many supporters of the radical, Big Bang approach to transition) and, in particular, the three shocks – shock liberalisation, shock stabilisation, shock privatisation – that weakened firms, leading to serious demand and supply failures, and ultimately to bureaucratic erosion and declining state capacity.

Four other explanations include Rodrik (1994) who identifies the collapse in foreign trade arising from the Soviet trade shock and the abandonment of the discredited CMEA as a significant factor in explaining the output decline; Atkeson and Kehoe (1996), whose model is based on sectoral shifts in the presence of labour market frictions or imperfections; Li (1999), who focuses on monopoly behaviour and pricing, and, in particular, the switch from a controlled monopoly under state socialism to uncontrolled monopolies in the initial years of transition as liberalisation policies are adopted; and Winiecki (2002), who claims that it is due to the legacy of the communist economic system and the ending of the pure socialist output (that is, the 'system-specific output not demanded under more normal systemic conditions') of the past.

The above explanations focus primarily on economic phenomena as factors accounting for the fall in output. If we broaden our discussion to include the political and institutional dimensions of transition, it is argued that the output decline was caused by the political and institutional structures that existed at the start of transition. In particular, countries with a longer tradition of sovereignty had, on average, more developed public sector institutions, a greater history of civil societies and a stronger tradition of collective action influencing the political process. These countries suffered less from the venal state capture that was rampant in many of the newly established successor states of the former Soviet Union. These new states, while adopting market reforms *and*, at the same time, building the institutions of a modern state, were weakened by the actions of powerful vested interests, comprising both the old *nomenklatura* and new private business groups. Moreover, the symbiosis of politics and economics that was a central feature of the socialist system resulted in, at great social cost, a lack of separation between government and business, and a blurring of the distinction between public and private interests. It is these historical legacies of politics and institutions in conjunction with insufficient economic and political contestability that determine the policy choices, and in turn, explain the (variation in) performances and outcomes in transition countries (World Bank 2000).

It is difficult to establish the relative importance of each theory. However, it is likely that the decline in output was not due to one factor alone (whether it was the slow response in supply, the decline in demand, systemic reasons, policy errors or trade implosions) but was more likely due to some combination of these factors. The following section sets out to test empirically the relative importance of a number of factors that explain output performance, both in the recessionary phase and the ensuing recovery period.

Determinants of performance outcomes in transition countries

In the context of transition from plan to market, this section attempts to address two key questions. First, what factors account for the evolution or pattern of output during transition and, in particular, the initial decline and the subsequent recovery in output, as evident in the GDP growth rate data reported in Table 7.1? Second, what explains the considerable cross-country differences in performance (as measured by changes in output) reported in Figure 7.2?[13] For example, what factors might explain the differences in performance between those countries with the highest GDP level as of 2008 and those economies with the lowest, relative to the 1989 level? To begin with, nearly all of the transition countries close to the bottom of Figure 7.2 (with the lowest GDP levels, relative to 1989) were engaged in conflict or war at some period during the 1990s. A priori, we would expect regional tensions to be a contributing factor in cross-country performance. Other factors, which may also account for these outcome differences and explain why, for example, Poland and Azerbaijan (or, indeed, Mongolia and the Slovak Republic) – transition countries that are not often grouped together – have the highest 2008 GDP levels relative to 1989 levels, include market and structural policies (including economic and financial integration), institutional reforms, resource endowments and initial conditions.

In order to help the reader understand the transition process and, in particular, how performance in TEs is determined, we present a heuristic model first developed by Sachs *et al.* (2000).[14] The model is outlined in Figure 7.3.

It consists of three blocks: determinants, reforms and performance. The reforms block, comprising macro, structural and institutional reforms, was dealt with in Chapters 5 and 6. Our focus here is primarily on the determinants and performance blocks. A number of performance determinants are identified, namely initial conditions, external factors, political constraints, foreign assistance and factor inputs (for a discussion on some of these

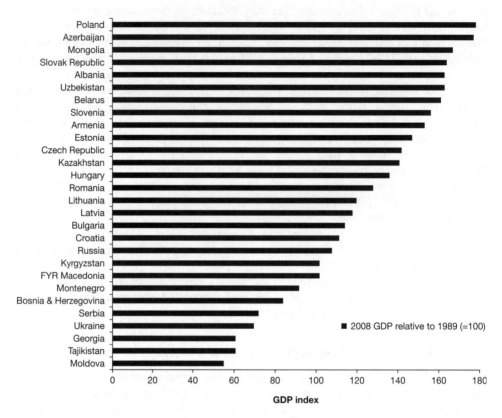

Figure 7.2 Growth in real GDP.
Source: EBRD.

determinants, see section below). Although reform is a separate block in the model, i.e. separate from the determinants block (although an arrow from reform to performance indicates the premise that reform determines performance), the empirical studies that follow specify reforms as a determinant of performance while at the same time acknowledging the policy reform endogeneity problem, i.e. reform policies may not be exogenous but may themselves depend upon output or growth. The two-way causation between outcomes and reform, or more generally, the feedback from performance to policy choices, is captured by the arrow from performance to reforms, and is mentioned again later in our summary of the regression analysis. There is also an arrow from the determinants, and particularly the initial conditions, to reforms, as the actual different policy reform strategies adopted (in terms of composition, speed and sequencing) may partly be explained by the circumstances and country-specific conditions that TEs faced on the eve of transition.

With respect to accounting for differences in economic outcomes, various studies in transition have identified and empirically tested the significance of explanatory factors, such as:

- the initial conditions and the legacy of the socialist system
- macroeconomic stabilisation

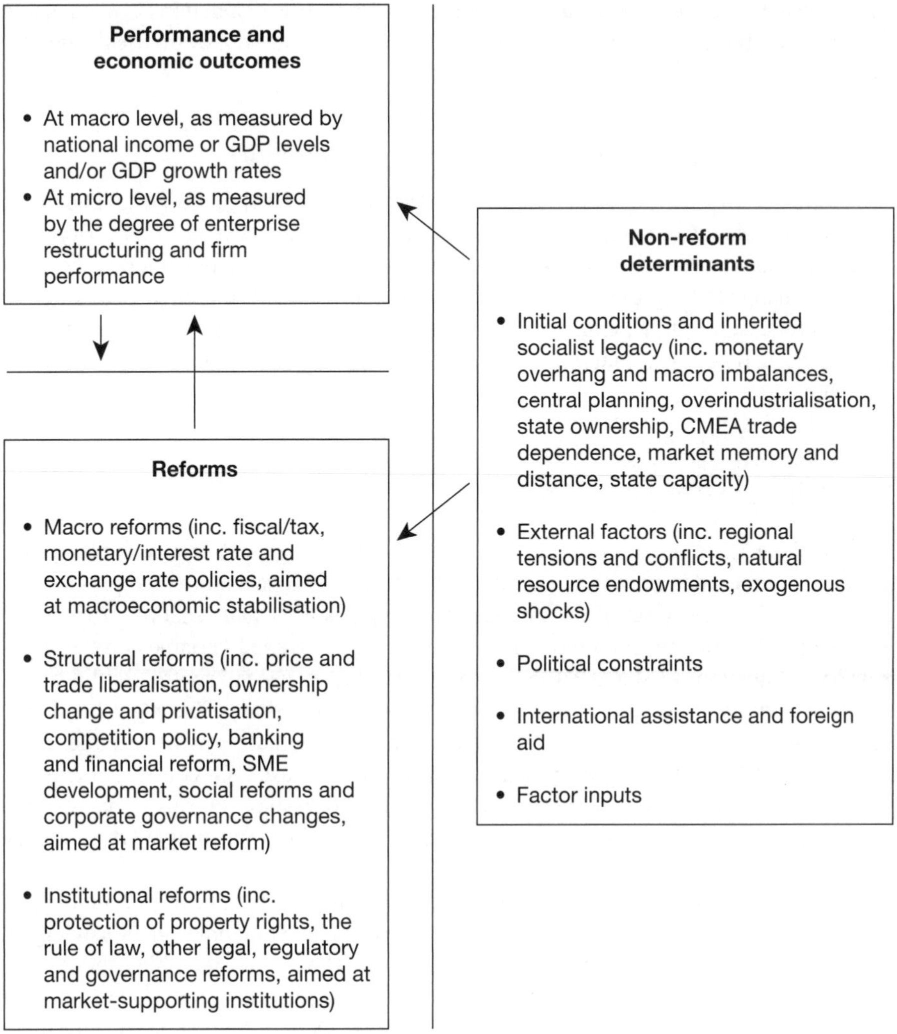

Performance and economic outcomes

- At macro level, as measured by national income or GDP levels and/or GDP growth rates
- At micro level, as measured by the degree of enterprise restructuring and firm performance

Reforms

- Macro reforms (inc. fiscal/tax, monetary/interest rate and exchange rate policies, aimed at macroeconomic stabilisation)

- Structural reforms (inc. price and trade liberalisation, ownership change and privatisation, competition policy, banking and financial reform, SME development, social reforms and corporate governance changes, aimed at market reform)

- Institutional reforms (inc. protection of property rights, the rule of law, other legal, regulatory and governance reforms, aimed at market-supporting institutions)

Non-reform determinants

- Initial conditions and inherited socialist legacy (inc. monetary overhang and macro imbalances, central planning, overindustrialisation, state ownership, CMEA trade dependence, market memory and distance, state capacity)

- External factors (inc. regional tensions and conflicts, natural resource endowments, exogenous shocks)

- Political constraints

- International assistance and foreign aid

- Factor inputs

Figure 7.3 A model of transition.

- institutions
- policy reforms (that is, market liberalisation and structural reforms)

while controlling for wars and regional strife, region/geography and external economic shocks. The purpose of the statistical exercise is to try to establish the relative importance of these explanatory variables so as to arrive at accurate estimates that measure the separate effects of these determinants. With respect to reforms and outcomes, a priori, it is argued that the more rapid and more extensive the reforms, the smaller the decline, the fewer the number of years in decline and the greater the recovery. Here, there are issues over the endogeneity of reforms (i.e. reforms may not be exogenous but in fact determined by other factors, such as inherited conditions, political constraints or pre-transition performance), the extent to which reforms can be measured accurately, and the nature of reforms (the distinction between macro reforms, structural reforms and institutional reforms). We now turn to the empirical evidence on growth in TEs.

The empirics of growth in transition countries

'Differences in per capita growth rates across countries are large and relate systematically to a set of quantifiable explanatory variables' (Barro and Sala-i-Martin 2004). Both the traditional neoclassical growth theory and the new growth models relate labour, capital and technological change to long-run economic growth. The empirics of growth in TEs is a more short-run exercise: growth depends not so much on human and capital investment as on changes in the efficiency of labour and capital used, i.e. reallocation and efficiency improvements.

The regression analysis is as follows:

$$Y = \alpha + \beta_1 X + \beta_2 C + \varepsilon$$

where Y, the dependent variable, is either GDP levels or GDP growth rate with preference for the latter as unrecorded economic activity may affect GDP levels more, X represents the exogenous variables, C is a set of control variables and ε is the usual random error term.[15] Further, we can also include contemporaneous and one-year lagged variables on the right-hand side of the equation. As stated before, dummy variables are used to control for the effects on economic activity of regional differences and armed conflicts. The right-hand-side variables are assumed to be exogenous to the performance (output growth) variable. If so, the econometric technique of Ordinary Least Squares (OLS) is used. Of course, some of the right-hand-side determinants of output – macro variables or policy reforms – may depend upon output themselves. If so, other statistical techniques, rather than simple OLS, may be used to derive better estimates.

In the mid-1990s, over half a decade after transition began, results from a number of quantitative studies examining the determinants of performance outcomes in TEs emerged. Findings for these and other early studies need to be treated with considerable caution for a number of reasons. First, the data (which in and of itself may be problematic) were only for the first few years (capturing only very short-run effects). Second, finding proxies for these variables is not an easy task and sometimes proxies are used that do not measure what they supposedly represent.[16] Third, in the regression equation there may be misspecification of the model (due to omission of relevant variables) and many of the variables used may be correlated with each other leading to biased estimates. There may also be measurement error, as official GDP data are underestimates due to the failure to capture much private sector activity in the early years of transition. To repeat: the results should be treated with caution and are merely indicative of the relative effects of some policy and non-policy variables on growth in TEs.

Table 7.8 lists 37 studies on the determinants of growth in transition countries. Coverage is mainly on the non-Asian countries, i.e. CEE and FSU countries. All these studies are cross-country, as we do not consider country-specific cases. This summary covers published studies over a 12-year period, from 1996 to 2007, and is adapted from an earlier summary in Havrylyshyn (2001).[17] The growth determinants identified are initial conditions, macroeconomic stabilisation, market reforms, institutions and factor inputs, with the latter

Table 7.8 Summary of empirical studies on the determinants of growth in transition countries

Author(s)	No. of TEs	Period	Initial conditions	Macro-stabilisation	Reforms	Institutions	Factor inputs	Others/control variables	Key findings
Fischer, Sahay and Végh (1996a)	25	1992–1994	✓	✓	✓				1. initial conditions (income and trade dependency) matter; 2. macro stability and structural change impact positively on growth
Fischer, Sahay and Végh (1996b)	20	1992–1994		✓	✓			Official External Assistance	1. macro stability (low inflation, fiscal discipline) is conducive to growth
Åslund, Boone and Johnson (1996)	23	1989–1995		✓	✓			Rouble zone and war dummies	1. a substantial loss of output is inevitable, and more so in FSU countries where the initial conditions were worse; 2. no robust significant correlation between output change and any measure of reform; 3. no evidence that radical reform leads to a greater fall in output; 4. cross-country differences in output fall reflect underlying structural factors as well as reform strategies
Sachs (1996)	25	1989–1995			✓				1. economic growth is positively correlated with reform progress.
Selowsky and Martin (1997)	25	1990–1995	✓		✓			war dummy	1. positive impact of policies on growth; 2. differences between FSU and CEE reflecting worse initial conditions in FSU countries
Brenton, Gros and Vandille (1997)	25	1989–1994		✓				speed of transition	1. significant positive correlation between output decline and average inflation; 2. significant positive correlation between output recovery and speed of transition

(*Continued*)

Table 7.8 Continued

Author(s)	No. of TEs	Period	Initial conditions	Macro-stabilisation	Reforms	Institutions	Factor inputs	Others/control variables	Key findings
Hernández-Catá (1997)	26	1990–1995		✓	✓			a set of control variables	1. strong liberalisation leads to a comparatively steep fall in output early in the transition, but a relatively strong recovery later on
Brunetti, Kisunko and Weder (1997)	20	1993–1995	✓	✓	✓	✓	✓	openness, government secure consumption	1. institutional reliability explains differences in performance; 2. property rights and political stability are important for growth; 3. the indicator of credibility is significant
Loungani and Sheets (1997)	25	1991–1994		✓	✓			war dummy	1. negative correlation between inflation and subsequent growth; 2. coefficient of reform index is positive and significant, indicating that increased reform is growth enhancing
Krueger and Ciolko (1998)	21	1989–1995	✓		✓			FSU and war dummies	1. if liberalisation index is endogenous to output decline, previous conclusions (with biased estimates) might overstate the role of policy; 2. in particular, while economic policies may have an effect on the recovery phase in transition, it is unlikely to have had a huge impact on the initial decline in output
Havrylyshyn, Izvorski and van Rooden (1998)	25	1990–1997	✓	✓	✓	✓		size of government	1. although adverse initial conditions hurt growth, the effect is small compared to the effect of

	No.	Period		Variables	Findings
					other factors; 2. macro stabilisation and structural reforms are key to achieving growth; 3. with respect to structural reform, there is no single reform that provides a magic solution for growth; 4. a reduction of government size and expenditure has a positive and significant effect on performance; 5. the impact of reform is different in the decline and recovery phase, with clear evidence of pain at the start of reforms
Havrylyshyn, Wolf, Berengaut, Castello-Branco, van Rooden and Mercer-Blackman (1999)	25	1990–1998	✓	openness, FDI, private sector share, IMF programme implementation	1. initial conditions matter but less so than policy reforms; 2. financial stabilisation is a necessary but not sufficient condition for sustained growth; 3. market reforms matter i.e. the initial output decline is greatest where reform is bolder, but so too is the subsequent recovery; 4. there is no one panacea as comprehensive progress on all elements of reform is needed
Heybey and Murrell (1999)	26	first 4 years	✓	speed of reform	1. initial conditions have a substantial affect on economic growth; 2. initial conditions are more important than policy changes in the first four years of transition; 3. the coefficients of speed of liberalisation and the policy level are insignificant; 4. no direct effect of speed of liberalisation on growth but growth performance (in the early years of transition) has a strong effect on liberalisation speed

(Continued)

Table 7.8 Continued

Author(s)	No. of TEs	Period	Initial conditions	Macro-stabilisation	Reforms	Institutions	Factor inputs	Others/control variables	Key findings
Moers (1999)	25	1990–1995	✓	✓	✓	✓	✓	control variables including a war dummy	1. (state) institutions (particularly formal ones) matter for growth; 2. institutions, as a determinant of growth, is more important than many others; 3. growth and institutional building are a two-way process rather than a one-way process; 4. inflation, war and institutions matter the most, implying that macrostabilisation, peace and (closely followed by) institution building are the transition policy priorities
Wolf (1999)	25	1989–1995	✓	✓	✓		✓	FSU and war dummies	1. a positive link between the liberalisation index and growth, but none between the speed of liberalisation and growth; 2. initial conditions do not exert an effect beyond an influence on the included growth determinants
Berg, Borensztein, Sahay and Zettelmeyer (1999)	26	1990–1996	✓	✓	✓			a set of control variables	1. the pre-eminence of liberalisation and structural reforms over both initial conditions and macro variables in explaining cross-country differences in performance and timing of the recovery; 2. countries that reform

Study		Period			Other variables	Findings
						faster, recover faster; 3. the U-shaped pattern in output is explained by the combination of a) post-communist initial conditions that, by themselves, generate a contraction in output and b) structural reforms, which are the driving force of the recovery; 4. fast liberalisation benefits growth; 5. findings support a 'radical' approach to reforms
Sachs and Woo (2000)	25	1989–1995	✓			1. faster reform is associated with higher growth
Fischer and Sahay (2000)	25	To – 1998	✓	✓	war dummy	1. stabilisation polices and structural reforms contribute to the growth recovery; 2. more and faster reform is better than less and slower reform i.e. the faster is the speed of reforms, the quicker is the recovery and the higher is growth; 3. with respect to initial conditions alone, the number of years under communism and the rate of secondary school enrolment were significant
Christoffersen and Doyle (2000)	22	1990–1997	✓		export market growth, war dummy	1. export market growth is strongly; associated with growth in transition 2. inflation is associated with weaker output only above a threshold inflation rate; 3. structural reform is associated with weaker output initially, but then it stimulates higher growth thereafter; 4. no evidence that disinflation necessarily incurs significant output costs

(Continued)

Table 7.8 Continued

Author(s)	No. of TEs	Period	Initial conditions	Macro-stabilisation	Reforms	Institutions	Factor inputs	Others/control variables	Key findings
Campos (2000)	25	1989–1997				✓			1. rule of law is the most important institutional factor in determining per capita growth; 2. there are differences in terms of FSU and CEE countries
Abed and Davoodi (2000)	25	1994–1998	✓	✓	✓			corruption index, control variables	1. macro policies, initial conditions and structural reforms are all important; 2. structural reforms tend to dominate the corruption variable
Katchanovski (2000)	28	1990–1998	✓	✓	✓			war, corruption, culture, ethnicity	1. The inclusion of a culture variable increases the explanatory power: there are direct and indirect (through policy, corruption, war) effects of culture, and it is difficult to determine which aspects of culture are the most important in explaining cross-country variation in performance; 2. macrostabilisation policy has an effect on growth, initially negative and then positive; 3. initial conditions and ethnicity are negatively associated with growth
Popov (2000)	28	1989–1996	✓	✓	✓	✓		FSU and war dummies	1. initial conditions matter: the higher the distortions the worse the performance; 2. whereas macroeconomic stability matters, liberalisation index is not significant; 3. institutional capacity

Study	N	Period		Additional variable		Findings
De Melo, Denizer, Gelb and Tenev (2001)	28	first 5 years	✓			matters; 4. liberalisation alone, without strong institutions, does not ensure good performance; 5. the focus on speed (gradualism vs. shock therapy), and on liberalisation per se, was misplaced as the primary issue is one of institutional strength
				regional tension dummy	✓	1. initial conditions are important; 2. relationship between economic liberalisation and performance is nonlinear overtime (initially negative, positive later on); 3. initial conditions and economic policy jointly determine economic performance; 4. policy (economic liberalisation) is the most important factor determining growth differences
Grogan and Moers (2001)	25	1990–1998		a set of control variables	✓	1. institutions (particularly formal state ones) matter for growth; 2. institutions, as a determinant of growth, is more important than many others; 3. inflation, liberalisation and institutions matter the most, implying that marostabilisation, liberalisation and institution building are the transition policy priorities
Raiser, Haerpfer, Nowotny and Wallace (2001)	19	1989–1998		social capital	✓	1. civic engagement is positively associated with growth; 2. trust in public institutions (particularly the legal system and the police) is also positively correlated with growth

(*Continued*)

Table 7.8 Continued

Author(s)	No. of TEs	Period	Initial conditions	Macro-stabilisation	Reforms	Institutions	Factor inputs	Others/control variables	Key findings
Radulescu and Barlow (2002)	25	1991–1999	✓	✓	✓			exchange rate regime and war dummies	1. macrostabilisation has a robust positive effect on growth; 2. a significant long-term effect of liberalisation on growth is not found, although the effects may be indirect; 3. results so far of empirical growth studies need to be treated with caution
Falcetti, Raiser and Sanfey (2002)	25	first 8 years	✓	✓	✓				1. the positive effects of reforms on growth, although evident, are smaller and less robust than previously thought and need considerable qualifications; 2. adverse initial conditions have a strong negative direct effect on growth, but their importance diminishes over time; 3. over the entire period, the initial conditions dominate the impact of reforms on growth
Havrylyshyn and van Rooden (2003)	25	1991–1998	✓	✓	✓	✓			1. the inclusion of an institutional variable adds to the explanatory power of the equation; 2. the effects of the indicators of institutional development are in the direction expected, statistically significant but not overwhelmingly i.e. a significant positive impact of growth; 3. confirmation of earlier findings i.e. stabilisation is a necessary but not sufficient

condition; eventual positive impact of liberalisation and related structural reforms; dispute on the impact of initial conditions; conventional factor input and technology determinants are not statistically significant; 4. good economic policies remain the dominant determinant of growth in TEs i.e. macrostablisation and broad-based economic reforms

Study							
Merlevede (2003)	25	To – 2000	✓	✓	✓		1. reform has a non-linear effect i.e. current level effects growth negatively, lagged reform effects growth positively; 2. stabilisation is significant in terms of its effect on growth (and its recovery)
Fidrmuc (2003)	25	5 yr moving avs.	✓		✓	democracy, war and location dummies	1. changing patterns of growth over time, with variables losing their significance in later period, reflecting the influence of external factors; 2. liberalisation is an important positive determinant of growth; 3. initial conditions and external environment also affect growth; 4. if democracy is included as a right-hand-side variable, the marginal impact of democracy on growth changes, initially negative and eventually positive. It does however reinforce liberalisation which in turn leads to better growth performance. Thus, there are merits to simultaneous democratisation and liberalisation

(Continued)

Table 7.8 Continued

Author(s)	No. of TEs	Period	Initial conditions	Macro-stabilisation	Reforms	Institutions	Factor inputs	Others/control variables	Key findings
Staehr (2005)	25	1989–2001	✓	✓	✓			war dummy	1. broad-based reforms are good for output growth in the medium term, but with a negative effect in the short-term; 2. inflation is negatively correlated with growth; 3. policy of liberalisation and small-scale privatisation (even without structural reform) is good for growth indicating that such a sequence is beneficial; 4. conversely, large-scale privatisation without other reforms affects growth negatively i.e. there is a complex pattern of reform complementarities; 5. the speed of reforms appears to have little effect on growth in the short and medium term.
Falcetti, Lysenko and Sanfey (2006)	25	1989–2003	✓	✓	✓			oil prices, external growth	1. progress in transition in one period has a significant positive effect on growth in subsequent periods; 2. higher growth, in turn, is associated with further reform efforts i.e. strong, contemporaneous feedback effects from growth to reforms; 3. initial conditions is an important determinant but has declined over time; 4. fiscal discipline, oil prices, recovery and trade links are all important

Study	No.	Period				Other variables	Findings
							determinants of a country's growth performance
Godoy and Stiglitz (2006)	23	1990–2001	✓	✓	✓		1. no evidence that fast privatisation has a positive effect on growth. Indeed, contrary to the earlier literature, the speed of privatisation is negatively associated with growth; 2. importance of the institutional strength measure. Consistent with earlier literature, property rights enforcement has a positive and very significant effect; 3. other variables, including initial conditions, appear to have little effect on growth after ten years, possibly because of the longer time dimension
Beck and Laeven (2006)	24	1992–2004	✓	✓	✓	speed of reform, ethnicity	1. a strong and positive relationship between institutional development and GDP per capita growth; 2. the robustness of the institutions-growth relationship to controlling for other growth determinants; 3. controlling for institutions, initial conditions, macro policies and speed of reform do not explain differences in growth across TEs
Popov (2007)	28	1989–2003 (2 periods)	✓	✓	✓	war dummy	1. initial conditions matter for the initial phase, as does the collapse of institutions; 2. recovery phase can be treated as standard growth theory, with liberalisation playing a positive role, and institutional capacity measure also;

(Continued)

Table 7.8 Continued

Author(s)	No. of TEs	Period of TEs	Initial conditions	Macro-stabilisation	Reforms	Institutions	Factor inputs	Others/control variables	Key findings
									3. liberalisation alone, when it is not complemented with strong institutions, cannot ensure good performance; 4. institutional capacity and macro policy are important prerequisites for performance; 5. overall, recessionary phase explained by initial conditions, institutional collapse and fast liberalisation whereas recovery phase explained by liberalisation and institutional capacity
Miller and Tenev (2007)	20	start – 1995	✓		✓	✓		regional tension	1. initial conditions are negatively associated with growth performance; 2. the effect of privatisation (when controlling for other factors) tends to be negative, although not statistically significant; 3. state strength or capacity has a strong and positive impact on growth performance. Indeed, it has the strongest impact on growth performance of all indicators

Note
To is defined as the year in which transition began in each country.

included in very few studies (for reasons outlined below). A number of studies include a variety of other (less important) exogenous variables and these are also listed, alongside control variables such as regional tensions and FSU membership. Table 7.8 also reports the main findings for each of the 37 studies listed.

We end with a short summary of the importance of the growth determinants as indicated by the empirical evidence that is reported above.

Factor inputs

In the traditional theory of economic growth, explanatory factors normally include physical and human capital accumulation, and other long-run factors such as innovation and political stability. Growth in TEs is not likely to be related to these standard determinants of growth found in the general empirics of growth literature but has more to do with improved resource allocation, i.e. reallocation of inputs within and across sectors rather than expansion of factor inputs. The general conclusion arising from the empirical research on growth in TEs is that traditional factor analysis plays very little or no part. More particularly, when investment (in the early years of transition) is tested for significance as an explanatory variable the results are the same, i.e. investment has not been a significant determinant of growth in transition. Over time, however, this is likely to change with some indication that the post-1999 recovery in many TEs and, in particular, the CIS countries was associated with a pick-up in investment.

Macroeconomic stabilisation

Macro stabilisation is usually measured by price stability and sound public finances. The respective proxies used are the inflation rate and the fiscal balance. Overall, the conclusion with respect to the relative importance of macro stabilisation is that it is significant in terms of explaining growth and, in particular, in accounting for the recovery phase. TEs that have achieved macro stability have also experienced a recovery in output. Although it is viewed as a necessary condition for recovery, it alone is not a sufficient condition for growth. Other reforms, both structural and institutional, are required in order for recovery to be sustained. One of the more controversial issues relating to the preconditions for growth is the extent of macro stability required. In particular, how low need the inflation rate be for economic growth to take off? As was stated above, was there a need for transition countries that were experiencing enormous structural and institutional change to push, within a short period of time, for single-digit inflation rates (in line with pre-conditions as set out for eurozone membership)? As with the empirical findings, there are mixed views on this issue, with no clear consensus emerging.

Liberalisation and structural reforms

The analysis suggests considerable variation in the nature of the relationship between economic policy reforms and growth. One view is that a minimum critical mass of reforms is required before policies begin to have the desired effects on growth. The evidence appears to indicate that the actual effects of policy reforms on growth are nonlinear, namely initially negative and then positive. Differences appear when comparing FSU countries and CEE countries, with the latter showing more positive effects of policy on output than the former group of countries. Overall, the conclusion with respect to the response to output of policy

261

reforms in transition countries is that reform policies are associated with higher growth rates (World Bank 2002a). In terms of speed (of reforms), there is some criticism of the findings in support of 'the faster, the better'. Such findings, it is argued, may be due to a number of methodological problems, including failure to address the difference between the speed of reform and the level of reform, the omission of initial conditions, the endogeneity of policy reforms and the multicollinearity among different measures of reform (Godoy and Stiglitz 2006). As with the speed of reform, testing for the importance of policy complementarities and/or sequencing is also difficult. Nonetheless, whereas early empirical studies generally found in favour of comprehensive reforms (that is, in support of reform complementarities), some later studies provide support for some form of policy sequencing.

Initial conditions

In the very early empirical studies on output performance and determinants of growth in TEs, initial conditions and the distorting effects of the inherited legacy of central planning were not included in the regression analysis. This often reflected a view that the important explanatory variable in explaining growth performance was policy reforms. By the mid- to late 1990s, the majority of studies on economic performance in TEs did include initial conditions as a determinant of output growth. In turn, the findings indicate that initial conditions do matter in terms of output performance and explaining cross-country differences. In general, countries with the most adverse initial conditions (that is, most of the FSU republics) performed the worst in terms of output growth, whereas countries with the most benign starting point have performed the best (namely CEE countries). There are also some findings to indicate that the importance of initial conditions has waned as the legacy of the Soviet system dissipates (Falcetti *et al.* 2006).

Institutions

As with initial conditions, a measure for institutions was not included in the earlier regression studies on the determinants of output performance in TEs (nor, for that matter, in many of the earlier regression studies for non-transition countries). Although this may have been due to a problem in accurately measuring institutions and institutional reforms, it was more likely to be as a result of a lack of appreciation of the importance of institutions in explaining output performance and cross-country differences. In more recent times, many of the regression studies accounting for growth differences have included institutions as an explanatory variable and, despite problems with using suitable proxies, the conclusion is that institutions, and institutional reform, matter and that institutions, along with initial conditions and policy reforms (both macro and structural), explain cross-country differences in output performance, particularly between CEE countries and CIS countries. With respect to transition, debate still continues over a number of specific issues relating to institutions including the identification of the most important institutions (is there a critical mass?), the design of a package of practical and implementable institutional reforms, the timing of market reforms versus institutional reforms, the determinants of institutional change (and whether institutions are inevitably slow moving or can they be built quickly), and the channels through which institutions affect growth.

After two decades of transition *and* reform, the authors are now in a position to identify what mattered most (what you might call first-order conditions) in terms of explaining or

Table 7.9 Determinants of performance and outcomes in transition countries

What mattered most for growth and performance	What mattered less for growth and performance
Certain initial conditions (e.g. proximity to markets, history of markets and market institutions)	Certain initial conditions (e.g. pre-transition reforms, natural resource endowment)
Structural reforms (e.g. enterprise restructuring, financial sector reforms)	Speed of reform
Entry and competition	Ownership and privatisation
Macroeconomic stability	Single digit inflation rates
International trade, exports	Exchange rate regimes
Absence of war and conflict	Factor inputs
Institutions and institution building	Best-practice institutions
Political constraints	Capital account convertibility and exchange controls
Good governance and effective State capacity	Democracy

accounting for growth, performance and outcomes in transition countries. Likewise, and possibly more controversially, we can identify what mattered less (or, expressed in a different way, what does not matter as much), some of which may be described as second-order conditions. In doing this, we do not distinguish between circumstances and policy choices. Furthermore, this tentative assessment is based only on the transition experience of former socialist countries and there is no suggestion (at least for now) of applicability to other countries and their respective experiences.

Some if not all of these issues arise in the context of changes in education and labour market reforms, which is the topic of the next chapter.

Summary

1   For CEE and FSU countries the first few years of transition were traumatic, with falling output, soaring prices, rising unemployment, and particularly in CIS countries, falling life expectancy rates. CEE countries were the first to recover, followed eventually by a rebound in FSU countries. However, these recoveries were uneven and erratic, with setbacks in some transition countries. By the beginning of the second decade, CEE countries and the Baltic States were performing well, acceding to the EU in 2004 and 2007. For many, this was a sign that transition was over. For others, namely the FSU countries, the data indicate that they, despite a surge in economic activity and GDP levels in the early to mid-2000s, have a long way to go.

2   With the exception of China and Vietnam, output in all former socialist countries declined in the early years of transition. Despite the recovery that followed, this output decline was a great surprise. Explanations for the fall in output vary, from systemic reasons, to policy mistakes and external shocks. Although it is difficult to establish the relative importance of each theory, it is likely that the decline in output was not due to one factor alone but was more likely due to some combination of factors.

3   The empirical research on the determinants of output growth in TEs identifies a number of factors, including initial conditions, macro stabilisation, institutions and policy reforms. Although the evidence is mixed, it appears that there is no one key factor in explaining cross-country differences in economic performance. Initial conditions matter,

but less so over time. Macro stability is important but excessive pursuit of low inflation and fiscal restraint may be costly. Market reforms matter but are not a sufficient condition for output recovery. Institutions are important, but differences exist as to which institutions are important and the timing of institutional reforms vis-à-vis economic policy reforms.

Key terms

Convergence effect
Credit crunch
Determinants of growth
Disorganisation
Endogeneity of reforms
Evolution of output
Factor inputs
Growth theory

Hyperinflation
Initial conditions
Institutions
Macro stabilisation
Policy reforms
Regression analysis
Transformational recession

Review questions

1 Identify factors that might explain differences between the economic performance of China and Vietnam and the performance of CEE/FSU countries in transition from plan to market.
2 Account for the output collapse in the early years of transition.
3 In the empirical literature on cross-country differences in output growth during transition, what are the key determinants identified? How are they measured in the regression analysis?

8

LABOUR MARKETS IN TRANSITION
A focus on Russia and China

The aim of this chapter is to explore how labour markets in Russia and China have moved in the direction of becoming labour markets as they are known and understood in mature Western economies. We focus on the two major and key transition economies by way of comparison as to how transition within their respective labour markets fundamentally differed and, in some cases, matched one another. The reader is advised to read this chapter in conjunction with Chapter 9, which also focuses on Russia and China but from the wider perspective as to how the economies travelled and are travelling the transition path.

Given the scope of the various areas that could be covered in this chapter – discrimination, gender wage gaps, poverty and inequality, segmented labour markets, the informal sector, the role of trade unions and so on – we have deliberately decided to focus on a few selected areas which will hopefully nevertheless highlight common areas between the two countries and at the same time some major differences.

We start by highlighting the main differences between labour markets as they existed under centrally planned economies and those that exist under market economies. We next examine the situation within the Russian labour market in the 1990s by exploring in some detail why there was a very large drop in output within the economy which was not accompanied by an equally proportionate fall in employment. We compare this labour hoarding to the surplus labour in China in the 1990s, both within an urban and a rural setting, and look at the major reforms of transition within China as it relates to the labour market. Unlike under central planning, education is a key element in any labour market that is market orientated. We next examine to what extent individuals in Russia and China could expect, as transition proceeded, to receive a wage which reflected their educational qualifications. Finally, we describe and explain the internal and external migration of labour that has taken place and is taking place within both countries. Linked into migration are the demographics of both countries which we briefly examine in order to see what the future holds for labour market development in both countries.

Labour under central planning and market economies

It may be useful for the reader if we start with a brief summary of the major differences between labour 'markets' as they existed under the classical Soviet system and labour markets as they exist under market systems. As noted in the introduction, we explore some of these differences in more detail later in the chapter.

Wage formation

- Very importantly, wages under the classical Soviet system did not act as a primary signal for the allocation of labour resources. Wages were not set through the free play of supply of and demand for labour, as broadly happens in market economies, but through bureaucratic fiat. The preceding, while correct in principle, masks a *degree* of free market forces that did occur in wage setting under central planning.[1]
- Wages differentials are considerably less in comparison with wage ranges in market economies. The wages of manual workers and of those in regions with harsh climates or 'pioneer' regions tended to be given greater weight in comparison to those of professionals or service workers.

Education and wages

- The link between education, which acts as a signal or indicates the degree of productivity of the individual in market economies, and is hence linked with the wage of the individual, is broken under the Soviet classical system.
- As a consequence, so-called 'returns to education' (discussed below) are far lower under the classical Soviet system in comparison to market economies. The tenure – length of service in a workplace – along with status and seniority are more important in determining the wage.

Labour market participation

- Labour market participation by individuals, as a percentage of the population of working age, is much higher under the Soviet system than under market economies.
- In particular, female labour market participation was, on average, higher under the classical Soviet system than in market economies. Both of these points are linked in with what was described in Chapter 1 as an extensive use of resources to develop the economy – rather than making the existing supply of labour (and capital) more productive (intensive use of resources) the central planners simply drew more and more sections of the population into the labour force. People who did not work were seen in the official media eye as 'parasites' living on the backs of others who did work.

Unemployment

- Open unemployment is virtually non-existent under the classical Soviet system. Due to the needs and demands of the overall planning system for factors of production under the Soviet-style system, the tendency was for local factory managers or directors to hoard labour (and other factors of production) just in case unexpected increases in production targets came through from channels above.
- Under market economies, not only has unemployment traditionally been an integral part of a market economy, but one can argue that it is part of the 'corrective process' whereby the degree of unemployment can influence how an economic boom turns into recession and recession then gives way to the next economic upswing.[2]

Labour mobility – both geographic and occupational

- Geographic labour mobility existed under the classical Soviet system especially when new areas of a country, far from already mature developed centres of the economy, were targeted by the planners for opening up. This mobility (notwithstanding the discussion on wages and mobility below) was largely directed from above and not on the same scale as exists under market economies, where individuals themselves will become mobile in reaction to the perceived benefits and costs of doing so.

- The degree of geographic mobility within market economies varies from one country to the next, with countries like the United States, for example, having quite extensive intra-state mobility. However, relatively speaking mobility is far greater in market economies in comparison with Soviet-style economies.
- Occupational mobility is also limited, again in comparison to market economies. The first job held could often be the last job.

Trade unions

- Trade unions under the Soviet-style system were an integral part of the system. Trade unions were expected to actively assist in achieving state-set production targets for five-year plans, working as they did so closely with the factory director. This differs from market economies where there is usually a high degree of independence between trade unions, employers and the state.
- In market economies, even where trade unions come under the control, or are pressurised by state bodies, the pressure from the state is for the trade unions to *desist* from participation in the economic process: they should not push for higher wages or campaign for better health and safety legislation, to give two examples, or in general interfere with management prerogatives.[3]

Wage formation and labour allocation

In Figure 8.1 (and in a simplified way) we describe wage formation under a market economy.[4] Once this has been done it should be easier to grasp the main differences with wage formation/setting under the classic Soviet system.[5]

Under a market economy, if we suppose that there are just two labour markets – one for college teachers and the other for university lecturers – *and* we assume that there is free mobility of labour between the two labour markets, *and* we assume that the job characteristics of the two occupations are roughly the same, *and* the skill levels of the workers in each factor market is the same, *and* there are no employee associations to fix wages at particular levels *or* impede entry to the profession by outsiders, then the wage paid in both markets should tend to equalise.

If the assumptions listed above hold, the wage differential between the two occupations should not last for any length of time. Assuming the demand curves do not shift, there would be a flow of college teachers moving to become university lecturers. This implies that the $S1_L$ shifts to the right and $S2_L$ shifts to the left. Both labour supply curves continue shifting until the wages of both professions equalise.[6]

If we now turn to the situation that had existed in the FSU, it may be thought by those who have had a cursory glance at wage setting in the FSU that the state set the going rate for a job or occupation: end of story. The preceding is only partly correct. The state certainly determined the overall amount of roubles available for distribution in the form of wages (the wage fund) and in that sense, even if supply and demand forces had free reign, they could only operate within certain parameters.

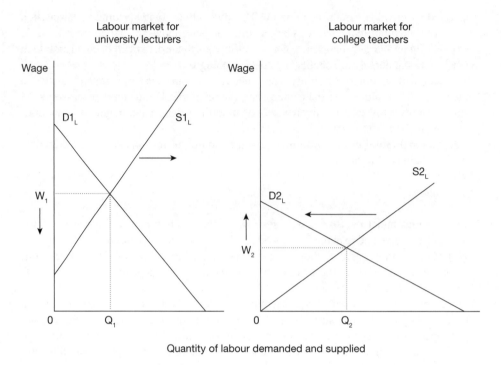

Figure 8.1 The wage equilibrium process under a market economy.

In theory the setting of wages and labour allocation proceeded as follows: economic (and political) goals were set by the Politburo – the all-powerful committee of the ruling Communist Party. Further down the command chain these priorities would be translated into production targets; this implied setting the level of inputs for different economic units not just of raw materials such as iron ore, copper, electricity and so on, but of the quantity and quality of labour needed to fulfil such targets, i.e. to turn input into output. Existing quantities and qualities of such labour could be compared to what would be required. Any shortfall would then have to be made up by either new additions to the workforce or by retraining the existing workforce.[7]

This then had implications for the education system in terms of the courses and degrees that were offered – you would not channel more students into chemical engineering courses, say, if there was already, or projected to be, a glut of such specialists; so cut back on these courses and/or lower the relative wages of this profession to make it less attractive to individual students. The opposite also held: professions in demand should have their respective courses at vocational, college or university institutions expanded and the relative standing of the salaries of these people would require an increase.

The above gives the appearance of a straightforward mechanical application of a command system. In reality, as outlined in Chapter 1, there was much coming and going as managers at all levels of the bureaucracy bargained with both the bureaucracy above and with the bureaucracy below it. Such bargaining involved the lower level echelons pleading for lower targets. In turn the same strata of bureaucracy which had argued for slack targets from above would cajole, threaten and entice those below it to achieve the targets agreed upon with the layer of bureaucrats above it.

The state set the actual wage scales and in the process determined the wage differentials between different occupations and professions. Originally, in the early stages of planning in the Soviet Union, there were as many as 1,900 different wage scales for workers. However, within each wage scale there could be a multitude of wage rates depending on the degree of perceived skill. Nove (1986b) reports that between 1933 and 1955 these scales were effectively set in stone with very little variation. Only with the creation of the State Committee on Labour and Wages in 1955 was there a significant overhaul of the wage scales with a drastic reduction in the number of scales by the mid-1960s, down to around 10. As can be seen, initially there was a high degree of inflexibility in how wages were determined in contrast to the relatively far more quick adjustments of real wages (and in many cases nominal wages) under market economies.

The other point to emphasise is the impossibility of a central planner being able to take into consideration the huge number of local factors when setting wage scales at a planning ministry. This was compensated for to a certain degree with an amount of discretion in how the 'pie' was distributed at a lower level. This is where a certain amount of market forces did operate in the short run. In brief, the setting of wages for particular grades of occupations or for specific professions and *ensuring* that individuals received such a wage was another matter. Flexibility of either an official or unofficial nature existed in the FSU within parameters laid down by the state.

The ultimate 'market force' assisting workers under the FSU to press for higher wages or, more accurately, for higher relative wages was the chronic shortage of labour that existed in many of the mature communist economies of the FSU and the Eastern bloc in general.[8] This shortage of labour existed even when there existed reserves of labour yet to be brought into the productive system. This combined phenomenon of both a labour shortage and a labour surplus existed for several reasons.[9] First, there is a lack of skills among those workers who could have been drawn into economic activity – the labour is then of the wrong type. It takes time to train and it takes time to gain quality experience. Second, much of the labour is in the countryside. Schools, hospitals, and of course housing need to be built first in the cities before such labour can even be transferred to the cities. The added problem then exists that if this process is rushed, agricultural output could decline, with food shortages leading to price hikes (in the black market) and unfulfilled queues. This could then lead to social unrest – something the bureaucracy of the FSU and other communist regimes wished to avoid at all costs.

Local managers also had a degree of discretion as to how a worker should be graded. Nove (1986b) makes the point that there were so few typists officially in the FSU since, with their pay scales being so low, they needed to be reclassified in some better paid occupation. He adds the humorous caption taken from a cartoon from the satirical Soviet magazine, *Krokodil*, 'She is an excellent secretary, and so I appointed her as a turner of the 5th grade'.

In addition, although in theory regional development could be planned and should not proceed in a haphazard manner, the reality was different with political priorities if not political whims deciding major economic policy issues. While labour from the gulags could, under Stalin, be marched into the tundra to open up the wilderness, by and large labour, under other Soviet rulers, had to be enticed into regions that were far from the centres of commerce and culture. Wages and living conditions (in terms of amenities) would have to be higher and of better quality. The promises to deliver such quality improvements in life were not always delivered. Nikita Khrushchev's adventure in opening up, or attempting to open up the Siberian wilderness is a case in point. Held back, in large part, by the difficulties in attracting and retaining labour to this region, it is also an example of regional development gone awry.[10]

Turning briefly to labour markets within China following the 1949 revolution, a feature of the wages system in contrast to market economies mentioned above is the compressed nature from the highest to the lowest paid workers. Within the People's Republic of China (PRC), after 1949 incomes within enterprises were reduced from a 40- to 50-fold difference between the highest and lowest paid, to a four- to seven-fold difference after the revolution. (Howe 1973, quoted in Knight and Song 2006). Nove (1986b) cites figures for the FSU where the ratio between the top 10 per cent of wage earners and the bottom 10 per cent stood at 7:1 in 1946, but by 1970 this had fallen to 3:1 with the respective figures for the top 5 per cent and bottom 10 per cent for the same years coming in at 10:1 and 3.5:1.[11]

Wage scales, as per the reform in the FSU, were streamlined in the PRC such that all administrative personnel were placed in 20 salary grades; technicians into 17 and manual employees into eight grades. In addition, while Kornai and Nove (see note 1 of this chapter) have emphasised the important role that supply and demand factors played in the Soviet system of labour allocation along with wage setting, Knight and Song (2006) emphasise that the system in China was far more rigid in the direction of labour where 'The first job was often the last.'

As with the FSU, many social benefits within the PRC were attached to the job – housing, childcare, medical services, pensions, etc. This-cradle-to-grave state protection went by the name of the 'iron rice bowl' (*tie fan wan*) whereby employees and many of those in collective farms had secured tenure of employment along with the accompanying benefits that were attached to the job. This state social protection also acted as a huge disincentive towards labour mobility in the limited number of cases where it was possible. Like the FSU, the PRC also had restrictions on who could live where. Within China from 1958 *and even during the current reform period*, every citizen is required to have a *hukou*. This is an official document stating one's legally recognised place of residence. With this *hukou* one may then obtain certain rights including the right to work in certain professions, health care, and sending your children to schools within the area of residence. Knight and Song (2006) argue that as a result of this tight control on internal migration, one major difference between the PRC and the USSR was in the sharpness of the rural–urban divide which, in terms of 'the ratio of urban to rural average household income and consumption per capita exceeded 2 to 1 and was sometimes as high as 3 to 1 throughout the period of central planning'. In contrast, Nove (1986b) informs us that for 1965 and 1984 the respective figures for sovkhozy and kolkhozy agricultural workers are as shown in Table 8.1. As may be seen, the rural–urban gap was not as wide as existed in China under central planning. In addition, the figures in Table 8.1 probably overplay the differences between town and countryside given that those living off the land had access to private plots of land and living costs in general should have been lower in rural areas.

Table 8.1 Average monthly pay as a percentage of urban workers' wage

	1965	1984
Sovkhozy	72	86.2
Kolkhozy	49	72.2

Source: Nove (1986b) and references cited therein.

Knight and Song (2006) conclude that in

the period prior to urban economic reform China had an administered labour system but no labour market. There was bureaucratic allocation of labour and determination of wages. Labour mobility, whether between jobs or between localities, was strictly controlled and severely restricted. The centralized control of enterprises provided no inducement for the efficient use of labour, and indeed surplus labour was imposed on enterprises. Workers had few material incentives to acquire human capital, to work efficiently, or to improve work methods. The system enabled the state to pursue its egalitarian objectives.

Labour hoarding during the transition in Russia

In the normal state of affairs it might be expected that under a market economy when a firm is faced with lower orders for its product or service, steps will be taken to cut back on the economic activities of the firm. In terms of labour input this usually refers to, first, cutting back on hours (less overtime, a shorter working week); if economic difficulties persist, those on temporary contracts may not have their contracts renewed; this could be followed by short-time working combined with those on full-time contracts being placed on work rotation – working only every alternative day or alternative week; extended periods of mass lay-offs – either paid or unpaid – could follow; usually, but not always, redundancies are the last step. The speed with which each of these potential steps can be taken will depend on the severity of the economic conditions facing the firm. If the onset of economic recession is gradual, each of the above steps may occur sequentially; if the difficulties are sudden and severe the initial steps will in all probability be bypassed and the firm will move straight to redundancies. January 1992 in the FSU stands out as a period when economic circumstances changed suddenly and severely – for the worse.

One would have expected not only the inevitable downturn in economic activity in terms of lost output of goods and services but an accompanying reduction in employment levels and so an increase in unemployment. Employment did fall but, in comparison to output, not nearly to the same extent. This is shown in Figure 8.2. The dashed-dotted line represents output and the solid line employment. The two time-series have been normalised to start in 1991. It may be seen that while output fell quite precipitously, employment did not match this fall, with output and employment only beginning to recover after the financial crisis of 1998.[12]

As for *registered* unemployment, for Russia this stood at 2.1 per cent as a percentage of the labour force at the year end in 1994, 2.7 per cent in 1998 and 1.4 per cent in 2000 (United Nations Economic Commission for Europe, Common Database 2001 cited in Nesporova 2002). If such figures are taken at face value this is a truly remarkable achievement given the widespread economic dislocation that occurred. As the reader might suspect, one should take these figures with the proverbial pinch of salt.

Standing (1996), based mainly on a series of Russian Labour Force Surveys (RLFS) between 1991 and 1994 of 340 to 500 enterprises, writes that in September 1991 managers of enterprises visited reported that only 10 per cent of their workforce had too little work in the *previous* year for periods of a month or more, although this average conceals differences between economic sectors of 7 per cent in textiles to 21 per cent in chemicals. By the second RLFS, however, in mid-1992 this figure had risen to an average of 62 per cent for all sectors with 55 per cent of all establishments reporting that they could produce the same level of

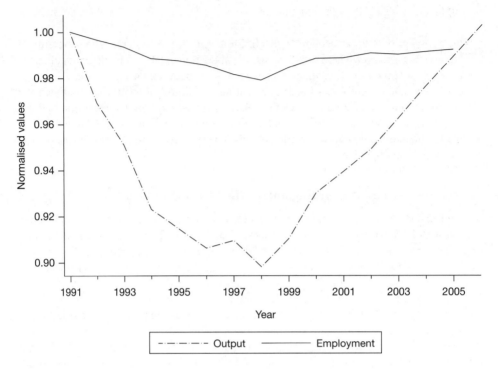

Figure 8.2 Russian employment and output dynamics, 1991–2005.*

Source: UNECE Database. See http://w3.unece.org/pxweb/DATABASE/STAT/Economics.stat.asp (accessed 23 January 2008). Rebasing of years, normalisation and graph are author's own calculations. The method of measuring GDP from the database was the output approach. Employment data for 1991 from Klein *et al.* (2001).

Note
*Normalised output is the method whereby the actual value of output at a particular year (in this case 1991) is divided by the output at that year. Other years' output figures are also divided by this original output figure. The same process is done for employment. This then allows the *relative* changes of the variables which have been normalised to be observed more easily.

output with fewer workers than currently employed. The estimated number of workers that could be cut by these firms, without affecting output, totalled 18 per cent.

Far from firms bypassing the stages mentioned above and proceeding to proportionate employment cuts, various measures short of outright redundancies were taken. The approach taken by many enterprises is shown in Table 8.2, derived from the third RLFS.

The high figure of approximately 40 per cent for unpaid leave is worth dwelling on and needs to be seen in the context of management, at the time, having a legal responsibility to pay two to three months' severance pay in the event of making someone redundant; if you hadn't actually sacked the person there was no need to pay redundancy money. For the employee on unpaid leave there was always the hope of being taken back on into paid employment at some stage. In addition, access to many social and cultural amenities was tied to one's employment status. Firms provided, even after several years of transition, many benefits of a non-monetary kind. Finally, from the management side there was always the possibility that the laid-off employee would simply 'drift away' with then no need to pay statutory severance pay.

Table 8.2 Main and second main measures taken in response to surplus labour, besides retrenchment and transfer, 1992–1993

	Main measure	Second main measure
None	0.5	0.0
Cut normal hours	20.7	20.3
Cut overtime	0.8	1.6
Paid leave	3.3	3.1
Unpaid leave	41.3	21.9
Partially paid leave	15.7	26.6
Cut wages	1.7	6.3
Cut production	9.9	15.6
Other	1.7	4.7

Source: Copyright © International Labour Organization (1996).

Table 8.3 Indicators of surplus labour or concealed unemployment in Russian industry, mid-1994

Indicator	Percentage
Could produce the same amount with fewer workers:	
% employment cut possible, if yes	20.3
% employment cut possible, all firms	9.8
Labour unused due to complete production stoppages	4.0
Labour unused due to partial production stoppages	2.8
Unpaid administrative leave	3.0
Partially paid administrative leave	12.2
Fully-paid administrative leave	0.3
Short-time working – fewer days or hours per day	12.3
Maternity leave:	
% of women	5.9
% of all workforce	4.0
Unpaid employment	?

Source: Copyright © International Labour Organization (1996). See the cited reference for the details of the assumptions necessary to make such a calculation.

By the time of the RLFS4 in mid-1994, 48.2 per cent of workplaces said they could maintain output at current levels with fewer employees. For all managements, including those that said they did not believe they could cut jobs, they estimated they could cut employment by 9.8 per cent.

Standing (1996) attempts to quantify the nature of the concealed unemployment that existed in Russian industry in 1994. Table 8.3 presents his estimates based on the RLFS4 conducted in mid-1994.

Excluding maternity leave and unpaid employment, Standing estimates that suppressed unemployment in Russian industry stood at approximately 35 per cent in May 1994 which, expressed alternatively, is one in three of the workforce.[13] Even allowing for the fact that (as Standing himself admits) this is a snapshot of the *industrial* labour market in Russia at a certain point in time, covering as it does a limited number of regions within Russia, *and* even if we allow a certain degree of overestimation, he argues that 'plausibly' one in five workers (i.e. 20 per cent) were in effect surplus to requirements in Russian industry in May 1994. This is still a very large percentage and should be compared to the estimated figure for hoarded *labour hours* in US manufacturing of 4 per cent during an economic downturn.

Little wonder that labour productivity languished at low levels for most of the 1990s in most economic sectors. It also helps to explain why, when economic recovery started – after the 1998 financial crisis – labour productivity increased strongly in many economic sectors (see Ahrend and Tompson 2005). That said, actual labour productivity increases started in 1997 and averaged 8 per cent each year up until 2003, perhaps indicative that economic recovery may have been on the way even without the assistance of a devalued rouble.

Were there any other reasons why employment did not appear to fall proportionately as much as output; and second, why did open, registered unemployment not rise by anything like what might have been expected? First, on open unemployment, it should be stressed that those without a job and registered as unemployed is not the same thing as unemployment as understood by economists and by conventions laid down by, for example, the International Labour Organisation.

(The internationally accepted definition is that the individual should be seen as unemployed if the person fulfils three criteria. First, that the person is without a job; second, that the person has been searching actively for work over a given period; and finally, that the individual is prepared to start work if a job is offered.)

Many household surveys (usually conducted quarterly) throughout the world tend to use a series of questions based on the ILO definition to uncover the employment status of the individual. These household surveys along with the ILO definition are often seen to be a more reliable indicator of the true level of unemployment. In the case of Russia in the early to late 1990s, survey unemployment is usually much larger than registered unemployment. For example, in the fourth quarter of 1993 and 1997 survey unemployment reached 5.6 and 9.0 per cent respectively against end-of-year officially registered unemployment of 1.1 and 2.8 per cent (OECD various years).

Layard and Richter (1995) list a number of possible reasons why registered unemployment in Russia in the early to mid-1990s was so much lower than survey unemployment. These are:

- Benefits paid by the state were very low; for many the bureaucracy of registering was hardly worth the end result.
- In the early 1990s most of the job vacancies on the books of the labour exchanges of the Federal Employment Service (FES) were of a manual character. These positions would not be attractive to the more educated jobless. As a result, job placement of those registered with the FES amounted to only about 1 per cent of the workforce per year; this is small when compared to the then hiring figure of 20 per cent of the workforce each year.
- In the early years of transition at least, the FES provided little formal training to the unemployed registered with them. Layard and Richter (1995) report that only 3 per cent in September 1994 received any kind of formal training. This acted as an additional disincentive to register.
- There was, among some individuals at the outset of transition, a distaste for claiming benefits. It should be recalled that under communism it was illegal not to work; people who did not work (but were able) were perceived not just by the state but by many people within society to be 'parasites'. Claiming benefits was seen by some as having a certain stigma attached to it.
- The network of FES branches was still developing in the 1990s and some people would not have had easy access to a local branch. It was probably perceived by some to be not worth the effort to travel in order to register.

- Some unemployed people within the survey were actually working but did not say so for fear of attracting the attention of the tax authorities. Only this last point above would tend to have exaggerated survey unemployment.

Real wage flexibility

As may be seen from Table 8.2, only 1.7 and 6.3 per cent of firms saw cutting wages as a main or secondary response respectively to surplus labour; given the proportion that saw unpaid leave as the main response this is hardly surprising. However, the data in Table 8.2 may give the impression that wage flexibility was not something that occurred within Russia in the early years of transition: this is not the case. First, even if it was the case that few enterprises actually cut the wages paid to their employees, inflation within the system did the job for them.

At the end of 1995, average real wages had, according to Goskomstat (1996, cited in Lehmann *et al.* 1999), fallen to around 34 per cent of the level observed before transition began in January 1992. The drop in real wages levelled off in 1996. However, a new mechanism took over from real cuts in wages brought about by either nominal cuts in wages or through inflation eating away at the value of nominal wages; this was the tide of wage arrears which swept Russia.[14] The above should be contrasted with real wages in China during the series of economic reforms that impacted upon urban workers. Below we show that with the beginnings of economic reform moving towards placing firms on a more market-oriented footing, real wages for urban workers rose, and rose very strongly.

Standing (1996) presents both qualitative and quantitative data for Russia on the proportion of firms which found it difficult to pay wages in 1993 and 1994. In 1993 46.9 per cent of all firms and 53.8 per cent of state firms reported in the 1993 RLFS that they had difficulty in paying the wages they had already agreed to pay their employees. Interestingly, Standing (1996) reports that the firms that were least likely *not* to pay wages were those firms where the managers had been elected by the workers (40.6 per cent of those firms having difficulties) against 56.5 per cent and 60 per cent where the manager had been appointed by a ministry or a local authority respectively.

By the time of the 1994 RLFS, 47.3 per cent of all firms admitted to not paying wages on time. The larger the firm (by employment), the more chance there was of it paying wages late; the more the firm had attempted to cut employment, the greater the chance of the firm having wage arrears. On average, of the firms who were in arrears, these arrears amounted to 78 per cent of the wage bill of the firm. While it may have been inconvenient (to put it mildly) for those employees not receiving their wages on time, one might be tempted to argue that they would/did get their wages eventually. First, this was not necessarily the case as was admitted off the record by many managers to Standing; and second, in a country where inflation was substantial, delays in receiving wages amounted to wage cuts.

Finally, we turn to the issue of how the assets of the state were privatised, and in the process we raise the issue of insider-power as a partial answer to the question as to why employment did not fall as fast as output in Russia in the 1990s.

Insider power

Why then did employment not fall as much as output? Why were, in effect, large sections of the workforce kept on when they were surplus to requirements? First, it should be pointed out that even under market economies, during an economic recession, it has been documented that some employees will be kept on when – in terms of the absolute needs of the firm for labour – they are not needed (see e.g. Fair 1985; Fay and Medoff 1985; Darby *et al.* 2001). Fay and Medoff (1985) calculate for a sample of US manufacturing plants that 4 per cent of the blue-collar labour hours paid for by the typical plant at the trough of a recession should be classified as hoarded.

This labour hoarding is different from the labour hoarding that occurred in the Russia of the 1990s, being due to the costs of firing, hiring, and training costs associated respectively with getting rid of 'excess' employees (e.g. redundancy payments); then having to find and hire replacement workers during the economic upswing (advertising vacancies, interview costs, and the general human resource department upkeep); followed by a costly time period when any new hands are either trained up and/or they need to get acquainted with firm-specific practices (there is no guarantee that those fired during the downturn will still be around to be taken on). These costs have given the basis to various theories of 'insider-power' as they relate to market economies (see Lindbeck and Snower 1988, 2002; Lindbeck 1992). Keeping on surplus labour in firms during a recession is costly but presumably not as costly as getting rid of skilled workers only to have to replace them several months later.

In terms of what transpired within the FSU during the early years of transition, from an economic perspective one may approach this question from many directions. We approach it from the point of view of the type of ownership that emerged with privatisation during the 1990s, and the concomitant change in corporate governance to which this has led.

The critical assumption of all versions of insider–outsider theories is that the respective wages of insiders and outsiders are linked (Romer 1996). The first group, the insiders, are workers who have had some connection with the firm at the time of bargaining, and whose interests are therefore taken into account in the contract. The second group, the outsiders, who have had no initial connection with the firm, may be hired after the contract with the insiders is set.

The literature dealing with insider theory as applied to Western economies implicitly (if not explicitly) gives the impression that insiders are to be seen as 'the workers'. In the context of transition economies this is not the case. Earle *et al.* (1996) suggested that insiders dominate a firm if the insiders hold more shares than outsiders do and the insiders hold at least an equal amount to the state. In their turn insider firms are seen as dominated by managers if management hold more than the workers do; and worker dominated if vice versa. Management, then, can be seen as insiders whose agenda may coincide or conflict with those of workers and/or outside investors. Further, outsiders may mean other groups of workers seeking employment or groups of financial investors looking to take a stake in the company that may or may not be of a controlling nature.

In general it would be expected a priori that *de novo* firms would act in a completely market-oriented fashion; that insider privatisation would be superior to state ownership but inferior to majority outsider ownership. However, as Earle *et al.* (1996) point out, regardless of the form of ownership, if competition within the product market is great enough, then this on its own may be sufficient to force firms to restructure and so to maximise profits. Given the last point above, privatisation in and of itself will *not* necessarily lead to an improvement in corporate governance. Of interest below is to explore whether ownership type played a role in firm behaviour despite the large-scale quasi-monopolisation that existed with privatisation in the 1990s (and still exists) in large sections of the Russian economy.

Simon Commander and the World Bank's Economic Development Institute developed the idea of insider-power as applied to transition economies. Due to the method of privatisation, which favoured those already working inside the enterprise, the chance for a controlling investment from outside the firm was limited. This resulted in labour hoarding since, in order to restructure, employees would have to be laid off. Which employee, however, was going to vote for himself or herself to be laid off? The ability of enterprises to put off restructuring was reinforced by soft budget constraints from the government either directly or indirectly by the refusal/inability to pay federal and regional taxes, and later, not to pay wages where management as the insiders dominated the firm.

As applied to economies in the West, insider–outsider theories are usually used to explain why wages are kept above market clearing levels and hence why the labour market does not clear. This leads to a persistence of unemployment and may be approached theoretically through the concept of hysteresis. Alternative explanations of unemployment build on labour turnover costs may be found in Lindbeck and Snower (1988) and Lindbeck (1992).

In a transition economy like Russia in the early to mid-1990s, labour turnover costs (of hiring, training and firing) were not seen by Commander (1998) as the main source of insider-power. Insiders in the context of the Russian economy in the 1990s exerted more market power because of the then unresolved ownership question (an incomplete privatisation programme or the *manner* of privatisation) and of past socioeconomic relations. It cannot be assumed that all firms will behave in a completely market-oriented fashion. Insiders have their power enhanced further if it is perceived by them that policy makers in their respective countries fear the potential social strains of too sudden a rush of unemployment in the drive to transform the economy along market lines.

Due to the method of privatisation within Russia, insider ownership over the period of the early 1990s had become quite widespread (Bim 1996; Earle *et al.* 1996). In 1992 the government of Russia began the privatisation of medium- and large-scale enterprises. The two main routes selected for this privatisation programme were management and employee buyouts and voucher auction sales of shares in state firms. The second variant in particular was popular, since it allowed employees – workers or management – to acquire up to 51 per cent of the shares.

Blasi and Shleifer (1994) found that insiders held about 65 per cent of enterprise shares in their survey material in 1993. Bim (1996), through his survey material, found, however, that it very soon became substantially dispersed and differentiated. At the end of 1993, non-managerial employees possessed more than 50 per cent of shares in only 16.7 per cent of the companies surveyed. In the majority of joint stock companies (66.7 per cent) non-managerial employees held 30 to 50 per cent of the shares, with a good proportion of the companies quite far from the upper margin of this range. The implication of this was that without the support of other interest groups non-managerial employees could not attain effective control of the workplace.

In the much larger sample of 439 enterprises, Earle *et al.* (1996) find that on average across privatised companies workers held 48 per cent of the shares, managers 21 per cent and outsiders 20 per cent. Both surveys found that even where workers held shares there was little active involvement in decision making. Indeed, Gurkov and Maital (1996) report that more than 40 per cent of the workers in their sample had their capacity to influence decision making reduced *after* they became shareholders. Furthermore, 38 per cent indicated 'no change'; 46 per cent of the worker shareholders even mentioned that their access to information about the performance of their company had also become worse following privatisation. Finally, about

50 per cent of the workers reported playing no role in any kind of distribution including that of dividends.

Does this imply that insider–outsider theory is irrelevant? Not quite. First, it cannot be assumed that even though the managers of firms were in effective control that the influence of workers did not have some impact, even implicitly, especially in the early years of transition. This is the influence of paternalism. Broadman and Recanatini (2001), for example, examine enterprise restructuring in Russia since 1996 (when it might have been thought that paternalism had waned) and note several factors to explain the apparent lack of restructuring. Observing that job destruction has taken place to a limited extent in some sectors and regions, they explain this by institutional and incentive constraints and a still widespread 'socialist' corporate culture. As they note, 'many managers have acted paternalistically in maintaining employment inasmuch as significant lay-offs would increase poverty among their workers, particularly as the unemployment insurance system does not have adequate resources or sufficient capacity to channel resources to particular groups' (Broadman and Recanatini 2001).

Below, when we look at the very low *official* level of unemployment in China during the mid- to late 1990s – despite millions of workers being laid off from SOEs – we will see that a form of paternalism also existed in Chinese workplaces (the *danwei* work unit). This paternalism (Chinese style), however, is more useful in explaining why real wages *rose* strongly and not in helping to explain the retention of workers, who, as noted, were laid off in their millions, although technically many of them – so-called *xia gang* workers – still retained ties to their old workplaces.

Second, as touched on above, it is possible that the managers themselves should be regarded as insiders who had their own agenda that did not necessarily coincide with profit maximisation and the concomitant need to restructure. Even Bim (1996), while effectively dismissing insider-power of *workers*, remarks that employees still more often support management in conflicts between managers and outsiders because they consider 'even tough managers less radical and more tolerant towards employees than "strangers" could potentially turn out to be'.

In 72 per cent of the cases in 1993 and 73 per cent in 1994 of Bim's survey, the response of workers interviewed showed clearly that managers had succeeded in creating an 'enemy image' with respect to outsider shareholders throughout the workforce. A case of 'better the devil you know', perhaps.

Commander *et al.* (1996) attempted to test for paternalism. They use an ordered logit estimation relating firm objectives to firm and other attributes. When profit objective is ranked high, employment and worker welfare objectives will tend to be of low importance. By contrast the predicted probability of holding sales in high importance rises in step with high importance being attached to worker objectives. The implication of their findings was that for those firms who do not rank profit highly or who are not located in the private sector, worker welfare is more important) Despite this and other studies, Commander (1998) concluded that estimating the extent of insider influence had been elusive. Commander argues elsewhere that workers exerted *indirect* influence (Commander and McHale 1996).

Standing (1996), on the other hand, placed the emphasis not on insider-power per se, but on wage flexibility. He argued that the Russian labour market suffered from *too much* wage flexibility. Flexible wages helped to sustain labour hoarding by state and former state enterprises. This removes the incentive of enterprises to restructure. Writing about the attempts of successive Russian governments to limit wage increases using tax-based income policies, he criticises the 'excess-wage tax' for distorting wage incentives.[15]

The tax has encouraged firms to shift into fringe benefits and thus has hindered them from developing the wage mechanism as an incentive and reward for labour productivity. Without productivity growth, economic restructuring will be painfully unrewarding for many years, and without a restructuring of the wage system productivity is unlikely to improve.

(Standing 1996)

Commander (1998), however, directed attention at the labour market rigidities highlighted by labour hoarding brought on by insider-power; at the same time Layard and Richter (1995) welcomed the flexibility of wages, which gave employees the choice between a job, albeit at low pay, or moving on to a new position. This flexibility of wages was a sign that the labour market was working, not that there were rigidities.

The differences between the three positions was well summarised by Clarke (1996):

Within the liberal camp there are two sharply contrasting interpretations which declare Russia to be the ultimate negative or positive example. On the one hand, it is argued that Russia is plumbing the depths of recession because of labour market rigidities, which impede structural adjustment. On the other hand it is argued that Russia has developed a perfectly flexible labour market, which is the key to a structural adjustment without mass unemployment. The third sceptical position combines the latter view that Russia has an extremely flexible labour market with the former view that Russia has undergone little structural adjustment, while contesting the position common to both that Russia has avoided mass unemployment.

(Clarke 1996)

In conclusion, is the above mere historical nit-picking which, while of interest to labour and transition economists, is ultimately an arcane subject area not really worthy of much attention today? In short, no. There was (and is) a debate within economic and political circles as regards the flexibility of labour markets within Europe and, indeed, within developing economies especially *before* the world economic turmoil of 2007 to 2009. If only, so the argument went, labour markets in countries such as Germany and France were more flexible, unemployment would not be so high and firms would not have the fear of being unable to fire workers during any economic downturn. Consequently firms would hire more workers.[16]

While this is not the time and the place to repeat the various arguments advanced (both for and against), it should be clear, especially from a reading of developments in Russia in the early 1990s by Standing (1996), that *too much* wage flexibility can be just as counterproductive to economic restructuring as *too little*. In addition, while it is recognised that the legal and economic situation between Russia at the start of transition and the European Union differs, one thing that Russia has demonstrated in the early to mid-1990s is that if firms wish to reduce their personnel levels short of making them actually redundant or to obviate employment legislation, they will find all sorts of ways to do so.

Labour hoarding in China and real wage increases during the transition period

What of China during the transition in the urban part of China? (See below for surplus labour in rural China both before and after transition started in 1978.) Here it is important to realise

279

that whereas surplus labour or labour hoarding took place in the Soviet Union under central planning and in Russia of the 1990s under a form of market capitalism, they did so for different reasons. The reasons for the former are outlined in Chapter 1 and the latter both above and, to a lesser extent, in Chapter 9.

With the PRC, while transition was well under way in the countryside by the mid-1990s, a fully fledged market economy as per Western Europe or even the rudimentary form of 1990s Russia was not present in China. Neither, however, was a pure central planning system! (See Chapter 9 for an explanation of the dual-track pricing system, for example.) Nevertheless, the surplus labour inside workplaces that did exist in urban areas of China in the early to mid-1990s must be seen to have existed for two main reasons. First, as outlined in more detail in Chapter 1, managers of firms under central planning always preferred labour resources over and above what was absolutely necessary just in case additional demands were placed on them by the planners. This might be seen as a micro reason; a macro reason was the belief held by the leadership of the CCP that the urban workers posed a political threat to their continued rule if and when the relatively privileged lifestyle of the urban workers (relative to the peasantry) should come under threat. Only with the success of rural reforms (see Chapter 9 for details) did the leadership become emboldened to turn its reformist agenda to the workers in the towns and cities. As such our second reason could tenuously be seen as a kind of collective insider-power held by the urban working class. However, this power was and is very much a latent power which during the transition period has never, on a nationwide basis, been expressed in open conflict with the CCP.[17] Even where localised disputes over unpaid wages have occurred they have not as a rule of thumb turned into political disputes to threaten the power of the ruling order.

Knight and Song (2006) cite various studies carried out in the early 1990s for estimates of surplus labour. By surplus labour they mean in the sense of output being unaffected by an x per cent cut in the workforce. The estimates cited vary from 10 to 12 per cent (a Ministry of Labour survey of 15,000 enterprises) to 25 per cent (by officials in charge of planning and systems reform), and 23 to 32 per cent in Wuhan province with other surveys scattered in between. How then was this surplus labour eventually released into open unemployment? While, of course, the immediate cause was in effect compulsory redundancies, there was a buildup of reforms in the state industrial sector which impacted both directly and indirectly upon the labour market. We outline some of the more important reforms and institutional developments taken from Knight and Song (2006).

- 1983: SOEs allowed to redistribute after-tax profits for employee welfare and bonuses, subject to maximum percentages.
- 1984: Bonus ceiling repealed and bonuses subject to a hefty tax which had the effect of ruling out bonuses in excess of three months' salary. The following year an alternative was tried whereby a SOE's wage bill was linked to its tax and profit remittances. Clearly the state was attempting some experimentation to 'get it right'.
- 1985: A system of labour contracts introduced for new workers as opposed to older workers who were regarded as permanent. This had no immediate effect until the mass layoffs of the mid-1990s. The Labour Law of 1994, however, required all employees to have work contracts including permanent employees.
- 1988: By this stage the wage of the worker is composed of (1) basic wage (from centrally laid down wage scales); (2) the functional wage (relating to seniority and status); and (3)

the floating wage relating to bonuses, which it would seem tended to be distributed evenly within a workplace, thus working against individual worker motivation.

- 1990s: Unemployment insurance system introduced. By 2000, 103 million workers covered.
- 1992: Growth in the wage bill would be linked strictly to the enterprise's economic performance measured by after-tax profits and labour productivity. SOEs would be free to determine how the wage bill would be distributed.
- 1994: The bank reform of 1994 forbade loss-making enterprises to borrow from banks to pay the wages of their workers.
- 1994: Labour Law introduced and became operative in 1995. Among its provisions were the promotion of labour exchanges; enforceable labour contracts; vocational training arrangements; the formal outlawing of discrimination; and the development of social insurance for unemployment and retirement.
- 1995: With the apparent success of rural reforms and a degree of urban labour market support institutions in place, mass layoffs begin in earnest. SOEs at their height in the mid-1990s number 80,000 but are down to 26,101 by the end of 2006 (Naughton 2008b).

With the move by the Chinese leadership in the mid-1990s to close loss-making SOEs millions of workers were made redundant. These workers became known as *xia gang* workers. Like Russia in the early to mid-1990s there was one parallel of a small registered number of unemployed in urban areas hovering as it did for many years at around 3 per cent even during the mass layoffs of the mid- to late 1990s and into the early 2000s. This official figure of 3 per cent 'does not reflect the true unemployment situation because of restrictions on registration' according to Knight and Song (2006), who note:

- the upper age limit of 50 for men and 45 for women to officially register;
- the exclusion of *xia gang* workers who are treated as laid off and nominally part of their former work units, and so do not qualify for unemployment benefits;
- excluded also are those forced into early retirement and in receipt of a pension;
- migrants without an urban *hukou*.

One measure of unemployment is a combination of official figures and *xia gang* workers which, although not the same as the ILO measure of unemployment, gives us a better picture of urban unemployment. Knight and Xue (2003), using a variety of sources such as the census, estimate that total administrative urban unemployment (*xia gang* plus registered unemployed) for the years 1990, 1995 and 2000 was 2.5, 4.3 and 7.9 per cent respectively. The corresponding figures using census data are 2.9, 5.6 and 11.5 per cent respectively.

Given that the 'true' level of unemployment was much larger and given the increasing rural to urban migration (see below) one would imagine that like the Russia of the 1990s real wages would be falling. For the urban wage in China in the 1990s this was *not* the case. In 1978 at the start of reforms the average real wage was only 110 per cent of its 1952 level, reflecting how real wages had inched forward during the planning period; by the year 2000 it was 319 per cent of its 1978 level. Table 8.4 shows the average real wage increase for urban China both before and during the reform period. (For more recent trends in wages within China see Chapter 9 and the section on the 'fly-wheel economy'.) Table 8.4 is indicative of just how far the labour market in China still had to travel before one could speak of a labour market as understood in a mature Western economy.[18] As Knight and Song (2006) note, 'Real wage

Table 8.4 Average percentage real wage increases for urban China before and during the reform period

Period	Average percentage annual real wage increase	Description
1952 to 1978	0.4	Real wages kept low during planning period aided by cheap food and welfare services linked to the workplace
1978 to 1980	6.4	Policy change by the government: two years after Cultural Revolution ends plus Deng Xiaoping now in charge
1981 to 1983	0.5	Consolidation period
1984 to 1986	9.4	Reflects the initial reform of SOEs
1987 to 1989	−1.6	Slow reaction to inflation in China by government
1990 to 1994	6.9	Inflation slows, wages make up for lost ground, plus government reaction to events in Tiananmen in 1989
1995 to 1997	2.9	Moderate increases due to serious level of inflation
1998 to 2000	13.6	High wage increases reflects negative inflation, rising profits after radical SOE reform

Source: All data and brief descriptions from Knight and Song (2006).

behaviour was largely a matter of changing government policy which was more exogenous than endogenous'; as such, 'The general rise in the urban wage was unlikely to be the result of market forces'. Given that real incomes per worker in rural areas were rising, but at only 3.4 per cent over the period of the urban economic reforms (1985–2000) in comparison to an equivalent 5.7 per cent over the same period for urban workers, if market forces were truly operating, real wage increases in urban areas should surely have been far more tempered than actually occurred. In addition, Knight and Song (2006) point to the very low turnover of workers during this period which again would militate against market forces operating.

For these authors the explanation is to be found not just in government economic policies which were in many cases conducive to rising wages, but also in the traditional Chinese work unit – the *danwei*. See Knight and Song (2006) for details on this institution based in the workplace, but it would probably be more accurate to describe this work unit (inside a factory, office, school, hospital, etc.) more as a social institution. In short, even after many years of a transitional process, management of these *danwei* identified with their employees and vice versa. Here we do see some similarity with the first period of reform in Russia where paternalism was a factor in keeping employees 'on the books'. Both sides of the urban work unit in China expected that any profits would be shared. It may well be that this was due to some form of insider-power on the part of the employees or a form of efficiency wages to encourage greater effort on the part of the employee or, perhaps, even a combination of the two.

As market forces became more prevalent in both Russia and China, how did this translate into rewarding well-educated workers? If a market system is operating effectively (and the education system which supplies new employees to the market system is also doing its job!), those with the skills and education in demand should command a proportionately higher salary to those who do not have the necessary skills. It is to this area that we now turn.

Education and wages

Why do people go to school, college, university, or any other educational institution for that matter? In some cases it is compulsory; this mainly concerns the lower levels of education such as primary and secondary. Where it is voluntary there must be some rationale as to why individuals give up – in some cases – many years of their lives without working and exist on low levels of income in order to study. While we acknowledge learning for learning's sake, most people enrol voluntarily in a higher educational institution because they believe that it will enhance their prospects within the job market, but by how much? The issue of 'returns to education' deals with this question:

> If I spend an extra year in full-time education or I attain a higher level of educational attainment, by how much will my wage improve over people who have fewer years of full-time education or a lower level of educational attainment?

The above question is important not only to the individual but to society in general. If one accepts that there is a direct link between the wealth created within a society and the education and skills needed to create such wealth (called human capital theory by economists), then if society wishes to maximise wealth it surely needs to encourage members of society to acquire the right education and skills in the right proportions. The absolute level of wages and the relative standing of wage levels compared to other wage levels are the main method (but not the exclusive way) within a market economy. If wages do not reflect the effort expended by the individual to acquire a certain level of education, individuals will ultimately explore alternative lines of career advancement which may not be wealth maximising for society (although rational and utility maximising for the individual).

The degree to which education is rewarded within transition economies reflected and reflects the degree to which such societies are starting to reward education to the individual and hence allowing society to maximise its wealth potential. In comparison with returns to education in Western mature, market economies it is an indication of the extent to which distortions within the labour market caused by central allocation of labour under the old regimes has given way to more efficient allocation of labour under market conditions.

Products which are in demand by consumers will lead to a greater demand by employers for those individuals who are able to make or provide such a good or service. If those with the right qualifications and skills are in short supply this will tend to raise their wages in the job market relative to other professions. This sends a signal to would-be job seekers to obtain the education and skills necessary to be able to do the job in question; the supply of such qualified and able candidates increases in the job market, leading to a slowing down in the rate of wage growth on offer for such professions (if not, in some cases, an outright fall).

There are ultimately two forces at work in determining the returns to education for an individual. On the supply side there is the effort expended in acquiring education and skills. However, the demand for labour is what economists call a derived demand – there must be demand for a product or service which labour produces for labour itself to be in demand by employers.

To give one example, the effort expended by teachers of Marxism-Leninism under the old communist regimes to acquire their knowledge of the political works of Marx, Lenin, Engels and so on was no doubt considerable. However, with the onset of transition the demand from consumers (i.e. students) for knowledge of Marxism-Leninism plummeted precipitously.

Regardless of the years of education acquired, the wage that could be commanded by such teachers fell. Therefore it should not be thought that years of education or educational attainment alone determine the returns to education, although for those readers new to this area it can often come across from reading the literature that this is the case.[19] In Box 8.1, *Returns to education and work experience*, we explore in a simplified way how such returns can be measured.

Box 8.1

Returns to education and work experience

How then do we measure returns to education? The normal method is through what are called Mincer equations named after the economist who first developed the method, Jacob Mincer. The relationship between the wage and the years of education takes the form given in equation 1 below.

$$ln\ wage = Intercept + (Returns \times Years\ of\ Education) \tag{1}$$

The term on the left-hand side represents the natural logarithm of the wage of the individual; the first term on the right is the vertical intercept; and the second term is the years of education of the individual multiplied by a coefficient – a number – which represents the 'reward' for all those years of education. The above equation may be easier to visualise if we present it diagrammatically in Figure 8.A.

A typical representation of equation 1 might be as follows:

$$ln\ wage = Intercept + 0.081(YrsEduc) \tag{2}$$

The above equation would be interpreted as saying that for each extra year of schooling the wage will rise (approximately) by 8.1 per cent where the coefficient 0.081 is simply multiplied by 100 to obtain the percentage figure.

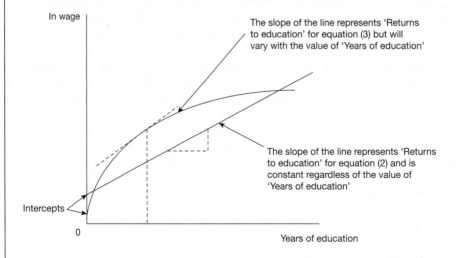

Figure 8.A A simplified returns to education.

As the reader might expect, the above is a simplification of the relationships estimated. If one believes that the effect of education gained at school or university 'deteriorates' over time, equation (3) is more appropriate. It implies that there are diminishing returns to education as one proceeds through an academic career – if you study more, then the payback will increase once you get a job but the rate of increase in the payback slows down with more and more education.

$$ln\ wage = Intercept + 0.124(YrsEduc) - 0.0034(YrsEduc)^2 \qquad (3)$$

Another important determinant of wages is the actual work experience of individuals either over the course of their working lives and/or the actual time spent in the current workplace.[20] People do not stop learning once they leave the education system; rather they learn 'on-the-job', picking up firm-specific expertise and general work habits and skills useful in other workplaces, not to mention any additional training they may undergo outside of their normal working hours. The relationship between the wage and years of work experience is, in practice, quadratic. This means that as the number of years of work experience increases so does the wage. However, the rate of increase slows down, eventually peaking and then gradually falling. Equation (2) then becomes:

$$ln\ wage = Intercept + 0.065(YrsEduc) + 0.0002(YrsWrkExp)$$
$$- 0.00004(YrsWrkExp)^2 \qquad (4)$$

In addition, other variables will usually be added to the right-hand side to reflect the industry or occupation the individual works in, the geographical location of the job, and other person-specific characteristics of the individual, for example, gender, marital status, the number of children and so on.

Finally, there are so-called 'sheepskin effects'. Rather than years of education being the key educational variable influencing the wage, some researchers have chosen to include variables representing the highest attained educational qualification.

$$ln\ wage = Intercept + 0.135(university) + 0.101(college) + 0.835(secondary)$$
$$+ 0.0002(YrsWrkExp) - 0.00004(YrsWrkExp)^2 \qquad (5)$$

'Years of education' is a continuous variable (assuming detailed measurement) whereas 'educational attainment' is discrete, usually taking the value of 1 when an individual has a particular educational attainment and 0 otherwise. In practice both approaches have been used. The attainment approach may be more appropriate where an education system in a country can 'branch off', leading to various educational routes running parallel to each other within the same age group; to select educational attainment implicitly recognises that an individual, say, graduating at 18 years of age from an academic route with the same years of education as someone graduating at 18 from a vocational route will have different wage prospects in the labour market (for better or for worse). To use years of education instead of educational attainment implicitly gives each year of education the same value regardless of educational route selected.

In terms of interpretation, equation (5) should be read as follows: if an individual goes to university, holding all other things equal (such as years of work experience being the same) then the wage of such a person will be 13.5 per cent higher (roughly) than someone who has attained the lowest form of education of primary schooling or illiterate (or whatever the 'base category' of education chosen). Due to the statistical technique used, a variable for those who have primary school education or are illiterate as their highest form of education is not shown. The coefficients then must be interpreted in relation to the category of education *not included*. Obviously many grades of education can be included depending on the nature of the education system.

By running Mincer-style wage regressions on data from transition economies in the 1990s, economists were able to compare the returns to education in these countries with those obtained by running similar regressions on labour market data in Western market economies. The degree or otherwise of the similarity of the returns to education could be seen as one indication of the extent to which a particular transition economy had travelled down the road to the market.

The situation with returns to education is made potentially more complicated in that the workforce at the start of transition has acquired its education and skills predominantly under an economy geared towards central planning. To show how this potentially complicates the picture take that of managerial expertise. The skills needed under central planning from a management perspective were entirely different from those managerial skills required under market conditions. One cannot simply assume that a manager with so many years of education gained from, say, Soviet educational institutions along with many years of work experience under central planning will receive the same returns to education or experience as his or her counterparts in mature market economies of the West.

Indeed, it may be that in the early years of transition entrepreneurs operating relatively large concerns would prefer the 'blank canvas' of relative youth and inexperience to that of 'old-hands' who may bring a degree of experience but also all the bad habits accumulated under the old regime. Alternatively, or additionally, as the education systems adapt during transition to the needs of the market one might expect that individuals who had been educated/trained during transition, and thereafter graduated, may be especially in demand from those enterprises which were orientated to the market.

Another factor worth noting concerns how females, under transition, may have fared in relation to their education and work experience; we do not pursue it here, but a 'reassuring' sign of transition economies moving to market-based economies was and is the *higher* returns to education but lower returns to work experience for females.[21] Yet another consideration is that even where individuals have been educated and gained work experience under the communist regimes, the oft-overlooked principle of 'who you know, and not what you know' might be important.[22] Within China this effect of networking is known as *guanxi*. Especially with this latter effect individuals may still exhibit relatively high salaries even when their work experience and educational qualifications might indicate that a lower wage might be expected.

Returns to education for an extra year are typically found to be between 6 and 9 per cent including work experience variables, with the United Kingdom, for example, being at the higher end of the range (see Harmon *et al.* 2000). Interestingly, using the same types of

Table 8.5 Returns to years of schooling in Europe (year closest to 1995)

	Men*	Women*
Scandinavia**	0.058	0.041
Germany (West) (95)	0.077	0.095
Netherlands (96)	0.057	0.042
Portugal (94)(95)	0.100	0.104
UK (94–96)	0.096	0.122
Ireland (94)	0.088	0.129
Spain (94)	0.069	0.079

Source: Harmon *et al.* (2001), cited in Walker and Zhu (2001).

Notes
* You need to multiply the above figures by 100 to get the approximate percentage increase in the wage for each additional year of education.
** Unweighted average for Denmark, Sweden, Finland, and Norway.

equations as shown in Box 8.1, they showed that different statistical techniques for estimation can increase the returns to education by about another 50 per cent. However, using the basic technique of ordinary least squares the following ranges of returns to schooling have been found for selected European countries (see Table 8.5).

A much larger grouping of worldwide countries using various country data between the years 1985 and 1995 puts the average male rate of return for an additional year of schooling at 4.8 per cent and 5.7 per cent for females (see Trostel *et al.* 2001 cited in Table 2 of Walker and Zhu 2001).

What then of transition countries in the 1990s? Newell and Reilly (1999) study nine transition countries and the returns to education over a number of different years using educational attainment rather than years of education which cover the early years of transition in the first half of the 1990s. The countries reviewed through either their own work or that of others are: Russia, Poland, Czech Republic, Slovak Republic, Hungary, the former Yugoslavia, Uzbekistan, Azerbaijan and Kazakhstan ranging from 1992 to 1996, although not all years are reviewed for some countries.

> The estimated returns to a university qualification are highest in Yugoslavia and the Central Asian Republics but lowest in the Czech and Slovak Republics. The remaining countries, including Russia, register estimates that are not that out of kilter with the estimated returns to higher education reported for high-income market economies.
>
> (Newell and Reilly 1999)

Munich *et al.* (2000) examine the returns to education within the Czech Republic both under communism and the transition period. They find that males' rate of return to a year of education was 2.7 per cent in the last year of communism (1989). However, by 1996 this had risen to 5.8 per cent. Ultimately, this or that percentage figure is not that important; what is important is that the findings of Munich *et al.* (2000) reveal a 'pattern to that found by the cross-sectional studies in other CEE countries, except East Germany. The pattern indicates that the rate of return on education was low under the communist wage grid and that it rose significantly during the transition.'

Table 8.6 Estimated rates of return to education in urban China, 1988–2001

Year	Years of schooling	College/above versus high school	Technical school versus high school	High school versus junior high	Junior high versus primary
1988	4.0	12.2	3.1	11.0	13.9
1989	4.6	14.4	5.8	11.6	17.3
1990	4.7	16.6	9.9	11.5	12.8
1991	4.3	15.9	8.0	9.7	13.4
1992	4.7	20.1	9.2	9.8	10.8
1993	5.2	20.4	7.0	11.5	13.6
1994	7.3	28.7	15.3	14.5	20.2
1995	6.7	24.4	12.0	15.3	18.9
1996	6.8	25.2	10.4	15.6	14.9
1997	6.7	22.3	12.0	17.3	10.9
1998	8.1	32.1	16.5	16.2	12.2
1999	9.9	38.1	17.0	21.0	14.8
2000	10.1	38.7	16.2	20.5	16.4
2001	10.2	37.3	17.8	21.4	13.8

Source: Zhang *et al.* (2005), cited in Cai *et al.* (2008).

Note
The results are based on a basic Mincerian equation, with gender and regional dummy variables using National Bureau of Statistics (NBS) urban household survey data from six provinces. Regressions are run separately for each year.

For China in the transition period we present Table 8.6. Notice that we are giving in column 2 the straightforward 'years of schooling' estimated results but presenting 'sheepskin effects' in the other columns. As may be seen from Table 8.6, regardless of whether one uses the years of schooling or the sheepskin approach, the returns remain fairly stable into the mid-1990s. Only from the mid-1990s onwards do rates of return increase markedly.

Can it be a coincidence that this parallels the reform to SOEs that occurred from the mid-1990s onwards with the laying off of millions of workers? That said, Cai *et al.* (2008) make the point that we should not immediately jump to the conclusion that the increase in returns to education can be placed at the door of labour market reforms. As Cai *et al.* (2008) note:

> Shifts in the demand for skilled versus unskilled workers, for example, due to skill-biased technical change, could also account for some of the change. However, the timing of the increases coincides with periods of economic liberalization, suggesting that institutional reforms were likely an important part of the story.

It is important to realise what is being reflected in these returns to education figures: the labour market is becoming more and more like a regular labour market one would see in mature Western economies. That is, the characteristics of the individual – to a large extent reflected in the individual's education – is being reflected in the wage he or she receives *relative to those individuals with a lower level of education*. This is a major turnaround from what we described above as regards how individuals were, on the whole, largely directed to a job under central planning and received the wage attached to the job.

Notice that the above is not in contradiction to what we described when we quoted Knight and Song (2006) as saying that the rise in real wages in urban China was unlikely to be the result of market forces. It is feasible for a combination of directives from central government, combined with economic reforms and the ethos of the *danwei* work unit to increase the *aggregate* level of real wages. The educational level of the individual would then determine the *relative standing* of that individual in comparison with his or her peers with those with more years of schooling or a higher qualification receiving a relatively higher wage.

The changes taking place during the transition period within China are also reflected by returns to education by ownership type. A priori, what would one expect? If private or privatised firms are operating to the principle of profit maximisation would they not try to keep costs down by paying a smaller real wage to their workers regardless of the level of education? State employees working for SOEs where there are soft budget constraints may, all other things being equal, receive higher returns for their education.

The theory of human capital, however, states that individuals under free market conditions are paid a wage which is commensurate to their productivity (technically equal to the value of their marginal product). It is assumed that individuals select educational courses based, in large part, on future anticipated earnings. These earnings will only be high if through the education gained the individual can be productive and assist in raising the profitability of the firm.

The actual evidence shows that returns to education have been consistently higher for non-public enterprises; and although returns to education started very low for state employees in 1988 at only 3 per cent (7.3 per cent non-public), this rose to 9 per cent by 2001 (although still below the non-public sector returns at 10 per cent). Again the returns to education in state concerns only increased markedly from the mid-1990s onwards. This may be no coincidence; as well as the restructuring that took place in SOEs in the second half of the 1990s, the SOEs that remained and which were not privatised increasingly operated under profit-orientated conditions. (See Chapter 9 for additional details.)

Migration within transitional labour markets – the cases of the CIS and China

We start by looking at migration *within* China during the transition period. Later we will look at migration *between* former countries that were once part of the Soviet Union. The issue of internal migration within China is linked intimately with the series of reforms that were undertaken by the leadership of the CCP from 1978 onwards. We have outlined these reforms in Chapter 9 and also specifically the reforms relating to the Chinese labour market above.

However, in brief, the transition in China began in the countryside where collective farming was replaced by the household responsibility system; basically, individual households now worked the land – not a group of families as a collective – and were allowed to retain the fruits of their labour. Not only did this give an enormous spurt to productivity and hence output, it also created a large pool of surplus labour. Surplus labour in the countryside was already a problem *before* the reforms started in 1978. The population of China increased between 1952 and 1978 by 388 million; with the rural labour force growing by 66 per cent but cultivatable land by only 6 per cent. Consequently the amount of land cultivated per rural worker fell on average by approximately 37 per cent. It was estimated that by the start of reforms surplus labour in the countryside represented some 30 per cent of the rural workforce, i.e. in principle one could cut the number of agricultural workers by almost one-third and output would not be affected. While per capita grain consumption remained virtually unchanged over this period for the peasantry, urban wages registered a very small average 0.4 per cent annual increase with economic development taking the form of capital accumulation (see the discussion on total factor productivity in Chapter 9) and through an average annual increase in urban employment of 5.3 per cent. (All preceding figures from Knight and Song 2006.)

Initially township and village enterprises were able to absorb part of this surplus labour. Of the total increase in the labour force in the 1980s, 71 per cent of this increase occurred within rural China, with TVEs accounting for 50 per cent of the total increase. Agricultural employment accounted for 21 per cent of the increase, and urban employment 30 per cent. Increasingly, however, there was a pull factor with the development of special economic zones (SEZ), in large part populated by foreign firms. Needing labour to staff the workplaces, the new SEZ drew not millions, but tens of millions of workers from the countryside to urban areas. Between 1980 and 2000, as can be seen in Table 8.7 (where we outline the changing nature of the Chinese labour force from 1980 to 2000), the urban share of the labour force increased from approximately 26 to 34 per cent. By the year 2000, as can be seen, less than 50 per cent of the labour force was primarily dependent on the land for a living.

In Figure 8.1 we outlined how under specific assumptions the wage rates between two similar occupations would *tend* to equalise over time. This analytical framework may also

Table 8.7 The labour force and its distribution, China, urban and rural, 1980–2000[a, b]

	1980	1985	1989	1990	1995	2000
Millions						
Labour force	429.0	501.1	557.1	651.3	689.3	737.8
Urban	110.6	130.5	147.7	174.2	199.0	248.4
Unemployed	5.4	2.4	3.8	3.8	8.6	16.9
Employed	105.2	128.1	143.9	170.4	190.4	231.5
SOEs	80.2	89.9	101.1	103.5	112.6	81.0
UCEs	24.3	33.2	35.0	35.5	31.5	15.0
Other employment	0.7	5.0	7.8	31.4	46.3	135.5
Rural	318.4	370.7	409.4	477.1	490.2	489.3
TVE employment	30.0	69.8	93.7	92.7	128.6	128.2
Private and Individual Enterprises	–	–	–	16.0	35.3	40.7
Household workers	288.4	300.9	315.7	368.4	326.3	320.4
Employment	423.6	498.7	553.3	647.5	680.7	720.8
Percentage of total						
Labour force	100.0	100.0	100.0	100.0	100.0	100.0
Urban	25.8	26.0	26.5	26.7	28.9	33.7
Unemployed	1.3	0.5	0.7	0.6	1.2	2.3
Employed	24.5	25.6	25.8	26.2	27.6	31.4
SOEs	18.7	17.9	18.1	15.9	16.3	11.0
UCEs	5.7	6.6	6.3	5.5	4.6	2.0
Other employment	0.2	1.0	1.4	4.8	6.7	18.4
Rural	74.2	74.0	73.5	73.3	71.1	66.3
TVE employment	7.0	13.9	16.8	14.2	18.7	17.4
Private and Individual Enterprises	–	–	–	2.5	5.1	5.5
Household workers	67.2	60.0	56.7	56.6	47.3	43.4
Employment	98.7	99.5	99.3	99.4	98.8	97.7

Notes

a. There was a major revision in the figures between 1989 and 1990, based on the 1990 census of population.

b. In the 1990s the number of urban employees who are attributed to particular ownership categories falls increasingly short of the total; the difference is included in the 'other employment' category. Table and notes from Knight and Song (2006) and sources as listed therein.

be used to demonstrate how pressures would exist between rural and urban areas for the same equalising tendency over time also; in Figure 8.1, instead of *university lecturers* we have *urban*, and instead of *college teachers* we have *rural*. Given, as already mentioned, that the disparities between rural and urban in terms of income and consumption grew ever larger, there would be generated a desire on the part of many in rural areas to migrate to urban areas. It might be thought that the *hukou* system would act as a brake on this equalising process and for many years it did just that. With the ending of food rationing in the early 1990s one impediment to mobility was removed. *On paper* at least, laws have been passed eliminating fees for temporary urban residence permits and allowing migrants to send their children to urban schools. Some fast-growing coastal areas also made it easier for urban *hukou* to be acquired by rural migrants as they increasingly saw a lack of labour as an impediment to growth (Cai *et al.* 2008). In Beijing itself as of 2010, there were six million registered migrants in the city based on the temporary residency permits introduced in 1985. This figure of six million makes up almost one-third of the entire population of the city (*China Daily*, 26 January 2010).

However, Knight and Song (2006) point out continuing discriminating practices by some city governments with labour bureaux in some cases actually imposing quotas on the number of migrants an enterprise can hire, such quotas then being enforced by inspection teams.

> The restrictions are sensitive to the state of the city labour market, being tightened if unemployment rises. Some city governments make price as well as quantity interventions. Enterprises must apply for their quotas, and they must pay an extra charge to exceed their quotas. Similarly enterprises receive subsidies, in the form of tax relief, if they recruit *xia gang* employees. It is clear that migrant workers are frequently treated as the residual supply which should be adjusted to match the excess demand for urban labour.
>
> (Knight and Song 2006)

Taking the above points into consideration it is clear that Figure 8.1, if it were to relate to rural-to-urban migration and wage rates, is an idealised version of how the labour market operates and should be seen as informing us of medium-term tendencies within the labour market between rural and urban areas. That is, over a prolonged period of time there will be forces at work tending to equalise wage rates for similar types of labour in rural and urban areas. However, given institutional restrictions, this equalising tendency will be much delayed.

How many internal migrants are there in China? We need to be careful about what we mean by an internal migrant: we could have rural to rural; urban to rural; urban to urban; although the one of main interest here is rural to urban. In addition, most researchers would not regard daily commuting as a form of migration or those who simply visit relatives; time is also a factor – for example, is someone who stays in a city for a week a migrant? Should we include only those whose change of residence was accompanied by a change of *hukou*? Finally, the stock of migrants should be distinguished from the flow of migrants where the former is a 'snapshot' of the number of migrants at any one time, and the latter the number of migrants over a set period of time. With so many ways in which to measure migration the numbers generated have varied both with the definition and the nature of the research question. Table 8.8 lists some of the main studies.

However, as Cai *et al.* (2008) point out, the data source with the most consistent picture of migration comes from the government of China itself. Since 1996 an annual survey of rural

Table 8.8 Estimates of internal migration within China during the transition

Author(s) and year	Description	Result
Li and Hu (1991)	25 large cities surveyed in 1988 of 'temporary' migrants.	Estimated at 23 per cent of *permanent population*, having been 9 per cent in 1980.
Knight and Song (1999)	Using information on labour force participation and origin of individual estimates for the above 25 large cities made.	Temporary migrants estimated at 12 per cent of the *labour force* of these cities.
Knight and Song (1999)	Used a rural household survey conducted in 1993. Migrants defined as individuals going to urban area for at least one month.	Flow of migrants in 1993 estimated at 39 million with the stock in urban areas at any one time in 1993 of 22 million (with average work duration of 205 days).
Rozelle *et al.* (1999)	Used a survey of 200 villages in 6 provinces in 1995. Migrants defined as people who left the village for at least a month in any one year but retained ties with the village. (No distinction was made between urban and rural destinations.)	Number of migrants estimated at 20 million in 1988 to 54 million in 1995.
Cai *et al.* (2008)	Use is made of the 2000 census to estimate the number and the division between *hukou* and non-*hukou* migration. Migrants defined as the total number who have moved from their current residence to another residence between 1995 and 2000 for at least 6 months in the prior year	Total number of migrants was 131 million of which 65.1 per cent were non-*hukou* migrants; 49.14 per cent of the non-*hukou* migrants were rural to urban migrants. Of the 34.9 per cent *hukou* migrants, 25.34 per cent were rural-to-urban migrants.

Sources: Cai *et al.* (2008) in Brandt and Rawski (2008); all other studies cited in Knight and Song (2006).

labour has been conducted by the Ministry of Agriculture and the Ministry of Labour and Social Security which records all those who migrate for at least one month in the previous year out of their township or out of their province. In 1997 the total number of rural migrants stood at 38.9 million but by 2003 it had reached 98.3 million; the survey indicates that from 1998 onwards about 40 per cent of these migrants went to destinations outside their home province. The National Bureau of Statistics also conducts an annual survey at the village level covering family migration: 'In 2004, there were 93.5 million individual rural migrants and 24.7 million persons in families that migrated, for a total of 118.2 million rural migrants' (Cai *et al.* 2008). Using such data from the aforementioned governmental bodies, Cai *et al.* (2008) conclude that TVEs played the dominant role in absorbing surplus labour in the countryside up until the late 1990s. Thereafter, however, migration is poised to surpass TVEs as the main destination of those leaving agriculture. What all this migration means for the people themselves is shown in Box 8.2, 'Behind the statistics are real people . . .'.

Box 8.2

Behind the statistics are real people . . .

A major theme in labour economics is poverty and inequality which we have *not* tackled in this chapter. However, we can catch a glimpse of the two Chinas that co-exist when we look at the housing market in urban China. Huge fortunes are being made by developers, and for some urban Chinese property price increases are leading to large capital gains. For migrant workers the situation is very far from this 'easy' money with long hours, low pay and limited living space. We start by looking briefly at the urban housing boom in China which at the time of writing has not yet stabilised.

Land in both the city and in rural areas is in great demand from property developers in order to provide both commercial and residential units for the market – for those who can afford to buy. The demand for property is being fed not just by China's new rich (and by 'average' people simply wanting somewhere to live) but by money coming in from other parts of Asia as inward investors 'park' their money awaiting, in some cases, not just a rise in property values but an anticipated appreciation of the Chinese currency. It costs the average couple in Beijing 20 years' salary to buy an apartment around the fifth ring road; 18 years of a Shanghai couple's salary for an apartment in the outer ring; and 16 years' income for a couple in Shenzhen's outskirts (figures from *China Daily*, 4 January 2010.) While the bulk of rural–urban migration is economically driven through migrants heading for higher paid work in the cities and towns of China, the removal of individuals from their homes and land – whether peasants or not – is not an insignificant phenomenon. A particular feature of this modern 'land grab' is that many local officials are motivated to sell land under their control. The *China Daily* (4 January 2010) reports that

> Local governments are widely seen as the largest beneficiary of the property boom. Statistics from China Index Academy show that as of November 23, the revenue of land sales in China's major 70 cities doubled from a year earlier, with Shanghai (82.1 billion yuan), Beijing (63.9 billion yuan), and Hangzhou (52.3 billion yuan) topping the first three places. Selling land in the third quarter in 2009 alone has earned the Shanghai local government 49.2 billion yuan.
>
> 'It's not practical to persuade local governments to rein in the housing market because that is equal to killing their biggest revenue contributor, and this is essentially the case in a country where GDP is still a leading indicator to gauge the performance of local officials,' said an analyst who spoke on condition of anonymity.

While *China Daily* deserves much credit for their article in exposing some of the issues, the article does not ask the question, '*Who or what was on all this land that was and is being sold?*'

Not all individuals in China are part of the housing bubble. Below we present an edited version of an article which appeared in the *China Daily* on 26 January 2010 entitled 'Facing the burden of growth'.

WUHAN: Like many other farmers-turned-migrant workers, Jia Changhua headed to the city last July to look for work and give his family a better life. 'In July, my mother was hit by a stroke . . . we needed money badly so my father went to the city,' said Jia Zijian, his son. The elder Jia, 59, a farmer of Hubei's Suixian county, managed to find work as a porter in Wuhan, capital of Hubei province. But on Jan 16, Jia died from work exhaustion. An urban inspector said there are more than 10,000 porters working in the city's Hanzheng Street alone. 'We carry about 75 kg for about 300m on average to make 5 yuan ($0.73),' a porter surnamed Hu from Bofan village in Anlu, Hubei, told *China Daily*. Jia himself died after hauling 1,500 kg of rice. Passers-by found him pale and lying on his trolley.

Jia's fellow porters remember him as a diligent and thrifty porter. 'Every day at 4 am, we head to the market to help carry food stuff until about 8 am, before going to Hanzheng Street for a simple breakfast that helps fuel us until we knock off at 4 or 5 pm,' said another porter surnamed Zhang, who was also Jia's roommate in the city. 'I never saw Jia himself eating any meat and he was always looking for more work,' Zhang said. Jia's daily expenses reportedly never went beyond 10 yuan, on top of the 8 yuan he spent every day on steamed bread and rice gruel or noodles. During days with brisk business, porters said they would make up to 80 yuan a day.

'A lot of people come from my home area to work in Wuhan,' Hu said. Hu said after the farming season, he could not find any way to make money. 'I am 43, without any other technical skills,' he said. 'A man should not remain idle.' He decided to leave for Wuhan every August for work until the planting season. His wife also found work brushing shoes for people in the city. The couple rent a 3-sq-m room.

Many residents said the living conditions of porters like Jia are deplorable. A room less than 10 sq m is typically divided into two partitions, with a bunk bed placed in each. Jia slept on the lower bed, which was soon occupied by another porter after his death. Hu and Zhang said they were both greatly saddened by Jia's death, which reminded them of their plight and the fear that their children would discontinue their studies and become labourers themselves.

What of the future for the labour market in China? Anyone who has visited China will be struck by the prodigious amount of shop assistants in shopping malls; by the peppering of young individuals every 10 or 20 feet in supermarkets eager to offer their services and advice on what products to buy; by the large number of waiters and waitresses in restaurants, coffee shops and fast food retailers; if you require your car *hand* washed, cleaned – inside and out – a seeming army of young people appear as if from nowhere to descend on one car to give it their full attention. Higher up the labour market the amount of graduates from Chinese universities each year is measured in millions. And yet whether as an employer in China you require unskilled labour or educated labour, the cost of attracting such young labour will be increasingly more expensive over the next few decades.

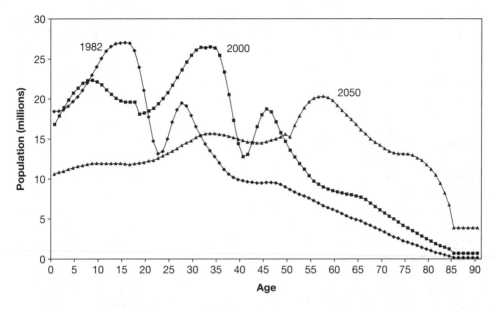

Figure 8.3 Population by age, China 1982, 2000, and 2050.

Source: Feng and Mason (2008).

In Figure 8.3 we present the work of Feng and Mason (2008). It shows the age composition of the Chinese population at three points in time: 1982, 2000 and 2050. Naturally the 2050 picture is a projection. As can be seen, while even as late as 2000 the vast majority of the Chinese population was young, this will change by 2050. In the passing years the population-age profiles contain within them the imprint of both recent Chinese history and changes in fertility. For the years 1982 and 2000 at the ages of about 23 and 41 respectively, the reader will notice distinctive dips followed by a new peak. This is the result of the famine created in large part by the Great Leap Forward of 1959 to 1961 (see Chapter 9 for details). The famine was followed by a surge in births for much of the 1960s which in 1982 and 2000 resulted in an excess of those in the 15 to 20 and 30 to 35 age ranges for these respective years. With a decline in fertility in the 1970s (which occurred *before* the one-child-policy per couple in urban areas was announced in 1980 – rural couples and minorities within China had and have a more relaxed policy, relatively speaking) there is a corresponding dip in the proportion of the population in 1982 and 2000 aged below 10 and 30 years respectively.

The upshot of the above is that it is projected that the effective labour force will start to decline by 2020. As Feng and Mason (2008) note:

> These broad demographic trends conceal important subnational variation. In urban China, where population aging is more rapid, the supply of new labour market entrants from within the cities has started to shrink. In rural China, a more lenient birth-control policy and a later start of fertility decline imply a slower aging process and a stronger labour supply. Thus, better job growth in urban China combined with urban–rural demographic differences will continue to fuel urban–rural migration.

This phenomenon of a predominantly young China as represented by the age-population profiles in 1982 and 2000 led to what demographers call a 'demographic dividend'. Since younger people of working age tend to produce more than they consume, there is more for society of all ages to consume and this can be a powerful support for economic growth in general. It is estimated that 15 per cent of China's economic growth between 1982 and 2000 is due to this demographic dividend, a dividend which over the next few decades will gradually disappear. Initially, the above will force employers to increase the productivity of existing workers whether within the services or the manufacturing side of the economy, and from that perspective this could be seen in a positive light.

However, younger people within the labour market – regardless of educational level – will increasingly be able to command higher wages. Only if employers are able to offset the shift in the supply curve of labour to the left (notwithstanding continued rural–urban migration) with higher productivity will this ameliorate higher labour costs. A glimpse into the future may already be seen in the Beijing university entrance examinations where, in 2010, 20,000 fewer middle school students sat the exams compared to 2009; and in 2009 the figure of 101,293 middle school students who sat the entrance exams in that year was 15,000 less than in 2008 (*China Daily*, 9 February 2010).

Another option would be for a certain cultural shift in the outlook of some businesses to the age of personnel they hire. While the traditional view of the elderly in China is one of respect, a cursory glance at advertising within China demonstrates an almost total fixation on youth and beauty. Those occupations that have traditionally relied on young people to staff the various positions could move up the age bracket ladder and simply employ older workers as a partial way of counteracting the reduction in younger sections of the workforce. If the marketing industry in China is anything to go by, business may need some time to revert back to the traditional Chinese reverence for the elderly both as consumers and workers.

What of Russia, in terms of migration both external and internal? In terms of Russia's standing in the world as regards migrants, despite less than friendly immigration policies from the government, Russia has the second largest number of migrants in the world with the United States having the largest number, followed in descending order by Germany and Ukraine, with two other transition countries – Kazakhstan and Poland – coming in at ninth and tenth. When the Soviet Union fell apart, this created many 'statistical migrants'; these individuals may even have been born in the new countries that emerged from the Soviet Union's demise, but because they identified with another country and so held foreign citizenship (and in some cases no citizenship at all), they became classified as migrants. One can think, for example, of the large ethnic Russian minorities in the Baltic States of Estonia, Lithuania and Latvia.

As the World Bank report *Migration and Remittances – Eastern Europe and the Former Soviet Union* (2006) notes, there have been two distinct patterns in terms of migration in the former communist regimes. First, within Europe and Central Asia (ECA[23]), then within the Western part of ECA, 42 per cent of all emigration is towards Western Europe; second, within CIS countries 80 per cent of emigration remains within CIS countries. Germany is the most important country outside of ECA for migrants and Russia the most important destination country for migrants within ECA. In the early to mid-1990s there was huge ethnic conflict, nation building and, as a result, much of the migration that took place was of a 'one-off' character. In addition, many migrants within the countries of ECA are illegal and undocumented. For example, it is estimated that there are in the region of 3 and 3.5 million undocumented migrants within Russia. What is clear, however, is that the scale of movement of personnel relative to what was and is being witnessed in China is not as great.

At the same time Russia – like China – is facing a radical demographic change to its population. It is predicted that the population of Russia will decline by 20 per cent up until 2050, giving the country a population of 110 to 112 million. On the surface it would appear that 'Russia needs an annual inflow of 1 million immigrants – 3 times as many as the official annual flow over the last 15 years, and 5 times as many as in the recent years after tightening the migration legislation' (Andrienko and Guriev 2005). In terms of how this will impact upon the Russian labour market in 2050, Andrienko and Guriev (2005) report that the share of the population of working age – 16 to 55 and 16 to 60 for females and males respectively – will be approximately 50 per cent, which is similar to the share in the 1939 census; the major difference is that the proportion of elderly in the population will rise to 34 per cent compared to 9 per cent in 1939.

As well as immigration *into* Russia, Andrienko and Guriev (2005) point out that much could be done through internal migration. Even after several decades now of transition, one can think of the mono-industrial towns inherited from the FSU which were based, as the name implies, on the production of one type of good which then 'fed into' the central plan. With the advent of market relations many of these towns discovered that their *raison d'être* no longer existed as the good produced just was not in demand; millions of people are located in the wrong place producing goods which, in part, are kept in demand through Russian government subsidies (see e.g. the *Financial Times* article 'Russian one-company towns face decline' by Charles Clover, 28 October 2009.) The above is important when we look below at the demographic challenge facing Russia. Much 'surplus labour' *if* it could be mobile would solve the shortage of labour in other parts of the country. However, unlike China where internal migration is an option actively pursued by tens of millions, this is not the case – at least up until now – in Russia.

Summary

Labour under central planning and according to Marxist theory was not a commodity, but given its central direction under the socialist economic system it was treated very much as a commodity. With the development of market forces in many transition economies, supply of and demand for labour are far stronger in ultimately influencing the setting of wages between workers and employers. This does not make the employee the only master of his or her own fate; demand for labour (or lack thereof) may overwhelm the wishes of the worker for this or that wage or for a particular employment position. Nevertheless, the supply condition of the worker – his or her education, work skills, social capital, work experience (as opposed to mainly tenure under central planning) – are now more important in determining the person's absolute wage and his or her relative standing to other groups of (non-)educated workers. Relatively speaking the possibility of influencing one's own career path is greater than under central planning. (Although not without obstacles: in this chapter we did not even touch on the huge subject area of poverty and wage inequality in transition economies which can be one of the biggest obstacles to acquiring an education.) The concept of a return to education and how this has increased since transition is evidence of more market-oriented economies.

We have mainly focused on Russia and China as they moved to market-based economies. That their respective labour markets appear to have developed differently should be no great surprise given the different transition paths that were taken (see Chapter 9 for a full explanation and discussion on gradualism and the Big Bang approach to transition). We can summarise the differences that we have covered in the following:

- (Surplus labour or labour hoarding developed as market relations were formed in Russia in the 1990s.) Only with the post-1998 financial crisis in Russia and the expansion of the Russian economy based in large part on the extractive side of the economy did surplus labour become fully absorbed into the production process. Within China, surplus labour was removed in the mid- to late 1990s in the process of creating the necessary conditions for market relations.

- (Paternalism in Russia helped keep many employees tied to a workplace over the first five to six years of transition in Russia, but at a cost of inefficient allocation of labour and of a huge real wage decline. Paternalism in China through the *danwei* work unit saw employment protection as secondary, but for those who remained in the workplace real wages improved strongly and consistently despite the increase in open (and concealed) unemployment.)

- The attempt at institution building within Russia in the early stages of transition as it relates to labour markets and the wider economy was at best patchy; within China there appears to have been a degree of institution building *ahead* of the mass layoffs that took place within SOEs in the mid-1990s. (These last points are more fully explored in Chapter 9.)

- On migration, Chinese peasants and workers have shown great flexibility (at much personal cost) in migrating in search of paid work within China; much of the migration into Russia that has and does occur is from other non-resource CIS countries.

- The one thing which both countries did have in common when SOEs were set free from the plan was implausibly low official unemployment rates.

Given that we have not covered all aspects of labour markets in China and Russia, we fully accept that there will be areas where they have much in common: an increase in the Gini coefficient, for example, and the number of well-qualified Russians who have emigrated abroad having received their higher education *in* Russia are similar, but not identical, to a large number of young Chinese who, having received their higher education *outside* China and have as yet not returned but are pursuing economic advancement elsewhere.

But ultimately the urban labour markets of Russia and China will depend to a large extent on how their respective economies develop. Russia has increasingly been seen as a resource-based economy, whereas China's is seen as being more diversified. This, if it continues, will surely be reflected in the future composition of the workforces in terms of the education and skills possessed, and the likely remuneration on offer to reflect the job openings of the two economies.

Key terms

Danwei	Output fall
Human capital	Paternalism
Insider-outsider theories	Returns to education
Insider-power	Unemployment
Internal and external migration	Wage arrears
Labour hoarding	Wage flexibility
Labour mobility	Wage formation

Review questions

1   An alternative to human capital theory and the concept of returns to education is the idea of 'signalling'. In brief, an individual's level of education sends a signal to a potential future employer about the person's productivity; the level of education, however, does not – in some versions of the theory – contribute anything to the person' productivity. Knowledge of the job and acquiring a skill will be learned on the job and not before one joins the workplace. Draw up a list of occupations which might lend support to the theory of signalling and those that lend support to human capital theory. Could the idea of signalling be used – even in part – to help explain labour allocation under central planning?

2   If employees and/or managers in Russia in the early to mid-1990s had 'insider-power' to influence and shape events in the workplace, how does one explain the rise of the oligarchs in Russia? Did not and do not the oligarchs generally determine how large sections of Russian industry are run?

3   If the Chinese *hukou* system of residency registration had not been introduced, the personal freedom of individuals to move around China would have increased; the labour market would potentially have been more flexible which in turn may have promoted job creation and helped enterprises keep their costs down. Can you think of any advantages to the individual or to society of having the *hukou* system?

9

ECONOMIC TRANSITION
Russia versus China

This chapter aims to explore the divergent paths of the two main transition regimes of Russia and China as they travelled, and continue to travel, very different paths to market-style economies. Such an examination of paths travelled usually revolves around the central issue of gradualism versus the Big Bang approach to transition. While we do not avoid such a discussion, we do explore alternative perspectives.

However, we start with a question raised by the United Kingdom-based newspaper the *Financial Times*, namely 'What is the point of economists?' The question, posed in a blog, ran in the newspaper over the summer of 2009 and had been inspired by a question posed by Her Majesty the Queen (of the United Kingdom) to a London School of Economics Professor in November 2008.[1] Her Majesty, referring to the then financial and economic crisis, posed the question, 'Why did no one see it coming?'

As the *Financial Times* (26 July 2009) reported, a selection of the great and the good of Her Majesty's loyal subjects composed a letter in reply.[2]

> The group, which includes economists and constitutional experts, explains that although the protagonists were 'bright', they failed to see the bigger picture.
>
> The letter, whose contents were leaked to newspapers on Sunday, says: 'Everyone seemed to be doing their job properly on its own merit. And according to standard measures of success, they were often doing it well.'
>
> However, 'the failure was to see how collectively this added up to a series of interconnected imbalances over which no single authority had jurisdiction'.
>
> 'In summary, your majesty', the authors conclude, 'the failure to foresee the timing, extent and severity of the crisis and to head it off . . . was principally a failure of the collective imagination of many bright people, both in this country and internationally, to understand the risks to the system as a whole.'

The reader is referred to the comments in the blog as to whether this explanation was agreed upon by *Financial Times* readers. Interesting as the above may be, what has this to do with the transition to market-based economies? Crises in the real economy brought about by crises within the financial sector are several hundreds of years old and yet the majority of observers (including economists) keep failing to predict when the bubble will burst.

Now along comes a *first*: the transition from centrally planned economies to market-based economies; not something that has happened before – ever. If the economics profession has persistently been unable to predict the onset of economic calamity out of financial crises over the past several hundred years one might argue, what hope for the transition path from socialism to capitalism?

In what way did the economics profession get the transition wrong? One could quote many commentators. Here we quote mainly Svejnar (2008) who, in comparing the performance of various transition economies, writes:

> In the case of China, economic growth has from the start *exceeded* most *expectations*. In the case of Central and East Europe (CEE) and the Commonwealth of Independent States (CIS), there was a precipitous and *unexpected* economic decline in the first three to eight years, with impressive growth thereafter.

And later in the same article,

> In terms of GDP growth, China's performance since 1978 has been *unexpectedly* strong, while that of the CEE and CIS was *disappointing to disastrous* in the early-to-mid 1990s and fairly strong thereafter.

. . . And finally from Svejnar in his article,

> The strength and persistence of growth in China and the depth and length of the early transition depression in the CEE and CIS countries were both *unexpected*. [All emphases added]

In addition, the OECD in a publication (Ahrend and Thompson 2005) writing about the Big Bang in Russia and the collapse in output:

> The immediate results of the reform package were a spike in inflation and a large drop in GDP. What was *unexpected*, however, was that the output fall carried on far longer than expected. With the exception of a weak pick-up in 1997, the economy continued to contract until 1999 . . . The initial output drop must to a large degree be seen as the result of dramatic changes that resulted from the attempt to transform a command economy into a market economy . . . Yet while the continuation of the downturn in 1993–94 was to a significant degree part of an *unavoidable* transition shock, there were other factors at work. [Emphasis added]

The 1995 *Economic Survey of Europe* published by the United Nations Economic Commission for Europe comments on the sharp fall in output and of Russia, finding this 'intriguing', since:

> the very collapse of communist regimes was supposed to bring about a substantial and rapid improvement in economic performance and standards of living . . . Removal of the command system and transition to a market economy was thus seen as an efficiency- and welfare-improving socio-economic innovation. It is therefore somewhat surprising that most experts tend to regard the registered falloff in output in the transition economies as something quite *natural* and largely *inevitable*.[3] [Emphasis added]

As may be seen, the main surprises have been in the area of the significant output fall for many transition economies but the sustained output increase on the part of China. (We return below to the inevitability or otherwise of what transpired.) With such diverse outcomes so far on their respective transition paths for Russia and China, a number of immediate questions arise: To what extent, if any, did the smoother transition path travelled by China – at least up until now – stem from the incremental reforms adopted as opposed to the more radical approach taken in many other transition economies? Were there any unique circumstances in China that allowed for a smooth transition, circumstances, perhaps, which could not have been repeated in other transition economies? Or is it more appropriate to say that unique circumstances in some transition economies, such as Russia, led to a transition process which made a difficult situation much worse?

Where to begin to answer so fundamental a series of questions? First, we emphasise that China was going through not one but two great social and economic transformations: transition and development.[4] The first is the obvious one of the movement from plan to market. The second is that of a society that was once overwhelmingly rural (and agrarian) in nature and composition and is now increasingly (but not overwhelmingly) urban; a rural–urban shift in population to match and exceed any in history where, although the majority of the population still lives and works in rural areas, the specific gravity of power and influence has shifted decisively to the city and the urban conurbation, with the rise of industry and eventually the service sector. Of course, the political power may, in pre-communist times and following the ascent to power of the communists, have always been in the major cities of their time. But by specific gravity we are referring not only to political power but to the rise of both the urban consumer and the the the urban middle class.

Russia, on the other hand, had conducted its rural to urban or agricultural to industrial transformation much earlier than its attempted transition to the market, with the forced collectivisation of the peasantry and the forced industrialisation of the Soviet Union throughout the 1930s to the early 1970s. (See Chapter 1 for a description.)

What then of initial conditions in both the former Soviet Union and China? We consider these below, but first we will look at the transition to date in each of the respective countries followed by a discussion on lessons that can be learnt from a joint comparison of the two countries' progress to date, and briefly, where they are likely to head in the near future.

The situation pre-transition in the Soviet Union[5]

In Chapter 1 we touched on the deteriorating situation facing the economy of the Soviet Union in the run-up to its dissolution.[6] While we cannot wind the clock back and see what might have been, the intriguing question to pose is whether Mikhail Gorbachev could have followed the example of Deng Xiaoping. That is, could he have led the Soviet Union out of its economic, social and political quagmire if he had pursued the goal of a ('socialist') market economy to the same degree as the leadership of the Chinese Communist Party did under Deng Xiaoping? The question is interesting not only for what might have been, but also for helping us to understand and explain the transition process that did eventually emerge from the failed attempts of Gorbachev to rescue the Soviet economy and, indeed, the Soviet Union.

Gorbachev as the new General Secretary of the Communist Party of the Soviet Union (CPSU), elected to the position on 11 March 1985 – at the relatively young age of 54 – may be said to have attempted the start of the reform process in April 1985 at the Plenum of the Central Committee of the CPSU. Here he spoke of three major themes relating to the economy: (1) acceleration of economic growth; (2) restructuring; and (3) the greater development of scientific and technical progress. This was followed by a widely publicised speech in Leningrad (now St Petersburg) in May 1985 where the issue of the need for radical reform was raised. This gave a 'green light' to the media to begin to tentatively explore the problem issues both within the economy and society at large which had been kept out of the limelight up until then.

The reforms would start, however, on the political front with changes in the top echelons of the Soviet government when Andrei Gromyko – the Foreign Affairs Minister for 28 years – was replaced by Eduard Shevardnadze. This, in many ways, was to be the start of Gorbachev's most successful reform – that of changing Soviet foreign policy – and marked a radical departure from previous Soviet foreign policy. Indeed, one could go so far as to say that Gorbachev's success in the international arena in bringing an end to the Cold War, earning (international) accolade after accolade including the Nobel Peace Prize, was in inverse relation to his record of success on the domestic front.

While the first two years were spent on issues such as corruption, nepotism and an anti-alcohol campaign (more on this below) and the opening up of Soviet society, these areas may be seen as preparing the ground for the economic reforms that were to come later. However, another view would be that they were two years of a missed opportunity. Gorbachev, for example, again proclaimed the need for reform at the February 1986 Plenum of the Central Committee. The ground was further prepared in January 1987 when, in another speech before the Central Committee, Gorbachev attacked 'lingering dogmas' from the 1930s. This was yet another signal to civil society that the reform debate could and should be 'heated up'. While this meeting did not yet introduce the radical reforms that were to come later, political reforms were introduced, including proposals for the appointment of non-Communist Party members to positions within the government both at a regional and federal level. Revolutionary for its time, it was also suggested that more than one candidate should be allowed on to election lists. Later in 1987 many of the former opponents of Joseph Stalin were rehabilitated which had its main symbolism in distancing the Gorbachev regime even more so from the Stalin period and sending yet another signal to civil society that this regime was not a continuation of the ones gone before. If further proof of this was needed Andrei Sakharov, the Soviet dissident and Nobel Prize-winning nuclear physicist, had been invited the previous December by Gorbachev to return to Moscow from internal exile in the closed city of Gorky (now Nizhny Novgorod) where he had been forced to live for six years due to his dissident ways.

All of the above would culminate in Gorbachev introducing the policy of *glasnost*, or political openness. Freedom of speech blossomed and the press which had tentatively followed the lead of Gorbachev in being more critical of faults in the system became a lot more critical. This was combined with the release from custody of thousands of political prisoners. Gorbachev was, he later claimed, partly inspired by Alexander Dubček, leader of the Czechoslovakian Communist Party, who had attempted to introduce 'socialism with a human face' in 1968 during the so-called Prague Spring; a spring which turned to winter with the invasion of Soviet tanks. Ultimately, however, the political openness was *intended* as a form of leverage; leverage on the conservative hardliners both within the Communist Party and within the *nomenklatura* as a whole, the idea being that opponents of economic reform would find it difficult to defend the status quo if other sections of civil society and, indeed, of government were pushing for change.

Ironically, such moves towards a more open and democratic society would be used by conservative forces as sticks to beat the back of Gorbachev for the 'chaos' that it had unleashed through the centrifugal forces of pent-up nationalism in the various republics. As open dissent became more and more acceptable the 'War of Laws' would also break out towards the end of the 1980s and the start of the 1990s when the constituent parts of the Soviet Union – the Soviet Socialist Republic of wherever – would declare that republic law took precedence over Soviet law; in theory and in practice up until that time, Soviet law superseded laws passed by the lower constituent parts of the Union. It would also no doubt give 'justification' to the Chinese leadership that their policy of an iron grip on political power while opening up the economy was the right approach. The above set the scene or gave the necessary excuses for the attempted coup d'état in August 1991 by hardline elements of the Communist Party.

The press were not the only ones to unearth faults within the system. Well-known economists within the Soviet Union, Vasilii Selyunin and Grigori Khanin, published an article in February 1987 in *Novyi Mir* (New World) where they demonstrated that far from economic growth in the Soviet Union reaching an average of 3.9 per cent in the 1970s and 3.1 per cent in the first half of the 1980s, the correct respective figures were 1.0 per cent and 0.6 per cent. Similar articles followed by other academics to the extent that Gorbachev felt able to declare at the June 1987 Central Committee meeting that the Soviet Union had reached a pre-crisis stage, i.e. on the *eve* of a full-blown economic and social crisis within society. As a consequence radical reforms were necessary, it was argued.

What were these radical reforms, which comprised *perestroika* (reconstruction), of Gorbachev's? Perhaps the most successful, and indeed the most popular economic reform was that on the Law on Cooperatives. This law came into force in May 1988 and allowed, for the first time since the New Economic Policy (NEP) of Lenin in 1922, private ownership of businesses (in the form of cooperatives) in the service, manufacturing and foreign trade sectors. While initially there existed restrictions on such cooperatives in terms of employment size, these were later relaxed. The service sector in particular enjoyed a relative boom with the appearance of many new family-run restaurants. This may be seen as the high end of the economic reform process.

However, a recurrent theme of the economic reforms pushed forward by Gorbachev would be the triumph of form over content; what seemed radical at first glance would later appear to have limited 'bite'. We give examples below taken from Hedlund (1999). Continuing with the radical reforms announced by Gorbachev stemming from what might be called the 'Pre-crisis Central Committee' meeting, it was decided that a law was to be passed whereby the overriding priority of central planning in the economic process would be curtailed, with individual enterprises being allowed to take their destiny into their own hands and set their own business plans. At face value central planning was finished.

However, all was not what it seemed since, although centrally imposed targets would no longer exist, a system of state orders (*goszakaz*) would be introduced for strategic goods. There was no compulsion on the part of managers of enterprises to accept the state orders. However, those who did accept them would also receive the necessary inputs of raw materials. Given that economists believe that individuals are – by and large – rational in their behaviour, for the individual enterprise manager the choice was as follows: (1) accept the state orders sent down from above and receive, more or less, the necessary inputs to complete the order; or (2) break away from the umbilical cord of the state, and start producing goods/services for a market that is in its infancy *and at the same time* begin the hunt for raw materials in factor markets that were also in their infancy! Most managers, no doubt, took the least line of resistance and opted for course (1). In effect *goszakaz* replaced the old target system. This should be contrasted with the dual-track pricing system introduced in China (described in more detail below) where the plan was maintained but SOEs could also produce and sell, at market prices, any output above their allocated plan target.

To compound matters, Gosplan was delegated the task of completing the current five-year plan and drawing up the new system of state orders. A rational, self-interested planner would no doubt have simply changed the name but kept the old targets for what were perceived to be strategic goods sectors.

Another example concerns *Gospriemka*, a relatively new section added to the extensive state bureaucracy. Established in 1985 to probe into the quality of production within manufacturing, it started to approach its task with élan in the first half of 1987. In principle, given the appalling track record of quality of output, this was a welcome step; not necessarily one of market reform since it chose to improve the situation *within* the existing planning system but welcome nevertheless to hard-pressed Soviet consumers. In the longer term it could be argued that it would pave the way for placing enterprises on a firm footing for entry into a market system by raising the quality of output and hence ultimately giving consumers something they really wanted to buy.

However, such was the volume of goods rejected as not fit for purpose that both managers and workers on a widespread scale started to lose their monetary bonuses which, recall from Chapter 1, were linked to the quantity and not to the quality of output. The spontaneous strikes which erupted only helped to highlight the extent of the inadequacies in the field of quality. If Gorbachev had been serious about tackling the weakness within the system, and quality of output was certainly one of them, then, as Hedlund (1999) notes:

> A rational policy would have been to reduce output targets to a level that could be achieved without cheating on quality. Such a move, however, would have involved an open admission of the true production capacity of the Soviet economy. Given this dilemma, it was decided instead to put gospriemka on ice . . . At the first litmus test of dedication of the new policy, gospriemka made it clear to all that the reformers either did not dare or did not have the intention of staying the course. Their credibility was thus given a serious blow from which it did not recover. Meanwhile the economy continued to decline.

The main criticisms of Gorbachev's reforms lay not in what was being put forward, but in what was not being proposed. The old Soviet mentality of control and discipline still ruled; decrees, for example, would be passed stating which private activities were allowable (as opposed to saying all private business activities are allowed with the exception of, say, selling hard drugs, prostitution, etc.). There was nothing put forward to create independent market institutions which would have *started* to separate the state from the economy. The ultimate concrete measure which would have started the Soviet Union down a market road – market-based pricing – was not introduced, being far too politically sensitive. Another barrier lay in the refusal to recognise capital as a factor of production and hence the necessity for capital markets to be formed. How could enterprises even consider breaking free of the state order system if they could not raise the necessary funds for investment? Indeed, how could various investment projects be adequately appraised for potential return and for risk without a market to weigh up these issues? And while the Law on Cooperatives did allow for small-scale private ownership of certain businesses, the principle that the 'means of production' (i.e. the large-scale industrial concerns which produced the wealth of the country) should not be allowed to be owned by individuals unconnected with the state was never – at least formally – up for discussion.

Finally, we present the anti-alcohol campaign. This must stand out as a good example of an attempt to achieve something laudable, but with unintended consequences. Equivalent consumption of pure alcohol per head of population had increased from 4.6 litres to 10.5 litres per year between 1960 and 1984. While there had been previous attempts at curtailing alcohol consumption by the Communist Party in 1958 and by Brezhnev in 1972 along with further attempts in the early 1980s, it was Gorbachev who declared war on alcohol and had the most success, at least initially. The intended effect of the campaign was not simply to improve the general health of the population but in the main to ensure that a large percentage of the workforce who did not at the time turn up for work or turned up inebriated would through the anti-alcohol campaign turn up to work sober and on time.

Naturally, the price of alcohol increased, twice to be precise; first in August 1985 and second in August of the following year. Access to alcohol sales were also substantially curtailed to just four hours per day between 4 p.m. and 8 p.m. through a drastically curtailed number of state shops – by 1987 the number of stores selling wine and vodka in the Soviet Union was five times lower than in 1984. Alcohol sales were banned near railway stations, on trains, at official functions, in public places, and party officials and managers who drank heavily risked being sacked, while in restaurants no alcohol could be served before 2 p.m. Even the foreign tourists with their hard currency, normally exempt from such issues, faced the same restrictions, demonstrating the seriousness of the campaign.

The initial results were impressive: recorded alcohol consumption between 1985 and 1987 dropped 56 per cent. That said, illicit brews – *samogon* – increased over time especially when, with the onset of *glasnost*, making one's own beer/vodka at home became a non-criminal offence. It became increasingly difficult to find any store that sold sugar, as shelves were cleared by shoppers looking to go into the alcohol home-brew industry. While it is generally accepted that public health did improve, with life expectancy increasing, and that absenteeism from work dropped substantially, along with a large fall in road fatalities from drunk drivers, the campaign was not popular. Starting in Moscow in the winter of 1988 the Moscow authorities opened extra outlets and kept stores open longer in response to Muscovite complaints. This was the thin end of the wedge; other cities and regions followed suit.

What then is the significance of Gorbachev's reforms? In the short to medium term the budget deficit increased significantly. No one it seems had thought about what the state was going to do to fill the void left by the missing billions of roubles brought about by the collapse in revenue from alcohol sales. In addition, given that expenditure on alcohol made up quite a large percentage of total expenditure by Soviet/Russian citizens, with less to spend their roubles on, they simply saved them. As a result, the anti-alcohol campaign contributed to the rouble overhang which would burst forth once prices were liberalised.

To all of the above, we must add the individual animosity that developed between Gorbachev and Yeltsin before transition proper commenced. We touch on it here, since it directly impacts upon the start of the transition process in 1992.

Yeltsin himself owed his initial elevation up the ranks of the CPSU to Gorbachev, an irony that would not be lost on Gorbachev at a later date. In December 1985 Yeltsin was appointed to the Politburo, and also to the powerful and prestigious position of First Secretary of the Communist Party's Moscow City Committee in which positions he would remain until 21 October 1987 when he resigned. During this time Yeltsin cultivated a man-of-the-people image, often travelling by public transport to work; he would also conduct unannounced visits to department stores which while selling little on the shelves would have backrooms filled with goods. This one-man crusade against corruption (at the lower levels of Soviet society) made Yeltsin both well known and popular with Muscovites.

On 21 October 1987 at the Plenary session of the Central Committee of the CPSU, Yeltsin, without prior warning to or approval from Gorbachev, criticised the Politburo and announced his resignation, adding that the City Committee would decide whether he should resign from the post of First Secretary of the Moscow City Party Committee. The trigger for this had been an apparent (heated) disagreement with Yegor Ligachev who aspired to be second in the country only to Gorbachev, over, it is said, Raisa Gorbachev's 'meddling' in politics. Feeling, perhaps, that support from Gorbachev was ebbing away, he no doubt felt it better to jump before being pushed. The timing of the 'jump', however, was provocative, being as it was only a matter of days before the seventieth anniversary of the 'Great October Revolution'. Despite attempts by the party leadership to keep the resignation under wraps, word got out and the celebratory events were tarnished by talk and rumours of splits within the leadership.

Gorbachev was to have his revenge; on 11 November, despite the fact that Yeltsin was at the time hospitalised, he was summoned to appear before the ruling body of the Communist Party within Moscow – the Moscow City Committee – to explain his actions and to hear accusations against him. Gorbachev accused Yeltsin of 'political immaturity' and 'absolute irresponsibility'. With no one backing Yeltsin, he was relieved of his position as First Secretary. Under such pressure from all in attendance and still weak from his hospital stay, Yeltsin 'recanted' and declared that his speech to the Politburo criticising it and the slow pace of reforms had been a mistake.

Unlike the show trials of the 1930s, times had moved on and Yeltsin, while not imprisoned or shot, was moved to a lowly position in government as minister for the construction industry where he worked for 18 months while he figured out his next move. His chance came, ironically, with Gorbachev's policy of *glasnost* and the establishment of the Congress of People's Deputies. This half-way house between fully democratic convention and rubber stamp body had two-thirds of its seats open, in principle, for anyone to stand, whether a member of the Communist Party or not, with the other one-third being kept for important individuals from public organisations. Standing for a seat in Moscow, Yeltsin secured 89 per cent of the vote. From this body he then secured a position in the Supreme Soviet – the highest legislative body constitutionally within the USSR.

Not finished yet, Yeltsin went on to stand for Russia's Congress of People's Deputies in March 1990 where again he won in his home town of Sverdlovsk (now Yekaterinburg) with 84 per cent of the vote. From that body he then went on to be selected for its supreme ruling body, in effect its executive arm. He had managed to 'hedge his bets'; he now had a channel through which to re-energise his political career either at an all-Union level or at a regional level through political bodies within Russia. The culmination of Yeltsin's long march within the regime of the Soviet Union came on 12 June when Yeltsin became the first democratically elected President of Russia.

We have mentioned the attempted coup d'état in August 1991 in Chapter 1, and do not repeat the details here. Suffice to say that with the coup's defeat Yeltsin was in a dominant position and it was his turn to administer the humiliation to Gorbachev. However, we run ahead of ourselves. The purpose of this section is to explain how the bitter rivalry between Yeltsin and Gorbachev impacted upon the start of the transition process. As Yeltsin jockeyed for position throughout 1990 and 1991, and hence ultimate power, this was to be no time for fiscal rectitude. Friends and allies, and more importantly waverers to the cause needed to be won over to Yeltsin's side. If one makes promises of higher wages and pensions, more subsidies, better access to goods – as Yeltsin did in the autumn of 1990 – then if this is not to be seen as mere talk, money must be found to back up the promises.

Even though Yeltsin did not control Gosbank – the then all-Union Soviet bank – he was able, as President of Russia, to influence the Russian branch of Gosbank. One would think that a branch bank of Gosbank – even one as large as that which covered Russia – would not be able to print money without prior approval from the head bank, i.e. Gosbank; it would be like the Bank of Italy deciding to print as many euros as it wished without recourse to consultation with the President of the European Central Bank. And yet this is exactly what happened between Gosbank and the branch within Russia. The end result was that the budget of Russia by the end of 1991 had run into deficit to the equivalent of 31.9 per cent of the GDP of Russia. That deficit was covered by the printing of money. As Hedlund (1999) notes:

> during the course of 1991 the monetary authorities in Moscow succeeded in creating no less than 137.3 billion roubles, which may be compared to an accumulated total of 133.8 billion roubles created between 1961 and 1990. During a single year, they thus managed to print more money than in the preceding three decades put together.

This was a financial weapon of mass political destruction which was to be a death blow to the USSR. Hedlund (1999) quotes a Russian economist, Andrei Illarionov, who writes:

> The populist macroeconomic policy of the Russian government dealt a fatal blow to the financial and monetary system of the USSR, and thence to its political structures. From an economic perspective, the USSR was finished not in December 1991, when the Belovezh accords were signed, and M. Gorbachev was forced to resign, nor in September, when the Union Parliament was dissolved, but in April 1991, when the weapon of financial destabilisation was trained upon the Union authorities.[7]

While we discuss in more detail below the various arguments put forward for the 'true path' to transition, it does not go amiss to mention here one obvious *similarity* between Russia and China pre-transition: both countries had been through several years of internecine political conflict. We have only touched on the above situation briefly between Yeltsin and Gorbachev, a conflict which culminated in an attempted coup d'état by hardline communists, but it is clear that with so much energy being directed by the antagonists at either holding on to power or gaining power, could it be said that the day-to-day running of the country was getting the attention that it should have got, never mind an actual attempt at transformation?

Within China such political infighting had also taken place; the period when this occurred was known as the Cultural Revolution (more in the next section) and devastated the country socially, politically, economically and culturally over a ten-year period. Officially ending on 10 October 1976 with the arrest of all members of the so-called Gang of Four, the reform process in China would start, even if tentatively, in 1978 two years later. Yeltsin's reform process would begin in early 1992 shortly after the USSR had been dissolved. We outline in more detail the condition of Chinese society pre-1978 below; however, the internecine struggle for power that took place in China was, as we will see, even more bitter and intense than anything that had been witnessed in the old Soviet Union. If anything, such conflict between various factions of the Chinese Communist Party with the disastrous spill-over effects into everyday Chinese life should have made the transition process for China *more difficult* than the path travelled in Russia, all other things being equal. That it did not is explained below.

The situation pre-transition in China

Before the war with Japan in 1937, one is struck by the level of development that had taken place with modern (for its time) industrial practices occurring in some of the major cities and regions of China. One is also struck in the sense of how similar this was to the situation that existed in Tsarist Russia before the Bolshevik Revolution, at least qualitatively if not exactly quantitatively. While Brandt and Rawski (2008) can rightly talk of Chinese industry in the 1930s that 'had developed a modern sector spanning industry, communications, transportation, banking, and finance, in which domestic ownership predominated', as they themselves point out, this 'nascent modern sector never surpassed one-tenth of GDP'. In essence there was the beginning of capitalist development, as in Tsarist Russia, but these were islands of the future stuck in the sea of the past.

After eight years of fighting the Japanese invaders in an uneasy alliance between Mao's communist forces and those of the Chinese nationalists – the Kuomintang – led by Chiang Kai-shek, the Japanese were defeated both in China and on the international scene. The loose alliance inevitably disintegrated and full-scale civil war commenced. With the defeat of the nationalist forces by Mao's communist peasant army, and the fleeing of the remnants of the Kuomintang to Formosa (now called Taiwan), China was established on 1 October 1949.[8] Yet again, a communist victory had occurred not in an advanced capitalist economy as Karl Marx had originally envisaged, but in a *relatively* backward economy. One crucial difference between Lenin and Mao, however, is that while Lenin used the battering ram of proletarians to smash Tsarism and the nascent capitalist class that was emerging in Russia, Mao used the peasantry.

Be that as it may, the leadership of China had at least an 'off-the-shelf model' on which to begin to construct their new Chinese order. This was Stalin's dash for growth through the development of heavy industry at the expense of light industry and, as a consequence, a dearth of consumer products be that for the city or for the countryside. Indeed, not only would Chinese citizens, like their Soviet cousins of the 1930s, not get the consumer goods they might desire, but this rapid industrialisation – as occurred in Stalin's Russia – would come through forced saving, and again mainly at the expense of the peasantry within China. For urban workers, their contribution to forced savings would be through a subsistence wage brought about by low-priced food and social benefits attached to the workplace such as subsidised housing, health care, childcare and pensions. Rural households were collectivised into production teams, brigades and from 1958, communes, which distributed incomes based on a 'highly egalitarian work-point system.' (Cai *et al.* 2008)

While Chapter 1 has rightly emphasised the inadequacies of the command economy and of central planning, it should be recalled that in the early stages of planning in less developed countries when the economy is relatively non-complex it is easier to coordinate production of goods and services through the central allocation of inputs and outputs. So too with central planning in China in the early years where the recorded annual average growth rate for per capita GNP over the period 1950 to 1975 was of the order of 4.2 per cent according to World

Bank estimates (Brandt and Rawski 2008). As Brandt and Rawski point out, this figure 'was surpassed by only ten of seventy-seven nonindustrialised nations, most of them oil exporters. During these years, China's planned economy outperformed other populous developing nations, including Brazil, Egypt, India, Indonesia, and Mexico, often by substantial margins.'

The Great Leap Forward

While Mao's Communist Party had come to power with the active assistance of the peasantry largely on the pledge to redistribute land from landlords and 'richer peasants' to poorer peasants or landless peasants, the land policy of Mao did not ultimately fulfil this original intent. Mao, like Stalin before him for the Soviet Union, wanted to raise the power and prestige of the country; this implied industrialisation; the way to quick industrialisation was through buying the agricultural surplus from the peasantry at low prices and selling either domestically or internationally at much higher prices. Just as within the Soviet Communist Party, some advocated within the Chinese Communist Party, notably Liu Shaoqi, that collectivisation should not be forced but introduced gradually to go hand-in-hand with gradual industrialisation which would provide the agricultural machinery to the peasantry and so act as an incentive for voluntary collectivisation.

Over a ten-year period from 1949 to 1958 progressively larger groups (200 to 300) of peasant families were brought together into collectivised units where animals and equipment which had been owned by individual families were now deemed the property of the group. Not popular with the peasants – forced collectivisation never is – there were still some within the ranks of the party who spoke out against it such as Zhou Enlai. In 1957 – some would say as a result of the disquiet in the party – Mao launched his 'Let a 100 flowers bloom' campaign. Ostensibly to allow open expression so that the party would learn from such criticism, and so move the country forward, the campaign came to a quick end either because it was seen to be getting out of hand or, as some suspected all along, it was simply a ruse to force those within the party and indeed anyone within society to 'expose' themselves in terms of their disquiet about Communist Party policies. As a result a mass purge was launched led by Deng Xiaoping, whereby hundreds of thousands of party members were expelled.

By the end of 1957 the first five-year plan had been completed. The next five-year plan, 1958 to 1963, is the one associated with the Great Leap Forward although only the first three years represent the Great Leap Forward proper, being formally announced by Mao in January 1958. For Mao, steel and grain were the two commodities that needed to be propelled up the list of priorities. The 'theory' was to use China's vast supply of cheap labour as a substitute or an alternative to capital industrialisation. One cannot help but think that this was Mao's illusion as to how to avoid the 'primitive socialist accumulation of capital' that the Soviet Union had gone through, and so the Great Leap Forward is remembered for two main thrusts by Mao. First, there would be another round of collectivisation whereby the scale would be increased – peasant families numbering 5,000 would be brought together; communal kitchens would be set up to 'emancipate' females from kitchen chores and allow them the liberty of working with their menfolk in the fields. Wages would no longer be paid, but points based on work effort would then determine reward. To that end an experimental commune was established at Chyashan in Henan in April 1958, which was quickly followed by 25,000 others by the year's end.

In addition, Mao, having reportedly visited a 'backyard' steel furnace in Hefei, Anhui in September 1958 where so-called high-quality steel was meant to have been produced, decided that this was the future. In reality he was probably shown what his underlings knew would please him given that, at the August Central Committee meeting, a decision had been taken to double steel production in one year. Mao distrusted intellectuals and specialists, any one of whom could have told him that to produce high-quality steel, large furnaces would be needed using superior fuel, i.e. coal or coking coal. Mao gave orders for backyard steel furnaces to be constructed in every commune and urban area. Trees were cut down from whole areas, and even doors were taken from the houses. Low-value pig-iron was the main result of the endeavours. In the meantime labour had been diverted from the fields where the crops needed tending in order to make and attend to the furnaces. Crops rotted in the fields. Officials, trying to please their superiors, reported crop yields way above actual numbers. Grain requisitions to feed the cities and to export were then set centrally, based in part on these inflated and false figures, which barely left enough for the peasants to live on. Hunger began to set in.

While the weather had been favourable in 1958, it turned for the worse in the next two years with drought affecting many areas. Supplementary to this, major rivers flooded, devastating crops. Local officials, again under pressure from above to deliver grain, exaggerated crop production. While natural disasters such as drought and flooding played a major role in the famine that developed, the policies of the Great Leap Forward were also decisive. Not only was grain exported when people were going hungry so that 'face' could be saved, but new totally untested farming techniques were tried out on a mass scale which led to yet more reduced yields. Every piece of metal that could be found in the kitchen along with metal farming implements were smelted down to produce pig-iron. The whole thing was compounded when early on in the Great Leap Forward campaign orders were given from the party to 'kill a sparrow' since sparrows ate grain; but they also ate locusts. Swarms of locusts duly arrived in biblical proportions to add to the misery of the peasantry. Disputed figures are still discussed to this day but anywhere from 14 million to 43 million died of starvation before the Great Leap Forward policies were reversed in 1961 with grain even being imported from abroad to make up for losses within China.

At Lushan, the Plenum of the Central Committee was held in July 1959. Here Mao made what must rank to be one of the most memorable admissions of errors from any politician of any communist state not under duress. Despite this confession of 'errors' regarding small-scale steel production, the agricultural policies of the Great Leap Forward would continue for another two years with the losses recorded above.

> I understand nothing about industrial planning . . . But comrades, in 1958 and 1959, the main responsibility was mine, and you should take me to task . . . Who was responsible for the idea of the mass smelting of steel? I say it was me . . . With this, we rushed into a great catastrophe, and ninety million people went into battle . . . The chaos caused was on a grand scale, and I take responsibility. Comrades, you must all analyse your own responsibility. If you have to shit, shit! If you have to fart, fart! You will all feel much better for it.
>
> (Mao 1974)

With this 'confession' Mao gives us a glimpse, perhaps, as to why he so distrusted intellectuals and specialists.[9]

The Cultural Revolution

China had just about time to catch its breath before Mao, and others, launched the country into the Cultural Revolution, which although starting in 1966 and peaking in 1968 to 1969, officially ended in 1976 with the arrest of the so-called 'Gang of Four' who had sought in effect a continuation of Maoist-style policies. The disruption caused by this 'Revolution' led to a paralysis of decision making at all levels of society.

Mao alleged that 'liberal bourgeois' elements were taking control of the Communist Party and that a restoration of capitalism was a possibility. The battering ram against these 'bourgeois' elements was to be China's youth who formed Red Guard groups around the country, and, in some cases, going so far as to seize weapons from the regular army. The movement itself spread to all sections of society including urban workers, the government and Communist Party, and even the military.

What, in brief, lay behind this upsurge of mass political activism? Mao had already indulged in self-criticism over the Great Leap Forward; he certainly had nothing to lose by doing so given that it was seen by the Party leadership to be directly his fault that this adventure had gone wrong. As a result, in 1959 Mao resigned as Chairman of China even though he insisted that the Great Leap Forward had been 70 per cent correct. The day-to-day running of the country and government was then carried out by the new Chairman Liu Shaoqi, the Premier Zhou Enlai, and the General Secretary of the Communist Party Deng Xiaoping. While Mao had been weakened politically he was still enormously powerful; he remained Chairman of the Communist Party. In 1959 Mao was criticised in a letter over the Great Leap Forward fiasco by Marshall Peng Dehuai. Peng himself was a distinguished Red Army commander, having earned his spurs fighting both the Japanese and the Kuomintang. Faced with the choice at that stage of supporting Mao or Peng, the Politburo came out against Peng. He was removed from his posts and placed under house arrest, and was later to face brutal treatment at the hands of the Red Guards and to face public humiliation and beatings in front of large crowds.

Perhaps, also, this had been a convenient excuse to purge the People's Liberation Army (PLA) of Peng. Peng had turned the PLA into a more professional army with political influence kept to a minimum, and with Peng removed Lin Bao took over. Lin, who also distinguished himself in the civil war and in fighting against the Japanese, reversed this de-politicisation process, bringing the PLA securely back under more direct political oversight.

Lin is remembered today in China as one of two of the 'counter-revolutionary' figures in the Cultural Revolution, the other being the last wife of Mao, Jiang Qing, who led the Gang of Four. The Gang of Four apart from Jiang Qing consisted of three of her close associates, Zhang Chunqiao, Yao Wenyuan and Wang Hongwen. They would all later be arrested in 1976 after Mao's death. Lin, himself, was to die in suspicious circumstances in 1971 when fleeing to the Soviet Union after an attempted coup d'état failed, his plane crashed, apparently running out of fuel. Rumours abounded at the time and since that his plane was shot down in Mongolia, either on Mao's orders or on orders from Moscow. (Neither version of events has ever been confirmed.)

The uneasy balance between Mao on the one hand and Liu, Zhou and Deng on the other was to last until the Cultural Revolution. Liu with the support of Deng had partially reversed some of the policies of Mao enacted during the Great Leap Forward period including disbanding the communes. No doubt Mao could feel both the political and ideological ground slipping from beneath him. Through the Cultural Revolution Mao gained the upper hand: Liu Shaoqi was sent to a detention camp where he died in 1969; Deng Xiaoping was sent to be 're-educated' on three separate occasions and ended up working in an engineering factory. Zhou Enlai had been lukewarm towards the Cultural Revolution but had gone with the flow. However, by the early 1970s, what with a deteriorating border conflict with the Soviet Union, the military as a group had pushed for the chaos to end. In this situation in 1973 Zhou Enlai felt strong enough to bring Deng Xiaoping back into the affairs of state at the highest level.

Zhou Enlai died in January 1976. Hua Guofeng was named acting Premier to the disappointment of the Gang of Four which was perhaps an indication that their position was weakening. Deng Xiaoping, who had given the eulogy to Zhou Enlai, came under attack after rioting took place in Tiananmen Square – rank-and-file citizens had been angered at the arbitrary removal of wreaths in honour of Zhou Enlai. The subsequent burning of vehicles and destruction of office property was conveniently used to remove Deng yet again from any positions of power. With Mao's death in September 1976, the Gang of Four had expected the Cultural Revolution to be continued by Hua. Instead, less than a month after Mao's death they were arrested and put on trial. Jiang Qing and Zhang Chunqiao were sentenced to death but later had this reduced to life imprisonment. Wang Hongwen and Yao Wenyuan were given life and 20 years in prison respectively. They were all subsequently released after having served several years in prison.

Deng himself was again called back by Hua into government in 1978 as, regardless of differences, Deng was recognised as someone who could run affairs of state which Hua had difficulty doing.

The above might appear at first glance to be simply a power struggle between individuals. However, the difference in particular between Deng and Hua is more than one of personalities. Hua had wanted to turn the clock back to Soviet-style industrial planning whereas Deng had argued for a more market-oriented system. Hua, while disposing of the Gang of Four, had sought a continuation of Maoist policies under the so-called 'Two Whatever' policy: whatever Chairman Mao said was correct; and whatever policy Chairman Mao enacted was also correct (and should be continued). Deng eventually became strong enough to oust Hua from power in 1980 when he was replaced as Premier, and in 1981 Hua was replaced as Chairman.

It was, perhaps, Deng's good fortune that Mao had anointed Hua as his successor since Hua appeared ill-equipped to run government, turning as he then did to Deng. With political hindsight Hua may have stood more chance of holding on to power if he had sided with the Gang of Four. In reality one had the impression that no matter which side he selected he would have been deposed. That said, it is doubtful whether Jiang Qing would have been as lenient as Deng, who allowed Hua following his fall from power to remain in the Central Committee until Hua stepped down in 2002, with Hua even being invited to the seventeenth Party Congress in 2007 as a special delegate.

Why then are the Great Leap Forward and the Cultural Revolution directly relevant to the reforms initiated in 1978? The above were crucially instrumental in laying the change of *mentality* in parts of the leadership of the Chinese Communist Party that a new direction was needed. The old faith in the power of central planning and of economic direction from the centre had been shown not to be all-powerful. As Brandt and Rawski (2008) note,

> the winding down of the Cultural Revolution disruptions failed to resolve chronic food supply problems. During the first half of the 1970s, rising numbers of grain-deficit households, reductions in grain stocks and in cross-provincial shipments, numerous reports of local shortages, and demands that the state return grain procurements to avoid 'repeating the errors of 1959' – an obvious reference

to the Great Leap Forward famine – all point to a system near the brink of a serious food crisis, with no indication of sustained progress. With this background, it is not surprising that the story of China's reforms begins in the farm sector.

In addition, with the elimination of the Gang of Four in 1976 and with much of the Chinese Communist Party leadership itself having been victims of the Cultural Revolution, the leadership in 1978, when it embarked on reform, could distance itself from the previous 20 years of turmoil by blaming the Gang of Four and, to a degree, Mao himself. Mao had, however, through the Cultural Revolution, usefully removed most serious contenders for power that might have stood in the way of the reformers. In addition, the reformers increased their constituency following by rehabilitating many tens of thousands of purged factory managers and party apparatchiks who had also suffered during the Cultural Revolution. Hua, in arguing for a return to Soviet-style central planning, had the deadweight of the Great Leap Forward and the Cultural Revolution on his back – two major catastrophes in the recent history of the Chinese people that seemed in the eyes of many to be linked to central planning.

At this point we are also able to partially answer our query posed at the end of the last section where we noted that the internecine struggles within China would in all likelihood make the transition process more difficult in China. In reality the survival of a unified Communist Party in China – once the internal conflict was over – with roots into the fabric of society may have been decisive in taking reforms forward once they had been agreed on. That there were heated discussions within the Chinese Communist Party on the way forward is taken as read; but such a body should be contrasted with the collapse and, indeed, proscription of the Soviet Communist Party. What constituency bodies did President Yeltsin have to fall back upon to build up support for his reforms once transition had been launched? (Or indeed what constituency bodies did he try to build?)

The above may seem a difficult concept to accept for those readers who have Western democratic ideals as part of their belief systems. However, one should not confuse *conjecture* with *advocacy* or, indeed, with *fatalism*. That it appears that a unified Chinese Communist Party may have expedited the reform process – compared to a situation where one was absent – in no way means that one is advocating the continuation of such a party indefinitely or that no other transition path was possible. However, in the absence of democratic institutions in China and the failure to establish them (Tiananmen 1989), the initial road to transition – with a reform-orientated leadership in place – seems to have been served by the Communist Party *remaining* in place. For how long the Chinese Communist Party will remain a positive force, in a relative sense, in taking Chinese society forward is an open question.

According to Huang *et al.* (2008), the reforms that came after 1978 in China can only be understood in relation to what went before. This much is self-evident. However, while the events within the Soviet Union would develop on the basis of what was happening in urban areas and among the industrial sector of the economy, within China it would be the stagnation in rural areas and in the agricultural sector of the economy that would lead – in a haphazard way – to the gradualist process of reform. Development economists have argued that the agricultural sector has traditionally, in developing economies, played a key role in helping the rest of society to reach a higher level of development. These are:

- Supplying high-quality labour to factories, construction sites and the service sector;
- Producing low-cost food which will assist in keeping wages low for industrial workers (and hence keeping export prices competitive on world markets);

- Producing fibre and other crops that can be inputs into production in other parts of the economy;
- Supplying agricultural exports to earn foreign exchange which then allows for the importation of capital goods for further economic and country development;
- Raising rural incomes.

Huang *et al.* (2008) conclude that during the socialist or Mao era agriculture was not able or not allowed to fulfil *any* of the above objectives. As the authors note:

> Although output per person rose slightly, the sector was not even able to provide the nation with 2,300 calories per capita per day (a level near the UN-established minimum) and emergency grain imports almost always were needed to meet food deficits through the 1970s . . . Most damning, incomes per capita were almost the same in the mid-1970s as they were in the mid-1950s.[10]

Between 1973 and 1980 China imported on average more than six million tons of cereals, mostly grain, each year. That said, agricultural output *did* rise during the socialist era, and it rose faster than the rate of population increase. However, it did not rise sufficiently to allow a sufficient surplus to aid the development of a rapidly growing modernising economy.

Why then this poor performance? Soon after Mao came to power the land was divided among rural households usually on a per-head basis. This has been described as 'one of the most comprehensive land reforms in the history of the world' (Perkins 1994, cited in Huang *et al.* 2008). No sooner had this private ownership of land been established than in 1953 farmers started to be organised into collective farms; by 1958 the Communist Party directed that the collective farms be turned into communes which, although similar to the kolkhozy in the Soviet Union, were in many cases on a larger scale. Small individual household plots were allowed. The main problem within the commune system – as within socialist industry – was the lack of incentives. In the case of agriculture, farmers did not keep what they had worked to grow, and indeed there are some indications that effort was directed at the small individual plots at the expense of the communal ground along with the presence of some free-riding.[11]

As mentioned above, following Mao's death in 1976 and the arrest of the Gang of Four many thousands of Communist Party members at all levels of society but especially so within the state planning system and within industry were rehabilitated, including Deng Xiaoping. The leadership attempted to jump-start economic growth through a 'Great Leap Outwards' which involved spending – or more accurately the commitment to spend – millions on the importation of Western-style technology. By 1978, however, this ambitious plan (given how scarce foreign hard currency reserves were) had come to naught.

That said, when we look at the statistics in Table 9.1 we see that GDP growth during the pre-reform period appears to have been remarkably resilient in that during the first five-year plan GDP growth was actually 6.5 per cent per annum. This, as mentioned previously, may in part be ascribed to the relative ease of managing and planning on a small scale. In addition, Perkins and Rawski (2008) make the point that the first five-year plan came after the long war with Japan followed by civil war: 'Recovery from war typically unleashes a quick productivity surge due to the reactivation of capital and labor idled by military strife and the associated chaos. Under these circumstances, simple measures such as restoring electricity

Table 9.1 Average annual growth of GDP, fixed capital, labour, and TFP, with contributions to TFP growth, 1952–2005

| Period | GDP | Average growth of inputs | | | Average TFP growth | Percentage shares of GDP growth attributable to | | |
		Fixed capital K	Raw labour L	Education enhanced H		K	Education enhanced labour H	TFP
1952–2005	7.0	7.7	1.9	2.6	2.1	47.7	21.4	30.9
1952–1978	4.4	5.8	1.9	2.5	0.5	56.3	32.7	11.0
1978–2005	9.5	9.6	1.9	2.7	3.8	43.7	16.2	40.1
1952–1957	6.5	1.9	1.2	1.7	4.7	12.7	14.9	72.4
1957–1978	3.9	6.7	2.0	2.7	-0.5	73.7	39.7	-13.4
1957–1965	2.4	5.2	1.5	2.1	-1.0	93.1	49.5	-42.6
1965–1978	4.9	7.7	2.4	3.1	-0.2	67.7	36.7	-4.4

Source: Perkins and Rawski (2008). Notes contained within original source state that values are in percentages; calculations assume that 1952 capital stock is two times that year's GDP; and assumed depreciation rate is 9.6 per cent. See Perkins and Rawski (2008) for details as to how they calculate their measures of enhanced labour.

and reopening transport routes can deliver major jumps in output.' The above, combined with the authorities' suppression of hyperinflation, led to additional increases in productivity and the resumption of much agricultural and trading activity.

When one considers, however, that from 1958 to 1961 China endured the Great Leap Forward that 'left much of industry in a shambles and caused a steep decline in agricultural output' (Perkins and Rawski 2008); that technical assistance from the Soviet Union was withdrawn in 1960 after Mao refused to roll over and become another satellite of the Soviet Union; that the Chinese leadership deliberately refused to use imported foreign technology; and finally that the Cultural Revolution which, while peaking in 1967 to 1968 continued to impede effective economic management of the country until the arrest of the Gang of Four, the wonder of it is that the average growth rate of GDP stood at just under 4 per cent from 1957 to 1978.

As may be seen from Table 9.1, the relatively high rates of GDP growth were made possible due to the accumulation of capital which substituted for the ability of the economy to increase the productivity of labour as an input. Capital accumulation was 1.9 per cent, 5.2 per cent and 7.7 per cent for the periods 1952 to 1957, 1957 to 1965 and 1965 to 1978 respectively. After the relative success of the first five-year plan, the 20 years until the start of the reform period witnessed capital formation contributing, respectively, 93.1 and 67.7 per cent of the GDP growth over the periods 1957 to 1965 and 1965 to 1978.

That total factor productivity (TFP – see Box 9.1, *Total factor productivity for China before and during transition*) is negative whether measured by growth rates or by percentage share contributions to GDP over the 20-year period up until 1978 indicates that productivity within the economy was going *backwards*.[12] As Naughton (2008a) concludes, referring to the communist leadership of the country, 'the near collapse of the state capacity after ten years of the Cultural Revolution threatened their efforts to stabilise the system'. Something needed to be done.

We now turn our attention to that something, namely the period following the breakup of the Soviet Union, and the start of reforms in China: what we call transition.

Box 9.1

Total factor productivity for China before and during transition

Total factor productivity (TFP) is a term which seeks to measure the growth in the economy due to other factors other than to the growth of factors of production, i.e. GDP growth not connected with simply increasing the amount of land, labour and capital used in the economy. The concept is important since, it may be argued, it was the failure of the Soviet Union to raise its TFP that led to its ultimate collapse. The Soviet Union (and indeed other communist regimes of CEE) had engaged in *extensive* use of resources; they had brought more and more land, labour and capital into productive use but had not improved the *intensity* or efficiency of the existing productive resources.

The primary 'other factors' that contribute to growth are technical change and the accumulation of human capital. By human capital we mean labour which has received education and/or training, both of which make labour more productive in comparison with its pre-educated and pre-training state. (This is what is referred to as Education Enhanced Labour in Table 9.1.) As for technical change, as Lipsey and Carlaw (2000) illustrate by means of a 'constant-technology experiment', imagine you take the year 1900 as your starting point and 'freeze technology' at that point. Then, a century later in 2000, you measure output and compare it with the actual output when technology is not frozen. The difference would be very large indeed. As they point out, 'Feeding 6 billion people with the agricultural technologies of 1900 would have been literally impossible'.[13]

In terms of a relationship between output and the factors of production following Perkins and Rawski (2008) we can use a production function approach to convey the basic idea.

$$Y = f(K,H,t)$$

where Y is GDP, K is the stock of fixed capital, H is the education-enhanced labour force which includes human capital, and t represents shifts over time in the production function or changes in the productivity of the factor inputs. To estimate this relationship one can differentiate with respect to time, which gives us:

$$g_y = s_k^* g_k + s_l^* g_h + a$$

where g_y is the growth rate of GDP, g_k is the growth rate of the capital stock, g_h is the growth rate of the education-enhanced labour force, and a is the increase in TFP. The terms s_k^* and s_l^* are the shares of capital and labour in national income.

Looking at the growth within Asian economies in the post-war period, Krugman (1994) draws an interesting parallel with the development of the Soviet economy in the initial post-Second World War period. At that time many economists in the West thought the impressive growth rates within the Soviet Union were the future and that the USSR would soon catch up with and overtake the American economy. Once, however, the growth in factor inputs had been taken into account, TFP was virtually zero. There was growth but, given the finiteness of factor inputs – and the law of diminishing returns – it was a growth that could not go on indefinitely. Krugman wondered whether economists were making the same mistake in looking at the Asian

317

Tigers' economic miracles. Perhaps the growth of the Asian economies is simply factor-driven. By implication the high growth rates witnessed will, at some stage, come to an end.

While looking at all economies in South East Asia, he concentrates on Singapore and Japan and makes passing reference to China. Nevertheless, Krugman's (1994) general conclusion applies to all countries in the region:

> The newly industrialising countries of the Pacific Rim have received a reward for their extraordinary mobilization of resources that is no more than what the most boring conventional economic theory would lead us to expect. If there is a secret to Asian growth, it is simply deferred gratification, the willingness to sacrifice current satisfaction for future gain.

While to write and speak about the whole of the Asian Tigers is beyond the scope of this book, as may be seen from Table 9.1, for China, recorded TFP was an annual average growth of 3.8 per cent between 1978 to 2005 which is certainly not zero. Furthermore, Perkins and Rawski (2008) go on to forecast the future state of the economy. Using 'uncontroversial assumptions to project the growth of fixed capital, labor, and education to 2025' they conclude that the growth of these factors alone would imply a growth rate of just under 5 per cent.

Turning to productivity increases Perkins and Rawski's (2008) focus

> on the likelihood that China can attain sufficient TFP growth to drive the economy forward at an average annual rate in the neighbourhood of 6–8 per cent during the two decades ending in 2025. That range does seem feasible over the next decade to 2015, but the upper end of this range appears to be unrealistically high for the second decade from 2016 to 2025.

The authors themselves admit that these growth projections are not 'sure things', based as they are on the assumptions of China continuing to enjoy a stable economic *and* political environment, *and* that economic reform will continue to be advanced by the Chinese government, *and* that China will continue to maintain high savings *and* high investment rates over the two decades up until 2025. As the old saying goes, there is many a slip between cup and lip.

Krugman, admittedly, does make the point, writing in 1994, that it would be a mistake to overstate the case that the Asian economies are following step-for-step à la the Soviet Union and that continued high rates of growth are likely for 'the next decade and beyond'. His main point is that Asian supremacy and dominance on the world stage cannot be taken for granted through simple extrapolation of past growth rates. In addition, Krugman may not actually be far of the mark: Heston and Sinclair (2008) make the point that estimates of TFP depend crucially on the rate of growth. Other authors, such as Maddison, have the growth rate for China coming in at lower rates (see Box 9.3, *Lies, damn lies and the environment*). So if China's GDP growth was 6.5 per cent instead of the normally used figure of 9 or 10 per cent, TFP would drop to zero or close to 1 per cent per year. Heston and Sinclair (2008) conclude that 'At worst, then, China has maintained respectable productivity growth; at best, it has had a stellar record. That said, by any estimate the majority of China's growth has been the result of increased use of inputs rather than increased productivity in the use of these input.'

The transition process in Russia

As mentioned above, the dissolution of the Soviet Union was the result of a growing economic and political crisis within the Union; in turn, however, the dissolution of the Union may be said to have moved the crisis along and up to a new level as we will see below.[14] GDP was falling precipitously *before* the start of the transition to a market economy – between 8 and 17 per cent in 1991. Inflation in the wholesale and retail sector reached 138.1 and 90.4 per cent respectively combined with a dire situation as regards exports and imports (a fall of 40 and 80 per cent respectively in dollar terms). Furthermore, Soviet external debt stood at $67 billion, and foreign exchange reserves at $60 million.

> An appreciation of these conditions is crucial to understanding why the early stages of the transition unfolded as they did . . . Faced with such an acute crisis, the Russian authorities at the end of 1991 concluded that they must act decisively and without delay.
>
> (Ahrend and Thompson 2005)

The above looks, and indeed was, a dreadful situation whether one considers it purely from an economic perspective or, indeed, for the political and social implications. However, another complementary perspective is that at this stage we start to see the involvement of Western interests. Recalling how Lenin had repudiated all Tsarist debts, Western governments were keen that Soviet external debts should be honoured by the *Russian* government – recall that formally the Soviet Union was still in existence towards the end of 1991. However, 'By insisting that the servicing of the debt should continue until a rescheduling could be worked out, the West pushed Russia into a position where its dollar reserves ran out. By mid-December payments were unilaterally suspended' (Hedlund 1999). Hedlund goes on to quote John Parker and Richard Layard, the latter being a prominent foreign economic adviser to the then Russian government: 'This incompetent outcome, which blocked the dollar accounts of many Russian firms, was the first notable failure of the reform Government, and it was due directly to Western advice and pressure.'[15]

Be that as it may, the above economic situation was 'justification' for the team led by the late Yegor Gaidar, who had been appointed by Yeltsin, to head down the road of what many at the time thought would be a short-sharp-shock transition to a market economy. (See Box 9.2, *Yegor Gaidar, 1956–2009: architect of radical market reforms in post-Soviet Russia*.) On 2 January 1992, 90 per cent of retail prices and 80 per cent of producer prices were allowed to find their own level in the 'market'. This was followed quickly by the abolition of the state monopoly on foreign trade, and the removal of quantitative controls on exports in the same month coupled with a 5 per cent import tariff in July 1992 (Ahrend and Thompson 2005).

Interestingly, Ahrend and Thompson (2005) make the point that the great bang of price liberalisation was not as loud as many thought at the time or after; many regional authorities were wary of liberalising prices on foodstuffs and other basic necessities and as a consequence enforced local controls. The federal authorities followed suit by muting the impact of the liberalisation process on energy prices. Naturally this was intended to assist industry since, if Russian industry had to pay world market prices large sections would have gone under (notwithstanding that large sections of Russian industry *did* go under but for the very different reason of the abrupt ending of 'planning' and the 'sink or swim' transition to market conditions). That said, it had the added spin-off of limiting price increases of energy in January – one of the coldest months of the year in Russia! Even as late as 1995, 30 per cent of Russian GDP was covered by price controls; and in 2002, a full ten years after the start of the 'Big Bang', 'the domestic price of oil was still under 30 per cent of the world market price of Urals crude and the average domestic wholesale price of natural gas was about 12.5 per cent of the export price' (Ahrend and Thompson 2005).

Box 9.2

Yegor Gaidar (1956–2009): architect of radical market reforms in post-Soviet Russia

Yegor Timurovich Gaidar was born on 19 March 1956 into a distinguished Russian family. Part of the Muscovite intelligentsia, his paternal grandfather, Arkady Petrovich Gaidar, was a famous Red Army field commander and author of children's books, while his maternal grandfather, Pavel Petrovich Bazhov, was a famous Soviet author of fairytale stories and member of the Supreme Soviet of the USSR. He attended the prestigious Moscow State University where he graduated with a doctorate from the Faculty of Economics. After working in a number of research institutes, he became economics editor of the Communist Party journal *Kommunist*, and, later, economics editor of the official Communist Party newspaper *Pravda*, for which his father, Timur Gaidar, had also worked. Although a member of the Communist Party, he had become disillusioned with the socialist system, politically, after the Soviet invasion of Czechoslovakia in 1968 and economically, with the stagnation that set in during the later stages of the Brezhnev era. He was heavily influenced by the writings of Milton Friedman and Friedrich von Hayek, while much earlier admitting to reading, among others, Adam Smith's *The Wealth of Nations* and Paul Samuelson's *Economics*.

He soon became convinced that the socialist system could not be reformed but had to be replaced. As founder of the Institute of Economic Policy (later the Institute for the Economy in Transition) he was the author of a number of documents that formed the basis of the radical reforms that were later to be adopted following the collapse of the Soviet Union. He rejected the notion of a special path for Russia, and was critical of the other groups of reformers, including Grigory Yavlinsky and Stanislav Shatalin (both authors of the earlier '500 Days program'). The core of the 1991/1992 programme, later to be dubbed shock therapy, was rapid and comprehensive marketisation using policies of liberalisation, financial stabilisation and privatisation, combined, on the political front, with the creation of a Russian nation state with all its institutions (currency, tax and budgetary system, Central Bank, etc.).

Introduced to Yeltsin by Gennady Burbulis, Gaidar, then only 35 years old, was appointed deputy Prime Minister, and Minister for Finance and Economy, in early November 1991. Considered the intellectual leader, his team of young radical economists, labelled the Chicago boys (following on from the Chilean example), or their detractors often referring to them as 'the little boys in pink pants', included Anatoly Chubais (Privatisation Tsar), Sergei Vasiliev (Government Minister) and Pyotr Aven (banker and Government Minister). On 2 January 1992, prices for most goods were freed up as price controls were lifted, but with some exceptions (including energy and fuel, transport, staple foods). In June 1992, Gaidar became acting Prime Minister (of the Council of Ministers, i.e. the Russian government). Six months later, he was ousted by the Congress of People's Deputies and replaced by the industrialist Viktor Chernomydrin. Following this, he took up a position as economic adviser to President Yeltsin while retaining directorship of the Institute for the Economy in Transition.

Gaidar became leader of the pro-market liberal party, Russia's Democratic Choice (winning 15 per cent of the popular vote in the 1993 elections) and returned to government as first deputy Prime Minister in September 1993, only to resign four months later. Worse was to come in the 1995 elections when his Russia's Choice party failed to meet the 5 per cent parliamentary threshold required to qualify for party representation in the Duma. He later became Co-Chairman of the political bloc Union of Right Forces and remained a deputy of the Russian Duma up until 2003. Gaidar was the author/editor of a number of books, including *Days of Defeat and Victory* (1999), *The Economics of Russian Transition* (2003), *State and Evolution: Russia's Search for a Free Market* (2003), and *Collapse of an Empire: Lessons for Modern Russia* (2007). On 16 December 2009, at the age of 53, he died of complications arising from blood clots. He will be remembered as the person who, in the words of Michael McFaul (in his Foreword to Gaidar's memoirs) introduced the 'most ambitious economic reform program ever attempted in modern times'. He remained a divisive figure right up until his death with the liberals crediting him as the saviour of modern Russia (from, in the words of Anatoly Chubais, 'starvation, civil war and collapse'), whereas the majority of Russian citizens blamed him as the person most responsible for the hyperinflation that wiped out people's savings and the economic turmoil that followed well into the mid-1990s. Quoting from the obituary in *The Economist*,

> Few people make such a difference. In 1991 Yegor Gaidar took responsibility for one of the worst messes in the history of economics, in the largest country in the world. The Soviet planned economy had collapsed amid grotesque shortages of everything from food to matches. Queuing for essential goods took many hours. Hard currency reserves had vanished, international trade had all but stopped. Few Russians had the faintest idea of how capitalism worked – and nobody knew if it could be made to work in Russia . . . In his few months in power, Mr Gaidar and his team demolished the Soviet economy and laid the foundations of capitalism in Russia.

Whether one is for or against the policies that he advocated, Yegor Gaidar will certainly be remembered and long associated with the transformation from socialism to capitalism and the transition from socialist USSR to capitalist (of some sort) Russia.

Soon after price liberalisation, privatisation on a mass scale was implemented via the voucher system, which continued until mid-1994 when the state's average holding in industrial enterprises – whether privatised or not – had fallen to 38 per cent, and to only 15 per cent in privatised firms. As Ahrend and Thompson (2005) note: 'According to Goskomstat data, 57.9 per cent of the workforce (including 76 per cent of the industrial workforce) was employed in privatised or new private firms. Over 70 per cent of small-scale enterprises had been transferred to private ownership.' Although intended to spread ownership among the masses, most shares held by the ordinary citizen were quantitatively small in nature. Given, however, the need by those on fixed incomes to raise their incomes during the inflationary period up to the mid-1990s, there followed a consolidation of share ownership with many shares ending up in 'insider' hands, i.e. under the ownership and control of factory managers or groups of employees.[16] (See Chapter 8 for a discussion on how this may have led to labour hoarding within enterprises.)

In embarking on the shock therapy approach to transition and in drawing up the mass privatisation programme through the voucher scheme, the group of young Russian reformers led by Gaidar had two potential objectives: first, they knew that transition to a market economy would require *real* money – the finance sector, for example, would need to be put on to a firm footing, i.e. banks would need to be properly capitalised and a large percentage of the non-performing 'loans' to former state enterprises written off; in addition, not all enterprises were adding 'negative value' to the production process. Deciding which enterprises had a potential future would be difficult to establish, and fraught with problems such as pressure from vested groups representing non-viable firms for soft budget constraints, but in theory the state could intervene to help the more promising firms 'ride out the storm' of transition. Then there was the general state of the infrastructural supports of the economy to the potential private sector, both the soon-to-be privatised and the *de novo* sector. Here we have in mind everything from the national rail network, the telecommunications sector, to the state of the roads and ports.

The second goal they had in mind was overtly political rather than economic and perhaps helps us to begin to understand the nature of the Big Bang approach to transition. While the country called the USSR had imploded, and people were – at all levels of society – becoming desperate, it should not be thought *ex post* that any measures advanced by a pro-reform government or group of reformers would be 'swallowed whole' by the populace. A one-day protest called by the trade unions in the mid-1990s (and backed by the Russian Communist Party) to protest against wage arrears, for example, had hoped to attract 20 million on to the streets. In the event, two million Russia-wide turned out. One can look back now and see the apparent resignation of large sections of the populace to their apparent inability to influence events, but at the time it was not so obvious that the public at large would simply 'take it'.

Ex ante, however, there was a stated need to build support for the privatisation process and the whole transition process. Many Western economic advisers and not a few Russian ones also have openly admitted that the eventual opting for a give-away in the early stages was an attempted co-opting of the various interested parties, namely the workers and managers inside the various concerns that would be privatised. There was a genuine fear that the communists would or could again assume power. True, a hardline communist coup d'état had been defeated by the courage of the protesters who took to the streets, and, it must be said, of Yeltsin himself, but that had literally been months before the transition process started. With the failed coup fresh in everyone's minds, the obvious question to pose was: Would there be another attempted coup? Would it attract more support this time especially if sections of the population felt 'left out' from the benefits of the transition to a market economy? That the majority of the Russian population *was* left out of the benefits of the transition process for much of the 1990s is neither here nor there. *Ex ante*, before the transition proper, the young Turks of reform had the neo-liberal vision of the promised land of free markets in front of them from which all sections of society would benefit. Indeed, Yeltsin himself had gone on television to say that by the autumn of 1992 a recovery would be underway from which all would benefit.

One cannot help but think that while the transition process of a Big Bang for the neo-liberal Western economists was a *means to an end* – with the end being a functioning market economy – for the Russian reformers perhaps, and most certainly for Yeltsin himself, a *different* end was being aimed for: the blocking of a return of the communists to power; the *means* to do that would be a fully fledged working market economy . . . and the sooner they could arrive at this stage the better lest they give the communists time to 'regroup'. The transition process, a market economy and the consequent raising of living standards would be the economic and social buffer against a return of the communists. Given that the output collapse, the rise in poverty and inequality within Russia, and the general deterioration of the health of the population did not give 'fuel' to the communists and lead to their return says as much about the communist opposition as it does about Yeltsin's ability to mobilise powerful support both within the country – the financial institutions who bankrolled his 1996 presidential election campaign and the oligarchs in general who controlled the media – and from outside the country, the additional financial support that would be needed from Western governments, the IMF and the World Bank.

Returning to our narrative, real GDP continued its fall through the period until 1994, dropping by about 32 per cent with additional falls in 1995 and 1996. Only in 1997 was there a modest increase in output and even then it was followed by a further drop in 1998, admittedly heavily influenced by the financial crisis of August 1998, itself – in part – the result of the Asian financial crisis but due also to the inappropriateness of fiscal and monetary policies in Russia.

Why did this output drop take place? In the short run the matter-of-fact reason was that the state ceased to place orders with state industries and refused to cover any losses incurred by many of these state enterprises.[17] State enterprises were then left to 'get on with it', that is, to find new non-state orders for their products and if nobody wished to buy their products it was then up to the respective enterprises to manufacture products and services that people did want to buy. The mindset or mental mode of many 'red' directors of enterprises was one of disbelief that the government would simply leave them to fend for themselves.

Another question that arises in relation to the output drop is why did the output decline take place for so long in comparison with other transition economies in Central and Eastern Europe? In other countries an output fall certainly took place but it 'only' lasted, on average, for less than four years or so before output started to recover. Here it is necessary to distinguish between the path chosen and how one chose to walk down that path. While the debate rages even now among politicians and economists as to whether a Big Bang approach to transition was the correct path to take, most are agreed that having chosen the path that was taken in Russia, the handling of it could have been carried out much better. Jeffrey Sachs, another prominent Western economic adviser, eventually resigned as an adviser to the Russian government 'in frustration' at what he saw as the continuing policy mistakes of successive Russian governments to implement good macroeconomic policy. We return to these points below.

Another point that needs to be borne in mind is that in talking about the Russian government this gives the impression of a unified body striving to carry out the tasks at hand. This was not the case. While the hardline communists had been defeated on the streets, there existed the Russian Parliament, technically still the Supreme Soviet, which had been elected when the old Soviet Union was still in place. It did contain (many) individuals who were not at all in favour of the transition process. Then there was the Central Bank of Russia which began to influence events through the emerging commercial banking sector of Russia with policies which were counter to the stabilisation process of the government. Finally there were the directors of the enterprises within Russia. While not at the apex of decision making within Russian society, their scope for influencing events would still be considerable taken as a group, given that many of these directors of the larger concerns from the days of the Soviet economy began to legally set up there own commercial banks, the very same commercial banks which would receive soft loans from the Central Bank; the commercial 'banks' would then lend to the enterprises which had set them up in the first place, so prolonging soft budget constraints which enabled many firms to survive *without* the need for active restructuring.

Consequently attempts to impose hard budget constraints were sidestepped. Even when fiscal discipline was hardened in the mid-1990s, 'loans' were taken out by enterprises through the non-payment of gas and electricity bills and by simply not paying employees their wages, and also by not paying government taxes.

Government policy, however, was not as consistent as it should have been in the light of the decision to make a dash for the market. Attempting to impose a hard budget constraint on enterprises and bringing down inflation would, one would think, involve both tight fiscal and monetary policies. However, while tighter monetary policy did assist in appreciating the rouble and so exerting downward pressure on inflation, the loose fiscal policy tended to push the economy in the opposite direction, assisting many unviable Soviet-era enterprises to stay afloat.

Recent developments

While most of the 1990s was not a good time for transition within the FSU, since 1998 (but before 2009) the growth record in both Russia and other FSU countries has been the polar opposite of the 1990s. Why? Was there a sudden change or development of institutions that complemented and gave succour to market development? Were the reforms advocated by the World Bank, the IMF and others accelerated?

Following the financial crisis of 1998 when the Russian government defaulted on its sovereign debt, 'Growth has consistently exceeded expectations since the financial collapse' (OECD 2004). Åslund and Kuchins (2009) state that the Russian economy has averaged annual growth of 7 per cent between 1999 and 2008 measured in *constant* roubles. If measured in *current* US dollars it has increased 27 per cent per year over the same period.[18] Given the depreciation of the rouble over the financial crisis of 2007 to 2009, the absolute amount of Russian GDP in current US dollars is always going to be subject to the vagaries of the exchange rate. That said, if one uses purchasing power parity measures which take into account prices of goods and services within an economy, the Russian economy *is* the sixth largest in the world.

Income-wise, Russia's GDP per capita in 2008 was roughly four times that of China at $12,000 and $16,000 in current dollars and purchasing power parity respectively. This income level is about one-third of the 15 EU member states before enlargement of the Central and East European countries in 2004 (Åslund and Kuchins 2009). Russia is seen as 'slightly more advanced than Brazil and Mexico but head and shoulders above China and India'. While the statistics quoted are no doubt correct, and indeed GDP per head *is* a better way to gauge a country's wealth rather than simply the absolute amount of GDP, the focus here is on a snapshot of the countries mentioned at a point in time. Of equal interest are the trends within the economy and where the economies of Russia and China are heading in the future. We are also trying to understand, recall, why it was that, initially at least, there was a deep and prolonged transitional recession in Russia but not in China.

What then has spurred on the growth within the Russian economy, and, indeed, other former Soviet states? OECD (2004) records the following factors in contributing to the growth of the Russian economy since 1998:

- Immediately following the financial crash and the rouble devaluation the main contribution came from exports net of imports.[19]
- From mid-1999 net exports became slightly negative or very weak. This does not imply that export growth fell; rather that side-by-side with export growth there was a surge in imports to satisfy consumer demand which took over as the driver of economic growth from mid-1999.
- Industry and construction led the increase in growth post-1998 but increasingly from 2002/2003 service sector growth became more important accounting for one-third of economic growth.
- Economic growth has been relatively broad-based but industrial growth has been driven by resource sectors and related industries. Referring to the years 2001 to 2003 inclusive, the OECD (2004) concludes: 'The fuel, non-ferrous metals and forestry sectors account for almost 70 per cent of industrial production over the last three years, with the oil sector accounting for around 45 per cent.'

Åslund and Kuchins (2009), on the other hand, see the economic growth since 1999 as being due to three factors:

- Capitalist transformation;
- Free capacity and structural change;
- Energy rents (by which they are referring to the rise in oil prices over the period since 1999).

It is not clear from their narrative why the first – capitalist transformation – is a major source of growth post-1998 but was not one before 1998 or why other transition economies which had restructured their economies faster than Russia should have experienced different growth rates pre- and post-1998.[20] Indeed, for Åslund and Kuchins (2009), of the three reasons mentioned, the first is the most important: 'The *primary reason* for growth has been European or capitalist convergence, which Russia has enjoyed thanks to the hard-fought introduction of a market economy in the 1990s' (emphasis added). This, however, only seems to beg the question as to what caused and is causing 'capitalist convergence'. The authors' reasoning appears to be analogous to saying that the reason the child grew into a man was because the child was born. Of more concern and interest is why the growth of the child was so stunted in the first few years of life, only then to spurt in later years.

Of more relevance is their point about spare capacity and structural change. On the spare capacity issue, throughout the 1990s much of Russian industry had excess labour and capital (factories and machinery) which lay idle as demand for enterprises' output collapsed. Rather than prune back both labour and capital to the level that was needed for the then current low level of output in Russia in the 1990s, many owners both hoarded labour and kept capital instead of scrapping it. (See Chapter 8 for more discussion on labour hoarding.) In the early years of the recovery owners of enterprises could call on unused capacity of both capital and labour to expand production relatively quickly. Notwithstanding possible misallocations of both labour and capital that remained fixed in workplaces rather than being mobile, with hindsight it is fortunate that this hoarding did occur, since presumably the growth that came after 1998 would not have been as robust (initially at least). Indeed, Ahrend and Thompson (2005) note that,

> While industrial production slowed in 2001–02, it recovered to around 6–7 per cent in 2003–04. The main reason for this resilience – apart from the dominant role of the oil sector – appears to be the significant labour productivity increases in a large majority of sectors. Average industrial labour productivity has been increasing strongly and steadily since 1997 (with the exception of 1998), and the average increase between 1997 and 2003 was around 8 per cent.

Not all, or even a majority, of this spurt in labour productivity should simply be seen as more effective use of labour. By 2002 the 'easy' gains from making better use of any idle capital and labour within the enterprise combined with the gains from the devaluation had largely been exhausted. At this stage active restructuring appears to have taken place in many industrial enterprises.

> In 2002–04, industrial output grew relatively strongly while industrial employment fell. Thus, despite rapidly rising wages, unit labour costs (ULCs) in industry in 2003 remained about 25 per cent below the levels of 1997, although wages were significantly higher. The major exception to this was . . . the gas sector, where ULCs were about 107 per cent above the pre-crisis levels.
>
> (Ahrend and Thompson 2005)

As regards structural change, 1998 to 2002 did witness a series of reforms:

- The introduction of a flat rate tax at 13 per cent;
- A law on the purchase and sale of agricultural land;
- Major legislation on judicial reform;
- Legislation on pension reform and on money laundering;
- New laws on bankruptcy, joint stock companies and a code on corporate governance;
- Virtually all capital controls phased out;
- A new customs code.

The verdict on this period of reform is mixed; the new laws and codes are seen as being definite improvements on what had gone before. The main weakness, however, is not the quality of the laws themselves but the quality of the institutions implementing the laws.

After 2002, reforms, whether aimed at the state apparatus or the better functioning of the market, slowed markedly. Indeed, there has been a more pro-active interventionist stance on the part of the Putin-Medvedev leadership with key 'strategic' sectors of the economy being taken either completely back into state ownership or the state taking a controlling stake:

> since 2005 renationalisation has prevailed, reducing economic efficiency and thus further growth. The renationalization of major companies such as Yukos, Sibneft, Vankor, United Heavy Machineries, VSMPO-Avisma, Sakhalin Energy, and Rusia (Kovykta) has aggravated corporate governance and political risk. The state now

accounts for 83 per cent of gas production and 45 per cent of oil production, and the Kremlin is utilizing the financial crisis to promote renationalization that is economically unfounded and harmful. Strangely, in the midst of the financial crisis, the Russian government is preoccupied with further nationalization.

(Åslund and Kuchins 2009)

It is probably the case that the nationalisations which Åslund and Kuchins (2009) speak of *during* the recession of 2008/2009 within Russia are linked more to keeping potential social unrest under control and not to the longer term strategic state control of key sectors; the two need to be separated out.

It would be tempting to see in this creeping state capture of *key* economic sectors a Russian version of the Chinese 'grasping the large, and letting go of the small' or perhaps a 're-grasping of the large, and letting go of the small'. However, it is not so clear to what extent the Russian state has an overall economic 'vision' of what it wishes to do with these strategic sectors now that they are under state control. The impression garnered of the Chinese state is a state that knows what it wishes to achieve – economic development and concomitantly a continual re-legitimisation of the Chinese Communist Party. It is more probable that the Russian state's interests in key economic sectors has more to do with (1) genuinely not wishing to see the 'threat' of foreign takeover of its key industries as perceived by the Russian state; and (2) through the Russian state's control of energy resources it hopes to increase its leverage over other countries but primarily the European Union. One wonders whether the recurrent head-to-head confrontations in recent years between Russia and Ukraine over unpaid gas bills which in turn have the potential to cut off gas supplies to Europe (since the gas pipe from Russia runs through Ukraine) is more to do with the firing of 'warning shots' to the EU.

What then of the drive for modernisation pushed in 2009 by President Medvedev? While we touch on this in future prospects for Russia and China at the end of this chapter the situation as regards efficiency perhaps encapsulates the problems facing any Russian administration determined to push Russia down the path of modernisation. In a report by McKinsey (*Lean Russia: Sustaining economic growth through improved productivity*) the consultancy firm (reported in the *Financial Times* of 13 October 2009, 'Red tape and Soviet ways slow output') measured five sectors of the Russian economy accounting for half of Russia's GDP finding that on average these sectors have levels of efficiency only 26 per cent that of comparable industries in the United States.

> Building a power plant, for example, costs 28 per cent more in Russia than it does in the EU, and building a distribution centre in Moscow costs 34 per cent more than in London. Part of the problem is regulation and corruption. Another stumbling block is the Soviet era bureaucratic culture that permeates most Russian companies, even private ones – paperwork is endemic.
>
> (*Financial Times*, 13 October 2009)

As an example, the article quotes the time taken to obtain permission to commence a construction project in Russia, taking on average 704 days which is six times longer than in Sweden. The long-running disputes between the Swedish home retailer IKEA and various Russian concerns – whether utility companies, fire or building inspectors or what have you – has led to IKEA's exasperation as to business ethics within Russia and highlights the problems in building a business-friendly environment within Russia.

Be that as it may, we now turn to the transition process within China, although we do return to future prospects for Russia towards the end of this chapter as to whether there is a realistic chance of any modernisation drive succeeding.

The transition process in China

That Chinese economic reforms have been gradual should in no way lead us to expect an economy that is still dominated by state-owned enterprises, with the OECD estimating that the private sector accounted for just under 60 per cent of China's gross domestic product in 2003 (OECD 2005). That said, neither should we expect a fully functioning market economy that one would see in Western mature economies. In addition, as we will see below, SOEs remain and are anything but insignificant or *un*profitable. In addition, while the figures on economic growth that we have quoted in this chapter and elsewhere in this book are indeed impressive, it should be noted that the growth has come at a cost in terms of environmental degradation. There is also a question mark over the accuracy of the GDP growth rate figures. Both aspects – the environmental concerns and the validity of the statistical figures – are explored in Box 9.3, *Lies, damn lies and the environment*.

Box 9.3

Lies, damn lies and the environment

The statistical figures for the Chinese growth rate of GDP, GDP per capita and level of GDP are not without some controversy. The late Angus Maddison specialised in estimating the level of wealth along with the growth rates of wealth for various countries across the millennia. He makes the point (Maddison 2006) that until 1985 China used the Soviet national accounting method of net material product which while systematically overstating growth also gave a false impression of the composition of that growth by excluding the 'unproductive' service sector.

In addition, according to Maddison, the heritage of the Cultural Revolution continued to make itself felt many years later after it officially finished in 1976. The national statistical office was closed down in 1968 and the entire staff dispersed. Even when it was reformed in 1972 virtually none of the old (experienced) staff were available to be taken on and most statistical records were gone. In addition, no new graduates in the field of statistics had been produced while the universities had been closed during the Cultural Revolution. Maddison reports that in 1981 the statistical office had 200 staff in comparison to 1966 when it had 400.

There are additional problems with the use, or non-use, of constant and current prices which tends to inflate official statistics (see Maddison (2006) for details). Finally, backward extrapolation of the official data from 1990 (recall that most data for the Mao era were lost) produces a per capita income far below subsistence level in 1952. However, with forward extrapolation from 1990 a GDP level of 85 per cent of the US GDP per capita level is seen as implausibly high.

We reproduce Maddison's tables as Tables 9.A to 9.C from Maddison (2006).[21] Even accepting the revised figures on growth for wealth creation, they nevertheless remain impressive by whatever standards one decides to use.

Table 9.A Official and alternative estimates of Soviet growth (annual average compound growth rates)

	Official			Alternative		
	1913–1950	*1950–1978*	*1978–1990*	*1913–1950*	*1950–1978*	*1978–1990*
NMP/GDP	6.1	7.7	2.4	2.1	4.4	1.2

Source: Maddison (1988b), cited in Maddison (2006).

Table 9.B Official and Maddison estimates of Chinese GDP and GDP per capita (1990 International Geary-Khamis $)

	Official GDP million $	Maddison GDP million $	Official per capita GDP $	Maddison per capita GDP $
1950	139,197	239,903	255	439
1952	177,401	305,742	312	537
1978	748,811	935,884	783	979
1990	2,109,400	2,109,400	1,858	1,858
2003	7,177,032	5,659,200	5,570	4,392

Source: Official volume movement 1952–1978 from Maddison (1998a), 1978–2003 from *China Statistical Yearbook* (2005). Maddison estimates for 1950–1990 from Maddison (1998a), updated from 1990 for agriculture, construction, transport and communications, and commerce from *China Statistical Yearbook* (2005); industrial value added from the latest estimates by Harry Wu, and value-added in non-productive activities assumed to move parallel to mid-year employment in this sector. The official estimates do not include 1950. The italicised 'official' figures for 1950 are based on Maddison's estimate of the 1950–1952 movement. All sources cited in Maddison (2006).

Table 9.C Official and alternative estimates of Chinese GDP growth (annual average compound growth rates)

	Official	Maddison	Wang and Meng
1952–1978	5.9	4.4	4.0
1978–1997	9.8	7.5	7.9
1952–1997	7.6	5.7	5.7

Source: Wang and Meng (2001) and Maddison (2003). All sources cited in Maddison (2006).

That there still exist problems in measuring the statistics of China – at least at a local level – was illustrated when the *China Daily* (30 January 2010) reported, 'Ma Jiantang, head of the National Bureau of Statistics (NBS), has criticised some local officials who inflate the GDP figures they report to the NBS'. The practice up until 2010 was for local governments to calculate their own local GDP figures and send them to Beijing for verification. It turns out that for Chinese GDP the sum of the parts (provincial GDP reported to the centre) is greater than the whole (GDP calculated centrally by the NBS).

> According to the bureau, in the first half of 2009, the sum of provincial GDP figures exceeded the national GDP figure, calculated by the bureau independently, by more than 1.4 trillion yuan, or about 10 per cent of the total GDP. In 2004, the difference was 3 trillion yuan, or 19.3 per cent of the national GDP that year, which was the biggest gap in history.
> Ma said that some provinces reported 18 to 20 per cent year-on-year GDP growth amid the country's economic slowdown in 2009. This has raised an

alarm for statisticians, because the national GDP growth in that year was only 8.7 per cent.

The problem would seem to arise from local officials being appraised by superiors of their performance by the degree to which regional or local GDP growth has increased or the level that has been achieved. The plan announced by the NBS is to relieve local governments of their data calculations and centralise all such future calculation by the NBS.

Whether one accepts the official statistics or the revised statistics from Maddison (and others), there are some more serious issues of Chinese economic and social development which lie behind these statistics such as the environment and inequality.[22] Woo (2007) quoting Elizabeth Economy (2004) summarises the economic impact of the failure to take the environment into consideration.[23]

> China has become home to six of the ten most polluted cities in the world. Acid rain now affects about one-third of China's territory, including approximately one-third of its farmland. More than 75 per cent of the water in rivers flowing through China's urban areas is [unsuitable for human contact] . . . deforestation and grassland degradation continue largely unabated . . . The [annual] economic cost of environmental degradation and pollution . . . are the equivalent of 8–12 per cent of China's annual gross domestic product.

One of the greatest environmental threats – brought on by the rapid economic expansion – is the shortage of water. China currently uses an estimated 67 to 75 per cent of the 800 to 900 billion cubic metres of water available to it. However, by 2030, if present trends in consumption rates continue, this will rise to 78 to 100 per cent. Woo makes the point, however, that water shortages are already critical within the country due to the distribution of water, with northern China faring the worst since the economic expansion has combined with semi-drought conditions for over a decade and a half. All in all, about '400 of China's 660 cities face water shortages, with 110 of them severely short' (Becker 2003, quoted in Woo 2007).

In response to this, the Chinese government began the construction of three canals to bring water north from various parts of China: 'an eastern coastal canal from Jiangsu to Shandong and Tianjin, a central canal from Hubei to Beijing and Tianjin, and a western route from Tibet to the northwestern provinces and each canal will be over a thousand miles long' (Woo 2007). This, in turn, has raised controversy, with some scientists saying it 'would cause more ecological damage than good' (*Wall Street Journal* 2006 quoted in Woo 2007).

One of the ways in which China's economic expansion has contributed to its own environmental damage is through the emission of 'black carbon' – particles of carbon which have not burnt up completely. This has allegedly caused a change in climate with northern droughts and southern flooding. The above, combined with desertification and soil erosion (3,900 square miles a year[24]) along with deforestation, leads Woo to a rather pessimistic (or realistic?) assessment of China's chances of combating environmental problems:

1 China's massive reforestation programme will not succeed in reducing sandstorms in the north because trees cannot survive if the amount of rainfall is declining over time; and

2 The number of south-north canals will have to be increased over time in order to meet the demand for water in northern China, until China reduces its emission of black carbon significantly (presuming no new large emissions from neighbouring countries like India).

Apart from the economic transformation that has been carried out in the country, the other major and striking difference between China and the other transition economies of the FSU and of CEE is that the CCP remains in power; arguably the CCP is stronger in China today than at any time in its past. The extent to which the CCP can claim responsibility for the emerging economic power of China is touched on below. Certainly in the initial period even one of the major architects of the reform process – Deng Xiaoping – was himself taken aback at the early success of the reforms.

'All sorts of small enterprises bloomed in the countryside, as if a strange army appeared suddenly from nowhere', remarked Deng Xiaoping, reflecting in 1987 on the first eight years of China's economic reforms (Zhou 1996). These startup firms drove China's reform momentum; they were arguably the single main source of China's growth. But their rapid emergence, Deng said, 'was not something I had thought about. Nor had the other comrades. This surprised us.'

(McMillan and Woodruff 2002)

For the transition process in Russia there is a clear break between the days of central planning and the start of the transition process, i.e. January 1992 and the introduction of shock therapy. (We acknowledge the earlier partial but ultimately unsuccessful attempts at reform by Gorbachev.) For China we have, to give two examples, Naughton (2008a) who distinguishes two periods of transition, namely 1978 to 1993, and the second period thereafter to the present. Other writers such as Clarke *et al.* (2008) talk persuasively of 1978 to 1984; 1985 to 1989; 1989 to 1992; and 1992 to the present as four periods which delineate the transition in China so far, although the 1989 to 1992 period is described by the authors as an 'interlude' when the most noticeable event was the so-called 'Southern Tour' (*nanxun*) by Deng Xiaoping where he rallied support for further reform. In part, it seems, different authors delineate different periods of reform depending on what perspective they have adopted – political or economic, for example.

What then are the factors in the Chinese 'success story', economically speaking? While reform in CEE and in the FSU would start with the macroeconomy and with the liberalisation of prices and stabilisation policies, followed quickly by privatisation of state concerns, the Chinese experience started in the countryside with the reform of the commune system or of what could be called loosely collective farms.

From 1978 to 1983 the household responsibility system (HRS) in agriculture was introduced. While previously farmers – as part of the commune – had received a small share of the collective output, now responsibility for what would be produced and how it would be produced was returned to the household unit within the villages. Importantly the HRS ensured that any profits rested with the household and not with the state. Increased procurement prices from the state in 1978 and 1983 combined to increase the returns greatly to farm activity and gave an enormous boost to agricultural productivity. While the above overcame incentive problems associated with the previous collective or commune system of agriculture, it did reduce the average size of landholdings by each household. That said, the smaller-sized farms do not appear to have suffered through lack of scale economies to the extent that farming in China seems to 'enjoy' constant returns to scale for small farms and not increasing returns to scale.[25]

With farm productivity increasing and labour beginning to appear as a surplus, the need for alternative employment outlets arose. With the government openly encouraging rural labourers to 'leave the land without leaving the village' (Cai *et al.* 2008) in 1983 and 1984 regulations were relaxed which allowed farmers the right to travel long distances to sell and market their products and to work freely in nearby towns or in the township and village enterprises (TVEs). These are businesses located in townships and villages that are owned collectively, or later when privatised, mainly by rural units and individuals.

While collective ownership dominated in the early stages, by the 1990s many had changed over to private ownership. That said, Naughton (2008a) makes the point that in reality many of these TVEs were established by entrepreneurs who struck deals with local officials that allowed them to maintain a pretence of collective ownership. The contribution of TVEs to China's success story may be seen in the statistics that while TVEs added 6 per cent to China's GDP in the early 1980s, this rose to about 30 per cent, with rural employment in TVEs rising from 9 to 27 per cent between 1980 and 2002.[26] Heston and Sinclair (2008) report that income from non-agricultural employment in rural areas now makes up approximately half of total rural household net income, a position which Taiwan reached in the 1970s and Japan by the mid-1960s.

The development of TVEs had several important results, apart from the obvious one of increased employment and higher rural incomes. First, the higher employment was not simply a transfer of workers from one occupation to another; TVEs, as touched on in Chapter 8, 'soaked up' the surplus labour in the countryside of both landless labourers and of labour which had become partially underemployed due to the rise in labour productivity on the land. This prevented large-scale migration to the cities and major towns by rural labour at a time when it is doubtful that these population centres would have been able to absorb the labour given the then limited job opportunities. Second, since TVEs faced less government legislation, paid lower wages, and received little in the way of state subsidies, they were far more competitive and could survive in market conditions. Where the output of goods and services overlapped with SOEs this placed pressure on the SOEs to reform and adapt to this new internal challenge (Cai *et al.* 2008).

Interestingly, while the first *draft* law on TVEs was circulated within China in 1984, it was to be 1996 before the National People's Congress was to pass this law. This typifies the actions of the ruling CCP in the first period of reform, inasmuch as it was not unknown for the law to 'catch up' with the economic reality on the ground. This was a combination of spontaneous movements from below (as in the redistribution of land among peasants that led to the HRS *without* prior approval from above) and conscious direction from the top without, in either case, laws being passed in advance to give a legal foundation to such initiatives. In both cases, if things were to go wrong, it would then be more straightforward for the leadership of the CCP and the government of China to declare any venture to be the result of 'rogue elements', so distancing the leadership from any failures at the grass roots.

This steady-as-you-go approach was to last until 1993. For example, the special economic zones (SEZ), established in 1979, were originally permitted in only four geographic zones: Shenzhen which lay across the border from Hong Kong, Zhuhai which was over the border from Macau (at that time a colony of Portugal), Shantou on the Guangdong coast facing Taiwan, and Xiamen which lay directly opposite Taiwan over the Taiwan Straits. Increasingly, however, as the success of the policy became evident – both to the central CCP leadership and to those areas *without* SEZ status – the number of areas increased to 14 'open cities' in 1984. (A Big Bang approach would have been to declare the whole of China open to inward investment.) Further, permission to approve FDI projects was delegated to the opened cities as long as the FDI project remained under $30 million, later increased to $50 million, although there appears to be evidence that local officials, to ensure the swift implementation of a FDI project and obviate the need for central government involvement, would parcel up higher value projects into projects under the required threshold. In 1986 the so-called '22 Regulations' were introduced which were applied throughout China and meant that foreign invested enterprises (FIE) were able to benefit from reduced business income tax rates regardless of location. (From 1 January 2008 the tax paid by domestic firms was lowered from 33 per cent to 25 per cent to bring it into line with tax paid by FIEs.) Complementary to these measures, controls on the remittance of profits in foreign currencies were lifted. To qualify, a FIE had to export at least 50 per cent or more of their production value or the FIE had to be a technologically advanced project (see Branstetter and Lardy 2008).

Given the locations of the initial four SEZs it should, in some ways, not be a surprise that much of the FDI in the initial years was due to entrepreneurs from Hong Kong and Taiwan. Emerging in the 1950s as low-cost bases for labour-intensive, small-scale manufacturing exports, by the 1970s both land and labour costs had started to rise – fortuitously for the leadership of mainland China. As Brandt and Rawski (2008) note with the new open-door policy, 'The offshore entrepreneurs uncoupled the pipeline they had established to world markets from their original home bases and reconnected it to China's new export zones.' China supplied the land and labour, and the incoming businessmen supplied the capital and the entrepreneurship and knowledge of world connections to distant export markets.

Japanese, American and European investors followed in the 1990s, but whereas the early FIE had see the SEZs as bases for exporting out of China, the FIE firms that came next increasingly saw it as a way to tap into the growing domestic market in China. The impact of this much-needed inward investment on the composition of Chinese industry in terms of sector and export share may be seen in Table 9.2 for the year 2002.

However, it should not be thought that this turning outward by China and its embrace of globalisation was all plain sailing either for the Chinese government or for those multinational firms tempted into the Chinese market. FDI actually peaked in 1993 and declined up until 1999, only starting to resume its upward trend thereafter. Rapid credit creation in the early 1990s had brought on a demand-led boom that in turn led to a burst of inflation when in 1994 alone prices increased by 24 per cent. The central bank stepped in with contractionary fiscal and monetary policies. No sooner, however, had the threat from a runaway demand boom abated in 1996 than the Asian crisis hit – not as hard as it did other countries but it did have an effect on the Chinese economy. Growth slowed along with export growth, and price deflation set in. It would appear that many inward firms had taken the unsustainable boom of the early 1990s as the future and had entered the Chinese market on that basis with revenue projections which were now of course completely out of date. In addition, many entrants had underestimated the difficulty of (1) setting up a subsidiary in China, and (2) in running day-

Table 9.2 Chinese industry in 2002: ten sectors receiving largest FDI inflows

Manufacturing sector	Sector share of industry FDI	FIE share of sector exports	Sector share of China's industrial exports
Instruments and meters	10.64	93.83	13.11
Electronics and telecommunications	7.88	91.12	19.01
Medical and pharmaceutical	7.03	56.34	3.42
Transportation equipment	6.50	64.03	2.78
Nonmetal mineral products	6.14	76.48	2.74
Ordinary machinery	5.56	58.13	4.66
Garments	5.07	61.40	10.63
Beverages	4.30	58.93	0.48
Textiles	3.52	50.41	5.54
Paper products	3.37	77.85	0.86
Total (for top 10)	60.01		63.23

Source: China Industrial Microdata for 2002. Values are in percentages. Coverage includes the entire state sector and other firms with annual sales in excess of Rmb 5 million (about US$600,000). Source and notes cited in Brandt, *et al.* (2008).

to-day business operations. The Chinese law at the time required that entering firms set up a joint venture with a Chinese SOE. The Chinese government naturally wished for some of the technological and management know-how to 'rub off' on to the SOEs and the management of these firms: however, 'many Western investors were unprepared for the cultural clashes, administrative difficulties, and operational inefficiencies created by their "forced marriages" to Chinese SOEs' (Branstetter and Lardy 2008). In addition, many incoming firms found that any kind of distributional network was not in place for the selling of their product or service throughout China, adding more complications to the daily running of the business. Over time, however, that has changed as experience and the necessary infrastructure have developed.

The other major strand of reform at this time was the 'dual-track' price system whereby SOEs were still allocated targets under the central plan of production, but any output above the target set for individual SOEs could be sold on the open market with enterprises being allowed to keep much of the resultant profit beyond the base figure – more than 50 per cent as a minimum and often 100 per cent. It should be added that this also applied to inputs. That is, enterprises would receive a guaranteed allocation of inputs sufficient, presumably, for the allocated output target, but additional inputs could be purchased on the open market if an enterprise so desired.

Greatly assisting the development of markets 'at the margin' was the freezing of the plan which allowed predictability from year to year and so increased incentives. As a result of this, planned prices set by bureaucrats had largely disappeared as a distinct feature of the Chinese economic landscape by the mid-1990s. The share of producer goods bought and sold at market prices rose from zero in 1978 to 13 per cent in 1985, 46 per cent in 1991, and 78 per cent in 1995 (see Brandt *et al.* 2008). In this sense, as various writers have said, the market *grew out of the plan* (Byrd 1989; Naughton 1995).

The retention of profits by individual enterprises above fixed plan levels increased incentives. Incentives were also introduced within the administrative apparatus of government with large cash bonuses being on offer to those who could cut costs on existing operations. One follow-on from the above was a marked increase in decentralisation to lower levels of government who were allowed to keep additional tax revenues generated by local enterprise successes in their local government budgets. Indeed, some would claim that this measure was crucial in generating a climate for the development of private enterprise in the absence of firm property rights; local officials, far from being mainly predatory in their behaviour to local businesses in the initial stages of business formation, encouraged their development, knowing that they would reap rewards later with increased tax revenues and the possibility for financial reward at that stage (Zhuravskaya 2000).[27]

In 1981 individual family firms (*getihu*) within the cities and towns were placed on a legal footing and limited by the number of employees or family members to eight or fewer. The private sector, however, received its biggest endorsement in 1982 when the constitution was altered to say that the Chinese economic system was based on socialist public ownership of the means of production and the state sector would be the leading sector in the economy. The crucial addition, however, was the part that now declared the 'individual economy' to be a complement to the socialist public economy. The following year saw this complementary nature of the individual economy extend to rural areas. The other private firm category is privately operated enterprises (*siying qiye*) which are able to employ more than eight employees. Industrial enterprises as a whole had grown from 936,000 in 1980 to 7.34 million in 1995, many of these being TVEs.

Reform in the industrial sector

Success in reforming agriculture and opening up the economy to inward investors undoubtedly raised the confidence of the leadership of the country. Eventually in the mid-1990s attention was turned to the urban areas and the SOE industrial sector. From 1995 the policy towards SOEs may be summarised as 'grasping the large, and letting go of the small' (*zhuada fangxiao*). Initially about 1,000 large SOEs were kept under central government control but local government would be encouraged to privatise or restructure most of those under their control since almost three-quarters of such firms under local government control were loss making in 1995 compared to just under a quarter of central government firms. By 2006 the number of state enterprises had been reduced by 3.8 million and, of the 1.8 million that remained, this only constituted 10 per cent of all firms.[28]

State enterprises, which had employed 147 million in 1995, saw this number fall to 122 million people in 1998, to 97 million in 2004 and to 76 million in 2006. Of the remaining workers in state employment this stood at just over one-quarter of all non-farm employment.[29] Consequently the state's share of economic output declined from 57 per cent of non-farm GDP to 35 per cent between 1998 and 2006 (Wildau 2008). If one focuses on industrial production, SOEs' share fell from 77.6 per cent in 1978 to 54.6 per cent in 1990 and 34.0 per cent in 1995 (Brandt *et al.* 2008).

That said, the picture can sometimes be confusing since state firms come in various legal guises: there are in the official statistics state enterprises which are non-listed and by and large unreformed; then there are shareholding companies, limited liability companies and collectives. The above can be important when trying to fathom what may be going on in various branches of the economy. For example, official data would lead one to believe that state-owned banks account for just 48 per cent of industry revenues and state-owned insurance revenues comprise just 5 per cent of the overall industry total. The reason for this, however, is that some state-owned banks and insurers have restructured as shareholding companies or as limited liability companies. Given the miniscule foreign participation in the Chinese banking sector, and the strong connections between the government and the appointees to the boards of these companies, they are still, in effect, part of a state monopoly of banking and insurance. Once these are taken into account, the state share from revenues within the banking sector and insurance rises to 97 and 94 per cent respectively. Within the service sector in general, Chinese-owned private firms in 2006 accounted for 27 per cent of service sector revenues even though they made up 63 per cent of service sector companies. The respective figures for the state service firms are 63 per cent and 35 per cent (all figures from the *Financial Times*, 14 July 2008: 'Large and in charge' by Arthur Kroeber and Rosealea Yao).

Going in the opposite direction are the so-called collective firms, such as the TVEs mentioned above, and which were often in the past – and to a degree currently – registered as collective concerns even though for all intents and purposes they were under private control. This was especially useful when private enterprise was still in the minority or was only beginning to be tolerated as an adjunct to the planning process. Entrepreneurs registering their firm as a collective firm stood to gain a degree of political protection from local party and government officials that out-and-out private firms would lack. They could also enter into certain business which was forbidden to private firms. Because of this these firms were and are known as red-hat firms.

As Haggard and Huang (2008) note, the definition of what is private and non-private as far as business entities are concerned can depend on who is reporting the 'facts' and what their intention is in doing so. The State Planning Commission (SPC) in wishing to demonstrate the extent of economic reform counted 'people-run enterprises' as being in the private sector. On the other hand, the National Bureau of Statistics (NBS) in attempting to show that reforms have not undermined state control assigned firms usually 'classified as nonstate, such as collective firms and shareholding firms in which the state maintains a substantial equity interest, to the state sector'. By the SPC's definition,

> the share of the nonstate sector in industrial output (by value) was 68.4 per cent in 1997. Under the NBS's definition, the nonstate sector accounted for only 21.2 per cent of industrial value added in the same year. Even if we acknowledge the substantial difference between output and value added, the difference between these two definitions of the nonstate sector is obviously quite large.
>
> (Haggard and Huang 2008)

Notwithstanding the above as to what constitutes the private sector and what the state sector (and acknowledging that many SOEs are loss-making entities), Naughton (2008b) informs us that in 1997, the low point for SOEs, once losses from the state-owned industrial sector were offset against gross profits, net profits came in at just 0.6 per cent of GDP. In 1999, profits from SOEs came in at 2 per cent of GDP, and by 2007, RMB1trn of profits were being made net or 4.2 per cent of GDP with non-industrial SOEs adding an additional 2 per cent of GDP in profits (Naughton 2008b). For 2009, the *China Daily* (21 January 2010) reported that SOEs increased profits by 14.6 per cent over 2008 coming in at 797.72 billion yuan ($116.8 billion).

What then of efficiency?

How has this profitability come about? Does it imply that state-owned enterprises have become more efficient? Is it then possible to improve the performance of state-owned firms without the need to privatise? Does the above mean that state-owned enterprises have found an elixir of vitality to rival the private sector?

Well, not quite. First, credit where credit is due: the above situation is a remarkable turnaround; the thought, in the mid-1990s, that state-owned enterprises would become profitable would have been on the fringes of any debate on SOEs within China. The main government body responsible for leading the turnaround has been the State-owned Assets Supervision and Administration Commission (SASAC). We use the word 'responsible' here in the sense of being given the charge or the responsibility by the government to lead on this policy aim. As mentioned above, bolstered by its success in the rural sector, the government then proceeded to close down loss-making firms, concentrating the remaining industrial state firms in strategic sectors such as military-industrial enterprises, telecommunications, energy, large-scale machinery building and transport.

However, as Wildau (2008) notes, most academic research focusing on the narrow economic criteria of efficiency would conclude that the private sector is 'better' in that the return on equity is higher in the private sector in comparison to the state sector. Between 1998 and 2003 the return on equity for all state-controlled firms rose from 0.4 per cent to 6.7 per cent. The respective figures for private firms are 2 per cent and 10.2 per cent. It may well be, of course, that there are other objectives for SOEs that have a higher political priority for the state apart from maximising profits.

Ultimately, however, of interest is to what extent the increase in profits has resulted from SOEs being better run and to what extent it is due to external factors. Wildau (2008) usefully lists the factors which are not connected with improved management of the SOEs but have nevertheless contributed to raising profits:

- The transfer of social welfare costs from SOEs to households and the government. Non-productive assets – such as schools, housing and health clinics – fell from 30 per cent of all SOEs assets in 1992 to 11 per cent in 2004. By getting rid of assets which generated negative cash flow, return on assets was automatically improved. Second, depreciation charges fell, also helping to boost profits. Third, when housing stock was purchased by employees from enterprises there was a flow of cash to enterprises, again helping to improve profitability.
- An improving economy, 'whose rising tide has lifted all boats'.
- The elimination of bank lending to many defunct SOEs, which gave the remaining SOEs access to more credit. The elimination of these non-viable SOEs led to an almost automatic increase in reported efficiency.
- Explicit or implicit subsidies. Included in this section would be the restructuring of SOE debts which led to reduced interest payments, given that the interest on one-year loans also fell from 11 per cent in August 1996 to 5.9 per cent in June 1999, and remained below 6 per cent until September 2006.

Summing up the interest costs and financial fees paid by all industrial enterprises and dividing this by aggregate liabilities, one discovers that the implied cost of capital for industrial SOEs fell from 4.8% in 1995 to 2.1% in 2003, and that it stayed at around this low level through (to) 2006.

(Wildau 2008)

In addition, the reform process itself *outside of* the SOE sphere increased the pressure on SOEs to become more efficient and profitable. With TVEs springing up through the 1980s and into the 1990s, combined with the presence of foreign-owned multinational enterprises operating on Chinese soil, this began the process of competition that was to place extra pressure on the weaker SOEs to adapt and survive or go under – when indeed they were eventually allowed to do so. While it may be objected that many SOEs produced products and services not produced by TVEs, at the very least the SOEs were now in competition for labour and raw materials and increasingly for skilled labour.

The government has in so doing tried to 'have its cake and eat it'; it has tried simultaneously to create reasonably sheltered environments for those firms operating in these sectors to carry on making handsome profits, but at the same time it has tried to inject a degree of competition. Barriers to entry are fairly high (through government red tape with high capital requirements that can be offputting) even in sectors where entry is allowed by law or in some cases (such as within the oil, telecoms sector, electricity generation and military equipment) it is simply forbidden by law for non-state firms to enter the market.

The competition element has come from the creation of oligopolies within the remaining SOE sector. Three national oil companies produce all of China's oil and gas; four telecom firms provide all the basic telecom services; and three airline companies carry 82 per cent of internal civilian air traffic. 'These companies enjoy enough protection that they can earn rich profits, but not so much protection that they can enjoy a "quiet life", the ultimate, stagnant reward of a pure monopolist' (Naughton 2008a). As an illustration of how well-off SOEs are, the top 15 state enterprises and the top 15 private firms, in terms of reported revenues, are listed in Table 9.3.

Recent developments

What then of recent developments?

> Impressively, many manufacturing enterprises were able to a) increase real wages by 10–15 per cent a year after 2000 while reducing unit labour costs, b) maintain or reduce export prices to gain market share (at least until 2006, when many Chinese export prices began to rise), and c) increase profitability.
>
> (*Financial Times*, 'The Flywheel Economy' by China Economic
> Quarterly (CEQ) staff 3 March 2008)

The argument is such that for much of Chinese manufacturing a virtuous circle has set in over the past ten years or so whereby rapid productivity gains have led to increased profitability, which allows increased investment, which leads to increased productivity gains, and so on.

The *Financial Times* article goes on to report that average annual labour productivity growth in large and medium-sized enterprises within China rose by a hefty 20.4 per cent per year over the 1995 to 2003 period. While this figure is not a Chinese government figure – and is probably an overestimate – it chimes with other independent research carried out by Peking University researchers. The official government figure for national labour productivity gains is 'only' 7.3 per cent per annum between 1995 and 2004. To put this into some kind of perspective, for the same period in the United States, we are informed, the respective figure was 2.4 per cent per year; the EU(15) 1.4 per cent; India 3.9 per cent, and for Japan 2 per cent.

Part of this massive productivity improvement occurred through a one-off increase in productivity brought about by the initial shedding of excess labour from SOEs in the mid- to late 1990s.

Table 9.3 A comparison of the 15 largest state and 15 largest private businesses in China, 2006/2007

15 biggest state enterprises by revenue 2007	Rmb (bn)	15 biggest private enterprises by revenue 2006	Rmb (bn)	Main business
China Petroleum & Chemical Corp (Sinopec)	1,065	Gome	87	Retail
China National Petroleum	894	Suning	61	Retail
State Grid	855	Jiangshu Shagang	59	Steel, Pharmaceuticals
China Mobile	286	Huawei Technologies	53	Telecoms Equipment
China Southern Power Grid	223	Midea	46	Household appliances
China Telecom	198	Shanghai Fosun	39	Steel, catering, retail
Shanghai Baosteel	181	Guansha Holding	32	Construction, real estate
China Railway Engineering Corporation	164	Wanxiang	31	Autoparts
China Railway Construction Corporation	149	Orient Group Industrial	30	Finance, building materials
First Automobile Group	149	Sichuan Huashi	29	Real estate Construction
China State Construction Engineering Corporation	145	Minsheng Bank	29	Banking
China National Cereals, Oils and Foodstuffs Corporation	143	Jiangsu Yuran Food	28	Food, retail, real estate
Dongfeng Automobile Corporation	142	Tianjin Rockcheck Steel	25	Steel products
China Minmetals	135	Gree	24	Household appliances
China National Offshore Oil Corporation (CNOOC)	132	Wumart	23	Retail
Total	**4,859**	**Total**	**592**	

Sources: State firms data from SASAC, company reports; private firms' data from industry associations, Forbes, Dragonomics research. All sources cited in Naughton (2008b).

Of course, the most recent developments concern the relationship between the US and China through international trade relations. While the 'Flywheel economy' may be ongoing within China a far larger form of this flywheel was being carried out at the international level between China and the US. Figure 9.A in Box 9.4 summarises the relationship. It should be noted that while we have focused on the US and China with Russia and the EU 'tagged on', it would be wrong to think, in the case of the European Union at least, that it was a minor player in terms of trade relations with China. In 2008, for example, 20 per cent of all Chinese exports went to the European Union with a value equal to 7 per cent of China's GDP. This compares to a figure of 17 per cent of China's exports headed for the US. For the EU, on the other hand, exports to China amounted to only 0.7 per cent of the EU combined GDP in 2008 (European Chamber of Commerce, Beijing).

Nevertheless, the interconnectedness of the relations between China and the US prior to the financial and economic crisis of 2007 to 2009 shows the degree to which both sides were supporting each other. While Beijing complains of its US assets being devalued by a falling dollar and Washington complains of an undervalued renminbi, there is an element in each side's accusations of the 'pot calling the kettle black'. The imbalances, of course, stem from the high savings in China in contrast to the high spending that (used to) take place in the US. These imbalances in turn stemmed from China – a country rich in *labour* resources and at a lower stage of development than the US – exporting *capital* to the US which enabled US consumers, via the housing bubble and equity withdrawal, to live beyond their means by buying, in many cases, goods made in China (in many cases manufactured by US subsidiaries). The dollar proceeds from these sales by China to the US then allowed China to invest/lend the money to the US, which allowed the US to buy from China, and so on. All it needed was for the housing bubble to burst, which it did, followed by the financial crisis to spread to the 'real economy', which it did, and the chain of interconnectedness would be broken, which it was; or at least up to a point. This 'tango' between China and the US did have supporting players or dancers but they were supporting and not leading.[30]

By June 2009 the Chinese government had amassed $2.13 trillion-worth of foreign exchange reserves. Initially the State Administration of Foreign Exchange (SAFE) had been established in 1978 to oversee foreign exchange market activities and directing and managing any foreign currency exchange reserves. In September 2007 the new sovereign wealth fund, China Investment Corporation (CIC), was established with assets of $200 billion; this had increased by about another $100 billion by the end of 2008. It is not known exactly how the reserves under the control of the two institutions have been directed (it is a state secret). The majority are located in US dollars, perhaps 60 to 70 per cent, followed by euros and other currencies, and while the lion's share has gone to the US and US Treasury bonds in particular, other assets have been acquired including shares in Royal Bank of Scotland, Tesco, the UK supermarket chain (0.5 per cent stake), Barclays, Diageo the drinks group (1.1 per cent stake) and British Petroleum.

Investments by both bodies have not been without controversy. CIC made large paper losses on investments in Blackstone and Morgan Stanley of roughly $4 billion and SAFE shifted about $270 billion into riskier stocks and shares in 2007, even as the subprime crisis was unfolding. Only with the near collapse and rescue of the US mortgage finance providers Freddie Mac and Fannie Mae in July 2008 did SAFE switch back to buying US government bonds. By that time stock markets internationally had suffered severe falls. Chinese losses are estimated to have been about $80 billion (*Financial Times*, 15 March 2009, 'China lost billions in diversification drive' by Jamil Anderlini).

We return to the possible future of the Chinese (and Russian) economies at the end of this chapter. However, many observers outside China – and increasingly within China – are agreed that there needs to be a reorientation by Chinese firms away from exports and towards the domestic Chinese market. That implies Chinese consumers raising consumption levels above where they currently stand. An appreciating yuan would help in that regard by making the real value of money held by Chinese consumers higher through cheaper imports.

In June 2010 the Central Bank of China did indeed announce that it would henceforth no longer be pegging the Chinese currency to the American dollar (conveniently just days before a G20 summit where the exchange rate issue would have been raised), although within days the bank was also at pains to announce that there would be no great one-off revaluation.

Most observers expect the speed of adjustment to resemble that which occurred in the three-year period after July 2005 when the real effective exchange rate appreciated by 20 per cent. Whether the size of the appreciation against the dollar will be near 20 per cent, however, is another matter. For one, if the Central Bank of China uses a basket of currencies to determine the exchange rate, the yuan, in theory, could actually depreciate against the dollar given that against the euro, for example, it appreciated in the first half of 2010 by approximately 18 per cent. Second, opposition to an appreciating Chinese currency remains strong in some quarters of the Chinese government: 'For the past few months the Ministry of Commerce has been conducting a battle to avoid any appreciation at all against the dollar' (*Financial* Times, 25 June 2010).

A complementary route to raising consumer purchasing power also started to unfold in China in May and June 2010. This alternative route started when workers in a host of factories started industrial action (i.e. strikes) with a view to obtaining higher wages. Reading the Western media reports at the time, one would come away with the impression that China was on the eve of some kind of full-blown General Strike, with revolution just around the corner, something which was far from the reality on the ground. That said, the strike activity was significant.

In many cases the strikes achieved media attention owing to the high-profile names of the companies involved, many of them Japanese or Taiwanese companies. In most cases the workers appeared to have been relatively successful in securing very large wage increases. Interestingly, while one does not know what went on behind the scenes, the Chinese Communist Party, far from rushing to crack down on any strike activity, appears to have allowed the action to take its course, mindful, perhaps, that labour's share of GDP in the form of wages dropped from 57 per cent in 1983 to 37 per cent in 2005. In general, wages for both urban and rural residents in China did rise in the first quarter of 2010 by 9.7 and 16.3 per cent respectively, but at the same time profits of industrial enterprises doubled in the same period, helping to push the Gini coefficient (a measure of inequality in society) up to 0.47 (*China Daily*, 13 May 2010).

Whether an appreciating currency, and a 'stand-offish' approach to workers pressing for increased wages constitutes part of the Chinese leadership's 'exit strategy' from the current export-led development model of the country is unclear. While the beginnings of a rudimentary welfare state have been and are being put in place, it is probably not sufficient as it stands to discourage, at this stage, excessive precautionary saving for old age among the Chinese people. Wages as a share of GDP will probably need to rise *consistently* before the Chinese consumer becomes the engine of Chinese economic growth. At the conclusion of this chapter we examine briefly the future prospects of the Chinese economy.

Box 9.4

Global imbalances: for every saver, the world economy needs a spender

In Figure 9.A we show the picture in the world economy prior to the financial and economic crisis of 2007 to 2009. The diagram – in a highly simplified way – conveys the interconnections between the US and China and, indeed, resource-rich countries including Russia. A continued large influx of foreign direct investment (FDI) into China combined with a high saving rate within China, allowed rapid and high investment in new capacity, much of it for export. The low export prices, in effect, exported low inflation to the rest of the world including the US. This allowed central banks internationally to keep interest rates low as low-cost labour in emerging markets helped

341

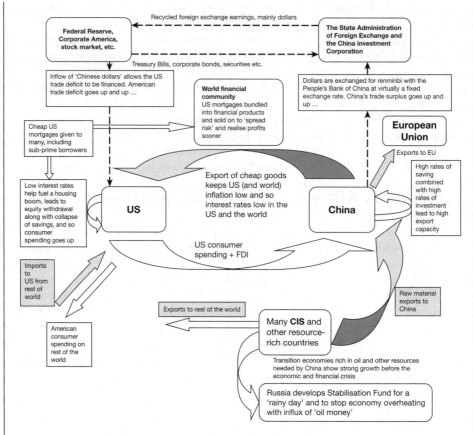

Figure 9.A Global imbalances before the 2007–2009 financial and economic crisis (or the 'US-China Tango' before the music stopped).

to moderate wage claims in developed market economies. Low or even falling prices of imported consumer goods also helped moderate wage claims. As such it can be argued that inflation was subdued for much of the period thanks to the entrance of emerging economies onto the world economic scene and not *primarily* through the independence of central bankers using inflation targeting.

Low interest rates, however, would help to fuel an asset bubble within the sphere of housing, not just in the US but in many other countries. As ever when bubbles start to expand, policy makers and those directly involved believe a new form of economic perpetual motion has been discovered with some thinking that 'boom and bust' has been consigned to the history books. Increasingly, financial institutions within the US started lending to people who really shouldn't have been lent money. These subprime mortgages would be the Achilles Heel of the perpetual motion cycle which would snap first.

However, the lenders in the US 'infected' the financial community internationally with the creation of CDOs – collaterised debt obligations. The purpose behind these extraordinarily complicated products was to bundle mortgages (and other financial assets) together and sell onwards. The buyers would receive an income stream of payments over many years until the mortgages (in this case) were paid off. Naturally, the original lenders of the mortgage money would not make as much money if they had 'waited' for the full redemption of mortgages but they (1) spread risk of default among many more financial institutions, and (2) receive money 'upfront' without the need to wait. As it turned out the assets bought by international financial institutions proved to be worthless in many cases (due to the mass default of subprime borrowers) which led to the fall and near collapse of many financial institutions internationally and within the US itself. This would necessitate government intervention on a massive scale which some in the US thought smacked of socialism but others saw simply as a life-saving exercise for financial capitalism.

As financial capitalism collapsed, the real economy became affected as (1) banks and other financial institutions stopped lending to each other and stopped lending to individuals and companies, and (2) individuals and companies lost confidence and cut back on spending either for direct consumption or for investment. With the downturn in economic activity internationally, governments of the world 'rediscovered' Keynes and began huge fiscal interventions, especially after interest rates had in many cases been driven to as low a point as possible, i.e. not far off zero.

Russia, which had initially thought that it would be immune from the financial crisis, soon discovered otherwise as demand for its oil and other resources fell precipitously. Not only was the volume demanded down from China and other oil-importing countries, but the price of oil dropped from about $150 per barrel to roughly $40 per barrel. The weakness of an economy biased heavily in favour of resource exports was laid bare. The impact of this was that the rouble should have slid in value, i.e. depreciated. Luckily or wisely for Putin, Russia had created a Stabilisation Fund in January 2004 whereby revenues from oil exports had been saved. (The Fund was split in two in early 2008 between a Reserve Fund which is used for investments in low-yielding, low-risk assets and a National Welfare Fund which invests in riskier assets.) The Stabilisation Fund was called upon to prop up the rouble which allowed the Russian Central Bank to *gradually* depreciate the rouble. Nevertheless, personal incomes of the Russian people fell by about 10 per cent in 2008 after several years of growth. In China growth fell, but by the standard definition of recession – two consecutive quarters of economic contraction – China did not enter into recession. Some took the slowdown in growth as evidence that China had not 'decoupled' from the West and the US in particular; others saw the glass as being half-full and viewed the non-recession in China as a partial decoupling and a growing internal economic vigour.

While the housing bubbles have popped, the dance between the US and China continues, if at a slower pace. China continues through its sovereign wealth fund to buy American assets (and indeed international assets) with dollars from its exports. This in turn allows the American people and government to live beyond their means. Meanwhile the US Federal Reserve has allowed 'benign neglect' of the dollar in the hope that a depreciation of the dollar will help American exporters and so the US economy as a whole. The Chinese complain of this since it means that the American assets they have purchased are no longer as valuable. Many believe China currently to be in a 'dollar trap'. By committing so much money to American assets, if China suddenly diversifies to other assets – gold, euros, etc. because of the sliding value of the dollar – it will precipitate an even bigger fall in the dollar making the American assets it has left even less valuable.

However, the Americans complain of Beijing's semi-fixed exchange rate policy between the yuan and dollar whereby the Chinese currency is pegged to the dollar, at what many consider an undervalued rate. This, it is claimed, allows Chinese exporters an unfair advantage in American markets. Beijing did allow a gradual appreciation of the yuan between June 2005 and July 2008 of 20 per cent (partly to help curb rising domestic inflation) before re-pegging to the dollar. As mentioned in the main text, the recent announcement at the time of writing of a relaxation of the peg to the dollar is unlikely to see dramatic improvements in the dollar–renminbi exchange rate.

A correct path for transition?
(Or, Умный человек в горы не пойдет, умный гору обойдет?)[31]

The object of this section is not to repeat what has been said elsewhere in other chapters. Rather it is to examine the transition process within Russia from the perspective of deciding whether anything that was done was 'sub-optimal' (we do the same for the Chinese transition path below); was there a better way of approaching the transition to a market economy? Much of what follows is therefore highly subjective: there are no right or wrong answers since ultimately the questions we are posing are counterfactual. That is, if we could turn back the clock of history and do this or that slightly, or even radically, differently, would the quality of the outcome be improved? This unfortunately simply passes the question one stage down the line, since what do we mean by 'improved'? Do we mean from a Pareto perspective? Could we have made all or some of the actors in our story better off without making any of them worse off since ultimately the whole point of moving from centrally planned to market-oriented economies *was* and *is* to improve human welfare? This is doubtful given the way in which wealth within Russia was and is skewed towards a minority (personified by the oligarchs): rerunning history would not result in a pure Pareto improvement since, by the strict definition of a Pareto improvement, such an improvement is only Pareto enhancing if at least one person/group within society is made better off, but no individual/group is made worse off. However, we leave a formal discussion of this until later and concentrate on events and developments over the first 20 years of transition.

Despite the fine intentions – for no one doubts that Gorbachev did want to tackle the problems of the system and not simply pay lip-service to them – the initial attempts at reform failed. Looking at Gorbachev's reforms and the process of trying to implement his reforms, one could come to the conclusion that, first, he missed an opportunity to tackle the main issues within Soviet society and the economy when such an attempt was still feasible, i.e. without the need for any kind of shock therapy. Second, the expression 'wanting your cake and eating it' springs to mind: Gorbachev wanted to rid the system of its problems but the ultimate solution – to replace the system – was one step he was not prepared to take.

The reader may be disappointed that we do not give a strict definition as to what would count as a 'better road' to transition. Most observers, for example, would agree on the *desirability* of the following for the FSU and countries of CEE: a smaller drop in output during the transitional recession; or the avoidance, if at all possible, of a transitional recession; less unemployment, less poverty; and a functioning market economy with functioning institutions working within the framework of agreed laws, rules, customs and procedures which enhance market participation and wealth creation. Ultimately, the only question worth posing is whether there was the *realistic* possibility of an alternative.

In the case of China the questions we are posing are slightly different, since there has been – up until now – no transitional recession; poverty *has* been reduced; a functioning market economy (with unfinished work) has been created; and unemployment, as a consequence, has been muted. Consequently, it would be hard to think of a set of policies which could have generated sustained economic growth *greater* than what has been observed up until now. Indeed, with the move to the HRS mentioned above, this was one of the few transition policies which could probably claim to be a Pareto improvement. Naughton (2008a) has described the first period of Chinese reform up until 1993 as a period of reform without losers.

The questions for the PRC are slightly different, but do tie in with the question we pose for the FSU and countries of CEE: Was and is the transition path followed by China a working model that could have been adopted in the other transition economies? Other questions arise in relation to the PRC such as the issue of democracy: to what extent, if at all, are Western-style democratic institutions necessary for the transition to a market-style economy *and* for continued economic development? Even if the answer to the previous question is No – Western-style democracy is not needed for transition and growth – individuals within China may still believe it is desirable to live in a Western-style democracy, but that is a separate issue which we do not pursue at this stage, although we do touch on the issue of democracy below.

Be that as it may, the 'debate' as to the rights and wrongs of the transition process has generated strong, even heated points of view. One particularly heated debate revolves around the costs of transition. Box 9.5, *The costs of transition – small or great?*, takes up this issue where we review an article that appeared in the *Lancet* medical journal and the reply it provoked from the *Economist* magazine. From the economics profession itself the opinions have not been slow in coming and punches have not been pulled. Below, for example, we present a view from John Kenneth Galbraith (1994):

> The history of the second great Russian revolution is not complete as this is written. Nor is that of the other countries that once composed the Soviet Union. It will not, one can already say, be celebrated as a compelling exercise in human intelligence. This was a transition that demanded restraint, careful analysis and, above all, thought. In place of these, there was action according to metaphor and doctrine.
>
> The hope was that a sudden dramatic change – shock therapy – would bring the magic transformation to capitalism. A brief period of pain, and the new system would be successfully in place. Many, including a sizable number of western advisers, believed that this should not be the mixed economy of Western Europe, the United States and elsewhere in the developed world but rather the idealised capitalism of free enterprise, of Friedrich von Hayek, Ludwig von Mises and Milton Friedman. Ideologically motivated scholars from the West found allies in enthusiastic new converts in the East.

In the opposite corner we have Jeffrey Sachs who, in reviewing a book on the Russian reform process by one of the Russian architects of that very reform process, Yegor Gaidar, takes issue with a number of economists and with the US itself: [32]

> Gaidar's re-telling reminds us of his lucidity, boldness, and persistence. We are also reminded of the shameless naivete or cynicism of many of Gaidar's critics, both in

Russia and the United States, who argue to this day that Russia's tumultuous decade was the result of misjudged economic reform ideas championed by Gaidar (and outside economists such as myself). Finally, we are reminded, implicitly, if we care to reflect on it, how much the United States lost by hardly lifting a finger to help Gaidar and his reform compatriots during the harrowing first years of their struggle.

This book is an instant antidote to those such as outgoing World Bank Chief Economist Joseph Stiglitz who somehow confuse Russia's revolution with an academic seminar. Stiglitz leads a group of American academics who think that Russia's reforms suffered mainly because Gaidar and other advocates of 'shock therapy' somehow forgot that market economies are based on institutions and laws, and not just on textbook pictures of supply and demand. Duh! Readers of Gaidar's memoirs will quickly learn that Russia's reform struggle was not mainly about the niceties of sequencing market reforms. The real issues were elemental and urgent. Would there be bread in Moscow in the winter of 1991–92? Would private property be legal? Would Russia lurch towards a violent, revanchist politics? Would Russia have a national currency and when? Would there be civil war in Moscow in 1993? In each case, Gaidar's cool pragmatism and power of analysis helped to find a way out of a near catastrophe.

(*Washington monthly*, online, March 2000)

Box 9.5

The costs of transition – small or great?

Commentators have often remarked about the remarkably peaceful nature of the transition from communism to capitalism within the former Soviet Union and the satellite countries of the former Soviet bloc. In the sense of open civil war or the direct military intervention of neighbouring countries to either support or prevent market transformation of a country's economy, they no doubt have a point. Indeed, Kornai (2006a) when referring explicitly to the countries of CEE makes this very point as regards the peaceful nature of the transition.[33]

However, what makes the area controversial is the *implication* that the policy recommendations of those Western economic advisers of the early 1990s to various transition economies led directly or indirectly to the deaths of hundreds of thousands if not millions of people. The controversy was sparked again in 2009 when the *Lancet*, a British medical journal, published an article by Stuckler *et al.* (2009) which claimed to demonstrate a link between rapid, mass privatisation of state enterprises (one part of the shock therapy advocated by many economists) and the increased mortality rates in Russia and other transition economies.

Examining the situation for *male* mortality rates they find that for all countries in their study adult male mortality increased by a mean of 12.8 per cent for 25 countries that introduced mass privatisation programmes compared to those which did not over the period 1989 to 2002.

The authors use two measures of privatisation: first, a so-called dummy variable which takes the value of one if the state had privatised at least 25 per cent of large state-owned enterprises into the private sector through vouchers and giveaways to firm insiders over a two-year period; and second, privatisation indices developed by the European Bank for Reconstruction and Development (EBRD) which ranged from 1 (little private ownership) to 4.3 (standards and performance typical of advanced industrial economies: more than 75 per cent of an enterprise's assets in private ownership with effective corporate governance).

Their complete model took the following form:

$$AMR_{it} = \alpha + \beta_1 PRIV_{it} + \beta_2 GDP_{it} + \beta_3 LIB_{it} + \beta_4 TRADE_{it} + \beta_5 DEM_{it} + \beta_6 WAR_{it} + \beta_7 DEP_{it} + \beta_8 URBAN_{it} + \beta_9 EDUC_{it} + \mu_i + \varepsilon_{it}$$

where i represents the individual country and t is the year. A description of the other variables is given in Table 9.D.

In reaching the conclusion that mass privatisation is associated with such an increase in male mortality rates the authors write, 'Although mass privatisation might be justified by enhanced economic growth, and thus subsequent mortality reductions, even a doubling of GDP per head would not be enough to offset the increase in mortality rates resulting from mass privatisation' (Stuckler *et al.* 2009).

While the article published in the *Lancet* went through the usual rigorous checks of anonymous reviewers, the *Economist* (22 January 2009) objected to the *Lancet* article and the conclusion it reached. Describing Stuckler *et al.*'s (2009) article as a 'statistical analysis', it goes on to claim that the article in the *Lancet* comes to the

Table 9.D The model of Stuckler, King and McKee (2009) in determining the effect of mass privatisation on adult male mortality rates in post-communist societies

	Description		*Description*
AMR	The natural logarithm of adult male standardised mortality rates (working ages of 15 to 59 years)	*PRIV*	One of two privatisation measures
GDP	The natural logarithm of the gross domestic product per head of population in current US$	*LIB*	The degree to which prices had been liberalised as measured by the EBRD
TRADE	The degree of foreign exchange and trade liberalisation as measured by the EBRD	*DEM*	A measure of the degree of democratisation within the country as measured by Freedom House*
WAR	A dummy variable as to whether military conflict existed in the country	*DEP*	The population dependency ratio which measures the ratio of total working-age adults to elderly people and children
URBAN	The percentage of the population living in urban settings	*EDUC*	The percentage of the population with a tertiary education
μ	Variables (dummies) which represent the individual countries and so model issues specific to an individual country not captured in the authors' model	(i) α, (ii) ε	(i) the constant or intercept term, (ii) the error term which captures random influences not detailed in the model

Source: Stuckler, King and Mckee (2009).

Note
* 'A non-profit organisation that advocates for democracy and publishes surveys of civil liberties, political rights, and measures of economic freedom' (Stuckler *et al.* 2009).

conclusion that 'in effect, mass privatisation was mass murder. Had Russia adopted more gradual reforms, those lives would have been saved'. It should be pointed out that at no place in Stuckler *et al.*'s (2009) article do the authors accuse anyone of mass murder and indeed, when Stuckler *et al.* (2009) pose the question, 'But were these excess deaths inevitable?' they answer, 'Probably not' in contrast to the more strident tone of the *Economist*.

In taking issue with the *Lancet* article the *Economist* makes two rather more substantial points which are worthy of attention. First, the blame for any rise in mortality rates lies with the decrepit state of the planned economy under communism; tracing, as they do, the blame for such planned economies not working all the way back to Stalin and Lenin (although as shown in Chapter 1, given Lenin's opposition to a *detailed* economic plan before his death, perhaps working all the way back to Stalin and Trotsky would have been more appropriate). The implication is clear from this and the accompanying graph shown as Figure 9.B: mortality rates were rising well before the advent of shock therapy. The only temporary blip in the slide in life expectancy was when General Secretary Gorbachev severely restricted alcohol sales for a three-year period between 1985 and 1987. (See body of text for a fuller description.) Much more blame for a rise in Russian mortality rates should be linked, according to the *Economist*, to alcohol: 'After 1992 the state monopoly on alcohol (and health checks on its quality) collapsed. As anybody who lived in Russia at the time will recall, the effect was spectacular – and catastrophic. Death rates returned to their long-term trend.'

And indeed the graph from the *Economist* magazine (online edition) clearly shows that in 1992 life expectancy for both males *and* females in Russia was lower than at any time since the graph starts measuring life expectancy in 1962. No mention is made in the *Economist* article that the study they criticise looked *only* at male mortality rates or that the country dummy variables (the μs in Table 9.D) would partially take into account country-specific issues.

Interestingly, when we come to look at the graph from the United States government's Department for Health and Human Services (Figure 9.C) it appears to

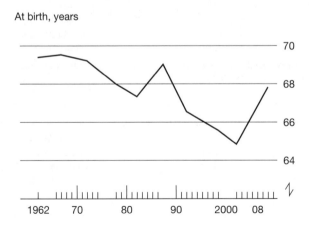

Figure 9.B Russia life expectancy, 1962–2008.

Source: *The Economist*.

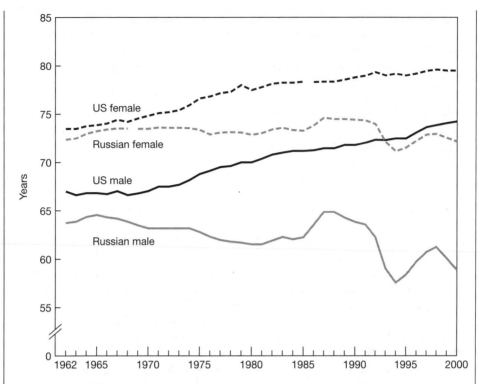

Figure 9.C Russia and United States life expectancy, 1962–2000.
Source: US Department of Health and Human Services.

be the case that in 1992 life expectancy for Russian *males* was at a comparable level to 1974. Indeed, although there is a gradual decline in life expectancy for males from 1962 it is far more gentle a decline than the *Economist* graph which is entirely plausible, given that we are measuring two different series. Indeed, a visual examination of Figure 9.C would seem to indicate that for male life expectancy in Russia, it stabilised in the late 1970s to the mid-1980s. Once transition gets under way there begins a precipitous drop in male life expectancy and a drop, if less precipitous, for Russian females.

Do the U.S. Department of Health and Human Services put the rise in mortality rates among Russian males *only* down to excessive alcohol consumption? They comment in their article:

> Economic conditions can affect health status in a variety of ways, creating a cascade of events that can lead to improvement or deterioration in health. Hyperinflation, wage reductions, and unemployment pushed many middle-class Russians below the poverty level during the 1990s. Declines in living standards were especially dramatic for retirees, whose pensions failed to keep pace with rapid price increases. The economic turmoil and rise in poverty that characterized, in particular, the first half of the decade and the end of the decade led to a profound deterioration of the health care system, an inability to obtain necessary medication, increasing nutritional deficiencies, and a sharp rise in stress and depression. The accompanying decline in governmental and

social controls may have played a key role in the rise of homicides and suicides in Russia, along with the sharp increase in per capita alcohol consumption. The economy clearly is not the only factor accounting for these problems, but it is an important part of the story. In addition, many of these problems tend to reinforce each other through a negative feedback loop.

The article then goes on to discuss the other relevant causes of falling life expectancy such as tobacco, alcohol, the collapsing health care system, nutrition, and stress and depression which act through the 'negative feedback loop'.

The *Economist* also states,

> Furthermore, countries that successfully applied shock therapy, such as Poland, saw improved life expectancy. So did the then Czechoslovakia, which plumped for mass privatisation, albeit not very successfully. Mistakes were made, but Russia's tragedy was that reform came too slowly, not too fast.

It may well be that Poland applied shock therapy successfully (although see this note[34]). However, Stuckler *et al.* (2009) defined a country as a mass privatiser if at least 25 per cent of state-owned assets were privatised *in a two-year period*. The authors write (pp. 4–5), 'Outside the former Soviet Union, only one of nine countries – the Czech Republic – had implemented a mass privatisation programme by 1994; overall, the privatisation process was more gradual than in the former Soviet Union, and handled on a firm-by-firm basis.' Indeed when they turned their sample of 25 countries into two samples – one made up of countries of the former Soviet Union and the other of non-former Soviet Union countries – they found that greater progress in privatisation is associated with either a neutral or *positive* influence on mortality rates.

Stuckler *et al.* (2009) attempt to explain this through the incidence of 'social capital' that existed or did not exist in a country. By social capital is meant the percentage of a country's population who are members of at least one social organisation such as a trade union, church, sports club, or a political organisation. The authors find that, 'In countries in which more than 45% of the population was a member of a social organisation, mass privatisation had no adverse association with mortality rates.'

The intuition here is that individuals who have 'somewhere to turn' when things get tough for them – as it certainly did in the period of transition – are more able to survive; people helping people when they are down on their luck keeps them alive.

They conclude,

> This finding might help to explain why, in addition to its effect on unemployment, mass privatisation programmes in the Czech Republic, which had the second highest social membership (48 per cent, which is equal to western Europe's average level) of all the former communist countries, had no significant negative association with mortality, but in the former Soviet countries, where social membership was much lower (about 10 per cent), rapid privatisation had very adverse results.
>
> (Stuckler *et al.* 2009)

Stuckler *et al.*'s (2009) paper was to produce other papers at a higher level of sophistication than the *Economist* article which took issue with the findings of their paper. In keeping with this area of controversy the debate generated was at times heated. See later issues of the *Lancet* (e.g. Vol. 372, 11 April 2009; and Vol. 375, 30 January 2010) for a debate, through correspondence, between John S. Earle, Scott Gehlbach and Stuckler *et al.* The reader is warned that the debate here becomes technical, and a reasonably good understanding of statistics and econometrics is probably needed to come to any firm opinion one way or another. In short, neither side would appear to give ground to the other and the verdict remains 'not proven'.

Five to six years into the transition process (the mid-1990s), in CEE and the FSU, comparisons were inevitably made between the Chinese approach to transition and the process that had emerged within CEE and the FSU. As Jeffrey Sachs and Wing Thye Woo (1996) commented,

> The most remarkable difference between reforms in China and in countries of Central and Eastern Europe and the former Soviet Union (CEE and FSU) is that China succeeded in producing more than a decade of phenomenal growth, while countries of CEE and FSU, no matter which reform strategy has been tried, have seen a sharp initial downturn in production, usually with a significant rise in unemployment.[35]

Sachs and Woo were and are far from those group of economists who would have urged the CEE and FSU transition countries to travel down a Chinese path. In their World Bank note they usefully categorise their position on the impossibility of the FSU and other CEE countries of adopting the Chinese path. For them there is no doubt that initial conditions combined with fundamentally different historical and cultural backgrounds of both sets of countries would have made any attempt by CEE and FSU countries to follow the Chinese path futile. As they put it, 'Supporters of introducing Chinese gradualism in Russia might as well advise Russia to solve its agricultural problems by shifting from wheat to rice.'

Sachs and Woo (1996) make several points regarding initial conditions (and reforms) which helped to shape the very different paths of CEE and FSU as opposed to China.

1   First, the composition of the labour force was very different in the two camps. At the start of reform in China in 1978 the urbanised, subsidised, industrial state sector made up about 18 per cent of the workforce compared to the non-subsidised agricultural sector's 71 per cent. Due to the welfare and social benefits which were attached to the state sector, workers were reluctant to give up this security which came with state sector jobs and jump into the fast-flowing river of new enterprise employment. Agricultural peasants-cum-land workers, on the other hand, did not have much to lose and much to gain by moving out of low-income-generating agricultural work into expanding, higher income, non-state jobs exemplified by the TVEs (see above). 'Thus the nonstate sector grew despite the preservation of the state sector.'

This contrasted with the countries of CEE and the FSU that had already completed the transition from largely rural to urban societies – the majority of these societies had no mass rural hinterland to draw on to develop a non-state sector as the state sector declined in size and importance. Russia itself, the authors point out, had 90 per cent of its population employed in state-owned enterprises, the vast majority of whom relied on the welfare and social benefits which came with such attachments. Like their Chinese proletarian cousins they were not about to voluntarily transfer over to the nascent private sector with the lower income, benefits and security that this entailed. The Russian workers on state farms and state collective farms, moreover, unlike their Chinese cousins in the rural communes, were receiving, claim the authors, income and benefits similar to urban workers in SOEs. The incentive to move out of agriculture and into the *de novo* private sector was just not there.

2   Sachs and Woo's second point centres on the maturity versus immaturity of the planned economies of the FSU and China. The planned economy within China basically did not have the same time as the old Soviet Union to mature and consequently – it is inferred – to develop the diseases of old age that come with mature planned economies: complexity leading to an overload of processible information; leading to economic bottlenecks, negative value-added; and ultimately to stagnation and falling living standards. As they note, the Soviet central plan controlled 25 million commodities whereas the Chinese central plan controlled only 1,200 commodities.

With respect to industry and output, Sachs and Woo (1996) write:

> Market reforms in the CEE (and) FSU countries *necessarily* involved an initial decline in industrial production . . . The experience of China and the CEEFSU countries suggests that the marketization of a planned economy *inevitably* shifts resources toward the service sector: from the agricultural sector in China, and from industry in the countries of the CEEFSU. Seen this way, much or all of the initial drop in industrial production in the CEEFSU countries after the start of reforms was a *natural* part of the needed reallocation of employment and resources. [emphases added]

3   While the above points relate to conditions pre-transition, Sachs and Woo (1996) develop other points as regards the transition reforms carried out at the macro level. Following on from the composition of the respective economies, the relatively small size of the state industrial sector within China meant that when, during the reform period, tax revenues declined, its impact on the general government budgetary position was minimal. Expansion in other sectors within China (i.e. the private sector) also assisted in minimising underreporting of profits from state sector Chinese enterprises. CEE and FSU countries, especially Bulgaria, Poland and the former Soviet Union, had 'deeper structural problems' and suffered from 'gross macroeconomic mismanagement' during both the communist reform period, for example, under Gorbachev, and well into the post-communist reform period in much of the FSU.

4   Social spending – be it on pensions, unemployment benefits, disability payments and so forth – is a key expenditure of governments. However, that 'burden' did not fall upon successive Chinese governments to the same extent as it did on countries within CEE and FSU. In China only about 20 per cent of the workforce was covered by such expenditures, whereas within CEE and FSU countries almost the entire population was covered. Combined with the fact that China's reforms did not start at a time of macroeconomic crisis or of severe external debt meant that an austerity programme was not required in the same way as it was for many CEE countries and for countries of the FSU thus helping to avoid, it is implied, a transformational recession within China.

5   With the Chinese saving rate being high both by Western levels and by East Asian levels this helped to stabilise the Chinese economy. Chinese governments could finance budget spending and, indeed, subsidies to the relatively small sector of SOEs as savings rose) from 3.4 per cent of GDP in 1980 to 11.7 per cent in 1991; savings which were, in the main, channelled through the state financial system. This predilection on the part of the Chinese citizen to save rather than spend helped to keep inflationary pressures down; unlike CEE and FSU where the reluctance of households to hold cash contributed to inflationary pressures and macro instability.[36]

6   The Great Leap Forward when Mao attempted a crass industrialisation programme (which contributed greatly to millions starving to death) and the Cultural Revolution, undermined belief in socialist planning as a superior way in which to organise the economy. Deng Xiaoping was able as a result to transfer a significant amount of formal and informal economic policy-making power and resources to the provinces when he returned to power in 1978. While sections of what could be called the Stalinist bureaucracy within Beijing looked to re-impose central planning after the Tiananmen events, Deng prevented such a move partly because this section of the Chinese leadership was discredited by the events of the Great Leap Forward and the Cultural Revolution, and partly through the support that Deng had built up in the provinces.

7   The one 'benefit' of the Cultural Revolution had been the breakdown of the national distribution system during the decade over which the Cultural Revolution ran. This forced local authorities to promote small and medium-size industrial enterprises in order to meet local demand.

8   As mentioned above in the main text, the luck of having a pool of talented entrepreneurs 'sitting next door' in Hong Kong (and, indeed, in South Korea) meant that when the policy of SEZs was announced, there was a ready supply of businesspeople ready to exploit it. These individuals could speak and write the local language; had in many cases family connections in the neighbouring Chinese provinces to Hong Kong; could quickly garner inside information on local legislation and to what extent limits of the legislation could be pushed; and, of course, they had knowledge of overseas markets and the right connections to shift products made in the SEZs. In many cases managers/owners could commute between their homes and factories. There was no sizeable diaspora of ethnic Russians with entrepreneurial skills waiting on the fall of the Iron Curtain to nip back into Mother Russia to reinvigorate the economy.[37]

For others the situation is the complete opposite. For these economists it may well be the case that initial conditions played a role, but to categorise the last 30 years of continuous high economic growth in China as being merely down to initial conditions or special Chinese circumstances beggars belief. A good example is Kotz (2000) who argues that the main problem lies, in effect, with many mainstream economists' fixation with the official 'ideology' of economics which has been and currently still is taught in Western universities. Kotz terms this ideology, as it relates to the transition of planned to market economies, the neo-liberal transition strategy (NLTS). As Kotz comments,

This strategy, designed by Western neoclassical economists, calls for limited government involvement in the transition process, relying primarily on individual self-interested initiatives to transform the economy. The other countries that emerged from the former Soviet Union, and the former Soviet Bloc countries in Central and Eastern Europe, have also been following the NLTS.

In contrast to the NLTS, Kotz categorises the situation in China as a state-directed transition strategy (SDTS) where, as the name suggests, the Chinese state has taken a very active role in the transition process.

Kotz (2000) outlines a litany of poor – even shocking – statistics for the Russian transition process. For example, according to Kotz, the human cost of this economic decline has been enormous. Russia's death rate rose from 11.4 per thousand population in 1991 to 15.5 in 1994, before falling to 14.3 in 1996. The increased death rate between 1992 and 1996 produced an estimated 2.1 million premature deaths in Russia during that period. The SDTS, however, was more than simply a matter of speed (with the NLTS arguing for rapid privatisation and the SDTS adopting the more gradualist approach). 'Rather than seeking to directly convert the state-owned, planned economy into a private, market-based one, China sought to use its state-owned planned economy as a base for launching a new non-state, market-based sector.'

We do not repeat the long list of statistics that Kotz marshals to argue his case. Of more interest is his view as to why the majority of the mainstream economics profession fell behind the NLTS and continue to do so even after it is 'apparent' that the shock therapy strategy in the FSU and (less so in) the CEE states was a 'failure' in comparison to the success of the Chinese path followed. According to Kotz (2000), most of the critics of the NLTS have been drawn from the margins of mainstream economics, particularly those who specialised in the Soviet economy, institutional economics and historical problems of economic development. The defining reason, for Kotz, is the almost naive belief in the textbook model of static market equilibrium produced by the competitive model of the economy. For the non-economist reader, recall the appendix to Chapter 1 where, using the example of the market for oil and motor vehicles, it was explained how the market has a *self-correcting mechanism* induced through the information contained within market prices of the goods on sale. Roughly speaking, it is this model which Kotz takes issue with. (The reader will also note that in Appendix 1 we are also very careful to mention the importance of institutional factors in this self-correcting mechanism, a feature that is not at all emphasised in introductory textbooks on economics.)

For Kotz, the idea that one can simply free prices from state control, privatise industry and then let the market 'get on with it' is ultimately a set of ideas which are as much rooted in an ideology as in the science of economics. More specifically, Kotz (2000) lists five points of criticism of the NLTS, especially as applied to Russia:

1   Building a market system takes many decades and requires an active state role in the process.
2   Dismantling the old centralised system of economic coordination before an effective market system can be built leads to economic chaos.
3   Sudden liberalisation in a formerly tightly controlled economy sets off inflation that is very difficult to contain.
4   Tight fiscal and monetary policies ensure a long depression and also prevent the restructuring and modernisation of industry, which requires substantial state spending and adequate credit.
5   A free trade policy in a transition economy exposes domestic producers to superior foreign competition before they are ready to compete.

It is worth pointing out that the above five points are themselves as much assertions as they are facts. Kotz (2000), while listing an apparently impressive list of statistics at the start of his article for both Russia and China, does not link in these statistical facts to his five asserted points. The reader is left to make the jump between cause and effect.

It would be tempting to simply say that the above two positions, those of Sachs and Woo (1996) contrasted with that of Kotz (2000), are extremes of the two limiting positions, and so the truth lies somewhere in between. In reality the situation may be more complex. Take, for example, Sachs and Woo's claim that people within the transition countries of the FSU were not willing to save to the same extent that citizens in China did, thus contributing to the inflationary pressures. Yet at the same time, the claim is also made by Sachs and Woo that part of the problem within the FSU lay in the fact that there was gross macro mismanagement of the economy towards the end of the communist period of power and 'well into the transition period' within Russia. In our opinion, the former situation – the unwillingness of households to hold increased money balances – is a result of the latter, the gross economic mismanagement and lack of policy credibility.[38]

To continue with the theme of economic mismanagement and in particular the rouble overhang that we touched on earlier, Hedlund (1999) makes a good case for the view that effectively politics trumped economics. In a situation where prices were immediately liberalised, policies could and should have been put in place whereby the impact of such a 'cold turkey' approach would be supplemented by policies such as a currency reform, an incomes policy and reform of the tax system. To prolong the cold turkey analogy, this would be the economic equivalent of giving the heroin addict methadone to wean him off the harder drug.

An example of what might have been done by an early transitional government in Russia is shown by what happened in Estonia over a three-day period from 20 to 22 June 1992. Determined to introduce an overtly Estonian currency, the Estonian government of the day allowed holders of roubles within Estonia to change up to 1,500 roubles at a rate of 1 new Estonian kroon per 10 roubles. Between 26 June and 30 June larger amounts could be converted at the rate of 50 roubles to 1 kroon. With the banking system on guard to prevent transfers of roubles from abroad into Estonia to take advantage of this currency reform, all went smoothly.

However, Anders Åslund, who was a prominent Western adviser to the Russian government in the first few years of the transition process before resigning, and like Stefan Hedlund also a fellow Swede, argues that the result of not going for a currency reform must be laid at the door of the IMF, not the reformers – whether Russian or Western.

Indeed, Åslund argues that 'the preservation of the ruble zone was the *worst* single mistake in the post-communist transition in terms of its costs' (Åslund 2002b, emphasis added). Given this statement, the reader will forgive us if we spend a little more time recounting this episode (briefly mentioned in Chapter 7) and what, according to Åslund, went wrong. First, the problem of the common rouble zone was one which led, in Åslund's view, to hyperinflation in 10 of the 15 successor states to the Soviet Union. Indeed, hyperinflation was so serious an issue that it

> can be blamed for the initial failure of the market economic reform in the twelve members of the CIS (Commonwealth of Independent States). It bred extreme rent seeking with a few gaining greatly, while most suffered, leading to great inequality. Bad payments practices were permeated the economy (*sic*), and disorder and corruption were aggravated.
>
> (Åslund 2002b)

Most economists would probably have no difficulty with the description of the consequences of hyperinflation recounted by Åslund as it impacted upon the then independent
countries of the FSU. Given his belief that the maintenance of the rouble zone was the
single biggest mistake of the transition process in the FSU, more controversially he asks:
'and the question is what role the IMF played in this mistake'. Åslund takes issue with a paper
by John Odling-Smee and Gonzalo Paster – 'The IMF and the Ruble Area, 1991–93' –
published in 2002. The reader will be relieved that we do not give a full account of Åslund's
views as regards this paper although it does from a historical distance make interesting
reading.

However, and in brief, there would have appeared to be three theoretical possibilities open
as regards the rouble currency: (1) a cooperative rouble zone in which all participating central
banks (of the now independent states of the FSU) would take part, (2) national currencies,
and (3) a Russian-dominated rouble area in which the Central Bank of Russia would alone
be responsible for monetary and exchange rate policies. Åslund appears to agree with Odling-
Smee and Pastor that option (3) was politically impossible. Åslund takes issue over what he
sees as the IMF's decision – through Odling-Smee – to back option (1), that is, the idea of a
cooperative rouble zone.[39]

For Åslund, given that each (new) central bank, including the Central Bank of Russia, was
able to issue its own credits (i.e. effectively money in the form of roubles), a 'Prisoner's
Dilemma' would be created – it would be in all central banks' interests to refrain from issuing
too much money as the result of not refraining would be inflationary. If all central banks could
have agreed to do this, *and* found a mechanism to enforce it, all would have benefited from
a stable currency combined with reduced economic transaction costs among member states
of the common currency zone. However, there would always be a temptation to cheat – to
issue more money than had been collectively agreed – and by so doing to effectively obtain
a larger share of total GDP. Since all central banks (and their respective governments behind
them) knew this, every bank would cheat. Knowing that other central banks would be
cheating, the logic would be to out-cheat everyone else! Hyperinflation would be the result:
'This prediction was made by Jeffrey Sachs and shared by most market reformers, tacitly
even by the research department of the IMF. However, the IMF also argued that the
cooperative solution was conceivable' (Åslund 2002b).

The issue came to a head at a meeting in Tashkent on 21–22 May 1992, where, according
to Åslund, 'the IMF had drafted a cooperative ruble arrangement for which it pushed actively
in Tashkent. It did so with the support of ignorant or inert heads of central banks against the
Russian reformers, well represented by Ignatiev.' Sergei Ignatiev was Deputy Chairman
of the Central Bank of Russia, and 'the Gaidar man at the CBR' who, according to Åslund,
saw the Tashkent meeting as an attempted 'coup'.

The IMF was, however, to change its position on the rouble zone in 1993 only
after inflation had taken off in many of the countries of the FSU. As Åslund (2002b)
concludes,

> The broader point is that the IMF did little to establish conditions that would
> impede hyperinflation in the former Soviet Union, although hyperinflation was
> widely expected from the end of 1990, and it mostly erupted in 1993 rather than
> 1992. Ample time was at hand to finish the ruble zone earlier. The IMF played an
> active role in possibly the biggest mistake of post-communist economic
> transformation.

So there we have it: the IMF should take primary responsibility for why the transition process in the FSU went awry, at least for far longer than expected. Is this fair comment? Probably not. The notion of a dominating IMF, able to stage or attempt 'coups', at least in post-Soviet Russia, implies an IMF that was able to dictate the course of events. And yet returning to Hedlund and reading through his account of events (and those of others, for example, the articles in Klein and Pomer (2001)), one is left with the impression of an IMF incapable of or unwilling to get a grip on the situation, at least until the mid-1990s onwards. The criticism from Hedlund, if anything, is of an IMF being 'sucked into' the politics of the region as much as the transition process proper such that the policies of the IMF adapted to the political desire to keep the West's man – Yeltsin – in power, and the communists out of power.

In the above sense, the so-called attempted coup in Tashkent fits more into a picture of a desire on the part of the IMF to bolster the person of Yeltsin, who, caring little for the minutia of economic policy, would certainly have cared a great deal about the power-politic implications of allowing the rouble zone to disintegrate.

The West also had an interest in maintaining a rouble zone if at all practical, even if there was only a small chance of doing so. The member countries of the CIS were in many cases rich in resources. The more this diffuse collection of countries could be influenced by a central authority like Russia, the easier the West could influence the influencer through their support for Yeltsin. And the more the West bet on Yeltsin (having switched from Gorbachev when his personal position was lost), the more they threw good money after bad. By the time the IMF did put their collective feet down and did expect certain conditions to really be met in the mid-1990s as conditions for its loans, one wonders whether in the first half of the 1990s it was the West who used Yeltsin, or whether it was Yeltsin (and his coterie) who used the West.

The role of institutions

A more complex account as to why the whole process went 'pear-shaped' in Russia (at least until the prolonged period of growth post-1998) revolves around the issue of institution building or lack thereof within the new Russia given the collapse and then annihilation of the remnants of the previous Soviet ones. Here we return to the ideas tentatively raised in the section 'Institutions' in Chapter 2 (p. 129) and elsewhere, where we touched on the concept of organisations and institutions. The general idea of institutional economics is that every society has two sets of rules by which all individuals participate: there are formal rules laid down, for example, by law, a government, a sovereign, a parliament or a president, and informal rules or more accurately informal norms. While the formal rules of a society are often backed up by 'armed bodies of men' (i.e. state power), non-coercive but nevertheless powerful informal norms can also exist and co-exist with the formal rules of society. Within any existing social order – feudalism, capitalism, communism. etc. – formal rules and informal norms usually end up in some sort of equilibrium with one another. The two sets of rules – one formal and one informal – result in 'mental modes' whereby the individual, through the medium of the rules/norms, comprehends society at large. Often there is some degree of conflict between the informal norms and the formal rules governing society. It should be emphasised that these rules/norms exist not just within the realm of the economy but more broadly touching on all aspects of society. In Box 9.6, *Anecdotes of Russia*, some personal reminiscences of Russia from the 1990s are recounted which hopefully help to shed some light on these norms and mental modes of thought as they pertain to Russia in the 1990s and perhaps even today.

Box 9.6

Anecdotes of Russia

In the context of Russia, how do the ideas of institutions and norms fit in? We freely admit the following is not scientific evidence as to the processes that were at work but it may help illustrate the issues; it is at best anecdotal but worthy of comment. Three personal incidents are recalled: first, when in conversation with a Russian friend the issue of bribe taking within Russian society in the late 1990s was discussed. The response was, '*It always surprises me what foreigners find strange about Russia.*' For my friend, if individuals within Russia wanted to take bribes then this was seen as perfectly normal; why the big fuss? In this, the mental mode of the individual had been 'conditioned' into thinking that it was a normal and socially acceptable activity; yes, it was known that bribe taking was against the law, but the fact that 'everybody did it' gave the individual 'comfort in numbers'. The formal rules of Russia at that time, and one suspects even now, are still weakly observed, with informal norms predominant.

The second occasion revolves around an international project operating within Russia in the early 2000s, whereby a relatively junior member of the project office was instructed to seek quotations for the purchase of computer equipment from the relevant suppliers in town. It then came to light that visits to each potential supplier had taken place and '*otkat*' (pronounced at-cat) had been asked for. The procedure worked as follows: You are the agent of the firm requesting quotations for the supply of this or that, in this case computers and ancillary equipment. You, as the agent, say to the potential supplier: '*If I get my firm to accept your quotation, what percentage of the order will you give me?*' Of course the agent of the firm is in a win-win position as he or she says this to every potential supplier; when the firm he or she works for then accepts the lowest bid, he or she will still receive a percentage. While the suppliers know this, they are nevertheless drawn in just in case the agent has some influence on the tendering process.

The third occasion concerns another acquaintance who when quizzed by one of the authors of this book, again in the mid- to late 1990s, as to why he did not pay tax on his work income – 'Think of the teachers with unpaid salaries', I ventured to him – replied in justification: 'Рыба гниёт с головы' (*The fish rots from the head*). By this he meant that if it was good enough for the top echelons to thieve from society then what he was doing was merely following in the example set by the leadership of the country.[40] The point being that while everyone has free will (in a non-religious sense of the term) to select the course of conduct that he or she desires, then, employing the language of game theory from economics, if everyone is 'at it', it becomes a dominant strategy to participate in the socially acceptable norm of thieving. Given the 'game' is a repeated one – be that of business affairs, paying or not paying taxes, paying or not paying wages, asking for bribes or not asking, etc. – and if the participant sees that not only others who participate in the game but (s)he can also 'get away with it', the players naturally become emboldened, and what might have been an occasional foray into a one-off bribe taking through a chance encounter turns increasingly into sought-after illegal activities.

While, rightly, observers have pointed to many of the above activities as existing under the Soviet regime (i.e. they did not simply start to flourish with the introduction of market-based relations in the economy), the equilibrium between informal and formal norms which had existed among the former Soviet institutions and norms was destroyed with the start of transition. Naturally, the above should not be viewed as any kind of retrospective excuse to have postponed transition; more that it should be seen as a reason to build the necessary countervailing institutions and formal norms of behaviour – difficult as that surely would have been in the Russia of the early 1990s – that balanced or subjugated the informal norms.

The point of the anecdotes in Box 9.6 is to illustrate that throughout the 1990s and into the new century, it was not just at the summits of power – both political and economic – that Russian society had degenerated into rent-seeking activities; it was an activity that *permeated* society at virtually all levels. One can think of the oligarchs and the dubious means by which privatised property fell into their hands such as the book deal that netted the authors – who happened to be in charge of privatising state property – $100,000 each (a book incidentally that had not even been written) paid for by a firm owned by a bank which then won the privatisation 'fight' to secure control of this or that business, but our point is that such was the predominance of informal norms over formal rules that society *as a whole* had become involved. The question arises: How does one build a 'normal' functioning market economy under such conditions? The question, of course, makes the implied assumption that the Russian actors involved in the reform process in the 1990s wanted to construct a market economy whereby the rule of law would dominate.

When society as a whole is faced with a radical shock brought on by forces from within or from outside, the formal rules break down either consciously or otherwise. The informal norms, however, can continue since the shock is directed at the rules of the game in a formal sense. The informal norms having adapted themselves to the old formal rules of the game can either adapt again – through a voluntary or not so voluntary move – or society can carry on as before. The informal norm system, having suffered an external shock of radical change in the formal rules from above, will either adapt to the new rules of the (formal) game or remain in the previously conditioned norms of behaviour.

It should not be thought that having set out on a path the economy or even a section of it is stuck on it for ever: what we may call path dependency. The idea of formal rules, informal norms, mental modes and path dependency does *not* imply determinism. As an example we present James Dyson and the humble vacuum cleaner. Dyson developed the bagless vacuum cleaner using centrifugal force to expel the dust from the container. Initially he approached all the major manufacturers with his invention, only to be turned down by each. Adoption of such a new innovation would imperil the £200-million-a-year bag market within the United Kingdom – a classic example of perfectly rational behaviour from a private perspective being at odds with the social good. Indeed on a BBC *Money Programme* the Hoover UK representative who had been originally approached by Dyson (half-) joked that he now wished that he had bought up the idea and 'shelved it'. Having been blocked by the incumbent manufacturers, Mr Dyson set up his own concern and launched into production. Now having 'swept' the market before him (along with copyright-infringing imitators) he is able to concentrate on the development of new products and innovations such as the bladeless fan.

The above examples raise some important issues. First, the role of the individual and the role of history matter in determining the directions to be taken by technological development, economies, and societies in general. This is in sharp relief to one variant of Marxism which holds that the individual plays a subordinate role in history: if the forces of production have 'ripened' such that new social relations either have or are in the process of emerging based on these new productive forces, then 'sooner or later' someone will emerge to provide the needed leadership or innovation necessary to take the forces of production forward. (See Plekhanov's classic essay *The Role of the Individual in History*.) In Chapter 1, we mentioned this in passing when describing the historical materialism of Karl Marx. Even if one were inclined to accept the above argument, such a person may take two or three (or more!) generations to emerge. This may seem trivial in the 'grand scheme of things' but for the individual with his or her three score and ten, such a wait can seem, and end up being, an eternity. In contrast to the Marxist way of thinking, the example of James Dyson (in a relatively mundane sector of the economy – apologies to Mr Dyson) demonstrates that individuals *do* matter. There would have been nothing automatic in moving from bag to bagless vacuum cleaners.

The conclusion from all of the above is that having a Boris Yeltsin or a Deng Xiaoping in charge of the country did make a difference. Individuals do matter to the course of developments and this was illustrated in the transition paths of both Russia and China. Naturally one can argue over the *degree* of importance that an individual makes, but not that they have an impact.

In general, if individuals get into a habitual way of conducting their affairs and learning costs for new ways of thinking and doing are not insignificant, lock-in effects can be created whereby it is difficult to break from established informal norms of behaviour. The above should be contrasted with the modern economics profession. It is perhaps at this stage that our opening anecdote about Her Majesty the Queen is now most relevant: why didn't anyone see the financial crisis coming? Because history, culture, politics, sociology, psychology have been stripped from the orthodox economist's toolkit. In the same way, it was a big surprise that output dropped so unexpectedly in transition economies of the FSU and CEE (unless with 20:20 vision in hindsight you now argue it was inevitable and natural). Most of the Western economics advisers to successive Russian governments would no doubt have shared the view of Lawrence Summers who declared as Chief Economist of the World Bank in October 1991, 'Spread the truth – the laws of economics are like the laws of engineering. One set of laws work everywhere.'

Lawrence Summers' statement

> would oft be repeated, as a sort of Clarion call for shock therapy. In February 1992, for example, the very same was proclaimed by Pyotr Aven, who was then Russian minister for foreign economic relations: 'There are no special countries from the point of view of economists. If economics is a science, with its own laws – all countries and all economic stabilization plans are the same.
>
> (Hedlund 1999)

Stiglitz (1999) took an opposing view to Mr Summers:

> I have tried, so far, to argue that there is a nexus of institutions that make capitalism work. It is not just 'private ownership,' but financial institutions and legal structures, and these were deficient in the economies in transition. Privatizing without effective financial institutions and legal structures was entering into *terra incognita* – a bold experiment where already existing theory indicated strong reservations.

Referring to the output fall observed in all FSU and CEE transition economies that was so unexpected as per the quotations at the start of this chapter, we agree with Roland (2000) when he writes that:

> For traditional economic analysis, whether markets are already present or not would be irrelevant, since the existence of markets with their institutional underpinnings, communication channels, and information networks is a priori *assumed*. Traditional analysis is very misguided in this particular context of transition because it cannot lead to predicting the output fall associated to price liberalization. In effect, the output fall was not predicted by economists advising transition countries because their thinking was based on traditional market analysis and on the neglect of the initial institutional conditions of liberalization in transition economies. [emphasis added]

That said, if we were to pose the question: 'Is there a correct transition path?' it would be the wrong question. Implicit in the question is that we are referring to a correct *economic* transition path. However, a more appropriate initial question is, 'Which actor or actors are involved in the transition process?' This is just as important an issue, if not more important, than the original question. The reason for this is that political issues were dominant over economic ones in the context of the FSU and China (and the countries of CEE); the then current political situation was more important in the eyes of leaderships as the actual economic destination. For the Western economic advisers in Russia in the early 1990s they no doubt genuinely and sincerely believed that the policy advice they were giving was with the intent of arriving at a market economy in as quick a time as possible where the efficiency and welfare of society would be raised; for them the market economy was an end in and of itself.

However, for individuals such as Boris Yeltsin, one is left with the impression that a market economy was of second order importance; that it – a market economy – was a means to an end and not the end itself. The end for Yeltsin was to ensure that the communists would have no way back into power and that his personal position and those of his immediate and extended family would remain secure even after he left office. This implied the destruction of all power bases of the old order from the Supreme Soviet to the red directors within the former SOEs.

How do the ideas of norms and institutions fit in with the transition path in China? As touched on above, it may be argued that the fact that the structures of the Chinese Communist Party were intact at the start of the transition process was an advantage (at least in the short to medium term); the equilibrium between informal and formal norms of behaviour was not radically disturbed. Further, the institutions on which they rested were also intact; change was imposed within the loosening of a straitjacket. Paradoxical as it may seem, the turmoil of the Cultural Revolution predisposed the leadership of the CCP to avoid at all costs any kind of repetition and so led them away from what Stiglitz has called 'market bolshevism'.

> They knew that institutional shock therapy destroys the old institutions and that new market institutions do not automatically arise out of the ashes. While Russia chose that path, China did not and the difference shows . . . China had one great advantage . . . it followed pragmatic policies, not the dictates of 'market bolshevism.' They knew the dangers into which ideological approaches to economic policies can lead; they were unwilling to exchange Mao's ideology for Milton's (Friedman).
>
> (Stiglitz 2001)

The above is not to say that the equilibrium has remained static within China. Indeed, as market forces gathered and continue to gather strength within China, potential powerful groupings can emerge outside of the normal channels of CCP-dominated structures that are not dependent on CCP patronage for their survival. It has been a success story for the CCP that over the period of reform they have not only contained alternative power groupings but in many ways subsumed them into an almost reinvented CCP. It could be no other way if the CCP was and is to survive: traditional patronage within the CCP (and any Communist Party in power) came ultimately from control of the economy. As that control slips away (in a relative sense), the leaders of the economy – managers, directors, shareholders – are no longer beholden to the CCP to the extent that they would have been in the 1960s, 1970s or 1980s. The reader is advised to consult Naughton (2008a) for a detailed description and explanation as to how the rules of the game within China have changed over the transition period, what Naughton calls 'transition within transition'. As Naughton (2008a) notes,

> For the CP to retain power and survive the economic transition process, it needed to protect and recreate a system of political patronage . . . To achieve their objectives, leaders of the regime had to both shape the reform policy package and reshape the rules of the authoritarian hierarchy.

For the current and previous communist leadership within China, a market economy was and is also a means to an end. This particular end, however, is about the attempt to permanently renew the legitimacy of the Chinese Communist Party in the eyes of the Chinese people. As with the Western economic advisers to Russia we have no reason to doubt the leadership's sincerity in wishing to make China a great power and to raise up the Chinese people to new levels of prosperity; we also have no reason to doubt that they wish to play a central and guiding role in this process. A Big Bang approach to transition would have released too many unknowns into the political mix of calculating the likelihood of the Chinese Communist Party's survival. To argue that the Chinese Communist Party leadership (or equivalently Boris Yeltsin in Russia) should have adopted a Big Bang (or equivalently for Yeltsin a gradualist) approach is like asking them to have gambled with their position of power and leadership. In both cases – in Russia and in China – both leaderships came to the conclusion that heading down the road to the market – at different speeds – offered the best chance of securing their *personal* and *group* futures given the localised political conditions and circumstances that they faced. Economists discuss and debate whether a Big Bang approach or a gradualist approach is and was the best way forward for transition to enhance the welfare of *society*; it was, however, not the welfare of Russian or Chinese society that was being consciously set out to be maximised in the first place. Once that is recognised, the economics becomes secondary to the politics.

In conclusion, we sympathise with Naughton (2008a) that:

> Today, the remaining supporters of the big bang approach recognise that Chinese gradualism was indeed feasible, but sometimes argue that what was possible in China was not possible in Europe. An alternative explanation is much more persuasive, namely that gradualist transition paths were possible in either environment but that political considerations were more important than economic considerations in determining the transition path adopted.[41]

Ultimately the reader must make up his or her own mind: there is no correct answer (since there is no such thing as a retrospective proof – time, as far as we know, only flows forward) as to why most transition economies suffered severe downturns with Russia in particular suffering prolonged recession while China did not. The above has touched on the various arguments, you must decide on whether an alternative transition path for both Russia and China would not only have been *feasible* but would have led to greater welfare enhancement for society.

What does the future hold for China and for Russia?

While this chapter is about the transition paths followed by Russia and China it would be remiss if we did not say a few words at least on future prospects. That said, we do so warily. In 1990, just a year before the downfall of the Soviet Union, a book was published in which the author wrote of the FSU and the countries of CEE (which he termed socialist societies) and of social democratic societies such as the Scandinavian countries (that he termed socialistic):

> The idea of 'burying socialism' is a fantasy of some conservative politicians, mainly in Britain and the United States. In the wider world there are many socialist or socialistic societies, of diverse kinds which for the most part function adequately and in some cases very well.
>
> (Bottomore 1990)

The author continues some pages later, on the same theme, and referring to communist East Germany (GDR):

> the GDR, for example, has a relatively efficient socialised agriculture (whatever may be the case in the Soviet Union) and industry, and its GNP per capita is probably higher than that of Britain, which is admittedly one of the least successful capitalist countries.
>
> (Bottomore 1990)[42]

Later, writing of unfolding political developments in Eastern Europe, Bottomore comments,

> Of course, it is customary in the predominantly Western media to interpret the changes now going on in Eastern Europe as some kind of 'return to capitalism', but that is very wide of the mark, at least in most of the countries concerned. For the most part public ownership and central planning are likely to remain, along with the emphasis in their policies on full employment, social welfare and a substantial degree of economic equality; to which may now be added greater democratic participation in all spheres of life.

The purpose of these quotations is not to disparage the author – a very distinguished author at that – from the safe vantage point of historical hindsight; it takes a brave person to not only describe what is happening but also to predict what *will* happen. That authors can and do get it wrong (see the end of Chapter 10 for another illustration) only goes to show that society at large is unpredictable to a very great extent and that the social sciences, of which sociology and economics are part, are not exact sciences like mathematics and physics. It is much easier, as we have seen with the *lack* of prediction on the economic and financial crisis of 2007 to 2009, for commentators to keep their heads below the parapet, to 'go with the flow' and not to run against the tide of conventional wisdom.

Consequently the authors of these concluding remarks are wary of making rash predictions as to the future of these two great countries. Tentative remarks proceed as follows, first on China and then to an extent on Russia: China has over a 30-year period successfully used a combination of export-based development policies combined with an increasing use of indicative planning methods (as opposed to classic Soviet-style central planning methods) to enter the world stage as a *potential* economic and political superpower. Such an approach was sufficient to 'prime the pump' of economic growth to keep the economic and social development of the country on course with growth rates in double-digit territory.

However, if we briefly turn our gaze Westward, in an article in the *Financial Times* newspaper of 26 November 2009 headed 'Taxpayers face a generation of pain', the fiscal measures which many countries adopted during the 2007 to 2009 financial and economic crisis and helped prevent global recession turning into global depression are now seen to be the barrier to the future growth prospects of these very same countries. 'Public sector gross debt is expected to explode from an average across advanced economies of 78 per cent of national income in 2007 to 118 per cent in 2014. Emerging economies with their faster economic growth and greater constraints on borrowing expect much lower build-up of debt.'[43] As the article notes, the difficulty for most advanced economies (i.e. Western economies) is that just as they attempt 'fiscal consolidation' (i.e. reduce government debt by cutting government services and/or raising taxes), the 'baby-boomer' generation will be retiring; the dependency ratio – the number of retired people to be supported by the number of working people – is going to get worse. More taxes will need to be raised from fewer people to support those not working *and* to pay off the huge debts run up during the economic crisis of 2007 to 2009. As a consequence the continued route adopted by China in the past of relying on the American and European consumer to keep growth in double-digit figures or even at 7 to 9 per cent is made more problematic.

Even if the above two problems were not present, the imbalance between spending in the West and saving in the East would end up *forcing* a change in China's development model. Vociferous calls will come from Western governments and will have – publicly at least for domestic Chinese consumption – zero impact on Chinese government thinking (privately of course it may be a different matter). Of greater impact on government thinking is and will be the huge disparities that have opened up between China's regions, between those who have and those who do not, between the rich and the poor. China risks a three-class society of the super rich, a large middle class, and a class which exists both within and without society at the same time; for example, working-class migrants who travel many hundreds of miles to work but at the same time cannot have the same rights as those with legal registration in the main cities. Even if this anomaly is removed, in what way are these transient workers part of Chinese society if they can look through shopping mall windows but cannot enter through the front door to buy the goods?

That said, encouraging signs are present. Increasingly China is moving away from its export-led only development model, if not quite at the pace that many Western governments would like. Speaking at the World Economic Forum in Davos, Vice-Premier Li Keqiang commented that economic strategies had become 'excessively reliant on investment and exports'. According to *China Daily* Li said, 'China would look to increase employment and increase income levels of its poorer people, hoping to unleash the huge potential of the Chinese consumer' (*China Daily*, 29 January 2010).

China needs 'economic spontaneous combustion' of consumer spending within its heartlands in a manner that occurred within the continent of the Americas in the late nineteenth century such that exports – while still important – play a progressively less vital role in taking the Chinese economy forward. This would lead over time to a reorientation of investment by domestic Chinese companies away from export markets and, indeed, 'simple' infrastructure projects to aligning the economy to the needs and desires of consumers. Much will depend on the development of safety nets such that consumers do not feel the need to save large proportions of their income for the future and can spend at a higher, and hopefully sustainable level. This may or may not impact upon the US and the EU countries, as the Chinese consumers' marginal propensity to import increases, and may allow a degree of growing out of debt rather than simply taxing one's way out of debt.

As for Russia, it is highly dependent on what happens outside its own borders. For better or for worse it has turned increasingly into a resource-based economy. This, of course, is a generalisation and no doubt this or that area of manufacturing or service sector business prowess could be pointed to (see e.g. Hare *et al.* 2004, in particular the section entitled 'FDI in Russia: More than just oil and natural resources'). However, to say that it does not have the economic diversity of the Chinese economy is not controversial. Ex-President Putin had enormous good fortune with a large and sustained rise in the price of oil for most of his Presidency. Notwithstanding the possibility of economic spontaneous combustion within China's heartlands, a lack of economic vigour in Western economies (in which we include Japan) will temper oil price increases (but not hold them down at recession levels!). This will have an adverse impact on the Russian economy; the room for manoeuvre will not be as great as it was during the Putin Presidency era of the early 2000s. The dependency of Russia on its resource-based economy was demonstrated when it entered into recession in the first half of 2008, re-emerging from recession in the third quarter of 2009 but not before the economy shrank by 8.7 per cent.

For China, however, notwithstanding the scouring of the globe for secure sources of energy, higher oil prices would impact upon growth prospects but not to the extent of causing the economy to go into reverse.[44] Quite by how much it is difficult to say. First, it depends on the development of the renewable sectors of the Chinese economy. It would also imply that far from winding down fossil fuel extraction as renewables and cleaner sources of energy come on stream, this source of energy *may* even be intensified, which is not such good news for the global environment. An additional implication is that if the price of oil does start to climb ever upwards (again we are talking about the next 5 to 20 years) then notwithstanding slower growth in mature Western economies, this could act as a spur for greater economic efficiency within Chinese enterprises.

In Russia much will depend on whether there will be a political struggle for power at the top of the state apparatus. (Politics trumps economics again?) The current Russian President Dmitry Medvedev in 2009 started to 'make noises', writing in his blog of 'An ineffective economy, a semi-Soviet social sphere, a weak democracy, negative demographic trends and an unstable Caucasus. These are very big problems even for a state like Russia' (*Guardian* newspaper, 11 September 2009). The current Russian President has also bemoaned the inefficiency of the remaining state-run enterprises and warned them that they cannot take state aid for granted. Whether this is all intended simply as a show – that he is his 'own man' and not simply following what Putin instructs him to do – or whether it is the start of a play for power and so the beginnings of a genuine attempt to break the mould of Russian economic and social development since the start of transition, time will tell.[45]

The above is not to say that the Russian government is devoid of plans or goals to change the economy. Goals for the year 2020 were set by Putin himself back in 2007 to 2008. There are three basic scenarios that the Russian government has laid before itself as possibilities for the future development of the economy. The three scenarios are: (1) the innovation scenario; (2) the energy and raw materials scenario; and (3) the inertia scenario (see Åslund and Kuchins (2009) for more details). In brief, as the first scenario implies, the government is looking for reasonably high and consistent growth of 6.5 per cent per year up until 2020 based on the development of innovative businesses backed by government at both the Federal and Regional level; this in turn will require the development of human capital and the movement away from an overbearing dependency on the resource sector of the economy.

As one proceeds to scenario (2) and then to (3), the picture for the future development of the economy becomes less rosy. Scenario (2) sees what in effect is a continuation of what has already taken place; the Russian economy continues to rely on its extractive sectors of the economy although with increased modernisation. This scenario sees growth at 5.3 per cent per year on average which by the standards of mature economies would still be respectable, although it would mask the lack of diversification within the economy. The final scenario is the bleakest, with growth forecast at 'only' 3.9 per cent (although one can think of many a European government that would be more than happy with such 'bleak' growth forecasts!).

While clearly the Russian government would prefer scenario (1), this scenario will also require the continuation of structural reforms to both the economy and government. The difficulty is that 'it has only been laid out in general reasoning in public speeches' (Åslund and Kuchins 2009). As Aleksei Pushkov, a political talk host in Moscow, commented to the *Financial Times* (12 November 2009) and referring to Medvedev, 'He is really infatuated with modernisation. This is not just talk, he really wants to do something. But while the goals are clear, where are the mechanisms? That's the problem.' In the absence of oil returning to a *consistent* price of $80+ per barrel, and in the absence of open and transparent 'mechanisms', it is doubtful whether scenario (1) can be achieved.

What of democracy? What of it, indeed? Given that this book is an economics textbook about transition, then what of democracy in the sense of it promoting and reinforcing economic reform and hence welfare advancement of the individual and society? This is a contentious area. Implicit in some writings on transition there has been the inclusion of Western-style democracy and the necessary democratic institutions as part and parcel of the transition process. However, this is not necessarily the case. The reader should not confuse *normative* with *positive* economics, the former being based on opinion or the desire to see something happen, and the latter being based on fact and observation. The economics profession attempts to keep itself positive in the sense of being fact-based or based on empirical foundations; if the economic theory is not supported by empirics, then the theory may need to be amended in the light of what is happening in the real world.[46] We quote Nicholas Stern (1997):

> The building of new institutions involves critical strategic approaches by government. In each case they involve basic interactions between government and the private sector in enforcing and generating creative and responsible market behaviour . . . Let us, however, dispose immediately of an overmechanical or

dogmatic approach to these issues. Some are tempted to argue that political liberalism, in the form of democracy, is an essential precondition for economic liberalism. Theoretical arguments are sometimes proposed in terms of political authoritarianism automatically leading to a command economy, or that political and economic freedoms are inseparable; sometimes empirical associations are offered.

There are sufficiently many, and major, examples in contradiction to this position to make for great scepticism concerning any inevitability in the relationship. Indeed, both the theoretical and empirical arguments are unconvincing. One can provide examples of political authoritarianism with economic liberalism, democracy with extensive public ownership and direction of the economy, political authoritarianism with a command economy and of democracy with economic liberalism.

Åslund and Jenish (2006) provide a neat contrast of the nature between democracy and economic growth in transition economies. Writing of the CIS and the CEE countries in the first period of transition, they note, 'With regard to politics, the 1990s evidenced strong, positive correlation between democracy, comprehensive market reforms, and economic growth.' However, after 1998 there is an about-face:

> While growth and democracy were nicely correlated in the 1990s, we see the opposite picture after 1998. A simple plot of growth against a Freedom House index suggests a negative correlation between these two indicators. The CIS countries, which are by and large authoritarian, have grown faster than the democratic countries in Central Europe.

As for democracy within Russia itself, elections are held along Western lines although, given the tight control of the media by the state, not to mention the hounding, persecution, and, indeed, the frequent murder of investigative journalists, the word *democracy* is used in an extremely relative sense. Such has been the slide to a more authoritarian style of state, started under the former President Putin, that even current President Medvedev 'has championed modest electoral reforms and harshly criticised the hegemonic United Russia political party, headed by Mr Putin, for rigging local elections' (*Financial Times*, 16 December 2009).

Some authors distinguish clearly between democratic institutions and the rule of law (see Clarke *et al.* 2008), the implication being that it is possible to have law and order – which would allow enterprise to develop – without necessarily having democracy. For enterprise to flourish economic agents must believe that political, economic and social conditions are such that their property is safe from other individuals and from expropriation by government. Further, another aspect of the rule of law is that contracts established between economic agents can be enforced under the rule of law. This then allows them to get on with creating wealth and consequently promoting economic growth without the need to be constantly looking over their shoulders.

The rule of law in generating such expectations is seen as crucial. However, Clarke *et al.* (2008) come to the conclusion that, 'In sum, the experience of the reform era in China seems to refute the proposition that a necessary condition for growth is that the legal system provide secure property and contract rights.' It would seem that not only is democracy not an absolute requirement, but the rule of law itself is not sacrosanct, at least as far as the specific and the important example of China is concerned up to the time of writing.[47]

That said, Woo (2007) not only sees the Chinese leadership as moving in the direction of democracy – represented by the Harmonious Society programme – but regards such moves as essential to the further development of the Chinese economy and of society in general. According to Woo (2007), the Harmonious Society programme, passed by the Sixth Plenum of the 16th Central Committee of the CCP, aims to establish by 2020:

- a democratic society under the rule of law;
- a society based on equality and justice;
- an honest and caring society;
- a stable, vigorous and orderly society;
- a society in which humans live in harmony with nature.

Woo (2007) sees the adoption and future implementation of this programme as not simply due to increased social unrest, which he documents, but also due to the rise of more affluent and better educated Chinese who, aware of the deficiencies of government at all levels, will have raised expectations of what government should deliver. Naughton (2007b), however, in the debate with Woo begs to differ as to the leadership's commitment to Western-style democracy: 'The Chinese Communist Party doesn't commit itself to democracy and hasn't committed itself to sharing power. It has committed itself to a kind of paternalistic role in solving the income distribution and corruption problems that it itself created' (Naughton 2007b).

As George Bernard Shaw once said, if you laid all the economists in the world end-to-end they still wouldn't reach a conclusion! What do *you* think is going to happen?

Summary

The transition paths followed by Russia and China remain controversial even today, and will, no doubt, for the foreseeable future. They are controversial since from the debates that have taken place it is asserted that alternative paths could have been followed in both the case of Russia and China. In the case of Russia, while some commentators have taken the *Tina* approach (**T**here **i**s/was **n**o **a**lternative), it is precisely because many other commentators feel that is not true that the area is controversial. If the former group of commentators are correct, then end of discussion. However, if the latter group of commentators are correct, then *potentially* much human suffering could have been avoided in the early stages of transition. Ultimately this is a subjective area since we cannot rerun history in either of the countries concerned.

In China's case, while it is difficult to imagine an alternative set of policies expediting a faster rate of *economic development*, it is possible that a faster *transition to a market* (of sorts) could, like Russia, have taken place more quickly through a more radical turn similar to the Big Bang approach. That said, some would argue that even if we focus on economic development the examples of South Korea, Taiwan and Japan show that fast economic development in China could have been possible even without an overbearing state presence. (Although the countries mentioned – part of the Asian Tigers – were themselves not wholly free from government indicative planning.)

The debate has focused in the past on what seems to be a remarkable degree of economic development with no transitional recession in China and hence, if it was possible in China why not Russia, which experienced one of the deepest and prolonged transitional recessions? As outlined here, many would counter that the initial conditions of the two countries were so at odds with one another that the comparison is meaningless, which leads them to adopt the *Tina* stance. Supporters of the Big Bang approach to transition, however, are not uncritical of successive Russian governments in their failure to implement correct fiscal and monetary policies. The point is that if the transitional recession was more intense in comparison to other transition countries of CEE this was due as much to successive inept Russian government policies as to the principle of a Big Bang itself. Western governments and institutions do not escape their ire either.

While the debate has often been posed in terms of gradualism versus a Big Bang approach there are other nuances to the discussion that are often lost, such as the institutional backdrop and the supremacy of politics over economics. The main critique of those who can – loosely – be placed in the gradualist camp is that market economies do not operate in an institutional vacuum. To plunge directly into a free market within Russia was to ignore the fact that institutions take time to develop; without the scaffolding of institutions around the building of a market economy the informal rules and norms (carried over in large part from Soviet times and epitomised by rent seeking) would come to dominate society at all levels in the new Russia post-1991. Whether there would have been time to develop such institutions is debateable, although some would contend that it was not even tried.

Finally, those involved in the drama, such as Boris Yeltsin and Deng Xiaoping (and behind him the Chinese Communist Party), had their own agendas which interacted with the desire/necessity to move towards a market economy. In this perspective the transition should be seen in both countries as being dominated by politics and not by economics. For Yeltsin a transition to a market was a battering ram against any attempted come-back of the communists in Russia, and the sooner the market could be introduced, and the institutions destroyed on which Soviet Communist power rested, the better. From Yeltsin's perspective transition in the 1990s was ultimately successful. For the Chinese Communist Party leadership the only hard truth was and is development, but development that can be controlled. Such a controlled approach leant itself towards adopting a more gradualist transition path. With the chaos of both the Cultural Revolution and the Great Leap Forward in the minds of many of the leadership, a radical rupture was to be avoided. In the process the CCP has reinvented itself over the years, symbolised by the opening up of Communist Party membership to entrepreneurs. Whether this makeover for the twenty-first century will be enough to keep them in power in the long run is, to borrow a phrase, too early to say.

Key terms

Big Bang	Institutions
Cultural Revolution	*Perestroika*
Dual-track pricing	Rouble zone
Formal and informal norms	Special economic zones
Gradualism	Total factor productivity
Great Leap Forward	Township and village enterprises
Household responsibility system	

Review questions

1   Do the experiences of China and Russia demonstrate that privatisation or competition is more important in the transition to a market economy?

2   Please answer the following questions:

- Do you agree that politics did indeed dominate economics in the decision to adopt a big bang approach in Russia and a gradualist approach in China?
- If you agree with the above, does this mean that the economy of a country is always secondary in the major decisions that governments take?
- Or can it not be argued that it was the respective crises in the centrally planned economies of Russia and China that provoked the political crises which in turn led to the changed economic path?

3   For the students of economics who have been weaned on the marginal concept and the theory of rational economic agents, discuss the following: 'The eventual collapse of Gorbachev's anti-alcohol campaign brought about in large measure by popular discontent and pressure from the drinking masses indicates that it is not always the case that consumers are the best judges of their welfare. While the marginal private (and social) cost of an extra 50 grams of vodka far outweighed the marginal benefits from its consumption, consumption proceeded nevertheless. *Ipso facto*: consumers are not rational economic agents.'

10

LESSONS FROM TRANSITION

Taking stock of transformation

With two decades of transition complete, it is an appropriate time to take stock of transformation. In doing so, we join a distinguished yet surprisingly small number of economists who have recently assessed the record of transition, and, more importantly, outlined what the economics profession has learnt from the transition experience (Havrylyshyn 2001, 2006; Kolodko 1999, 2006; Kornai 2000b, 2008; Roland 2001, 2002). Some of these conclusions are outlined in Appendix 7.

After two decades of economic transformation in the so-called transition economies, what lessons can be learnt from transition? What can the economics profession learn from the experience of transition countries?[1] What does the transition literature and the extensive body of research on transition now tell us about the capitalist system and economic reform in general? Can other countries undertaking similar changes in economic systems, rules and behaviour learn from the transition experience? In previous chapters we included some brief assessments of the individual topics and specific issues covered. In this final chapter, we present what we consider to be the main general lessons that the economics profession (both from a policy and non-policy perspective) can learn, acknowledging that our task is not straightforward, since disagreements among economists and policy makers persist over precisely what lessons are to be learned, and that two decades (and a little longer in the cases of China and Vietnam) is a short time given the enormous changes that were involved in transition.

At the outset of transition, there was no theoretical model or conceptual framework and no policy blueprint for transformation from plan to market. Indeed, expectations of almost everything, from the time period involved to the amount of external assistance and FDI flows to the accrued benefits from transition, were excessive. With respect to insights from economic theory, the study of what is called comparative economic systems tended to compare the functioning of different systems – socialism and capitalism – as opposed to the transition from one to another, as took place in 1917 (or 1928 to be more precise with the first five-year plan) and in 1989 to 1991 with the dissolution of the Soviet system and the transition to a market economy.[2] Likewise, as alluded to in the Introduction, development economics focused on low-income developing countries (what was called the Third World) and the alternate paths from underdevelopment to development, as opposed to transition economics that focuses on predominantly middle-income socialist countries (what was referred to as the Second World) and the transformation from the command system to the market system. That is not to say that there were no historical precedents or that no economic fundamentals could be applied (see below).

Transition, however it is defined, is extraordinarily complex, involving wholesale systemic changes or, as Dewatripont and Roland (1997) describe it, as 'large-scale institutional change'. Economic transition, combined with the political and social transition of the 1990s, was unprecedented. One consequence of this systemic change is that the discipline of economics now has a greater understanding of capitalism and its institutional foundations, the interplay of politics and economics, and the importance (and unpredictability) of dynamic change. We now appreciate more the difficulties involved in creating a market economy (and all its institutional underpinnings), since that is what transition (to market, from plan) entailed.

In TEs, policy makers were confronted with the dual problems of transition and development, of emerging markets and destatisation, of market reform and institutional reform, of structural adjustment and reconstruction, of political change and economic change, resulting in outcomes that included, for the majority of transition countries, a large fall in output, rapid inflation, social disruption, and, for many CIS countries, disturbing demographic trends. From an economic theory perspective, the lesson here is the inadequacy of any one school of economic thought (neoclassical or institutional) to fully explain transition or to adequately inform policy makers of the complexities of the transition process. Over two decades on, institutions are now considered mainstream, and institutional reform is considered to be as important (if not more important, according to its supporters) to the success of transition as the market reforms that were advocated by the IFIs, policy makers and the majority of influential Western academic economists at the outset of transition. This is a lesson that has relevance beyond transition and transition countries, to topics such as the determinants of economic growth, governance of developing and emerging markets, the role of IFIs and the suitability (and conditionality) of market reforms, etc.

The remainder of this concluding chapter is organised around markets, the degree of presence or absence of which is the defining characteristic of the market regime and the essential difference between the centrally planned system and the market system (that is, states versus markets). However, as transition is a complex process, we need to discuss markets in the context of a number of important issues, namely politics, policy reforms, institutions, states and firms. We will also examine transition and markets in the two largest, most populated and, geopolitically, most important TEs, that is, Russia and China. We end with some concluding remarks.

Markets and politics

If there was ever an event in the twentieth century that required a political economy perspective, it was the transition from socialism to capitalism and from plan to market. The interplay between politics and economics is crucial in helping to understand the policy reforms, performance and outcomes in transition countries. The experience of TEs clearly illustrates the importance of political constraints. Politics matters and the political economy of reform is central to an understanding of transition. Indeed, this practice, and growing trend, of integrating the political process into an analysis of economic issues is more widespread now in economics, into areas such as international trade, public finance, regulation and so on (Roland 2002).[3] In reforms, political considerations dominate as much as, if not more than, economic deliberations. More generally, the events and outcomes during transition simply reinforce the need for the economics profession today, as was the case in earlier times when the discipline was known as political economy, to emphasise and reiterate the link between economics and politics, as Adam Smith and Karl Marx did centuries ago.

Reforms were often not the exogenous choice of policy makers (despite the rhetoric of many) but instead were endogenous, subject to political constraints. Feasibility as opposed to ideology was, in the end, often what determined actual policy reforms. In the tradition of political economy, reforms were designed based on what was politically feasible and acceptable (alongside what was technically implementable and socially enforceable). Two good examples include macro-stabilisation in Russia which was first introduced in 1992 but was subsequently blocked and delayed until 1995, and the mass privatisation programme (MPP) in Poland which was initially introduced in 1991 but was delayed for up to five years in the face of much opposition both outside and within the Sejm.

Markets and policy reforms

Prior knowledge, and expectations, of market reforms, in the context of former socialist countries where market-supporting institutions were, at best, weak and at worst absent, was overstated. Moreover, it is now clear from the transition experience, from what worked and what did not work, that there are no one-size-fits-all reforms.[4] In general, policy reforms need to be tailored to the reforming country, with its history, culture and local conditions. This is not to say that there are no economic fundamentals (what one might call 'good economics') that can apply regardless of location, custom or tradition. The evidence from transition countries, and elsewhere, indicates that economic growth is associated with macro-stability and a conducive business environment (where entry and competition is free and unrestricted), well-defined property rights and suitable enforcement mechanisms, openness to foreign trade and participation in world markets, and a sound, well-functioning banking and financial system.[5] Transition countries that have failed to correct macro imbalances, to secure and enforce property rights, to reap the gains from international trade and to support and regulate the financial sector are preventing improvements in economic growth.

We will briefly mention here two of these preconditions, namely macro-stability and a sound banking system. Macro (that is, fiscal and monetary) stability, is, as argued by many including Hare (2010) and Berglöf and Bolton (2002), a precondition for economic growth. With respect to the former, in a very entertaining account of transition countries (and the author's own experiences therein), Hare (2010) argues strongly for sound macroeconomic conditions (but in noticeably moderate language such as 'manageable levels' of inflation, a budget balance 'under control' and avoidance of 'excessive and unsustainable external debt') to be put in place in order for economic growth to be sustained. In the case of the latter and despite the prominence of financial architecture given in their 2002 'Great Divide' paper, they conclude that it is not financial reform that explains the differences in performance between CEE and CIS countries but, indeed, the fiscal and monetary discipline (which, in turn, is determined by historical legacy and initial conditions, location, state legitimacy and accountability) that explains why some countries, most notably CEE countries, have crossed the Great Divide while others are left behind, namely many of the CIS countries. For CEE countries, a return to Europe was both an anchor and a commitment device. It was a source of inspiration and more concretely, of institutions, technical assistance, finance and trade. This goes some way in explaining the outcome differences between CEE and CIS countries.

As if the reader needs any reminding (given the adverse contribution of banks and their ill-advised and unregulated lending to the global economic crisis of 2007 to 2009), a sound banking system, well-functioning credit markets and a properly regulated financial sector are, literally, at the heart of the market and capitalist system. In the early days of transition, financial sector reform was primarily concerned with the establishment of financial intermediation and involved the setting up of a two-tier banking system, liberalisation of interest rates and credit allocation, a new payments system, investment in monitoring and screening of loans, and recapitalisation of some banks. As time progressed, and with the onslaught of the global financial crisis (where many Eastern European countries, most notably Hungary, Latvia and Ukraine, were badly affected owing to excessive foreign borrowing and private sector lending), it was evident that proper regulation and prudential supervision, in conjunction with better corporate governance and improved lending practices, of the (traditional and otherwise) banking and non-banking financial sector was required for economic growth to resume.[6] In that context, among other changes, a well-resourced and independent Financial Regulator is vital, with recent developments in transition and non-transition countries alike proving how difficult a task it really is.

With respect to reform in general, speed may not be as important an issue as was originally argued (in the early 1990s), but phasing or sequencing is probably of significant importance. Of course, some reforms, by their very nature, can and should be implemented early and rapidly. A good example is macroeconomic stabilisation. In contrast, other reforms require more time: these reforms can be staged, and done slowly. An example is enterprise restructuring and corporate governance changes. A corollary of this is the importance of phased or sequenced reforms. It is generally agreed that, at the outset of transition for those countries with a macro crisis or serious imbalance, macroeconomic stabilisation is a priority: it must be done quickly and is required in advance of other reforms. Liberalisation is also required at an early stage, although there is some debate over how quick and comprehensive it needs to be and whether a single track (as was adopted in the CEE/FSU countries) or a dual track (as adopted in China and Vietnam) is preferable. Legal and regulatory reform is also required at an early stage, although it is likely that such reform will be continuous throughout transition. With other reforms, from ownership structure to infrastructural reforms, initial change may be minimal and will only accelerate as transition progresses, and beyond.

Interestingly, despite the predictions of many who advocated (radical) policies that would ensure irreversibility and the cross-country trend for early-reforming governments to be defeated at subsequent elections as they faced electoral backlash, market reforms were followed and adopted by the vast majority of incoming governments, whether (centre) right-wing or (centre) left-wing parties, two-party coalitions or multi-party coalitions, presidential or parliamentary regimes. Despite the setbacks, public opposition and growing concerns over social issues such as unemployment, public health, poverty and inequality, there were no sharp policy reversals in the vast majority of countries.[7]

Finally, and not unique to TEs, is the realisation that although policy and policy reform are important, so too is implementation. It is a serious mistake to underestimate the importance of implementation. Adopting and designing a policy is only half the story: effective implementation – political and administrative – is the other, equally important, half of the story. Indeed, the ability to implement policies should be, it is argued, a key determinant of policy and policy design itself (Barr 2001; Ellerman 2001).

Overall, with respect to transition and market reforms, the evidence from transition (and non-transition) countries is that there is no panacea – no single reform that will ensure a resumption of sustainable economic growth. Although reforms are complementary, it is not an exact science. It is difficult to predict the precise effect of one reform change relative to another policy change. Benefits from one reform may be contingent on implementation of other reforms. In warning against hubris, the late John McMillan (2004) noted,

Reform is hard to do because we cannot predict its effects. The big bang approach presumes we know where we are going and how to get there. We may know where we should be headed, but there is much we do not know about how to get there. No recipe for success has yet been written. Acknowledging our ignorance means moving step by step rather than betting everything on a comprehensive blueprint. The whole point of the market economy, after all, is that it handles, better than any more centralised alternative, the unforeseen and the unforeseeable. If we could plan the reforms, we could have planned the economy.

With respect to transition and market reforms, a broader issue is its impact on the set of policies commonly known as the Washington Consensus. The experience of reform, and outcomes in TEs, as in Latin America a decade earlier, raised serious concerns about the applicability, comprehensiveness and (in)adequacy of the list of policy recommendations included in the Washington Consensus. The disappointing early outcomes in CEE/FSU countries as against the impressive economic record in China further weakened the supremacy of the Washington Consensus and accelerated the search for an alternative, or at the very least, a post-Washington Consensus that would include many of the original ten policy recommendations but augmented to include reforms – often more institutional in nature than the market reforms that comprised the original ten policies – relating to poverty reduction, inequality and income distribution, corporate governance, regulation and prudential supervision, and so on. Over two decades on from the collapse of the Soviet system and, coincidently at the same time, the emergence of the Washington Consensus, one of the most important effects of transition and the outcomes that ensued in TEs is the contribution it made, especially in policy circles, to the ongoing debate on the relevance, or otherwise, of the Washington Consensus (a paradigm that, although at its peak at the time of the demise of the socialist system, had its critics at the outset of transition) and the move away (or transition, if you so wish) from the so-called Washington Consensus to a post-Washington Consensus era where consensus, as in 1989 despite claims to the contrary, is still difficult to reach.[8]

Markets and institutions

Although market reforms have a significant role to play in increasing a country's level of economic activity and ultimately improving the standard of living for a country's citizens, it is evident from the transition experience, and elsewhere, that the institutional and legal arrangements that support market transactions matter a great deal. In any setting, transition or otherwise, some set of rules and social norms for behaviour is essential for a stable society and economy. These are what we call 'institutions'. They can be legal, financial, political, economic or social in nature. They can be formal or informal, slow moving or fast moving, evolving or designed, perfect best practice or imperfect second-best. Whatever form they take, rules of the game need to be credible and have the support of the population. Although many of these rules are enforced through legal institutions, formal legislation is not enough to guarantee social and economic order. Law is often based on moral standards accepted by a country's citizens. What are these institutions? Qian (2003), in describing institutional reforms in China, outlines a list of important best-practice institutions, to include 'secure private property rights protected by the rule of law; impartial enforcement of contracts through an independent judiciary; appropriate government regulations to foster market competition; effective corporate governance; transparent financial systems'. Likewise, Stiglitz and

Ellerman (2001), in defending the so-called Stiglitz Perspective on reform and transition, outline the institutional infrastructure, to include 'banking and financial systems, effective judicial systems to enforce contracts, competition, bankruptcy laws fairly and efficiently, and regulatory systems'.

Market reforms without institutional reform will not improve economic prosperity. Given the circumstances of each country, market reforms in the absence of institution building may undermine future economic development. Indeed, in the early years of the transition from plan to market, what was more apparent than institutional building was institutional destruction (of Soviet-type institutions). As capitalism and its institutions had taken centuries to evolve in the advanced market economies of the West, it was a misjudgement to think that they could be introduced to former socialist countries in a short period of time. Moreover, existing institutions need to be (or made) suitable to available policy instruments. However, depending on a country's historical, cultural and social circumstances, the evidence from transition countries indicates that the transplantation of best-practice institutions may be inferior to the adoption of transitional institutions. Qian (2003) argues that it is the adoption of so-called transitional – imperfect, unconventional but novel, sensible and complementary to initial conditions – institutions that explains why Chinese reforms worked, and ultimately explains China's impressive growth record. The importance of institutions is also evident in an earlier EBRD assessment, a decade into transition, when it concluded that 'The evidence now shows clearly that the central lesson in transition is that markets will not function without supporting institutions, a state that carries through its responsibilities and a healthy civil society' (EBRD 1999).[9] Institutions, not an established part of the reform agenda at the outset of transition, are now an accepted element of the mainstream. This is a fundamental change in economics in less than two decades. Indeed, it was Nobel Laureate Ronald Coase who wrote in 1992 that

> The value of including . . . institutional factors in the corpus of mainstream economics is made clear by recent events in Eastern Europe. These ex-communist countries are advised to move to a market economy, and their leaders wish to do so, but without the appropriate institutions no market economy of any significance is possible. If we knew more about our own economy, we would be in a better position to advise them.[10]

One of these institutions is the state itself. In addition, it is the state that is responsible for building, resourcing and regulating many of the essential market-supporting institutions.

Markets and states

Another lesson from the transition experience is the role of the state in the modern capitalist system. It was inevitable that transition from a centrally planned economy to a market economy would involve a change in the role of the state. Given the extent of state control in the socialist system (and the lack of the market mechanism and profit motive), and given the prevailing economic orthodoxy at the time of the collapse of the Soviet system (what might be called the neo-liberal agenda), there was inevitably going to be a significant reduction (and reorientation) in state involvement, both in terms of size and scope. Some commentators, admittedly those closest to the neo-liberal perspective, even argued for a dismantling of the state.[11] In cases where this occurred (deliberately or otherwise), state collapse and the problem of a weakened state emerged.

No doubt, reform of government was necessary. A reconstituted state was required. However, as learnt from elsewhere (particularly in the post-Second World War era and in the NICs of South East Asia), markets and governments complement each other. Lessons from individual transition countries, both positive and negative (whether it is decentralisation in China, enterprise restructuring in Poland or state collapse in Georgia and Russia), indicate the important role of the state (and government reforms) in the capitalist system. Despite the tendency during transition to dismantle the state, it became clear that, in many respects, a strong and effective state was required, albeit playing a much more different (and limited economic) role than before. Again, it was the Chief Economist of the EBRD who, when assessing the achievements and challenges of the first decade of transition, acknowledged that 'Markets, if they are to function well, need a state with the strength to regulate responsibly, tax effectively, and provide its people with basic services, including the rule of law' (Stern 2001).

In the final few years of the socialist regime (especially in Poland and the Soviet Union), the state was weakened. This was further exacerbated by war and internal conflict in many former socialist countries and most especially in the Balkans and Caucasus States. With the onset of transition, the state was weakened even further, manifesting itself in declining revenues, the rise of the mafia and the ability of vested interest groups to capture aspects of public policy, i.e. the phenomenon of state capture. Although much destatisation was required and was considered welfare enhancing, these other phenomena were neither intended nor desirable. One difficulty was how to establish an effective administrative state capacity – the quality of public administration in many TEs was very low – while, at the same time, preventing predatory government action: short of revenues, state officials in many CIS countries predate on the non-privileged new private sector SMEs. There was a need to recognise that although the state was less required in many cases (e.g. subsidies from profit- to loss-making firms, foreign trade monopolies setting prices, extensive state ownership), other roles for the state were required (e.g. policing competition policy, supporting SME development, implementing counter-cyclical macro policy, ensuring social protection). As we know from international experience, both now and in the past, it is a difficult task to achieve the right balance between a state that is, on the one hand, strong and competent and, on the other hand, constrained and non-predatory.

With respect to government changes, reform of the organisation of government is important. Indeed, it is probably the key reform in the transformation from plan to market. Incentives that local government officials face, the design of intergovernmental fiscal relations, the meritocracy (and otherwise) of the bureaucracy, etc. are all examples of important government reforms. For reforms to work, the state must have the administrative capacity to implement policy changes, to oppose vested interest groups from capturing the policymaking process, and to have the legitimacy and support of the public.[12]

In sum, markets (i.e. spontaneous market forces) and states (i.e. state guidance and planning) are not mutually exclusive. In the context of TEs, although it was both inevitable and desirable that the market's role would increase while the role of the state would decline, excessive moves in either direction can be costly. When writing about the importance of time and state guidance in transition, and specifically in Russia, Nobel Laureate Kenneth Arrow (2001) concluded, 'Although the role of government in directing economic activity in a healthy economy is limited, transition does require guidance. The only source of general guidance for the economy is the state, and there is no denying that appropriate policy and leadership could considerably smooth transition.'[13] Although the private sector in many TEs is now bigger in size (measured as a percentage of GDP) than the private sector in many well-established Western European countries, there is a recognition that the public sector, and the government's role, either in the case of macro policy, support of SMEs, income and wealth redistribution, are required. For instance, although the creation of a social safety net was part of the early reform agenda, it was not sufficient given the enormous dislocation and social upheaval of the first transition decade. The state, newly established in many countries within the CIS, had an important role in protecting the most vulnerable groups in society and cushioning the social impact of transition. With depleting resources, there was a need for better targeting (partly a legacy of the old system when benefits were universal) especially in CIS countries. These former republics of the Soviet Union tended to be the very same countries that were captured the most, by powerful vested interests, both from the *nomenklatura* and from the emerging private sector business elites (among them the oligarchs and FIGs).

Given the enormous disruption during the early years of transition (at least in the former Soviet republics) and the inevitable decline in government, and given the starting point for most socialist countries (where poverty was low and inequality was less than in the West), a rise in poverty and inequality was likely. However, the increase that took place in the 1990s was very large indeed, and may, in modern times, be unprecedented in terms of the short time period involved. Happily, the recovery in output from the mid- to late 1990s onwards did lead to a part-reversal of the trend in poverty rates in most TEs, and in some cases an improvement in income distribution (i.e. a tendency for less inequality) in the countries that had witnessed the largest increases in inequality in the preceding decade. Policies aimed at continued economic growth in conjunction with better targeting of social protection will further improve the poverty and inequality situation. This is vital in order to ensure social cohesion and to improve the legitimacy of governments (and their market reforms) in these newly established states. Unfortunately, in many TEs the human costs of transition did not receive the attention that was required, or deserved. This is one of many challenges still confronting future governments in transition countries, and most especially in many of the CIS countries.

Markets and firms

With respect to the enterprise sector, a number of lessons are worth noting. First, when addressing the issue of enterprise performance and privatisation, the evidence from many transition countries indicates that although ownership is important, without complementary reforms the benefits from privatisation – primarily in the form of improved enterprise performance – have been small (measured as a percentage of GDP) and less than anticipated. Proper corporate governance mechanisms, enterprise restructuring, the hardening of the budget constraint and product market competition are all significant determinants of enterprise performance. Of these, there is some evidence that free entry and competition is of paramount importance. For example, McMillan (1997) claims that 'Perhaps the most important – and most elementary – lesson from the various countries' transitions is the power of competition.' Empirical studies on firms in TEs, including those by Brown and Earle (2000) and Carlin *et al.* (2001) support this claim. In terms of country experiences, entry and competition was certainly emphasised more in China whereas in Russia the focus was more on ownership and privatisation (see below).

As for privatisation itself and contrary to most expectations (where some claimed at the outset of transition that almost any privatisation is better than no privatisation), privatisation outcomes were partly determined by the form or method of privatisation (direct sales, voucher schemes, MEBOs) and whether the privatisation process favoured insiders or outsiders, and/or dispersed or concentrated ownership and/or domestic or foreign investors. Even Åslund, a strong advocate for rapid reforms – including privatisation – accepts that the early results from privatisation were disappointing. Åslund (2002a) writes: 'In the short term, privatisation might not be of vital economic importance for enterprise performance', although he counters by arguing that '[it] certainly is in the long term'.[14] Likewise, fellow supporters of rapid reform Fischer and Sahay conceded that 'the slower more individualised (by firm) Hungarian approach appears to have been more successful than the more rapid Czech voucher system' (Fischer and Sahay 2000).

A related issue is the role of the SME sector. Again at the beginning of transition, the need for start-ups was outweighed by (claims of) the importance of closing down unviable SOEs, enterprise restructuring, changes in ownership and privatisation. Evidence indicates that a vibrant and growing enterprise sector is more likely to come from new SMEs rather than from the privatisation and breakup of existing SOEs. The public policy lesson is that attention to the business environment and, in particular, addressing barriers to entry, competition policy and supports to entrepreneurship and SME development is more likely to generate a dynamic business sector than policies designed solely to restructure and privatise SOEs. Unfortunately, it was the latter policy that dominated the enterprise reform agenda in CEE and FSU countries. According to the World Bank study on the first decade of transition, the optimal policy reform at the enterprise level is a combination, the relative weights depending on country circumstances, of both encouragement of new firms and discipline of older enterprises. It concluded that 'Creating an environment that disciplines old enterprises into releasing assets and labour and encourages new enterprises to absorb those resources and undertake new investment, without tilting the playing field in favour of any particular type of enterprise, is central to economic growth' (World Bank 2002a).

The majority of the new enterprises will be SMEs, and we believe that the state's role with respect to the SME sector is critical, and often misunderstood. In order for the state to create a conducive business environment, it is required to make changes on a number of fronts. On the one hand, it needs to reduce its (arbitrary) interventionist role in the economy. Among other things, this often requires less regulation of business, fewer, simpler and less discretionary forms of taxation, less corruption and fewer bailouts of loss-making firms. On the other hand, the state needs to play a more supportive role in terms of securing private property rights (and providing proper enforcement mechanisms), ensuring a stable and responsible macro environment (that is, stable prices, low interest rates, fiscal prudence), supporting SME development, and policing and enforcing competition policy. There is no consensus on a role for the state in respect of industrial policy, although this is often for firms larger than the average-sized SME.

We can see from this list that it is, with respect to the state–enterprise relationship, not simply a case of reducing the role of the state but, indeed, of reconstructing and transforming the role of the state so that it enhances (as opposed to obstructs or distorts) the market mechanism.

Markets and discipline

We wish to emphasis here the importance and the general applicability (to non-transition countries) of a concept that was most prevalent in the socialist system. János Kornai's soft budget constraint refers to the persistent or recurring expectation of a bailout of loss-making enterprises (Kornai 1980). This incentive problem was inherent in the socialist system when the state would consistently bail out troubled firms. Given that a paternalistic state and public ownership of firms were viewed as reasons for the budget softness in the socialist system (and, thus, less common in the market system where the state is less paternalistic and public ownership is not as prevalent), the expectation was that privatisation, in conjunction with other reforms including new bankruptcy laws, would harden the budget constraint. Unfortunately, during the early years of transition, the soft budget constraint persisted, often in new and different guises, including the unusual (in a market economy) phenomenon of tax and wage arrears.[15]

The lesson learnt from this costly experience is that political will and reductions in budgetary subsidies alone will not harden the budget constraint. Aside from the ownership and legal changes already alluded to, other necessary reforms include greater product market competition, improved enforcement of tax and other contract obligations, reform of government, and more complete banking sector reform. It requires institutional changes in order for the commitment to a no-bailout policy to be credible. Moreover, the soft budget constraint has relevance far beyond transition and loss-making enterprises. Seemingly diverse economic issues such as state bailouts (and the EU state aids to industry debate), fiscal federalism (intergovernmental fiscal relations and subnational borrowing), devising bankruptcy laws and the design of fiscal discipline in monetary unions can all be framed in the context of the soft budget constraint syndrome. The broad lesson here is that the general incentive problem first identified in the socialist system over three decades ago has relevance for various different economic relationships, whether it be between superiors and subordinates, funding organisations and recipients, or government and business (whatever the setting, transition or otherwise).

Markets and Russia

Russia is, by all accounts, a market (or, perhaps more accurately, a quasi-market) economy. The market is the main coordination mechanism with prices for the majority of goods and services determined by market forces of demand and supply. The private sector share of GDP is close to 70 per cent. However, the post-socialist path to the market economy was difficult and, for many, traumatic. Given Russian and Soviet preconditions (rule of men as opposed to rule of law, absence of private property rights, importance of patronage, privileges, personal contacts and political connections, arbitrary and discretionary state power, etc.), transition from plan to market in Russia was inevitably going to be complex and arduous; indeed it was. The interesting question is whether it could have been done any less painfully. What, if any, were the alternatives?[16] We will never know the answer to these questions but what we can do is identify some lessons and policy mistakes of the past two decades. With respect to Russia, the lessons from transition are many and controversial (with no real consensus). Many of the general lessons have been alluded to already in this and previous chapters. From our analysis of transition in Russia (and other CIS countries), the important specific lessons are:

- Politics matters (the 1992 Gaidar government faced many more demanding political constraints than CEE governments of that time).
- Market reforms need to be tailored to local conditions (Russian culture and its peculiarities, in addition to a Soviet legacy, required careful and imaginative decisions by reforming policy makers) and, despite often wrenching circumstances, need to be socially tolerable.

- The significance of macroeconomic stability (the 1992 to 1995 macro environment was not conducive to FDI inflows, private sector SME development and overall was costly in terms of economic growth).
- The danger of an institutional vacuum (the old institutions of state socialism were dismantled and/or disintegrated but for some time were not replaced by the institutions of the market system as reformers almost exclusively focused on market reforms in the belief that institutional reform simply takes too long and that priority given to market reforms would, when completed, create, from the new private owners, a demand for such institutions).
- The importance of effective state capacity (the already weakened state had to confront powerful vested interest groups seeking rents and state capture. Moreover, both now and in the past, there is the additional problem of a serious mistrust of the state and its institutions, whether it is legal, executive, administrative, or otherwise).
- The importance – or absence in the case of Russia – of legitimacy (many policies, particularly later phases of privatisation, were not viewed by the population as legitimate, further undermining public support for market reforms and damaging the long-term prospects of the sort of capitalism characterised by free enterprise and secure private property rights protected by the rule of law).

Markets and China

In our view, the important lessons from the Chinese reforms are not, contrary to some opinions, related to the (gradual, if that is the correct label, as some reforms in China were anything but slow) speed of reform, since we believe speed is not the big issue, or to ownership, as the Chinese record on privatisation has neither, in our view, caused nor prevented (an even more) impressive output growth. The interesting and more relevant reforms in China are as follows:

- change in openness to foreign trade and participation in world markets;
- emphasis on changing incentives (of households, enterprises, subnational governments, local government officials);
- willingness to, and emphasis on, experimentation, bottom-up reforms (despite one-party rule), the evolutionary nature of change;
- decentralisation and competition;
- pragmatism and emphasis, ironically not on ideology but on what works (for economic growth and development).

Concluding remarks

Given the extent of surprises evident during transition (some already alluded to in Chapter 7 and in a more complete list below), one of the most important lessons learnt is the need for the economics profession to show a greater degree of humility. The main surprises, of which the vast majority are negative, include the following (in no particular order and all discussed in previous chapters):

- the collapse in output in the early years of transition;
- the sharp rise in prices, with hyperinflation in many countries;

- the worsening demographics in CIS countries, in the form of falling population numbers (falling fertility and rising mortality) and deteriorating life expectancy for males in the Slavic CIS countries;
- the collapse in state revenues, the weakening of the state and the degree of state capture and rent seeking;
- the rise in corruption, the mafia and the unofficial economy;
- the extent of disorder, disruption and dislocation;
- the number of failed privatisation outcomes, and associated asset stripping and tunnelling;
- the extent of the rise in poverty and inequality in the first decade of transition;
- the persistence of the soft budget constraint, often in the form of payment arrears (to workers, suppliers, utilities, banks, government);
- the overall disappointing economic performance of transition countries (with some notable exceptions). Related to this is the very large cross-country and regional variation in performance and outcomes, most notably the relatively poor performance of Russia as compared with the impressive outcomes achieved in China.

Although they relate primarily to the first decade (and more so to the CIS countries than to the CEE countries), and with a notable improvement thereafter, it still raises questions about the excessive expectations and forecasts made at the start of transition and the need for the economics profession, particularly those who are fortunate enough to find themselves in the position of policy advisers and even policy makers, to learn from the transition experience.

An appropriate way to conclude this chapter and our review of two decades of transition is to quote J.M. Keynes (very much in fashion again, not surprisingly, given recent global economic and financial conditions), who wrote:

> The ideas of economists and political philosophers, both when they are right and when they are wrong, are more important than is commonly understood. Indeed the world is ruled by little else. Practical men, who believe themselves to be quite exempt from any intellectual influence, are usually the slaves of some defunct economist.

> (Keynes 1936)

This claim is as appropriate to the transition economies of the turn of the century as it was to the era that Keynes was commenting on, namely the post-1930s Great Depression. Indeed, it may be another century before economists and economics, both 'good' and 'not-so-good', have the same incredible opportunity to influence public policy and society. But then again, as with reforms, we just do not know, do we? Remember, more humility, less hubris! In a final exercise in humility, let the reader not forget that less than ten years before the Soviet Union collapsed, two of the most distinguished scholars on Russia and the Soviet Union, namely Abram Bergson (of the Harvard Russian Research Centre) and Herbert S. Levine, edited a book entitled *The Soviet Economy: Toward the Year 2000*. Although we now know it to be an unfortunate title (which had as its theme the long-term perspective growth of the Soviet economy), it does reflect the consensus at the time, namely that the Soviet Union, although stagnating, was not, according to the majority of leading experts in the field, in any imminent danger of disintegrating.[17] Of course, by the year 2000, the Soviet Union, not to mention the socialist system, the Soviet bloc and the CMEA, no longer existed. Indeed, by 2010, we have had two decades of transition. Who knows what 2020 will bring us! On that note, we leave the last few words, appropriately, to the playwright, former dissident and politician Vaclav Havel (the last President of Czechoslovakia and the first elected President of the Czech Republic) who, in an address on 4 July 1994 in celebration of American Independence Day, remarked, 'In short, we live in the postmodern world, where everything is possible and almost nothing is certain.'[18]

APPENDIX 1

The crux of the market

We herewith outline the principles underlying capitalistic or market economies. For those readers (most of you) who engage daily in market transactions – buying milk or bread, occasionally a television set or a car, clothes from a retailer, etc. – it may seem unnecessary. However, simply because we engage in an activity does not mean we fully understand why we do so or, indeed, the consequences of the actions we undertake. In addition, having grasped the essentials of the market mechanism it is then easier to understand the mechanism of central planning – the engine – of a command economy, and the foundations of Soviet-style communism. Inevitably in what follows we generalise. However, there are many excellent textbooks on introductory economics from which the reader can select if he or she requires additional details. We start with a famous quote from Adam Smith, regarded by many as the founder of modern economics:

> every individual necessarily labours to render the annual revenue of the society as great as he can. He generally, indeed, neither intends to promote the public interest, nor knows how much he is promoting it. By preferring the support of domestic to that of foreign industry, he intends only his own security; and by directing that industry in such a manner as its produce may be of the greatest value, he intends only his own gain, and he is in this, as in many other cases, led by an *invisible hand* to promote an end which was no part of his intention. Nor is it always the worse for the society that it was no part of it. By pursuing his own interest he frequently promotes that of the society more effectually than when he really intends to promote it. I have never known much good done by those who affected to trade for the public good. [emphasis added]

In short, individuals act in their own self-interest but in doing so they promote the welfare of all. Again, quoting Smith (1776):

> It is not from the benevolence of the butcher, the brewer or the baker, that we expect our dinner, but from their regard to their own self interest. We address ourselves, not to their humanity but to their self-love, and never talk to them of our own necessities but of their advantages.

While later writers such as Marx saw uncoordinated chaos with periodic crises, Smith saw a self-correcting mechanism that needed as little government intervention as possible. In the same way that a thermostat in a room detects changes in temperature and regulates the central heating accordingly, the thermostat of a market economy is the *price mechanism*. As long as prices are freely determined by the supply and demand of a particular good or service, the market will respond to the desires, needs and whims even of the consumer.

Let us suppose that consumers' demand for a particular product changes. For example, as the price of oil climbed to ever new heights through the early part of the new century, due, in part, to economic expansion in emerging markets, this led to higher gasoline prices at the pumps for American motorists.[1] This new high price for gasoline in America (and elsewhere of course) has several effects. In the short run the tendency is for consumers to cut back on gasoline consumption. In the longer term consumers switch to cars with lower fuel consumption; demand for 'gas guzzlers' drops, prices for these cars falls also but ultimately if the price needed to clear the market is so low as to make the production of these high-fuel-use cars unprofitable, production will be curtailed at best or completely stopped.

Manufacturers of fuel-efficient cars will see demand for their product rise. The initial excess of demand over supply will allow them to raise prices until they can respond in the longer term with an increase in the supply of these types of vehicles. Labour which was engaged in the manufacture of the 'gas guzzlers' will not be in demand to the same extent and some if not most will be made redundant. Some of this labour, if it is geographically mobile enough, may find employment in the expanding sector of the car industry that makes fuel-efficient cars. It would be up to the receiving car firms of this laid-off labour to determine whether they had the right skills or could be trained up in good time to be used productively within the firms making fuel-efficient cars. Other segments of this laid-off labour may find (eventually) alternative sources of employment in other industries.

What we have described above is nothing less than the reorganisation of an industry brought about by the change in price of, first, oil and then ultimately of different types of cars. Through prices being either sustainable or not (what economists call being in or out of equilibrium) this economic butterfly effect has rippled through the markets to eventually bring a new equilibrium. No one has coordinated the restructuring of the industry; the interaction of consumers with producers has done that. Each of them has reacted to the market situation in their own self-interest: the consumer switches to more fuel-efficient cars and manufacturers, seeing that prices for gas guzzlers are unsustainable, either adapt by switching production to more fuel-efficient cars or they go bust.

Diagrammatically we have Figure A1.1 which shows how various markets interact with one another. At first glance the diagram seems complicated. It would be tempting to omit it from the book. However, it serves two purposes. First, it explains – complicated or not – how indeed a market and industries adjust when the price of a commodity changes, admittedly in a major way; but second, and more importantly, we are trying to explain how such a restructuring occurs, by and large, *without* government or any other purposeful intervention. That is not to say that governments do not step in to ameliorate the worst excesses of market outcomes. (Mass unemployment, for example, or, if they feel it appropriate, they sometimes lend a helping hand if they believe that the firm in difficulties is 'sound' but just needs time to restructure.) True, our example has not introduced the oil cartel OPEC but over the last period (the early part of this new century) their impact has been limited given, *inter alia*, the economic expansion of the BRIC economies – Brazil, Russia, India and especially China, dragging much of South East Asia up with it.

Now imagine a world with no markets, or, at least, no oil market, no gasoline market and no market for cars. All of these assets are controlled and owned by a new world government. Anyway, the new world government must somehow estimate demand for oil in different parts of the world – what will the needs for oil of developing countries be? What of motorists in all parts of the world, what will their demand for gasoline be if the price is increased by 10 per cent or 20 per cent? How will this affect the demand for fuel-inefficient and fuel-efficient cars? What instructions should they issue to manufacturers of such cars? Cut back production of fuel-inefficient cars? Yes, but by how much? 5 per cent, 10 per cent or what? Likewise for fuel-efficient cars; by how much should their production be expanded? And then there is the labour that will be needed to build such vehicles; can it simply be transferred from the factories which made the fuel-inefficient cars to new factories which will make the fuel-efficient cars? Is it of the right type? That is, suitably trained and flexible to simply be transferred over? Or will additional labour be required? And if additional labour is required how will that impact upon other industries which may need similar types of semi-skilled labour? And we haven't even started on how the capital needed for the production of these new fuel-efficient cars will be found and again its impact on demand for capital in other industries. Likewise we haven't considered how oil supply could be expanded in the longer term.

In private markets (even with or without OPEC) profit was the incentive and new oil reserves would be opened up if it was felt to be profitable based on the current *and* the expected market price of oil over the lifetime of the investment.

However, for non-market economies, what now? On what basis should a 'marginal field' (one barely profitable under markets and profit motivation) be developed? What is the yardstick to determine whether society's resources are being used the most effectively if we no longer use the profit motive or market prices to determine whether production goes ahead or not?

Someone, somewhere (and quickly) must make his or her mind up to all of these questions and a million more not even yet touched on before society's resources can be utilised. Put in this perspective Figure A1.1 becomes a lot more straightforward. By and large, if markets are operating using price signals and the profit motive, what should be produced, where it should be produced, in what quantities, and when it should be produced, and for whom, will be decided without having to resort to all of the above questions. Individuals who legally own the resources which are capable of enhancing society's wealth will take decisions guided by whether any such course of action will be profitable and that will in large part be determined by the price they can expect in the market for their product or service. In turn that price will be determined by whether consumers find the product or service on sale gives them any satisfaction or gratification (what economists call utility) and so makes it worth buying.

In one sense we have simplified the market mechanism shown in Figure A1.1 While resource allocations are decided ultimately in the unconscious manner in which Figure A1.1 is displayed, what is not displayed are the institutions that underpin the apparent unconscious movement of resources throughout a market-based system.

What do we mean by institutions? At first glance we might be thinking of such organisations as trade or unions employers' organisations. In Britain, the Confederation of British Industry, the Church (of whatever denomination) within a community, the London Stock Exchange, and the Russell Group of leading Universities within the United Kingdom would be some examples that spring to mind. One ultimate institution is, of course, government whether at national or local level.

In giving the above examples of organisations it would be easy to confuse them with the term 'institutions'. Strictly speaking, institutions are the rules by which individuals and social bodies conduct their interactions. As such the existing legal system of laws – be that on

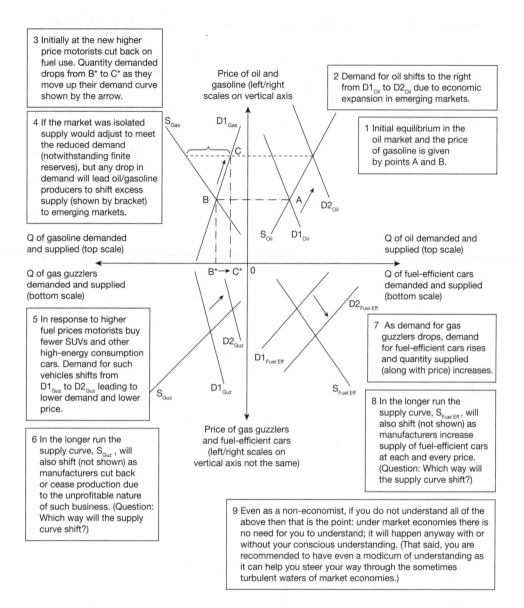

3 Initially at the new higher price motorists cut back on fuel use. Quantity demanded drops from B* to C* as they move up their demand curve shown by the arrow.

4 If the market was isolated supply would adjust to meet the reduced demand (notwithstanding finite reserves), but any drop in demand will lead oil/gasoline producers to shift excess supply (shown by bracket) to emerging markets.

Price of oil and gasoline (left/right scales on vertical axis)

2 Demand for oil shifts to the right from $D1_{Oil}$ to $D2_{Oil}$ due to economic expansion in emerging markets.

1 Initial equilibrium in the oil market and the price of gasoline is given by points A and B.

Q of gasoline demanded and supplied (top scale)

Q of oil demanded and supplied (top scale)

Q of gas guzzlers demanded and supplied (bottom scale)

Q of fuel-efficient cars demanded and supplied (bottom scale)

5 In response to higher fuel prices motorists buy fewer SUVs and other high-energy consumption cars. Demand for such vehicles shifts from $D1_{Guz}$ to $D2_{Guz}$ leading to lower demand and lower price.

7 As demand for gas guzzlers drops, demand for fuel-efficient cars rises and quantity supplied (along with price) increases.

8 In the longer run the supply curve, $S_{Fuel\ Eff}$, will also shift (not shown) as manufacturers increase supply of fuel-efficient cars at each and every price. (Question: Which way will the supply curve shift?)

6 In the longer run the supply curve, S_{Guz}, will also shift (not shown) as manufacturers cut back or cease production due to the unprofitable nature of such business. (Question: Which way will the supply curve shift?)

Price of gas guzzlers and fuel-efficient cars (left/right scales on vertical axis not the same)

9 Even as a non-economist, if you do not understand all of the above then that is the point: under market economies there is no need for you to understand; it will happen anyway with or without your conscious understanding. (That said, you are recommended to have even a modicum of understanding as it can help you steer your way through the sometimes turbulent waters of market economies.)

Figure A1.1 The invisible hand or how the market adjusts when the world price of oil increases.

enforcing property rights in a market system or limited liability of a business owner in the event of bankruptcy (to give two examples) – may be described as institutions. These would be the formal rules. However, the custom and practice of how one conducts business or how one interacts culturally, built up over many years (what might be called informal social norms) which may not be encoded in formal law would also be another part of what we term 'institutions'. (Think of how business might be conducted in, say, the People's Republic of China where *guanxi* is very important, and the United States of America where business can be conducted with total strangers knowing that the law is always there in the background to assist in the enforcement of business contracts.)

Chapter 9 on the situation with the transition from plan to market in both the Russian Federation and within the People's Republic of China, we examined this issue of institutions. The above example of institutional conflict, as will be seen, is very pertinent in particular to the Russian transition path where some have argued that formal rules of the game were 'transplanted' from the West to Russian soil . . . without due preparation of the soil.

Continuing with our example of the car industry, then, this also provides an example of how institutions, and one in particular, namely the United States government, has intervened to 'smooth out' the worst excesses of market adjustment. A bailout package for the big three car makers in the US of approximately $17 billion was put forward towards the end of 2008 and at the start of 2009 subject to the three US car firms bringing forward comprehensive plans for restructuring.[2] This is not uncontroversial. Proponents of a rescue package (of whatever sort eventually emerges) argue that if it is fine to rescue the financial system with hundreds (not tens) of billions of dollars then why not the 'real economy'.

'Pure marketeers' counter that the crisis with the US car manufacturers, or at least some of them, has not come about through the credit crunch but ultimately because they could not adapt in the face of competition from more low-cost and more fuel-efficient manufacturers such as Toyota and Honda cars. As such the law of the market should prevail – the less efficient should go to the wall and the strongest should take over. In other words government in general should keep at arms' length from the market.[3]

What side is correct is not really the purpose of this appendix or, indeed, this book. However, notice that the debate is over the degree of government intervention. Under a centrally planned economy the debate – if there was one – would be over the degree of allowing private markets to operate at all.

Another simplification which has been introduced is the lack of market failures. This concerns the question of externalities. Externalities, in short, are a form of market failure; failure in the sense that markets have not found the optimal level of output of a good or service from the point of view of *society*. Note that such output may be optimal from the viewpoint of the economic agent producing the good or service but not of society. This could be because the market is producing too much of a good or too little of a good and as such may be detracting from the optimal welfare of society as a whole.

The classic example is the steel mill discharging waste products into the nearby river which when it flows downstream kills fish which fishermen depend on for their livelihood. The steel mill owners have not *internalised* the cost they impose on the fishermen; if they had factored in this extra cost then their output decisions would have led them to reduce their output, since the increased cost (of compensating the fishermen) makes the previous production levels (and consequent pollution) less profitable. The individual welfare of the owners of the steel mill is maximised by ignoring this negative externality of pollution but the welfare of society as a whole which includes the fishermen is reduced.

It is worth quoting Nobel Laureate Joseph Stiglitz at length for his views on externalities:

> Adam Smith, the father of modern economics, is often cited as arguing for the 'invisible hand' and free markets: firms, in the pursuit of profits, are led, as if by an invisible hand, to do what is best for the world. But unlike his followers, Adam Smith was aware of some of the limitations of free markets, and research since then has further clarified why free markets, by themselves, often do not lead to what is best.

As I put it in my new book, *Making Globalization Work*, the reason that the invisible hand often seems invisible is that it is often not there.

Whenever there are 'externalities' – where the actions of an individual have impacts on others for which they do not pay or for which they are not compensated – markets will not work well. Some of the important instances have been long understood – environmental externalities. Markets, by themselves, will produce too much pollution. Markets, by themselves, will also produce too little basic research. (Remember, the government was responsible for financing most of the important scientific breakthroughs, including the internet and the first telegraph line, and most of the advances in bio-tech.)

But recent research has shown that these externalities are pervasive, whenever there is imperfect information or imperfect risk markets – that is always.

Government plays an important role in banking and securities regulation, and a host of other areas: some regulation is required to make markets work. Government is needed, almost all would agree, as a minimum to enforce contracts and property rights.[4]

Having given that extensive caveat as regards how markets can sometimes fail, it is worth stressing that there was not one non-market economy under (any type of) communism which approached the level of development and sophistication shown by the advanced industrialised countries of Western Europe, North America and Japan in the post-war period. Everything in life is relative, and relatively speaking market economies were more successful than non-market economies; hence the reason, ultimately, why the USSR lost the Cold War and the People's Republic of China, despite its communist political system, has headed down a market road.[5]

That said, why mention the issue of institutions and externalities at all? For the former, the better to understand in the body of the text, and especially Chapter 9, what may have gone wrong in the transition from plan to market (by some interpretations) in many former centrally planned economies, the principal one being the Soviet Union.

It is still an area of heated debate; however, the method of transforming the Soviet Union's economy from plan to market involved a Big Bang approach, i.e. the sudden liberalisation of the majority of state-controlled prices, a fast privatisation route of state industries, and macroeconomic stabilisation policies (all discussed in more detail in Chapter 5). It is uncontroversial to say that the majority of the economics profession was caught unawares by the precipitous drop in output when this 'shock therapy' was applied. One school of thought (there are counterposing views) contends that it was the failure to recognise the need for institutions and to prepare the ground for them that led to such an output collapse. Market relations, so the argument goes, do not work in a vacuum but need the bedrock of institutions to ensure ultimately their smooth functioning. Alternative explanations for this output drop are discussed in Chapter 7.

APPENDIX 2

Transition countries vs. the rest of the world

Using the 2009 IMF *World Economic Outlook* database, here we report data (for GDP growth, inflation and investment) for different regions of the world, including the transition countries. It again illustrates the trends in transition countries already alluded to with respect to output, prices and investment but, in addition, it shows the relative position of transition countries vis-à-vis other regions (based on geography and income/development) of the world. It is evident that TEs fared badly (with CIS countries doing worse than CEE countries) in the first decade of transition, even against other emerging and developing countries. As regards output, whereas the group of CEE countries (14 in total, including the Baltic States) – embarking on transition in 1989/1990 (1992 for the Baltics) – suffered, on average, three years of negative growth (that is, 1990–1992), the CIS countries (13 in total, including Mongolia) – with transition beginning in 1992 – witnessed, on average, seven years of economic decline (1991–1996 and 1998). Not even the continent of Africa fared as badly in the 1990s. Fortunately, what is also clear from the data is the extent of the recovery in transition countries throughout the second decade of transition (or, at least up until the global crisis of 2007–2009). Here the CIS countries, led by the rebound in Russia, outperformed not only the CEE countries but all other country groupings, with the exception of China. This pick-up in economic activity was associated with an improvement in the business climate in the TEs, and a rise in investment (from a low, relative to GDP, of 16 per cent in 1999 and 20 per cent in 1994, for CIS and CEE countries respectively), as evident from Table A2.1.

With respect to inflation, the outcome and performance of TEs is equally poor, relative to the other country groupings. Since 1992, the average yearly inflation rate for both CIS and CEE countries has exceeded the annual average inflation rate for any other group of countries (excluding Emerging and Developing Economies as this group includes CIS and CEE countries). Indeed, the average annual inflation rate in both the CIS and CEE groups of countries did not fall below 20 per cent (with one exception; that is, 1997 for CIS countries) until the year 2002: it actually exceeded 100 per cent in both 1990 and 1992 in the CEE countries, and, in the four-year period 1992 to 1995 in the CIS countries. Again, the record, as regards inflation, was remarkably better in the second decade, despite impressive levels of economic growth across the region. Inflation rates remained moderate until the late 2000s when a number of transition countries, both CEE and CIS countries, began to witness a rise in inflation rates, reflecting in some cases overheated economies fuelled by short-term inflows, rising property and asset prices and mounting levels of debt (see Table 7.3 for the 2008 inflation rates for individual TEs).[1]

Table A2.1 Two decades for the transition countries vs. the rest of the world

	1989	1990	1991	1992	1993	1994	1995	1996	1997	1998	1999	2000	2001	2002	2003	2004	2005	2006	2007	2008
GDP constant prices, annual percentage change																				
CIS + Mongolia	2.8	1.4	–63	–13.6	–9.7	–14.1	–5.5	–3.7	1.4	–3.6	5.4	9.1	6.1	5.2	7.8	8.2	6.7	8.4	8.6	5.5
CEE	0.5	–0.8	–6.4	–1.0	2.9	0.0	6.0	5.1	5.0	3.2	0.5	5.3	0.0	4.4	4.9	7.3	6.0	6.6	5.4	2.9
Russia	–	–	–5	–14.5	–8.7	–12.7	–4.1	–3.6	1.4	–5.3	6.4	10	5.1	4.7	7.3	7.2	6.4	7.7	8.1	5.6
China	4.1	3.8	9.2	14.2	14.0	13.1	10.9	10.0	9.3	7.8	7.6	8.4	8.3	9.1	10.0	10.1	10.4	11.6	13.0	9.0
Advanced Economies	4.0	3.0	1.3	2.1	1.4	3.4	2.9	3.0	3.5	2.5	3.5	4.0	1.2	1.6	1.9	3.2	2.6	3.0	2.7	0.9
World	3.7	2.9	1.5	2.0	2.0	3.4	3.3	3.7	4.0	2.5	3.5	4.7	2.2	2.8	3.6	4.9	4.5	5.1	5.2	3.2
European Union	3.5	2.4	0.7	0.7	–0.2	2.9	3.0	2.0	2.8	3.0	3.0	4.0	2.1	1.4	1.5	2.6	2.2	3.4	3.1	1.1
Newly Industrialised Asian Countries	6.8	7.4	8.1	6.5	6.8	8.1.	7.4	6.5	5.6	2.7	7.3	7.7	1.2	5.6	3.1	5.9	4.7	5.6	5.7	1.6
Emerging and Developing Economies	3.3	2.8	1.7	1.8	3.1	3.3	4.0	5.1	5.0	2.5	3.6	6.0	3.8	4.8	6.3	7.5	7.1	8.0	8.3	6.1
Africa	3.4	2.7	0.7	–0.8	0.5	2.4	2.8	5.8	3.3	3.3	2.7	3.5	4.9	6.5	5.5	6.7	5.8	6.1	6.2	5.2
Asean-5	8.6	7.7	6.4	6.5	7.1	7.8	8.4	7.5	3.9	–8.4	3.2	6.0	2.8	5.1	5.8	6.1	5.5	5.7	6.3	4.9
Investment, per cent of GDP																				
CIS + Mongolia	–	–	–	31	20	25	25	23	21	17	16	19	22	20	21	21	21	22	25	26
CEE	28	28	26	20	22	20	22	22	23	23	21	23	20	20	20	22	21	24	25	25
Russia	–	–	–	–	–	–	–	–	–	–	–	–	–	–	–	–	–	–	–	–
China	–	–	–	–	–	–	–	–	–	–	–	–	–	–	–	–	–	–	–	–
Advanced Economies	24	24	23	22	22	22	22	22	22	22	22	22	21	20	20	21	21	21	21	21
World	–	–	–	22	22	22	22	22	22	23	22	23	22	21	21	22	23	23	24	24
European Union	24	23	22	21	19	20	20	20	20	21	21	21	20	20	20	20	20	21	22	22
Newly Industrialised Asian Countries	22	29	29	30	33	30	31	27	31	43	29	28	25	25	25	26	26	26	26	27
Emerging and Developing Economies	–	–	–	25	25	25	26	25	26	25	24	24	24	25	26	27	27	28	30	31

(Continued)

Table A2.1 Continued

	1989	1990	1991	1992	1993	1994	1995	1996	1997	1998	1999	2000	2001	2002	2003	2004	2005	2006	2007	2008
Africa	19	20	20	20	19	20	20	19	19	21	21	20	21	22	22	23	22	23	25	25
Asean-5	–	–	–	–	–	–	–	–	–	–	–	–	–	–	–	–	–	–	–	–
Inflation, average consumer prices, annual																				
CIS + Mongolia	2	5	92	1530	1206	455	228	53	18	25	72	24	20	14	12	10	12	9	10	16
CEE	87	139	93	101	88	73	49	45	64	41	30	28	24	19	11	7	6	6	6	8
Russia	–	–	93	1526	875	308	197	48	15	28	86	21	21	16	14	11	13	10	9	14
China	18	3	3	6	15	24	17	8	3	–1	–1	0.4	1	–1	1	4	2	1	5	6
Advanced Economies	6	6	5	4	3	3	3	2	2	2	1	2	2	2	2	2	2	2	2	3
World	24	26	22	37	35	28	15	9	6	6	5	5	4	4	4	4	4	4	4	6
European Union	18	29	16	15	11	7	5	5	10	3	2	3	3	3	2	2	2	2	2	4
Newly Industrialised Asian Countries	6	7	7	6	5	6	5	4	3	4	0	1	2	1	1	2	2	2	2	4
Emerging and Developing Economies	66	74	59	128	119	90	40	21	13	13	13	8	8	7	7	6	6	5	6	9
Africa	19	14	27	35	34	42	36	32	13	9	11	12	11	9	9	7	7	6	6	10
Asean-5	11	5	13	8	7	7	8	6	5	25	9	2	6	6	4	5	7	8	4	9

Source: IMF World Economic Outlook Database (2009).

CIS + Mongolia (13) = Armenia, Azerbaijan, Belarus, Georgia, Kazakhastan, Kyrgyzstan, Moldova, Mongolia, Russia, Tajikistan, Turkmenistan, Ukraine, Uzbekistan
CEE (14) = Albania, Bosnia and Herzegovina, Bulgaria, Croatia, Estonia, FYR Macdonia, Hungary, Latvia, Lithuania, Montenegro, Poland, Romania, Serbia, Turkey
Advanced Economies (33), including Czech Republic, Slovak Republic and Slovenia
World (182)
European Union (27), including the 10 TEs accession countries
Newly Industrialised Asian Countries (4) = Hong Kong, Korea, Singapore, Taiwan
Emerging and Developing Economies (149) including China, Mongolia, Vietnam, all CIS countries and most of the CEE countries
Africa (50)
Asean-5 = Indonesia, Malaysia, Philippines, Thailand, Vietnam

APPENDIX 3

World Bank Corruption Index

The World Bank Corruption Index measures perceptions of the extent to which public power is exercised for private gain, including petty and grand forms of corruption, as well as 'capture' of the states by elites and private interests. The index is calculated based on responses given by a large number of firm, household and expert (from private sector, NGOs and public sector) survey respondents. As with other WGI, the Corruption Index is based on subjective or perceptions-based data reflecting the views of the aforementioned stakeholders. The index ranges from –2.5 to 2.5 with higher values corresponding to better governance outcomes. The index for 1996 to 2008, again for four-year intervals, is given in Table A3.1.

Somewhat similar trends to the CPI, in terms of regional differences and intra-group differences, are found herein. In 1996, the first year of the World Bank Corruption Index, corruption levels in TEs are relatively high. Of all the CEE/FSU countries, only the Visegrád-4 (the Czech and Slovak Republics, Hungary and Poland) and Slovenia had a corruption index that was greater than zero (implying less corruption). Of the others, eight countries had a corruption index of –1 or lower (implying more corruption). Three transition countries, namely Georgia, Tajikistan and Turkmenistan, were ranked in the bottom 5 per cent (with only the war-torn African countries of Dem. Rep. of Congo, Liberia, Sierra Leone and Somalia below them) in terms of corruption, i.e. these were among the most corrupt countries in the world, according to the World Bank. We know from elsewhere that corruption levels increased with the disintegration of the Soviet system and continued to rise until the mid-1990s when levels in some TEs, predominantly CIS countries, were comparable to levels found in the most corrupt countries in the world. As for changes over time since the mid-1990s, countries that showed much improvement in tackling corruption during the transition period include Bulgaria, Croatia, Estonia, Georgia, FYR Macedonia, Latvia and Serbia, whereas for some others, namely the Slavic countries and Central Asian states, little or no improvement is evident. Indeed, the majority of CIS countries, in addition to the East Asian countries, still face enormous challenges in trying to confront corruption at all levels of government and society. On a more positive note, and using the WGI over the period 1998 to 2008, 13 countries witnessed significant changes in corruption, as measured by the Corruption Index. Of these 13, four countries – all non-transition – experienced an increase, with the remaining nine witnessing a significant decrease in corruption. Of those nine, four (that is, Albania, Estonia, Georgia and Serbia) were transition countries.

Table A3.1 World Bank Corruption Index, 1996–2008

Country	1996	2000	2004	2008
CEB				
Czech Republic	0.63 (76)	0.3 (64)	0.4 (67)	0.37 (67)
Estonia	0.0 (56)	0.66 (74)	1.0 (83)	0.94 (79)
Hungary	0.66 (77)	0.77 (77)	0.75 (75)	0.55 (72)
Latvia	–0.6 (28)	0.11 (59)	0.27 (63)	0.29 (65)
Lithuania	–0.1 (52)	0.42 (67)	0.39 (67)	0.18 (63)
Poland	0.44 (72)	0.56 (70)	0.21 (61)	0.38 (68)
Slovak Republic	0.39 (70)	0.31 (64)	0.49 (70)	0.43 (69)
Slovenia	1.1 (84)	0.85 (80)	1.07 (83)	0.95 (80)
SEE				
Albania	0.03 (59)	–0.8 (23)	–0.75 (26)	–0.45 (39)
Bosnia and Herzegovina	–0.3 (46)	–0.6 (33)	–0.34 (45)	–0.32 (46)
Bulgaria	–0.8 (24)	–0.1 (53)	0.19 (60)	–0.17 (52)
Croatia	–0.6 (31)	0.07 (57)	0.21 (60)	0.12 (62)
FYR Macedonia	–1.1 (12)	–0.5 (37)	–0.44 (43)	–0.11 (55)
Romania	–0.2 (47)	–0.3 (46)	–0.25 (49)	–0.06 (57)
Serbia and Montenegro	–1.0 (18)	–1.1 (9)	–0.45 (42)	–0.16 (53) / –0.28 (48)
CIS				
Armenia	–0.8 (24)	–0.8 (26)	–0.7 (29)	–0.54 (35)
Azerbaijan	–1.1 (11)	–1.1 (9)	–1.11 (12)	–1.00 (14)
Belarus	–1.0 (17)	–0.6 (34)	–1.02 (14)	–0.79 (24)
Georgia	–1.3 (5)	–0.9 (17)	–0.62 (31)	–0.23 (51)
Kazakhstan	–0.9 (20)	–1.0 (16)	–1.13 (11)	–0.95 (16)
Kyrgyzstan	–0.7 (26)	–0.8 (25)	–0.99 (16)	–1.06 (13)
Moldova	–0.3 (46)	–0.7 (29)	–1.01 (15)	–0.64 (31)
Russia	–0.8 (23)	–1.0 (14)	–0.75 (26)	–0.98 (15)
Tajikistan	–1.3 (4)	–1.2 (7)	–1.18 (10)	–0.99 (14)
Turkmenistan	–1.7 (2)	–1.1 (10)	–1.39 (4)	–1.34 (5)
Ukraine	–0.8 (25)	–1.0 (12)	–0.89 (20)	–0.72 (28)
Uzbekistan	–1.0 (16)	–0.9 (19)	–1.15 (11)	–1.08 (11)
East Asia				
China	–0.1 (54)	–0.2 (48)	–0.58 (34)	–0.44 (41)
Mongolia	0.37 (69)	–0.3 (45)	–0.38 (44)	–0.62 (32)
Vietnam	–0.6 (32)	–0.8 (27)	–0.8 (23)	–0.76 (25)
Others				
Afghanistan	–	–1.9 (0)	–1.51 (2)	–1.64 (1)
Finland	2.29 (100)	2.32 (100)	2.43 (100)	2.34 (100)
Myanmar	–1.2 (6)	–1.4 (4)	–1.69 (0)	–1.69 (1)
United Kingdom	2.19 (96)	2.1 (97)	1.95 (94)	1.77 (93)
USA	1.72 (92)	1.73 (93)	1.73 (93)	1.55 (92)

Source: World Bank Governance Indicators (www.govindicators.org).

APPENDIX 4

Tackling poverty and income inequality

1 Building effective national institutions

- Increasing political accountability;
- Strengthening institutional restraints within the state;
- Strengthening civil society participation and media oversight;
- Creating a competitive private sector;
- Reforming the public sector.

2 Key Policy measures to promote poverty-reducing growth (Table A4.1).

Table A4.1 Tackling poverty and income inequality

(a) Key policy measures to promote poverty-reducing growth

Type of country	Policies to improve the competitive environment	Policies to strengthen fiscal reforms	Policies to enhance social development
Advanced market reformers	Develop adequate legal and regulatory frameworks for infrastructure and utility privatisation. Promote entry and exit. Improve competition policies. Support financial sector development. Promote export competition Improve labour market policies.	Reduce contingent fiscal liabilities. Improve the system of intergovernmental finance. Strengthen public administration.	Reform pensions. Introduce social programmes to upgrade workers' skills. Improve delivery of education services.
Less advanced market reformers	Introduce hard budget constraints. Remove barriers to entry and exit and enhance competition policies. Reduce transaction costs for small businesses. Improve labour market policies sector. Promote incentives for export growth.	Reduce deficits through appropriate expenditure cuts and revenue increases. Re-orient public expenditures towards human and physical capital investments. Manage external borrowings carefully. Improve systems for	Consolidate social assistance. Improve poverty targeting and cost-effectiveness of social assistance services. Improve quality and cost-effectiveness of education services.

Undertake agriculture land   budget and public
reforms.   expenditure
Liberalise agriculture   management.
marketing and pricing.
Introduce greater efficiency
in the use of irrigation.

(b) Policy measures to reduce inequality, by subregion

Policy	CEE and the Baltics	Southern Europe and the Balkans	CIS	Caucasus and Central Asia
Building transparent and efficient product markets	Fairly advanced but taxes and regulation burdensome for new firms.	More progress needed. Licensing, regulations, and anticompetitive practices hamper expansion of private firms.	High priority. Anti-competitive practices, licensing, regulations, and corruption hamper entry and expansion of new private firms.	High priority. Anti-competitive practices, licensing, regulations, and corruption hamper entry and expansion of new private firms.
Expanding financial markets	Shallow by OECD and East Asia standards, but comparable to Latin America and the Caribbean. New firms and especially small enterprises still face difficulties accessing long-term finance.	Very shallow credit markets; private/small firms and SOEs have differential access.	Very shallow credit markets; unequal access for private/small firms and SOEs; connections are important.	Very shallow credit markets; unequal access; small firms face problems financing even working capital.
Raising the incomes of those at the bottom through labour market reforms	Focus on raising incomes of low-skilled workers while maintaining wage flexibility. Anti-discrimination policies.	Focus on raising incomes of low-skilled workers while maintaining wage flexibility. Anti-discrimination policies.	Wage inequality high. Product markets and governance are key. Skills upgrading for poorest important in medium term.	Wage inequality high. Product markets and governance are key. Skills upgrading for poorest important in medium term.
Using distributive fiscal policy	Large scope for using fiscal policy. Focus on improving targeting of transfers. Policies to foster accumulation of public capital and education in poorest regions (within countries).	Scope to improve taxation and tax compliance, as well as targeting of transfers. Restoring fiscal balance is key. Possible scope for regional policies.	Scope to improve tax compliance and budget execution (arrears). Improve targeting of transfers. Possible scope for regional policies.	Priority is improving tax compliance, expenditure prioritisation, and budget execution. Limited role for transfers in short to medium term (too poor).

Source: World Bank (2000).

APPENDIX 5

Hard budget constraint (HBC) and enterprise restructuring in Romania[1]

In spring 2000, several firms in Romania were shortlisted for a HBC case study on the basis of their financial position, i.e. highly indebted, loss-making firms are strong candidates for 'budget softness'. A list of unprofitable firms was drawn up. Roman S.A. and Tractorul UTB S.A. were chosen from the list on the basis of a number of criteria. First, both firms were in a poor financial position. Sales were falling and losses were quickly mounting up. Second, both firms employed a large workforce. This can strengthen a firm's bargaining position if it wishes to seek financial or state aid. Third, both firms had overdue tax liabilities to the state and have had debt rescheduled in the past.

We begin our case study with a description of the geographical region where Roman and Tractorul are located.

Brasov region

Brasov is Romania's second-largest city and is located in the central part of Romania. The county accounts for 2.3 per cent of the whole surface of Romania and, with a population of 636,434 inhabitants in 1997, accounts for 2.8 per cent of the country's population. The city (municipality) of Brasov in 1997 had a population of 317,772. Table A5.1 shows a selected number of indicators for Brasov county, as compared to Romania as a whole.

Apart from the government, the biggest single employers in the Brasov region in 1999 were Roman S.A. with 10,600 employees, Tractorul S.A. with 10,112 employees and Rulmentul S.A. Between them, they accounted for a very large percentage of total employment in the region. All three firms paid wages above the average wage level in Brasov. Other important firms in Brasov include Hidromecanica and IAR Ghimbav. Hidromecanica Brasov, a manufacturer of pumps, was one of the 64 companies (along with Roman and Tractorul) shortlisted for privatisation under the World Bank PSAL (Private Sector Adjustment Loan) programme. IAR Ghimbav was the Romanian airplane and helicopter manufacturer that was embroiled in the Bell Helicopters affair. The proposed sale of IAR Ghimbav to Bell Helicopters fell through when the Romanian government refused to buy the military helicopters from Bell.

The task of enterprise restructuring in transition countries is not easy. Romania is no exception. Despite the economic benefits that accrue from restructuring the enterprise sector, policy makers are well aware of the costly social and political consequences that are associated with restructuring. Brasov with its truck- and tractor-making factories is a good example. With its history of strikes and demonstrations by its workforce, combined with a small number of very large employers, in what are declining industries beset with over-capacity worldwide, it makes for an interesting case study.

Table A5.1 Selected indicators for Brasov (county) and Romania, 1997

	Brasov County (thousands)	Romania (thousands)
Population, mid-1997	636.4	22545.9
Labour force	289.1	9904.4
Employment, end 1997	265.6	9023
of which		
State-owned	n.a.	2633
Private	n.a.	5186
Other	n.a.	1204
Agriculture	46.1	3384
Services	77.4	2580
Construction	22.9	439
Industry	115.1	2450
Manufacturing	108.2	2079
Other	4.1	170
Registered unemployed	23.5	881.4
Unemployment rate	8.1	8.9
Av. net monthly salary in lei/economy	692.8	632.1
Av. net monthly salary in lei/industry	767.8	693.4
Av. net monthly salary in lei/manufacturing	748.6	628.8

Source: Romanian Statistical Yearbook 1998, National Commission for Statistics, Bucharest.

Tractorul UTB S.A.

Based in Brasov, Tractorul UTB S.A. makes tractors. It was set up in 1925 as a Franco-Romanian aircraft company. The first tractor was manufactured in 1946. A licensing agreement with FIAT dates back to 1968. In 1991 it became a joint-stock company. In 1999 its corporate status was as a state-owned commercial company with 75 per cent of shares owned by State Ownership Fund (SOF) and the remainder owned by private shareholders (18 per cent in a Private Ownership Fund and 7 per cent owned by individual investors). As a firm in the automotive industry, the relevant ministry for Tractorul was the Ministry of Industry and Trade. As it produced tractors, Tractorul also had relations with the Ministry of Agriculture. Along with 63 other companies, Tractorul was shortlisted for privatisation, with the support of the World Bank.

At its peak in the mid-1980s, Tractorul was manufacturing close on 50,000 tractors per annum with a workforce of 20,000. Average production in the period 1990 to 1998 was 17,000 tractors per year. By 1999, the number of tractors sold had fallen to less than 5,000. The full-time workforce in 1999 was 10,112, down from just over 19,000 in 1990. In recent years, Tractorul's sales of new tractors have been almost exclusively for the foreign market, as domestic demand has been very weak. Instead of purchasing new machines, cash-poor farmers have repaired old machines. Whatever home market existed, Tractorul was virtually the sole producer.

From 1994 to 1999, the company was making heavy losses. Management puts much of these losses down to external factors, such as the weak state of the home demand, exchange rate losses and certain high costs, such as electricity prices. The company did admit that layoffs had not been high enough to offset the fall in demand. Partly in response to these conditions and to prepare for the privatisation of the company under the World Bank's PSAL programme, Tractorul S.A. was split into 10 separate companies at the end of 1999. Tractorul UTB S.A. remained the largest, manufacturing tractors with a workforce of 5,600 workers. The activities of the other nine companies varied from the manufacturing of engines, machine tools and spare parts to the design of cabs and to general repairs. In addition, a new management team took over in September 1999, replacing the old management team that had been in place since 1990. It consisted of a new general manager and nine managers responsible for specific functions ranging from finance to quality. On further investigation, it transpired that the change in management team was initiated because the outgoing general manager had asked to be replaced. The general manager is the firm's representative on the Administrative Council, a body comprising three representatives from SOF, one from the POF and the firm's representative.

Tractorul's foreign customers came from countries as far apart as the USA, Canada, Egypt, Pakistan, Turkey, France, Hungary, Slovenia and Croatia. In general, Tractorul had no payment problems with its clients. As its customer base is foreign, Tractorul, on average, got paid on time, in cash and in foreign currency. This was a fortunate position for Tractorul as many Romanian companies had overdue receivables and often got paid in kind rather than in cash. Like all companies that sell on world markets, they faced competition. Earlier, their main competitors came from other CEE countries, including Poland, the Czech Republic and Belarus. Currently (in 2000, when the case study was first written), it is the view of management that foreign competition for its product range is quite limited.

The average monthly wage was 1.8 million lei ($100) in December 1999. This is net (after tax and social security contributions) and includes bonuses. It compared favourably with the average monthly wage for the sector. On the question of strikes and late payment of wages, management was insistent that there were no strikes at Tractorul and that wages were always paid on time. When questioned about the strikes in Brasov in the summer of 1999, the Tractorul management was adamant that the workers on strike in June 1999 were not employees of Tractorul and that the press reports were incorrect. Like other state-owned companies, Tractorul UTB has divested itself of most of its social assets, in this case to the local municipality. All that remained were a number of flats that were occupied by unmarried personnel.

The next issue raised was finance and payments. When questioned about the firm's creditors and the ordering of payment, management said that in practice (and contrary to legislation where payments to the state have priority) the ordering was as follows: utilities (paid in cash) followed by banks (paid in cash), suppliers (paid in mix of cash and goods) and, finally, government. This, in turn, explained the breakdown of the firm's outstanding debts. By January 2000, Tractorul UTB S.A. had debts amounting to 1,400bn lei ($76.3m), of which a high proportion was interest and penalties for late payment. Of the total, 745bn lei ($40.6m) were owed to the state (comprising state budget, social security and special funds). 500bn lei ($27.2m) of this were penalties and interest charges. An amount of 360bn lei ($19.6m) was debt to banks, of which two-thirds was principal. Tractorul's main bank was the Romanian Development Bank, subsequently bought by Société Generale. Close to 160bn lei ($8.7m) were owed to suppliers, who normally extend 30 days' trade credit to Tractorul. It appeared that Tractorul had little or no debts to the electricity or gas companies. In response to a question relating to deferrals or write-offs of debt, management admitted that the company had debt rescheduled in the past.

The financial situation for Tractorul looked bleak. In every year between 1994 and 1999 except one, that is, 1997, the firm was making operating losses. This suggested that Tractorul was having difficulty covering basic costs, such as materials and labour costs. In addition, the large losses accumulating since 1994 indicated a debt overhang problem. In 1990, Tractorul owed 9bn lei, of which the majority was owed to banks. Debts to suppliers (of power, materials and components) and to the state were insignificant, at less than 5 per cent of the total debt. By 1998, the debt owed to the state had ballooned. Of a total debt of over 1,100bn lei ($127m), almost 540bn lei ($60.5m) were owed to the state. Of this, almost half was penalties and interest on overdue debt.

Tractorul did receive some aid from the state, largely in the form of low interest rate loans and injections of capital from SOF. On account of the difficult financial and trading situation that Tractorul found itself in, management wanted the government to dissolve the debts owed to the state. At a minimum, it wanted the interest charges and penalties on late tax and contribution payments to be written off and the principal to be rescheduled. On a follow-up visit to Tractorul, it was learnt that Tractorul was one of a number of debt-ridden firms whose debts were to be rescheduled by the government. Although agreed by the Cabinet, the plan was abandoned after unfavourable press coverage.

Roman S.A.

Roman S.A. is a truck-making company, based in Brasov. At the time of the case study (that is, in early 2000) it was a state-owned commercial company, with 94 per cent of its shares owned by SOF and the remaining 6 per cent owned by local investors. It was one of the 64 Romanian companies that were shortlisted for privatisation, with the support of the World Bank. It was founded in 1921, manufactured the first Romanian truck in 1954 and became a joint-stock trading company in 1990. At its peak it employed over 26,000 workers. In 1980 it manufactured 30,000 trucks, mainly for the domestic market. In 1999 it employed 10,600 workers and sold 1,000 trucks, virtually all (in excess of 90 per cent) for the home market. On further investigation, it transpired that the fall in production was gradual between 1980 and 1990, with 12,000 sold in 1990. Between 1990 and 1999, the downward trend was more dramatic, with a large fall in sales reported in the earlier part of the decade. This period (1990–1992) coincided with the early years of economic transition in the Romanian economy when the fall in national output was substantial. In spring 2000 the workforce was 9,150 workers. All 9,150 workers were full-time employees and close on 90 per cent were unionised. The average monthly wage before tax and social security contributions was 2 million lei ($110). All wage payments were made on time and the firm had no wage arrears.

Strikes have played an important part in Roman's (and Brasov's) history. Under Ceausescu's regime, workers in Roman (known then as the Red Flag factory) and elsewhere went on strike in November 1987. Riots ensued in response to the workers' demands for an end to shortages and pay cuts. In the more recent past, there were demonstrations in June and, again, in November 1999. The November 1999 strike was resolved when a government military order for Roman trucks was agreed. In return for this, Roman had some of its tax debt reduced. By 1999, Roman had divested itself of all its social assets with the exception of two blocks of flats that were occupied by unmarried employees. Its other social assets were sold to local firms and investors.

Historically, Roman sold primarily to the home market, with domestic sales accounting for over 90 per cent. Since the demise of the CMEA market and with Europe being dominated by large competitors (the likes of Scania and Volvo from Sweden, Man and Mercedes from Germany, Iveco from Italy), Roman's main external market was Asia. Sales to the Asian market were hit by the Asian crisis of 1997 and market conditions improved only slowly. As for the composition of the domestic customers, 60 per cent of buyers were small private firms and the remaining 40 per cent were state owned. As ties and relations are important, Roman's customer base has not changed much over the years, with one exception. In early times, the military sector was a reliable customer but this has changed with the cuts in military spending and the downsizing of government. In recognition of these market changes, Roman sought new markets and new ways of selling its product. One option was leasing and with a bank credit guaranteed by SOF, Roman managed to lease 45 trucks in late 1999 and early 2000. Despite this, management felt that this market was constrained by buyers' limited access to finance. Management also expressed its concern over the granting of favourable tax conditions by the Romanian government to foreign firms operating in Romania.

As for Roman's suppliers, the majority of them were Romanian and, like its customers, were traditional trading partners of Roman. The components and engines that are imported came from different countries, namely Germany, Italy, France, UK and Hungary.

By 1999, Roman's debts amounted to close on 1,500bn lei ($97.8m), of which 85 per cent was owed to the state. In 1999 alone, the company made a loss (after exceptional items) of 750bn lei ($48.9m). The debt to the state comprised both principal and interest, with the latter accounting for a greater percentage. In 1999, Roman paid off the outstanding principal that was due to the state budget and to social security, leaving penalties and interest charges of 650bn lei ($42.4m). The total debt to the local budget and to the special funds by the end of 1999 amounted to close on 1,000bn lei ($65.2m). The management of Roman was insistent that interest charged on late payment to the state was excessive and could not be paid. It also complained that due to the mounting interest charges, it was not in a position to take advantage of the 1999 government scheme allowing firms to pay off their principal due as of August 1999 in return for a writing-off of interest charges. On further questioning, Roman admitted that in return for its payment of outstanding principal, the government did agree to a rescheduling of interest over a five-year period. In response to questions relating to government subsidies and regional aid, Roman was insistent that it was not in receipt of any such aid. It did admit, however, that the government (by tolerating late or non-payments) was helping the firm to avoid bankruptcy and in doing so, was ensuring (for the short term, at least) its survival. In its defence, the management of Roman argued that a closure of the firm would cost the government billions in welfare and other payments. In addition, Roman was an important employer in Brasov, with one job in Roman affecting 2.5 jobs elsewhere in Brasov, it claimed.

Unlike its debt to government, Roman had only a small amount of debt owed to its banks and no debt to the utility companies. As for its trading partners, amounts due on receivables and payables were similar, close on 120bn lei ($7.8m). There was a deliberate policy on behalf of the company to keep trade receivables and payables in line with each other. Of the amount due to suppliers, the majority of it was less than three months old. As for the utilities (gas and electricity), payments were generally made on time and in cash. The reason for prompt payment, or the absence of late payment, was the threat of a power cut. Roman believed that late or non-payment would result in disconnection. In addition, any late payment to the utility company was subject to an interest charge.

When settling with its creditors, Roman paid in cash. Sometimes, depending on the creditor, Roman paid in trucks, in other firms' goods (received by Roman in exchange for trucks) or in vouchers issued by the utilities (received by Roman in lieu of payment for delivery of trucks/components to clients). The normal period of trade credit given by Roman to its customers was 15 to 30 days. Trade credit extended to Roman by its suppliers was normally 30 days. On average, Roman received 60 per cent of its payment in cash and 40 per cent in goods/vouchers via the compensation scheme. This so-called compensation scheme was common in Romania and worked as follows. Suppose Roman sells a truck to customer A. A has no cash to pay for the truck but he has a receivable from B. This receivable is paid to Roman, in exchange for the truck. Likewise, Roman's domestic suppliers will accept payment from Roman in goods, either its own products or others'. The utility companies also take part in this scheme, accepting payment in goods and/or vouchers. In this scheme, invoices are exchanged and taxes accrue (VAT). Although these transactions only required the trading parties involved, large transactions in excess of 100 million lei were centralised, involving an agency within the Ministry of Industry and Trade. This clearing of inter-firm arrears function by the Ministry was not unusual in Romania where, since transition began, various enterprise surveillance or isolation programmes were initiated by government with the aim, among other things, of clearing the financial payments 'blockage' brought about by the buildup of trade credit arrears in the enterprise sector.

As for banks, Roman had reasonably good relations with its two main banks, Banca Comerciala Romana (Romanian Commercial Bank) and the Romanian Development Bank (owned by Société Generale). Roman's outstanding debt to these and others (including a German Bank) was close on 120bn lei as of the end of 1999. A small amount was overdue. Likewise, it had a small bank debt rescheduled by the bank-restructuring agency, AVAB (Agentia pentru Valorificarea Activelor Bancare). In response to a question relating to overdue bank debt and penalties, management inferred that the penalties imposed by these (often state-owned) banks were large and acted as a deterrent. In addition, late or non-payments would threaten any extension of credit in the future and would harm its relations with the bank. Although the government did have the power to block the bank accounts of delinquent firms, in practice it was not in the banks' interests to have their clients' accounts seized. Roman indicated that, in terms of payment priorities, the banks were paid first, followed by workers. This is contrary to legislation, which stated that wages should be paid first, followed by payments to the state budget.

In response to a question relating to government assistance, Roman was insistent on the need for some state aid. It expected credits from government for R&D spending and general investment spending. In addition, it hoped that the government would provide finance for leasing and instalment schemes. Roman felt that government aid provided to foreign investors (Renault-Dacia was mentioned) should also be made available to domestic producers. This assistance would help Roman to reach its target of 55–60 per cent of the domestic market. At that time, Roman had 45 per cent of the home market. When questioned about the marketing and possible identity of these new buyers, management did not appear to have many ideas, only commenting that it would be private buyers. Although it did not state it explicitly, there is a suspicion that it would turn to the government, and the military in particular, for new orders. Roman felt that it would be unable to capture market share beyond 60 per cent owing to foreign competition (in receipt of government assistance) and its own inability/unwillingness to supply certain types of trucks. Despite the relatively low labour costs in Romania, the price of trucks manufactured and exported by Roman was close to world levels. According to management, this was because the engines in the trucks were imported (from France, Germany and the USA). Management also admitted that further cuts in wage levels and/or the workforce were unlikely due to trade union opposition. Without a change in market conditions, the breakeven point of 1,700 sales (with sales of components) or 2,700 sales (without sales of components) would not be reached.

Summary and conclusions

In the socialist system, firms were subject to a SBC. Under that regime, fiscal subsidies and tax concessions were (aside from their role in the pricing mechanism) instruments by which budget constraints were softened. With a paternalistic state, the source of the budget softness was government. In the transition period, new instruments for budget softness emerged, as did new or alternate sources of budget softness. In some transition countries, tax arrears, overdue bank credit and inter-firm trade credit arrears were often used as ways of softening the budget constraints of enterprises. In addition to the state, banks and other firms were sometimes the sources of budget softness.

In this case study, we chose two firms operating in the Romanian enterprise sector that, on initial investigation, were strong candidates for budget softness. In order for there to be evidence of budget softness, firms must be (1) loss-makers and (2) in receipt of ex-post subsidies, i.e. the losses *result* in a net flow of financing to the deleterious firms. From our case study of Roman and Tractorul, we know that both firms were loss makers. It would appear that they were also in receipt of government subsidies, either in the form of tax concessions or cheap loans. Are these subsidies conditional, paid over to guarantee the survival of these loss-making firms?

We attempt to answer this question by examining the conduct and behaviour of government. It does appear from this case study that there was some evidence of a recurring government rescue or bailout of the two big Brasov firms. The government was well aware of the difficult political and social factors that surrounded the big Brasov firms. As for the position of the firms themselves, the likelihood of state aid (based on past experience and on current bargaining power) weakened the incentive or motivation to restructure. This was evident in the case of Roman and Tractorul where, despite the collapse of their markets, employment numbers were still high, organisational changes were slow to evolve and the search for new markets, products and suppliers was sluggish. Well-publicised strikes resulted in much media attention, often ending with the government conceding to the demands of the workforce.

In these cases, the government's role as creditor is counterpositioned by its role as owner and employer. These concessions, if repeated, tend to undermine the government's commitment to enforce hard budget constraints on delinquent firms. The credibility of its 'no bailout' commitment is weakened by recurring infringements of financial discipline. In the context of ex-post bailouts, there is little doubt that the two firms in our case study were in a strong bargaining position *because of* their poor financial situation. In the case of both firms, the government tolerated late payment of taxes/social security contributions (at favourable penalty charges to the delinquent firms) and rescheduled debt (principal or interest). It is also true in both cases that it was the government that behaved (and was viewed by its debtors) as the softest creditor. Other creditors, whether banks or suppliers, were unlikely to accept late or non-payment to the same degree as did the government. For the two firms in question, the risks associated with late or non-payment to banks and/or suppliers were considered too great. It was likely that non-payment to banks would result in high penalty charges and a loss of banking services. Non-payment to certain utilities might have resulted in disconnection. Suppliers were likely to stop shipping goods if they were not paid. Delayed payment to workers was not considered an option due to a combination of factors (militant workforce, strong trade union membership, little precedence). When in trouble, these state-owned firms (already a drain on the public finances) turned to the softest creditor for help, namely the government. Although the state purported to be tough in its commitment to ensuring financial discipline in the enterprise sector, its actions suggested otherwise. In the case of both Roman and Tractorul, government assistance in the form of government orders, injection of cash, toleration of late payment of taxes and social security contributions, debt relief (rescheduling of principal and a writing off of penalties) and favourable tax treatment (similar to the concessions given to foreign investors) was sought. The evidence, outlined in this case study and elsewhere, suggests that, in most cases, the external assistance was given.

This summary completes our case study analysis. Whether Roman, Tractorul and the machine-building industry in general, no doubt constituting part of Romania's financial black hole, can restructure sufficiently to meet the demands of a market economy, remains to be seen.

APPENDIX 6

Human Development Index 1990–2005

Table A6.1 Human Development Index, 1990–2005

		1990	*1995*	*2000*	*2005*
High human development					
27	Slovenia	0.851	0.857	0.891	0.917
32	Czech Republic	0.845	0.854	0.866	0.891
36	Hungary	0.813	0.817	0.845	0.874
37	Poland	0.806	0.822	0.852	0.870
42	Slovak Republic	..	0.827	0.840	0.863
43	Lithuania	0.827	0.791	0.831	0.862
44	Estonia	0.813	0.792	0.829	0.860
45	Latvia	0.804	0.771	0.817	0.855
47	Croatia	0.812	0.805	0.828	0.850
53	Bulgaria	0.794	0.785	0.800	0.824
60	Romania	0.777	0.772	0.780	0.813
64	Belarus	0.790	0.755	0.778	0.804
66	Bosnia and Herzegovina	..	..	..	0.803
67	Russia	0.815	0.771	0.782	0.802
68	Albania	0.704	0.705	0.746	0.801
69	FYR Macedonia	..	..	..	0.801
Medium human development					
73	Kazakhstan	0.771	0.724	0.738	0.794
76	Ukraine	0.809	0.756	0.761	0.788
81	China	0.634	0.691	0.732	0.777
83	Armenia	0.737	0.701	0.738	0.775
96	Georgia	..	..	..	0.754
98	Azerbaijan	..	..	..	0.746
105	Vietnam	0.620	0.672	0.711	0.733
109	Turkmenistan	..	..	..	0.713
111	Moldova	0.740	0.684	0.683	0.708
113	Uzbekistan	0.704	0.683	0.691	0.702
114	Mongolia	0.654	0.638	0.667	0.700
116	Kyrgyzstan	..	..	..	0.696
122	Tajikistan	0.703	0.638	0.640	0.673
Regional groupings					
	Central and Eastern Europe + CIS				0.808
	OECD				0.916
	East Asia and the Pacific				0.771
	Latin American and the Caribbean				0.803
	Least Developed Countries				0.488
	World				0.743

Source: United Nations Development Report.

APPENDIX 7

Policy conclusions and lessons from transition

Here we present a summary of the policy conclusions and lessons from a selected number of experts on transition.[1] In recognition of the two broad approaches to transition and reforms, we include findings that are reasonably representative of both views. The findings listed below from Fischer and Sahay (2000), Havrylyshyn (2001, 2006) and Linn (2001) reflect, broadly speaking, the orthodox, conventional view of transition (in support of early, rapid, comprehensive and simultaneous reforms) whereas, in contrast, the findings from Kolodko (1999, 2006), Kornai (2000b, 2008) and Roland (2001, 2002) represent, by and large, the views of the alternate. Although there are similarities, the differences between the two sets of views, with respect to overall conclusions and lessons, are not trivial.

The conventional perspective

Fischer and Sahay 2000

- The most successful transition economies are those that have both stabilised and undertaken comprehensive reforms, and that more and faster reform is better than less and slower reform.
- Small-scale privatisation was generally successful. The imposition of hard budget constraints is an important determinant for successful privatisation. Insider privatisation does not seem to have led to self-induced restructuring, as was expected. Productivity in private enterprises is higher than in state enterprises.
- With respect to institutions and governance, the absence of a predictable legal framework has hindered growth.
- Foreign assistance at the early stage helps sustain reform, but on its own it is not enough. Growth was facilitated by foreign private financing but only in those countries that had successful stabilisations and reforms.
- Among CEE/FSU countries, the Russian transition experience stands out as unique. Given its size and power, that was inevitable. Reforms were stalled. The resource curse did not help.
- In terms of output performance, the outliers of Uzbekistan and Belarus may be largely explained by country-specific factors, namely cotton exports and energy self-sufficiency in the case of Uzbekistan and close trade ties to Russia in the case of Belarus.
- The extent of reform is partly explained by initial conditions and partly by the prospects of joining the European Union.

Linn 2001

- Changes in the countries involved are fundamental and far-reaching, encompassing all aspects of life, notably social, political, economic and institutional.
- Central European and Baltic countries have managed to stabilise their economies and to bring them back to market-oriented systems.
- Poorer, small countries of the Caucasus and Central Asia are vigorously continuing economic and political reforms, despite the enormous initial shock caused by the breakup of the Soviet Union.
- Despite the breakup of the former Yugoslavia and the warfare which ensued, the countries in that region have managed to rebuild.
- Neglect of institutional reforms can be detrimental to further economic reforms (as the case of Russia clearly demonstrates).
- Although Russia and Ukraine economies have not performed well, which had a serious impact on the political and social conditions in those countries, the influence of these events on the world economy remained very limited.
- Market-oriented reforms, together with institutional strengthening and social reforms, have worked and have put the formally centrally planned economies (at least a large number of them) on a sustainable path of economic growth and social inclusion.

Havrylyshyn 2001

No royal road to growth exists but a wide range of good policies is needed, including financial stabilisation, market liberalisation, and market-friendly government rules and institutions.

Five points of consensus

1 Traditional factor inputs have no role in explaining growth over time and across countries.
2 The decline in output was inevitable.
3 Financial stabilisation is a necessary first step before sustainable growth can occur. Stabilisation is not sufficient and market liberalisation or structural reform is the most important factor.
4 Initial conditions have some, at least initially, minor impact.
5 Good institutions are one of the necessary components in the reform package.

Five continuing debates

1 The timing and sequencing of institutional reforms.
2 Speed of reforms (gradualism vs. Big Bang).
3 Does distance from the market matter, and if so, how does it matter?
4 Can 'badly done' privatisation be harmful?
5 How much pain may be caused in the early part of the transition?

A handful of puzzles

1 Why was the transformational recession quite as deep as it was?
2 Why do the two variables, exports and foreign direct investment, appear (in the econometrics) insignificant?
3 How can the low decline and high growth of Belarus and Uzbekistan be explained?

Havrylyshyn 2006

- With respect to the large output decline in TEs, there is no consensus on the reasons for it, or indeed for how excessive it was. Although the official estimates may exaggerate the magnitude, there is no doubt that it was historically very high. On the reasons for this, it is, at a minimum, clear that the magnitude of decline was greatest for countries with slower progress in transforming their economic systems.
- In relation to privatisation, there is no technical method of privatisation that has worked better than any other. All forms of privatisation appear to have some beneficial effect in efficiency, but in a clear rank order as follows: new enterprises, small and medium enterprises, large enterprises and traditional state-owned enterprises. Private ownership alone has a limited effect, but adding a favourable institutional and competitive environment gives much greater results. A high degree of ownership concentration may not in the short run preclude improved efficiency, but in the long run it is problematic if its leads to state capture by a handful of powerful business groups, or oligarchs.
- With respect to institutions, the pace of institutional development is broadly related to the pace of economic reform which is not consistent with the conclusion that rapid reform went too far ahead of institutional changes. As for identifying the critical institutions, they include a minimal degree of property rights security, and a liberal free entry environment equal for large and small enterprises. There is a clear difference between Central Europe and the Baltic countries and many of the CIS countries in terms of the development of these important market-enhancing institutions, and this, in turn, partly explains the variation in performance.
- As regards social costs, theory and cross-country evidence would indicate that costs in transition were inevitable. Despite the tendency for the early assessments to overstate the costs (as they were done too soon, and owing to data biases) considerable economic and social costs were indeed incurred in transition countries, varying from significant to enormous. Critics of the transition who attribute such social costs to rapid economic reforms are mistaken. It is precisely the opposite: too-gradual reforms, allowing new capitalist elites to capture the process, abuse it for their own interests and neglect the negative impacts on the larger populace. The evidence shows that the faster reformers experienced much lower negative effects, and even for the lagging reformers, the effects over time bottomed out and partially recovered.
- As for the diverse outcomes and performance assessment (is transition over?), the transition journey for Central European and Baltic countries is essentially complete; in Southeast Europe it is clearly not over yet but steady progress is evident; as for the reforming CIS countries, they are not only further behind but are stalled at a stage of partial, frozen transformation. In three CIS countries – Belarus, Turkmenistan and Uzbekistan – reforms have barely begun, with their economic system resembling a Soviet-type regime. These four groups can more or less be categorised respectively as liberal societies, intermediate regimes, captured states and lagging reformers. The different outcomes can be explained largely by three proximate causes: reforms, proclivity to state capture and rent seeking, and the prospect of a safe haven (such as EU membership).

The alternative view

Kolodko 1999

1 Institutional arrangements (by design rather than by chance) are the most important factor for progress toward durable growth.
2 The size of government is less important than the quality of its policy and the manner of the changes of government size.
3 Institution building by its nature must be a gradual process.
4 If institutional arrangements are neglected and left to the spontaneous processes and unleashed forces of liberalised markets, then informal institutionalisation fills the systemic vacuum.
5 In transition economies the policies must transform and streamline the judiciary system to serve the needs of the market economy.
6 A shift of competence and power from the central government to local governments is necessary for deregulation of the post-socialist economy.
7 There is an urgent necessity to accelerate the development of non-government organisations (NGOs).
8 During transition incomes policy and government concern for equitable growth has great meaning.
9 Post-socialist transition to the market is taking place at a time of worldwide globalisation, hence opening and integration with the world economy is an indispensable part of the whole endeavour.
10 International organisations should not only support but also assist in further regional integration and cooperation.
11 The Bretton Woods organisations should reconsider their policies towards transition economies.
12 These interactive processes of learning-by-monitoring and learning-by-doing continue and will last for several years.

Kolodko 2006

Lesson One: Economic reforms that increase the flexibility of markets and at least partially contribute towards the building of institutions necessary for the efficient functioning and development of a market economy always come in handy when a bolder and more profound structural shift is subsequently made. Even if certain reasons – for instance, of a political or cultural nature – prevent changing too much at one go, it makes sense to change things little by little, since in time this is likely to bring about the desired results.

Lesson Two: Only a proper mix of two policies – a system change policy and a development policy oriented towards the accumulation and efficient allocation of capital – offers a chance for a rapid economic growth. Neglect of either of these components precludes good results.

Lesson Three: Confusing means and ends in economic policy backfire, increasing the social costs of development and decreasing its attainable scale.

Lesson Four: Institution building, that is, the creation of new rules of the market economic game and a legal and organisational framework for their implementation, is of fundamental importance. But policy is also vital. Ever-improving institutions do not by themselves entail – at least not in the short-term perspective – an ever-improving policy. Institutions matter, but so do policies.

Lesson Five: The main source of development finance in all types of so-called emerging markets has been and is domestic capital accumulation. Therefore, the formation of this capital should be given the priority it requires in the macroeconomic policy and in the system of microeconomic incentives. What is important, in particular, is the appropriate design of the financial – both fiscal and monetary – policy.

Lesson Six: Globalisation creates additional development opportunities and additional development threats to everyone. Therefore, the art of economic policy making consists today in the apt handling of the dilemmas that crop up under the new circumstances.

Kornai 2000b, 2008

- In the capitalist system as compared with the socialist system, technological development is faster, due primarily to the pursuit of innovation by the capitalist system.
- There is no universal prescription. There are no specific, practical recommendations equally valid for each country. It would be a mistake to follow mechanically the path of any other country.
- There is no convincing theory or model for calculating an 'optimum speed' of transition.
- Legal reform and the creation of institutions and organisations for a state of law call for circumspection and precision, which in turn require quite a lot of time. Every sphere of the transformation – the political process, the business world, the arts or the sciences – requires an adequate legal or legislative background.
- For a healthy and strong private sector:

  – barriers to free entry need to be dismantled (with some minimum conditions remaining);
  – a strategy to assist the new private sector and SMEs;
  – pragmatic and open approach to foreign capital and FDI, but with conditions.

- With respect to privatisation, there is no one simple, universal applicable answer. The privatisation process must be preceded by a minimum level of institutional reform.
- There are some common features in the approach to preparing the transformation programme, namely:

  – the strong political charge in any essential change must not be forgotten;
  – it is illusionary to expect any tasks to be purely professional and 'politics-free' (after all, the change in system is a political process);
  – the ethical aspects of the changes planned have to be conscientiously considered.

Roland 2001, 2002

- Reforms have not delivered uniformly good outcomes or economy-wide efficiency gains.
- The importance of the political economy perspective on transition and reforms. Policies are endogenous and depend on political constraints. These political constraints have been less strong in Central Europe compared with the former Soviet Union. Geopolitics plays

an important role here and elsewhere. Political economy arguments can also explain different transition paths and variations in transition outcomes.

- Ability to enforce the law and protect property rights seems to be a first-order effect in explaining why Central European countries recovered from their output fall quicker than did Russia and other countries (with these CIS countries not facing the prospect of entry into the European Union).
- The importance and relevance of aggregate uncertainty.
- A great majority of the population suffered from transition, and have resented the strong concentration of wealth created by a privatisation process viewed as illegitimate and corrupt.
- Sequencing of reforms does not necessarily stall the reform process but may be used to create momentum for further reform. However, insufficient attention has been given to the issue of partial reform, and the conditions under which it creates momentum or, on the contrary, creates vested interests that block further reform.
- The need for further research on the dual-track approach to transition.
- Although many important laws were adopted, law enforcement was a big problem, especially in Russia.
- The adequate institutions, including social norms, for a market economy have not yet fully emerged.
- With respect to ownership, the emphasis on both the speed of privatisation and insider privatisation was unfounded.
- Reform in the organisation of government is important. In China, this took the form of decentralisation, fiscal federalism arrangements and the development of different forms of competition between local governments. In Russia, reform of the organisation of government was relatively neglected, as the main focus of reform was the implementation of mass privatisation.
- Hardening the budget constraints is not just a matter of political will but of devising institutional mechanisms that create credibility for hardening. Here again, the geopolitical factor may have played an important role in shaping expectations early on in accession countries, where there was a rapid hardening of the budget constraint.
- The institutional-evolutionary approach is more complete and adequate than the Washington Consensus view. This is associated with a shift in economic thinking, from an emphasis on standard price theory and market reforms towards a focus on contracting, and institutional reforms.

Finally, a fascinating policy debate on transition, published in 2000/2001, took place between the high-profile Nobel prize-winning economist and critic of neo-liberalism and rapid reformers, Joseph Stiglitz (joined subsequently by David Ellerman, a colleague of Stiglitz) and three Polish economists (all involved in policy advice) who were associated with the early (rapid) reforms in Poland. The relevant publications are as follows:

Dabrowski, M., S. Gomulka and J. Rostowski. *Whence Reform? A critique of the Stiglitz perspective*, 2001.
Stiglitz, J. *Whither Reform? Ten years of the transition*, 2000.
Stiglitz, J. and D. Ellerman. *Not Poles Apart: 'Whither reform?' and 'whence reform?'*, 2001.

You are encouraged to read these enthralling journal articles and the ensuing debate between the two policy camps. Detailed citations are given in the Bibliography.

411

NOTES

INTRODUCTION

1 Balcerowicz (2002) writes that 'Post-communist transition in Europe and the former USSR was one of the most important transformations in modern history'. Gregory and Stuart (2001) refer to the transition experience as '. . . the greatest social science experiment of recorded history'. Similarly, Campos and Coricelli (2002) write that 'this transition will join the Great Depression as one of the most important economic events of the last century. Like the Great Depression, it will be intensely studied for years to come because it marks a fundamental break in the ways of organising and going about economic life.' One obvious connection between the Great Depression of the 1930s and the collapse of the socialist system at the end of the twentieth century is that the former came about because of certain weaknesses in the capitalist system whereas the latter came about because of the relative strengths of the capitalist system and its defeat of communism.

2 For a historical account of what is meant by Central and Eastern Europe (and within that region, differences between Central Europe and Eastern Europe), and how it has differed throughout history from Western Europe, see Berend (2005).

3 A good account of the differences between development and transition, and between developing countries and transition countries is given by Ofer (2001).

4 Although this extract, taken from *The Concise Encyclopedia of Economics* at the Library of Economics and Liberty, is a good critique of transition, it contains some disputed points. Many of these are dealt with in other parts of the book. The author is a well-respected expert on the Soviet socialist system and economic transition in the former Soviet bloc countries and was (and still is) one of radical reform's most vocal advocates. He has served as economic adviser to governments in Russia, Ukraine and Kyrgyzstan, and is currently a Senior Fellow at the Peterson Institute for International Economics. Here, as elsewhere, Åslund, in explaining transition in former socialist countries, highlights the role of rent seeking. Indeed, he describes rent seeking as the key problem in post-communist countries and particularly in Russia and other CIS economies. While rent seeking was undoubtedly a problem, many commentators, including the authors of this book, would not agree that it was the 'key problem'.

5 Mongolia was often referred to as the 16th republic of the USSR as it was highly integrated into the Soviet system. As is common with other commentaries on transition, East Germany (GDR) is omitted as it was no longer a separate state following the reunification of Germany in 1990. We also do not include Kosovo in our analysis as it has been an independent state only since 2008, with the world community still divided (at the time of writing) on the issue of the international recognition of Kosovo. As for the Federal Republic of Yugoslavia (FRY), formed in 1992 following the breakup of the former Yugoslavia, we use the common name of Serbia and Montenegro (although officially the FRY was only reconstituted as Serbia and Montenegro in 2003), which split in 2006 after Montenegro seceded from the federation and declared independence, with Serbia declaring itself a republic almost immediately afterwards.

6 Inevitably, given the history, size and geopolitical importance of the Soviet Union's largest and most populated successor, much of the attention in transition has focused on Russia at the expense of other CIS countries. Indeed, it is often the case that any analysis of Russia, either in the context of heritage, economic structure, political constraints, reforms or outcomes is assumed to equally apply to the other

CIS countries. Although there are undoubted similarities between the CIS countries, the 12 member states of the CIS are very different in many respects and since transition began have witnessed large variations in cross-country reforms and performance. It is often the case that any analysis of the CIS is divided into three country groupings: the Slavic countries of Russia, Belarus and Ukraine (with Moldova often included), the three Caucasus states (Armenia, Azerbaijan and Georgia) and the five Central Asian countries (Kazakhstan, Kyrgyzstan, Turkmenistan, Tajikistan and Uzbekistan). This classification, largely based on geography, although at times useful, often hides important intra-regional differences (e.g. as between non-reforming Belarus and uneven reforming Russia and Ukraine; oil-rich Azerbaijan as against remittances-dependent Armenia or war-torn, rebellious Georgia; autocratic but resource-endowed Turkmenistan versus gradual reformer Uzbekistan as against rapid reforming (at least initially) Kyrgyzstan). One of the better studies of the CIS, based not on the usual cross-country empirical research but on country case studies, is Ofer and Pomfret (2004).

7 In his concluding chapter of his memoirs, Kornai (2006b) writes 'I did not try to do what I had done with my course on the socialist system a decade earlier and put the message of my lectures in book form. Although there is a need for summarizing monographs on the transition, they have been left to a younger generation to supply.' As members of the 'younger generation', our hope in writing this book is that we have supplied an accurate and fair account of transition's first two decades.

1 PRE-TRANSITION: THE SOCIALIST SYSTEM

1 The classic example that would often be cited by Menshevik and Bolshevik alike as a bourgeois-democratic revolution was the French Revolution. That Napoleon did not introduce a democratic system and stamped on any beginnings of open and free debate is neither here nor there – in their view. He preserved the fundamental 'gains' of the revolution by not going back to the *ancien régime* and allowed, in effect, the class based on the ownership of wealth-producing assets in the towns and cities – the bourgeoisie and petty bourgeoisie – to start its rise to dominance which had been blocked by the old feudal order. The development of industry and the working class in France then paved the way for forces of the left to make inroads into French society which enabled them at the appropriate moment (a failed war of France against Prussia) to intervene in urban-based revolts such as in Paris in 1871. This was the famous Paris Commune of 1871. Another example of a so-called bourgeois-democratic revolution would be the English civil war which comprised a series of wars over the period 1642 to 1651 between the forces of absolute rule by the King, Charles I, and the republican and parliamentary forces of Oliver Cromwell. The view that feudalism would be replaced by capitalism and then succeeded by socialism was seen by Lenin and others on the Bolshevik wing of Russian social democracy as being mechanistic, i.e. too rigid. The genius, or perhaps ruthlessness, of Lenin – recognised by supporters and detractors alike – is that he was flexible in his tactics and would not let a little bit of Marxist theory stand in his way of taking power.

2 Indeed some revolutionaries at the time, both within Russia and other countries, saw trade unionism as the way to overthrow 'wage slavery' without the need for centralised parties. (Names associated with this view that the reader will encounter are Pierre-Joseph Proudhon and Mikhail Bakunin.) The ultimate weapon against capitalism was not the power of the party machine to 'lead the masses' but the weapon of the General Strike organised by the leadership of the trade unions. Those individuals who followed this line often went by the name of syndicalists or anarcho-syndicalists and they saw their role as turning what might start as a classic trade union struggle into a political struggle for power for the trade unions. Bolsheviks and Mensheviks alike were dismissive of this approach; after all if the anarcho-syndicalists were correct, what role would be left for them! As Lenin noted, 'Nothing like the ridiculous transfer of the railways to the railwaymen, or the tanneries to the tanners' (cited in Nove 1986a). A more pertinent criticism from the RSDLP would be that trade union leaders themselves had either a conscious vested interest in working within the capitalist system or that they just simply didn't have a 'revolutionary consciousness'. As such they would always draw back from using their leadership of trade unions to turn what might have started as a trade union fight over demands for rights such as higher wages and shorter working hours into a more overt political fight to replace the system completely with one based on their members 'running the show'.

3 Lenin, V. I. (1902) *What is to be Done?* Published 1978 by Progress Publishers, Moscow.

4 One major difference between Lenin and Mao, and simplifying no doubt, was that whereas Lenin's vanguard party would primarily rest on the urban workforce, Mao's armed communists would build

support on the peasantry winning them over by dividing the land of the landlord among them as they advanced, only eventually taking control of the towns and cities once the countryside had been won.

5 Such footnotes of history on these parties may seem unnecessary. First, however, these were organisations which had, in their day, potentially real power at their disposal if properly coordinated and so for an understanding of events that transpired their existence and views are worthy of note. Today they will best be remembered by the people of virtually all countries as the organisations which openly declared 1 May as International Workers' Day and 8 March as International Women's Day. Campaigns then ensued over the decades for governments to recognise these two days and allow national holidays on them. While the two days started off as overtly political days to celebrate 'the power of the workers' and the role of women in society they are now largely simply seen as holidays.

6 China and India are the two countries that stand out whose respective governments are not content simply to be the world's cheap labour assembly workshop for everything sold in Wal-Mart, Carrefour or Tesco.

7 The Russian Soviet Federative Socialist Republic was the largest component of the USSR – the Union of Soviet Socialist Republics – which you sometimes see written on T-shirts worn by young people as 'CCCP'. The Russian Revolution has gone down in many textbooks and in the propaganda of the USSR as the Great October Revolution. Was it October or November? Well, both. By the Julian calendar it took place on 25 October 1917; by the Gregorian calendar it took place on 7 November 1917. The Bolsheviks later adopted the Gregorian calendar. However, in their propaganda it was still referred to as the October Revolution.

8 Peter Fryer (1956) *Hungarian Tragedy*, London. Quoted in Harman (1974). A more up-to-date edition of Peter Fryer's book may be obtained from Beekman Books (2001). Peter Fryer's dispatches from Hungary to the *Daily Worker* with regard to the Hungarian Revolution were at first heavily censored and then simply discarded. For writing the book *Hungarian Tragedy* he was expelled from the Communist Party of Great Britain. Just days before his death in 2006 he learned that the Hungarian President had awarded him the Knight's Cross of the Order of Merit of the Republic in recognition of his 'continuous support of the Hungarian revolution and freedom fight'.

9 The work of E. H. Carr springs to mind as a definitive account of the Soviet Union not just in terms of economics but all related and relevant issues from social to political. Encompassing 14 volumes it takes the reader from the Bolshevik revolution of 1917 through to 1929.

10 The decree was actually issued by Sovnarkom – the Council of People's Commissars – the informal name given to the government of the Russian Soviet Federative Socialist Republic. Vesenkha was then given responsibility for organising the administration of these nationalised industries.

11 Strictly speaking the Red Army was not created from absolutely nothing. Leon Trotsky who headed the Red Army introduced a policy of using former Tsarist army officers at all levels of the army not only to advise but to lead as well. This was a controversial policy among Bolshevik members as it was seen as a retreat to the old order. Trotsky and Lenin were more pragmatic, keen as they were to use the skills of such officers in the art of war; they were also pragmatic enough to appoint a political commissar with each former Tsarist officer with orders to summarily execute him at the first sign of treachery.

12 In addition, see Chapter 9 for a discussion with regard to *possible* casualties from the transition process.

13 One month after Lenin made this remark in *Pravda* (22 February 1921), Stalin was to write to Lenin attacking Party leaders Trotsky and Rykov – who were highly supportive of the idea of an all-encompassing and detailed economic plan for the economy – and informing Lenin that 'the one and only "economic plan" is the plan of "electrification", and all the other "plans" mere chatter, idle and harmful' (Carr 1984). As so often happens in politics, Stalin would later take the clothes of the 'Left Opposition', as Trotsky's grouping was termed, and implement the very thing he denounced to Lenin.

14 Before turning to a description of the economic system under the Soviet Union any reader who has a very limited understanding of the economic principles underlying *market economies* is urged to read Appendix 1. How can one know what good health really is without having experienced bad health? In a similar vein, we outline the crux of the market in Appendix 1, the better to understand the main mechanisms at work under the socialist economic system known as central planning.

15 It should be added that for every country that can claim to have made good use of indicative planning in its economic development there are probably two or three that can be quoted that did not. India is probably a case in point. In short, indicative planning is not a cure-all for countries seeking rapid economic development.

16 Laissez-faire: the belief that the best option for government if it wishes the economy to flourish is to do as little as possible save ensure a level playing field for all players in the market and to uphold the necessary judicial structures that ensure the rule of law and protect the sanctity of property in the market.

17 Legend has it that at the Moscow trade fair in 1959 Khrushchev, the leader of the Soviet Union at the time, sampled eight bottles of Pepsi at the Pepsi stand guided there by the then Vice-President of America Richard Nixon after the head of Pepsi's International Operation Donald M. Kendall persuaded Nixon to steer Khrushchev in the direction of the Pepsi stand. Twelve years later (things moved slowly in those days) a barter deal was agreed whereby Pepsi supplied the equipment and bottles to the Soviet Union to make Pepsi. In return Pepsi obtained the rights to sell Russian Stolichnaya vodka and wine in America. The vodka retailed in America at $2 more than the then bestselling American brand of Vodka – Smirnoff. (*Source*: http://www.time.com/time/magazine/article/0,9171,918632-1,00.html, accessed 5 October 2008.)

18 Nove lists a number of individuals at that time as examples, which through their work were *ahead* of economists who were to follow in the West. For example, Feldman 'whose growth model has been introduced to Western readers by E. Domar' (op. cit.); and 'Popov and Groman created the "grandfather" of the input-output tables of later years. They invented a new idea, without which planning could hardly begin' (op. cit.); 'The issue of balanced *versus* unbalanced growth, known to most economists from the (recent) work of Hirschman, Rosenstein-Rodan and Nurkse, was also discussed in the Soviet Union at this period' (op. cit.).

19 For a more complete explanation of the input-output method – from where this box presentation drew inspiration – see Chiang (1974) *Fundamental Methods of Mathematical Economics*.

20 Think of the Politburo as a cabinet of a government or the board of directors of a large company. Strictly speaking, of course, the Politburo was the executive of the *party* and not the government. The Politburo was drawn from the central committee of the Communist Party and the central committee was 'elected' by the party congress, made up of 'elected' delegates from party cells in workplaces or geographic branches in the towns and cities. However, there was in effect a dual structure of party and government where the party 'shadowed' the government to ensure the decisions arrived at in the party were carried out in the government. In places and at times the two would often blur into one nexus of party and state.

21 As developed in the later chapter on labour markets, under central planning, this partly explains why open unemployment was not an issue for much of the existence of the Soviet Union. Full utilisation of labour on the shop-floor was another matter and this is often referred to as hidden unemployment under the Soviet style of central planning.

22 Of course it does not explain why female employment for much of the twentieth century was so low relative to male employment in market economies within the West. We leave that to the reader to ponder.

23 For further details of this joint venture see Hamill and Wersun (1996).

24 Slabbered = covered thickly, probably deriving from concrete slabs.

25 Note that Churchill's spelling of Romania, namely Roumania, is no longer in use. The spelling Rumania can also be found in certain documents.

26 One cannot put a clear dividing line historically in place when the ideals of the revolution in Russia gave way to the totalitarianism of Stalin. Some might say the defining event was on the day that the democratically elected Constituent Assembly was dispersed by Bolshevik forces in 1918; others when the revolt of the Kronstadt sailors – who had previously supported the Bolsheviks – in 1921 was put down. Others would argue that it was a process and that there was a slide into totalitarianism, culminating in the Great Purges of Stalin from 1936 to 1938. So, for example, as noted in the main text, it was still possible throughout the 1920s for heated discussion within the Russian Communist Party to take place and also within various governmental organs.

27 See https://www.cia.gov/library/center-for-the-study-of-intelligence/csi-publications/books-and-monographs/watching-the-bear-essays-on-cias-analysis-of-the-soviet-union/index.html. Accessed 1 February 2009. The cartoon presented here is inspired by its use in this document.

28 Figures cited in Naimark (1995).
29 Strictly speaking, East Germany was the GDR – the German Democratic Republic which existed between 1949 and 1990.
30 Figures from Harman (1974) and sources cited therein.
31 It is true that the price differential for oil in internal Soviet bloc trade compared to world market prices was also to be greatly increased by the quadrupling of oil prices by OPEC in 1974. Thus it could be argued that much of the subsidy in later years was 'accidental', having been caused by events outside the control of the USSR. However, as slow as the bureaucracy in the USSR could be to act, it strains credulity to think that they would 'allow' their satellite neighbours to benefit from this disparity in oil prices for so long unless there was another pressing reason. In passing, this subsidy towards CEE countries is also cited sometimes as one reason why Gorbachev was willing to allow these communist regimes to go their own way. Given the economic dire straits of the USSR, Gorbachev wished to relieve the Soviet economy of this financial commitment.
32 Think of the (inexact) parallel with American troops in Iraq following the second Gulf War.
33 'The first Declaration of the underground Polish Workers' Party (PWP) of March 1943, 'What Are We Fighting For?', included nationalisation of the banks and of large-scale industry and called for a comprehensive planning system in all branches of the national economy. These parts of the declaration came under criticism from the Secretary of the Executive Committee of the Communist International, Georgi Dimitrov, because '[such policies] forfeited the support of those who could be attracted into a broad national front . . . the Polish experience seems to have repeated itself in other countries' (Brus 1986). By national front Dimitrov means an alliance between parties of the Left and non-fascist Right.
34 For a detailed account of the nationalisations that took place in CEE after the Second World War see Brus (1986).
35 This summary draws on Brus (1986) to which the reader is referred for more detail.
36 *Source*: http://blogs.iht.com/tribtalk/business/globalization/?p=177 (accessed 27 September 2008).

2 STYLISED FACTS OF TRANSITION: TWO DECADES ON

1 It is often argued by supporters of market reform that the relatively better performance of Belarus and Uzbekistan in the early years of transition is not due to the avoidance of disorder and disruption as a result of a retention of central plan discipline but simply down to the maintenance of old statistical methods or due to the socialist legacy manifesting itself in the persistence of pure socialist production (Balcerowicz 1995; Winiecki 2002; Djankov *et al.* 2003).
2 Although the average growth rate for Albania is high (at 3.5 per cent) we do not report it in the text, as the Albanian economy in the 1990s was affected by the unprecedented (relative to the size of the economy) rise and fall of the financial pyramid schemes. Although difficult to establish, output figures for Albania in the mid- to late 1990s were no doubt affected by the initial rise and subsequent collapse (followed by civil unrest) of these huge pyramid schemes.
3 Surpassing Georgia's 1994 inflation rate is Yugoslavia's (Serbia and Montenegro) traumatic bout of inflation in 1993 to 1994, where inflation, according to one commentator, amounted to what was the 'second-highest and second-longest hyperinflation in world history' (Hanke 2007).
4 Bruno and Easterly (1998) show that periods of high inflation (taken as a 40 per cent annual rate or more) are harmful to economic growth, i.e. growth falls sharply during high inflation crises. Although there is some arbitrariness in the choice of a threshold of 40 per cent, Bruno and Easterly (1998) claim that '40% seems like a natural breakpoint between low and high inflation because it is where the risk of even higher inflation rises sharply'.
5 A similar measure used is the sectoral share of employment. The stylised pattern of development mentioned in the text also applies to the sectoral share of employment.
6 For an alternative critique, see Will Hutton's *The Writing on the Wall: China and the West in the 21st Century*, who argues the case for 'Made in China', but not 'Made by China'. Mr Hutton writes,

> The reason why so few Britons can name a great Chinese brand or company, despite China's export success, is that there aren't any. China needs to build them, but doing that in a one-party authoritarian state, where the party second-guesses business strategy for

ideological and political ends, is impossible. In any case, nearly three-fifths of its exports and nearly all its hi-tech exports are made by non-Chinese, foreign firms, another expression of China's weakness. The state still owns the lion's share of China's business and what it does not own, it reserves the right to direct politically.

(http://www.guardian.co.uk/business/2007/jan/07/bookextracts.china)

7   These reforms were largely a success, unlike the earlier agrarian reforms in the CEE/FSU countries (which are more rural than countries in Western or Northern Europe) where progress in agricultural reforms and the privatisation of land was, at least initially, very limited (see Jeffries 2004; Berend 2009).

8   Of course, others view it quite differently, arguing that public investment was not the solution, but instead what was needed was an emphasis on private spending and/or supply-side measures. This is part of a larger debate in transition, and elsewhere, on the role of the state vs. the market, public spending vs. private enterprise and demand management vs. supply-side policies. The global crisis of 2007 to 2009 has seen a vigorous debate emerge, yet again, between supporters of Friedman and market forces and advocates of Keynes and government counter-cyclical policies with the latter returning to prominence after almost 40 years.

9   Corruption was also evident in pre-Soviet times (and not just in Russia, of course). When writing about the developmental role of the state in nineteenth-century Russia and its economic backwardness (a term that has also been applied to the countries of Central and Eastern Europe, relative to Western Europe), Gerschenkron (1962) noted, 'the standards of honesty in business were so disastrously low, the general distrust of the public so great, that no bank could have hoped to attract even such small capital funds as were available'.

10 In terms of taxation and corruption, it is not necessarily the level of taxation per se that matters but the arbitrary and discretionary nature of the tax and powers of tax officials, the number of taxes and frequency of payments, the relationship between taxpayer and tax official, the transparency (and otherwise) of the tax laws and regulations, the relative wages of employees of the tax administration agency, etc. With respect to government spending and regulation, what matters is less the size of total government expenditure and more the size of individual investment projects, the existence and prevalence of extra-budgetary funds and off-balance sheet activities, and the procurement procedures (Tanzi 1998, 1999).

11 It was the New York Times columnist William Safire who, writing in 1999, described corruption in Russia as 'congenital'.

12 It cannot be ruled out that given the large inefficiencies that existed in the old Soviet industries, firms in the post-Soviet enterprise sector which became more efficient would *reduce* electricity consumption *and* produce more. However, in the initial transition period such firms were probably few and far between. The sharp fall in electricity consumption witnessed in the first few years was associated with large declines in output and production.

13 Trust is viewed as an important aspect of the institutional framework of a market economy. Akin to 'social capital', it is one of many important informal institutions that facilitate trade and exchange. For interesting accounts of the importance of trust (including, *inter alia*, as a determinant of economic growth and cross-country performance) and the post-communist legacy of distrust in former socialist countries and transition economies, see Rose (1994), Raiser (1999) and Raiser *et al.* (2001).

14 This neglect of social issues, and the rapid deterioration in social conditions during the early years of transition, was noted by UNICEF in many of its Regional Monitoring Reports. For example, in 1993, it wrote,

While a number of comprehensive regional reviews and periodic reports have appeared in recent years on several aspects of the 'Eastern European transition', particularly on the issues of stabilization, privatization, taxation and labour market adjustment, demographic, distributive and welfare issues have received far less attention. However, the gravity and extent of changes recorded in these latter areas – whatever their origins – are both unprecedented and more pronounced, in relative terms, than those observed in Latin America and Africa during the 'lost decade' of the 1980s. Notwithstanding the severity of the crisis and the efforts of several national and international institutions – including the United Nations, the European Community and the World Bank – transition concerns have generally remained narrowly economic or geo-political.

(UNICEF 1993)

15 With respect to market reforms and transition, one of the more controversial policy questions is the effect of enterprise privatisation (most especially, mass/voucher or insider privatisation) on inequality. Although there are a number of papers on the vexed topic of privatisation and the distribution of income and wealth (see McHale and Pankov 1999; Alexeev 1999), any assessment based on quantitative analysis is very difficult to give owing to the dearth of reliable data and empirical evidence. Although the World Bank (2000) finds a negative association between privatisation (and stronger if insider privatisation is used as the index) and income inequality (not surprising given the concentrated ownership that resulted), much more research, both quantitative and qualitative, is required here before any general conclusions can be reached.

16 Although commonly referred to as $4 per capita per day, it is actually $4.30 per capita per day, in 1996 purchasing power parity terms.

17 Although Armenia and Georgia were not included in Milanovic (1998), estimates of poverty numbers for both countries were included in World Bank (2000). Using a 1999 survey and a $4.30 per person per day poverty line, the poverty headcount index was 86 for Armenia and 54 for Georgia.

18 Although the education and health services in former socialist countries were better than in countries of similar income per capita, the quality of state services has declined with transition while access, in terms of cost, is more difficult. In respect of health, a frightening (one of a number) statistic from the World Health Organisation (WHO) is the estimated number of deaths in transition countries from cardiovascular diseases. Indeed, per 100,000 population, TEs have the highest deaths from heart disease anywhere in the world, of countries where reporting is reliable. In 2002, transition countries filled the first 18 places (of which the first nine were FSU republics) in terms of countries in the world with the highest number of deaths from heart disease, Ukraine occupying number one spot with 686 deaths per 100,000 population. Taking the percentage change in the period 1988 to 1998 (roughly corresponding to the first decade of transition), former socialist countries witnessed large increases, for both male and female, in coronary heart disease death rates. For example, whereas Portugal (male/female) and Greece (male/female) witnessed declines of 19/29 and 11/15 per cent respectively, Croatia and Romania recorded increases, for the same period, of 62/61 and 20/26 per cent respectively. For more data, the WHO *Atlas of Heart Disease and Stroke* may be found online at http://www.who.int/cardiovascular_diseases/resources/atlas/en/, accessed 11 September 2009.

19 In the context of inequality and transition countries (and most especially CIS countries), income may not be the best measure to use. First, in Soviet times, Party members and elites received not so insignificant non-wage benefits in the form of dachas, foreign holidays and hard currency, access to state stores, etc. During transition, phenomena such as barter, non-monetary payments, wage arrears and unofficial activities were all common. These and other measurement problems associated with income reporting may make income estimates inaccurate and suggest the use of a consumption-based measure which tended to be less volatile. Notwithstanding this observation, it does appear that income-based and consumption-based estimates are not too dissimilar, although there are greater differences between the two measures for the CIS countries where the use of a consumption-based measure may be more accurate. If the income-based estimate is used, there is not much difference between gross and disposable income as personal income taxes are not very large.

20 A common criticism of time-series data for transition countries is that before and after transition comparisons are not meaningful. With respect to income equality estimates and the underlying data and household surveys, it is indeed the case that there are methodological problems with comparing these countries pre- and post-transition as pre-transition surveys were often not representative of the entire population. Notwithstanding this valid criticism, the evidence on the whole indicates that there was a large increase in inequality, with some CIS countries by the mid-1990s witnessing very large income inequalities.

21 Although Armenia and Georgia were not included in Milanovic (1998), estimates for both countries for 1996 to 1999 were included in World Bank (2000). The Gini index (of income) for 1996 to 1999 was 0.59 for Armenia and 0.43 for Georgia. The estimate for Moldova was 0.42. With respect to Russia, Commander *et al.* (1999), using a large household dataset, claim that official figures have 'grossly understated the degree of inequality'.

22 With respect to self-employment in CIS countries, it is not in retail or services as one might expect but largely in agriculture – often no more than a household plot – and petty trade. This indicates a coping mechanism for survival rather than any medium- to long-term strategic business decision that one often associates with self-employment and entrepreneurial activity.

23 Yao *et al.*'s (2004) estimates include a figure, of 5.5 to 15 million and rising, for urban poor. Although small relative to rural poverty, the authors recommend action, not only the promotion of economic growth but also the reduction of inequality, against urban as well as rural poverty. The authors also conclude that poverty overall is bigger than official estimates.

24 An indication of the difference between poverty trends during transition in CEE/FSU countries and China is given in the World Bank 2000/2001 World Development Report *Attacking Poverty*. Using a $1 per day poverty line and applying it to the global regions as categorised by the World Bank, we can see that for the East Asia and Pacific region (including China) the number of people living on less than $1 a day fell from 417.5 million in 1987 to 278.3 million in 1998 whereas for the same period in Europe and Central Asia (including the TEs of CEE/FSU), the number of people living on less than $1 per day rose from 1.1 million to 24 million. In terms of a share of the world's population living on less than $1 a day, Europe and Central Asia's share increased from 0.2 per cent in 1987 to over 5 per cent one decade later.

25 For example, migrant workers are not included in the analysis, as the official household surveys, based on China's registration system as opposed to any population census, usually only include rural residents and urban dwellers with residency permits. Their inclusion is likely to increase urban inequality and reduce the urban–rural divide.

26 With respect to reforms more generally in China, Naughton (2007a) concludes that although 'China's experience shows that markets work and should be at the heart of any country's development effort', it is also clear that 'China's experience provides no support for "market fundamentalism".' but, on the contrary, 'shows that steady expansion of human and institutional capabilities, consistent and predictable incentives and property rights, and some government coordination to make up for market failures are as important as the steady expansion of markets'. In an earlier article, co-authored with the late John McMillan, he wrote, 'China shows the potency of the fundamental market forces of entry and competition. China's example does not, however, justify *laissez-faire*: the state must monitor firms during the transition' (McMillan and Naughton 1992).

27 UNECE (2004) reaches a similar finding. It concludes:

> Stimulating growth that will benefit the poor and reduce income inequalities will require confronting the vested interests that are holding back restructuring, stifling small-scale private enterprise and frustrating efforts to improve public expenditure management. Poor governance remains an issue at all levels of society ... It is unlikely that real improvements in material and capability poverty will be achieved unless, and until, governance is improved. This will require strengthening systems of public governance administration and financial management, transparency and political accountability and enabling greater community involvement in decision-making, as well as the creation of a competitive and buoyant private sector. Renewed emphasis on institution building – financial and judicial – and continued capacity-building at both national and local levels to ensure delivery of reforms remain essential.

28 The turnover tax, essentially the difference between the administratively set wholesale price and retail price, was a highly differentiated, product-specific tax. The rates (both positive and negative – subsidies were paid in the form of negative turnover tax rates), often in the thousands, were not legislated and were often changed subject to negotiation between enterprise and planner. As in the case of the enterprise profit tax (and its analogous tax, namely corporate income tax), the turnover tax had very little in common with its nearest equivalent (i.e. sales tax/VAT) in modern market-based tax systems.

29 The structure and profile of tax administration that existed in the USSR just before the start of transition, namely the State Tax Service (STS), is discussed in Chapter III.I of *A Study of the Soviet Economy*, Vol. 1. One indication of how straightforward and unsophisticated tax collection was in pre-transition days is the number of staff employed in the Union Ministry of Finance's Department of Main State Tax Inspectorate (MSTI). In 1990, of a total staff of 40,000 in the STS, only 91 worked

for the MSTI (IMF 1991). This tendency to understaff central headquarters continued throughout the 1990s. For example, by the mid-1990s in Russia, less than 1 per cent of the total STS staff worked in headquarters.

30 Taking 1989 as an example, defence expenditure, as recorded in the USSR state budget, amounted to 8 per cent of GDP. It may even have been higher. Comparable figures for the US and for industrial countries as a whole are 5.9 per cent and 4.4 per cent respectively (IMF 1991).

31 Indeed, fiscal policy becomes more important during and post-transition because as the role of the state is reduced vis-à-vis liberalisation and privatisation and with an independent Central Bank in charge of monetary policy, discretionary macroeconomic policy is conducted largely through the government budget.

32 The World Bank report did acknowledge that transition 'may have aggravated' possible contributors (especially substance abuse and the deterioration in healthcare) to the rise in mortality (World Bank 1996).

33 Much of the literature on the Russian mortality crisis has focused on the effects, or otherwise, of alcohol consumption on male life expectancy rates. There appears to be some consensus that excessive consumption of alcohol, and, in particular, the binge drinking that is common in Russia, is related to the excess deaths of working-age males. It remains to be seen what the authorities can do to address this complex social issue. Of course, Russia is not unique in this respect. Other countries have problems with excessive alcohol consumption but the rise in mortality rates that was evident in Russia (and most FSU countries) is prevented elsewhere by other factors, including better health care systems, higher taxes on alcohol sales, better law enforcement, and more stable societies with stronger civil society groups. For more on mortality rates in Russia and the demographic crisis in the post-Soviet era, see the various journal articles in *World Development*, vol. 26, issue 11, 1998.

34 In terms of the possible negative impact of radical reform on mortality rates, it is interesting to note that Russia and Ukraine, despite different speeds of reform with Russian reforms being much quicker and more intensive than the earlier stalled reforms in Ukraine, both experienced a large fall in male life expectancy rates in the early 1990s. What does that tell us about reforms and mortality rates? As one commentator succinctly put it, 'A neoliberal economic viewpoint tells us that it is an object lesson on Soviet ways of doing things and on the deleterious effect of corruption. A sociological perspective believes it is a warning against pushing any nation into radical economic changes without adequately considering its culture' (Anderson 1997).

35 The decline in institutional quality is not the same for all countries. For example, whereas the decline in Hungary is from a position where the institutional quality was relatively high in the mid-1990s, the decline in Kyrgyzstan and Moldova reflects a continuous deterioration from levels that were already very low at the outset. The Chinese case is different again as many of its institutions (for example, dual price liberalisation and local government-owned firms) differ from the standard institutions, and this is reflected in its low scores.

36 Murrell (2005) does distinguish between CEE and FSU countries with the 'institutions in Eastern Europe . . . better than expected on the basis of the level of economic development' whereas 'institutions in the former Soviet Union are worse than would be expected'.

3 INITIAL CONDITIONS AT THE OUTSET OF TRANSITION

1 We need to distinguish between the different features of the socialist system. As Kornai (1992) outlined in his classic book *The Socialist System: The Political Economy of Communism*, the key explanatory factors in the socialist system were one-party rule, state ownership and bureaucratic coordination. These, in turn, led to, *inter alia*, bargaining, the soft budget constraint and the quantity drive. The results of all these factors were shortages, unemployment on the job, forced growth and so on.

2 The 2001 published paper originated from a 1997 working paper by De Melo, Denizer and Gelb, based on a presentation at the first Dubrovnik Conference on Transition, in 1995.

3 As Godoy and Stiglitz (2006) point out, these are mainly economic and structural variables and do not directly measure, as they employ in their article, institutional variables.

4 Regional tensions, war and civil strife was captured in the De Melo *et al.* (2001) study by the inclusion of a dummy variable.

5 Sachs *et al.* (2000) define initial conditions as those that 'describe the situation a country finds itself at the start of the process and are a mixture of geographic fixed characteristics, hard-to-change institutional and economic conditions, and relatively easy-to-change policy conditions' and, furthermore, make a distinction between initial conditions that are fixed (those that are invariant and hard to change, e.g. geography, climate), hard (those that can be changed but not quickly, e.g. quality of institutions, industrial structures) and soft (those that can be changed quickly, e.g. government policy, international relations).

6 This result, namely the important role of initial conditions in explaining differences in growth performance, was a finding in a number of studies, including Heybey and Murrell (1999) and Stuart and Panayotopoulos (1999). The diminishing effect of initial conditions on cross-country performance is highlighted in World Bank (2002a) *Transition – The First Ten Years* report, and, later, in a paper by Godoy and Stiglitz (2006) who conclude that, over a longer period of analysis, initial conditions have an insignificant effect on cross-sectional growth.

7 Murrell (1996) later observes that policies may have 'become increasingly homogeneous over time but outcomes have become more varied, suggesting that initial conditions greatly determine the effectiveness of policies'. Similarly, in a response to a paper by Åslund, Boone and Johnson, Barry Ickes notes, 'My argument is simply that the initial conditions that a transition country faces affect its choice of liberalization strategy and the success of its reforms' (Åslund *et al.* 1996).

4 PARADIGMS OF TRANSITION

1 Taking a political economy approach, Marangos (2004) identifies five different models of transition, namely the Neoclassical Gradualist model, the Shock Therapy model, the Post Keynesian model, the Pluralistic Market Socialist model and the Non-pluralistic Market Socialist model (the Chinese approach). The first two approaches are neoclassical in outlook, and broadly coincide with the two paradigms outlined in this chapter; whereas the third is a post-Keynesian approach, the other two are perspectives from market socialism, with and without political democracy.

2 Havrylyshyn (2006) outlines a somewhat different paradigm, the Kornai-Blanchard (KB) framework where he combines Kornai's (1994) transformational recession analysis with Blanchard's (1997) work on reallocation and restructuring. By doing so, transition involves four key changes, namely (adopted from the Kornai model) the move from a sellers' to a buyers' market and the hardening of the budget constraint, and, from the Blanchard model, the reallocation of resources combined with restructuring existing firms (or to use World Bank speak, encouragement and discipline). Although useful as a model, we do not see the KB framework as an alternative to the two well-established paradigms outlined in this chapter.

3 The term 'Washington Consensus' dates back to a background paper on policy reform for Latin America prepared by John Williamson for a conference organised by the Washington-based Institute for International Economics in November 1989, the same month, coincidentally, that the Berlin Wall collapsed in Eastern Europe (see Williamson 1990).

4 The demise of the state socialist system at the end of the 1980s coincided with, as Vito Tanzi, the former Director of the Fiscal Affairs Department at the IMF, put it, a 'universal rediscovery of the market' (Tanzi 1997). Throughout the Western world, neo-liberalism had been on the rise since the previous decade and had reached a high point in the mid-1980s with the reign of Ronald Reagan and Margaret Thatcher in the US and UK respectively. For a highly charged and polemical account of the neo-liberal shock therapy agenda see Naomi Klein's *The Shock Doctrine: The Rise of Disaster Capitalism*, Penguin, 2007.

5 Marangos (2007) distinguishes between what he calls the Washington Consensus proper (as was originally constituted by John Williamson), the Washington Consensus neo-liberal manifesto, and shock therapy.

6 Kolodko (1999), in his attack on the Washington Consensus, describes it as the 'half-baked advice according to which the sooner government becomes small, the sooner the market economy can begin to rise and expand'. Easterly (2006), in his attack on mega-reforms and Big Push strategies, argued, 'the top-down solutions do not translate well into fixing whole societies that are at one-sixtieth of U.S. per capita income and with very different institutions, social norms, and economic arrangements'. He also argues that the debate between supporters of the Big Bang and supporters

of incrementalism is but a modern-day version of the long-standing intellectual debate concerning social and economic change, and, in particular, dates back to the 1950s and 1960s within development economics when supporters of the Big Push strategy (see Rosenstein-Rodan 1943) clashed with advocates (including Albert Hirschman) of the Unbalanced Growth strategy. One difference between the Big Push theory of development economics and the Big Bang theory of transition economics is that the former argued for state planning and greater public investment while the latter strategy supported state withdrawal and less public investment.

7 Poznanski (1995) explains that unlike neoclassical economics which is primarily concerned with the scarce allocation of resources, evolutionary economics is largely concerned with the shortage of information. Institution building is the principal method of maximising information flows, with evolutionary theorists advocating a gradual, organic type of institutionalisation. Differences between the market system and the planned system can be measured in terms of respective information costs. For an interesting use of evolutionary metaphors in the context of evolution and transition (with transition described as a 'mass extinction process') see Ickes (2003).

8 Along similar lines to our two paradigms, Kornai (2000a) in his self-evaluation of *The Road to a Free Economy* outlines two strategies to ownership reform and the development of the private sector. He calls Strategy A, the strategy of organic development and Strategy B, the strategy of accelerated privatisation. His strategy A is similar to the institutional-evolutionary approach whereas strategy B is analogous to the Washington Consensus approach. Similarly, Miller and Tenev (2007) outline two distinct approaches to transition. One view, what might be coined the ideological approach, focuses on ownership change and privatisation, with little role for the state and where welfare considerations are secondary. The second perspective, referred to as the pragmatic approach, highlights, in contrast, welfare and development, with the reform – as opposed to the destruction – of the state and the alignment of incentives at all levels of government bureaucracy being an important priority (Miller and Tenev 2007).

9 Murrell (1993) provides the reader with a critique of the shock therapy approach and the early radical reforms that were undertaken in Poland and Russia. As elsewhere, Murrell (1993) advocates an alternative approach to the revolutionary top-down reforms, one based on evolutionary change. In the same *Post-Soviet Affairs* issue, Brada (1993) provides an alternative perspective, and a defence of radical reform. Later Murrell (2005) gives an account of the role of new institutional economics in understanding, and influencing, transition.

10 A more detailed table outlining the differences between the two approaches to transition is given in Roland (2000, 2001). Gabrisch and Hölscher (2006) also include the differences in tabular form. Although these are now regarded as the two broad theories of transition, there were other views at the outset of transition. For example, Berend (2009) draws attention to the policy recommendations made both by the Research Institute of the Ministry of International Trade and Industry, in Japan, and the Viennese Agenda Group, in Austria. In advocating a more government-led, gradual approach, both sets of recommendations were closer to the institutional-evolutionary approach than the Washington Consensus approach. For a recent Japanese perspective on transition, and the differences between the European (CEE) and (East) Asian experiences, see Ichimura *et al.* (2009).

11 Michael Ellman, in Admiraal (1993), distinguishes, in the context of economic transition, between two approaches or schools of thought. The constructivists are utopians who are system builders and advocate rapid change whereas Popperians emphasise gradual change conditional on local conditions and circumstances. Popper and his support of gradualism and change by trial and error gets a favourable mention, in the context of transition in both Europe and Asia, in Dahrendorf (1990) and Nolan (1995). Still further, Murrell (1993), in claiming that the 'radical and organic views are modern economic variants of wider, older traditions', sees a similarity with, among others, the debate between the teleologists and the geneticists that took place in the 1920s in the USSR. More generally, he writes, 'the divide between radicals and evolutionists is not simply a matter of technical judgments about narrow economic issues. Rather, that divide reflects fundamental disagreements about the way human societies function, differences in judgments on matters of politics, psychology, and society, as well as economics' (Murrell 1993).

12 It was the Nobel laureate Robert M. Solow of MIT who wrote, 'There is not some glorious theoretical synthesis of capitalism that you can write down in a book and follow. You have to grope your way' (*New York Times*, 29 September 1991).

13 In one of the first volume studies on transition, published in 1994 but based on a NBER conference held in 1992, Lawrence Summers refers to the 'striking degree of unanimity' on the advice given to transition countries. Among some notable detractors to this 'consensus' was Peter Murrell who, in 1995, wrote, 'Inherited arrangements, functional and pathological, Eastern and Western, had a profound influence on outcomes, reminding us that history and society, as well as sensible economics, are important actors on transition's stage' (Murrell 1995).

14 As outlined in its Articles of Agreement, the purpose of the IMF is to promote international monetary cooperation, exchange stability, and orderly exchange arrangements; to foster economic growth and high levels of employment; and to provide temporary financial assistance to countries to help ease balance of payments adjustment. According to the World Bank, its mission is to fight poverty and improve the living standards of people in the developing world.

5 TRANSITION REFORMS AND ECONOMIC POLICIES

1 For a taxonomy of major societal transitions, including the post-communist transition in Eastern Europe, see Balcerowicz (1995, 2002).

2 As the reader can see from the figure, institutional and legal reforms were part of the reform package as recommended by mainstream economists. However, with respect to the role of institutions in the context of transition reforms, the difference between advocates of the Big Bang and those who favoured gradual reform was not the absence or presence of institutional reform (as was often claimed) but the degree, timing and importance of institutional change. In the first decade of transition, the emphasis was on the trinity (not surprisingly given the crisis in many former socialist countries at the outset of transition, and, the prevalence, at that time, of the neo-liberal agenda worldwide) and less on institutional and legal reform. Well before the second decade, institutional design had become the key element of reform.

3 Marangos (2004) uses a variation of the reform policies outlined in Figure 5.1 to distinguish between the gradualist approach and the shock therapy approach. Differences relate not to the package of reforms itself (as both approaches, according to the author, agree on the essential elements, namely stabilisation and price liberalisation, privatisation, monetary, financial and fiscal reforms, foreign trade, social policy and institutional reform) but to the priorities, sequencing and speed of these reform elements.

4 It is claimed that the concept of mass voucher privatisation was first formulated at the end of the 1980s by Janusz Lewandowski and Jan Szomburg, members of the so-called Gdańsk-based liberals. Their proposal for mass privatisation based on vouchers was published, in Polish, in 1989/1990.

5 With respect to the privatisation scheme in the Czech Republic, Portes (1993) noted that 'this is as pure an application of the 19th century French economist Léon Walras's iterative price-setting procedure (*tâtonnement*) on as large a scale as we are likely to see in economic policy – and correspondingly risky'. With respect to Russian privatisation, many accounts, the majority of an unfavourable nature, have been given of its privatisation programme. For a particularly critical insiders' account of the process (and outcomes), see Black, Bernard, Reinier Kraakman and Anna Tarassova 'Russian Privatisation and Corporate Governance: What Went Wrong?', *Stanford Law Review*, vol. 52, 2000. It neatly describes the rapid mass voucher privatisation, insider self-dealing, tunnelling and asset-stripping activities commonly associated with the Russian privatisation of the 1990s.

6 Willem Buiter, former Chief Economist of the EBRD, in a 2004 address entitled 'What have we learnt from fifteen years of transition in Central and Eastern Europe', to an International Policy Conference in Vietnam, commented, 'In a world with high transaction costs, there is no "Coase theorem" supporting privatisation on a first-come first-served basis: ownership and the initial allocation of property rights can have a major impact on efficiency.'

7 China's reforms were the big exception to the rulebook. As Mukand and Rodrik (2005) note, 'China's reforms have been marked by partial liberalisation, two-track pricing, limited deregulation, financial restraint, an unorthodox legal regime, and an absence of clear private property rights.'

8 In more recent years (and since the publication of the 2007 Transition Report) the EBRD has classified reforms into three categories: market-enabling, first-stage reforms (comprising market liberalisation and small-scale privatisation), market-deepening, second-stage reforms (comprising large-scale privatisation and financial sector reform) and market-sustaining, third-stage reforms (comprising governance and enterprise restructuring, and reform to competition policy and infrastructure).

According to the EBRD in 2008, the first-stage reforms were complete except in Belarus, Turkmenistan, and Uzbekistan, the second-stage reforms, requiring 'more than just political will . . . need to be supported by institutional reforms', are complete in EU accession countries but elsewhere much remains to be done, and the third-stage reforms are unfinished even in the more advanced TEs.

9 In their interdisciplinary work *Institutional Design in Post-communist Societies: Rebuilding the Ship at Sea* (note that this is not the first time that the ship at sea analogy is used: see Havrylyshyn (2006)), Elster *et al.* (1998) identify a similar taxonomy of reforms. Whereas the initial retreat of the state from the economy (akin to the initial phase reforms) comprised curtailing state expenditures, divestiture of state-owned assets, wage and capital markets, liberalisation of prices, and market entry, the furnishing of capitalism and new markets (analogous to the second-phase reforms), included the adoption of a legal framework, enterprise restructuring and banking sector reform. Interestingly, the EBRD uses an average of a specific set of transition indictors of second-phase reforms (comprising privatisation, governance and enterprise restructuring, competition policy, infrastructure reforms, banking and interest rate liberalisation and non-bank financial institutions) as a metric for 'institutional reforms'. As the reader will see later, we prefer to use broader measures, including Weder (2001) and Kaufmann *et al.* (2009), which we believe are more comprehensive measures of institutional reform.

10 More worryingly, Berglöf and Bolton (2002) note that

> Even though the basic financial architecture of a market economy is now in place in the countries on the right side of the great divide, banking and other financial institutions do not yet perform their intended functions of channeling savings to the most productive investments.

11 In some cases, more than two groups are identified. For example, Havrylyshyn (2006) classifies the 27 CEE/FSU countries into five groups on the basis of reform strategies. They are Advanced Start, Steady Progress; Sustained Big-Bang; Big-Bang Unsustained; Gradual, Delayed Reforms; and Limited or Reversed Reforms. In addition, the former East Germany's (GDR) transition to a market economy was different as it fully adopted the West German economic and legal system on reunification.

12 Solimano, in his concluding comments on reform in post-socialist and post-dirigiste transition, writes,

> the different country experiences . . . show the enormous variety in the possible routes to a reformed market economy, both across and within the group of socialist and nonsocialist countries. Universally valid blueprints showing how to conduct reform hardly exist. However, other countries' experiences – of both success and failure – provide important information and analysis for those embarking on reform. Systemic transformation in real life ultimately requires informed judgment, political vision, and good luck.
>
> (Solimano *et al.* 1994)

13 According to the World Bank's review of reform in the 1990s, 'economic policies and policy advice must be country-specific and institution-sensitive if they are to be effective' (World Bank 2005b). Back in 1999, the EBRD wrote, 'the development of institutions that support markets and private enterprise is at the heart of the transition' (EBRD 1999). Interestingly, as Rodrik (2006) and others note, the IMF appears to be less revisionist. For example, in 2003, Stanley Fischer, a former First Deputy Managing Director of the IMF and advocate of rapid and comprehensive market reforms, wrote, 'After ten years of experience, the evidence is clear: the basic economic reform and growth strategy recommended by mainstream economists . . . works'.

14 In terms of foreign aid, Jeffrey Sachs, an early advocate of the Big Bang approach to transition, argued strongly in favour of a large financial package to transition countries and was critical of the international community when no Marshall-type Plan materialised. In terms of an investment strategy, as early as the mid-1990s advocates of market reforms acknowledged that 'the key to rapid growth in the transition economies is . . . investment and the policies that promote it' (Fischer *et al.* 1996b). The difference, however, between the alternative policy camps was in terms of the state's role, with respect to investment, and the need, or otherwise, for an active industrial policy.

15 In the case of institutions and TEs, laws could be created from scratch (deliberately in order to match the specific cultural, social, economic and political characteristics of the country), copied from other jurisdictions or, in the case where old (pre-communist) laws and codes existed, revived. In some

cases all three options were followed. Often, however, the problem was not the law itself but its enforcement.

16 The lack of emphasis in the first decade of transition on institutional arrangements was eventually recognised by many of the mainstream policy advisers, including the IMF. In its *World Economic Outlook* Report 2000, there was an acknowledgement that, 'although the need for an institutional infrastructure to support the nascent market economies was recognised from the beginning, in practice such institution building was not always given adequate attention' (IMF 2000). In the same year, John Williamson (of the Institute for International Economics, and the Washington Consensus), wrote, 'The major advance of the 1990s stemmed from the recognition that the central task of the transition from communist to market-based economies involved building the institutional infrastructure of a market economy. This realization was complemented by a growing recognition that bad institutions can sabotage good policies' (Williamson 2000). The UNECE 2003 *Economic Survey of Europe* report was more critical when it noted that 'the general underestimation and even neglect of the importance of adequate institution building for the general success of the transition process was a major weakness of the reform efforts in the early stages of transition' (UNECE 2003).

17 On a related matter, North (2000) writes: 'We are still a long way from having a theory of economic change and the accumulated evidence we have from fragmented stories of different countries does not add up to giving us firm convictions.' To illustrate the importance of institutions, a recent paper by Djankov *et al.* (2003) argues that differences in institutions and how they account for differences in economic performance are the subject of what the authors call the 'new comparative economics'.

18 In the words of Kornai (2000a), 'The "trinity" of privatization, liberalization and stabilization will not suffice for a successful transition.' In the same article and in the context of what he refers to as accelerated privatisation, he writes, 'a more solid foundation for an irreversible advance of capitalism would be provided if a broad bourgeoisie developed, property rights and private contracts applied consistently, democracy was institutionalized, and the market economy enjoyed political support from the majority of voters'.

19 Murrell (2005), in describing transition in the context of new institutional economics, refers to the 'institutional earthquake' that transition countries and state enterprises experienced when the old socialist system collapsed, with 'mammoth institutional destruction and construction . . . on the agenda'.

20 A variant of this methodology is the composite institutional index, comprising five components from the *International Country Risk Guide* (ICRG). Of the five, three are common to the two indices, namely rule of law, corruption and bureaucracy quality. The other two are repudiation of contracts by government and expropriation risk. More details on the use of this index may be found in Burki and Perry (1998) *Beyond the Washington Consensus: Institutions Matter*, World Bank. The role of institutions – or, more precisely, the institutional dimensions of governance – their measurement, the construction of a panel dataset and the testing for their effect on cross-country performance are also dealt with, in the context of transition economies, in Campos (2000). Earlier, Knack and Keefer (1995) use institutional data compiled by two private international investment risk services: ICRG and Business Environmental Risk Intelligence (BERI) to test for the effects on economic growth over the period 1974 to 1989. For statistical reasons, the different ICRG and BERI variables are aggregated into two composite indices, measuring the security of contractual and property rights, i.e. indices of institutional quality.

21 In their account of large-scale social change in *The Grand Experiment*, Pickel and Wiesenthal (1997) go on to write, 'Historically, today's successful market economies have not emerged by establishing in a simultaneous fashion the core institutions of the market as defined by the radicals. Evidently, the transition to the market can be successfully accomplished in a variety of piecemeal, and perhaps at times even disjointed and coherent, ways.'

22 For a very interesting historical account of the 'rights' to property in Russia ('rule by law') as compared with the West ('rule of law'), see Hedlund (2001). It is here that Hedlund describes the process of Russian reform as more like 'destructive creation' than (Schumpeter's) 'creative destruction'. For a more comprehensive account of the Russian tradition and path dependency, see *Russian Path Dependence* (Hedlund 2005).

23 The Czech Republic is not included in Figure 5.3 as it graduated from the EBRD (due to '. . . its advanced stage of transition . . .') at the end of 2007, with no new investments by the EBRD in the Czech Republic thereafter.

24 Although quite dated now, Richard Portes' early analysis of the policy mistakes in Eastern Europe is still worth repeating. In his 1994 *Transformation Traps*, he identified nine policy errors. They were (1) programmes of restitution of physical property; (2) overemphasis on macroeconomic relative to microeconomic policies; (3) excessively tight monetary policy; (4) excessive devaluation and inadequately specific exchange rate policy; (5) misunderstanding of the capacities and behaviour of the SOEs; (6) overly complex and ambitious plans to privatise SOEs; (7) sequencing errors; (8) deliberate early dissolution of CMEA, and (9) inadequate emphasis on debt reduction and excessive delays in all cases (Portes 1994).

6 ENTERPRISE REFORM AND RESTRUCTURING

1 Blanchard (1997) identifies the basic mechanisms of microeconomic change as, alongside the process of disorganisation and reorganisation, the reallocation of resources (from old to new, both in terms of firms and activities) and the restructuring (of state firms).

2 Priority was given to industry (and, within that, heavy industry over light industry) over agriculture, military production over civilian production, producer goods over consumer goods, material goods over services, and large enterprises over small enterprises. More generally in terms of enterprise preferences, in a centrally planned system priority was given to state ownership as opposed to private ownership, acquisition of inputs as opposed to disposition of output and domestic production over production for foreign markets.

3 With the exception of Yugoslavia and the USSR during Khruschev's reign of the early 1960s.

4 It may also be argued that pre-transition reforms exacerbated the problems in the socialist system and the state enterprise sector. In particular, early reforms in the Soviet socialist system meant that branch ministries lost control of their SOEs, resulting in, among other things, ever-increasing wage concessions at the micro level and, at the macro level, rising budget deficits.

5 Roland (2008b) notes that traditional economic theory does not have much to offer in terms of public vs. private ownership of firms and the transfer of ownership rights from public to private. In general equilibrium theory what matters is that firms are profit maximisers and operate in competitive markets. More recently, economic theory has been more enlightening with regard to public and private ownership, with the advance of modern microeconomic theory and, in particular, the development of contract theory and the incomplete contracts approach. In the same publication, Stiglitz writes that the 'theoretical case for privatization is, at best, weak or nonexistent' (Roland 2008b).

6 The authors of this article and the book *Privatising Russia*, namely Maxim Boycko, Andrei Shleifer and Robert Vishny, were involved in designing the Russian mass privatisation scheme of the early 1990s. For a different insiders' account, see Black *et al.* (2000) 'Russian Privatisation and Corporate Governance: What went wrong?', *Stanford Law Review*, 52.

7 The best example of a country with direct sales as the primary form of privatisation was East Germany (GDR). Treuhand, the privatisation agency set up to sell off state-owned enterprises, sold over 13,800 firms (or parts of firms) between 1990 and 1994, primarily to West German investors. Although it managed a very rapid privatisation, it did so at a large financial cost, selling off many enterprises cheaply and, at the same time, amassing a large debt in the process (Brada 1996).

8 Interestingly, authors of an earlier World Bank study concluded that privatisation outcomes were determined by a number of factors, of which the two most important were country conditions and the nature of the market into which the firm was being divested, i.e. competitive or non-competitive (Shirley *et al.* 1992).

9 Its sister organisation, the World Bank, also accepts the failings with respect to the design of privatisation in transition countries. In its 2005 review of a decade of reform, it writes,

> Advocates of rapid privatisation won the day, but critics now question the haste and point to mistakes that were made: assets were sold to cronies at low prices, and the many institutions that were vital to supporting the market have been slow to develop. Minority shareholders have few protections, and privatisation sometimes resulted in the new owners stripping assets and spiriting them abroad rather than investing to improve their working.
>
> (World Bank 2005b)

10 As we are only focusing here on the enterprise-level impacts of privatisation, we exclude the literature on the possible macro effects of privatisation on the economy and society at large.

11 A later study by the same authors, for a range of transition countries, was equally unimpressed by the effects of privatisation on firm performance. When controlling for potential endogeneity/ selection of ownership, the positive results of earlier years are less evident, and particularly so for domestic – as opposed to foreign – private ownership. Their 'relatively sobering assessment' was that privatisation 'did not have the strongly positive effect on economic performance that was expected' (Hanousek *et al.* 2008).

12 Aghion and Blanchard (1998), on the basis of the first few years of transition, claimed that enterprise restructuring requires outsider ownership whereas political constraints require insider privatisation. There is much evidence from transition countries to support these propositions.

13 In the 37 studies that the two authors examined for results of privatisation, Murrell contributed as a co-author on two papers relating to the mass privatisation programme in Mongolia. In one of these papers the authors conclude that firms with residual state ownership are more efficient than all other firms, including privatised firms (Anderson *et al.* 2000).

14 In accounting for the problems with the Czech mass privatisation scheme, Claessens and Djankov (1999a) conclude that 'Our results lend more support to the alternative view . . . that the Czech government fell victim to its own success in privatisation by not introducing proper institutions to oversee the development of capital markets.'

15 Lieberman and Kopf (2008) offer a defence of privatisation, and the involvement of the World Bank as part of the external advisory community, in transition countries. For example, one of the contributions concludes that 'Privatisation therefore achieved what was expected of it as a leading structural reform in the region' (Lieberman *et al.* 2008). Another, invoking the *realpolitik* argument used by reformers and policy makers, concludes that 'the ultimate conclusion is that while privatisation could have and probably should have been done better, it nonetheless had to be done. The Czech Republic and Russia, and others in the region, are better off after the flawed privatisations they carried out than they would have been had they avoided or delayed divestiture' (Nellis 2008).

16 Stiglitz (2000) reaches a similar conclusion when writing that 'economists, who should have known better, had a hand in helping create these interests, believing somehow – in spite of the long history to the contrary – that Coasian forces would lead to efficient social outcomes'.

17 For example, in 1992, Dusan Triska (Head of the Czech Privatisation Agency, later renamed and known as the National Property Fund) wrote, 'Privatisation . . . is not just one of the many items on the economic program. It is the transformation itself . . . Privatisation is the element that distinguishes transformation from reform. That is why privatisation must be conceived of and viewed as an end in itself' (Lieberman and Kopf 2008).

18 According to one renowned expert on enterprise reform and transition, 'privatisation has rarely led to effective corporate governance mechanisms' (Estrin 2002).

19 The use of the terms 'market' and 'market structures' in the context of state socialism is somewhat of a contradiction, as no real markets existed in the pre-reform era (Lavigne 1999).

20 In terms of accounting for cross-country performance, Miller and Tenev (2007) claim that the role of government (underpinned by contrasting ideological beliefs), and in particular, the incentives and capabilities of (all levels of) bureaucracy partly explains the differences in economic performance in Russia and China. Whereas Russia gave priority to economic reform and privatisation, China focused on administrative reform and state restructuring. The authors claim that these differences help in explaining 'arguably the most salient fact of transition', that is, the 'different economic performance of transitioning Asia versus Central and Eastern Europe and the FSU' (Miller and Tenev 2007).

21 Zhuravskaya (2000) claims that the lack of entrepreneurial activity and new business formation in Russia, as compared with China, is related to fiscal federalism, intergovernmental fiscal relations and most particularly the fiscal incentives (especially revenue-sharing relations between local and regional governments) that exist in both countries. Her results, based on budgetary data for Russian cities and regions, provide evidence in support of the hypothesis that the number of newly formed businesses is positively correlated with the government's fiscal incentives.

22 According to the Eurostat Structural Business Statistics (SBS) database for 2004 and 2005, of the 10 EU accession (former socialist) countries, the Baltic States have the highest SME shares of value-added (well above the EU average and similar to levels found in the EU Mediterranean countries), followed by, in order, Slovenia, the Czech Republic, Bulgaria, Romania, Hungary, Poland and the

Slovak Republic. When expressed in terms of employment, Bulgaria, the Czech Republic, Hungary and Poland do much better in terms of SME contribution.

23 The number of small businesses in Russia is both relatively low and underdeveloped. In the late 1990s, according to official statistics, Russia's small businesses accounted for 11 per cent of total GDP, as compared with levels close to 50 per cent for many market economies. The percentage of the population employed in these businesses is estimated at somewhere below 20 per cent, well below the 50 to 70 per cent levels observed in many developed market economies (Goskomstat, OECD). Even if we allow for the number of small businesses that may be operating in the informal economy and include an estimate for the number of individual entrepreneurs, the total figure for small businesses is still well below the average for mature market economies. It is also the case that the definition of a small business may differ from country to country as there is no universal size definition. According to the European Commission definition, a small enterprise (as opposed to a medium-sized enterprise, defined as having fewer than 250 employees) is one whose workforce is fewer than 50 employees. In Russia, according to the Federal Law No. 88–Ф3 of 14 June 1995, 'On State Support for Small Business in the Russian Federation' the small business definition comprises (1) small enterprises – legal entities; (2) farms, and (3) individual entrepreneurs without legal status. For Russia, using the number of persons employed as the criterion for a small business, the maximum number of employees is 100 for industry, building and transport, 60 for agriculture, science and technological fields, and 30 for retail trade and consumer services.

24 This raises the important issue of identifying a suitable or appropriate benchmark for the transition countries, and particularly the former socialist CEE/FSU countries. Often it is the case that, at least in terms of reforms and outcomes, they are compared to OECD or EU countries, when the result is often unfavourable. This is indeed the case when, in terms of the ease of doing business, we compare Eastern Europe and Central Asia with the OECD high-income region. However, when we compare the region to regions comprising low- and middle-income countries (with similar levels of development), the result is reversed, i.e. CEE/FSU countries do relatively well, as evident in the relatively low average rank for *doing business*. This applies elsewhere, and arises again in Chapter 7 when we examine the economic record and performance of transition countries.

25 Meta-analysis is a statistical technique that integrates, for the purpose of synthesising findings, the results of different comparable quantitative studies. As an alternative to the traditional narrative literature reviews, it is widely used in some of the social and medical sciences.

26 In another (co-authored) paper by Djankov examining the effect of management turnover on enterprise performance, Claessens and Djankov (1999b) find evidence, for the Czech Republic over the period 1993 to 1997, of a positive relationship between profitability and appointments of new managers, indicating the importance of new human capital for transition countries.

27 A more recent study (covering both the early and late transition period) of privatisation effects in transition economies is by Estrin *et al.* (2009). It differs from Djankov and Murrell (2002) in that it distinguishes separately the impact of privatisation on performance indicators such as efficiency, profitability, sales and revenues. Estrin and colleagues also distinguish between effects on the level of performance and effects on growth. Unlike many previous surveys, China is included in the study, although the authors do acknowledge that privatisation started late in China and, partly as a result, there are relatively few convincing, at least econometrically, studies on privatisation effects in China. Overall, they conclude that privatisation and performance are indeed related, but the relationship is 'more complicated than has been assumed' and the policy implication is that privatisation 'per se does not guarantee improved performance, at least not in the short to medium run'. Their concluding remarks, that 'type of private ownership, corporate governance, access to know-how and markets, and the legal and institutional system matter for firm restructuring and performance', confirm much of the material in our chapter on enterprise reform and restructuring.

28 This Djankov and Murrell extract is taken from the first draft of the paper, in April 2000, and the shortened volume published by the World Bank later that year. A slightly different wording is contained in later versions of the paper and in the version published in the *Journal of Economic Literature* in September 2002. It reads,

> Privatisation to outsiders is found to have the largest positive effects on enterprise restructuring, both in Eastern Europe and in the CIS. Hardened budgets are also economically significant in explaining restructuring. Increased competition is associated with positive results in Eastern

Europe but not in the CIS. . . . Finally, privatisation to workers has not enhanced restructuring in Eastern Europe and has had negative effects in the CIS.

7 PERFORMANCE AND TRANSITION OUTCOMES

1 Other difficulties faced by the national statistical offices in transition countries included the move from the Material Product System (using as its main indicator Net Material Product, with its exclusion of non-material output, i.e. services) as used in the Soviet era to the UN System of National Accounts as used in market economies, the choice of base year for constant-price series, deflating nominal output when inflation rates are exceedingly high (and rising), how to account for non-monetary transactions (particularly common in the early years and most especially in the CIS countries) and the ability to survey, monitor and report data in countries devastated by economic disruption, wars and regional conflicts.

2 United Nations Economic Commission for Europe, *Economic Survey of Europe*, no. 1, 2004.

3 Eichengreen (2007) then proceeds to point out a number of caveats, including the observations that previous output contributed little to living standards, that the fall in production (as measured against the decline in electricity consumption) may have been overstated, and that the statistical agencies failed to capture much of the new private enterprise, amounting to a view that 'all these are reasons for thinking that welfare rose even as output was falling'. While these are all valid, it is debatable whether welfare actually did improve (even in the better performing CEE countries) in the early years of transition.

4 Bunce (1999) refers to the 'remarkable diversity' in economic performance and the striking 'intraregional contrast in postsocialist economic and political pathways'. As for an explanation for this variation in outcomes, and unlike economic reform which 'seems to be shaped by proximate politics', the variation in 'economic performance seems to be heavily influenced by distal economics', i.e. initial conditions and the socialist past (Bunce 1999).

5 Although Russia retained sole right to print roubles, republican Gosbanks still had the authority to grant credits. This gave the republics an incentive to adopt more expansionary policies than otherwise, with the knowledge that the resulting inflation would be spread to other countries in the rouble zone. This is a good example of the free-rider problem in economics (Pomfret 2002).

6 For example, male life expectancy in Russia, from a peak of 65 years in 1986 to 1988, was falling in the years immediately prior to the dissolution of the USSR in December 1991 and the start of market reforms in January 1992. However, the largest fall in life expectancy, from 62 years to 59 years, was in 1992 to 1993, coinciding with the first two years of transition and market reforms. In addition, not surprisingly given the size of the country, there are large regional differences in life expectancy at birth in Russia. These inter-regional differences increased in the early years of transition and despite some convergence after that, diverged again after the 1998 crisis (Ellman 1997a; Shkolnikov *et al.* 1998).

7 The increase in inequality has been acknowledged by the IMF, the international organisation most associated with, and supportive of, market reforms in transition. In its 2000 *World Economic Outlook*, it admits, 'there is little doubt that inequality has risen substantially and the economic situation for a substantial number of people, particularly those at the lower end of the income scale or whose savings were wiped out by high inflation at the start of transition, has worsened' (IMF 2000).

8 At the same time, he also acknowledges that, 'from the perspective of everyday life, the result is different. Deep economic troubles are experienced by a considerable portion of the population', resulting in 'pain, bitterness and disappointment for so many people' (Kornai 2006a). It must be remembered here that, as he states in this article, his overall positive assessment is based on a number of particular values, and most especially, democracy and human rights.

9 When compared with the growth rates recorded in the East Asian NICs or Tiger countries of Japan, South Korea and Taiwan, the growth performance of China is less remarkable. With Japan's per capita GDP growth of 490 per cent between 1950 and 1973, South Korea's per capita GDP growth of 680 per cent between 1962 and 1990 and Taiwan's per capita GDP growth of 600 per cent between 1958 and 1987, China's GDP per capita growth rate of 337 per cent between 1978 and 2003 has been 'far from spectacular by the standards of its smaller Asian neighbours' (Wolf 2005).

10 When it became evident that all transition countries, with the exception of China and Vietnam, were experiencing sharp initial falls in output, many in the economics profession claimed that the fall in

output was both inevitable and unavoidable. This may very well be the case (although there is some evidence to the contrary), but these claims often contradicted what the majority of mainstream economists were predicting at the outset of transition. More admission of mistakes in forecasting the possible outcomes of systemic change or a failure to properly understand the institutional underpinnings of the market system from a more humble profession would have been more welcome.

11 In 2000, he wrote, 'My prognosis was wrong. I did not predict the deep recession that followed; I was too optimistic in my expectations of future growth' (Kornai 2000a).

12 Robert Mundell, the 1999 Nobel Prize in Economic Sciences winner, was more forthright in his views. Writing in 1995, he had this to say about the fall in output. 'One of the most remarkable economic events of the twentieth century has been the tremendous contraction of output experienced by the economies of Eastern Europe and the former Soviet Union as they underwent the transition from communism to postcommunist or market economies.'

13 The variation in cross-country performance may be different, and, indeed reduced, when estimates of economic activity in the informal economy are taken into account. China and Vietnam are not included in Figure 7.2, as economic transition in both of those countries started before 1989. Turkmenistan is omitted, as the data are unreliable.

14 A similar schematic framework can be found in Balcerowicz (1995) and Sachs *et al.* (2000), with the former including an interesting account of his personal reflections on the early days of transition in Poland.

15 Many of the cross-country regression studies in transition are based on Barro's (1991) initial study where growth is a function of initial income, policy variables and structural variables. For a more complete and up-to-date account of economic growth, both theory and empirical evidence, see Robert J. Barro and Xavier Sala-i-Martin, *Economic Growth*, 2nd edition, MIT Press, 2004.

16 For example, measures of reform are imperfect, as both the EBRD transition indicators and the World Bank liberalisation index are both subjective indices (as, indeed, are many of the institutional measures that are commonly used in regression analysis) rather than directly observable variables. Another example would be, when measuring speed of policy reform, we need to distinguish between policy and policy change.

17 Havrylyshyn (2001) concludes: 'It is agreed that no royal road to growth exists but that a wide range of good policies is needed, including financial stabilization, market liberalization, and market-friendly government rules and institutions.' In their account of output performance, World Bank authors (2002a) concluded,

> Although policies and initial conditions account for more than half the variability of output growth across countries and years, they still leave substantial room for other factors influencing growth. A full explanation of output performance would have to include more country-specific factors – as well as shocks and other omitted factors – and a detailed analysis of individual countries or smaller groups of countries.

8 LABOUR MARKETS IN TRANSITION

1 'Market coordination has a substantial influence on the allocation of labor and on wages. However, the assertion is true insofar as the market influence is secondary; the influence of bureaucratic coordination is far stronger than that of the market' (Kornai 1992). According to Nove (1986b),

> There are, however, ample statistics showing that millions of people change their jobs annually of their own volition, as they have the formal right to do, and migrate from area to area in total disregard of the planners' intentions. Labor mobility is far from perfect (where *is* it perfect?), but enough mobility exists to ensure that very serious problems would arise if the wage rate in an industry, profession, or region were such that the necessary labor force could not be attracted and retained . . . forces of supply, and demand are an important influence on actual earnings.

2 There was a period of 25 years or so in a small number of advanced market economies shortly after the Second World War when unemployment was negligible. From a historical perspective that has been the exception rather than the rule for market economies throughout the world.

3 Occasionally the opposite process may be seen, especially in relation to the so-called corporatist model where there is a 'tripartite' arrangement between the trade unions, management and the state whereby what can be afforded by the economy in terms of wage increases is discussed centrally between all three parties and then all sides are expected to honour such an agreement.

4 Naturally, for the interested reader, there are quite a few theories to explain wage formation under market economies apart from the elementary supply-and-demand diagrams that you will come across in introductory textbooks: efficiency wages; insider–outsider models; implicit wage contracts; dual labour markets; segmented labour markets; internal labour markets, etc. Nevertheless, the starting point of supply and demand diagrams for labour is ultimately a general framework which approximates most labour markets over time.

5 To this author the word 'setting' implies a *conscious decision* on the part of an individual or individuals to fix the wage (in this case) at a fairly precise moment in time after due deliberation. The word 'formation' (in relation to how a wage is determined) implies a *process* that occurs over time and not necessarily a process that is consciously determined at formal meetings between individuals. Rather it occurs as the unintended consequence of countless decisions that are taken by individuals in their everyday economic activities who may have no knowledge of the eventual impact that their activities have on the wage in this or that occupation.

6 Of course under market conditions, when all of these 'and' conditions are not met, this can help us to understand why wages do not equalise in a short period of time between occupations (and within occupations) but in many cases only *tend* to equalise over time with wage differentials between (and within) occupations reflecting labour immobility, differing skill and educational levels, and differences in job characteristics, such as how dangerous or dirty it may be. This mirrors the situation in the FSU where in theory labour wages, mobility, occupational choice and so on were in the hands of a bureaucracy. In reality many factors intervened to modify this control.

7 Economists speak of *replacement demand* for labour and *expansion demand*. The former covers people who have died (while in employment); have retired; have removed themselves from the workforce before retirement (child-rearing, full-time students in higher education, prisoners, army conscripts, professional criminals and so on); and people who have emigrated. Some of these were less likely than others under the classical socialist system (emigration, for example, to outside the socialist bloc). However, emigration to an area within the system that had been targeted for 'opening up' was always possible, although the overall totality of labour within that system remained the same at any point in time. Expansion demand comes about when the planners envisage a growth of the economy and forecast that there will need to be an x% increase in labour input over and above any replacement demand. Under market conditions – and depending on the stage of the economic cycle – one type of demand can dominate the other. Under central planning, at least in the formative period of high growth rates, expansion demand dominated.

8 Some groups of workers were in greater demand by a factory director than others. The so-called wage fund was divided more favourably for these workers at the expense of other professions, occupations or skills. Now and then the bureaucracy from above may have sanctioned a general increase in wages for all workers in the system. However, planned economies are not immune from the dictum of 'too much money, chasing too few goods'. Unlike, however, in market economies where this normally leads to inflation, under communist central planning this led to even longer queues and to a black market for the goods in demand by the population. If the relative wages of groups of workers had remained unchanged after the general wage increase, then the ability of the better-off groups to purchase the goods available remained unchanged. So-called repressed inflation, then, showed up as longer queues and/or higher prices in the black market.

9 Even under market economies one can observe both a shortage of labour and a surplus of labour co-existing at the same time. This apparent paradox comes about when we recognise that labour is not homogeneous but has varying skill levels; is located in the 'wrong' place for economic activities; is of the 'wrong' age; is not geographically mobile; lacks access to affordable housing even when it is mobile, and so on. The modern-day example of India and China, with labour currently in abundance but with acute shortages of *skilled* labour, springs to mind. The labour market of the United Kingdom with shortages of skilled and unskilled labour in the southeast of the country but with a relative abundance of labour in the north is another example.

10 See, for a brief appraisal of this policy, a transcript of a broadcast by Radio Free Europe on 20 February 1958, held online at the Open Society Archive at the following URL (accessed 29th January

2008): http://files.osa.ceu.hu/holdings/300/8/3/text/55-2-69.shtml. The article chronicles the lack of success of the regime in attracting and retaining labour in that particular harsh environment of Siberia. The lack of a coherent development programme led to the disastrous harvest in 1953 to 1954 in Ukraine (the breadbasket of the FSU) which was caused in large measure by a shortage of harvesting equipment which had been moved to Siberia in anticipation of the grand results expected from opening up Siberia. See the following URL of Time magazine/CNN accessed 29 January 2008 which reports the harvest or lack thereof: http://www.time.com/time/magazine/article/0,9171, 807019,00.html.

11 It should be noted that all of these figures exclude the very senior echelons of the Communist Parties of the FSU and the PRC.

12 Indeed, if one took as the starting point the year 1989 – two years before the dissolution of the USSR – the drop in GDP from 1989 to 1997 was in the order of 41.4 per cent (United Nations Economic Commission for Europe 1998). Figure 8.2, between 1992 and 1998, shows an approximately 30 per cent fall in output.

13 Maternity leave is included in this table as many female employees were given *extended* maternity leave. It was difficult, however, to quantify this in terms of full-time equivalent jobs. On the question of unpaid leave we touch on this below when looking at wage arrears.

14 Nominal wages are the physical pieces of paper and coins that an employer actually pays his or her employees. Real wages are what can be bought by the wages. So, to give an example to clarify the nature between the two, if a trade union negotiates a 10 per cent rise in nominal wages of its members but inflation is running at 10 per cent also, then the real wage negotiated by the trade union is 0 per cent – the increased wages cannot buy any more goods and services than the old wages due to the effects of inflation. Even where the actual wages stayed the same in Russian industry, if inflation was substantial in Russia in the early years of transition – which it was – then real wages can fall, even though the actual wage or the wage rate has not been cut by the employer.

15 Eventually abolished, from 1994, if the firm's wage bill divided by the number of employees was more than four times the statutory minimum wage, the wage was subject to a 35 per cent excess wage tax. The incentive to the firm was then to keep people 'on the books' to avoid paying the tax.

16 The significance of emphasising that the debate raged before the world economic recession of 2008 to 2009 is that the rigidities of the European labour market – for so long seen as a barrier to job creation – may have turned out to have partially ameliorated the job losses during the recession by making it harder for employers to shed labour. In America by contrast unemployment rose much faster, a situation aided, it would appear, by a more laissez-faire approach that successive US governments have had to the labour market. It also appears that many (not all!) labour markets in European countries turned out to be more flexible than might have first been thought with groups of workers accepting a freeze on wage increases or even nominal wage cuts to preserve jobs. The view of labour hoarding being an obstacle within the Russian labour market may also have been premature; when an economic upswing did eventually come in Russia – post-1998 – the upswing was assisted, at least initially, by the hoarding of labour that had taken place throughout the 1990s. As demand increased, the necessary (underutilised) labour (and capital) was on hand to be put to work (see Chapter 9 for more details).

17 The Tiananmen events of 1989 were not led by workers – sympathetic as some may have been – but were in the main organised by radicalised students and sections of the intelligentsia.

18 Although one immediately concedes that there are various models of labour markets in the West based on general economic models of capitalism such as the Anglo-Saxon, Social-Market, Scandinavian, and the Mediterranean model. It is, however, difficult to imagine any of these models 'engineering' such a sustained rise in real wages for so long when market fundamentals were not always favourable.

19 Again we realise that there are all sorts of other factors which can influence wage levels in the *short to medium term*. The wages of many lecturers and professors in transition economies whose skills *were* in demand did not keep up relatively speaking with other professions (unlike, say, the salaries of lecturers in Western Europe). That *eventually* market forces might solve the problem is, of course, one main reason why governments still have a role to play through career guidance schemes at schools, prioritising budget expenditures on groups of workers to enhance their pay and so on. 'Eventually' is not much consolation to most people, since they eventually grow old and retire. Market forces do work – but not instantaneously.

20 Often in datasets, where these relationships are examined, information may not be present on the actual years of work experience. In this situation, researchers will often use the age of the individual less the years spent in full-time education as a proxy for years of work experience. Naturally, this is only a good proxy if the individual has not spent several years inactive through prolonged periods of unemployment or through child-rearing, for example.

21 This does not imply that females are better paid where returns to education are higher than those of males. Say, because of gender discrimination, a female with basic education receives €60 per day, but a male with the same basic education receives €100 per day. With secondary education a female can expect, say, €100 per day, but a male with secondary education will get on average €160 per day. For the female on €100 per day there has been an increase in her pay by just over 66 per cent in comparison to the lower educated female; for the male with secondary education, his pay is 60 per cent higher than a male with lower education. Running separate wage regressions (Mincer regressions) for females and males can show higher returns for females compared to males.

22 This is sometimes referred to as 'network effects' or the influence of social capital. While no doubt there are differences between all three terms, the expression 'who you know, and not what you know' overlaps with these more technical terms.

23 These countries grouped together by the World Bank for their report are: Albania, Armenia, Azerbaijan, Belarus, Bosnia and Herzegovina, Bulgaria, Croatia, the Czech Republic, Estonia, Georgia, Hungary, Kazakhstan, Kyrgyzstan, Latvia, Lithuania, the former Yugoslav Republic of Macedonia, Moldova, Poland, Romania, the Russian Federation, Serbia and Montenegro, the Slovak Republic, Slovenia, Tajikistan, Turkey, Turkmenistan, Ukraine, and Uzbekistan. As can be seen, the only country that is *not* a former socialist transition country is Turkey. The reader is directed to this World Bank report (which at the time of writing was freely accessible online) for a far more detailed account of migration in many of these transition countries.

9 ECONOMIC TRANSITION: RUSSIA VERSUS CHINA

1 See http://blogs.ft.com/arena/2009/07/28/economists-what-is-the-point/#comments. Accessed 26 August 2009.

2 It is not reported why it took roughly eight months to reply to Her Majesty.

3 Quoted in Hedlund (1999).

4 The alert reader will notice that we do not include political transformation in our list of major changes. We return to this later in the text when we discuss democracy and its relation to transition.

5 We willingly acknowledge our debt to two books used as bibliographical material within this chapter. The first is by Hedlund (1999), *Russia's Market Economy*, which approaches the transition to a market economy within Russia with a combination of political economy and historical perspective. We feel it provides valuable insights into an understanding of the course of events that transpired throughout the 1990s as Russia stumbled towards a market economy. The second book is a compendium of articles by leading authors in their respective fields concerning the transition within China. *China's Great Economic Transformation* edited by Loren Brandt and Thomas G. Rawski (2008) is a 'one-stop shop' for those who wish to have a deeper understanding of events – be it economic, political or social – within the People's Republic of China. Weighing in at 906 pages, the collection of articles will no doubt remain an invaluable reference guide and study book for many years to come.

6 We deliberately say dissolution rather than collapse since it may be argued that it was the agreement between Boris Yeltsin, with the Ukrainian President Leonid Kravchuk and the leader of Belarus, Stanislav Shushkevich, in Belovezhskaya Pushcha, on 8 December 1991 which led to the announcement of the dissolution of the Soviet Union. In its place they would establish a voluntary Commonwealth of Independent States (CIS). That said, it may also be argued that they only formalised the de facto collapse of the old Soviet Union.

7 The original quotation comes from Voprosy Ekonomiki, vol. 7, from an article entitled 'Popytki provedeniya politiki finansovoi stabilizatsii v SSSR i v Rossii' ('Attempts at implementing financial stabilisation policies in the USSR and in Russia'). Mr Illarionov himself was at one time an economic adviser to President Putin and currently (at the time of writing) works at the US think-tank Cato in Washington, DC.

8 The issue of Taiwan is an extremely sensitive one for the leadership of the PRC, and, indeed, for many ordinary citizens of mainland China. Regarded as a 'renegade province', Taiwan, strictly

speaking, has never declared formal independence from PRC, perhaps believing that at some stage (with outside assistance?) it would retake the mainland. That never happened, and it seems unlikely that Taiwan would now wish to launch a full-scale invasion of mainland China with or without outside assistance. The leadership of PRC has, however, made it clear that in the event of Taiwan declaring formal independence this would be treated as an act of war.

9 Mao had occasion to make use of the shit metaphor on at least one other occasion. 'Marxism-Leninism has no beauty, no mystical value; it is simply very useful.' He went on to explain to those who regarded Marxism-Leninism as a dogma that 'Your dogma is less useful than excrement. We see that dog excrement can fertilize the fields and man's can feed the dog. And dogmas? They can't fertilize the fields, nor can they feed a dog. Of what use are they?' (in Boyd Compton, ed., *Mao's China: Party Reform Documents, 1942–44* (Seattle: University of Washington Press, 1952, quoted in Bianco 1986). As is relatively well known, Mao eventually graduated from a pedagogical school at the age of 25 and was attracted to the ideas of Marxism at 27. No value judgement is passed on Mao by reciting these anecdotes of shit and of his own educational standing. Many a great leader has come from both a humble background and lowly educational status. (One can think of Sir Winston Churchill who, while not of humble origins, certainly was no academic genius at school, famously failing his exams but going on to lead his own country during the Second World War.) Rather we see in these small glimpses that Mao was more a 'fighter than a thinker' to borrow Bianco's phrase. While this would stand him in good stead during the fight against the Japanese and during the civil war (and indeed in the internecine party warfare of the Cultural Revolution), it would not be such an advantage in times of peace when considered, insightful analysis would be required rather than decisive action.

10 In the 1970s, in urban areas, average calorie intake was 2,328 per capita. In the countryside it stood even lower at just under 2,100 calories (see Huang *et al.* 2008). By comparison, during the Siege of Leningrad (now called St Petersburg) where approximately 1.5 million people starved to death when in 1941 German troops besieged the 'Northern Capital' of the USSR, industrial workers were limited to 600 grams of bread per day at the start of the siege: 100 grams of bread contains about 220 calories. Doing the arithmetic, that comes to 1,320 calories per day. Thus rural peasants in Mao's China were receiving only about 50 per cent more calories than those under siege.

11 Free-riding refers to the situation here, whereby individuals working in a group can shirk on their effort to the group as a whole through difficulties in monitoring from above or from their fellow collective farmers (see note 5 in Chapter 7). It may well have been that given the presence of small individual private plots, the group *as a whole* restricted effort since as Huang *et al.* (2008) make the point, the 'concentration of decision making (was) in the hands of collective leaders who often were somewhat removed from day-to-day production and had limited access to information'. So not only could they not observe what the farmers on the ground were actually doing, but the lack of this first-hand knowledge often led to ill-informed decisions as to the future direction of the commune.

12 The situation is a bit like a car which is travelling along a road with a hole in the petrol tank leaking petrol; the car only keeps going because the rate at which new petrol is being poured into the tank (by a passenger, let us assume!) is greater than the rate at which the petrol is leaking from the car! At some stage, however, the reserves of petrol in the back seat of the car are going to run out.

13 The whole article, 'What does total factor productivity measure?' may be downloaded at http://www.csls.ca/ipm/1/lipsey-e.pdf. The reader will quickly see that TFP is actually rather more controversial than at first glance. That said, we ignore the esoterics of the debate and stick with our generalised statement that TFP is a measure of technical change and consequently of productivity within the economy.

14 Interestingly, Ahrend and Thompson (2005) as well as pointing to the implosion of the command economy within the Soviet Union also note three external factors which assisted in the slow-motion collapse of the Soviet Union and its economy: (1) the Chernobyl nuclear accident which, 'in addition to its enormous human cost, arguably wrecked the 12th Five-Year-Plan'; (2) the international oil price collapse of 1986 which meant that more oil needed to be exported from the Soviet Union to buy the same quantity of imports – in effect the economy had to run faster simply to stand still; and (3) a sharp decline in the value of the dollar in 1986 to 1987 which reinforced the oil price collapse since oil was and is priced in American dollars. Imports, however, into the Soviet Union at that time tended to be invoiced in Western European currencies, especially the German Deutschmark.

15 Layard, Richard and John Parker (1996) *The Coming Russian Boom: A Guide to the New Markets and Politics*. New York: The Free Press. At the time, Layard was a prominent foreign economic adviser to the Russian government. He was not the only foreign economic adviser to see 'betrayal': 'the G-7 governments disgracefully pressed the Russian government to continue servicing the Soviet foreign debt, at a time when the G-7 should have been working hard to provide the new government with fiscal breathing space' (Sachs, Jeffrey (1994) Betrayal, *The New Republic*, 31 January. Both quotes in Hedlund (1999).

16 Privatisation was also to receive a bad name in the 'loans-for-shares' programme where blocks of shares in state enterprises were offered in return for loans to the Russian government. In theory the Russian government could reclaim the shares at a later period. This did not happen and many suspect it was yet another way in which to sell off relatively valuable state assets to a favoured few.

17 Notice that in Chapter 8 the main focus was on why employment had not dropped as fast as output. Here we simply concentrate on the output collapse.

18 GDP measured in *constant prices* takes account of price increases in the economy which if not accounted for can give a false impression of growth in the economy. Changes in GDP measured in *current prices* do so without taking into account inflation.

19 For the non-economist reader, if the rouble trades at 5 roubles for 1 dollar (say) and the government, in effect, devalues the currency, then we may have 10 roubles to 1 dollar. A manufacturer in Russia of, say, pens who makes a pen for 5 roubles (including reasonable profit) sells in the US before the devaluation at 1 dollar (we ignore transport costs). After the devaluation the pen will still cost 5 roubles to make using materials sourced and purchased inside Russia, but can now sell in the US for 50 US cents. All other things being equal, Russian exports should then expand as Russian exporters take a larger market share.

20 In Åslund and Jenish (2006), however, the authors give a more detailed analysis and explanation as to why there was this sudden volte-face in growth between the two groups of countries. In a paper entitled 'The Eurasian Growth Paradox', the paradox referred to is the fact that

> The lesson from 1989–98 was that market economic reform worked. The more radical and the earlier the economic reform efforts were, the sooner a country would return to economic growth and the greater the upturn would be . . . Strangely everything was turned upside down from 1999 on. From 1999 to 2004, 11 CIS countries had an average annual growth of 7.8 per cent (Russia, Ukraine, Belarus, Moldova, Armenia, Azerbaijan, Georgia, Kazakhstan, Kyrgyzstan, Tajikistan, and Uzbekistan), while the four Central European Visegrad countries (Poland, the Czech Republic, Slovakia, and Hungary) recorded annual growth of only 3.6 per cent. The three Baltic countries came closer to the first group with 7.1 per cent growth, and Romania and Bulgaria closer to the Central Europeans with 5.4 percent.
>
> Åslund and Jenish (2006)

The supremacy of the latter group of countries up until 1999 (compared to the 11 CIS countries) lay not only in their faster implementation of market reforms but 'privileged access to the large EU market' (Åslund and Jenish (2006). Post the 1998 financial crisis the Russian rouble was devalued significantly. 'The ensuing commodity boom, driven by Chinese commodity imports, allowed the CIS countries to boost their exports despite stagnant EU markets and EU protectionism . . . Increased investment followed the export boom, as would be expected, which has further reinforced economic growth' (Åslund and Jenish 2006). Using regression analysis, with a limited number of right-hand-side variables, the authors conclude that 'the sharp rise in the growth rate in CIS countries can mainly be explained by a drastic reduction in public spending and budget deficits in these countries. A second explanation, unsurprisingly, is that the commodity boom on world markets boosted that growth as well' (Åslund and Jenish 2006). While we do not find the conclusion of a commodity boom controversial in boosting growth, it may well be that two factors have been overlooked. First, there may be a simultaneity problem (as distinct from an endogeneity problem) with the variable capturing government spending as a share of GDP not only influencing the GDP growth rate, but itself being influenced by the growth in the economy – if the economy grows but the growth in government spending is lower, then, of course, it would appear that lower government spending is correlated with higher growth, but it could be the higher growth – and hence higher government revenues – driving the reduction in deficits and not the other way round, or perhaps mutually reinforcing each other. Second, some of the non-CIS countries experiencing lower economic growth post-1999 had effectively pegged their currencies to the euro so as to enhance their prospect for eurozone membership. Given the appreciation of the euro over this period this may also have contributed to slower growth in some cases.

21 Note that the term 'Geary-Khamis' in the tables refers to adjustments that are made to the value of currencies, such as the renminbi, when one wishes to make international comparisons between countries. One cannot simply use what economists refer to as the *nominal* exchange rate in order to convert so many renminbi into dollars and then make comparisons. One needs also to take into account what a unit of the currency can buy in each country. For example, if per capita GDP in the US in a particular year is $30,000 but in China, in the same year, using the nominal exchange rate, we find per capita GDP stands at $5,000, this *does not* mean that the standard of living for an 'average' citizen in China is one-sixth that of an 'average' American. If services in China – haircuts, laundry, taxi fares, restaurant meals – along with prices of goods in general are far cheaper than in America, then in effect one's money in China 'goes further' than one's money in America. This means the nominal GDP per capita in China needs to be adjusted upwards in order to reflect the cheaper cost of goods and services in order to give a fairer or more accurate comparison of standards of living between the US and China. Benchmark years which are often chosen from which to work out international comparisons are 1990 and 2000.

For those interested in the minutia of this subject, Maddison (2009) is also worth studying. For many years the World Bank used Geary-Khamis dollars (or what is also called International dollars) but in a 2005 World Bank International Comparison Study (ICP) of per capita GDP across countries the use of the Geary-Khamis dollar was replaced by an alternative statistical technique, much to Maddison's chagrin. 'A major shortcoming of the recent World Bank study is its disparaging attitude to the five previous ICP global studies . . . These are dismissed by the World Bank as being "based on very old and very limited data," implying that any discrepancy with early findings cannot cast doubt on its implausible results for China, India, and some other Asian countries' (Maddison 2009). The implausible results Maddison writes of – and linked with Box 9.3 on statistical accuracy within China – is that whereas Maddison for the year 2005 estimates China's per capita GDP at 18.3 per cent of the US figure, the World Bank, having adopted a new methodology, estimates it at only 10 per cent – a drop of just over 45 per cent.

Even if one accepts Maddison's critique that the World Bank has got it wrong, then in fairness to the World Bank it would appear – from Maddison's article – that the World Bank based its calculations on data received from Chinese statisticians. The hypothesis advanced by Maddison after discussion with others is that the Chinese statisticians in calculating the 'true' price level for China used consumer goods at the higher end of the price range, since they may have been 'aiming at comparability with advanced countries' (Maddison 2006). If this hypothesis is indeed accurate, then the Chinese statisticians will have also unintentionally, as a by-product, made it easier for politicians, if they so desired, both inside and outside China to argue the case that China is still very much a developing country, a fact which should be taken into account when examining, say, international trade issues through the WTO or, indeed, the merits of whether the exchange rate is undervalued or not with the US dollar.

As if on cue when writing the above, an article appeared in *China Daily* (30–31 January 2010) entitled 'Is China still a developing nation? No doubt'. Quoting a senior reporter from Xinhua News Agency, Gao Qiufu – an expert, we are told, in international studies – said, 'Some people in the West try to prove China is a developed country . . . because they want it to shoulder greater responsibility in coping with global issues, such as climate change.' But he goes on to point out: 'China's per capita GDP is only $3,000, which ranks 104th in the world.' We presume that Gao is using a nominal exchange rate here to arrive at a figure of $3,000. What exchange rate and at what point in time is not mentioned. Gao goes on (although the lack of quotation marks in the *China Daily* article makes it hard to tell apart direct speech from reported speech): 'people who claim China is already a developed country evade the crucial points and dwell only on what is favorable to their argument, Gao said. Such people have a secret motive: To force China to bear a heavier burden in order to retard its development.'

22 For the record there are some authors who dispute Maddison's revisions, in particular Holz (2006a, 2006b).

23 Space prevents more coverage of Woo's comments on China's environmental problems. The reader is recommended to peruse Woo's full remarks for an eloquent description of the environmental travails facing China.

24 See Woo (2007) and references cited therein.

25 Heston and Sinclair (2008), reporting other authors, state the household farm size in China as being directly proportional to family size with average size, based on the Chinese census data, of 0.67 hectares, although China's National Bureau of Statistics reports average size as being 1.2 hectares in 2002 with 98 per cent of landholdings being less than 2 hectares. By comparison we have average landholdings by hectare in India of 1.55, 1.20 in Japan, the Philippines at 2.16, and Thailand at 3.36. By way of visualisation, FIFA, the world governing body of football (soccer in American English), stipulates that all international games must be played on a football pitch between 100 metres and 110 metres long and 64 to 75 metres wide. That is, the smallest international football match is played on a surface area of 0.62 hectares and the largest on 0.82 hectares with 1 hectare being 10,000 square metres. American baseball fields come in at between 0.83 hectares to 1.12 hectares. (See http://metricviews.org.uk/2007/11/how-big-hectare, accessed 1 November 2009.)

   The significance of economies of scale to our non-economist reader is as follows: if one doubles the use of land, labour and capital in the production of whatever (in the case of farming, rice and other crops) will output more than double (increasing returns to scale or economies of scale, and the one to be hoped for); will it less than double (decreasing returns to scale or diseconomies of scale); or will it output simply double (constant returns to scale)? The 'blame' for collectivisation of agriculture in all communist societies, from Stalin's Soviet Union to Mao's People's Republic of China, can be partly laid at the door of the belief in the concept of economies of scale; that is, if we make the size of the farm really big there will be increasing returns to scale. Research quoted by Heston and Sinclair (2008) would seem to suggest constant returns to scale, although 'the apparent lack of scale economies may reflect uniquely Chinese circumstances' (Heston and Sinclair 2008).

26 In terms of absolute numbers: 28 million were employed by TVEs in 1978; 70 million in 1985 and 123 million in 1993. (Cai *et al.* 2008)

27 It would be wrong, however, to give the impression that such manoeuvres are without risk. Haggard and Huang (2008) recount an interesting example:

> A private entrepreneur registered his firm as a collective, and in a side – and most likely under-the-table – agreement, he gave 30 per cent of the equity stakes to the local government, even though he provided all the equity capital. After paying out all the agreed dividends and taxes, he used a portion of the residual profits to settle a loan, which led to an embezzlement charge. He was sentenced to death by a lower-level court. The case went all the way to the country's Supreme Court and his life was spared only when the State Administration of Industry and Commerce, the branch in charge of registering firms, confirmed that the firm was in fact privately owned.

28 Sometimes the reader may come across the statement that the peak in 1995 was not 5.6 million but 7.6 million enterprises. This would seem to be due to adding the number of collective enterprises to the number of 'genuine' state enterprises. As noted in the main body of the text, collectives were sometimes merely collective in name, but in spirit were market entities. Consequently a degree of ambiguity may exist with the figures depending what is 'lumped in' as originally being state or non-market in nature. However, the overall conclusion that there was a massive reduction in enterprises controlled and owned by the state is not ambiguous. Indeed, when local regional governmental bodies were encouraged to privatise at the local level, it has been argued that they merely recognised the de facto situation that already existed within many of these collectives.

29 Sachs and Woo (1996) write, 'in China the proportion of the labor force employed by state-owned units was 18 per cent in 1978 and was still 18 per cent in 1993. This means that there were actually 35 million more Chinese working in state-owned units in 1993 than in 1978. The state-owned sector is not "withering away." ' This statement as regards the state sector not withering away was absolutely correct for its time and, indeed, if one includes the TVEs as 'state' entities then the comparison between 1978 and 1993 is also correct. With the very easy benefit of hindsight we can see this statement is not appropriate today. True, as we relate in the main body of the text, the *importance* of the state sector is still as great as ever even if the quantitative size of the state in terms of its formal ownership and control of firms within the economy is not. That said, a comparison of

remaining state firms today with their predecessors in 1978 is not that appropriate given that many of them are now run on commercial lines and operate within a market environment. Does it matter then that the remaining state firms are just that: state firms? Does it matter what colour the cat is as long as it catches the mouse? We tackle this issue when we come to look at the efficiency of state firms in comparison with the private sector.

30 Russia for example, along with many other resource-rich nations, benefited handsomely from the commodity boom prior to the 2007 to 2009 financial and economic crisis. In doing so it wisely created an oil stabilisation fund. This prevented the large amount of oil money from seeping into the economy, and while it could be argued that Russia does need to upgrade much of its infrastructure, a large influx of money into the economy without proportionate and simultaneous expansion of both labour and capital resources would have seen most of the money generating price increases rather than solid real wealth increases. Further, such a fund could be used for a rainy day in the future when the outlook for the Russian economy was not so rosy. That rainy day eventually came for Vladimir Putin when, with the onset of the Great Recession of 2008 to 2009, the rouble came under heavy pressure for a market-led depreciation. Anxious not to be seen to be following in the footsteps of Boris Yeltsin who precipitated the last major devaluation of the rouble in 1998, a large chunk of the stabilisation fund went on supporting the rouble. Whether this was money well spent for the Russian economy or simply a very expensive way of saving the face of Putin is open to discussion.

31 Умный человек в горы не пойдет, умный гору обойдет: This old Russian proverb can be translated as 'A clever person doesn't go through/over the mountain, a clever person goes around the mountain.' Perhaps given the metaphors that have been adopted by some observers that transition to a market economy in Russia is like leaping over a canyon – it needs to be done in one giant leap – a modern equivalent might be: не стоит пытаться перепрыгнуть каньон - лучше его обойти!, (It's not worth attempting to leap over the canyon – better to go around it).

32 The Washington Monthly, March 2000. http://www.washingtonmonthly.com/books/2000/0003. sachs.html accessed 16 November 2009.

33 Although about 1,100 people did die in the Romanian revolution of 1989 which overthrew Nicolae Ceausescu. It may also be seen by some as a peaceful transformation to market relations if we do not count the succession of failed uprisings against Soviet rule in various countries in Central and Eastern Europe after the Second World War which resulted in many deaths. Likewise, the civil wars and secessionist movements which erupted in the Caucuses in the 1990s would need to be seen more as a result of pent-up nationalism under the Soviet Union than of the establishment of market relations proper.

34 The reader may sometimes come across conflicting claims as to whether Poland was a fast-track transition economy or pursued a more gradualist line. The issue revolves around the distinction between bringing inflation under control once prices have been liberalised *and then* carrying out the necessary steps to a market economy. Stiglitz (2001), for example, referring to Poland's attempt to bring prices under control once they had been liberalised, writes, 'I use the term "radical reform" rather than the more frequently used term "shock therapy" since the latter is sometimes used to discuss the necessity of rapidly bringing down hyperinflation. Poland had "shock macro-therapy" but followed a more incremental process of reform (including privatization).'

35 See *China's Transition Experience, Reexamined* at it http://www.worldbank.org/html/prddr/trans/m&a96/art1.htm accessed 3 October 2009. The article makes it clear that it is taken from various other articles written by the authors, although these are not specified.

36 Not mentioned by Sachs and Woo, but this high savings rate was (and is) ironically to protect themselves, i.e. the Chinese citizen from the inadequacy of the Chinese state's social safety net in old age, not to mention the pay-as-you-go health service along with other pay-as-you-go services such as quality higher education. The lack of such a social burden, as Sachs and Woo categorise it, contributed to the success of the 'Chinese path'. In addition, it is also debateable as to whether the reluctance on the part of the citizens of the FSU, for example, to hold money balances (i.e. not to save but to spend and so add to inflationary pressures) was a cause of the macro-instability in the early 1990s or whether it resulted from the macro-instability brought on by governmental policy – was reluctance to hold money balances a cause or an effect? We explore this further in the main text.

37 Russian entrepreneurial flair had either been shot during the War Communism period; suitably re-educated in labour camps; or had fled abroad. Unfortunately for the transition to a market economy

in Russia, all the re-educated capitalists from the labour camps or exiled capitalists in Paris and elsewhere had died out.

38 It should be noted that Professor Sachs is not an entirely impartial observant being as he was an economic adviser to the Russian government in the early years of transition. Professor Sachs eventually resigned 'in frustration' that his policy recommendations to the governments in Moscow had, he claimed, not been followed. That said, Professor Sachs himself wrote of himself in a book review of the transition process in Russia,

> Advisors such as myself don't even get a bit role. This, I've always tried to explain, is how I actually felt when in Moscow. After helping to devise and introduce Poland's reforms during 1989–91, and after conveying their significance to Russian colleagues such as Gaidar in late 1991, my actual influence on events was essentially zero. This was certainly true inside Russia, but also in the U.S., where both the U.S. government and the IMF simply rejected my criticisms of their inaction (to provide vital aid and debt relief) and policy recommendations (such as to maintain the Soviet-era ruble as a shared currency).
>
> (Russia's Tumultuous Decade – an insider remembers,
> *The Washington Monthly*, online, March 2000)

39 Åslund writes of the Odling-Smee and Pastor (2002) article, 'I welcome their interest in sorting this old issue out. While I have few disagreements on facts, I am surprised by how different our perspectives were, given that both John Odling-Smee and I were deeply engaged in this drama and met repeatedly during its course.'

40 It is interesting that when during the 1990s I discussed with some Russian friends the issue of corruption, bribe taking, etc. in Russian society, and while they all knew it took place, and took place at all levels of society, the President of Russia – Boris Yeltsin – was often exempted from these alleged activities. 'He is not involved in these things; it's the people around him. If only he could get rid of these people, he'd be able to run the country better.' One is struck in this attitude by the very similar attitude expressed by elements of the lower echelons of society in Tsarist Russia that if only they could petition the Tsar and get past the people who surrounded the Tsar, then the Tsar would listen to their problems and deal with them.

41 For a concise explanation of the role of politics on the gradualism versus Big Bang debate see the section *The Political Challenge of Transition* by Naughton (2008a, pp. 94–97 including fn. 3, 4, and 5 in the chapter 'A Political Economy of China's Economic Transition').

42 Tom Bottomore was a Professor at the University of Sussex, the United Kingdom, where he taught sociology from 1968 until he retired in 1985, whereupon he was given the honour of being made Professor Emeritus. 'He was perhaps Britain's best known and admired social scientist partly because his prolific as well as profound writings were read widely all over the world and also partly because of his sustained interest and intense engagement in building the international community of sociologists' (Dhanagare 1993).

43 *Financial Times*, 26 November 2009. Accessed online on 26/11/2009 at http://www.ft.com/cms/s/0/598f2426-d9f9-11de-b2d5-00144feabdc0.html.

44 China has announced a rash of investments around the world designed to secure access to hydrocarbons it needs to fuel its energy-thirsty growth. This week, it was learned, Beijing has offered the west African state of Guinea billions of dollars in infrastructure loans in return for rights to explore for offshore oil. CNOOC, one of China's three big energy groups, has made a pitch to prise Nigerian oil blocs away from western oil majors. This followed on from other loan-for-oil deals with Kazakhstan, Russia, Brazil, Venezuela and Angola.

> *Financial Times*, 15 October 2009, 'The state's dead hand returns to haunt China' by David Pilling)

45 There is one other possibly radical alternative future that could occur over the next 20 to 30 years (but sufficiently less certain that we relegate it to an endnote). Interestingly, it may well be the case that we are much closer to 'peak oil' than had at one time been assumed with peak oil being at that time when quite literally the amount of oil produced in the world reaches a maximum and then starts to decline. A report by the UK Energy Research Centre (UKERC) predicted that this could happen before 2020. 'Steve Sorrel, chief author of the report, said forecasts suggesting oil production will not peak before 2030 were "at best optimistic, and at worst implausible" ' (The UK *Guardian*

newspaper, 9 November 2009). This would seem to have been confirmed by a whistleblower at the International Energy Agency who claimed that the IEA had been deliberately downplaying a looming shortage for fear of triggering panic buying. 'The senior official claims the US has played an influential role in encouraging the watchdog to underplay the rate of decline from existing oil fields while overplaying the chances of finding new reserves' (The UK *Guardian* newspaper, 9 November 2009). If such a scenario is, indeed, proved correct then even with lower growth coming from the mature Western economies, the price of oil will rise despite this, and rise to new record highs over the next 20 to 30 years. This may just be enough to ensure the long-term stability of the Russian economy – if not the long-term prosperity – at least for a temporary period of several decades. For Russian policy makers who number their years in power by perhaps a single decade at the most (Mr Putin notwithstanding!), this temporary safety net of several decades brought on by high oil prices is more than long enough. Long enough in fact that any thought of taking on entrenched vested interests and having a radical makeover of the economy to root out corruption, improve corporate governance, and develop an atmosphere where genuine entrepreneurship can flourish without hindrance is postponed indefinitely.

46 One criticism of the economics profession, or parts of it at least, especially in the light of the financial and economic crisis of 2007 to 2009, has been that economists when confronted by real world events that *persistently* confound a particular theory are more inclined to 'blame' the real world for the theory being wrong than the theory itself.

47 It would be wrong to give the impression that Clarke *et al.* (2008) are in some ways primarily negative in their attitude to developments as regards the rule of law within China. If anything, reading their article one comes away with a very positive impression of the development of law in the sphere of the economy: 'Twenty-five years after reforms began, courts, despite their many deficiencies, were playing a significant role in dispute resolution. Survey evidence indicates that this role is much greater than would have been imagined, given the emphasis placed in the literature on the pervasive role of *guanxi* in economic life' (Clarke *et al.* 2008). So while the courts do not, in the opinion of Clarke *et al.* (2008), secure property rights for aspiring entrepreneurs within China, neither are they a negligible force to be reckoned with as regards contract dispute resolution. As mentioned in the main text, Clarke *et al.* (2008) would seem to agree with the idea of fiscal decentralisation having beneficial effects on growth – and property rights protection – through aligning local officials' outlook with the needs of business in their respective localities. In addition, however, they emphasise the 'cadre evaluation system' whereby local officials both within local government and within local Communist Party structures are monitored for effectiveness; in short, a form of job appraisal. If an official wishes to preserve his or her position or advance it then the criteria set by the evaluation system need to be met which may include local economic development.

10 LESSONS FROM TRANSITION

1 As one transition economist remarked, 'Economists often offer advice to transition economies based on their knowledge about economics. But economics has as much to learn from the experience of the transition economies as it has to teach them' (Qian 2000). As far back as 1994, Richard Freeman wrote: 'economics does not have sufficient compelling theory or empirical knowledge to answer questions about the institutional design of advanced capitalist economies, much less economies in transition' (Blanchard *et al.* 1994).

2 One of the implications of the transition is the change in comparative economic systems from simply comparing alternative systems to what is now considered to be the new comparative economics, that is, understanding institutional 'differences and their consequences for economic performance' (Djankov *et al.* 2003).

3 Despite this advance, our understanding of the interplay between politics and economics is still quite limited. As the economic historian and Nobel Laureate Douglas C. North remarks, 'The interface between economics and politics is still in a primitive state in our theories but its development is essential if we are to implement policies consistent with intentions' (North 2000).

4 The advice of no-one-size-fits-all applies not only to market reforms but also to institutional reforms. Neither best-practice market reforms nor first-best institutional reforms will necessarily work if transplanted elsewhere, where local conditions, circumstances and norms prevail.

5 Along similar lines, Rodrik (2008), in welcoming the Commission on Growth and Development and the Spence Report, writes that successful economies have many things in common: they all engage in the global economy, maintain macroeconomic stability, stimulate saving and investment, provide market-oriented incentives, and are reasonably well governed. It is useful to keep an eye on these commonalities, because they frame the conduct of appropriate economic policies.'

6 Two good sources for material on the 2007 to 2009 economic and financial crisis (or more general transition-related information) in transition countries are the *EBRD Transition Reports* of 2008 and 2009, and the July 2009 edition (issue 13/2009) of the newsletter *Development and Transition*, jointly published by the United Nations Development Programme (UNDP) and the London School of Economics and Political Science (LSE). The respective websites are www.ebrd.org and www.developmentandtransition.net.

7 Given the role of the state, and the universal benefits of the Soviet system, transition to a market economy was inevitably going to witness the emergence of unemployment, and a rise in both poverty and inequality. Due to wage decompression and higher returns to education, an initial rise in inequality was to be welcomed. The issue, and mounting public concern, was in relation to the extent of the rise in inequality (and poverty) witnessed in the first decade of transition. By all accounts, the increases recorded were indeed very large (see Chapter 2).

8 One such vision is from the Commission on Growth and Development, comprising leading practitioners (from government, business and international organisations) and independent academics, and chaired by Nobel Laureate Michael Spence. Published in summer 2008, its final report *The Growth Report: Strategies for Sustained Growth and Inclusive Development* is available online on the Commission's website http://www.growthcommission.org. See http://www.bepress.com/ev/vol5/iss3/art4/ in the e-journal *The Economists' Voice* for a favourable review of the report. An alternate is the so-called Beijing Consensus, popularised by former foreign edition of *Time* magazine, Joshua Cooper Ramo.

9 The thenn Chief Economist of the EBRD, Nicholas Stern, at an IMF conference in 1999 to commemorate the first decade of transition, wrote, 'perhaps the most important lesson from the Russian crisis and the first decade of transition has been that free trade and private ownership will not by themselves bring well-functioning markets, and that market-supporting institutions are fundamental' (Stern 2001). A decade later, Erik Berglöf, the EBRD Chief Economist, wrote in the Foreword to the *Transition Report 2009*,

> The crisis . . . has confirmed a view which has been gaining traction over the last decade, namely that transition to a market economy is about much more than building markets and shifting economic responsibilities from the state to the private sector. It also involves developing certain state functions, and improving how the state interacts with the private sector. The crisis has brought about the importance of market-supporting institutions and policies, particularly in the financial sector.
>
> (EBRD 2009)

The crisis referred to here is the economic and financial turmoil that many transition countries faced as a result of the global recession at the end of the 2000s. The concluding judgment of the EBRD was that although the transition region was indeed in deep crisis, with 2009 witnessing the 'worst output collapse since the great "transitional recession" that followed the end of communism', transition itself, and the underlying financial integration and development models pursued (although with some pitfalls), were not in crisis.

10 He went on to write in the same AER article, based on his lecture delivered on receipt of the Nobel Prize in Economic Sciences in 1991, that 'It makes little sense for economists to discuss the process of exchange without specifying the institutional setting within which the trading takes place, since this affects the incentives to produce and the costs of transacting. I think this is now beginning to be recognized and has been made crystal-clear by what is going on in Eastern Europe today.' The importance of institutions – both the institutional environment (rules of the game) and the institutional arrangement (institutions of governance) – was recognised more recently by the economics profession when the 2009 Nobel Prize in Economic Sciences was awarded (jointly) to Oliver Williamson for his work on institutions, governance and transaction cost economics. For Williamson's views on economic development and reform from the perspective of institutions and governance, read Williamson (1995). Included in the Proceedings of the 1994 World Bank Annual

Conference on Development Economics, it was later published in Williamson's 1996 *The Mechanisms of Governance.*

11 In the context of transition from plan to market and from communism to capitalism and the call by neo-liberals for a dismantling of the state (and what one might call the dictatorship of the market), it is worth pointing out that ironically it was, although from a different perspective, Marx, Engels and Lenin who wrote, in the context of transition from capitalism to communism (or in the case of Lenin, from Tsarist Russia to Soviet Communism), about the withering away of the state and the dictatorship of the proletariat.

12 Legitimacy is not only a requirement of government but also of the broader political system. Rayment (1995), when citing others, argues that there are three essential requirements of a new system: legitimacy, order and welfare. Clarifications of all three demands may be found in Rayment (1995) and, in a different context, in Schroeder (1994). Interestingly, in the context of markets and states, Rayment (1995) had this to say: 'the policy pendulum is already swinging back from the ultra free market, anti-government policies of the 1980s: . . . This shift in emphasis may help to suggest a more complex model of the market economy to the governments of Eastern Europe, one in which the state has an unavoidably important role to play in both sustaining and regulating market forces, as well as in the design of institutions and promoting economic growth.' A similar view is given by a fellow UNECE Secretariat member and colleague, Yves Berthelot (Executive Secretary of the UNECE for most of the 1990s when transition was under way). In Emmerij (1997 cited in Berthelot 1997), he writes, '[the] most important lesson to be drawn from the countries in transition is that at the heart of any development strategy there needs to be a proper division of responsibilities between government and market and that the balance between the two necessarily varies from one country to another.' In particular, what was witnessed in the 1990s was that 'the need for the state itself to manage the transition process was underestimated'. This perspective (on transition, and more generally, on markets and governments) is typical of the UNECE and is, in general, in sharp contrast to views often espoused by the IMF.

13 Kolodko (1999) writes, 'The erroneous assumption that emerging market forces can quickly substitute for the government in its role in setting up new institutions, in investing in human capital, and in developing infrastructure has caused severe contraction and growing social stress in transition countries.' In the same article, Kolodko, a critic of the neo-liberal agenda, cites George Soros who when writing in 1997, admitted, 'although I have made a fortune in the financial markets, I now fear that the untrammelled intensification of laissez-faire capitalism and the spread of market values into all areas of life is endangering our open and democratic society . . . Too much competition and too little cooperation can cause intolerable inequities and instability.' In conversations with Padma Desai on reforms in Russia, Soros further remarked, 'there was an excessive belief in the virtue and efficacy discipline among the Russian reformers and Western advisors . . . There was an excessive reliance on monetary policy and not enough attention to the structural changes that were necessary' (Desai 2006). Stiglitz has made the same point on numerous occasions. One example is from 1999 when he wrote, 'perhaps there has been excessive and unwarranted confidence in the previous conventional wisdom – a conventional wisdom that, unfortunately, continues to unduly influence policymakers in some circles' (Stiglitz 1999).

14 Åslund is still a strong supporter of early and radical reform. In his 2007 book *Russia's Capitalist Revolution: Why Market Reform Succeeded and Democracy Failed*, he argues that 'under revolutionary circumstances little but radical reform is likely to succeed, and the earlier and simpler the better. The focus must be on principles and speed, not on details.' With respect specifically to privatisation, he went on to say, 'Now, countries that undertook mass privatisation have actually grown faster than those that carried out case-by-case privatisation and mass privatisation appears to be the key explanation.' Interestingly, his deliberate use of the 'revolutionary' paradigm is a topic common in the transition literature, particularly among McFaul (2001), Mau and Starodubrovskaya (2001) and Gaidar (2003).

15 An essential difference between the wage arrears common in transition countries in the 1990s and the recent phenomena prevalent in the 2007 to 2009 global economic crisis of firms seeking workforces to take wage cuts or periods of unpaid labour is that, in the latter case, the salary cuts or unpaid work are voluntary, arising from negotiations between employers and employees, whereas during transition wage arrears tended to be imposed and were of an involuntary nature.

16 With respect to mass or voucher privatisation, alternatives in the form of stakeholder privatisations and lease buyouts (as per the Polish leasing privatisation by liquidation programme and the Soviet

enterprise leasing in Gorbachev times) were raised by some academics including Black *et al.* (2000), Ellerman (2001) and Stiglitz and Ellerman (2001).

17 The Harvard historian Richard Pipes, in conversation with Padma Desai, claims that he predicted the collapse of the Soviet system as far back as 1954 with the publication of *The Formation of the Soviet Union*. For this dialogue and for many other interesting conversations with distinguished economists and policy makers in Russia (including the late Yegor Gaidar, Anatoly Chubais, Sergei Dubinin, Grigory Yavlinsky and many others) see *Conversations on Russia: Reform from Yeltsin to Putin* by Padma Desai.

18 *The Need for Transcendence in the Postmodern World*, Independence Hall, Philadelphia, 4 July 1994.

APPENDIX 1

1 At the time of writing the price of oil has fallen to between approximately $50 to $70 a barrel compared to the heights of over $140 or thereabouts in 2007. This has been mainly due to two factors: the collapse in demand for oil brought about by the world slowdown in the second half of 2008; and also a speculative rush by investors with hot money to cash in on what was seen as a one-way bet. There is the possibility that some non-economists looking at the current price will think that the 'problem' of high oil prices has ended. It has not; with the resumption of an upswing in economic activity oil prices may resume an upward trajectory (along with speculative investment). The degree of increase in oil prices will be determined by the strength of the economic recovery but increase they probably will. That said, there is one other possibility: that some major economies will slip into deflation á la Japan in the 1990s when that country lost a decade. If that occurs – and one of those major economies happens to be America – then all bets are off and the price of oil could remain fairly 'sluggish'. Ironically, then, a continued low price for oil may be construed as a bad sign for world economic prospects.

2 The big three being, of course, Chrysler, General Motors and Ford. We are also assuming here that the reader will be familiar with the events leading up to the worldwide slowdown in economic activity in 2007 to 2009, namely the subprime crisis in America which generated the credit crunch which infected the real economy leading to the recession throughout many countries of the world.

3 For example, see the *International Herald Tribune* of 3–4 January 2009 where in a well-argued editorial entitled 'Chrysler's flimsy claim to a government bailout' the editorial staff conclude by writing,

> Chrysler has been an American fixture since 1925. It would be tough to close this company and cause pain for the thousands of workers and their families. But taxpayers' dollars would be better used for worker retraining and warranties for existing Chrysler vehicles than to prop up a company that has outlived its usefulness.

4 Source: http://blogs.iht.com/tribtalk/business/globalization/?p=177 (accessed 27 September 2008).

5 The sometimes subtle difference between the Chinese development of market-based capitalism and the development within the ex-Soviet Union countries is explored in Chapter 9.

APPENDIX 2

1 The IMF database includes Turkey in the CEE group and thus the CEE data in the table in Appendix 2 include data for Turkey. To view the data for Turkey and others, see http://www.imf.org/external/pubs/ft/weo/2009/01/weodata/index.aspx.

APPENDIX 5

1 We wish to thank members of CEROPE (Romanian Centre for Economic Policies), Bucharest for their assistance in compiling this case study. Our thanks also go to Alina Porter and Constantin Munteanu.

APPENDIX 7

1 Of the countless number of early reviews of transition, we wish to draw the reader's attention to a small number, including Portes (1994) and Ellman (1994), as they, in our view, have remarkably,

given the enormous changes that have taken place since their publication over 15 years ago, stood the test of time. We alluded to the Portes paper earlier in Chapter 5 when we addressed the issue of policy errors. As for Ellman's 1994 paper, 'Transformation, Depression and Economics: Some Lessons', he recognised, at that early stage, some of the defining lessons from transition, including the complexity of, and our failure to fully appreciate, the transformation process, not enough attention to institutions with too much faith in markets, the importance of banking reform (to include supervision), the overemphasis on irreversibility, the need for a growth policy and so forth. Equally impressive and relevant are the concluding remarks made by Nelson (1994) when examining the linkages between politics and economics. Concerned with achieving, simultaneously, both democratic consolidation and economic reform, the author argues for

> a broadened government agenda that included attention to equity and to restoring the capacity of the state to perform its basic functions. A second theme is likely to be a shift from the rather autocratic, executive-dominated style of early economic reforms toward much fuller consultation and coordination between state and society. Such consultation is important to prevent the erosion of democratic institutions and procedures. Consultation between government bureaucrats and networks of stakeholders is also crucial for the design, implementation, and fine-tuning of the complex institutional and regulatory reforms typical of later-stage economic transformation.
>
> (Nelson 1994)

Finally, an even earlier attempt to identify some tentative lessons from transition in Eastern Europe is given in Rausser (1992), with four general (and insightful) lessons relating to constitutional design and policy credibility, the legal and regulatory infrastructure, the political economy of public policy, and the need for jointly designing privatisation and anti-monopolisation policies.

BIBLIOGRAPHY

Abed, George T. and Hamid R. Davoodi. (2000) 'Corruption, Structural Reforms, and Economic Performance in the Transition Economies', *IMF Working Paper 00/132*, Washington, DC: International Monetary Fund.

Admiraal, P.H. (ed.). (1993) *Economic Transition in Eastern Europe. Michael Ellman, Egor T. Gaidar and Gregorz W. Kolodko*, Oxford: Blackwell.

Aghion, Philippe and Olivier J. Blanchard. (1998) 'On Privatization Methods in Eastern Europe and their Implications', *Economics of Transition*, 6 (1).

Ahrend, Rudiger and William Tompson. (2005) 'Fifteen Years of Economic Reform in Russia: What has been achieved? What remains to be done?', *OECD Economics Department Working Paper 17*, Paris: OECD.

Alam, Asad and Mark Sundberg. (2002) 'A Decade of Fiscal Transition', *Policy Research Paper No. 2835*. Washington, DC: The World Bank.

Alexeev, Michael. (1999) 'The Effects of Privatization on Wealth Distribution in Russia', *Economics of Transition*, 7 (2).

Amsden, Alice, Jacek Kochanowicz and Lance Taylor. (1994) *The Market Meets Its Match: Restructuring Eastern Europe's economies*, Cambridge, MA: Harvard University Press.

Anderson, David. (1997) 'The Russian Mortality Crisis: Causes, Policy Responses, Lessons', *IUSSP Policy and Research Paper No. 11*, Paris.

Anderson, H. James and Cheryl W. Gray. (2006) *Anti Corruption in Transition: Who is succeeding ... and why?*, Washington, DC: The World Bank.

Anderson, James H., Georges Korsun and Peter Murrell. (2000) 'Which Enterprises (Believe They) Have Soft Budgets? Evidence on the Effects of Ownership and Decentralisation in Mongolia', *Journal of Comparative Economics*, 28 (2).

Andrienko, Yuri and Sergei Guriev. (2005) 'Understanding Migration in Russia', *Center for Economic and Financial Research at New Economic School Policy Paper No. 23*, Moscow.

Andvig, Jens Chr. (2006) 'Corruption in China and Russia Compared: Different legacies of central planning', in Susan Rose-Ackerman (ed.), *International Handbook on the Economics of Corruption*, Cheltenham, UK: Edward Elgar.

Angelucci, Manuela and Saul Estrin. (2003) 'Ownership, Competition and Enterprise Performance', *Comparative Economic Studies*, 45 (2).

Angelucci, Manuela, Alan Bevan, Saul Estrin, Julian A Fennema, Boris Kuznetsov, Giovanni Mangiarotti and Mark E. Schaffer. (2002) 'The Determinants of Privatised Enterprise Performance in Russia', *CEPR Discussion Paper No. 3193*, London: Centre for Economic Policy Research.

Arrow, Kenneth J. (2001) 'The Role of Time', in Lawrence R. Klein and Marshall Pomer (eds), *The New Russia: Transition Gone Awry*, Stanford, CA: Stanford University Press.

—— (2000) 'Economic Transition: Speed and scope', *Journal of Institutional and Theoretical Economics*, 156.

445

Åslund, Anders. (2008) 'Transition Economies', in David R. Henderson (ed.), *The Concise Encyclopedia of Economics*, Library of Economics and Liberty, Liberty Fund, Inc. http://www.econlib.org/library/Enc/TransitionEconomies.html.

—— (2007) *Russia's Capitalist Revolution: Why market reform succeeded and democracy failed*, Washington, DC: Peterson Institute for International Economics.

—— (2002a) *Building Capitalism: The transformation of the former Soviet Bloc*, Cambridge, UK: Cambridge University Press.

—— (2002b) 'The IMF and the Ruble Zone', *Comparative Economic Studies*, 44 (4).

—— (2001a) 'The Myth of Output Collapse after Communism', *Carnegie Endowment for International Peace Working Paper No. 18*, Washington, DC.

—— (2001b) 'Russia', *Foreign Affairs* July–August.

—— (1994) 'Russia's Success Story', *Foreign Affairs*, September–October.

Åslund, Anders and Andrew Kuchins. (2009) *The Russia Balance Sheet*, Washington, DC: Peterson Institute for International Economics.

Åslund, Anders and Nazgul Jenish. (2006) 'The Eurasian Growth Paradox', *Institute for International Economics Working Paper 06–05*, Washington, DC: Peterson Institute for International Economics.

Åslund, Anders, Peter Boone and Simon Johnson. (1996) 'How to Stabilize: Lessons from post-communist countries', *Brookings Papers on Economic Activity*, 1.

Atkeson, Andrew and Patrick J. Kehoe. (1996) 'Optimal Insurance and Transition', *International Economic Review*, 37 (2).

Atkinson, Anthony B. and John Michelwright. (1992) *Economic Transformation in Eastern Europe and the Distribution of Income*, Cambridge and New York: Cambridge University Press.

Balcerowicz, Leszek. (2002) 'Post-Communist Transition: Some lessons', *IEA Occasional Paper No. 127*, London: Institute of Economic Affairs.

—— (1995) *Socialism, Capitalism, Transformation*, Budapest: Central European University Press.

Barberis, Nicholas, Maxim Boycko, Andrei Shleifer and Natalia Tsukanova. (1996) 'How Does Privatization Work? Evidence from the Russian shops', *Journal of Political Economy*, 104 (4).

Barr, Nicholas. (2001) 'Reforming Welfare States in Post-Communist Countries', in Lucjan T. Orlowski (ed.), *Transition and Growth in Post-Communist Countries: The Ten-year Experience*, Cheltenham, UK: Edward Elgar.

Barro, Robert J. (1991) 'Economic Growth in a Cross Section of Countries', *Quarterly Journal of Economics*, 106 (2).

Barro, Robert J. and Xavier Sala-i-Martin. (2004) *Economic Growth*, 2nd edn, Cambridge, MA: MIT Press.

Beck, Thorsten and Luc Laeven. (2006) 'Institution Building and Growth in Transition Economies', *Journal of Economic Growth*, 11 (2).

Becker, Jasper. (2003) 'The Death of China's Rivers', *Asian Times Online*, 26 August.

Berend, Ivan T. (2009) *From the Soviet Bloc to the European Union: The economic and social transformation of Central and Eastern Europe since 1973*, Cambridge, UK: Cambridge University Press.

—— (2005) 'What is Central and Eastern Europe?', *European Journal of Social Theory*, 8 (4).

—— (1998) *Central and Eastern Europe 1944–1993: Detour from the periphery to the periphery*, New York: Cambridge University Press.

Berg, Andrew, Eduardo Borensztein, Ratna Sahay and Jeromin Zettelmeyer. (1999) 'The Evolution of Output in Transition Economies: Explaining the differences', *IMF Working Paper WP/99/73*, Washington, DC: International Monetary Fund.

Berglöf, Erik and Gérard Roland (eds). (2007) *The Economics of Transition: The fifth Nobel symposium in economics*, Basingstoke, UK: Palgrave Macmillan.

Berglöf, Erik and Patrick Bolton. (2002) 'The Great Divide and Beyond – financial architecture in transition', *Journal of Economic Perspectives*, 16 (1).

Bergson, Abram and Herbert S. Levine. (1983) *The Soviet Economy: Toward the year 2000*, Boston, MA: Allen & Unwin.

Berkowitz, Daniel and David N. DeJong. (2005) 'Entrepreneurship and Post-socialist Growth', *Oxford Bulletin of Economics and Statistics*, 67 (1).

Berle, Adolf A. and Gardiner C. Means. (1932) *The Modern Corporation and Private Property*, New York: Macmillan.

Berliner, Joseph S. (1952) 'The Informal Organization of the Soviet Firm', *Quarterly Journal of Economics*, 66 (3).

Berthelot, Yves. (1997) 'Lessons from Countries in Transition', in Louis Emmerij (ed.), *Economic and Social Development into the XXI Century*, Washington, DC: Inter-American Development Bank.

Bevan, Alan A. and Saul Estrin. (2000) 'The Determinants of Foreign Direct Investment in Transition Economies', *William Davidson Institute Working Paper No. 342*, University of Michigan.

Bevan, Alan A., Saul Estrin, Paul G. Hare and Jon Stern. (2001) 'Extending the Economics of Disorganization', *Economics of Transition*, 9 (1).

Bevan, Alan A., Saul Estrin and Mark E. Schaffer. (1999) 'Determinants of Enterprise Performance during Transition', *CERT Discussion Paper No. 99/03*, Heriot-Watt University, Edinburgh.

Bhaumik, Sumon K. and Saul Estrin. (2005) 'How Transition Paths Differ: Enterprise performance in Russia and China', *William Davidson Institute Working Paper No. 744*, University of Michigan.

Bianco, Lucien. (1986) *Origins of the Chinese Revolution 1915–1949*, London: Oxford University Press. Originally published in French in 1967 under the title *Les Origines de la révolution chinoise, 1915–1949* by Editions Gallimard. Translated 1971 by the Board of Trustees of the Leland Stanford Junior University. The 1986 printing translated from the French by Muriel Bell.

Bim, Alexander. (1996) 'Ownership and Control of Russian Enterprises and Strategies of Shareholders', *Communist Economies and Economic Transformation*, 8 (4).

Black, Bernard, Reinier Kraakman and Anna Tarassova. (2000) 'Russian Privatization and Corporate Governance: What went wrong?', *Stanford Law Review*, 52.

Blanchard, Olivier. (1997) *The Economics of Post-Communist Transition*, New York and Oxford: Oxford University Press.

Blanchard, Olivier and Michael Kremer. (1997) 'Disorganization', *Quarterly Journal of Economics*, 112 (4).

Blanchard, Olivier, Kenneth Froot and Jeffrey Sachs (eds). (1994) *The Transition in Eastern Europe*, Chicago, IL: University of Chicago Press.

Blasi, Joseph and Andrei Shleifer. (1994) 'Corporate Governance in Russia: An initial look', paper presented at a conference on conversion of the defence industry in Russia and Eastern Europe, 10–13 August 1994, Bonn.

Blejer, Mario I. and Marco Škreb. (2001) *Transition: The first decade*, Cambridge, MA: MIT Press.

Boenker, Frank, Klaus Müller and Andreas Pickel. (eds) (2002) *Postcommunist Transformation and the Social Sciences: Cross-disciplinary approaches*, Lanham, MD: Rowman & Littlefield.

Boeri, Tito and Hartmut Lehmann. (1999) 'Unemployment and Labour Market Policies in Transition Countries', *Journal of Comparative Economics*, 27 (1).

Boeri, Tito and Katherine Terrell. (2002) 'Institutional Determinants of Labour Reallocation in Transition', *Journal of Economic Perspectives*, 16 (1).

Bornstein, Morris (ed.). (1965) *Comparative Economic Systems: Models and cases*, Irwin Series in Economics. Illinois: Richard D. Irwin Inc.

Bottomore, Tom. (1990) *The Socialist Economy: Theory and practice*, London: Harvester Wheatsheaf.

Boycko, Maxim, Andrei Shleifer and Robert Vishny. (1996) 'A Theory of Privatisation', *The Economic Journal*, 106 (435).

—— (1995) *Privatizing Russia*, Cambridge, MA: MIT Press.

Brabant, van, Jozef M. (1998) *The Political Economy of Transition: Coming to grips with history and methodology*, London and New York: Routledge.

Brada, Josef C. (1996) 'Privatization is Transition – or is it?', *Journal of Economic Perspectives*, 10 (2).

—— (1993) 'The Transformation from Communism to Capitalism: How far? How fast?', *Post-Soviet Affairs*, 9 (2).

Brandt, Loren and Thomas G. Rawski. (2008) 'China's Great Economic Transformation', in Loren Brandt and Thomas G. Rawski (eds), *China's Great Economic Transformation*, New York: Cambridge University Press.

Brandt, Loren, Thomas G. Rawski and John Sutton. (2008) 'China's Industrial Development', in Loren Brandt and Thomas G. Rawski (eds), *China's Great Economic Transformation*, New York: Cambridge University Press.

Branstetter, Lee and Nicholas R. Lardy. (2008) 'China's Embrace of Globalisation', in Loren Brandt and Thomas G. Rawski (eds), *China's Great Economic Transformation*, New York: Cambridge University Press.

Brenton, Paul and Daniel Gros. (1997) 'Trade Reorientation and Recovery in Transition Economies', *Oxford Review of Economic Policy*, 13 (2).

Brenton, Paul, Daniel Gros and Guy Vandille. (1997) 'Output Decline and Recovery in the Transition Economies: Causes and social consequences', *Economics of Transition*, 5 (1).

Broadman, Harry G. and Francesca Recanatini. (2001) 'Is Russia Restructuring? New evidence on job creation and destruction', *Policy Research Working Paper 2641*, Washington, DC: The World Bank.

Brown, Annette N. (ed.). (1999) *When Is Transition Over?* Kalamazoo, MI: W.E. Upjohn Institute for Employment Research.

Brown, David J. and John S. Earle. (2000) 'Competition and Firm Performance: Lessons from Russia', *William Davidson Institute Working Paper No. 296*, University of Michigan.

Brown, David J., John S. Earle and Álmos Telegdy. (2006) 'The Productivity Effects of Privatization: Longitudinal Estimates from Hungary, Romania, Russia, and Ukraine', *Journal of Political Economy*, 114 (1).

Brunetti, Aymo, Gregory Kisunko and Beatrice Weder. (1997) 'Institutions in Transition: Reliability of rules and economic performance in former socialist countries', *Policy Research Working Paper 1809*, Washington, DC: The World Bank.

Bruno, Michael and William Easterly. (1998) 'Inflation Crises and Long-run Growth', *Journal of Monetary Economics*, 41 (1).

Brus, Wlodzimierz. (1986) 'Postwar Reconstruction and Socio-economic Transformation', in Michael C. Kaser and Edward A. Radice (eds), *The Economic History of Eastern Europe 1919–1975, Volume II Interwar Policy, the War and Reconstruction*, New York: Oxford University Press.

Buiter, Willem. (2004) 'What Have we Learnt from 15 years of Transition in Central and Eastern Europe?', paper prepared for the International Policy Conference on Transition Economies, Hanoi, Vietnam.

Bunce, Valerie. (1999) 'The Political Economy of Postsocialism', *Slavic Review*, 58 (4).

Burki, Shahid Javed and Guillermo E. Perry. (1998) *Beyond the Washington Consensus: Institutions matter*, Washington, DC: World Bank.

Byrd, William A. (1989) 'Plan and Market in the Chinese Economy: A simple general equilibrium model', *Journal of Comparative Economics*, 13 (2).

Cai, Fang, Albert Park and Yaohui Zhao. (2008) 'The Chinese Labor Market in the Reform Era', in Loren Brandt and Thomas G. Rawski (eds), *China's Great Economic Transformation*, New York: Cambridge University Press.

Calvo, Guillermo and Fabrizio Coricelli. (1993) 'Output Collapse in Eastern Europe: The role of credit', *IMF Staff Papers*, 40 (1), Washington, DC: International Monetary Fund.

Campbell, Robert W. (1966) *Soviet Economic Power: Its organization, growth and challenge*, 2nd edn, Boston, MA: Houghton Mifflin Co.

Campos, Nauro. (2000) 'Context is Everything: Measuring institutional change in transition economies', *Policy Research Working Paper 2269*, Washington, DC: The World Bank.

Campos, Nauro F. and Fabrizio Coricelli. (2002) 'Growth in Transition: What we know, what we don't, and what we should', *Journal of Economic Literature*, 40 (3).

Campos, Nauro F. and Jan Fidrmuc (eds). (2003) *Political Economy of Transition and Development: Institutions, politics and policies*, ZEI Studies in European Economics and Law, vol. 5, Dordrecht: Kluwer Academic Publishers.

Carlin, Wendy, Steven Fries, Mark E. Schaffer and Paul Seabright. (2001) 'Competition and Enterprise Performance in Transition Economies: Evidence from a cross-country survey', *EBRD Working Paper No. 63*, European Bank for Reconstruction and Development.

Carr, Edward H. (1984) *A History of Soviet Russia: The Bolshevik revolution 1917–1923, Volume 2*, Harmondsworth, UK: Penguin Books.

—— (1980) *The Russian Revolution from Lenin to Stalin 1917–1929*, London: Macmillan.

Chang, Ha-Joon and Peter Nolan (eds). (1995) *The Transformation of the Communist Economies: Against the mainstream*, Basingstoke: Macmillan.

Chiang, Alpha C. (1974) *Fundamental Methods of Mathematical Economics*, New York: McGraw-Hill.

Christoffersen, Peter and Peter Doyle. (2000) 'From Inflation to Growth: Eight years of transition', *Economics of Transition*, 8 (2).

Claessens, Stijn. (2006). 'Corporate Governance and Development', *World Bank Research Observer*, 21 (1).

Claessens, Stijn and Simeon Djankov. (1999a) 'Ownership Concentration and Corporate Performance in the Czech Republic', *Journal of Comparative Economics*, 27 (3).

—— (1999b) 'Enterprise Performance and Management Turnover in the Czech Republic', *European Economic Review*, 43 (4–6).

Clague, Christopher and Gordon Rausser (eds). (1992) *The Emergence of Market Economies in Eastern Europe*, Oxford: Blackwell.

Clarke, Donald, Peter Murrell and Susan Whiting. (2008) 'The Role of Law in China's Economic Development', in Loren Brandt and Thomas G. Rawski (eds), *China's Great Economic Transformation*, New York: Cambridge University Press.

Clarke, Simon. (1996) *The Restructuring of Employment and the Formation of a Labour Market in Russia*, Institute for Comparative Labour Relations Research, Moscow and Centre for Comparative Labour Studies, University of Warwick, UK.

Coase, Ronald H. (1992) 'The Institutional Structure of Production', *American Economic Review*, 82 (4).

Cohen, Andreea Balan. (2007) 'Sobering Up: The impact of the 1985–1988 Russian anti-alcohol campaign on child health', Tufts University Discussion Paper.

Commander, Simon (ed.). (1998) *Enterprise Restructuring and Unemployment in Models of Transition*, Washington, DC: The World Bank, Economic Development Institute.

Commander, Simon and Sumana Dhar. (1998) 'Enterprises in the Polish Transition', in Simon Commander (ed.), *Enterprise Restructuring and Unemployment in Models of Transition*, Washington, DC: The World Bank, Economic Development Institute.

Commander, Simon and John McHale. (1996) *Worker Influence and Employment Bias in a Transitional Firm*, Washington, DC: The World Bank, Economic Development Institute.

Commander, Simon and Jan Svejnar. (2007) 'Do Institutions, Ownership, Exporting and Competition Explain Firm Performance? Evidence from 26 transition countries', *IZA Discussion Paper No. 2637*, Bonn.

Commander, Simon, Mark Dutz and Richard Stern. (2000) 'Restructuring in Transition Economies: Ownership, competition and regulation', in Boris Pleskovic and Joseph Stiglitz (eds), *Annual World Bank Conference on Development Economics 1999*, Washington, DC.: The World Bank.

Commander, Simon, Andrei Tolstopiatenko and Ruslan Yemstov. (1999) 'Channels of Redistribution: Inequality and poverty in the Russian Federation', *Economics of Transition*, 7 (2).

Commander, Simon, Sumana Dhar and Ruslan Yemtsov. (1996) 'How Russian Firms make their Wage and Employment Decisions', in Simon Commander, Qimiao Fan and Mark E. Schaffer (eds),

Enterprise Restructuring and Economic Policy in Russia, Washington, DC: World Bank, Economic Development Institute.

Commission on Growth and Development. (2008) *The Growth Report: Strategies for sustained growth and inclusive development*, Washington, DC: The World Bank on behalf of the Commission on Growth and Development.

Csaba, László. (2005) *The New Political Economy of Emerging Europe*, Budapest: Akadémiai Kiadó.

—— (1995) *The Capitalist Revolution in Eastern Europe: A contribution to the economic theory of systemic change*, Aldershot, UK: Edward Elgar.

Cuddy, Michael and Ruvin Gekker. (eds) (2002) *Institutional Change in Transition Economies*, Aldershot: Ashgate.

Dabrowski, Marek, Stanislaw Gomulka and Jacek Rostowski. (2001) 'Whence Reform? A critique of the Stiglitz perspective', *Journal of Policy Reform*, 4 (4).

Dahrendorf, Ralf. (1990) *Reflections on the Revolution in Europe: In a letter intended to have been sent to a gentleman in Warsaw*, New York: Times Books.

Daianu, Daniel. (2002) 'Whither Taxation in Transition Countries', presented at 'Beyond Transition' Conference, Warsaw.

Dallago, Bruno. (2007) 'Corporate Governance in Transition Economies: A Comparative Perspective', in Bruno Dallago and Ichiro Iwasaki (eds), *Corporate Restructing and Governance in Transition Economies*, Basingstoke: Palgrave Macmillan.

Dallago, Bruno and Ichiro Iwasaki. (eds) (2007) *Corporate Restructuring and Governance in Transition Economies*, Basingstoke, UK: Palgrave Macmillan.

Darby, Julia, Robert A. Hart and Michela Vecchi. (2001) 'Wages, Work Intensity and Unemployment in Japan, UK and USA', *Labour Economics*, 8 (2).

De Melo, Martha, Cevdet Denizer, Alan Gelb and Stoyan Tenev. (2001) 'Circumstance and Choice: The role of initial conditions and policies in transition economies', *The World Bank Economic Review*, 15 (1), Washington, DC: The World Bank.

Desai, Padma. (2006) *Conversations on Russia: Reform from Yeltsin to Putin*, New York: Oxford University Press.

Dewatripont, Mathias and Gérard Roland. (1997) 'Transition as a Process of Large-scale Institutional Change', in David Kreps and Kenneth Wallis (eds), *Advances in Economics and Econometrics: Theory and applications*, Seventh World Congress of the Econometric Society, Vol II, Cambridge, UK: Cambridge University Press.

Dewatripont, Mathias and Eric Maskin. (1995) 'Credit and Efficiency in Centralized and Decentralized Economies', *Review of Economic Studies*, 62 (213).

Dhanagare, Dattatreya N. (1993) 'Remembering Tom Bottomore', *Economic and Political Weekly*, 28 (48).

Djankov, Simeon and Peter Murrell. (2002) 'Enterprise Restructuring in Transition: A quantitative survey', *Journal of Economic Literature*, 40 (3).

—— (2000) 'The Determinants of Enterprise Restructuring in Transition: An assessment of the evidence', Washington, D.C: The World Bank.

Djankov, Simeon, Edward Glaeser, Rafael La Porta, Florencio Lopez-de-Silanes and Andrei Shleifer. (2003) 'The New Comparative Economics', *Journal of Comparative Economics*, 31 (4).

Dutkiewicz, Piotr and Vladimir Popov. (2006) 'Ahead or Behind? Lessons from Russia's postcommunist transformation', in Antoni Kuklinski and Bogusla Skuza (eds), *Turning Points in the Transformation of the Global Scene*, Warsaw: The Polish Association of the Club of Rome.

Dyker, David A. (2004) *Catching Up and Falling Behind: Post-communist transformation in historical perspective*, London: Imperial College Press.

Earle, John. (1998) 'Post-privatization Ownership Structure and Productivity in Russian Industrial Enterprises', *SITE Working Paper No. 127*, Stockholm Institute of Transition Economics.

Earle, John and Saul Estrin. (1998) 'Privatization, Competition and Budget Constraints: Disciplining enterprises in Russia', *SITE Working Paper No. 128*, Stockholm Institute of Transition Economics.

Earle, John, Saul Estrin and Larisa L. Leshchenko. (1996) 'Ownership Structures, Patterns of Control, and Enterprise Behaviour in Russia', in Simon Commander, Qimiao Fan and Mark E. Schaffer (eds), *Enterprise Restructuring and Economic Policy in Russia*, Washington, DC: World Bank, Economic Development Institute.

Easterly, William. (2006) 'The Big Push Déjà Vu: A review of Jeffrey Sachs's the end of poverty: economic possibilities for our time', *Journal of Economic Literature*, 44 (1).

EBRD. (2009) *Transition Report 2009: Transition in crisis?*, London: European Bank for Reconstruction and Development.

—— (2008) *Transition Report 2008: Growth in transition*, London: European Bank for Reconstruction and Development.

—— (2005) *Transition Report 2005: Business in transition*, London: European Bank for Reconstruction and Development.

—— (1999) *Transition Report 1999: Ten years of transition*, London: European Bank for Reconstruction and Development.

Economy, Elizabeth C. (2004) *The Rivers Runs Black: The environmental challenge to China's future*, Ithaca, NY: Cornell University Press.

Eichengreen, Barry J. (2007) *The European Economy since 1945: Coordinated capitalism and beyond*, Princeton, NJ: Princeton University Press.

Ellerman, David. (2003) 'On the Russian Privatization Debate', *Challenge*, 46 (3).

—— (2001) 'Lessons from Eastern Europe's Voucher Privatization', *Challenge*, 44 (4).

Ellman, Michael. (2000) 'The Social Costs and Consequences of the Transformational Process', Chapter 5 in *Economic Survey of Europe*, nos 2/3, Geneva: United Nations Economic Commission for Europe.

—— (1997a) 'Transformation as a Demographic Crisis', in Salvatore Zecchini (ed.), *Lessons from the Economic Transition: Central and Eastern Europe in the 1990s*, Dordrecht: Kluwer Academic.

—— (1997b) 'The Political Economy of Transformation', *Oxford Review of Economic Policy*, 13 (2).

—— (1994) 'Transformation, Depression, and Economics: Some lessons', *Journal of Comparative Economics*, 19 (1).

Elster, Jon, Claus Offe and Ulrich K. Preuss, with Frank Boenker, Ulrike Goetting and Friedbert W. Rueb. (1998) *Institutional Design in Post-communist Societies: Rebuilding the ship at sea*, Cambridge: Cambridge University Press.

Ericson, Richard E. (1998) 'Review: Economics and the Russian transition', *Slavic Review*, 57 (3).

Estrin, Saul. (2002) 'Competition and Corporate Governance in Transition', *Journal of Economic Perspectives*, 16 (1).

Estrin, Saul and Alan Bevan. (2003) 'Determinants of Russian Enterprise Performance: Conclusions from the symposium', *Comparative Economic Studies*, 45 (2).

Estrin, Saul and Jan Svejnar. (1998) 'The Effects of Output, Ownership, and Legal Form on Employment and Wages in Central European Firms', in Simon Commander (ed.), *Enterprise Restructuring and Unemployment in Models of Transition*, Washington, DC: World Bank, Economic Development Institute.

Estrin, Saul, Jan Hanousek, Evžen Kočenda and Jan Svejnar. (2009) 'The Effects of Privatization and Ownership in Transition Economies', *Journal of Economic Literature*, 47 (3).

Europa Regional Surveys of the World. (2008) *Central and South-Eastern Europe*, 8th edn, London: Routledge.

Fair, Ray C. (1985) 'Excess Labor and the Business Cycle', *American Economic Review*, 75 (1).

Falcetti, Elisabetta, Tatiana Lysenko and Peter Sanfey. (2006) 'Reforms and Growth in Transition: Re-examining the evidence', *Journal of Comparative Economics*, 34 (3).

Falcetti, Elisabetta, Martin Raiser and Peter Sanfey. (2002) 'Defying the Odds: Initial conditions, reforms, and growth in the first decade of transition', *Journal of Comparative Economics*, 30 (2).

Fay, Jon A. and James L. Medoff. (1985) 'Labor and Output Over the Business Cycle: Some direct evidence', *American Economic Review*, 75 (4).

Feng, Wang and Andrew Mason. (2008) 'The Demographic Factor in China's Transition', in Loren Brandt and Thomas G. Rawski (eds)., *China's Great Economic Transformation*, New York: Cambridge University Press.

Fidrmuc, Jan. (2003) 'Economic Reform, Democracy and Growth during Post-Communist Transition', *European Journal of Political Economy*, 19 (3).

Fischer, Stanley and Alan Gelb. (1991a) 'The Process of Socialist Economic Transformation', *Journal of Economic Perspectives*, 5 (4).

—— (1991b) 'Issues in Socialist Economy Reform', *Policy Research Working Paper 565*, Washington, DC: The World Bank.

Fischer, Stanley and Ratna Sahay. (2000) 'The Transition Economies after Ten Years', *NBER Working Paper 7664*, National Bureau of Economic Research.

Fischer, Stanley, Ratna Sahay and Carlos A. Végh. (1996a) 'Stabilization and Growth in Transition Economies: The early evidence', *Journal of Economic Perspectives*, 10 (2).

—— (1996b) 'Economies in Transition: The beginning of growth', *American Economic Review, Papers and Proceedings*, 86 (2).

Freeland, Chrystia. (2000) *Sale of the Century: Russia's wild ride from communism to capitalism*, New York: Crown Business.

Freidman, Eric, Simon Johnson, Daniel Kaufmann and Pablo Zoido Lobatón. (2000) 'Dodging the Grabbing Hand: The determinants of unofficial activities in 69 countries', *Journal of Public Economics*, 76 (3).

Fries, Steven, Tatiana Lysenko and Saso Polanec. (2003) 'The 2002 Business Environment and Enterprise Performance Survey: Results from a survey of 6,100 firms', *EBRD Working Paper No. 84*, European Bank for Reconstruction and Development.

Frydman, Roman, Cheryl Gray, Marek Hessel and Andrzej Rapaczynski. (1999) 'When Does Privatization Work? The impact of private ownership on corporate performance in the transition economies', *Quarterly Journal of Economics*, 114 (4).

Frye, Timothy and Andrei Shleifer. (1997) 'The Invisible Hand and the Grabbing Hand', *American Economic Review Papers and Proceedings*, 87 (2).

Gabrisch, Hubert and Jens Hölscher. (2006) *The Successes and Failures of Economic Transition: The European experience*, Basingstoke: Palgrave Macmillan.

Gaddy, Clifford G. and William G. Gale. (2005) 'Demythologizing the Russian Flat Tax', *Tax Notes International*, 37.

Gaidar, Yegor. (ed.). (2003) *The Economics of Russian Transition*, Cambridge, MA: MIT Press.

—— (1999) *Days of Defeat and Victory*, Seattle, WA: University of Washington Press.

Galbraith, John Kenneth. (1994) *The World Economy since the Wars – a Personal View*, London: Sinclair-Stevenson.

Gelb, Alan. (1997) 'Assessing the Transition from Plan to Market: What have we learned – about policies and economic theory?', *Journal of International Development*, 9 (4).

Gerschenkron, Alexander. (1962) *Economic Backwardness in Historical Perspective: A book of essays*, Cambridge, MA: Harvard University Press.

Godoy, Sergio and Joseph E. Stiglitz. (2006) 'Growth, Initial Conditions, Law and Speed of Privatization in Transition Countries: 11 years later', *NBER Working Paper 11992*, National Bureau of Economic Research.

Gomulka, Stanislaw. (2000) 'Macroeconomic Policies and Achievements in Transition Economies, 1989–1999', Chapter 3 in *Economic Survey of Europe*, nos 2/3, Geneva: United Nations Economic Commission for Europe.

—— (1998) 'Output: Causes of the decline and the recovery', in Peter Boone, Stanislaw Gomulka and Richard Layard (eds), *Emerging from Communism: Lessons from Russia, China and Eastern Europe*, Cambridge, MA: MIT Press.

Goskomstat. (1996) 'The Differentiation of Wages of Workers in Enterprises (Organisations) during the first half of 1996', *Informational Statistical Bulletin*, 13.

Gray, Cheryl. (1996) 'In Search of Owners: Privatization and corporate governance in transition economies', *The World Bank Research Observer*, 11 (2).

Gregory, Paul R. (1997) 'Has Russia's Transition Really Been Such a Failure?', *Problems of Post-Communism*, 44 (6).

Gregory, Paul R. and Robert Stuart. (2001) *Russian and Soviet Economic Performance and Structure*, 7th edn, New York: Addison Wesley Longman.

Grogan, Louise and Luc Moers. (2001) 'Growth Empirics with Institutional Measures for Transition Countries', *Economic Systems*, 25 (4).

Gros, Daniel and Alfred Steinherr. (2004) *Economic Transition in Central and Eastern Europe: Planting the seeds*, Cambridge, UK: Cambridge University Press.

Grosfeld, Irena and Gérard Roland. (1997) 'Defensive and Strategic Restructuring in Central European Enterprises', *Journal of Transforming Economies and Societies*, 3 (4).

Gross, Natalie. (1996) 'Farming in Former East Germany: Past policies and future prospects', *Landscape and Urban Planning*, 35 (1).

Guriev, Sergei and William L. Megginson. (2007) 'Privatization: What have we learnt?', in Francois Bourguignon and Boris Pleskovic (eds), *Beyond Transition: Annual World Bank Conference on Development Economics 2007*, Washington, DC: The World Bank.

Gurkov, Igor and Shlomo Maital. (1996) 'Perceived Control and Performance in Russian Privatized Enterprises', *European Management Journal*, 14 (2).

Haggard, Stephan and Yasheng Huang. (2008) 'The Political Economy of Private Sector Development in China', in Loren Brandt and Thomas G. Rawski (eds), *China's Great Economic Transformation*, New York: Cambridge University Press.

Hall, Robert and Alvin Rabushka. (1985) *The Flat Tax*, Stanford, CA: Hoover Institution Press.

Hamill, Jim and Alec Wersun. (1996) 'Joint Ventures in Russia – The Experience of Two Small Companies', *Journal of East-West Business*, 1 (4).

Hanke, Steve H. (2007). 'The World's Greatest Unreported Inflation', *Globe Asia*.

Hanousek, Jan, Evžen Kočenda and Jan Svejnar. (2008) 'Privatization in Central and Eastern Europe and the Commonwealth of Independent States', in Gérard Roland (ed.), *Privatization: Success and failures*, New York: Columbia University Press.

—— (2007) 'Origin and Concentration: Corporate ownership, control and performance in firms after privatization', *Economics of Transition*, 15 (1).

Hare, Paul. (2010) *Vodka and Pickled Cabbage: The Eastern European travels of a professional economist*, Twickenham: Athena Press.

—— (2001a) 'Institutional Change and Economic Performance in Transition Economies', Presented at the UNECE Spring Seminar, Geneva.

—— (2001b) 'Trade Policy During the Transition: Lessons from the 1990s', *The World Economy*, 24 (4).

—— (ed.) (1999) *Systemic Change in Post-Communist Economies*, London: Macmillan.

Hare, Paul and Alexander Muravyev. (2002) 'Privatization in Russia', *Russian-European Centre for Economic Policy Research Paper Series*, Moscow.

Hare, Paul, Mark E. Schaffer and Anna Shabunina (2004) 'The Great Transformation: Russia's return to the world economy', *CERT Discussion Paper No. 01/04*, Heriot-Watt University, Edinburgh.

Harman, Chris. (1974) *Bureaucracy and Revolution in Eastern Europe*, London: Pluto Press.

Harmon, Colm, Westergaard-Nielsen, Niels and Ian Walker. (2001) *Education and Earnings across Europe*, Cheltenham, UK: Edward Elgar.

Harmon, Colm, Hessel Oosterbeek and Ian Walker. (2000) 'The Returns to Education: A review of evidence, issues and deficiencies in the literature', *Centre for the Economics of Education Discussion Paper*, London School of Economics and Political Science.

Harper, Joel T. (2002) 'The Performance of Privatized Firms in the Czech Republic', *Journal of Banking and Finance*, 26 (4).

Havrylyshyn, Oleh (2006) *Divergent Paths in Post-Communist Transformation: Capitalism for all or capitalism for the few*, Studies in Economic Transition, Basingstoke: Palgrave Macmillan.

—— (2001) 'Recovery and Growth in Transition: A decade of evidence', *IMF Staff Papers*, vol. 48, Special Issue. Washington, DC: International Monetary Fund.

Havrylyshyn, Oleh and Donal McGettigan. (2000) 'Privatization in Transition Countries', *Post-Soviet Affairs*, 16 (3).

Havrylyshyn, Oleh and Saleh M. Nsouli (eds). (2001) *A Decade of Transition: Achievements and challenges*, Washington, DC: International Monetary Fund, IMF Institute.

Havrylyshyn, Oleh and Ron van Rooden. (2003) 'Institutions Matter in Transition, but so do Policies', *Comparative Economics Studies*, 45 (1).

Havrylyshyn, Oleh, Ivailo Izvorski and Ron van Rooden. (1998) 'Recovery and Growth in Transition Economies 1990–1997: A stylized regression analysis', *IMF Working Paper 98/141*, Washington, DC: International Monetary Fund.

Havrylyshyn, Oleh, Thomas Wolf, Julian Berengaut, Marta Castello-Branco, Ron van Rooden and Valerie Mercer-Blackman. (1999) 'Growth Experience in Transition Economies, 1990–1998', *IMF Occasional Paper No. 184*. Washington, DC: International Monetary Fund.

Hayek, Friedrich A. von. (1945) 'The Use of Knowledge in Society', *American Economic Review*, 35 (4).

—— (1944) *The Road to Serfdom*, London: Routledge.

Hedlund, Stefan. (2005) *Russian Path Dependence*, London: Routledge.

—— (2001) 'Property Without Rights: Dimensions of Russian privatisation', *Europe-Asia Studies*, 53 (2).

—— (1999) *Russia's "Market" Economy: A bad case of predatory capitalism*, London: UCL Press.

Hellman, Joel S. (1998) 'Winners Take All: The politics of partial reform in postcommunist transitions', *World Politics*, 50 (2).

Hernández-Catá, Ernesto. (1997) 'Liberalization and the Behaviour of Output during the Transition from Plan to Market', *IMF Working Paper 97/53*, Washington, DC: International Monetary Fund.

Heston, Alan and Terry Sinclair. (2008) 'China and Development Economics', in Loren Brandt and Thomas G. Rawski (eds), *China's Great Economic Transformation*, New York: Cambridge University Press.

Heybey, Berta and Peter Murrell. (1999) 'The Relationship between Economic Growth and the Speed of Liberalization During Transition', *Journal of Policy Reform*, 3 (2).

Hoen, Herman W. (1998) *The Transformation of Economic Systems in Central Europe*, Cheltenham, UK: Edward Elgar.

—— (1996) 'Shock versus Gradualism in Central Europe Reconsidered', *Comparative Economic Studies*, 38 (1).

—— (1994) 'Is there such a thing as "Transitology"?', paper presented at the Eleventh World Congress for Social Economics, France, June.

Holz, Carsten A. (2006a) 'China's Reform Period Economic Growth: How reliable are Angus Maddison's estimates?', *Review of Income and Wealth*, 52 (1).

—— (2006b) 'China's Reform Period Economic Growth: How reliable are Angus Maddison's estimates? Response to Angus Maddison's reply', *Review of Income and Wealth*, 52 (3).

Howe, Christopher. (1973) *Wage Patterns and Wage Policy in Modern China 1919–1972*, Cambridge: Cambridge University Press.

Huang, Jikun, Keijiro Otsuka and Scott Rozelle. (2008) 'Agriculture in China's Development: Past disappointments, recent successes, and future challenges', in Loren Brandt and Thomas G. Rawski (eds), *China's Great Economic Transformation*, New York: Cambridge University Press.

Hutton, Will. (2007) *The Writing on the Wall: China and the West in the 21st century*, London: Little, Brown.

Ichimura, Shinichi, Tsuneaki Sato and William E. James. (eds). (2009) *Transition from Socialist to Market Economies: Comparison of European and Asian experiences*, Basingstoke: Palgrave Macmillan.

Ickes, Barry W. (2003) 'Evolution and Transition', in Naura F. Campos and Jan Fidrmuc (eds), *Political Economy of Transition and Development: Institutions, politics and policies*, ZEI Studies in European Economics and Law, vol. 5, Dordrecht: Kluwer Academic.

—— (1996) 'Comment on Åslund-Boone-Johnson', *Brookings Papers on Economic Activity*, 1.

Illarionov, Andrei. (1999) 'The Roots of the Economic Crisis', *Journal of Democracy*, 10 (2).

IMF. (2009) *Government Finance Statistics Yearbook*, Washington, DC: IMF.

—— (2000) *World Economic Outlook: Focus on transition economies*, Washington, DC: IMF.

—— (1991) *A Study of the Soviet Economy*, IMF/World Bank/OECD/EBRD, Washington, DC: IMF.

Jackman, Richard. (1994) 'Economic Policy and Employment in the Transition Economies of Central and Eastern Europe: What have we learned?', *International Labour Review*, 133 (3).

Jeffries, Ian. (2004) *The Countries of the Former Soviet Union at the Turn of the Twenty-first Century: The Baltic and European states in transition*, London: Routledge.

Johnson, Simon, Daniel Kaufmann and Andrei Shleifer. (1997) 'The Unofficial Economy in Transition', *Brookings Papers on Economic Activity*, 2.

Johnson, Simon, John McMillan and Christopher Woodruff. (2002) 'Property Rights and Finance', *American Economic Review*, 92 (5).

Johnson, Simon, Daniel Kaufmann, John McMillan and Christopher Woodruff. (2000) 'Why Do Firms Hide? Bribes and unofficial activity after communism', *Journal of Public Economics*, 76 (3).

Jomo, K.S. (2008) 'A Critical Review of the Evolving Privatization Debate', in Gérard Roland (ed.), *Privatization: Success and failures*, New York: Columbia University Press.

Kaser, Michael C. and Janusz G. Zielinski. (1970) *Planning in Eastern Europe. Industrial management by the state*, London: The Bodley Head.

Katchanovski, Ivan. (2000) 'Divergence in Growth in Post-Communist Countries', *Journal of Public Policy*, 20 (1).

Kaufmann, Daniel and Aleksander Kaliberda. (1996) 'Integrating the Unofficial Economy into the Dynamics of Post-socialist Economies: A framework of analysis and evidence', *Policy Research Working Paper No. 1691*, Washington, DC: The World Bank.

Kaufmann, Daniel, Aart Kraay and Massimo Mastruzzi. (2009) 'Governance Matters VIII: Aggregate and individual governance indicators 1996–2008', *Policy Research Working Paper 4978*, Washington, DC: The World Bank.

Keen, Michael, Yitae Kim and Ricardo Varsano. (2006) 'The Flat Tax(es): Principles and evidence', *IMF Working Paper WP06/218*, Washington, DC: IMF.

Keynes, John Maynard. (1936) *The General Theory of Employment, Interest and Money*, London: Macmillan.

Khan, Azizur Rahman and Carl Riskin. (2005) 'China's Household Income and Its Distribution, 1995 and 2002', *The China Quarterly*, 182.

King, Lawrence P. (2003) 'Explaining Postcommunist Economic Performance', *William Davidson Institute Working Paper No. 559*, University of Michigan.

Klein, Lawrence R. (2001) 'What Do Economists Know about Transition to a Market System?', in Lawrence R. Klein and Marshall Pomer (eds), *The New Russia: Transition gone awry*, Stanford, CA: Stanford University Press.

Klein, Lawrence R. and Marshall Pomer (eds). (2001) *The New Russia: Transition gone awry*, Stanford, CA: Stanford University Press.

Klein, Naomi. (2007) *The Shock Doctrine: The rise of disaster capitalism*, London: Penguin.

Knack, Stephen and Philip Keefer. (1995) 'Institutions and Economic Performance: Cross-country tests using alternative institutional measures', *Economics and Politics*, 7 (3).

Knight, John and Xue Jinjun. (2003) *How High is Urban Unemployment in China?*. Department of Economics, University of Oxford, mimeo.

Knight, John and Lina Song. (2006) *Towards a Labour Market in China*, Oxford: Oxford University Press.

Kočenda, Evzen and Jan Svejnar. (2003) 'Ownership and Firm Performance after Large-scale Privatization', *William Davidson Institute Working Paper No. 471a*, University of Michigan.

Kolodko, Grzegorz W. (2006) *The World Economy and Great Post-Communist Change*, New York: Nova Science Publishers.

—— (2000) *From Shock to Therapy: The political economy of postsocialist transformation*, Oxford: Oxford University Press.

—— (1999) 'Ten Years of Post-socialist Transition: Lessons for policy reform', *Policy Research Working Paper 2095*, Washington, DC: The World Bank.

Kontorovich, Vladimir. (2001) 'The Russian Health Crisis and the Economy', *Communist and Post-Communist Studies*, 34.

Kornai, János. (2008) *From Socialism to Capitalism*, Budapest: Central European University Press.

—— (2006a) 'The Great Transformation of Central Eastern Europe: Success and disappointment', *Economics of Transition*, 14 (2).

—— (2006b) *By Force of Thought: Irregular memoirs of an intellectual journey*, Cambridge, MA: MIT Press.

—— (2001) 'Hardening the Budget Constraint: The experience of the post-socialist countries', *European Economic Review*, 45 (9).

—— (2000a) 'Ten Years After "The Road to a Free Economy": The author's self-evaluation', *Economic Systems*, 24 (4).

—— (2000b) 'What the Change of System from Socialism to Capitalism Does and Does Not Mean', *Journal of Economic Perspectives*, 14 (1).

—— (1998) 'Legal Obligation, Non-compliance and Soft Budget Constraint', in Peter Newman (ed.), *The New Palgrave Dictionary of Economics and the Law*, New York: Macmillan.

—— (1994) 'Transformational Recession: The main causes', *Journal of Comparative Economics*, 19 (1).

—— (1992) *The Socialist System: The political economy of communism*, Oxford: Clarendon Press.

—— (1980) *Economics of Shortage (Vols 1 and 2)*, Amsterdam: North Holland Publishing.

—— (1979) 'Resource-constrained Versus Demand-constrained Systems', *Econometrica*, 47 (4).

Kornai, János, Lászlo Mátyás and Gérard Roland (eds). (2008) *Institutional Change and Economic Behaviour*, Basingstoke: Palgrave Macmillan.

Kotz, David. (2000) 'Lessons from Economic Transition in Russia and China', in Bob Baiman, Heather Boushey and Dawn Saunders (eds), *Political Economy and Contemporary Capitalism: Radical perspectives on economic theory and policy*, New York: M.E. Sharpe.

Kozul-Wright, Richard and Paul Rayment. (1997) 'The Institutional Hiatus in Economies in Transition and its Policy Consequences', *Cambridge Journal of Economics*, 21 (5).

Krueger, Gary and Marek Ciolko. (1998) 'A Note on Initial Conditions and Liberalization during Transition', *Journal of Comparative Economics*, 26 (4).

Krugman, Paul. (1994) 'The Myth of Asia's Miracle', *Foreign Affairs*, 73 (6).

Lackó, Mária. (2000) 'Hidden Economy – An Unknown Quantity? Comparative analysis of hidden economies in transition countries 1989–1995', *Economics of Transition*, 8 (1).

Landesmann, Michael. (2000) 'Structural Change in the Transition Economies, 1989–1999', Chapter 4 in *Economic Survey of Europe*, nos 2/3, Geneva: United Nations Economic Commission for Europe.

La Porta, Rafael, Florencio Lopez-de-Silanes, Andrei Shleifer and Robert Vishny. (1999) 'The Quality of Government', *Journal of Law, Economics and Organizations*, 15 (1).

Lavigne, Marie. (2000) 'Ten Years of Transition: A review article', *Communist and Post-Communist Studies*, 33 (4).

—— (1999) *The Economics of Transition: From socialist economy to market economy*, 2nd edn, Basingstoke: Palgrave.

Layard, Richard and Andrea Richter. (1995) 'How Much Unemployment is Needed for Restructuring: the Russian Experience', *Economics of Transition*, 3 (1).

Lehmann, Hartmut, Jonathan Wadsworth and Alessandro Acquisti. (1999) 'Grime and Punishment: Job insecurity and wage arrears in the Russian Federation', *Journal of Comparative Economics*, 27 (4).

Lévesque Jacques. (1997) *The Enigma of 1989, the USSR and the Liberation of Eastern Europe*, Berkeley: University of California Press.

Levin, Mark and Georgy Satarov. (2000) 'Corruption and Institutions in Russia', *European Journal of Political Economy*, 16 (1).

Li, Wei. (1999) 'A Tale of Two Reforms', *RAND Journal of Economics*, 30 (1).

Lieberman, Ira W. and Daniel J. Kopf (eds). (2008) *Privatization in Transition Economies: The ongoing story*, Contemporary Studies in Economic and Financial Analysis, vol. 90, Amsterdam: Elsevier.

Lieberman, Ira W., Ioannis N. Kessides and Mario Gobbo. (2008) 'An Overview of Privatization in Transition Economics', in Ira W. Lieberman and Daniel J. Kopf (eds), *Privatization in Transition Economies: The ongoing story*, Contemporary Studies in Economic and Financial Analysis, vol. 90, Amsterdam: Elsevier.

Lindbeck, Assar. (1992) 'Macroeconomic Theory and the Labour Market', Presidential Address, *European Economic Review*, 36 (2–3).

Lindbeck, Assar and Dennis Snower. (2002) 'The Insider-Outsider Theory: A survey', *IZA Discussion Paper No. 534*, Bonn.

—— (1988) *The Insider-Outsider Theory of Employment and Unemployment*, Cambridge: MIT Press.

Lindblom, Charles E. (1959) 'The Science of Muddling Through', *Public Administration Review*, 19 (2).

Linn, Johannes F. (2001) 'Ten Years of Transition in Central Europe and the Former Soviet Union: The good news and the not-so-good news', in Mario I. Blejer and Marko Škreb (eds), *Transition: The first decade*. Cambridge, Mass.: MIT Press.

Lipsey, Richard G. and Kenneth Carlaw. (2000) 'What Does Total Factor Productivity Measure?', *International Productivity Monitor*, 1.

Lipton, David and Jeffrey Sachs. (1990) 'Privatization in Eastern Europe: The case of Poland', *Brookings Papers on Economic Activity*, 2.

Loungani, Prakash and Nathan Sheets. (1997) 'Central Bank Independence, Inflation, and Growth in Transition Economies', *Journal of Money, Credit and Banking*, 29 (3).

McFaul, Michael. (2001) *Russia's Unfinished Revolution: Political Change from Gorbachev to Putin*, Ithaca, NY: Cornell University Press.

—— (1995) 'State Power, Institutional Change and the Politics of Privatization in Russia', *World Politics*, 47 (2).

McFaul, Michael and Kathryn Stoner-Weiss. (2004) *After the Collapse of Communism: Comparative lessons of transition*, Washington, DC: Carnegie Endowment for International Peace.

McHale, John and Alexander Pankov. (1999) 'Post-Communist Privatization and Wealth Distribution: What do we know?', Harvard University and World Bank, draft.

McKinnon, Ronald I. (1991a) *The Order of Economic Liberalization: Financial control in the transition to a market economy*, Baltimore, MD: Johns Hopkins University Press.

—— (1991b) 'Financial Control in the Transition from Classical Socialism to a Market Economy', *Journal of Economic Perspectives*, 5 (4).

McMillan, John. (2004) 'Avoid Hubris and Other Lessons for Reformers', *Centre for Democracy, Development and the Rule of Law Working Paper No. 2*, Stanford Institute for International Studies.

—— (1997) 'Markets in Transition', in David Kreps and Kenneth Wallis (eds), *Advances in Economics and Econometrics: Theory and applications*, Seventh World Congress of the Econometric Society, vol. II, Cambridge, UK: Cambridge University Press.

McMillan, John and Barry Naughton. (1992) 'How to Reform a Planned Economy: Lessons from China', *Oxford Review of Economic Policy*, 8 (1).

McMillan, John and Christopher Woodruff. (2002) 'The Central Role of Entrepreneurs in Transition Economies', *Journal of Economic Perspectives*, 16 (3).

Maddison, Angus. (2009) 'Measuring the Economic Performance of Transition Economies: Some lessons from Chinese experience', *Review of Income and Wealth*, 55 (1).

—— (2006) 'Do Official Statistics Exaggerate China's GDP Growth? A reply to Carsten Holz', *Review of Income and Wealth*, 52 (1).

—— (2003) *The World Economy: Historical statistics*, Paris: OECD.

—— (1998a) *Chinese Economic Performance in the Long Run*, Paris: OECD.

—— (1998b) 'Measuring the Performance of a Communist Command Economy: An assessment of the C.I.A. estimates for the USSR', *Review of Income and Wealth*, 44 (3).

Malleret, Thierry, Natalia Orlova and Vladimir Romanov. (1999) 'What Loaded and Triggered the Russian Crisis?', *Post-Soviet Affairs*, 15 (2).

Mansoor, Ali and Bryce Quillin (eds). (2006) *Migration and Remittances: Eastern Europe and the Former Soviet Union*, Washington, DC: The World Bank.

Mao, Zedong. (1974) *Mao Tse-tung Unrehearsed: Talks and letters, 1956–71*, edited by Stuart R. Schram, London: Penguin Books.

Marangos, John. (2007) 'Was Shock Therapy Consistent with the Washington Consensus?', *Comparative Economic Studies*, 49 (1).

—— (2004) *Alternative Economic Models of Transition*, Aldershot: Ashgate.

Marer, Paul. (2010) 'The Global Economic Crises: Impacts on Eastern Europe', *Acta Oeconomica*, 60(1).

—— (1984) 'East European Economies: Achievements, problems, prospects', in Teresa Rakowska-Harmstone (ed.), *Communism in Eastern Europe*, 2nd edn, Manchester: Manchester University Press.

Mau, Vladimir. (2000) *Russian Economic Reforms as Seen by an Insider: Success or failure*, Chatham House: Royal Institute of International Affairs.

Mau, Vladimir and Irina Starodubrovskaya. (2001) *The Challenge of Revolution: Contemporary Russia in historical perspective*, Oxford: Oxford University Press.

Megginson, William L. and Jeffrey M. Netter. (2001) 'From State to Market: A survey of empirical studies on privatization', *Journal of Economic Literature*, 39 (2).

Megginson, William L., Robert C. Nash and Matthias van Randenborgh. (1994) 'The Financial and Operating Performance of Newly Privatized Firms: An international empirical analysis', *Journal of Finance*, 49 (2).

Merlevede, Bruno. (2003) 'Reform Reversals and Output Growth in Transition Economics', *Economics of Transition*, 11 (4).

Mickiewicz, Tomasz. (2005) *Economic Transition in Central Europe and the Commonwealth of Independent States*, Basingstoke: Palgrave Macmillan.

Milanovic, Branko. (1999) 'Explaining the Increase in Inequality during Transition', *Economics of Transition*, 7 (2).

—— (1998) *Income, Inequality and Poverty during the Transition from Planned to Market Economy*, Washington, DC: The World Bank.

Miller, Jeffrey B. and Stoyan Tenev. (2007) 'On the Role of Government in Transition: The experiences of China and Russia compared', *Comparative Economic Studies*, 49 (4).

Mincer, Jacob. (1974) *Schooling, Experience and Earnings*, New York: Columbia University Press.

Mitchell, Janet. (1998) 'Strategic Creditor Passivity, Regulation and Bank Bailouts', *CIPR Discussion Paper No. 1780*, London: Centre for Economic Policy Research.

Mitra, Pradeep and Nicholas Stern. (2003) 'Tax Systems in Transition', *Policy Research Working Paper No. 2947*, Washington, DC: The World Bank.

Moers, Luc (1999) 'How Important are Institutions for Growth in Transition Countries?', *Tinbergen Institute Discussion Paper No. 99-004/2*, Amsterdam.

Montias, John M. (1959) 'Planning with Material Balances in Soviet Style Economies', *American Economic Review*, 49 (5).

Mrak, Mojmir, Matija Rojec and Carlos Silva-Jáuregui. (eds) (2004) *Slovenia: From Yugoslavia to the European Union*, Washington, DC: The World Bank.

Mukand, Sharun and Dani Rodrik. (2005) 'In Search of the Holy Grail: Policy convergence, experimentation, and economic performance', *American Economic Review*, 95 (1).

Mundell, Robert A. (1997) 'The Great Contractions in Transition Economies', in Mario I. Blejer and Marko Škreb (eds), *Macroeconomic Stabilization in Transition Economies*, New York: Cambridge University Press.

Munich, Daniel, Jan Svejnar and Katherine Terrell. (2000) 'Returns to Human Capital under the Communist Wage Grid and During the Transition to a Market Economy', *IZA Discussion Paper No. 122*, Bonn.

Murrell, Peter. (2006) 'Institutions and Transition', in Lawrence Blume and Steven Durlauf (eds), *The New Palgrave Dictionary of Economics*, 2nd edn, Basingstoke: Palgrave Macmillan.

—— (2005) 'Institutions and Firms in Transition Economies', in Claude Ménard and Mary M. Shirley (eds), *Handbook on New Institutional Economics*, Dordrecht: Kluwer Academic.

—— (2003) 'The Relative Levels and the Character of Institutional Development in Transition Economies', in Naura F. Campos and Jan Fidrmuc (eds), *Political Economy of Transition and Development: Institutions, politics and policies*, ZEI Studies in European Economics and Law, vol. 5, Dordrecht: Kluwer Academic.

—— (1996) 'How Far Has the Transition Progressed?', *Journal of Economic Perspectives*, 10 (2).

—— (1995) 'The Transition According to Cambridge, Mass.', *Journal of Economic Literature*, 33 (1).

—— (1993) 'What is Shock Therapy? What did it do in Poland and Russia?', *Post-Soviet Affairs*, 9 (2).

—— (1992) 'Evolution in Economics and in the Economic Reform of the Centrally Planned Economies', in Christopher Clague and Gordon Rausser (eds), *The Emergence of Market Economies in Eastern Europe*, Oxford: Blackwell.

Nagy, Piroska M. (2000) *The Meltdown of the Russian State*, Cheltenham: Edward Elgar.

Naimark, Norman M. (1995) *The Russians in Germany: A history of the Soviet zone of occupation 1945–1949*, Cambridge, MA: Harvard University Press.

Naughton, Barry. (2008a) 'A Political Economy of China's Economic Transition', in Loren Brandt and Thomas G. Rawski (eds), *China's Great Economic Transformation*, New York: Cambridge University Press.

—— (2008b) 'SOE Policy: Profiting the SASAC way', *China Economic Quarterly*, 12 (2).

—— (2007a) *The Chinese Economy: Transitions and growth*, Cambridge, MA: MIT Press.

—— (2007b) 'Reframing China Policy: The Carnegie Debates – Debate 2: China's Economy. Motion: Without significantly accelerated reforms and major new policy actions, China's rapid growth will unravel before its economy overtakes the US', *Journal of Chinese Economic and Business Studies*, 5 (3).

—— (1995) *Growing out of the Plan: Chinese Economic Reform 1978–1993*, New York: Cambridge University Press.

Nellis, John. (2008) 'Leaps of Faith: Launching the Privatization Process in Transition', in Ora W. Lieberman and Daniel J. Kopt (eds), *Privatization in Transition Economics: The ongoing story*, Contemporary Studies in Economic and Financial Analysis, vol. 90, Amsterdam: Elsevier.

—— (2002) 'The World Bank, Privatization, and Economic Reform in Transition Economies: A retrospective analysis', Washington, DC: Operation Evaluation Department, The World Bank.

—— (1999) 'Time to Rethink Privatization in Transition Economies', *IFC Discussion Paper 38*, Washington, DC: The World Bank.

Nelson, Joan. (1994) 'Linkages between Politics and Economics', *Journal of Democracy*, 5 (4).

Nelson, Joan, Charles Tilly and Lee Walker (eds) (1997) *Transforming Post-Communist Political Economies*, Washington, DC: National Academy Press.

Nelson, Richard and Sidney Winter. (1982) *An Evolutionary Theory of Economic Change*, Cambridge, MA: Harvard University Press.

Nesporova, Allen. (2002) *Unemployment in the Transition Economies*, Employment Strategy Department, International Labour Office, Geneva.

Newell, Andrew and Barry Reilly. (1999) 'Rates of Return to Educational Qualifications in the Transitional Economies', *Education Economics*, 7 (1).

Nickell, Stephen J. (1996) 'Competition and Corporate Performance', *Journal of Political Economy*, 104 (4).

Nolan, Peter. (1995) *China's Rise, Russia's Fall: Politics, economics and planning in the transition from Stalinism*, New York: St Martin's Press.

North, Douglass C. (2000) 'Big-Bang Transformations of Economic Systems: An introductory note', *Journal of Institutional and Theoretical Economics*, 156.

—— (1997) 'The Contribution of the New Institutional Economics to an Understanding of the Transition Problem', *WIDER Annual Lecture*, Helsinki: UNU/WIDER.

—— (1991) 'Institutions', *Journal of Economic Perspectives*, 5 (1).

—— (1990) *Institutions, Institutional Change and Economic Performance*, Cambridge, MA: Cambridge University Press.

North, Douglass C., John Joseph Wallis and Barry R. Weingast. (2009) *Violence and Social Orders: A conceptual framework for interpreting natural human history*, New York: Cambridge University Press.

Notzon, Francis C., Yuri M. Komarov, Sergei P. Ermakov, Alexei I. Savinykh, Michelle B. Hanson and Juan Albertorio. (2003) 'Vital and Health Statistics: Russian Federation and United States, selected years 1985–2000 with an overview of Russian mortality in the 1990s', U.S. Department of Health and Human Services, Center for Disease Control and Prevention, National Center for Health Statistics, 5 (11).

Nove, Alec. (1996) 'Economics of Transition: Some gaps and illusions', in Mark Knell (ed.), *Economics of Transition: Structural adjustments and growth prospects in Eastern Europe*, Cheltenham, UK: Edward Elgar.

—— (1986a) *An Economic History of the U.S.S.R.*, Harmondsworth: Penguin Books.

—— (1986b) *The Soviet Economic System*, 3rd edn, London: Allen and Unwin.

Odling-Smee, John and Gonzalo Pastor. (2002) 'The IMF and the Ruble Area, 1991–1993', *Comparative Economic Studies*, 44 (4).

OECD. (2005) *OECD Economic Surveys: China*, Paris: OECD.

OECD. (Various years). *Short-term Economic Indicators: Transition economies*, National Labour Force Surveys, Paris: OECD.

Ofer, Gur. (2001) 'Development and Transition: Emerging, but merging?', *Revue D' Economie Financiere*, Special Issue.

Ofer, Gur and Richard Pomfret. (eds) (2004) *The Economic Prospects of the CIS: Sources of long term growth*, Cheltenham, UK: Edward Elgar.

Olson, Mancur. (1992) 'Hidden Path to a Successful Economy', in Christopher Clague and Gordon Rausser (eds), *The Emergence of Market Economies in Eastern Europe*, Oxford: Blackwell.

Orlowski, Lucjan T. (ed.) (2001) *Transition and Growth in Post-Communist Countries: The ten-year experience*, Cheltenham, UK: Edward Elgar.

Parker, Stephen, Gavin Tritt and Wing Thye Woo. (1997) 'Some Lessons Learned from the Comparison of Transitions in Asia and Eastern Europe', in Wing Thye Woo, Stephen Parker and Jeffrey D. Sachs (eds), *Economies in Transition: Comparing Asia and Eastern Europe*, Cambridge, MA: MIT Press.

Perkins, Dwight H. and Thomas G. Rawski. (2008) 'Forecasting China's Economic Growth to 2025', in Loren Brandt and Thomas G. Rawski (eds), *China's Great Economic Transformation*, New York: Cambridge University Press.

Pickel, Andreas and Helmut Wiesenthal. (1997) *The Grand Experiment: Debating shock therapy, transition theory, and the East German experience*, Boulder, CO: Westview Press.

Pohl, Gerhard, Robert E. Anderson, Stijn Claessens and Simeon Djankov. (1997) 'Privatization and Restructuring in Central and Eastern Europe: Evidence and policy options', *World Bank Technical Paper No. 368*, Washington, DC: World Bank.

Pomer, Marshall. (2001) 'Introduction', in Lawrence R. Klein and Marshall Pomer (eds), *The New Russia: Transition gone awry*, Stanford, CA: Stanford University Press.

Pomfret, Richard. (2002) *Constructing a Market Economy; Diverse paths from central planning in Asia and Europe*, Cheltenham, UK: Edward Elgar.

Popov, Vladimir. (2007) 'Shock Therapy Versus Gradualism Reconsidered: Lessons from the transition economies after 15 Years of reform', *Comparative Economic Studies*, 49 (1).

—— (2006) 'Life Cycle of the Centrally Planned Economy: Why Soviet growth rates peaked in the 1950s', paper presented at the American Economic Association Annual Meeting in Boston. Also published as Почему снижались темпы роста советской экономики в брежневский период in Неприкосновенный запас, 2 (52), 2007.

—— (2000) 'Shock Therapy Versus Gradualism: The end of the debate (explaining the magnitude of transformational recession)', *Comparative Economic Studies*, 42 (1).

Popper, Karl. (1945) *The Open Society and Its Enemies*, London: Routledge.

Portes, Richard. (1994) 'Transformation Traps', *The Economic Journal*, 104 (426).

—— (1993) 'From Central Planning to a Market Economy', in Michael Mandelbaum and Shafiqul Islam (eds), *Making Markets: Economic transformation in Eastern Europe and the post-Soviet States*, New York: Council on Foreign Relations Press.

Poznanski, Kazimierz Z. (ed.). (1995) *The Evolutionary Transition to Capitalism*, Oxford: Westview Press.

Qian, Yingyi. (2003) 'How Reform Worked in China', in Dani Rodrik (ed.), *In Search of Prosperity: Analytic narratives on economic growth*, Princeton, NJ: Princeton University Press.

—— (2000) 'The Institutional Foundations of China's Market Transition', in Boris Pleskovic and Joseph Stiglitz (eds), *Annual World Bank Conference on Development Economics 1999*, Washington, DC: The World Bank.

Qian, Yinygi and Jinglian Wu. (2008) 'Transformation in China', in János Kornai, Lászlo Mátyás and Gérard Roland (eds), *Institutional Change and Economic Behaviour*, Basingstoke: Palgrave Macmillan.

Qian, Yingyi, Gérard Roland and Chenggang Xu. (1999) 'Why is China Different from Eastern Europe? Perspectives from organization theory', *European Economic Review*, 43 (4–6).

Radulescu, Roxana and David Barlow. (2002) 'The Relationship between Policies and Growth in Transition Countries', *Economics of Transition*, 10 (3).

Raiser, Martin. (1999) 'Trust in Transition', *EBRD Working Paper No. 39*, European Bank for Reconstruction and Development.

Raiser, Martin, Mark E. Schaffer and Johannes Schuchhardt. (2003) 'Benchmarking Structural Change in Transition', *IZA Discussion Paper No. 727*, Bonn.

Raiser, Martin, Christian Haerpfer, Thomas Nowotny and Claire Wallace. (2001) 'Social Capital Transition: A first look at the evidence', *EBRD Working Paper No. 61*, European Bank for Reconstruction and Development.

Ransome, Arthur. (1919) *Six Weeks in Russia in 1919*, London: Faber Finds.

Rausser, Gordon. C. (1992) 'Lessons for Emerging Market Economies in Eastern Europe', in Christopher Clague and Gordon Rausser (eds), *The Emergence of Market Economies in Eastern Europe*, Oxford: Blackwell.

Ravallion, Martin and Shaohua Chen. (2004) 'China's (Uneven) Progress Against Poverty', *Policy Research Paper No. 3408*, Washington, DC: The World Bank.

Rayment, Paul. (1995) 'The Hard Road to the Market Economy: Realities and illusions', *MOCT-MOST: Economic Policy in Transitional Economies*, 5 (2).

Rodrik, Dani. (2008) 'Spence Christens a New Washington Consensus', *The Economists' Voice*, 5 (3), http://www.bepress.com/ev/vol5/iss3/art4/.

—— (2006) 'Goodbye Washington Consensus, Hello Washington Confusion? A review of the World Bank's economic growth in the 1990s: Learning from a decade of reform', *Journal of Economic Literature*, 44 (4).

—— (1996) 'Understanding Economic Policy Reforms', *Journal of Economic Literature*, 34.

461

—— (1994) 'Making Sense of the Soviet Trade Shock in Eastern Europe: A framework and some estimates', *NBER Working Paper 4112*, National Bureau of Economic Research.

Roland, Gérard. (2008a) 'Fast-moving and Slow-moving Institutions', in János Kornai, Lászlo Mátyás and Gérard Roland (eds), *Institutional Change and Economic Behaviour*, Basingstoke: Palgrave Macmillan.

—— (ed.). (2008b) *Privatization: Success and failures*, New York: Columbia University Press.

—— (2008c) 'Transposable and Non Transposable Lessons from the Transition Experience', *Seoul Journal of Economics*, summer.

—— (2002) 'The Political Economy of Transition', *Journal of Economic Perspectives*, 16 (1).

—— (2001) 'Ten Years After . . . Transition and Economics', *IMF Staff Papers*, vol. 48, Special Issue, Washington, DC: International Monetary Fund.

—— (2000) *Transition and Economics: Politics, markets, and firms*, Cambridge, MA: MIT Press.

Roland, Gérard and Thierry Verdier. (1999) 'Transition and the Output Fall', *Economics of Transition*, 7 (1).

Romer, David. (1996) *Advanced Macroeconomics*, New York: The McGraw-Hill Companies, Inc.

Rosati, Dariusz. (1994) 'Output Decline during Transition from Plan to Market', *Economics of Transition*, 2 (4).

Rose, Richard. (1994) 'Rethinking Civil Society: Postcommunism and the problem of trust', *Journal of Democracy*, 5 (3).

Rosefielde, Steven. (2007) *The Russian Economy: From Lenin to Putin*, Oxford: Blackwell.

Rosenstein-Rodan, Paul N. (1943) 'Problems of Industrialisation of Eastern and South-Eastern Europe', *The Economic Journal*, 53 (210/211).

Sachs, Jeffrey. (2005) *The End of Poverty: Economic possibilities for our time*, New York: Penguin.

—— (1996a) 'The Transition at Mid Decade', *American Economic Review, Papers and Proceedings*, 86 (2).

—— (1996b) 'China's Transition Experience, Reexamined', *Beyond Transition – The Newsletter about Reforming Economies*, 7, (3–4), March–April, Washington, DC: The World Bank.

—— (1993) *Poland's Jump to the Market Economy*, Cambridge, MA: MIT Press.

Sachs, Jeffrey and Wing Thye Woo. (2000) 'Understanding China's Economic Performance', *Journal of Policy Reform*, 4 (1).

Sachs, Jeffrey, Clifford Zinnes and Yair Eilat. (2001) 'The Gains from Privatization in Transition Economies: Is "change of ownership" enough?', *IMF Staff Papers*, vol. 48, Special Issue, Washington, DC: International Monetary Fund.

—— (2000) 'Patterns and Determinants of Economic Reform in Transition Economies: 1990–1998', *CAER II Discussion Paper 61*, Cambridge, MA: Harvard Institute for International Development.

Sampson, Steven L. (1987) 'The Second Economy of the Soviet Union and Eastern Europe', *Annals of the American Academy of Political and Social Science*, 493.

Santiso, Javier. (2000) 'Hirschman's View of Development, or the Art of Trespassing and Self-Subversion', *Cepal Review*, 70, United Nations.

Schaffer, Mark, E. (2000) 'Should We be Worried about the Use of Trade Credit and Non-monetary Transactions in Transition Economics?', *Economic Systems*, 24 (1).

—— (1998) 'Do Firms in Transition Economies Have Soft Budget Constraints? A reconsideration of concepts and evidence', *Journal of Comparative Economics*, 26 (1).

Schama, Simon. (1989) *Citizens: The Chronicle of the French Revolution*, New York: Knopf.

Schneider, Friedrich. (2006) 'Shadow Economies and Corruption All Over the World: What do we really know?', *IZA Discussion Paper No. 2315*, Bonn.

Schneider, Friedrich and Dominik H. Enste. (2000) 'Shadow Economies: Size, causes and consequences', *Journal of Economic Literature*, 38 (1).

Schroeder, Paul W. (1994) *The Transformation of European Politics 1763–1848*, New York: Oxford University Press.

Schumpeter, Joseph A. (1942) *Capitalism, Socialism and Democracy*, New York: Harper & Brothers.

Selowsky, Marcelo and Ricardo Martin. (1997) 'Policy Performance and Output Growth in the Transition Economies', *American Economic Review, Paper and Proceedings*, 87 (2).

Shiller, Robert J., Maxim Boycko and Vladimir Korobov. (1991) 'Popular Attitudes Toward Free Markets: The Soviet Union and the United States compared', *American Economic Review*, 81 (3).

Shirley, Mary and Patrick Walsh. (2000) 'Public versus Private Ownership: The current state of the debate', *Policy Research Working Paper 2420*, Washington, DC: The World Bank.

Shkolnikov, Vladimir M., Giovanni A. Cornia, David A. Leon and France Meslé. (1998) 'Causes of the Russian Mortality Crisis: Evidence and interpretations', *World Development*, 26 (11).

Shleifer, Andrei and Robert W. Vishny. (1998) *The Grabbing Hand: Government pathologies and their cures*, Cambridge, MA: Harvard University Press.

—— (1997) 'A Survey of Corporate Governance', *Journal of Finance*, 52 (2).

—— (1994) 'Politicians and Firms', *Quarterly Journal of Economics*, 109 (4).

—— (1993) 'Corruption', *Quarterly Journal of Economics*, 108 (3).

Simai, Mihaly. (2006) 'Poverty and Inequality in Eastern Europe and the CIS Transition Economies', *Department of Economic and Social Affairs Working Paper No.17*, United Nations.

Solimano, Andrés, Osvaldo Sunkel and Mario I. Blejer. (1994) *Rebuilding Capitalism: Alternative roads after Socialism and Dirigisme*, Ann Arbor: University of Michigan Press.

Staehr, Karsten. (2005) 'Reforms and Economic Growth in Transition Economies: Complementarity, sequencing and speed', *European Journal of Comparative Economics*, 2 (2).

Standing, Guy. (1996) *'Russian Unemployment and Enterprise Restructuring – reviving dead souls'*, Geneva: Macmillian Press.

Stern, Nicholas. (2001) 'Challenges for the Next Decade of Transition', in Oleh Havrylyshyn and Saleh M. Nsouli (eds), *A Decade of Transition:Aachievements and challenges*, Washington, DC: International Monetary Fund, IMF Institute.

—— (1997) 'The Transition in Eastern Europe and the Former Soviet Union: Some strategic lessons from the experience of 25 countries over six years', in Salvatore Zecchini (ed.), *Lessons from the Economic Transition: Central and Eastern Europe in the 1990s*, Dordrecht: Kluwer Academic.

Stiglitz, Joseph, E. (2002) *Globalization and Its Discontents*, New York: W.W. Norton.

—— (2001) 'Preface', in Lawrence R. Klein and Marshall Pomer (eds), *The New Russia: Transition gone awry*, Stanford, CA: Stanford University Press.

—— (2000) 'Whither Reform? Ten years of the transition', in Boris Pleskovic and Joseph Stiglitz (eds), *Annual World Bank Conference on Development Economics 1999*, Washington, DC: The World Bank.

—— (1999) 'Quis Custodiet Ipsos Custodes?', *Challenge*, 42 (6).

—— (1994) *Whither Socialism?*, Wicksell Lectures, Cambridge, MA: MIT Press.

Stiglitz, Joseph, E. and David Ellerman. (2001) 'Not Poles Apart: "Whither reform?" and "whence reform?" ', *Journal of Policy Reform*, 4 (4).

Stuart, Robert C. and Christina M. Panayotopoulos. (1999) 'Decline and Recovery in Transition Economies: The impact of initial conditions', *Post-Soviet Geography and Economics*, 40 (4).

Stuckler, David, Lawrence King and Martin McKee. (2009) 'Mass Privatisation and the Post-Communist Mortality Crisis: A cross-national analysis', *Lancet*, 373 (9661).

Svejnar, Jan. (2008) 'China in Light of the Performance of the Transition Economies', in Loren Brandt and Thomas G. Rawski (eds), *China's Great Economic Transformation*, New York: Cambridge University Press.

—— (2002) 'Transition Economies: Performance and challenges', *Journal of Economic Perspectives*, 16 (1).

—— (1978) 'Workers' Participation in Management in Czechoslovakia', *Annals of Public and Cooperative Economy*, 49 (2).

Syrquin, Moises and Hollis B. Chenery. (1989) *Patterns of Development 1950 to 1983*, Washington, DC: The World Bank.

Tanzi, Vito. (1999) 'Transition and the Changing Role of Government', *Finance and Development*, 36 (2), Washington, DC: IMF.

—— (1998) 'Corruption Around the World: Causes, consequences, scope and cures', *IMF Staff Papers*, 45 (4).

Tanzi, Vito and George Tsibouris. (2000) 'Fiscal Reform Over Ten Years of Transition', *IMF Working Paper, WP00/113*, Washington, DC: IMF.

Taylor, Lance. (1994) 'The Market Met Its Match: Lessons for the future from the transition's initial years', *Journal of Comparative Economics*, 19 (1).

Tenev, Stoyan and Chunlin Zhang (with Loup Brefort). (2002) 'Corporate Governance and Enterprise Reform in China: Building the institutions of modern markets', *World Bank and International Finance Corporation*, Washington, DC.

Thompson, Edward P. (1979) *The Making of the English Working Class*, London: Penguin Books.

Treisman, Daniel. (2003) 'Postcommunist Corruption', in Naura F. Campos and Jan Fidrmuc (eds), *Political Economy of Transition and Development: Institutions, politics and policies*, ZEI Studies in European Economics and Law, vol. 5, Dordrecht: Kluwer Academic.

—— (2000) 'The Causes of Corruption: A cross national study', *Journal of Public Economics*, 76 (3).

Trostel, Philip, Ian Walker and Paul Woolley. (2002) 'Estimates of the Economic Returns to Schooling for 28 Countries', *Labour Economics*, 9 (1).

Turley, Gerard. (2006) *Transition, Taxation and the State*, Aldershot: Ashgate.

UNECE. (2004) 'Poverty in Eastern Europe and the CIS', Chapter 7 in *Economic Survey of Europe*, no. 1, Geneva: United Nations Economic Commission for Europe.

—— (2003) 'Some Aspects of Labour Market Performance in Eastern Europe and the CIS', Chapter 7 in *Economic Survey of Europe*, no. 1, Geneva: United Nations Economic Commission for Europe.

—— (2000) 'Fertility Decline in the Transition Economies, 1989–1998: Economic and social factors revisited', Chapter 6 in *Economic Survey of Europe*, no.1, Geneva: United Nations Economic Commission for Europe.

—— (1999) 'Fertility Decline in the Transition Economies, 1982–1997: Political, economic and social factors', Chapter 4 in *Economic Survey of Europe*, No.1, Geneva: United Nations Economic Commission for Europe.

UNICEF. (1993) *Central and Eastern Europe in Transition: Public policy and social conditions*, Regional Monitoring Report, no. 1, Florence: Innocenti Research Centre.

Vining, Aidan R. and Anthony E. Boardman. (1992) 'Ownership versus Competition: Efficiency in public enterprise', *Public Choice*, 73 (2).

Wagener, Hans-Jürgen (ed.). (1993) *On the Theory and Policy of Systemic Change*, Heidelberg: Physica-Verlag.

Walker, Ian and Yu Zhu. (2001) *The Returns to Education: Evidence from the Labour Force Surveys*, Research Report RR313 for the Department for Education and Skills.

Wang, Xiaolu and Lian Meng. (2001) 'A Revaluation of China's Economic Growth', *China Economic Review*, 12 (4).

Weder, Beatrice. (2001) 'Institutional Reform in Transition Economies: How far have they come?', *IMF Working Paper WP/01/114*, Washington, DC: IMF.

Wildasin, David E. (1997) 'Externalities and Bailouts: Hard and Soft Budget Constraints in Intergovernmental Fiscal Relations', Department of Economics, Vanderbilt University, mimeo.

Wildau, Gabriel. (2008) 'Efficiency: Has anything really changed?', *China Economic Quarterly*, 12 (2).

Williamson, John. (2000) 'What Should the World Bank Think about the Washington Consensus?', *The World Bank Economic Observer*, 15 (2).

—— (1990) 'What Washington Means by Policy Reform', in John Williamson (ed.), *Latin American Adjustment: How much has happened?*, Washington, DC: Institute for International Economics.

Williamson, Oliver E. (1996) *The Mechanisms of Governance*, New York: Oxford University Press.

—— (1995) 'The Institutions and Governance of Economic Development and Reform', *Annual World Bank Conference on Development Economics 1994*, Washington, DC: The World Bank.

Winiecki. Jan. (2002) 'An Inquiry into the Early Drastic Fall of Output in Post-communist Transition: An unsolved puzzle', *Post-Communist Economies*, 14 (1).

—— (2000) 'Crucial Difference between the Privatized Sector and the Generic Private Sector in Post-Communist Privatization: Determinants of economic performance', *Communist and Post-Communist Studies*, 33.

—— (1988) *The Distorted World of Soviet Type Economies*, London: Routledge.

Wolf, Holger C. (1999) 'Transition Strategies: Choices and outcomes', *Princeton Studies in International Finance No. 85*, Princeton, NJ: Princeton University Press.

Wolf, Martin. (2005) 'Why is China Growing so Slowly?', *Foreign Policy*, 146.

Woo, Wing Thye. (2007) 'Reframing China Policy: The Carnegie Debates – Debate 2: China's Economy. Motion: Without significantly accelerated reforms and major new policy actions, China's rapid growth will unravel before its economy overtakes the US', *Journal of Chinese Economic and Business Studies*, 5 (3).

Woodruff, Christopher. (2006) 'Measuring Institutions', in Susan Rose-Ackerman (ed.), *International Handbook on the Economics of Corruption*, Cheltenham, UK: Edward Elgar.

World Bank. (2008) *Russian Economic Report No. 17*, World Bank Russia Country Office, Economic Management and Policy Unit.

—— (2006) *Migration and Remittances: Eastern Europe and the Former Soviet Union*, Europe and Central Asia Region, eds Ali Mansoor and Bryce Quillin, Washington, DC: The World Bank.

—— (2005a) *Growth, Poverty and Inequality in Eastern Europe and the former Soviet Union*, Washington, DC: The World Bank.

—— (2005b) *Economic Growth in the 1990s: Learning from a decade of reform*, Washington, DC: The World Bank.

—— (2002a) *Transition – The First Ten Years: Analysis and lessons for Eastern Europe and the former Soviet Union*, Washington, DC: The World Bank.

—— (2002b) *Building Institutions for Markets*, Washington, DC: The World Bank.

—— (2001) *World Development Report 2000/01: Attacking poverty*, New York: Oxford University Press.

—— (2000) *Making Transition Work for Everyone: Poverty and inequality in Europe and Central Asia*, Washington, DC: The World Bank.

—— (1996) *World Development Report 1996: From plan to market*, New York: Oxford University Press.

Wyplosz, Charles. (2000) 'Ten Years of Transformation: Macroeconomic lessons', *CEPR Discussion Paper no. 2254*, London: Centre for Economic Policy Research.

Yao, Shujie, Zongyi Zhang and Lucia Hanmer. (2004) 'Growing Inequality and Poverty in China', *China Economic Review*, 15.

Zecchini, Salvatore (ed.). (1997) *Lessons from the Economic Transition: Central and Eastern Europe in the 1990s*, Dordrecht: Kluwer Academic.

Zhang, Junsen, Yaohui Zhao, Albert Park and Xiaoqing Song. (2005) 'Economic Returns to Schooling in Urban China, 1988 to 2001', *Journal of Comparative Economics*, 33 (4).

Zhou, Katie Xioa. (1996) *How the Farmers Changed China*, Boulder, CO: Western Press.

Zhuravskaya, Ekaterina V. (2000) 'Incentives to Provide Local Public Goods: Fiscal federalism, Russian style', *Journal of Public Economics*, 76 (3).

INDEX

Abalkin, L. 187
accounting 43, 170, 208, 212, 219, 328
Administrative Council 399
administrative economy *see* central planning
Adriatic Sea 234
adverse selection 166, 211
Afghanistan 92
Africa 2, 134, 155; Corruption Index 393;
    growth 390
Agentia pentru Valorificarea Activelor Bancare
    (AVAB) 402
agriculture 7, 12, 27–8, 76; boosting 23–4;
    collectivisation 61–8; developing countries 4;
    informal economy 96; poverty/inequality
    395; Russia/China 314–15, 331–2, 352;
    socialist countries 5
Ahrend, R. 319, 321, 326
Albania 3, 57, 64, 67; Corruption Index 393; flat
    tax 120; initial conditions 140, 143; labour
    market 112; land reform/collectivisation 65;
    life expectancy 237; output 226; planning
    59–60; reforms 178–9
alcohol 128, 238, 303, 306, 348–50
all-Russian Congress of Soviets of Workers',
    Soldiers' and Peasants' Deputies 21
Allies 51
alternative view 409–11
America *see* USA
Americas 365
Amsden, A. 244
Andrienko, Y. 297
Andropov, Y. 90
Andvig, J.C. 95
anecdotes 357–8
Angelucci, M. 200, 210
Anglo-Saxon world 149, 187, 203, 207
Anhui 311
Armenia 3, 176, 181; agriculture 79;
    demographics 127; government
    revenue/expenditure 124; hyperinflation 74;
    inequality 103; initial conditions 140
arrears 162, 167, 382; expenditure 122;

inter-enterprise 161, 165–7, 244, 402;
    pension and transfers 104–5; tax 118, 165–7,
    212, 380; wage 102, 104–5, 116, 166, 231,
    275, 322, 380
Arrow, K. 377
Asia 2, 5, 30, 155; financial crisis 323, 333, 401;
    initial conditions 146; life expectancy 236;
    Romanian links 400–1; South 215; South
    East 30, 141, 158, 318, 377, 385; trade 140
Asian Tigers 317–18
Åslund, A. 5–8, 163, 185, 324–5, 327, 355–6,
    367, 379
asset-stripping 2, 164, 188, 206, 382
asymmetric information 166, 193, 207, 211,
    243
Atkeson, A. 244
austerity 229, 352
Austria 234
Austrian School 154
Aven, P. 320, 360
Axis powers 47–8, 64
Azerbaijan 3, 15; business regulation 215;
    demographics 127; FDI 109; growth 72;
    industry 79; inflation 76; initial conditions
    140; performance 245; reforms 176, 179,
    181; returns to education 287; unemployment
    233

backwardness 21–2, 142, 309
bailouts 165–6, 184, 193, 212, 379–80, 388, 403
bakeries 42–6
Baklanov, O. 15
balance of payments 155
Balcerowicz, L. 150
Balkans 47, 74, 105, 377; demographics 127;
    inflation 74, 229; reforms 167; trade 108
Baltic States 2, 5–7, 11, 15; demographics 124,
    127–8; flat tax 120; inequality 104; initial
    conditions 140–2; life expectancy 237;
    migration 296; negative growth 390; output
    226; performance 225, 238–9; policy
    conclusions/lessons 407–8; poverty 101;